Frommer's®

Virginia

Here's what the critics say about Frommer's:

"Amazingly easy to use. Very portable, very complete."
—*Booklist*

♦

"The only mainstream guide to list specific prices. The Walter Cronkite of guidebooks—with all that implies."
—*Travel & Leisure*

♦

"Complete, concise, and filled with useful information."
—*New York Daily News*

♦

"Hotel information is close to encyclopedic."
—*Des Moines Sunday Register*

♦

"Detailed, accurate and easy-to-read information for all price ranges."
—*Glamour Magazine*

Other Great Guides for Your Trip:

Frommer's Washington, D.C.

Frommer's Washington, D.C. from $70 a Day

Frommer's Portable Washington, D.C.

Frommer's Memorable Walks: Washington, D.C.

Frommer's Irreverent Guide to Washington, D.C.

Frommer's Washington, D.C., with Kids

The Unofficial Guide to Washington, D.C.

Frommer's Maryland & Delaware

Frommer's Carolinas & Georgia

Frommer's USA

*The Civil War Trust's Official Guide to the
Civil War Discovery Trail*

Frommer's®

Virginia

by Bill Goodwin

IDG Books Worldwide, Inc.
An International Data Group Company
Foster City, CA • Chicago, IL • Indianapolis, IN • New York, NY

ABOUT THE AUTHOR

Born and raised in North Carolina, **Bill Goodwin** has lived in northern Virginia since 1979. He was an award-winning newspaper reporter before becoming a legal counsel and speech writer for two U.S. Senators, Sam Nunn of Georgia and the late Sam J. Ervin, Jr., of North Carolina. Now a full-time travel writer, Goodwin is the author of *Frommer's South Pacific* and *Frommer's Portable Tampa & St. Petersburg,* and coauthor of *Frommer's Florida* and *Frommer's Florida from $60 a Day.*

IDG BOOKS WORLDWIDE, INC.

An International Data Group Company
919 E. Hillsdale Blvd.
Suite 400
Foster City, CA 94404

Find us online at **www.frommers.com**

ISBN 0-02-863517-5
ISSN 1058-4943

Editor: Matt Hannafin
Production Editor: Christina Van Camp
Photo Editor: Richard Fox
Design by Michele Laseau
Staff Cartographers: John Decamillis, Roberta Stockwell, Elizabeth Puhl
Page Creation: Marie Kristine Parial-Leonardo, David Faust, and Carl Pierce

SPECIAL SALES

For general information on IDG Books Worldwide's books in the U.S., please call our Consumer Customer Service department at 1-800-762-2974. For reseller information, including discounts, bulk sales, customized editions, and premium sales, please call our Reseller Customer Service department at 1-800-434-3422.

Manufactured in the United States of America

5 4 3 2 1

Contents

List of Maps

An Invitation to the Reader

In researching this book, we discovered many wonderful places—hotels, restaurants, shops, and more. We're sure you'll find others. Please tell us about them, so we can share the information with your fellow travelers in upcoming editions. If you were disappointed with a recommendation, we'd love to know that, too. Please write to:

Frommer's Virginia, 5th Edition
Frommer's Travel Guides
1633 Broadway
New York, NY 10019

An Additional Note

Please be advised that travel information is subject to change at any time—and this is especially true of prices. We therefore suggest that you write or call ahead for confirmation when making your travel plans. The authors, editors, and publisher cannot be held responsible for the experiences of readers while traveling. Your safety is important to us, however, so we encourage you to stay alert and be aware of your surroundings. Keep a close eye on cameras, purses, and wallets, all favorite targets of thieves and pickpockets.

What the Symbols Mean

✪ Frommer's Favorites

Our favorite places and experiences—outstanding for quality, value, or both.

The following abbreviations are used for credit cards:

AE	American Express	EURO	Eurocard
CB	Carte Blanche	JCB	Japan Credit Bank
DC	Diners Club	MC	MasterCard
DISC	Discover	V	Visa
ER	EnRoute		

Find Frommer's Online

www.frommers.com offers up-to-the-minute listings on almost 200 cities around the globe—including the latest bargains and candid, personal articles updated daily by Arthur Frommer himself. No other Web site offers such comprehensive and timely coverage of the world of travel.

Virginia

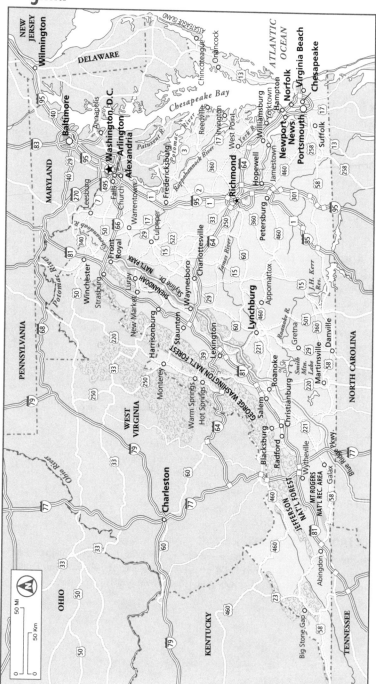

The Best of Virginia

America's first permanent English-speaking colonists had a rough start at Jamestown in 1607, but within a few years the beautiful and bountiful land they called Virginia had greatly rewarded them for their courageous efforts. They first set foot on a sandy Atlantic Ocean beach at Cape Charles, at the mouth of one of the world's great estuaries, the Chesapeake Bay. Beyond them lay a varied, rich, and highly scenic land. They settled beside one of the great tidal rivers whose tributaries led their descendants through the rolling hills of the Piedmont, over the Blue Ridge Mountains, and into the great valleys beyond.

Almost 400 years later, the history-loving Commonwealth of Virginia rewards today's traveler with glimpses back to the colonial era, to the stirrings of revolution and the great victory that sealed independence for the United States, and to the bloody battles that nearly tore the young nation apart during the Civil War. The state abounds with beautifully preserved historic homes and plantations, buildings that rang with revolutionary oratory, museums that recall the nation's storied past, and small towns that seem little changed since the earliest days of colonial times.

Fortunately, preservation hasn't been limited to historical landmarks. Conservation efforts have kept a great deal of Virginia's wilderness looking much as it did in 1607, making the state a prime destination for lovers of the great outdoors. Whether you like to hike, bike, bird watch, fish, take out a canoe, or just lie on a sandy beach, Virginia has a place to indulge your passion.

This chapter describes some of the best experiences Virginia has to offer. Bear in mind that it's just an overview, and you'll surely come up with your own "bests" as you travel through the state. See the destination chapters later in this book for full details on the places mentioned here.

1 The Best of Colonial Virginia

- **Old Town Alexandria:** Although Alexandria is today very much part of metropolitan Washington, D.C., the historic district known as "Old Town" evokes the time when the nation's early leaders strolled its streets and partook of grog at Gadsby's Tavern. See chapter 4.
- **Mount Vernon:** When he wasn't off surveying, fighting in the French and Indian War, leading the American Revolution, or

serving as our first president, George Washington made his home at a northern Virginia plantation 8 miles south of Alexandria. Restored today as it was in Washington's day, Mount Vernon is America's second most visited historic home (after the White House). See chapter 4.

- **Fredericksburg & the Northern Neck:** Not only did the Fredericksburg area play a role in the birth of a nation, it was also the birthplace of George Washington, the father of that new nation. Also born here was James Monroe, who as president kept European powers out of the Americas by promulgating the Monroe Doctrine. A generation later, the great Confederate leader Robert E. Lee was born here. Fredericksburg still retains much of the charm it possessed in those early days, and the birthplaces of Washington and Lee stand not far from town on the Northern Neck. See chapter 5.

- **Charlottesville:** Although Washington was the father of the United States, Thomas Jefferson was its intellectual genius. This scholar, lawyer, writer, and architect built two monuments to himself—his lovely hilltop home, Monticello, and the University of Virginia. Both still evoke memories of this great thinker and patriot. See chapter 6.

- **Richmond:** Although Richmond is best known as the capital of the Confederacy, it played a major role in events leading up to the American Revolution. It was in Richmond's St. John's Church that Patrick Henry shouted "Give me liberty, or give me death," thus inciting Virginia to join the rebellion. See chapter 9.

- **Williamsburg, Jamestown & Yorktown:** Known as the Historic Triangle, these three towns are the finest examples of colonial America to be found anywhere. Thanks to an infusion of cash from the Rockefeller family, Colonial Williamsburg has been restored and rebuilt as it appeared when it was the capital of Virginia from 1699 to 1780. The site of the original Jamestown settlement is now a national historical park, as is Yorktown, where George Washington bottled up Lord Cornwallis and won the American Revolution. See chapter 10.

- **James River Plantations:** America's first great wealth was created by colonists who fanned out from Jamestown and hacked huge tobacco plantations out of Virginia's pristine forests. Today, you can visit some of the great manses they built along the James River between Williamsburg and Richmond. Descendants of the colonial planters still occupy some of these mansions. See chapter 10.

2 The Best of Civil War Virginia

Some historians think the Civil War actually began in 1859 with John Brown's aborted antislavery raid on Harpers Ferry, then in Virginia. When the real fighting broke out in 1861 and the Confederacy moved its capital to Richmond, the state became the prime target of the Union armies. Consequently, Virginia saw more battles than any other state, as Robert E. Lee's Army of Northern Virginia turned back one assault after another aimed at Richmond. Today's peaceful visitor can visit the sites of many key battles, all of them national historical parks.

- **Harpers Ferry:** Now just over the West Virginia line, Harpers Ferry National Historical Park is dedicated to John Brown's raid. The forces that captured and hung him were led by Robert E. Lee, then a Union officer. The old stone town has been preserved, and the historical park has lovely hiking trails overlooking the gorge where the Potomac and Shenandoah rivers join and cut their way through the Blue Ridge. See chapter 4.

- **Manassas:** The first battle of the war occurred along Bull Run near Manassas in northern Virginia, and it was a shock to the Union when the rebels engineered a surprising victory over a disorganized Union force. They won again here at the Second Battle of Manassas. See chapter 4.

- **Fredericksburg:** No other town in Virginia has as many significant battlefields as does Fredericksburg. Lee used the Rappahannock River as a natural line of defense, and he fought several major battles against Union armies trying to cross it near Fredericksburg and advance on Richmond. Today, you can visit the battlefields in town and at Chancellorsville and the Wilderness all in a day. See chapter 5.
- **Appomattox Court House:** After the fall of Petersburg in April 1865, Lee fled for little more than a week until realizing that continuation of the war was fruitless. On April 9, he met Grant at Wilbur McLean's farmhouse and surrendered his sword. America's bloodiest conflict was over. The farmhouse is preserved as part of Appomattox Court House National Historical Park. See chapter 6.
- **New Market:** While Lee was fending off the Union near Fredericksburg, the war was ebbing and flowing up and down the Shenandoah Valley, the Confederacy's breadbasket. The town of Winchester actually changed hands 72 times. Perhaps the war's most poignant battlefield is at New Market, where the corps of cadets from Virginia Military Institute marched up from Lexington and helped stop a larger Union force. Ten of the teenagers were killed, and 47 were wounded. See chapter 7.
- **Richmond:** The capital of the Confederacy, Richmond is loaded with reminders of the great conflict, including the Museum of the Confederacy and its adjacent White House of the Confederacy, home of President Jefferson Davis. The city's Monument Avenue is lined with statues of the rebel leaders. Now suburbs, the city's eastern outskirts are ringed with battle sites, part of the Richmond National Battlefield Park. See chapter 9.
- **Petersburg:** After nearly 4 years of frustration in trying to capture Richmond, Union Gen. Ulysses S. Grant finally bypassed the southern capital in 1864 and headed for the important railroad junction of Petersburg, the lifeline of the Confederate capital. Even there he was forced into a siege situation, but finally, in April 1865, Grant broke through and forced Lee into retreat westward. See chapter 9.

3 The Best of the Great Outdoors

Virginia has hundreds of thousands of acres preserved in national and state parks, national forests, and national recreation areas. Especially in the mountains, you can find more than 1,000 miles of trails for hiking, biking, and horseback riding. The Chesapeake Bay offers fabulous boating and fishing, and the Atlantic beaches are among the best on the East Coast.

- **The W&OD Trail:** Even in Virginia's metropolitan areas, it's possible to get away from it all. One fine example is the Washington & Old Dominion (W&OD) Trail, which begins in Arlington and runs 45 miles across northern Virginia to Purcellville at the edge of the Blue Ridge Mountains. A rails-to-trails park, it follows an old railroad bed through the Washington, D.C., suburbs into the gorgeous Hunt Country. See chapter 4.
- **Shenandoah National Park:** Nearly two million visitors a year venture into the Shenandoah National Park, which straddles the crest of the Blue Ridge Mountains from Front Royal to Rockfish Gap between Charlottesville and Waynesboro. Many visitors merely ride along the 105-mile Skyline Drive, one of America's most scenic routes. Others come to walk more than 500 miles of

hiking trails, including 101 miles of Virginia's 450-mile share of the Maine-to-Georgia Appalachian Trail. Many trails start at the Skyline Drive and drop down into hollows and canyons, some of them with waterfalls. Even on the Skyline Drive, you're likely to encounter deer, and you might even see bear, bobcat, and wild turkey. See chapter 7.

- **Running the Rivers (Front Royal, Luray, Lexington, Richmond):** The South Fork of the Shenandoah River twists and turns its way between the valley towns of Front Royal and Luray, making it a perfect place for river rafting, canoeing, and kayaking—or just floating along in an inner tube. Likewise, the James River can be swift and turbulent as it crosses the Shenandoah Valley, cuts through the Blue Ridge Mountains, and courses its way across the Piedmont to Hampton Roads. Depending on the amount of rain, you can even raft down the James through metropolitan Richmond. See chapters 7 and 8.

- **Mount Rogers National Recreation Area:** While you won't be alone in Shenandoah National Park, you could have a hiking, mountain-biking, horseback-riding, or cross-country skiing trail all to yourself in Mount Rogers National Recreation Area. This wild wonderland in the Southwest Highlands occupies some 117,000 forested acres, including its namesake, Virginia's highest peak. Two of Virginia's finest rails-to-trails hiking, biking, and riding paths serve as bookends to the 60-mile-long recreation area: the New River Trail near Wytheville, and the Virginia Creeper Trail, from Abingdon to White Top Mountain. See chapter 8.

- **Back Bay National Wildlife Refuge/False Cape State Park:** You can't sunbathe or swim on the beach of Back Bay National Wildlife Refuge, a mere 15 miles south of the heavily developed resort area of Virginia Beach, but you can hike through the dunes or take a canoe into the marshes, an Atlantic Flyway landing zone for migrating birds. You can sunbathe and swim at the adjoining False Cape State Park, but it's so out of the way that you'll have to bring your own drinking water. See chapter 11.

- **Assateague Island:** Of all the natural areas in Virginia, none surpasses Assateague Island, which keeps the Atlantic Ocean from the back bays of Chincoteague. Here you will find the famous wild ponies grazing in Chincoteague National Wildlife Refuge, and relatively tame humans strolling some 37 miles of pristine beach. Assateague Island is also one of the nation's prime places to watch birds, for it, too, is situated directly on the Atlantic Flyway. See chapter 11.

4 The Best Scenic Drives

The best way—some of us think the *only* way—to see Virginia is by car, and with very good reason: the Old Dominion has some of America's most scenic drives.

- **George Washington Memorial Parkway:** Stay away from this route during rush hour, when it becomes a major commuter artery into and out of Washington, D.C. But any other time, the "G.W. Parkway" is a great scenic drive along the Potomac River from I-495 at the Maryland line all the way to Mount Vernon. The river views of Washington's monuments are unparalleled. See chapter 4.

- **Skyline Drive:** Few roads anywhere can top the Skyline Drive, which twists and turns 105 miles along the Blue Ridge crest in Shenandoah National Park. The views down over the rolling Piedmont to the east and the Shenandoah Valley to the west are nothing short of spectacular, especially during spring, when the wildflowers are in bloom, and in fall, when the leaves change color from green to brilliant hues of rust, orange, and yellow. See chapter 7.

- **Interstate 81 & U.S. 11:** Few interstate highways are as beautiful as I-81, which runs the entire length of Virginia from the Shenandoah Valley all the way through the Southwest Highlands to Tennessee. Alongside, the old Valley Pike (now U.S. 11) is a scenic excursion back to the 1950s, complete with old-fashioned gas stations, clapboard houses, and small-town restaurants. See chapters 7 and 8.
- **Lexington to Hot Springs:** While I-81 runs down the floor of Virginia's great valleys, other roads offer a very different scenic treat by cutting across the mountains. One of these is Va. 39, which runs from Lexington to Hot Springs via the Goshen Pass, a picturesque gorge cut by the Maury River. You can make a loop by continuing north from Hot Springs via U.S. 220 to the beautiful village of Monterey in "Virginia's Switzerland." From Monterey, you can cross the mountains via U.S. 250 to Staunton and I-81. See chapter 7.
- **Blue Ridge Parkway:** Actually a continuation of the Skyline Drive, this road continues along the Blue Ridge crest all the way south to the Great Smoky Mountains National Park in North Carolina. Of the 218 miles in Virginia, the most scenic are north of Roanoke, where you'll find it difficult to keep your eyes on the road, as the parkway often runs right along the ridgeline, with views down both sides of the mountain at once. See chapter 8.
- **Colonial Parkway:** It's not very long, but the Colonial Parkway between Jamestown, Williamsburg, and Yorktown has its scenic merits, especially the views of the James River near Jamestown and of the York River near Yorktown. The parkway goes through a tunnel under the heart of Colonial Williamsburg. See chapter 10.
- **Chesapeake Bay Bridge-Tunnel:** One of the man-made wonders of the world, the Chesapeake Bay Bridge-Tunnel runs for 17 miles over—and under—the mouth of the Chesapeake Bay between Norfolk and the Eastern Shore. You can barely see dry land when you're out in the middle. See chapter 11.

5 The Best Small Towns

Another good reason to see Virginia by car is its many lovely small towns, the best of them capturing and keeping alive the state's storied history. This is especially true in the Shenandoah Valley, where first the Valley Pike, then U.S. 11, and now I-81 string together Winchester, Strasburg, Staunton, and Lexington, all possessed of 18th- and 19th-century brick and stone buildings.

- **Waterford Village:** Founded by Quakers in the late 1700s, the little hamlet of Waterford went into a time capsule in 1870 when the railroad bypassed it in favor of nearby Leesburg. Today it looks very much like it did then, its houses carefully preserved by private owners. See chapter 4.
- **Middleburg:** The self-proclaimed unofficial capital of Virginia's horse-loving Hunt Country, Middleburg takes up barely 6 blocks along U.S. 50, making it small enough to be digested in an afternoon. Some of the world's wealthiest individuals keep their horses near Middleburg, and the town has a host of upscale shops in buildings dating back to the 1700s. See chapter 4.
- **Monterey:** Over Shenandoah and Bull Pasture Mountains from Staunton, the little village of Monterey appears more like New England than Virginia, with its white churches and clapboard homes nestled in a picturesque valley. Thousands of visitors make the trek over the mountains during the annual Highland Maple Festival in March. See chapter 7.

- **Lexington:** Not only one of Virginia's but also one of America's best small towns, Lexington has a lively college atmosphere in addition to a host of historical sights. It's home to Virginia Military Institute (VMI), where Gen. Thomas J. "Stonewall" Jackson taught; its student body went off to the Civil War at New Market. After the war, Robert E. Lee came here as president of Washington College, now known as Washington and Lee University. VMI was also the alma mater of Gen. George C. Marshall, winner of the Nobel Peace Prize for the post–World War II Marshall Plan to rebuild Europe. Jackson, Lee, and Marshall are buried here, and the town has three fine museums dedicated to these great leaders. On top of all that, Lexington's downtown looks so much like it did when Jackson and Lee were here that only dirt had to be added to Main Street's pavement to film the movie *Sommersby*. See chapter 7.
- **Abingdon:** Daniel Boone opened Virginia's Southwest Highlands to settlement in the 1770s, and it wasn't long before a thriving town grew up at Abingdon. Homes and buildings dating back to 1779 still line shady Main Street, making Abingdon a wonderful place for a stroll. The town's beauty has attracted a community of artists, craftspeople, and actors. The latter perform at the famous Barter Theatre, where, if you really insist, you can still barter for a ticket. See chapter 8.
- **Onancock:** Relatively isolated on the Eastern Shore, little Onancock was incorporated in 1690 and was for more than 2 centuries an important Chesapeake Bay shipping port. The great ferries don't run anymore between Norfolk and Baltimore, and U.S. 13 passes a mile east of town, leaving Onancock as a lovely reminder of the old days of planters and merchants. See chapter 11.

6 The Best Beaches

If you want to find a great beach in Virginia, just head east. The Atlantic Ocean surf beats all along the state's shoreline, from North Carolina to Maryland. Fortunately for conservationists, however, not all of this coastline is easily accessible to travelers.

- **Virginia Beach:** Okay, it's developed, but this resort still has a seemingly unending fine-sand beach with excellent surf. The resort itself is one of Virginia's best family destinations, with much more to do than sun and swim, including visiting one of the country's top science museums. See chapter 11.
- **Back Bay National Wildlife Refuge/False Cape State Park:** Also among the best of the great outdoors, these two preserves are just 15 miles south of—but a developed world removed from—Virginia Beach. You can't swim or sunbathe at the refuge's deserted beach, but you can hike or bike south to False Cape State Park. Carry your own drinking water—it's that isolated and undeveloped. See chapter 11.
- **Assateague Island:** This 37-mile-long barrier island is completely within the Assateague Island National Seashore, which has prevented all development along this stretch of golden sand. The National Park Service has been kind enough to build bathhouses and rest rooms on one end of the beach; otherwise, it belongs to the seagulls and to hardy souls who don't mind a hike. The Virginia end of the island is also home to Chincoteague National Wildlife Refuge, where the famous Chincoteague wild horses roam. See chapter 11.

7 The Best Family Vacations

A vast majority of Virginia's visitors arrive by car, and most of them are families. Accordingly, the state's major attractions and resorts are well equipped to entertain and care for children. It's a great place for kids to learn about American history while still enjoying a good time at the beach or at one of the state's three major amusement parks.

- **Northern Virginia:** A good place for a history lesson is in northern Virginia, especially at Mount Vernon, Old Town Alexandria, and Arlington National Cemetery. Of course, Arlington is just across the Potomac River from Washington, D.C., where the kids can roam the National Air and Space Museum and other key attractions. See chapter 4.
- **Shenandoah National Park:** Two lodges in the most popular part of Shenandoah National Park make this scenic wonderland a great place for family vacations. The kids can participate in ranger programs, hike to waterfalls, or go for a pony ride in the mountain forests. See chapter 7.
- **Richmond:** The state capital has several attractions of interest to children, including the hands-on Science Museum of Virginia. The big draws, however, are the wild rides and movie and TV characters at the huge Paramount's Kings Dominion amusement park north of the city. See chapter 9.
- **Colonial Williamsburg:** The historic area of Colonial Williamsburg is the best place of all for children to get a quick lesson in American history. On the streets, they might run into Thomas Jefferson and have a conversation about the Declaration of Independence, or perhaps practice marching and drilling with the 18th-century militia. As soon as they get bored, head for Busch Gardens Williamsburg or Water Country USA, two nearby theme parks. See chapter 10.
- **Virginia Beach:** First there's the beach, all 4 miles or so, with lifeguards during summer—but that's not all Virginia Beach has to offer. Rainy days can be spent at the local Virginia Marine Science Museum—the state's most popular museum. Norfolk's NAUTICUS, Hampton's Virginia Air and Space Center, and Colonial Williamsburg are all just short drives away. See chapter 11.
- **Chincoteague:** The little fishing village was the setting for Marguerite Henry's classic children's book *Misty of Chincoteague,* and there are plenty of wild horses (called "ponies" here) in Chincoteague National Wildlife Refuge on Assateague Island, which also has a lifeguarded beach for swimming during the summer. The best time to see the horses is during the annual pony swim the last week in July. See chapter 11.

8 The Most Unusual Travel Experiences

A museum devoted to hounds, a stalactite organ, an 18th-century version of today's Jacuzzi, a stuffed horse, and a cruise to Elizabethan times all make for unusual travel in Virginia.

- **Tally Ho! (Leesburg):** The Hunt Country gets its name from the hounds, horses, and very wealthy people who hunt foxes for sport here. You can learn all about the history of this aristocratic pastime at Leesburg's Morven Park, home to the Museum of Hounds and Hunting. See chapter 4.

- **Chimes Down Under (Luray):** There are several caverns under the Shenandoah Valley, but one of the most fascinating is at Luray. Through subterranean rooms more than 140 feet high comes beautiful organ music—but not from a man-made instrument. Well, almost not man-made. Thanks to modern technology, hammers striking million-year-old stalactites make this wonderful music. See chapter 7.
- **Ancient Hot Tubs (Warm Springs):** Eighteenth-century travelers couldn't climb into the hotel Jacuzzi after a rough day on the road—unless, that is, they pulled into Warm Springs. Since 1761, travelers have slipped their weary bodies into these natural rock pools whose circulating waters range from 94°F to 104°F. You can, too. See chapter 7.
- **Mounting Little Sorrel (Lexington):** After he died of wounds accidentally inflicted by his own men at the Battle of Chancellorsville, Gen. Stonewall Jackson was brought home and buried in Lexington, where he had taught at Virginia Military Institute before the conflagration. One of the key exhibits at VMI's museum is the bullet-pierced raincoat Jackson was wearing that disastrous night. And thanks to taxidermy, there stands the hide of his war horse, Little Sorrel. Nearby, Robert E. Lee's horse Traveller is buried just outside Lee Chapel, his master's resting place. See chapter 7.
- **Hoi Toide Tonoit (Tangier Island):** Out in the Chesapeake Bay sits remote Tangier Island, whose residents have been so isolated over the centuries that they still speak with the Elizabethan brogue of their forebears. Out here, "high tide tonight" is pronounced *hoi toide tonoit*—as in "hoity-toity"—and narrow 17th-century lanes barely can accommodate modern automobiles. Cruises leave from Onancock on the Eastern Shore and from Reedville on the Northern Neck. See chapters 5 and 11.

9 The Best Country Inns

With all of its old homes and gorgeous countryside, it's no wonder that Virginia is a hotbed of country inns and bed-and-breakfasts. Some have been in business since colonial times, and a few are among the best America has to offer. My picks barely touch the surface.

- **Tides Inn (Irvington):** Down by the Chesapeake Bay in Virginia's Tidewater, the Tides Inn is a sprawling resort complex beside a broad creek near the eastern end of the Northern Neck. The Stephens family has maintained a tradition of gracious service here since 1946. Guests can go boating on the Chesapeake Bay or play golf on a creekside course. See chapter 5.
- **Clifton, The Country Inn (Charlottesville):** You'll think you've arrived at Tara from *Gone With the Wind* when you first glimpse the tall white columns fronting this stately manse, built in 1790 by Thomas Mann Randolph, who married Thomas Jefferson's daughter Martha. Clifton today adds all the modern comforts, an energetic young staff, and chef Craig Hartman's gourmet cuisine to its Jefferson-era charms. See chapter 6.
- **Wayside Inn (Middletown):** Located in the tiny Shenandoah Valley village of Middletown, the Wayside Inn has been serving travelers since stagecoaches started prowling the Valley Pike (now U.S. 11) in 1797. Restored by an antiques collector in the 1960s, today's rooms are decorated with an assortment of 18th- and 19th-century pieces. The Wayside Theatre is virtually next door, lending entertainment to a stop here. Just down the pike is another antiques-laden historic relic, the Hotel Strasburg. See chapter 7.

- **Inn at Little Washington (Washington):** For the best, you need look no further than the tiny Blue Ridge foothill village of Washington, which everyone in Virginia calls "Little Washington." The rooms here were designed by an English decorator, but it's the romantic restaurant that draws the most raves, as co-owner and chef Patrick O'Connell relies on regional products to produce wonderful French cuisine. See chapter 7.
- **Fort Lewis Lodge (Millboro):** One of Virginia's most unusual country inns, the Fort Lewis Lodge occupies an old mill and a rebuilt barn on a farm beside the Cowpasture River, just over the mountain from Warm Springs. A spiral staircase winds its way to three rooms inside the old silo beside the barn, and there are two log cabins with their own fireplaces. It's a great place to show urban kids a bit of farm life in beautiful surroundings. See chapter 7.
- **Camberly's Martha Washington Inn (Abingdon):** Gracing Abingdon's historic district, the center portion of this Greek Revival inn was built as a private home in 1832. You can sit in white-wicker rocking chairs on the front porch and watch the traffic on Main Street—or imagine Daniel Boone's dogs being attacked by wolves nearby. See chapter 8.

10 The Best Luxury Accommodations

With deep enough pockets, you can enjoy some of the Mid-Atlantic's best luxury accommodations in Virginia. Here are some of the finest the Old Dominion has to offer.

- **Ritz-Carlton Pentagon City (Arlington):** Although this Ritz-Carlton was built in 1990 as part of a modern shopping mall, massive china cabinets, graceful wing chairs, plush sofas, Oriental rugs, crystal sconces, and a $2.5-million collection of 18th- and 19th-century paintings and antiques make it seem from another era. So does the superb service. See chapter 4.
- **The Homestead (Hot Springs):** Outstanding service, fine cuisine, and a myriad of recreational activities are the hallmarks of this grand old establishment, in business since Thomas Jefferson's day. In fact, Jefferson was the first of seven presidents to stay here. The Homestead offers accommodations ranging from standard rooms to plush suites. PGA pro Lanny Wadkins presides over its golf course, one of Virginia's finest. See chapter 7.
- **Hotel Roanoke & Conference Center (Roanoke):** The grand, Tudor-style Hotel Roanoke stood in a wheat field when the Norfolk & Western Railroad built it in 1882 as the centerpiece of its new town called Roanoke. It was closed in 1989, but a $42-million renovation has completely restored its grand public areas to their original appearance and rebuilt all its rooms to modern standards. See chapter 8.
- **Jefferson Hotel (Richmond):** A stunning beaux arts landmark with Renaissance-style balconies and an Italian clock tower, the Jefferson was opened in 1895 by a wealthy Richmonder who wanted his city to have one of America's finest hotels. A complete 1980s restoration renewed its original splendor. See chapter 9.
- **Williamsburg Inn (Williamsburg):** Another establishment with not one but three fine golf courses, the Williamsburg Inn was built as part of the Colonial Williamsburg restoration, but looks like it might have been here in 1750. If staying in the main inn with its superb service and cuisine won't do, you can opt for one of several restored colonial houses and taverns that have been converted into accommodations. See chapter 10.

11 The Best Moderately Priced Accommodations

Virginia has far too many fine, affordably priced lodgings to mention them all here. The following are some we like best.

- **Kenmore Inn (Fredericksburg):** George Washington's brother-in-law, Fielding Lewis, once owned the property where this 1700s mansion sits, right in Fredericksburg's Old Town historic district. A sweeping staircase leads to guest rooms furnished with four-poster beds and a mix of antiques. Four rooms have working fireplaces. See chapter 5.
- **Belle Grae Inn (Staunton):** Owner Michael Organ gave up teaching at Mary Baldwin College in the 1980s to convert an 1873 hilltop Victorian house into an inn. Today his establishment includes houses ringing an entire city block, all of them beautifully restored and furnished with period pieces. The cuisine here is the best in town. See chapter 7.
- **The Breakers Resort Inn (Virginia Beach):** Among the many cookie-cutter, high-rise buildings lining Virginia Beach's oceanfront, the Breakers stands out as a family-operated hotel that's friendly to families. Efficiencies here have fully equipped, money-saving kitchens. See chapter 11.
- **Hart's Harbor House (Wachapreague):** Unlike the hosts of many small-town bed-and-breakfasts (many of whom tend to be expatriates from big cities), Tom and Pat Hart of Hart's Harbor House are born-and-bred Wachapreaguers. Accordingly, their knowledge of the Eastern Shore is unsurpassed, and they are experts at arranging boat trips out to Parramore and Cedar Islands along the Atlantic. Accommodations are in two Victorian houses they have restored (one's called Burton House Bed-and-Breakfast), both with charming screened porches. See chapter 11.

12 The Best Inexpensive Accommodations

Virginia has a large number of clean, comfortable motels of the Econo Lodge, Super 8, and Motel 6 variety. But for something a little more unique, check out the following inexpensive choices.

- **Americana Hotel (Arlington):** When my parents brought my sister and me to Washington, D.C., in 1955, we stayed at an old-fashioned motel, one of many that lined U.S. 1 in Arlington. The Americana was built a few years after that, but it still stands among the high-rise buildings of what's now known as Crystal City. It's run by the same family, and it's as clean and comfortable as ever. See chapter 4.
- **Fredericksburg Colonial Inn (Fredericksburg):** Don't be surprised to see Blues and Grays toting Civil War rifles in the lobby of the Fredericksburg Colonial Inn, so popular is this establishment with reenactment buffs. An avid collector, the owner has laden the rooms with antiques. See chapter 5.
- **The Cardinal Inn (Luray):** Built in the 1950s and 1960s but recently remodeled by an energetic local couple, The Cardinal offers clean and comfortable rooms within an easy drive of the Shenandoah National Park's prime central area. See chapter 7.
- **Roseloe Motel (Hot Springs):** You don't have to pay a fortune to stay at the Homestead—just drive 3 miles north to the Roseloe, a clean family operation across U.S. 220 from the lovely sounds of the Garth Newel Chamber Music Center. The hot pools at Warm Springs are a short drive away, and you can pay

a lot less than the cost of a room to use the Homestead's superb recreational facilities. See chapter 7.

- **Alpine Motel (Abingdon):** Another holdover from the early 1960s, the immaculate, family-run Alpine Motel has extraordinarily large rooms—common in those days when cost-per-square-foot wasn't as high as today. Although they open to a parking lot, most of the rooms have mountain views. See chapter 8.

13 The Best Culinary Experiences

Author William Styron, a native of Newport News, once said that the French consider strong, salt-cured Virginia hams to be America's only gourmet contribution to the world's cuisine. Virginians love their ham (especially stuffed into piping hot biscuits), but they are also crazy about rockfish (sea bass) and crabs from the Chesapeake Bay and shad and trout from their rivers. Their farms produce a plethora of vegetables during the summer, and their orchards are famous for autumn apples. And let's not forget the peanut, one of Virginia's major crops.

You can dine on all types of cuisine in Virginia, but the highlights here are produced from recipes handed down since colonial times—dishes such as peanut soup and Sally Lunn bread—or those that put a modern spin on fresh local ingredients. You may have tourist company, but here are some of the best places to sample Virginia's unique and very historic cuisine.

- **Gadsby's Tavern (Alexandria):** George Washington said good-bye to his troops from the door of Gadsby's Tavern in Alexandria's Old Town historic district. This old rooming house and the tavern next door look much as they did then, and a wait staff in colonial garb still serve chicken roasted on an open fire, buttermilk pie, and other dishes from that period. See chapter 4.
- **The Green Tree (Leesburg):** Most of the dishes at the Green Tree are from faithfully reproduced 18th-century recipes garnered from the Library of Congress. A smoked-sausage pie, a green-herb soup, and an oyster-flavored cabbage pie are featured offerings. See chapter 4.
- **Inn at Little Washington (Washington):** Chef Patrick O'Connell constantly changes his basically French menu to take advantage of trout, Chesapeake Bay seafood, Virginia hams, and other local delicacies at the romantic dining room of the Inn at Little Washington. The service here is extraordinarily attentive and unobtrusive. See chapter 7.
- **Mrs. Rowe's Family Restaurant and Bakery (Staunton):** Every town has its favorite "local" restaurant, where you can clog your arteries with plain old Southern favorites like pan-fried chicken, sausage gravy over biscuits, and fresh vegetables seasoned with smoked pork and cooked to smithereens. In business since 1947, Mrs. Rowe's somehow manages to cook the golden oldies without all the lard you'll ingest elsewhere. See chapter 7.
- **The Roanoker Restaurant (Roanoke):** Another favorite "local" restaurant, the Roanoaker regularly changes its menu to take advantage of the freshest vegetables available, but every day it serves the best biscuits in Virginia, hot from the oven. See chapter 8.
- **The Log House 1776 Restaurant (Wytheville):** The name is appropriate at this particular restaurant, part of which is contained in a log house built in 1776. Here you can order Thomas Jefferson's favorite, chicken marengo, or a very sweet Confederate beef-and-apple stew like the one Robert E. Lee fed his troops. See chapter 8.

- **The Frog and the Redneck (Richmond):** The "Frog" stands for the French style of cooking learned and practiced by noted chef Jimmy Sneed. The "Redneck" refers to the local ingredients he uses in his gourmet interpretations of traditional French dishes. You'll get Virginia ham and cantaloupe here, not Bayonne and melon. See chapter 9.

- **King's Barbeque (Petersburg):** Like all Southerners, Virginians love their smoked pork barbecue, and it doesn't get any better than at the two branches of King's Barbeque. Pork, beef, ribs, and chicken roast constantly over an open pit right in the dining rooms, and the sauce is served on the side, not soaking the succulent meat and overpowering its smoked flavor. See chapter 9.

- **Trellis Café, Restaurant & Grill (Williamsburg):** Chef Marcel Desaulniers has been nationally recognized for his outstanding regional cuisine, all of which emphasizes fresh local produce. Desaulniers has written three cookbooks, including *Death by Chocolate.* They don't raise cocoa in Virginia, but you can definitely die by it here. See chapter 10.

- **Old Chickahominy House (Williamsburg):** Named for a nearby river, this reconstructed, antiques-filled 18th-century house is one of the best places to sample traditional Virginia fare, such as Brunswick stew and Virginia ham on hot biscuits. See chapter 10.

- **Lynnhaven Fish House (Virginia Beach):** Wonderful water views accompany some of the state's finest traditional seafood fare at this famous restaurant, built on a fishing pier over the Chesapeake Bay. See chapter 11.

Planning a Trip to Virginia

Whether you plan to spend a day, a week, 2 weeks, or longer in Virginia, you'll need to make many where, when, and how choices before you leave home. This chapter explains how best to plan your trip.

1 The Regions in Brief

Virginia has three distinct geographic regions. Along the eastern coast, the **Tidewater** (or coastal plain) is dominated by four rivers—the Potomac, Rappahannock, York, and James—that empty into the Chesapeake Bay, one of the world's largest estuaries. These rivers divide the Tidewater into three peninsulas, or *necks* in local parlance. To the south, the Chesapeake meets the Atlantic Ocean at the large natural harbor of Hampton Roads.

The rolling hills of the **Piedmont** run through central Virginia, from Richmond and Charlottesville to the Hunt Country and suburban sprawl of northern Virginia. This farm country gently rises to meet the foothills of the **Blue Ridge Mountains.** Between the Blue Ridge and the Allegheny Mountains to the west, gorgeous valleys—including the fabled Shenandoah—extend the length of the state, from the Potomac in the north to the Southwest Highlands near the borders of Tennessee and Kentucky.

NORTHERN VIRGINIA The fastest growing, most densely populated, and wealthiest part of the state, northern Virginia today is much more than a suburban bedroom for government workers in Washington, D.C. Areas such as Tysons Corner have become unincorporated cities in their own right, with employment in high-tech service industries outstripping federal government jobs. Long known for its famous cemetery just across the Potomac from the nation's capital, Arlington today is a melting pot of immigrants from around the world—with a marvelous mix of ethnic cuisines to show for it. Centered on its historic Old Town, Alexandria offers fascinating daytime walks as well as lively nighttime entertainment and good restaurants. Beyond are the beautiful Potomac plantations, including George Washington's Mount Vernon. In Virginia's Hunt Country, sightseers can enjoy Virginia's traditional historic inns and fine restaurants. Farther south is Manassas, site of the first major battle of the Civil War.

FREDERICKSBURG & THE NORTHERN NECK The quaint cobblestone streets and historic houses of Fredericksburg recall

America's first heroes—George Washington, James Monroe, John Paul Jones—as does the quiet Northern Neck farmland, where Washington and Robert E. Lee were born. Military buffs love to explore Fredericksburg's Civil War battlefields.

CENTRAL VIRGINIA   These rolling Piedmont hills are "Mr. Jefferson's country." Charlottesville boasts his magnificent estate, Monticello, as well as the University of Virginia, which he designed. From Lynchburg, you can visit Poplar Forest, his beloved retreat, as well as Patrick Henry's final home at Red Hill and Appomattox Court House, where the Civil War ended when Robert E. Lee surrendered to Ulysses S. Grant.

THE SHENANDOAH VALLEY   Some of Virginia's most striking scenery is along the **Skyline Drive,** which follows the crest of the Blue Ridge Mountains through Shenandoah National Park, where visitors will find a host of hiking paths, including part of the famed Maine-to-Georgia Appalachian Trail. Down below, charming towns like Winchester, Staunton, and Lexington evoke the Civil War, which ebbed and flowed over the rolling countryside of the Shenandoah Valley, the South's breadbasket. Across the mountains are the famous mineral waters of Warm Springs and Hot Springs.

THE SOUTHWEST HIGHLANDS   Beyond the vibrant city of Roanoke rise the highlands of Virginia's southwestern extremity, a land of untouched forests, waterfalls, and quiet streams. Here sits the state's highest point, Mount Rogers, surrounded by a national recreation area teeming with trails for hiking, mountain biking, and horseback riding. And down in the Great Valley of Virginia, the crossroads town of Wytheville still shows signs of Daniel Boone's famous trail to Kentucky, and the quaint town of Abingdon features the famous Barter Theatre, begun during the Great Depression when its company traded tickets for hams.

RICHMOND   The state capital has few rivals among U.S. cities for its wealth of historic associations, among them St. John's Church, where Patrick Henry made his famous "Give me liberty, or give me death" speech. Fine arts and science museums, cafes, lively concerts, and theater add to Richmond's cosmopolitan ambience. Military buffs can tour the Richmond and Petersburg battlefield sites, and children can get their kicks at nearby Paramount's Kings Dominion amusement park.

WILLIAMSBURG, YORKTOWN, & JAMESTOWN   Coastal Virginia's "Historic Triangle" is one of the country's most visited areas, and with good reason. Colonial Williamsburg's 173 acres re-create Virginia's colonial capital; Yorktown commemorates the last, victorious battle of the American Revolution in 1781; and Jamestown is where America's first permanent English settlers arrived in 1607. Adding to its allure are two theme parks and world-class discount shopping. From here it's an easy excursion to one of the nation's premier maritime museums in the shipbuilding city of Newport News, and to the state's modern air and space museum in historic Hampton, the country's oldest continuous English-speaking settlement.

HAMPTON ROADS & THE EASTERN SHORE   At the mouth of the Chesapeake Bay, Hampton Roads is ringed by Virginia's largest metropolitan area, highlighted by the resurgent cities of Norfolk and Portsmouth. Here you also can play in the surf on Virginia Beach, whose boardwalk and 20 miles of white-sand beach are lined with hotels, or commune with nature in Back Bay National Wildlife Refuge and the remote False Cape State Park. You can drive across the 17-mile-long Chesapeake Bay Bridge-Tunnel to Eastern Shore, an unspoiled sanctuary noted for the charming village of Chincoteague and nearby Assateague Island, whose wildlife refuge and national seashore have protected the famous wild ponies and prevented any development on almost 40 miles of pristine beach.

2 Visitor Information

The **Virginia Tourism Corporation,** 901 E. Byrd St. (P.O. Box 798), Richmond, VA 23219 (☎ **800/VISIT-VA** or 804/786-2051; fax 804/786-1919; www.virginia.org; e-mail: vainfo@vedp.state.va.us), is the best source for information about the entire state. It publishes or distributes a host of information, including a statewide travel planner containing up-to-date calendars of events; official state highway maps showing all roads or just the scenic routes; lists of all hotels and motels and those that accept pets; a list of country inns and bed-and-breakfasts; an outdoor guide to the state (call ☎ **800/827-3325** for a copy); a golf directory; a state park directory; a list of Virginia wineries and wine festivals; and a guide for travelers with disabilities.

The corporation also operates information offices in **Washington, D.C.,** at 1629 K St. NW (☎ **202/659-5523**); in **Canada** at 1 Eva Rd., Suite 302, Etobicoke, Ontario M9C 425 (☎ **416/626-3974;** fax 416/626-3171; e-mail: toronto@ discovertheworld.ca), and at 411 Antoine-Forestier, Vimont, Laval, Québec H7M 4G1 (☎ **514/967-2681;** fax 514/967-2684); in the **United Kingdom** at 1st Floor, 182/184 Addington Rd., Selsdon, South Croydon, Surrey CR2 8LB (☎ **181/ 651-4743;** fax 181/651-5702; e-mail: geoff@ttmi.democn.co.uk); in **Germany** at Fremdenverkehrsamt Virginia, Steinweg 3, D-60313 Frankfurt (☎ **69/291923;** fax 69/291904; e-mail: vawild@aol.com); and in **Japan** at Travel South USA, Koa Bldg. 3F, 2-38-14 Hakusan, Bunkyo-ku, Tokyo 112-0001 (☎ **3/3814-3140;** fax 03/3814-7889).

If you're driving into Virginia, you can stop at roadside **Welcome Centers** in Bracey, on I-85 near the North Carolina border; Bristol, on I-81 near the Tennessee border; Clear Brook, on I-81 near the West Virginia border; Covington, on I-64 near the West Virginia border; New Church, on U.S. 13 at the Maryland border; Fredericksburg, on I-95 southbound; Lambsburg, on I-77; Manassas, on I-66; Rocky Gap, on I-77; and Skippers, on I-95.

3 When to Go

Virginia is a gorgeous place in October, when the Indian summer weather is at its finest and the turning leaves blaze orange, red, and yellow across the state. October also is the most crowded time in the western part of the state, when throngs of visitors mob the mountains to see the autumn foliage during this "leaf season." (You can find out the approximate dates for peak color by calling ☎ **800/434-5323** for the Shenandoah Valley, ☎ **540/999-3500** for Shenandoah National Park and the Skyline Drive, and ☎ **704/298-0398** for Virginia's portion of the Blue Ridge Parkway.)

Otherwise, Virginia is busiest during summer, when the historic sites, theme parks, and beaches draw millions of visitors from around the world—and hotel rates are at their highest. The least crowded—and least expensive—time to visit is in spring. Fortunately, that's when the dogwoods, azaleas, and wildflowers are in a riot of bloom from one end of Virginia to the other.

THE CLIMATE

Virginia enjoys four distinct seasons, with some variations in temperature from the warmer, more humid coastal areas to the cooler climate in the mountains. Wintertime snows are usually confined to northern Virginia and the mountains. In summer, extremely hot and humid spells can last several weeks, but are normally short-lived. Spring and autumn are long seasons, and in terms of natural beauty and heavenly climate, they're optimum times to visit. Annual rainfall averages 46 inches; annual snowfall, 18 inches.

Virginia's Average Temperatures

	Jan	Feb	Mar	Apr	May	June	July	Aug	Sept	Oct	Nov	Dec
High °F (°C)	44 (6)	46(8)	56 (13)	68 (20)	75 (24)	84 (29)	90 (32)	88 (31)	81 (27)	69 (21)	57 (14)	47 (8)
Low °F (°C)	26 (–3)	27 (–3)	38 (3)	45 (7)	54 (12)	62 (17)	66 (19)	65 (18)	59 (15)	48 (9)	39 (4)	28 (–2)

Virginia Calendar of Events

January

- **Historic Birthday Parties,** Lexington. The historic town throws a birthday bash for its Civil War heroes, Robert E. Lee and Stonewall Jackson. Call ☎ **540/463-2552** or 540/463-8767. Mid-January.
- **Wildlife Arts Festival,** Newport News. Artists display and sell stained glass, carvings, oils, watercolors, and photography, all with a wildlife theme. Call ☎ **757/595-1900.** Mid-January.
- **Lee Birthday Celebrations,** Alexandria. Period music, plus house tours at Lee-Fendall House and Lee's boyhood home. Call ☎ **703/548-1789.** Fourth Sunday in January. Also, open house at Stratford Hall on the Northern Neck, Lee's birthplace. January 19.

February

- **Antiques Forum,** Williamsburg. Lectures and workshops on 18th-century life. Call ☎ **800/603-0948.** First week in February.
- **Maymont Flower and Garden Show,** Richmond. A breath of spring, with landscape exhibits, vendors, and speakers. Call ☎ **804/358-7166,** ext. 341. Early February.
- ✪ **George Washington Birthday Events,** Alexandria. Black-tie or colonial-costume Saturday evening dinner, followed by birth-night ball at Gadsby's Tavern, where George and Martha Washington attended balls in 1798 and 1799. On Sunday, Revolutionary War encampment at Fort Ward, featuring a skirmish between British and colonial uniformed troops. Parade on Monday. Call ☎ **703/838-9350** or 703/838-4242 for information and tickets. Presidents' Day weekend.
- **George Washington's Birthday Party,** Fredericksburg. Reduced rates at attractions. Call ☎ **800/678-4748** or 540/373-1569. Monday of Washington's Birthday weekend.

March

- **James Madison's Birthday,** Montpelier. Ceremony at cemetery and reception at house. Call ☎ **540/672-2728.** March 16.
- **Virginia Festival of the Book,** Charlottesville. Tributes, seminars, and readings by authors and poets, some famous. Call ☎ **804/924-3296.** www.vabook.org. Mid-March.
- **Patrick Henry Speech Reenactment,** St. John's Church, Richmond. "Give me liberty, or give me death," he said here. Call ☎ **804/648-5015.** Closest Sunday to March 23.
- ✪ **Highland Maple Festival, Monterey.** See maple syrup produced, pour it over pancakes, and visit one of the state's largest crafts shows. Call ☎ **540/468-2550** for information. Second and third weekends in March.

April

- **Thomas Jefferson's Birthday Commemoration,** Monticello, Charlottesville. Wreath-laying ceremony at gravesite, fife-and-drum corps, and a speaker. Call ☎ **804/984-9822.** April 13.
- ✪ **International Azalea Festival,** Norfolk. The brilliant beauty of azaleas in bloom is the backdrop for ceremonies in the Norfolk Botanical Garden saluting NATO countries, including the crowning of a queen who reigns at a parade and other festivities. Also features a military display that includes an air show, visiting of ships, and aircraft ground exhibits. Call ☎ **757/622-6647,** ext. 1. Second to third week in April.
- **Virginia Waterfront International Arts Festival,** Williamsburg, Hampton, Newport News, Norfolk, Virginia Beach. Famous performers appear at venues from Williamsburg to Virginia during month-long festival. Call ☎ **800/368-3097** (Norfolk) or 800/446-8038 (Virginia Beach). Mid-April to mid-May.
- **Virginia Horse Festival,** Virginia Horse Center, Lexington. All breeds are showcased with demonstrations, events, seminars, sales, and equine art and merchandise. Call ☎ **540/463-2194.** Third weekend in April.
- ✪ **Historic Garden Week in Virginia,** statewide. The event of the year—a celebration with tours of the grounds and gardens of some 200 Virginia landmarks, including plantations and other sites open only during this week. For information contact the **Garden Club of Virginia,** 12 E. Franklin St., Richmond, VA 23219 (☎ **804/644-7776** or 804/643-7141; www.vagardenweek.org). Last full week in April.

May

- ✪ **Shenandoah Apple Blossom Festival,** Winchester. Acres of orchards in blossom throughout the valley, plus 5 days of music, band competitions, parades, coronation of the queen, footraces, arts and crafts sale, midway amusements, and a carnival, with a celebrity grand marshal. Contact **Festival,** 5 N. Cameron St., Winchester, VA 22601 (☎ **703/662-3863**). Usually first weekend in May.
- **Virginia Gold Cup Race Meet,** Great Meadow Course, The Plains. Everyone dresses to the nines for the state's premier steeplechase event. Call ☎ **540/347-2612.** First Saturday in May.
- **Seafood Festival,** Tom's Cove, Chincoteague. All you can eat—a seafood lover's dream come true. You must get tickets in advance from **Eastern Shore Chamber of Commerce,** P.O. Drawer R, Melfa, VA 23410 (☎ **757/787-2460**). First weekend in May.
- **George Mason Day,** Gunston Hall, Lorton. All-day celebration with music and costumed role-players portraying Mason's daily life and concern for the Bill of Rights. Call ☎ **703/550-9220.** May 5.
- **Jamestown Landing Day,** Jamestown. Militia presentations and sailing demonstrations celebrate the first settlers. Call ☎ **757/253-4838.** Early May.
- **New Market Battlefield Historical Park,** New Market. Reenactment of battle. Call ☎ **540/740-3212.** Second Sunday in May.
- **New Market Day,** Virginia Military Institute Campus, Lexington. Annual roll call of cadets who died in the battle. Call ☎ **540/463-3777.** May 15.
- **Oatlands Sheepdog Trials,** Leesburg. Dogs compete in sheepherding contests. Crafts, food, and house and garden tours. Call ☎ **703/777-3174.** Late May.

✪ **Virginia Hunt Country Stable Tour,** Loudon County. A unique opportunity to view prestigious Leesburg, Middleburg, and Upperville horse farms and private estates. Ticket information at **Trinity Church,** Upperville (near Middleburg; ☎ **540/592-3711**). Late May.

• **Shenandoah Valley Music Festival,** Orkney Springs. Classical to country-and-western fill the mountain air. Call **Orkney Springs Hotel** at ☎ **800/459-3396.** Starts Memorial Day weekend, then weekends through August.

June

• **Vintage Virginia Wine Festival,** Great Meadows Steeplechase Course, The Plains. Taste the premium vintages from 35 wineries at this Hunt Country festival. Arts and crafts displays, food, and jazz, reggae, and pop music. Call ☎ **800/277-CORK** for information about this and many other wine festivals statewide. First weekend in June.

• **Harborfest,** Norfolk. Tall ships, sailboat races, air shows, military demonstrations, and fireworks. Call ☎ **757/441-2345.** First full weekend in June.

• **Boardwalk Art Show,** Virginia Beach. Works in all mediums, between 14th Street and 28th Street along the boardwalk. Call ☎ **757/425-0000.** Mid-June.

✪ **James River Bateaux Festival,** Lynchburg. Old-fashioned "bateaux" boats race to Richmond. Music at the riverfront, footraces, games, and historic crafts exhibits and demonstrations. The 8-day festival moves along the James, stopping each night at a historic town along the 200-year-old river route. Call ☎ **804/528-3950** or 804/847-1811. Second to third week in June.

✪ **Ash Lawn–Highland Summer Festival,** Charlottesville. James Monroe's home is the setting for opera, musicals, concerts, and a traditional bonfire finale. Tickets from the box office or in town (☎ **804/293-9539**). End of June to August.

• **Hampton Jazz Festival,** Hampton. Big names perform at Hampton Coliseum. Call ☎ **800/800-2202** or 757/838-4203. Late June.

July

• **Independence Day Celebrations,** statewide. Every town parties and shoots fireworks in honor of the nation's birthday. Contact local tourist information offices. July 4.

• **Stratford Hall Open House.** Honoring Richard Henry Lee and Francis Lightfoot Lee, the only two brothers to sign the Declaration of Independence. Call ☎ **804/493-8038.** July 4.

✪ **Pony Swim and Auction,** Chincoteague. Famous wild horses swim the Assateague Channel, and are later herded to carnival grounds and auctioned off. Return swim to Assateague on Friday. Call ☎ **757/336-6161.** Festival is last 2 weeks in July; swim on last Wednesday in July.

August

✪ **Virginia Highlands Festival,** Abingdon. Appalachian Mountain culture showcase for musicians, artists, artisans, and writers. Area's largest crafts show has antique market and hot-air balloons. Call ☎ **800/676-2282** or 540/676-3440; www.va-highlandsfestival.org. First 2 weeks in August.

• **Old Time Fiddlers' Convention,** Galax. Dating to 1935, one of the largest and oldest such conventions in the world. It also coincides with the Fiddlefest street festival. Call ☎ **540/236-8541** or 540/238-8130 for information. Early August.

• **Hot Air Balloon Festival and Flying Circus Airshows,** Bealeton. One of the largest regional conventions of hot-air balloons. Biplanes barnstorm and offer open-air cockpit rides. Call ☎ **540/439-8661.** Balloon Festival is mid-month; flying circus, weekends May to October.

Virginia's Vinos

When Thomas Jefferson returned home to Charlottesville in 1789 after 5 years in Paris as minister to France, he brought with him a keen appreciation for fine wine. Although Virginians had grown grapes since the early 1600s, there just wasn't enough good wine made here to satisfy Mr. Jefferson's tastes.

Too bad he can't come back to life today, for Jefferson would find his beloved commonwealth dotted with more than 140 vineyards and 50 wineries. Most turn out between 2,000 and 8,000 cases a year (if this were beer, we would call them microbreweries). Despite their small sizes, however, together they produce some 2.5 million bottles annually, ranking Virginia as the nation's fifth-largest wine-producing state behind California, Washington, Oregon, and New York.

Moderately good wines at moderate prices best describes Virginia's product. Vines require lots of sunshine to produce great grapes, so the state usually doesn't produce the quality of grapes grown in sunnier France, Italy, and California. And since the amount of rays falling on Virginia varies from year to year, so can the quality of its vintages. The relatively dry years of 1997 and 1998 produced good crops, and drought-stricken 1999 promised to do likewise.

Chardonnay is the most widely grown grape here, of which **Barboursville Vineyards'** 1997 Reserve and **Jefferson Vineyards'** 1998 Signature Reserve are among the most popular, but many experts say viognier is perhaps the best-suited white grape for Virginia. **Horton Vineyards'** viognier is one of the few local wines to reap international acclaim. You'll also find Riesling in good quantity. Among the reds, cabernet sauvignon is the most widely planted grape, with cabernet franc a rising star (Barboursville Vineyards' 1997 cabernet franc won the prestigious Governor's Cup as Virginia's best wine).

Most of the state's gourmet groceries and wine and cheese shops sell Virginia wines, and occasionally you'll find them in supermarket beer-and-wine sections. But the best places to sample them are in the state's better Virginia restaurants or by actually visiting the wineries that have tasting rooms (wine-logo road tour signs will show you the way). You can also taste them in August at the **Virginia Wine Festival,** at Great Meadow racetrack near The Plains in the Hunt Country (☎ **800/520-9670**), and at other festivals held every weekend, especially in October, the state's official Wine Month.

The **Virginia Division of Wine Marketing,** P.O. Box 1163, Richmond, VA 23218 (☎ **800/828-4637;** www.state.va.us/home/wine.html), publishes an annual directory of wineries and wine festivals. Copies are available from the Virginia Tourism Corporation (see "Visitor Information," above). The division and the corporation jointly offer specialized wine country travel packages; call ☎ **888/829-6437** for details.

Information also is online at the **Virginia Wine Country Web site** (www.va-wine.com), and you can order copies of the quarterly trade newspaper *Virginia Wine Gazette,* 17–19 Morristown Rd., Bernardsville, NJ 07924 (☎ **908/766-3900,** ext. 19; fax 908/766-6365).

September

- **American Music Festival,** Virginia Beach. Top entertainers perform on the sand. Tickets are first come, first served. Call ☎ **800/446-8030** or 757/491-SUNN. Labor Day weekend.

County Fairs

In addition to the fun-filled State Fair of Virginia in Richmond each September, the state has more than 50 local fairs featuring agricultural products, handcrafts, cooking, and, of course, a midway with carnival rides. For a complete annual schedule, contact the **Virginia Association of Fairs,** P.O. Box 886, Salem, VA 24153 (☎ **540/375-4013**).

- **Miller Genuine Draft/Autolite Platinum 200 Auto Race,** Richmond. Two-day stock-car event at the International Raceway. Call ☎ **804/345-7223.** Early September.
- **Apple Harvest Arts & Crafts Festival,** Winchester. Bookend to Winchester's apple festival; the fruit is made into butter, pies, and cobblers, but arts and crafts take the spotlight. Square dancing, mountain music, and food, too. Call ☎ **540/662-3996.** Third weekend in September.
- **Northern Neck Seafood Extravaganza,** Ingleside Winery, Oak Grove. Oysters, crabs, shrimp, and clams, all washed down with fine vintages. Call ☎ **804/224-8687.** Third Saturday in September.
- **State Fair of Virginia,** Richmond. Rides, entertainment, agricultural exhibits, pioneer farmstead, and flower shows. At Strawberry Hill Fairgrounds. Call ☎ **800/588-3247** or 804/228-3200. Ten days in late September.

October

- **Chincoteague Oyster Festival,** Chincoteague. A feast of oysters—but for advance ticket holders only. Call ☎ **804/336-6161.** Early October.
- **Michelob Championship at Kingsmill,** Williamsburg. PGA golfers compete in Virginia's top pro golf tournament. Call ☎ **757/253-3985.** Early October.
- ✪ **Waterford Homes Tour and Crafts Exhibit,** Waterford Village. The tiny Quaker town grows to some 40,000 on this one weekend. Call ☎ **540/882-3085** for tickets. First weekend in October.
- **Virginia Film Festival,** Charlottesville. Tribute to all things celluloid. Call ☎ **800/882-3378** for tickets, 804/924-3376 for information. www.vafilm.com. Starts mid-October.
- **Yorktown Day.** British surrender in 1781 celebrated with a parade, historic house tours, colonial music and dress, and military drills. Call ☎ **757/898-3400.** October 19.
- **International Gold Cup,** Great Meadows Course, The Plains. Fall colors provide a backdrop to one of the most prestigious steeplechase races. Call ☎ **540/253-5001.** Third Saturday in October.
- **Marine Corps Marathon,** Arlington. More than 18,000 men and women run the regulation 26.2-mile course from Arlington through Washington, D.C., and back. The U.S. Marine Corps' "People's Marathon" is open to all (there's even a wheelchair division). Call ☎ **800/786-8762** or 703/784-2225. Third or fourth Sunday in October.

November

- **The First Thanksgiving,** Charles City. Reenactment at Berkeley Plantation. Call ☎ **804/829-6018.** Early November.
- ✪ **Assateague Island Waterfowl Week,** Chincoteague. The only time of the year when visitors can drive to the northern end of Chincoteague National Wildlife Refuge on Assateague Island. Guided walks for pedestrians. Call ☎ **757/336-6122.** Thanksgiving weekend.

December
- **Mount Vernon by Candlelight,** Mount Vernon. See Washington's mansion as he would have, by the light of candles. Tickets required. Call ☎ **703/780-2000.** First week in December.
- **Grand Illumination,** Williamsburg. Gala opening of holiday season with fife-and-drum corps, illumination of buildings, caroling, dancing, and fireworks. Call ☎ **800/246-2099.** First Saturday in December.
- **Christmas Candlelight Tour,** Fredericksburg. Call ☎ **800/634-4118** or 540/ 371-4504. First weekend in December.
- **Monticello Candlelight Tour,** Charlottesville. Call ☎ **804/984-9822.** Early December.
- **Historic Michie Tavern Feast and Open House,** Charlottesville. The old tavern puts on two Christmastime feasts. Reservations required. Call ☎ **804/ 977-1234.** Second weekend in December.
- **Jamestown Christmas,** Jamestown. Call ☎ **757/253-4838.** Second to fourth week in December.

4 The Active Vacation Planner

Although Virginia is best known for its multitude of historic sites, it's also home to a host of outdoor activities. You'll find them described in the chapters that follow, but here's a brief overview of the best places to move your muscles, with tips on how to get more detailed information.

The Virginia Tourism Corporation publishes an annual *Virginia Outdoors* magazine that gives a comprehensive rundown of the activities available, a calendar of outdoor events, and a list of the many outfitters and tour companies operating in the state. Call ☎ **800/827-3325** for a copy, or see "Visitor Information," above.

BICYCLING & MOUNTAIN BIKING   Bicycling is popular throughout Virginia, and with very good reason. Most of the state's scenic highways are open to bicycles: the 17-mile George Washington Memorial Parkway between Arlington and Mount Vernon (see chapter 4), the 105-mile Skyline Drive above the Shenandoah Valley (see chapter 7), the 218-mile Blue Ridge Parkway in the Southwest Highlands (see chapter 8), and the 22-mile Colonial Parkway between Jamestown and Yorktown (see chapter 10), to name the most popular.

The state also has three excellent "rails-to-trails" parks, in which old railroad beds have been turned into biking and hiking avenues. In northern Virginia there's the Washington & Old Dominion Trail, which begins in Arlington and ends 45 miles away at Purcellville in the rolling hills of the Hunt Country (see the Arlington section in chapter 4). The Southwest Highlands boasts two dramatic trails that go through some of the state's finest mountain scenery (see chapter 8). The 34-mile Virginia Creeper Trail begins in the Mount Rogers National Recreation Area high up on the flanks of Whitetop Mountain, Virginia's second-highest peak, and descends to Abingdon (see the Abingdon section in chapter 8). Near Wytheville, the 55-mile New River Trail follows the New River, which actually is one of the world's oldest rivers (see the Wytheville section in chapter 8). Outfitters along both trails rent bikes and provide shuttle services so you don't have to ride both ways—particularly handy on the Virginia Creeper Trail, which drops more than 3,000 feet from Whitetop Mountain to Damascus, near Abingdon.

Down on the coast, bikers can ride along the Virginia Beach boardwalk, through the natural beauty of First Landing/Seashore State Park and Back Bay National

Wildlife Refuge, into the heart of the Great Dismal Swamp, and along all of the flat Eastern Shore roads (see chapter 11).

Statewide, Virginia is crossed by sections of three major Interstate bicycle routes. The Maine-to-Virginia Route 1 runs 150 miles from Arlington to Richmond and connects to 130 miles of the Virginia-to-Florida Route 17 from Richmond to the North Carolina line at Suffolk. Some 500 miles of the TransAmerican Bicycle Trail (Route 76) run from the Kentucky line to Yorktown, including a stretch through Mount Rogers National Recreation Area in the Southwest Highlands. For strip maps of these routes, contact **Adventure Cycling Association,** P.O. Box 8308, Missoula, MT 59807 (☎ **406/721-1776**).

Some of the state's bed-and-breakfasts are connected through inn-to-inn bicycle tours, in which you ride 20 to 30 miles a day, then stay overnight in B&Bs. **Eastern Shore Escapes** (☎ **888/VA-SHORE;** www.vashore.com/escapes; e-mail: esescapes@esva.net) has nature-oriented guided trips on the flat Eastern Shore. **Old Dominion Bicycle Tours** in Powhatan (☎ **888/296-5036** or 804/598-1808; www.olddominionbike.qpg.com) has excursions with lodging in tents and cabins as well as B&Bs. And **Pineapple Peddlers of Rockingham County** (☎ **800/893-2516**) will guide you through the Shenandoah Valley and along the Skyline Drive from its base in beautiful Lexington.

Mountain bikers can find plenty of trails, especially in Mount Rogers National Recreation Area and in the George Washington and Jefferson National Forests, which occupy large parts of the Shenandoah Valley (see chapter 7) and the Southwest Highlands (see chapter 8). For details about the latter, contact the **George Washington and Jefferson National Forests,** 210 Franklin Rd. SW, Roanoke, VA 24004 (☎ **540/265-6054**). *Mountain Bike Virginia,* by Scott Adams (Beachway Press, 1995), is a very handy atlas to Virginia's best trails, with excellent maps.

The **Virginia Department of Transportation's Bicycle Coordinator,** 1401 E. Broad St., Richmond, VA 23219 (☎ **800/835-1203** or 804/786-2964; www.vdot.state.va; e-mail: vabiking@vdot.state.va.us), publishes the annual *Virginia Bicycling Guide,* which describes Virginia's routes and trails and lists local bike clubs and relevant publications. Contact the department or the Virginia Tourism Corporation (see "Visitor Information," above) for a free copy.

BIRD WATCHING   The big bird-watching draws in Virginia are waterfowl nesting in the flatlands and marshes along the coast, all of them on the Atlantic Flyway. Chincoteague National Wildlife Refuge on Assateague Island and Back Bay National Wildlife Refuge below Virginia Beach offer first-rate bird-watching opportunities. Chincoteague is especially good on Thanksgiving weekend, the only time the refuge's back roads are open to vehicles. See chapter 11.

BOATING   The Chesapeake Bay and its many tributaries, including the Potomac, Rappahannock, York, and James rivers, are perfect for boating. In fact, you can come away from eastern Virginia with the impression that every other home has a boat and trailer sitting in the yard. Marinas abound on the Northern Neck (see chapter 5), and you can rent boats in Hampton Roads and over on the Eastern Shore, where the back bays of Chincoteague and Wachapreague await to be explored from a fish's-eye view (see chapter 11).

A detailed map showing public access to the Chesapeake and its tributaries is available from the **Virginia Department of Conservation and Recreation,** 203 Governor St., Suite 302, Richmond, VA 23219 (☎ **804/786-1712**).

CANOEING, KAYAKING & RIVER RAFTING   Kayakers and canoeists will find easy, quiet paddling on the backwater creeks of the Northern Neck (see chapter 5) and in Hampton Roads and on the Eastern Shore (see chapter 11). Outfitters in Reedville, Virginia Beach, and Chincoteague rent both canoes and kayaks and offer guided excursions of the creeks and back bays. **Atlantic Kayak Company,** 1201 N. Royal St., Alexandria, VA 22124 (☎ **703/838-9072;** www.atlantickayay.com), has kayaking packages on the local waters of Northern Virginia and to the Northern Neck and the Eastern Shore.

Up in the hills, the Shenandoah, James, and Maury rivers can be either quiet or raging, depending on how much rain has fallen recently. Depending on the state of the rivers, outfitters in Scottsville, near Charlottesville (see chapter 6); near Front Royal, Luray, and Lexington in the Shenandoah Valley (see "River Rafting & Canoeing" in chapter 7); and in Richmond (the only city in the country with white-water rafting right in town; see chapter 9) provide either canoe- or river-rafting excursions. White-water rafting is most likely during spring and late fall. When the water is low during summer, multitudes forget canoes and rafts and lazily float down the rivers in inner tubes.

FISHING   The same waters that are so great for boating are stocked with a wide array of fish. The best rivers for fishing include the South Fork of the Shenandoah near Front Royal for smallmouth bass and redbreast sunfish; the James between Richmond and Norfolk for smallmouth bass and catfish; the New near Wytheville for walleye, yellow perch, musky, and smallmouth bass; the Rappahannock from Fredericksburg to the Northern Neck for smallmouth bass and catfish; and the Chickahominy near Williamsburg for largemouth bass, chain pickerel, bluegill, white perch, and channel catfish.

The mountains have 2,800 miles of trout streams, many of them stocked annually. You can go trout fishing in Shenandoah National Park (see chapter 7), and guides are available in Lexington (see chapter 7) and Abingdon (see chapter 8).

From Virginia Beach and Chincoteague you can go deep sea fishing on charter and party boats in search of bluefish, flounder, cobia, gray and spotted trout, sharks, and other ocean-dwelling fish (see chapter 11).

The **Virginia Department of Game and Inland Fisheries,** 4010 W. Broad St., Richmond, VA 23230 (☎ **804/367-1000**), publishes an annual freshwater-fishing guide and a regulations pamphlet detailing licensing requirements and regulations. It's available at most sporting-goods stores, marinas, and bait shops. Licenses are required except on the first Saturday and Sunday in June, which are free fishing days throughout Virginia.

The most comprehensive book on the subject is *Virginia Fishing Guide* by Bob Gooch (University Press of Virginia, 1988, 1993). The monthly *Chesapeake Angler Magazine,* P.O. Box 233 Burgess, VA 22432 (☎ **804/453-7511;** www.chesapeake-angler.com), tells what's being caught in the bay and where.

GOLF   You can play golf almost anytime and anywhere in Virginia, given the state's mild climate and more than 130 courses, but serious duffers head to Williamsburg and the famous Golden Horseshoe, Green, and Gold courses at the Williamsburg Inn, and the links at Kingsmill Resort, home of the annual PGA Michelob Classic in October (see chapter 10). An hour's drive away, the PGA-owned Tournament Players Club in Virginia Beach is one of the country's best new upscale links (see chapter 11). Up in the mountains, the Homestead's beautiful course in Hot Springs has the nation's oldest first tee, in continuous use since 1890 (see chapter 7). Wintergreen Resort near Charlottesville also has an excellent course (see chapter 6).

The best source for statewide information is the Virginia Tourism Corporation's annual *Virginia Golf Guide,* which lists and describes all the state's courses (see "Visitor Information," above).

HIKING & BACKPACKING   The same trails that make Virginia so popular with bicyclists also make it a hiker's heaven. Both good and easy are the state's rails-to-trails paths along old railroad beds (see "Bicycling & Mountain Biking," above). Some 450 miles of the Appalachian Trail snake through Virginia, nearly climbing Mount Rogers and paralleling the Blue Ridge Parkway and the Skyline Drive in many places. The best backcountry trails are in Shenandoah National Park (see chapter 7) and Mount Rogers National Recreation Area (see chapter 8), with less-traveled trails in the George Washington and Jefferson national forests.

For information and maps of the Appalachian Trail, contact the **Appalachian Trail Conference,** P.O. Box 807, Harpers Ferry, WV 25425-0807 (☎ **304/535-6331;** www.atconf.org). Three good books give trail-by-trail descriptions. *The Trails of Virginia: Hiking the Old Dominion,* by Allen de Hart (University of North Carolina Press, 1995), is the most comprehensive. *The Hiker's Guide to Virginia,* by Randy Johnson (Falcon Press, 1992), is a slimmer, easier-to-carry volume, as is *Hiking Virginia's National Forests,* by Karin Wuertz-Schaeffer (Globe Pequot Press, 1994), which covers trails in the George Washington and Jefferson national forests in the Shenandoah Valley and Southwest Highlands.

HORSEBACK RIDING & RACING   Equestrians will find stables with horses to rent to ride on hundreds of miles of public horse trails in Virginia, the majority of them in the Shenandoah Valley (chapter 7) and the Southwest Highlands (chapter 8). The granddaddy of all trails, the Virginia Highlands Horse Trail, runs the length of Mount Rogers National Recreation Area, which has campgrounds especially for horse owners. Horses are also permitted on the Virginia Creeper Trail and the New River Trail. You can rent horses at the Mount Rogers National Recreation Area and along the New River Trail (see chapter 8). Shenandoah National Park has guided trail rides, as does the fine Jordan Hollow Farm Inn, near Luray and the park's central section (see chapter 7). Ironically, few stables rent horses in Northern Virginia's Hunt Country, since just about everyone who rides there owns his or her own horse (see chapter 4).

The **Virginia Horse Council,** P.O. Box 72, Riner, VA 24149 (☎ **540/382-4113;** e-mail: vahcouncil@aol.com), publishes a list of public horse trails and stables statewide.

The Hunt Country and the Piedmont have 25 steeplechase races from spring to fall. The biggest are the Virginia Gold Cup in May and the International Gold Cup in October, both at Great Meadow near The Plains, in the Hunt Country (see "Virginia Calendar of Events," above). For an annual schedule, write the **Virginia Steeplechase Association,** P.O. Box 1158, Middleburg, VA 22117 (no phone).

Colonial Downs, in New Kent County between Richmond and Williamsburg (see chapter 9), is the state's only thoroughbred track, with pari-mutuel betting and simulcast racing.

HOT-AIR BALLOONING   The rolling hills of the Hunt Country and central Virginia are beautiful—especially during leaf season in October—when seen from a basket suspended under a hot-air balloon. **United Balloon Ventures** in Midland (☎ **540/439-8621**) and **Balloons Unlimited** in Oakton (☎ **540/554-2002** or 703/ 281-2300; www.balloonsunlimited.com) both fly over the Hunt Country. You can also go up for a quiet ride over the hills near Charlottesville with **Balloon Adventures** (☎ **804/971-1757**); near Richmond with **Balloons Over Virginia** (☎ **804/ 798-0080**); and over the gorgeous countryside around Abingdon with **Sky High Balloon Promotions** (☎ **540/439-8621**). Call the companies well in advance, since reservations are essential and schedules depend on weather conditions.

SKIING   Four all-season resorts in Virginia's mountains have downhill ski slopes and cross-country trails, but don't look to the Old Dominion for your ultimate ski vacation. Frankly, you will glide downhill over more man-made ice than the real thing here, and Virginia doesn't get enough snow to make for reliable cross-country skiing. The slopes here are used primarily by weekenders to hone their skills before flying off to better conditions out West. If that's your plan as well, head for **The Homestead** in Hot Springs (☎ **800/838-1766;** www.thehomestead.com; see chapter 7); **Wintergreen Resort** near Charlottesville (☎ **800/325-2200;** www.wintergreenresort.com; see chapter 6); **Massanutten** between Luray and New Market (☎ **800/207-MASS** or 540/289-9441; www.massresort.com; see chapter 7); or **Bryce Resort** near Bayse (☎ **800/831-1444** or 540/856-2121; www.bryceresort.com). All have accommodations, restaurants, ski rentals, and lesson programs.

When it snows, you can ski cross-country along the Skyline Drive in Shenandoah National Park (see chapter 7) and on the backcountry trails in Mount Rogers National Recreation Area and along the Virginia Creeper and New River trails (see chapter 8). Outfitters in Abingdon rent equipment.

For a free ski packet, call ☎ **800/THE-SNOW.**

WATER SPORTS   To indulge your passion for surfing, jet skiing, wave running, sailing, or scuba diving, head for Virginia Beach, which has it all in abundance. Jet skis also rip up the waters of Chincoteague's back bays. See chapter 11.

5 Health, Insurance & Safety

HEALTH

Malaria may have been a curse of the colonists who settled Virginia, but today the state poses no unusual health threats. Although they don't carry malaria, mosquitoes are still rampant in the Tidewater during summer, especially in the marshes of Chincoteague and the Eastern Shore, so take plenty of insect repellent if you're going there. Hospitals and emergency-care facilities are widespread in the state, so unless you're in the backcountry mountains, help will be close at hand.

INSURANCE

Many travelers buy insurance policies providing health and accident, trip-cancellation and -interruption, and lost-luggage protection. The coverage you need will depend on the extent of protection in your existing policies. Some credit-card companies also insure their customers against travel accidents if the tickets were purchased with their cards. Read your policies and credit-card agreements carefully before buying additional insurance.

Many health insurance companies and health maintenance organizations provide coverage for illness or accidents for their patients while away (don't forget to bring your identification card), but you may have to pay the local provider up front and file for a reimbursement when you get home. You will need adequate receipts, so collect them at the time of treatment.

Trip-cancellation insurance covers your loss if you have made nonrefundable deposits, bought airline tickets that have no or partial refunds, or paid for a charter flight, but can't travel for some good reason. **Trip-interruption insurance,** on the other hand, offers refunds in case an airline or tour operator goes bankrupt or out of business.

Lost-luggage insurance covers your loss over and above the limited amounts for which the airlines are responsible, and some policies provide instant payment so that you can replace your missing items on the spot.

Your travel agent should know of a company that offers traveler's insurance. Some American companies are: **Access America** (☎ 800/284-8300 or 804/285-3300; www.worldaccess.com); **Divers Alert Network (DAN)** (☎ 800/446-2671 or 919/

684-2948; www.dan.ycg.org), which provides coverage for scuba divers; **Health Care Abroad (Wallach & Co., Inc.)** (☎ 800/237-6615 or 540/687-3166; www. wallach.com); **Travel Guard International** (☎ 800/782-5151 or 715/345-0505; www.noelgroup.com); and **Worldwide Assistance** (☎ 800/821-2828 or 202/ 331-1609; www.worldwideassistance.com or www.europ-assistance.com), the American subsidiary of the European company Europ Assistance Worldwide Services, Inc.

SAFETY

Most areas of Virginia are relatively free of street crime, but this is not the case in some areas of Richmond, Norfolk, Roanoke, and other large cities. Ask your hotel staff or the local visitor information office whether neighborhoods you intend to visit are safe. Arlington and Alexandria have low crime rates compared to Washington, D.C., across the Potomac River, but they aren't entirely free of it, either. Never leave anything of value visible in your parked car; it's an invitation to theft anywhere.

When heading into the great outdoors, keep in mind that injuries often occur when people fail to follow instructions. Believe the experts who tell you to stay on the established ski trails. Hike only in designated areas, follow the marine charts if piloting your own boat, carry rain gear, and wear a life jacket when rafting. Mountain weather can be fickle at any time of the year. And watch out for summer thunderstorms that can leave you drenched and send bolts of lightning your way.

For more information, see "Preparing for Your Trip" in chapter 3.

6 Tips for Travelers with Special Needs

FOR TRAVELERS WITH DISABILITIES

The *Virginia Travel Guide for the Disabled,* a 300-page guide for persons with disabilities, is available from the Virginia Tourism Corporation (see "Visitor Information," above). The corporation's TTD number for the hearing impaired is ☎ **804/371-0327.**

Nationwide resources include **Mobility International USA,** P.O. Box 10767, Eugene, OR 97440 (☎ **541/343-1284,** voice and TDD; www.miusa.org), which offers its members travel-accessibility information and has many interesting travel programs for the disabled. The **Moss Rehab Hospital** (☎ **215/456-9600**) has been providing friendly and helpful phone advice and referrals to disabled travelers for years through its **Travel Information Service** (☎ **215/456-9603;** www.mossresourcenet.org). You can join **The Society for the Advancement of Travel for the Handicapped** (SATH), 347 Fifth Ave., Suite 610, New York, NY 10016 (☎ **212/447-7284;** fax 212/725-8253; www.sath.org), to gain access to their vast network of connections in the travel industry. They provide information sheets on travel destinations, and referrals to tour operators that specialize in traveling with disabilities. Their quarterly magazine, *Open World for Disability and Mature Travel,* is full of good information and resources. In addition, **Twin Peaks Press,** P.O. Box 129, Vancouver, WA 98666 (☎ **360/694-2462**), publishes travel-related books for people with disabilities.

Travelers with disabilities may also want to consider joining a tour that caters specifically to them. One of the best operators is **Flying Wheels Travel,** 143 West Bridge (P.O. Box 382), Owatonna, MN 55060 (☎ **800/535-6790**). They offer various escorted tours and cruises, with an emphasis on sports, as well as private tours in minivans with lifts. Other reputable specialized tour operators include **Access Adventures** (☎ **716/889-9096**), which offers sports-related vacations; **Accessible Journeys** (☎ **800/TINGLES** or 610/521-0339), for slow walkers and wheelchair travelers; **The**

Guided Tour, Inc. (☎ 215/782-1370); **Wilderness Inquiry** (☎ 800/728-0719 or 612/379-3858); and **Directions Unlimited** (☎ 800/533-5343).

You can obtain a copy of *Air Transportation of Handicapped Persons* by writing to Free Advisory Circular No. AC12032, Distribution Unit, U.S. Department of Transportation, Publications Division, M-4332, Washington, DC 20590.

In addition, both **Amtrak** (☎ 800/USA-RAIL; www.amtrak.com) and **Greyhound** (☎ 800/752-4841; www.greyhound.com) offer special fares and services for the disabled. Call at least a week in advance of your trip for details.

Avis (☎ 800/331-1212; www.avis.com), **Hertz** (☎ 800/654-3131; www.hertz. com), and the other major car rental companies offer hand-controlled cars for disabled drivers. They require reservations, so call well in advance. **Wheelchair Getaways** (☎ 800/873-4973; www.blvd.com/wg.htm) rents specialized vans with wheelchair lifts and other features for the disabled in more than 100 cities across the U.S.

The **National Park Service** (www.nps.gov) issues free "Golden Access Passports," which waive admission fees into national parks, forests, and wildlife refuges for a disabled person and a companion. Get them at park entrances.

Vision-impaired travelers should contact the **American Foundation for the Blind,** 11 Penn Plaza, Suite 300, New York, NY 10001 (☎ 800/232-5463), for information on traveling with Seeing Eye dogs.

FOR SENIORS

Many Virginia hotels, motels, and attractions offer discounts to senior citizens. Always ask about senior discounts when making air or hotel reservations.

Choice Hotels, which includes Clarion, Comfort Inn, Econo Lodge, Friendship Inn, Rodeway Inn, Sleep Inn, and Quality Inn, gives a 30% discount to anyone 50 or over who books a room in advance through its toll-free reservations phone numbers. Rooms are limited, and the discount doesn't apply if you reserve directly with the hotels.

The **American Association of Retired Persons (AARP),** 601 E St. NW, Washington, DC 20049 (☎ 800/424-3410 or 202/434-2277), offers its members discounts on hotels, car rentals, air travel, and tours. The AARP Travel Service sponsors group worldwide tours and cruises; members must be 50 years or older.

Other helpful organizations include the nonprofit **National Council of Senior Citizens,** 1331 F St. NW, Washington, DC 20004 (☎ 202/347-8800), part of whose magazine is devoted to travel tips. **Mature Outlook,** 6001 N. Clark St., Chicago, IL 60660 (☎ 800/336-6330), offers discounts at select hotels, restaurants, and car-rental firms. **Golden Companions,** P.O. Box 5249, Reno, NV 89513 (☎ 702/324-2227), helps travelers ages 45 and over find compatible companions through a personal voice mail service. Contact them for more information. **Elderhostel,** 75 Federal St., Boston, MA 02110-1941 (☎ 617/426-7788), sponsors vacations on college campuses. Participants must be 55 or older; however, if two people go as a couple, only one has to be of the required age.

Companies specializing in travel for seniors include **Grand Circle Travel,** 347 Congress St., Suite 3A, Boston, MA 02210 (☎ 800/221-2610 or 617/350-7500); and **SAGA International Holidays,** 222 Berkeley St., Boston, MA 02115 (☎ 800/343-0273).

The National Park Service (www.nps.gov) issues a **"Golden Age Passport"** to any citizen or person who lives in the United States and is 62 or older, providing free admittance to all national parks. Get this lifetime admission permit for $10 at any Park Service property; proof of age is necessary.

FOR FAMILIES

Virginia has a host of activities ideal for families with children, from learning American history at Williamsburg to riding the exciting rides at Paramount's Kings Dominion near Richmond. I won't begin to tell you how to raise your children, but you might give them a stake in your trip by letting them help plan it. And since much of your travel in Virginia is likely to be by car, think about carrying a few simple games to relieve potential boredom. Many Virginia hotels offer baby-sitting services, and most resorts have children's programs.

Below are some of the highlights of the state that are particularly good for children.

HISTORIC ATTRACTIONS   Virginia will bring history to life for your kids (and you, too) with myriad associations involving America's first heroes—Washington, Jefferson, Madison, Monroe, and Patrick Henry among them. Be sure to take them to the first English settlement at **Jamestown;** to the picturesque village of **Colonial Williamsburg** and its crafts demonstrations, militia reviews, and tours designed especially for kids; and to **Yorktown,** where they can climb over the ramparts where Washington defeated Cornwallis. Other possibilities are the presidential homes of **Mount Vernon, Monticello,** and **Ash Lawn-Highland** (Monroe's home). **Civil War battlefield** tours portray crucial events with fascinating exhibits, scenic walks and drives, and multimedia programs.

THEME PARKS   Theme parks offer thrills and chills, not to mention food, fun, and entertainment, at **Paramount's Kings Dominion, Busch Gardens Williamsburg,** and **Water Country USA.**

MUSEUMS   In Arlington, kids and adults alike will get a kick out of seeing themselves on TV at the **Newseum,** a state-of-the-art museum that shows the history of journalism and how it works. Roanoke's museums, especially the **Museum of Transportation,** with its railroad cars, and **Science Museum,** featuring all sorts of interactive exhibits, rate high with kids. Richmond's **Children's Museum** and the **Science Museum of Virginia** will keep children enthralled with participatory activities and "touch me" exhibits.

Another family favorite is Virginia Beach's **Marine Science Museum,** where computers, exhibits, and the museum's own waterside setting explore the marine environment. Nearby in Norfolk, the new **NAUTICUS** has interactive and "virtual adventures" featuring make-believe U.S. Navy ships. Across the harbor in Hampton, kids can see real spaceships at the **Virginia Air and Space Center.**

It's not a museum, but children who have read the story of the pony in *Misty of Chincoteague* will adore a chance to see the action themselves at the **wild ponies' swim across Assateague Channel.** The wildlife refuge there also offers hikes, nature programs, and a sandy beach.

THEATER   Theater for young people is sponsored by **TheatreVirginia** (☎ 804/367-0831) in the Virginia Museum of Fine Arts, Richmond. Outdoor theater is appealing to kids of all ages—in Lexington, the **Theater at Lime Kiln** (☎ 540/463-3074) has folk music and other concerts, as well as musicals that kids will enjoy.

FOR STUDENTS

It's worthwhile to bring along your valid high school or college identification. Presenting it can mean discounted admission to museums and other attractions. And remember, alcoholic beverages cannot be sold in Virginia to anyone who is under 21, so if you're eligible and intend to imbibe, bring your driver's license or another valid photo identification showing your date of birth.

The best travel resource for students is the **Council on International Educational Exchange,** or CIEE. They can set you up with an ID card (see below), and their travel branch, **Council Travel Service** (☎ **800/226-8624;** www.ciee.com), is the biggest student travel agency operation in the world. It can get you discounts on plane tickets, railpasses, and the like. Ask them for a list of CTS offices in major cities so you can keep the discounts flowing (and aid lines open) as you travel.

From CIEE you can obtain the student traveler's best friend, the $18 **International Student Identity Card** (ISIC). It's the only officially acceptable form of student identification, good for cut rates on railpasses, plane tickets, and other discounts. It also provides you with basic health and life insurance and a 24-hour help line. If you're no longer a student but are still under 26 you can get a "GO 25" card, which will get you the insurance and some of the discounts, but not student admission prices in museums.

FOR GAY & LESBIAN TRAVELERS

Virginia is not without its intolerant contingent, but there are gay and lesbian communities in most cities here. For general information, *Out and About,* 8 W. 19th St., Suite 401, New York, NY 10011 (☎ **800/929-2268**), profiles the best gay or gay-friendly hotels, gyms, clubs, and other places and destinations throughout the world. *Our World,* 1104 N. Nova Rd., Suite 251, Daytona Beach, FL 32117 (☎ **904/441-5367**), is a slicker magazine devoted to options and bargains for gay and lesbian travel worldwide.

The International Gay & Lesbian Travel Association (☎ **800/448-8550** or 954/776-2626; fax 954/776-3303; www.iglta.org) links travelers up with the appropriate gay-friendly service organization or tour specialist. Members are kept informed of gay and gay-friendly hoteliers, tour operators, and airline and cruise-line representatives.

General gay and lesbian travel agencies include **Family Abroad** (☎ **212/459-1800;** 800/999-5500), gay and lesbian; **Above and Beyond Tours** (☎ **800/397-2681**), mainly gay men; and **Yellowbrick Road** (☎ **800/642-2488**), gay and lesbian.

7 Getting There & Getting Around

BY PLANE

Most international visitors will arrive at **Washington Dulles International Airport** (☎ **703/661-2700**), in northern Virginia about 25 miles west of Washington, D.C. Dulles is also a major regional hub for domestic flights, and fares generally are less to fly in and out of here than other airports in Virginia.

Washington Dulles is served by **Aeroflot** (☎ 800/955-5555), **Air Canada** (☎ 800/776-3000), **Air France** (☎ 800/321-4538), (☎ 800/255-3191), **AirTran Airlines** (☎ 800-247-8726), **All Nippon Airways** (☎ 800/235-9262), **America West** (☎ 800/235-9292), **American** (☎ 800/433-7300), (☎ 800/843-0002), **British Airways** (☎ 800/247-9297), **Continental** (☎ 800/525-0280), **Delta Airlines** (☎ 800/221-1212), **Ethiopian Airlines** (☎ 800/445-2733), **KLM Royal Dutch Airlines** (☎ 800/374-7747), **Korean Airlines** (☎ 800/438-5000), **Lufthansa Airlines** (☎ 800/645-3880), **Metrojet** (☎ 888/638-7653), **Northwest** (☎ 800/225-2525), (☎ 800/227-4500), **SAS Scandinavian Airlines** (☎ 800/221-2350), **Saudi Arabian Airlines** (☎ 800/472-8342), **Spanair** (☎ 888/545-5757), **Swissair** (☎ 800/221-4750), **TACA International Airlines** (☎ 800/535-8780), **TWA** (☎ 800/221-2000), (☎ 800/241-6522), **US Airways** (☎ 800/428-4322), and **Virgin Atlantic Airlines** (☎ 800/862-8621).

Cyber Deals for Net Surfers

It's possible to get some great deals on airfare, hotels, and car rentals via the Internet. Grab your mouse and surf before you take off—you could save a bundle on your trip. The Web sites highlighted below are worth checking out, especially since all services are free (you'll pay for the tickets, of course). Always call the airlines or a travel agent and ask the lowest published fare before you shop for flights online.

Frommers.com   Home of Frommer's and *Arthur Frommer's Budget Travel* magazine and daily newsletter, this site offers detailed information on destinations around the world, and up-to-the-minute ways to save dramatically on flights, hotels, car reservations, and cruises. Book an entire vacation online and research your destination before you leave. Consult the message board to set up "hospitality exchanges" in other countries, to talk with other travelers who have visited a hotel you're considering, or to direct travel questions to Arthur Frommer himself. The newsletter is updated daily to keep you abreast of the latest-breaking ways to save, to publicize new hot spots and best buys, and to present veteran readers with fresh, ever-changing approaches to travel.

Microsoft Expedia (www.expedia.com)   The best part of this multi-purpose travel site is the "Fare Tracker": You fill out a form on screen indicating that you're interested in cheap flights from your hometown, and, once a week, they'll e-mail you the best airfare deals on up to three destinations. The site's "Travel Agent" will steer you to bargains on hotels and car rentals, and with the help of hotel and airline seat pinpointers, you can book everything right online. This site is even useful once you're booked. Before you depart, log on to Expedia for maps and up-to-date travel information, including weather reports and foreign exchange rates.

Travelocity (www.travelocity.com)   This is one of the best travel sites out there, especially for finding cheap airfare. In addition to its "Personal Fare Watcher," which notifies you via e-mail of the lowest airfares for up to five different destinations, Travelocity will track the three lowest fares for any routes on any dates in minutes. You can book a flight right then and there, and if you need a rental car

Also in northern Virginia, **Ronald Reagan Washington National Airport** (☎ **703/685-8000**), located on the Potomac River midway between Arlington and Alexandria, is the region's busiest airport, but because of space and noise limitations, it takes international flights only from eastern Canada and only domestic flights originating no more than 1,250 miles away. National is served by **Air Canada** (☎ 800/776-3000), **America West** (☎ 800/235-9292), **American** (☎ 800/433-7300), **Continental** (☎ 800/523-3273), **Delta Airlines** (☎ 800/221-1212), **Midway Airlines** (☎ 800/446-4392), **Midwest Express** (☎ 800/452-2022), **Northwest** (☎ 800/225-2525), (☎ 800/221-2000), **United** (☎ 800/241-6522), and **US Airways** (☎ 800/428-4322).

You can get up-to-date information, including airlines and ground transportation, for both Dulles and Reagan National airports online at **www.metwashairports.com**.

Other major Virginia gateways are **Richmond International Airport** (☎ 804/226-3000), **Norfolk International Airport** (☎ 757/857-3351), **Newport News/Williamsburg Airport** (☎ 757/877-0221), **Charlottesville/Albemarle Airport** (☎ 804/973-8341), and **Roanoke Regional Airport** (☎ 540/362-1999). See the or hotel, Travelocity will find you the best deal via the SABRE computer reservations system (a huge travel agent database). Click on "Last Minute Deals" for the latest travel bargains, including a link to "H.O.T. Coupons" (www.hotcoupons.com), where you can print out electronic coupons for travel in the U.S. and Canada.

The Trip (www.thetrip.com)   This site is really geared toward the business traveler, but vacationers can also use The Trip's exceptionally powerful fare-finding engine, which will e-mail you every week with the best city-to-city airfare deals for as many as 10 routes. The Trip uses the Internet Travel Network, another reputable travel agent database, to book hotels and restaurants.

E-Savers Programs   Several major airlines offer a free e-mail service known as E-Savers, via which they'll send you their best bargain airfares on a regular basis. Here's how it works: Once a week (usually Wednesday), or whenever a sale fare comes up, subscribers receive a list of discounted flights to and from various destinations, both international and domestic. Here's the catch: These fares are usually only available if you leave the very next Saturday (or sometimes Friday night) and return on the following Monday or Tuesday. It's really a service for the spontaneously inclined and travelers looking for a quick getaway. But the fares are cheap, so it's worth taking a look. If you have a preference for certain airlines (in other words, the ones you fly most frequently), sign up with them first.

One caveat: You'll get frequent-flier miles if you purchase one of these fares, but you can't use miles to buy the ticket (look for the sites' frequent flyer links, if any).

The airlines' Web sites will provide details on these services.

Smarter Living (www.smarterliving.com)   If the thought of all that surfing and comparison shopping gives you a headache, then head right for Smarter Living. Sign up for their newsletter service, and every week you'll get a customized e-mail summarizing the discount fares available from your departure city. Smarter Living tracks more than 15 different airlines, so it's a worthwhile time-saver.

following destination chapters for details about these airports. With a few exceptions, most flights to these airports are of the commuter variety, and usually you'll pay higher fares to fly into them than into Washington Dulles (see above).

You can get around the state by air, but you are likely to change planes along the way. For example, US Airways offers the most flights around the state, but you may have to fly through its hubs at Ronald Reagan Washington National Airport or Charlotte, North Carolina, to get, say, from Roanoke to Norfolk. Check with the airlines or your travel agent for the most efficient and cost-effective routing.

For more information about getting here from other countries, see "Getting to & Around the U.S." in chapter 3.

SAVING ON AIRFARES   Always shop among the airlines, and don't forget the cut-rate carriers such as AirTran, America West, Metrojet, Midway, and Midwest Express. Ask for the lowest fare and if it's cheaper to book in advance, fly in midweek, or stay over a Saturday night. Always ask for the *lowest* fare. Don't stop at the 7-day advance purchase; ask how much the 14- and 30-day plans cost. Decide when you want to go before you call, since many of the best deals are nonrefundable. Also check travel sections of your local newspaper for special promotional fares or packages. Your travel agent can find out all available options.

Travel agents offer hundreds of **package tour** options, especially to Washington, D.C., and to Williamsburg. Quite often, a package tour will result in savings not just on airfares, but on hotels, transfers, and sometimes meals and other activities as well. The specifics vary a great deal depending on the package, so consult your travel agent to find out the best deals at the time you want to travel.

Consolidators, also known as "bucket shops," are a good place to find low fares. Consolidators buy seats in bulk from the airlines and then sell them back to the public at prices below even the airlines' discounted rates. Their small boxed ads usually run in newspapers' Sunday travel sections at the bottom of the page. Before you pay, however, ask for a confirmation number from the consolidator and then call the airline itself to confirm your seat. Be prepared to book your ticket with a different consolidator—there are many to choose from—if the airline can't confirm your reservation. Also be aware that bucket shop tickets are usually non-refundable or rigged with stiff cancellation penalties, often as high as 50% to 75% of the ticket price.

Among the consolidators, **Council Travel** (☎ 800/226-8624; www.counciltravel. com) and **STA Travel** (☎ 800/781-4040; www.sta.travel.com) cater especially to young travelers, but their bargain-basement prices are available to people of all ages. **Travel Bargains** (☎ 800/AIR-FARE; www.1800airfare.com) was formerly owned by TWA but now offers the deepest discounts on many other airlines, with a 4-day advance purchase. Other reliable consolidators include **1-800-FLY-CHEAP** (www.1800flycheap.com); **TFI Tours International** (☎ 800/745-8000 or 212/ 736-1140), which serves as a clearinghouse for unused seats; or "rebators" such as **Travel Avenue** (☎ 800/333-3335 or 312/876-1116) and the **Smart Traveller** (☎ 800/448-3338 in the U.S. or 305/448-3338), which rebate part of their commissions to you.

Another possibility is travel clubs such as **Moment's Notice** (☎ 718/234-6295) and **Sears Discount Travel Club** (☎ 800/433-9383, or 800/255-1487 to join), which supply unsold tickets at discounted prices. You pay an annual membership fee to get the club's hotline number. Of course, you're limited to what's available, so you have to be flexible. You may not even have to join these clubs to get the deals, however, since some airlines now unload unsold seats directly through their World Wide Web sites (see the "Cyber Deals for Net Surfers" box in this chapter).

If you live overseas, see "Getting to the United States" in chapter 3.

BY TRAIN & BUS

Amtrak trains (☎ 800/USA-RAIL; www.amtrak.com) are better for getting to and from Virginia than for getting around. Its Metroliner and other northeast corridor trains connect New York to Union Station in Washington, D.C., where riders can board the Metrorail subway to Arlington and Alexandria. All Amtrak trains between New York and Florida stop at Washington, D.C., and Richmond; some also stop at Alexandria, Quantico, and Fredericksburg. Another train follows this route from New York to Richmond, then heads east to Newport News via Williamsburg. From Newport News, Amtrak's Thruway bus service connects to Norfolk and Virginia Beach. Some east- and westbound trains to and from Washington stop at Charlottesville, Staunton, and Clifton Forge. From Clifton Forge, a Thruway bus connects to Roanoke.

Generally, you'll find **Greyhound/Trailways** bus service available to and from—as well as between—all Virginia cities and most towns (☎ 800/231-2222; www. greyhound.com).

Virginia Driving Times & Distances

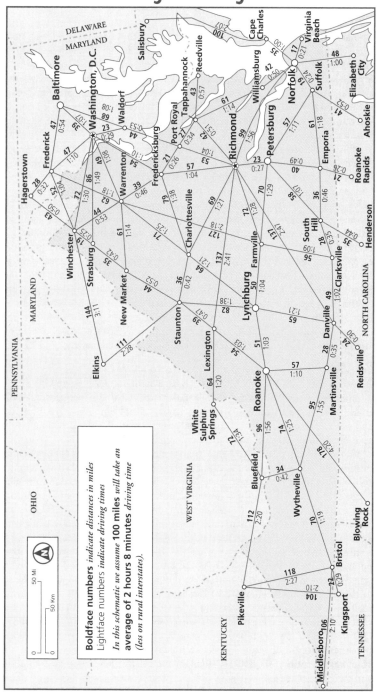

In this schematic we assume 100 miles will take an average of 2 hours 8 minutes driving time (less on rural interstates).

Boldface numbers *indicate distances in miles*
Lightface numbers *indicate driving times*

BY ESCORTED BUS TOUR

Several travel companies offer **escorted bus tours** of the historic sites in Virginia and Pennsylvania. These 1-week or longer tours usually start in Washington, D.C, and visit Mount Vernon, Fredericksburg, Williamsburg, Richmond, Charlottesville, the Shenandoah National Park, and Harpers Ferry. From there they go on to Gettysburg and the Amish Country in Pennsylvania before ending in Philadelphia. You'll have to pay extra to get to Washington and home from Philadelphia, but meals, lodging, and bus transportation are included in the tour prices, which start at around $1,000 per person double occupancy.

Most of the companies prefer that you book through a travel agent, but you can directly contact **Tauck Tours** (☎ 800/788-7855; www.tauck.com) and **Mayflower Tours** (☎ 800/323-7604; www.mayflowertours.com) to see what they're offering. **Globus and Cosmos Tours** require that you book through a travel agent, but you can order brochures on their Web site (www.globusandcosmos.com).

You can also make 1-day escorted bus tours from Washington, D.C., to Charlottesville or Williamsburg with the venerable **Gray Line** (☎ 800/862-1400 or 301/386-8300; fax 301/386-2024; www.grayline.com or www.dctourism.com/dc; e-mail: grayline@dctourism.com). The 14-hour Williamsburg tour usually runs on Wednesday and Saturday and costs $65 for adults, $55 for children. The 11-hour Charlottesville trip usually goes on Tuesday and Thursday and costs $65 per person regardless of age. Reservations are required at least a day in advance. Overnight trips from Washington to Williamsburg also are available.

From Norfolk, Gray Line has half-day bus trips to Williamsburg and to Hampton and Newport News. Call ☎ 757/853-6480 in Norfolk for details.

BY CAR

If at all possible, see Virginia by car. You'll have optimum flexibility to visit the rural beauties of the state, including the plantations and Civil War battlefields. And, of course, two of the state's most scenic attractions, the Skyline Drive and Blue Ridge Parkway, are motoring destinations. Only in northern Virginia, Richmond, and Hampton Roads will you encounter heavy rush-hour traffic.

Visitors arriving in Virginia by car from the northeast do so via **I-95,** which runs north-south across the state (note that I-95 is undergoing several major long-term construction projects, especially at the Capital Beltway (I-495) junction in northern Virginia and south of Petersburg near the North Carolina line). From western Maryland and eastern Tennessee, the major highway is **I-81,** which runs north-south the entire length of the state through the Shenandoah Valley and Southwest Highlands. Be aware that both I-95 and I-81 are heavy-duty truck routes, and accidents are common, so be especially careful while driving on them. Major western entrance points are from West Virginia via **I-77** and **I-64.** The latter runs east-west across the state between Covington and Norfolk. In northern Virginia, **I-66** traverses the state east-west between Arlington and I-81 at Strasburg. Be aware that I-66 can slow to a snail's pace during morning and evening rush hours in northern Virginia.

The **Virginia Department of Transportation,** 1401 E. Borad St., Richmond, VA 23219 (☎ 804/786-5731; www.vdot.state.va.us; e-mail: vdotinfo@vdot.state.va.us), publishes a free list of road construction projects, and it maintains a 24-hour-a-day **Highway Helpline** (☎ 800/367-ROAD) for information about road conditions and to report emergencies. It posts a winter weather road conditions map online at **www.vdot.state.va.us/roads/eoc.html**. Call ☎ 800/792-2800 to check on conditions in Hampton Roads' often-congested tunnels.

Driving the Civil War Trails

One advantage of touring Virginia by car is that you can easily follow the state's official Civil War Trails. These signposted driving tours follow the Shenandoah battles, the Peninsula campaign of 1862, the northern Virginia battles from Manassas to Fredericksburg, Lee vs. Grant as the Union drove south to Richmond in 1864, and Lee's retreat from Petersburg to Appomattox in 1865. Call ☎ **888/CIVIL-WAR** for free brochures and maps.

The Virginia Tourism Corporation distributes a detailed **state road map** as well as one that highlights the scenic drives (see "Visitor Information," above).

Most **car-rental companies** operate in Virginia's major metropolitan areas and at all but the smallest of airports.

8 Tips on Accommodations

Virginia has a vast array of accommodations, from rock-bottom roadside motels to some of the nation's finest resorts. Whether you spend a pittance or a bundle depends on your budget and your tastes. In the words of that well-worn phrase, you can enjoy "champagne tastes on a beer budget"—if you plan carefully and possess a little knowledge of how the hotel industry works.

The Virginia Tourism Corporation (see "Visitor Information," above) publishes a directory of all the state's accommodations. If you plan to take your **pet** along, ask the corporation for a list of hotels and motels that accept animals.

MONEY-SAVING TIPS

The rates quoted in this book are published (otherwise known as "rack" rates)—that is, the highest regular rates charged by a hotel or motel. Not long ago the rack rate was what you paid, unless you were part of a tour group or had purchased a vacation package. Today, most hotels give discounts to corporate travelers, government employees, senior citizens, automobile club members, active duty military personnel, and others. Most hotels usually don't advertise these discounted rates or even volunteer them at the front desk, but you can take advantage of them by asking politely if there's a special rate that might apply to you.

One company that does advertise a major discount is **Choice Hotels,** which gives a 30% discount to anyone over 50 at its chains (see "For Seniors" under "Tips for Travelers with Special Needs," above).

Computerized reservations systems have also permitted many larger properties to adjust their rates on an almost daily basis, depending on how much business they anticipate. Even if they don't officially reduce their rates, they may drop them rather than have beds go empty. Don't hesitate to ask if a less expensive rate is available on the days you plan to be there.

Most rack rates include commissions for travel agents, which many hotels will knock off if you make your own reservations and bargain a little.

Downtown hotels catering to business travelers during the week usually offer big discounts on Friday, Saturday, and Sunday nights. If you're staying in a city over a weekend, always ask about a weekend rate or package deal. Weekend rates don't apply in the resort areas such as Virginia Beach, nor in college towns like Charlottesville, but you should ask there about weekday or week-long vacation packages.

Parking fees can run up the cost at downtown hotels, especially for long-term stays, and many hotels jack up the price of long-distance phone calls made from your room. Accordingly, always inquire about the costs of parking, and use a pay phone or cell phone if the hotel tacks a hefty surcharge on calls.

Online, try booking your hotel through **www.frommers.com**, and save up to 50% off the rack rate. **Microsoft Expedia** (www.expedia.com) features a "Travel Agent" that will also direct you to affordable lodgings.

BED & BREAKFASTS

Virginia has several hundred bed-and-breakfasts, far too many to mention them all in this book. These aren't expensive country inns (of which Virginia has more than its share), nor are they the kind of old-fashioned "tourist homes" that used to provide inexpensive accommodation. In Virginia, today's B&Bs pretty much follow the same pattern: A couple sells their big city home, buys a Victorian house in a small town or rural area, fixes it up, and turns it into a charming B&B. Invariably they adorn the rooms with antiques or quality reproductions, throw in luxurious touches like fresh flowers and top-drawer linens and toiletries, and serve gourmet breakfasts. Some even add whirlpool tubs to their bathrooms. All these niceties have a price, so bed-and-breakfasts aren't inexpensive. On the other hand, you don't have to go out for breakfast, and the hosts usually are fonts of information about where to dine and what to see and do in their local areas.

More than 200 of the best belong to the **Bed & Breakfast Association of Virginia,** 6600 Belmont Rd., Chesterfield, VA 23832 (no phone; www.bbav.org), which publishes an annual directory of its members. Write for a copy or contact the Virginia Tourism Corporation (see "Visitor Information," above). The association inspects and approves all the establishments it promotes.

The Virginia Division of Tourism operates a **reservation service** for association members and other country inns and bed-and-breakfasts (☎ **800/934-9184**). In addition, most local visitor centers will send you a list of bed-and-breakfasts in their area.

Fast Facts: Virginia

American Express　Call customer service (☎ **800/528-4800**) to report lost or stolen traveler's checks or for locations of representatives in Virginia. The main Virginia office is in Richmond at 1412A Starling Dr. (☎ **804/740-2030**).

Car Rentals　See "Getting There & Getting Around" earlier in this chapter and in the destination chapters that follow.

Climate　See "When to Go" earlier in this chapter.

Embassies & Consulates　See chapter 3, "For Foreign Visitors."

Emergencies　Call ☎ **911** (no charge) for police, fire, and ambulance.

Information　See "Visitor Information" earlier in this chapter.

Liquor Laws　In Virginia, many grocery and convenience stores sell beer and wine, but only state-licensed Alcoholic Beverage Control (ABC) stores are permitted to sell bottles of hard liquor. Any licensed establishment (restaurant or bar) can sell drinks by the glass. The legal drinking age is 21, and a photo identification may be requested if you appear to be underage.

Newspapers/Magazines   Each major city in Virginia has its own daily newspaper, and the *Washington Post* is available at newsstands and coin boxes as far south as Richmond and as far west as Lexington.

Pets   Many hotels and motels accept small, well-behaved pets. However, a small fee is often charged to allow them into guest rooms. Many places, in particular bed-and-breakfast inns, do not allow pets at all (many B&B owners have pets, however, so ask before booking if you're allergic to animals). The Virginia Tourism Corporation publishes a list of the state's hotels and motels that accept pets (see "Visitor Information," earlier in this chapter). A good resource for pet owners is the book *On the Road Again with Man's Best Friend: Mid-Atlantic States,* which will steer you toward dog-friendly accommodations. Pets are allowed on short leashes in Virginia state parks, but they usually are restricted in national parks, so check with each park's ranger station before setting out.

Police   To reach the police, dial ☎ **911** from any phone (no charge).

Taxes   The Virginia state sales tax is 4.5% for most purchases, and a few local jurisdictions add another 0.5% to bring the total sales tax to 5%. Hotel taxes vary from town to town; in most communities it's 5%, which makes the total tax on your hotel bill 9.5% or 10%. Some local jurisdictions also add a restaurant tax, bringing the total tax on meal and drink bills to anywhere from 8% to 10%.

Time Zone   Virginia is on eastern standard time (EST), the same as New York and other East Coast cities. When it's noon in Virginia, it's 11am in Chicago, 10am in Detroit, 9am in Los Angeles, 8am in Anchorage, and 7am in Honolulu.

Weather   See "When to Go" earlier in this chapter for Virginia's climate. For current weather conditions in northern Virginia, call ☎ **703/936-1212;** in Richmond, call ☎ **804/268-1212;** in Roanoke, call ☎ **540/982-2303.** Elsewhere, check the front pages of the telephone directory for the local number.

3 For Foreign Visitors

The pervasiveness of American culture around the world may make you feel that you know the USA pretty well, but leaving your own country still requires an additional degree of planning. This chapter will help prepare you for the more common problems that visitors may encounter.

1 Preparing for Your Trip

ENTRY REQUIREMENTS

DOCUMENT REGULATIONS   Immigration laws have been a hot political issue in the United States in recent years, so it's wise to check at any U.S. embassy or consulate for current information and requirements. You can also plug into the U.S. State Department's Internet site at **www.state.gov**.

Canadians may enter the United States without passports or visas; you need only proof of residence.

The U.S. State Department has a **Visa Waiver Program** allowing citizens of the United Kingdom, Australia, New Zealand, Japan, and most western European countries to enter the United States without a visa for stays of up to 90 days. If you're from one of these countries, you will need only a **valid passport** and a **round-trip ticket** (air or cruise) in your possession upon arrival. Once here, you may then visit Mexico, Canada, Bermuda, and/or the Caribbean islands and return to the United States without needing a visa. Further information is available from any U.S. embassy or consulate.

If you're from any other country, you must have (1) a valid **passport** with an expiration date at least 6 months later than the scheduled end of your visit to the United States; and (2) a **tourist visa,** which may be obtained without charge from the nearest U.S. consulate.

To obtain a tourist visa, submit a completed application form with a 1½-inch-square photo and demonstrate binding ties to your residence abroad. If you cannot go in person, contact the nearest U.S. embassy or consulate for directions on applying by mail. Your travel agent or airline office may also be able to provide you with the visa application forms and instructions. The U.S. embassy or consulate where you apply will determine any restrictions regarding the length of your stay and whether you receive a multiple-entry or single-entry visa. This may take a few days or even weeks, so apply well in advance.

British subjects can obtain up-to-date passport and visa information by calling the **U.S. Embassy Visa Information Line** (☎ **0891/200-290**) or the **London Passport Office** (☎ **0990/210-410** for recorded information).

Foreign **driver's licenses** are recognized in Virginia, but you may want to get an international driver's license if your home license is not written in English.

HOW TO OBTAIN A PASSPORT   **Canadians** can pick up a passport application at one of 28 regional passport offices or most travel agencies. The passport is valid for 5 years and costs $60. Children under 16 may be included on a parent's passport but need their own to travel unaccompanied by the parent. Applications, which must be accompanied by two identical passport-sized photographs and proof of Canadian citizenship, are available at travel agencies throughout Canada or from the central **Passport Office, Department of Foreign Affairs and International Trade,** Ottawa, Ontario K1A 0G3 (☎ **800/567-6868;** www.dfait-maeci.gc.ca/passport). Processing takes 5 to 10 days if you apply in person, or about 3 weeks by mail.

Residents of the United Kingdom can pick up an application for a regular 10-year passport (the Visitor's Passport has been abolished) at passport offices, major post offices, or travel agencies. You can also contact the **London Passport Office** at ☎ **0171/271-3000;** www.open.gov.uk/ukpass/ukpass.htm. Passports are £21 for adults and £11 for children under 16.

Irish residents can apply for a 10-year passport, costing IR£45, at the Passport Office, Setanta Centre, Molesworth Street, Dublin 2 (☎ **01/671-1633;** www.irlgov.ie/iveagh/foreignaffairs/services). Those under age 18 and over 65 must apply for a IR£10 3-year passport. You can also apply at 1A South Mall, Cork (☎ **021/272-525**) or over the counter at most main post offices.

Australians can apply at the local post office or passport office or search the government Web site at www.dfat.gov.au/passports/. Passports for adults are A$126 and for those under 18 A$63.

New Zealanders can pick up a passport application at any travel agency or Link Centre. For more info, contact the Passport Office, P.O. Box 805, Wellington (☎ **0800/225-050**). Passports for adults are NZ$80 and for those under 16 NZ$40.

MEDICAL REQUIREMENTS   No inoculations are needed to enter the United States unless you are coming from, or have stopped over in, areas known to be suffering from epidemics, particularly cholera or yellow fever. Requirements for HIV-positive visitors entering the United States are somewhat vague and change frequently. For up-to-the-minute information concerning HIV-positive travelers, contact the Centers for Disease Control's **National Center for HIV** (☎ **404/332-4559;** www.hivatis.org) or the **Gay Men's Health Crisis** (☎ **212/367-1000;** www.gmhc.org).

If you have a disease that requires treatment with narcotics or syringe-administered medications, carry a valid signed prescription from your physician to allay any suspicions that you may be smuggling narcotics.

CUSTOMS REQUIREMENTS   Entering Country   Every adult visitor may bring in free of duty: 1 liter of wine or hard liquor; 200 cigarettes or 100 cigars (but no cigars made in Cuba) or 3 pounds of smoking tobacco; and $100 worth of gifts. You must spend at least 72 hours in the United States and must not have claimed the exemptions within the preceding 6 months. It is altogether forbidden to bring into the country foodstuffs (particularly cheese, fruit, cooked meats, and canned goods) and plants (vegetables, seeds, tropical plants, and so on). Foreign tourists may bring in or take out up to $10,000 in U.S. or foreign currency with no formalities; larger sums must be declared to Customs upon entering or leaving.

Penalties are severe for smuggling illegal narcotics into the United States, so if you have a disease requiring treatment with medications containing narcotics or drugs (especially those administered by syringe), carry a valid signed prescription from your physician to allay any suspicions that you're smuggling drugs.

For more specific information regarding U.S. Customs, call your nearest U.S. embassy or consulate, or the **U.S. Customs** office at ☎ **202/927-1770;** www.customs.ustreas.gov.

Leaving Country   U.K. subjects returning from the U.S. can bring back 200 cigarettes; 50 cigars; 250g of smoking tobacco; 2 liters of still table wine; 1 liter of spirits or strong liqueurs (over 22% volume); 2 liters of fortified wine, sparkling wine or other liqueurs; 60cc (ml) perfume; 250cc (ml) of toilet water; and £145 worth of all other goods, including gifts and souvenirs. People under 17 do not qualify for the tobacco and alcohol allowances. For more information, contact **HM Customs & Excise,** Passenger Inquiry Point, 2nd Floor Wayfarer House, Great South West Road, Feltham, Middlesex, TW14 8NP (☎ **0181/910-3744;** from outside the U.K. 44/181-910-3744), or consult their Web site at www.open.gov.uk.

Canadians get a $500 exemption, and you're allowed to bring back duty-free 200 cigarettes, 2.2 pounds of tobacco, 40 imperial ounces of liquor, and 50 cigars. In addition, you're allowed to mail gifts to Canada from abroad at the rate of C$60 a day, provided they're unsolicited and don't contain alcohol or tobacco (write on the package "Unsolicited gift, under $60 value"). All valuables should be declared on the Y-38 form before departure from Canada, including serial numbers of valuables you already own, such as expensive foreign cameras. Note: The $500 exemption can only be used once a year and only after an absence of 7 days. For a summary of Canadian rules, write for the booklet *I Declare,* issued by **Revenue Canada,** 2265 St. Laurent Blvd., Ottawa, Ontario K1G 4KE (☎ **613/993-0534**).

The duty-free allowance in **Australia** is A$400 (A$200 for those under 18). Citizens can bring home 250 cigarettes or 250 grams of loose tobacco, and 1,125ml of alcohol. If you're returning with valuable goods you already own, such as foreign-made cameras, you should file form B263. A helpful brochure, available from Australian consulates or Customs offices, is *Know Before You Go.* For more information, contact **Australian Customs Services,** GPO Box 8, Sydney NSW 2001 (☎ **02/9213-2000**).

The duty-free allowance for **New Zealand** is NZ$700. Citizens over 17 can bring in 200 cigarettes, or 50 cigars, or 250 grams of tobacco (or a mixture of all three if their combined weight doesn't exceed 250 grams); plus 4.5 liters of wine and beer, or 1.125 liters of liquor. New Zealand currency does not carry import or export restrictions. Fill out a certificate of export, listing the valuables you are taking out of the country; that way, you can bring them back without paying duty. Most questions are answered in a free pamphlet available at New Zealand consulates and Customs offices: *New Zealand Customs Guide for Travellers, Notice no. 4.* For more information, contact New Zealand Customs, 50 Anzac Ave., P.O. Box 29, Auckland (☎ **09/359-6655**).

INSURANCE   There is no national health-care system in the United States, and the cost of medical care here is extremely high; therefore, we strongly advise that you secure health insurance coverage before setting out. You may want to take out a comprehensive travel policy that covers sickness or injury costs (medical, surgical, and hospital), as well as loss or theft of your baggage, trip-cancellation costs, guarantee of bail in case you are arrested, and costs of accident, repatriation, or death. See "Health, Insurance & Safety" in chapter 2 for more information. Packages such as Europ

Assistance in Europe are sold by automobile clubs and travel agencies at attractive rates. **Worldwide Assistance Services, Inc.** (☎ 800/821-2828 or 202/347-2025), is the agent for Europ Assistance in the United States.

Canadians should check with their provincial health plan offices or call **Health-Canada** (☎ 613/957-3025) to find out the extent of their coverage and what documentation and receipts they must take home in case they are treated in the United States.

In Great Britain, most big travel agents offer their own insurance, and will probably try to sell you their package when you book a holiday. Think before you sign. **Britain's Consumers' Association** recommends that you insist on seeing the policy and reading the fine print before buying travel insurance. The **Association of British Insurers** (☎ 0171/600-3333) gives advice by phone and publishes the free *Holiday Insurance*, a guide to policy provisions and prices. You might also shop around for better deals: Try **Columbus Travel Insurance Ltd.** (☎ 0171/375-0011) or, for students, **Campus Travel** (☎ 0171/730-2101).

MONEY

The U.S. monetary system has a decimal base: one American dollar ($1) = 100 cents (100¢). Notes come in $1 (we call it a "buck"), $5, $10, $20, $50, and $100 denominations (the last two are not welcome when paying for small purchases and are not accepted in taxis or at subway ticket booths). There are also $2 bills, but since these are in limited circulation you're unlikely to see one. There are six denominations of coins: 1¢ (one cent, known here as "a penny"), 5¢ (five cents or "a nickel"), 10¢ (ten cents or "a dime"), 25¢ (twenty-five cents or "a quarter"), 50¢ (fifty cents or "a half dollar"), and the $1 piece, which is relatively uncommon.

Changing foreign currency in the United States is a hassle, so leave any currency other than U.S. dollars at home—it will prove more of a nuisance than it's worth. Even banks here may not want to change your home currency into U.S. dollars. The one exception is the exchange desks operated by **Thomas Cook Foreign Exchange** (☎ 800/287-7362; www.us.thomascook.com) at Washington Dulles International Airport and Ronald Reagan Washington National Airport (see "Getting There & Getting Around" in chapter 2).

Traveler's checks denominated in U.S. dollars are readily accepted at most hotels, motels, restaurants, and large stores. Do not bring traveler's checks denominated in other currencies. Sometimes a passport or other photo identification is necessary when cashing checks. The three traveler's checks that are most widely recognized—and least likely to be denied—are **Visa, American Express,** and **Thomas Cook.** Be sure to record the numbers of the checks, and keep that information separately in case they get lost or stolen.

American Express, Diners Club, Discover, MasterCard (EuroCard in Europe, Access in Britain, Chargex in Canada), and Visa (BarclayCard in Britain) **credit and charge cards** are the most widely used form of payment in the United States, and you should bring at least one with you—if for no other reason than to rent a car, since all rental companies require them.

Widespread in Virginia, some **automated teller machines (ATMs)** will allow you to draw U.S. currency against your bank and credit cards. When available, this is the easiest way to get U.S. dollars, and you get the bank's rate of exchange, normally better than you will receive at hotels and other businesses. Check with your bank before leaving home, and remember that you will need your personal identification number (PIN) to use this service.

SAFETY

While tourist areas are generally safe, large U.S. cities tend to be less safe than those in Europe or Japan. You should always stay alert. It's wise to ask your hotel front desk staff or the city's or area's tourist office if you're in doubt about which neighborhoods are safe.

Remember also that hotels are open to the public, and in a large hotel, security may not be able to screen everyone entering. Always lock your room door—don't assume that once inside your hotel you are automatically safe and no longer need be aware of your surroundings.

When driving, if you see someone on the road who indicates a need for help, you can telephone the police by dialing ☎ **911.** In Virginia, you can also call ☎ **800/ 367-ROAD** 24 hours a day to report an accident and seek emergency assistance statewide.

Park in well-lighted, well-traveled areas if possible. Always keep your car doors locked, whether attended or unattended. Never leave any packages or valuables in sight. If someone attempts to rob you or steal your car, do not try to resist the thief/carjacker—report the incident to the police department immediately.

2 Getting to & Around the U.S.

A number of U.S. and foreign airlines offer service from Europe and Latin America to Washington Dulles International Airport in northern Virginia (see "Getting There & Getting Around" in chapter 2). You can get to Virginia from Australia and New Zealand via **Air New Zealand, Qantas,** and **United,** with a change of planes in Los Angeles. Call the airlines' local offices or contact your travel agent, and be sure to ask about promotional fares and discounts.

Whichever airline you choose, always ask about **advance purchase excursion (APEX)** fares, which represent substantial savings over regular fares. Most require tickets to be bought 21 days prior to departure.

On the World Wide Web, the European Travel Network (ETN) operates a site at **www.discount-tickets.com,** which offers cut-rate prices on international airfares to the United States, accommodations, car rentals, and tours. Another site to click for current discount fares worldwide is **www.etn.nl/discount.htm#disco**.

When you arrive in the U.S., getting through immigration control may take as long as 2 hours on some days, especially summer weekends. Accordingly, you should make very generous allowances for delay in planning connections between international and domestic flights.

In contrast, travelers arriving by car or by rail from Canada will find border-crossing formalities streamlined to the vanishing point. And air travelers from Canada, Bermuda, and some places in the Caribbean can sometimes go through Customs and Immigration at the point of departure, which is much quicker.

For further information, see "Getting There & Getting Around," in chapter 2.

GETTING AROUND THE U.S.

BY AIR   The United States is one of the world's largest countries, with vast distances separating many of its key sights. From New York to Miami, for example, is more than 1,350 miles (2,173km) by road or train. Accordingly, flying is the quickest and most comfortable way to get around the country.

Some large airlines (for example, Northwest and Delta) offer travelers on their transatlantic or transpacific flights special discount tickets under the name **Visit USA,** allowing mostly one-way travel from one U.S. destination to another at very low prices. These discount tickets are not on sale in the United States and must be purchased abroad in conjunction with your international ticket. This system is the best, easiest, and fastest way to see the United States at low cost. You should obtain information well in advance from your travel agent or the office of the airline concerned, since the conditions attached to these discount tickets can be changed without advance notice.

BY TRAIN   Long-distance trains in the United States are operated by **Amtrak** (☎ **800/USA-RAIL;** www.amtrak.com), the national passenger rail corporation. See "Getting There & Getting Around," in chapter 2, for information about Amtrak's services to and within Virginia.

Be aware that with a few notable exceptions (for instance, the Northeast Corridor line between Boston and Washington, D.C.), intercity service is not up to European standards. Delays are common, routes are limited and often infrequently served, and fares are seldom significantly lower than discount airfares. Thus cross-country train travel should be approached with caution.

International visitors can buy a **USA Railpass,** good for 15 or 30 days of unlimited travel on Amtrak. The pass is available through many foreign travel agents, and with a foreign passport you can also buy them at some Amtrak offices in the United States, including Boston, Chicago, Los Angeles, Miami, New York, San Francisco, and Washington, D.C. The prices are based on a zone system: eastern, central, and western United States. At press time, prices for a 15-day pass were $295 off-peak, $440 peak; a 30-day pass cost $385 off-peak, $535 peak. (With a foreign passport, you can also buy passes at some Amtrak offices in the United States, including locations in San Francisco, Los Angeles, Chicago, New York, Miami, Boston, and Washington, D.C.) The highest prices are in summer and at holidays. Reservations are generally required and should be made for each part of your trip as early as possible.

If you'll be traveling in both the United States and Canada, Amtrak and VIA, the Canadian railway system, offer a joint **North American Rail Pass,** good for unlimited travel over 30 consecutive days anywhere the two systems go. One key restriction: You must travel by rail in both the United States and Canada. At press time, these cost about $650 from June to mid-October, $450 the rest of the year.

BY BUS   Although it's the least expensive way to get around the country, long-distance bus service here can be both slow and uncomfortable, so it's not for everyone. **Greyhound/Trailways** (☎ 800/231-2222; www.greyhound.com), the sole nationwide bus line, offers an **Ameripass** for unlimited travel for 7 days at $199, 15 days at $299, 30 days at $409, and 60 days at $599. Passes must be purchased at a Greyhound terminal. Special rates are available for senior citizens and students.

BY CAR   Traveling by car gives you the freedom to make (and alter) your itinerary to suit your own needs and interests. And especially in Virginia, it offers the possibility of visiting some off-the-beaten-path locations, places that cannot be reached easily by public transportation. For information on renting cars in the United States, see "Getting There & Getting Around," in chapter 2, and "Automobile Organizations" and "Automobile Rentals" in "Fast Facts: For the Foreign Traveler," below.

Please note that in the United States we drive on the **right side of the road** as in continental Europe, not on the left side as in the United Kingdom, Australia, and New Zealand.

You can call ☎ **800/367-ROAD** 24 hours a day to find out about road conditions in Virginia or to report an accident and seek emergency assistance statewide.

3 Shopping Tips

The U.S. government charges very low duties when compared to the rest of the world, so you could get some excellent deals here on imported electronic goods, cameras, and clothing. Of course, it all depends on the value of your home currency versus the dollar, and how much duty you'll have to pay on your purchases when you get home.

The national "discount" chain stores consistently offer some of our best shopping deals. For televisions, VCRs, radios, camcorders, computers, and other electronic goods, go to **Best Buy, Circuit City,** and **Radio Shack.** Best Buy also has a wide selection of music. **CompUSA, Computer City,** and **Micro Center** specialize in computer hardware, accessories, and software. **Service Merchandise** is one of our best chains for cameras, and it also has electronics, jewelry, and many other items.

Many computers and other electronic equipment sold here use only 110- to 120-volt AC (60-cycle) electricity. You will need a transformer to use them at home if your power is 220 to 240 volts AC (50 cycles). Be sure to ask the salesperson if an item has a universal power adapter.

Our major department store chains are **Sears, Macy's, Saks Fifth Avenue, Lord & Taylor, JCPenney,** and **Dillard's** anchoring many shopping malls. You get real deals in department stores only during sales, when selected merchandise is marked down 25% or more. The **Marshall's** and **TJ Maxx** chains carry name-brand clothing at department-store sale prices, but their stock tends to vary greatly from store to store.

Outlet malls are another source, where manufacturers operate their own shops, selling directly to the consumer. Sometimes you can get very good buys at the outlets, especially when sales are going on. Most lingerie and china outlets have good prices when compared to department stores, but that's not necessarily the case with designer clothing. In addition, some manufacturers produce items of lesser quality so they can charge less at their outlets, so inspect the quality of all merchandise carefully. The main advantage to outlet malls is that if you are looking for a specific brand—Levi's jeans, for example—the company's outlet will have it.

You'll find national chain stores, department stores, and outlet malls throughout Virginia; many are listed under "Shopping" in the following chapters. You can also look under their names in the White Pages of the local telephone directory for addresses and phone numbers, or under subjects such as computer dealers, television and radio dealers, stereo and hi-fi dealers, department stores, and discount stores in the Yellow Pages directory.

Fast Facts: For the Foreign Traveler

Automobile Organizations   Auto clubs will supply maps, suggested routes, guidebooks, accident and bail-bond insurance, and emergency road service. The **American Automobile Association (AAA)** is the major auto club in the United States. AAA has reciprocity agreements with the major auto clubs in the United Kingdom, Australia, and New Zealand; if you belong to an auto club in another country, inquire about AAA reciprocity before you leave. You may be able to join AAA even if you're not a member of a reciprocal club; to inquire, call AAA (☎ **800/222-4357**). AAA is actually an organization of regional auto clubs; in Virginia, look under "AAA Potomac" in the White Pages of the telephone directory. AAA has a nationwide emergency road service telephone number (☎ **800/AAA-HELP**).

Automobile Rentals   See "Getting There & Getting Around," in chapter 2 and in the following destination chapters.

Business Hours   See "Fast Facts: Virginia," in chapter 2.

Currency & Currency Exchange   See "Entry Requirements" and "Money" under "Preparing for Your Trip," above.

Electricity   Like Canada, the United States uses 110 to 120 volts AC (60 cycles), compared to 220 to 240 volts AC (50 cycles) in use in most of Europe, Australia, and New Zealand. If your small appliances use 220 to 240 volts, you'll need a 110-volt transformer and a plug adapter with two flat parallel pins to operate them here. Downward converters that change 220–240 volts to 110–120 volts are difficult to find in the United States, so bring one with you.

Embassies & Consulates   All embassies are located in Washington, D.C. Some consulates are located in major U.S. cities, and most nations have a mission to the United Nations in New York City. Some key embassies are:

- **Australia:** 1601 Massachusetts Ave. NW, Washington, DC 20036 (☎ **202/ 797-3000**). Australian consulates are located in New York, Honolulu, Houston, Los Angeles, and San Francisco.
- **Canada:** 501 Pennsylvania Ave. NW, Washington, DC 20001 (☎ **202/ 682-1740**). Other Canadian consulates are in Atlanta, Buffalo (N.Y.), Chicago, Cleveland, Dallas, Detroit, Los Angeles, Miami, Minneapolis, New York, and Seattle.
- **Republic of Ireland:** 2234 Massachusetts Ave. NW, Washington, DC 20008 (☎ **202/462-3939**). Irish consulates are in Boston, Chicago, New York, and San Francisco.
- **New Zealand:** 37 Observatory Circle NW, Washington, DC 20008 (☎ **202/ 328-4800**). New Zealand consulates are in Los Angeles, Salt Lake City, San Francisco, and Seattle.
- **United Kingdom:** 3100 Massachusetts Ave. NW, Washington, DC 20008 (☎ **202/462-1340**). Other British consulates are in Atlanta, Boston, Chicago, Cleveland, Dallas, Houston, Los Angeles, Miami, New York, and Orlando.

Emergencies   Call ☎ **911** to report a fire, call the police, or get an ambulance anywhere in the United States. This is a toll-free call (no coins are required at public telephones). If you're on the road in Virginia, you can call ☎ **800/ 367-ROAD** 24 hours a day to report an accident and seek emergency assistance statewide.

If you encounter traveler's problems, check the local telephone directory to find an office of the **Traveler's Aid Society,** a nationwide, nonprofit, social-service organization geared to helping travelers in difficult straits. Their services might include reuniting families separated while traveling, providing food and/or shelter to people stranded without cash, or even emotional counseling. If you're in trouble, seek them out.

Gasoline (Petrol)   Petrol is known as gasoline (or simply "gas") in the United States, and petrol stations are known as both gas stations and service stations. Gasoline costs about half as much here as it does in Europe (generally fluctuates between $1.30 and $1.60 per gallon). One U.S. gallon equals 3.8 liters or .85 Imperial gallons. A majority of gas stations in Virginia are now actually convenience grocery stores with gas pumps outside; they do not service automobiles. All but a very few stations have self-service gas pumps.

Holidays   Banks, government offices, post offices, and many stores, restaurants, and museums are closed on the following legal national holidays: January 1 (New Year's Day), the third Monday in January (Martin Luther King, Jr. Day), the third Monday in February (Presidents' Day, Washington's Birthday), the last Monday in May (Memorial Day), July 4 (Independence Day), the first Monday in September (Labor Day), the second Monday in October (Columbus Day), November 11 (Veterans' Day/Armistice Day), the last Thursday in November (Thanksgiving Day), and December 25 (Christmas). In addition, most Virginia state government offices are closed on the Friday preceding the third Monday in January for the Lee-Jackson Day (thus creating a 4-day weekend in conjunction with Martin Luther King, Jr. Day). "Super Bowl Sunday"—the last Sunday in January, when our two top professional gridiron football teams play for the national championship in the Super Bowl—is tantamount to a holiday. The Tuesday following the first Monday in November is Election Day and is a federal government holiday in presidential-election years (held every 4 years, including 2000).

Legal Aid   The foreign tourist will probably never become involved with the American legal system. If you are "pulled over" for a minor infraction (for example, of the highway code, such as speeding), never attempt to pay the fine directly to a police officer; this could be construed as attempted bribery, a much more serious crime. Pay fines by mail, or directly into the hands of the clerk of the court. If accused of a more serious offense, say and do nothing before consulting a lawyer or your embassy or consulate. Here the government must prove a person's guilt beyond a reasonable doubt, and everyone has the right to remain silent, whether he or she is suspected of a crime or actually arrested. If arrested, a person can make one telephone call to a party of his or her choice, and foreigners have a right to call their embassies or consulates.

Mail   If you aren't sure what your address will be in the United States, mail can be sent to you, in your name, **c/o General Delivery** at the main post office of the city or region where you expect to be. You must pick it up in person and must produce proof of identity (driver's license, passport, etc.).

Generally to be found at intersections, **mailboxes** are blue with a red-and-white stripe and carry the inscription U.S. MAIL. If your mail is addressed to a U.S. destination, don't forget to add the five-digit postal code, or ZIP code, after the two-letter abbreviation of the state to which the mail is addressed (VA for Virginia).

Our postal service has been raising its rates over the past several years and may do so again, but at press time **domestic postage rates** were 20¢ for a postcard and 33¢ for a letter. Airmail postcards to Canada cost 30¢, while letters were 46¢. Airmail letters to other countries were 60¢ for the first half ounce.

Measurement Conversions   To convert **miles to kilometers,** multiply the number of miles by 1.61 (example: 50 miles × 1.61 = 80.5km). Note that this conversion can be used to convert speeds from miles per hour (m.p.h.) to kilometers per hour (kmph). To convert kilometers to miles, multiply the number of kilometers by 0.62. To convert **U.S. gallons to liters,** multiply the number of gallons by 3.79 (example: 12 U.S. gal. × 3.79 = 45.48 liters). To convert liters to U.S. gallons, multiply by 0.26. To convert **U.S. gallons to Imperial gallons,** multiply the number of U.S. gallons by 0.83 (example: 12 U.S. gal. × 0.83 = 9.96 Imperial gal.). To convert Imperial gallons to U.S. gallons, multiply by 1.2. To convert **pounds to kilograms,** multiply the number of pounds by 0.45

Telephone Dialing Info at a Glance

- **To place a direct call from your home country to the United States:** Dial the international access code (0011 in Australia; 00 in Ireland, New Zealand, and the U.K.), plus the 3-digit area code and 7-digit local number (for example, 0011-804/000-0000). Calls from Canada to the U.S. do not require you to dial a country code.

- **To place a call within the United States:** Dial "1" followed by the 3-digit area code and the 7-digit local number (for example, 1-804/000-0000).

- **To place a direct call from the United States to your home country:** Dial the international access code (**011**) followed by the country code (Australia 61, Republic of Ireland 353, New Zealand 64, U.K./Northern Ireland 44). For calls from the U.S. to Canada, just dial 1 followed by the area code and local number.

- **To reach directory assistance ("information"):** Dial 411; for long-distance information, dial 1, then the appropriate area code and 555-1212.

(example: 90 lb. × 0.45 = 40.5kg). To convert kilograms to pounds, multiply by 2.2. To convert **degrees Fahrenheit to degrees Celsius,** subtract 32 from °F, multiply by 5, then divide by 9 (example: 85°F − 32 × 5 ÷ 9 = 29.4°C). To convert degrees Celsius to degrees Fahrenheit, multiply °C by 9, divide by 5, and add 32.

Newspapers/Magazines   Every city in Virginia has a daily newspaper, which you can buy at hotel gift shops, at convenience stores, and at coin boxes at many major street intersections. *USA Today,* the national daily, is widely available, as is *The Washington Post,* one of America's most highly respected dailies.

Safety   See "Safety" in chapter 2 and under "Preparing for Your Trip" in this chapter.

Taxes   In the United States there is no value-added tax (VAT) or other indirect tax at the national level. Every state, county, and city has the right to levy its own local tax on all purchases, including hotel and restaurant checks, airline tickets, and so on. For Virginia's sales taxes, see "Fast Facts: Virginia," in chapter 2. Virginia's hotel tax varies from county to county.

Telephone, Telegraph, Telex & Fax   The telephone system in the United States is run by private corporations, so rates, especially for long-distance service and operator-assisted calls, can vary widely. Generally, hotel surcharges on long-distance and local calls are astronomical, so you're usually better off using a **public pay telephone** (which you'll find clearly marked in most public buildings and private establishments as well as on the street), your cellular phone, or a **phone company credit card.** Hotel lobbies, convenience grocery stores, and gas stations usually have public phones. Many convenience groceries and packaging services sell **prepaid calling cards** in denominations up to $50; these can be the least expensive way to call home. With a few exceptions (the Wyndham chain is the most notable), hotels don't charge for calls to the toll-free numbers required to use phone company credit cards or pre-paid calling cards. Many public phones at airports now accept American Express, MasterCard, and Visa credit cards. Local calls made from public pay phones in Virginia cost 35¢.

Most **long-distance and international calls** can be dialed directly from any phone. For calls within the United States and to Canada, dial 1 followed by the area code and the seven-digit number. For other international calls, dial 011 followed by the country code, city code, and telephone number of the person you are calling.

Calls to area codes 800, 888, and 877 are toll-free. However, calls to numbers in area codes 700 and 900 (chat lines, bulletin boards, "dating" services, pornography, and so on) can be very expensive—usually a charge of 95¢ to $3 or more per minute, and they sometimes have minimum charges that can run as high as $15 or more.

For **reversed-charge** or **collect calls,** and for **person-to-person calls,** dial 0 (zero, *not* the letter O) followed by the area code and number you want; an operator (or one of those pre-recorded voices) will then come on the line, and you should specify that you are calling collect, or person-to-person, or both. If your operator-assisted call is international, ask for the overseas operator.

Telegraph and telex services are provided primarily by Western Union. You can bring your telegram into the nearest Western Union office (there are hundreds across the country) or dictate it over the phone (☎ **800/325-6000**). You can also telegraph money or have it telegraphed to you, very quickly over the Western Union system, but this service can cost as much as 15% to 25% of the amount sent.

Most hotels have **fax** machines available for guest use (be sure to ask about the charge to use it), and many hotel rooms are even wired for guests' fax machines. A less expensive way to send and receive faxes may be at stores such as **Mail Boxes Etc.,** a national chain of packing service shops (look in the Yellow Pages directory under "Packing Services").

There are two kinds of telephone directories in the United States. The so-called **White Pages** list private and business subscribers in alphabetical order. The inside front cover lists emergency numbers for police, fire, ambulance, the Coast Guard, poison-control center, crime-victims hotline, and so on. The first few pages will tell you how to make long-distance and international calls, complete with country codes and area codes. Government numbers usually are on pages printed on blue paper. Printed on yellow paper, the so-called **Yellow Pages** list all local services, businesses, industries, and churches and synagogues by type of activity, with an index at the front or back. The Yellow Pages also include city plans or detailed area maps, often showing postal ZIP codes and public transportation routes.

Time   The continental United States is divided into four **time zones:** eastern standard time (EST), central standard time (CST), mountain standard time (MST), and Pacific standard time (PST). Alaska and Hawaii have their own zones. For example, noon in New York City (EST) is 11am in Chicago (CST), 10am in Denver (MST), 9am in Los Angeles (PST), 8am in Anchorage (AST), and 7am in Honolulu (HST). Virginia observes eastern standard time.

Daylight saving time is in effect from 1am on the first Sunday in April through 1am the last Sunday in October. Daylight saving time moves the clock 1 hour ahead of standard time.

Tipping   Tipping is so ingrained in the American way of life that the annual income tax of tip-earning service personnel is based on how much they *should* have received in light of their employers' gross revenues. Accordingly, they may have to pay tax on a tip you didn't actually give them.

Here are some rules of thumb: Bartenders get 10% to 15% of the check; bellhops, at least 50¢ per bag, or $2 to $3 for a lot of luggage; cab drivers, 10% of the fare; chambermaids, $1 per day; checkroom attendants, $1 per garment; hairdressers and barbers, 15% to 20% of the bill; waiters and waitresses, 15% to 20% of the check; valet parking attendants, $1 per vehicle; rest room attendants, 25¢. We do not tip theater ushers, gas station attendants, or the staff at cafeterias and fast-food restaurants.

Toilets   You won't find public toilets (euphemistically referred to here as "rest rooms") on the streets in most U.S. cities, but they can be found in hotel lobbies, bars, restaurants, museums, department stores, railway and bus stations, and service stations. Note, however, that the restaurants and bars in heavily visited areas may reserve their rest rooms for the use of their patrons.

4 Northern Virginia

America's past and present meet in northern Virginia. Linked by bridges and three subway lines to the nation's capital, Arlington is very much in Washington's international, cosmopolitan orbit. Yet in nearby Alexandria, the cobblestone streets of the 18th-century Old Town historic district still ring with the footsteps of George Washington, James Monroe, and Robert E. Lee. South of Old Town on the Potomac, more visitors go through the doors of George Washington's beloved Mount Vernon than of any American home except the White House.

Northern Virginia is a vast suburban area stretching west and south from the nation's capital. Not long ago, Arlington, Alexandria, and the region's other municipalities were primarily bedroom communities for workers who headed across the river each morning. However, a boom of high-tech service industries and the arrival of major corporate headquarters have given this region its own thriving economy. Now its residents are just as likely to work in fast-growing Fairfax County, which wraps around Arlington and Alexandria and has one million residents, making it the most populous single jurisdiction in Virginia—almost twice the size of the District of Columbia. If it were incorporated, the Fairfax area known as Tysons Corner would be Virginia's wealthiest city (it has more office space than downtown Denver, Colorado). And the burgeoning strip running west through Reston and Herndon to Washington Dulles International Airport is one of the nation's leading high-tech corridors.

The downside to this rapid expansion is the nation's second-most gridlocked traffic, behind only Los Angeles. Accordingly, try to avoid being on the road here during weekday rush hours from 6:30 to 9:30am and from 3:30 to 6:30pm.

West of Dulles, however, the crowded highways eventually give way to the winding country roads, beautiful rolling hills, picturesque horse farms, charming country inns, and quaint villages of Loudon and Fauquier counties, heart of Virginia's renowned Hunt Country.

1 Arlington

Across the Potomac River from Washington, D.C.; 100 miles N of Richmond

Easy access to Washington, D.C., and its tourist attractions is Arlington's main draw for visitors, who can stay in less-expensive digs here and still be only minutes away from the capital via Metrorail, the region's clean and efficient subway system. Even visitors who stay across the Potomac River in D.C. eventually find their way here, too, for Arlington is home to the **Pentagon,** our national military headquarters; the **Newseum,** an interactive museum dedicated to journalism; and **Arlington National Cemetery,** our most hallowed national shrine.

As its straight land borders will attest, Arlington was once part of the District of Columbia, originally a square flanking the Potomac. Unneeded in the final planning, Arlington was returned to the state of Virginia in 1847.

Although it has always provided housing for federal government civilian workers and military personnel, Arlington now has a lively life of its own. Its subway stations, safe neighborhoods, and more affordable housing have attracted the type of young folk who used to live in the nation's capital. Some of the friendly pubs that have sprung up to offer libation and entertainment to these young residents have even put the county on the music map.

Nor do Arlingtonians have to cross the river for good food these days, for immigrants from overseas have not only given it Virginia's most diverse population, but have also opened many ethnic restaurants serving cuisines from around the world.

ESSENTIALS
VISITOR INFORMATION

Contact or visit the **Arlington Visitor Center,** 735 S. 18th St., Arlington, VA 22202 (☎ 800/677-6267 or 703/228-5720 for information, 888/743-8292 for hotel reservations; fax 703/892-9469; www.stayarlington.com; e-mail: avcs@co.arlington.va.us), for maps and information about events, accommodations, and restaurants, as well as answers to any questions about the entire Washington, D.C., area. The center is 2 blocks south of Pentagon City Metro station (go south on South Hayes Street, which becomes South 18th Street). Open daily 9am to 5pm.

GETTING THERE

BY PLANE   Ronald Reagan Washington National Airport (☎ 703/685-8000) is located on the Potomac River in Arlington. **SuperShuttle** (☎ 800/BLUE-VAN) operates frequent van service daily from 6am to 11pm to locations in D.C. and northern Virginia. Shuttle fares start at $6 one-way. Metrorail's Yellow and Blue lines stop at the airport's new main terminal (see "Getting Around," below).

International and long-distance domestic flights arrive at **Washington Dulles International Airport** (☎ 703/661-2700), about 25 miles west of Arlington via I-66 and the Dulles Access Road. **SuperShuttle** (☎ 800/258-3826) provides van service to Arlington and all other destinations in the D.C. metro area. Fares to Arlington range from $16 to $26 per person. **Washington Flyer** (☎ 703/685-1400) is the only taxi operator at Dulles airport; fares to Arlington range from $35 to $45. Washington Flyer also runs buses between Dulles and National airports and also shuttles between Dulles and the West Falls Church Metro stop, from which you can access all Metrorail route locations ($8 one-way, $14 round-trip).

All of the major car-rental companies are represented at both airports.

See "Getting There & Getting Around" in chapter 2 for more information.

BY CAR   I-95 and **I-395** are the major highways to Arlington from the north and south. From the north, follow I-95 south to Exit 19, for U.S. 50 west and Washington, D.C. Follow U.S. 50 west (John Hanson Highway), which will turn into New York Avenue. Follow signs for I-395 south toward Richmond and cross the 14th Street Bridge, leaving Washington, D.C. From the northwest, take **I-270** to **I-495** (the Capital Beltway) south to the **George Washington Memorial Parkway,** which runs through Arlington to Alexandria along the south bank of the Potomac River. In

Arlington

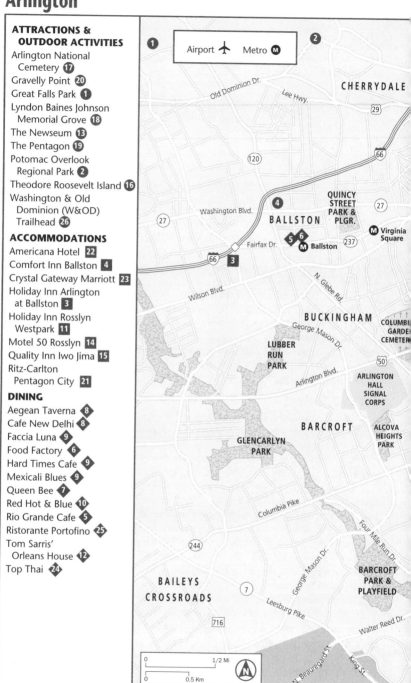

Airport ✈   Metro Ⓜ

CHERRYDALE

Old Dominion Dr.

Lee Hwy.

29

66

120

Washington Blvd.

QUINCY STREET PARK & PLGR.

27

BALLSTON

237

Ⓜ Virginia Square

Fairfax Dr.

Ⓜ Ballston

66

27

Wilson Blvd.

N. Glebe Rd.

BUCKINGHAM

George Mason Dr.

COLUMBIA GARDEN CEMETER

LUBBER RUN PARK

50

Arlington Blvd.

ARLINGTON HALL SIGNAL CORPS

BARCROFT

ALCOVA HEIGHTS PARK

GLENCARLYN PARK

Columbia Pike

Four Mile Run Dr.

BAILEYS CROSSROADS

244

7

George Mason Dr.

BARCROFT PARK & PLAYFIELD

Leesburg Pike

Walter Reed Dr.

716

0   1/2 Mi
0   0.5 Km

N. Beauregard St.

King St.

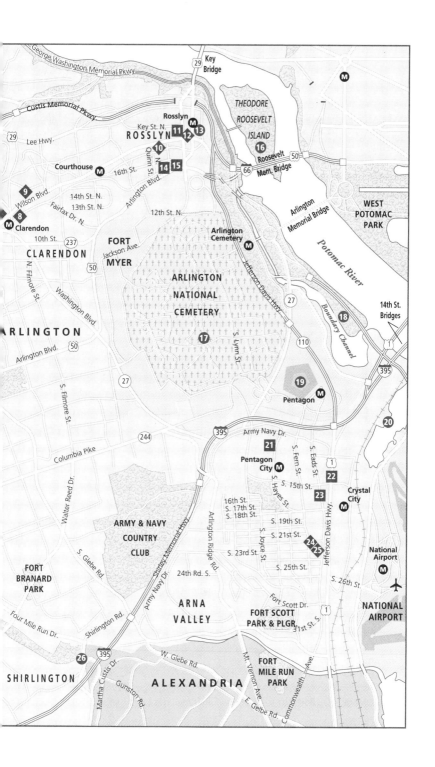

addition, **I-66, U.S. 50** (Arlington Boulevard), and **U.S. 29/211** (Lee Highway) run east-west through Arlington. **U.S. 1** (Jefferson Davis Highway) passes north-south through the county; it intersects with I-95 in Alexandria just west of the Potomac River.

BY TRAIN   Visitors arriving on Amtrak at Washington's **Union Station,** 50 Massachusetts Ave. NE (☎ **800/USA-RAIL**), can easily switch to the Metro stop there for a quick ride to Arlington. Alexandria also has an Amtrak station with adjacent Metrorail stop (see "Getting There" in section 2, below).

BY BUS   The **Greyhound/Trailways** bus station is at 3860 S. Four Mile Run Dr., near South Walter Reed Drive (☎ **800/321-2222**).

County Layout

The main thoroughfares radiate from the Potomac River bridges. I-395 runs southwest through the county from the 14th Street Bridge to Alexandria, where it connects with I-95. I-66 begins at the Theodore Roosevelt Bridge and runs from Rosslyn due west. Paralleling I-66, Wilson Boulevard begins at the Key Bridge in Rosslyn and runs due west. Jefferson Davis Highway (U.S. 1) extends due south from the 14th Street Bridge (I-395) to Alexandria. Columbia Pike starts at the Pentagon and heads southwest into Fairfax County.

Neighborhoods in Brief

Arlington is a county, not a city, and has no single downtown area. Instead, it's a place of neighborhoods. Most are of little interest, but those surrounding subway stations make convenient bases from which to explore Arlington, Alexandria (see section 2, below), and Washington, D.C. Stores, hotels, restaurants, and office and apartment towers have sprung up like glass-and-steel forests over and around several of the county's subway stations.

Easy to find if you're arriving via I-66, **Ballston** was once a weekend getaway for Washingtonians, but its older buildings are quickly giving way to new office towers and condos centered on its Orange line Metro station and modern shopping mall.

On the Blue and Yellow lines, **Crystal City** and **Pentagon City** straddle Jefferson Davis Highway (U.S. 1) between Ronald Reagan National Airport and the Pentagon on the county's eastern side. Here you'll find the area's "airport" hotels, plus a few good restaurants and Arlington's largest shopping complex. A multi-purpose development, Crystal City is tightly packed with hotels, offices, apartments, service shops, and the Crystal Underground, a shopping mall beneath the streets. Pentagon City is less crowded, and you can walk to the Pentagon from here.

Although it has no hotels, you should spend an evening in **Clarendon,** one of the Washington metropolitan area's prime destinations for good, inexpensive ethnic food and a mix of live music in its neighborhood pubs. You'll find more than a dozen cuisines within 2 blocks of its Orange line station (it has so many Vietnamese restaurants, in fact, that locals refer to Clarendon as "Little Saigon"). For the time being, most of its restaurants and lively neighborhood bars are housed in older, one-story storefronts.

Rosslyn is a rather unappealing center of hotels, offices, and condominium towers, but you can walk across the Key Bridge into Washington's trendy Georgetown neighborhood from here. Both the Orange and Blue lines run under Rosslyn.

Getting Around

Except during weekday rush hours, traffic moves smoothly on Arlington's highways and streets. All-news WTOP radio (AM 1500) gives traffic reports every 10 minutes.

The easiest way to get around is via Washington's **Metrorail** subway system, which offers efficient transport within Arlington and to Washington, D.C. The Orange line runs under Wilson Boulevard from Rosslyn west through Clarendon and Ballston. The Blue line runs southeast from Rosslyn to Arlington National Cemetery, the Pentagon, Pentagon City, Crystal City, and Ronald Reagan Washington National Airport to Alexandria. Sharing tracks with the Blue line in Arlington, the Yellow line also connects the Pentagon, Pentagon City, Crystal City, and National Airport to Alexandria. Metrorail operates Monday to Friday from 5:30am to midnight, Saturday from 8am to midnight, and Sunday from 10am to midnight. For information, call ☎ **202/ 637-7000.** You can also call that number for **Metrobus,** which has extensive (and complicated) 24-hour service throughout Arlington.

The best taxi company here is **Red Top Cab** (☎ **703/522-3333**).

THE TOP ATTRACTIONS

If you're in Arlington, you probably want to take the Metro over to D.C. and see some of the many attractions in the nation's capital. For complete descriptions, see either *Frommer's Washington, D.C.* or *Frommer's Washington, D.C., from $70 a Day,* available at your local bookstore.

✪ **Arlington National Cemetery.** Va. 110 at Memorial Circle. ☎ **703/607-8052.** Free admission. Tourmobile $4 adults, $2 children 3–11. Apr–Sept daily 8am–7pm; Oct–Mar daily 8am–5pm. Parking $1 per hour first 3 hours, $2 per hour thereafter. Metro: Blue line to Arlington Cemetery. From I-395 or I-66 take Va. 110 to entrance signs.

For more than a century, this famous cemetery on a ridge overlooking the Potomac River and Washington, D.C. has been a cherished shrine commemorating the lives given by members of the U.S. armed forces. Its seemingly endless graves mark the mortal remains of the honored dead, both the known and the unknown, who served in conflicts from the Revolutionary War through the Persian Gulf War.

This quiet expanse of green is a walker's paradise. Head first for the **Arlington Cemetery Visitor Center,** where you can get a free map—and if you have family buried here, find out where. If you're not hoofing it, you can purchase a **Tourmobile** ticket for a cemetery tour. Service is continuous, and the narrated commentary interesting. At the visitor center you can also purchase Tourmobile combination tickets ($12 for adults, $6 for children) that include Arlington and major Washington, D.C., sights, allowing you to stop and reboard when you're ready. Tourmobiles also depart here for Mount Vernon (see section 3, below).

Women in Military Service for America Memorial: At the cemetery's ceremonial entrance, you'll come to a fountain emptying into a reflecting pool backed by an imposing granite wall. This is the Women in Military Service for America Memorial, dedicated in 1997 to honor all women who have served in the military, from the Revolution to the present. The memorial's Hall of Honor has a block of Colorado marble virtually identical to that of the Tomb of the Unknowns (see below). On the terrace roof, 11 glass panels are etched with quotations about women who have served, and inside, there's a computerized registry of more than 250,000 women veterans.

The Kennedy Graves: Follow the paved pathways to the John F. Kennedy gravesite, marked by an eternal flame. Jacqueline Kennedy Onassis is buried next to her first husband. Nearby stands a simple white cross at the grave of Robert F. Kennedy. Looking north, you'll have a spectacular view of the capital city across the river (during his presidency Kennedy once remarked of this spot, "I could stay here forever"). A few steps below the gravesite is a wall inscribed with JFK quotations, including the one he's most remembered for: "And so my fellow Americans, ask not what your country

Arlington National Cemetery

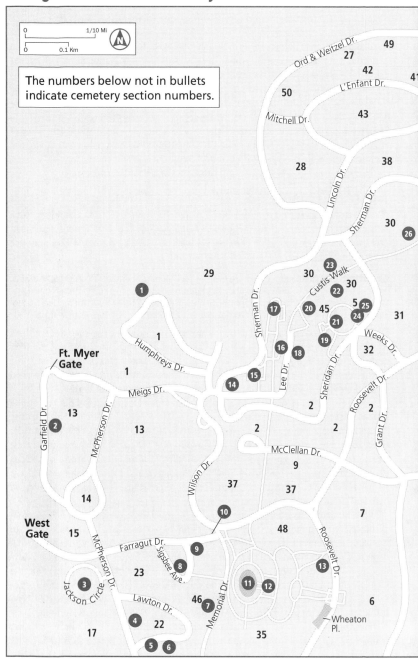

The numbers below not in bullets indicate cemetery section numbers.

Ord & Weitzel Gate

29 30

27

40

41

Ord & Weitzel Dr.

52

51

39

Custis Walk

110

53

Arlington Metro Stop Ⓜ 34

Jefferson Davis Hwy.

Schley Dr.

28

7

36

32

Memorial Dr.

Women Military Service Memorial

Visitor Center 33

31

Roosevelt Gate

Eisenhower Dr.

54

Halsey Dr.

Visitors' Parking

33

Leahy Dr.

55

McClellan Gate

59

12

York Dr.

Arlington House 16
Arlington Memorial Bridge 34
Bradley (Gen. Omar Nelson) grave 27
Byrd (Rear Adm. Richard, Jr.)
    statue 32
Challenger Memorial 10
Confederate Section/Confederate
    Monument 3
Douglas (Supreme Court Justice
    William O.) grave 22
Dulles (Sec. of State John Foster)
    grave 6
Evers (Medgar) grave 28
Holmes (Supreme Court Justice
    Oliver Wendell) grave 23
Visitor Center 33
Iwo Jima Memorial 30
Kennedy (Pres. John F. & Jacqueline
    Kennedy Onassis) grave 21
Kennedy (Sen. Robert F.) grave 19
Lee (Robert E.) Museum 17
L'Enfant (Pierre Charles) grave 18
Louis (Joe) grave 13
Marshall (Supreme Court Justice
    Thurgood) grave 25
Memorial Amphitheater 11
Murphy (Audie) grave 7
Netherlands Carillon 29
Old Amphitheater 14
Paderewski (Ignace Jan) marker 9
Parks (James) grave 2
Randolph (Mary) grave 20
Rickover (Adm. Hyman G.) grave 24
Rough Riders Monument 4
Taft (Pres. William Howard) grave 26
Tomb of the Unknown Civil War
    Dead 15
Tomb of the Unknowns 12
USS Maine mast 8
Wainwright (Gen. Jonathan)
    grave 1
Warren (Supreme Court Justice
    Earl) grave 5
Women in Military Service for
    America Memorial 31

can do for you—ask what you can do for your country. My fellow citizens of the world, ask not what America will do for you, but what together we can do for the freedom of man."

Arlington House: Commanding a gorgeous view of Washington, D.C., from atop the ridge above the Kennedy graves, the Greek Revival Arlington House (☎ 703/ 557-0613; www.nps.gov/arho) was built by George Washington Parke Custis, grandson of Martha Washington by her first marriage, after his daughter married a dashing young Virginian named Robert E. Lee. The Lees had lived in the mansion for 30 years when General Lee received word in April 1861 of the dissolution of the Union and Virginia's secession (see the "Born of Vengeance" box, below). After the U.S. government acquired it in 1883, Arlington House was used for several decades as office space and living quarters for cemetery staff. In 1925, Congress empowered the Secretary of War to restore the house to its pre–Civil War appearance and furnish it with original pieces (as much as possible) and replicas. Since 1955, it has served as a permanent memorial to Robert E. Lee. Servants' quarters and a small museum adjoin. Admission is free. You'll need a free ticket to tour the house from Thursdays to Mondays during summer, when volunteers in period dress conduct 10-minute tours (no tickets needed Tuesday and Wednesday). Staff distribute the tickets from 9:15am to 4:20pm at a tent near the mansion's Tourmobile bus stop. The tickets are timed, so go see other parts of the cemetery while waiting your turn. During the rest of the year, there's a self-guided tour, with volunteers on hand to give an introductory talk, hand out brochures, and answer questions. The mansion is open October to March, daily from 9:30am to 4:30pm; until 6pm April to September (closed Christmas and New Year's Day).

Tombs of the Unknowns: Beyond the mansion, America's most distinguished honor guard slowly marches before the Tombs of the Unknowns, a tribute to all members of the armed forces who have given their lives for their country in war. The 50-ton white-marble tomb rests above the remains of unidentified combatants slain during World War I. Unknowns from World War II and the Korean War are in the crypts on the plaza in front of it. There's also a crypt for an unknown killed in the Vietnam war, but modern forensic science is so sophisticated that the serviceman originally buried there with much ceremony was later identified as a U.S. Air Force pilot. His body was moved to another grave. Plan your visit to coincide with the changing of the guard ceremony—an impressive ritual of rifle maneuvers, heel clicking, and military salutes. It takes place daily every half hour April through September, every hour on the hour the rest of the year.

Memorial Amphitheater: Adjoining the tomb is the Greek Revival outdoor Memorial Amphitheater, used for special holiday services, particularly on Memorial Day when the sitting president or vice president attends. Free Tourmobile transportation from the visitor center parking lot is provided on these occasions.

U.S. Marine Corps War Memorial: On the northern periphery of Arlington National Cemetery, just off Va. 110 about 1½ miles north of the Kennedy graves, stands the U.S. Marine Corps War Memorial, better known as the Iwo Jima Memorial. The famous statue of Marines raising the American flag over Iwo Jima in February 1945 symbolizes the nation's esteem for the honored dead of the U.S. Marine Corps. News photographer Joe Rosenthal won a Pulitzer Prize for his photo of the flag-raising on Mount Suribachi, and sculptor Felix W. de Weldon, then on duty, was moved to create a sculpture based on the scene Rosenthal had captured. Two of the five servicemen who raised the flag were later killed in action; the survivors posed for de Weldon after the war. The sculpture took 3 years to complete and was dedicated in 1954 on the Marines' 179th anniversary. The Memorial grounds are used for military

---

Born of Vengeance

On April 20, 1861, Robert E. Lee crossed the Potomac River to a meeting at Blair House, opposite the White House in Washington, D.C. There he was offered command of all Union forces that would fight the Civil War. A distinguished career soldier and patriot, Lee nevertheless turned down President Abraham Lincoln and went home to his Custis-Lee mansion across the Potomac River in Arlington. Two days later he left for Richmond, where he took command of his native Virginia's rebel army.

The Union soon turned the Custis-Lee estate into a bivouac area for troops headed to war. Outraged at Lee's inflicting an unexpected defeat on them at the first Battle of Manassas, Quartermaster Gen. Montgomery Meigs ordered that Union dead be buried in the front yard of Lee's mansion. Thus was America's most hallowed national cemetery born of an act of vengeance.

Robert E. Lee never returned to Arlington. After many years and lengthy litigation, the U.S. Supreme Court finally returned ownership to his son. In 1883, George Washington Custis Lee sold the estate to the U.S. government for $150,000. Today you can visit Lee's old home, which has been restored and furnished to reflect its appearance during the Lee family's time of residence.

---

parades on Tuesday from 7 to 8:30pm in summer, and at all times many visitors picnic on the grass. There is a free shuttle from the visitor center starting at 6pm.

Netherlands Carillon: Adjacent to the Iwo Jima statue is the Netherlands Carillon, a gift from the people of Holland, with 50 bells, each carrying an emblem signifying a segment of Dutch society; for instance, the smallest bells represent Dutch youth. Verses cast on each bell were composed by poet Ben van Eysselsteijn. The carillon was officially dedicated on May 5, 1960, the 15th anniversary of the liberation of the Netherlands from the Nazis. The 127-foot-high open steel tower housing it stands on a plaza with steps guarded by two bronze lions. Thousands of tulip bulbs are planted on the surrounding grounds, creating a colorful display in spring. Carillon concerts are presented on Easter Sunday and every Saturday thereafter in April, May, and September, from 2 to 4pm. Concerts are held from 6 to 8pm June through August. Visitors are permitted into the tower after the carillonneur performs, to enjoy spectacular views of Washington.

The U.S. Marine Corps Memorial and the Netherlands Carillon are administered by the National Park Service as part of the George Washington Memorial Parkway (☎ **703/289-2500;** www.nps.gov/gwmp).

✪ **Newseum.** 1101 Wilson Blvd. (at N. Kent St.), Rosslyn. ☎ **888/NEWSEUM** or 703/284-3544. www.newseum.org. Free admission. Audio guides $1. Wed–Sun 10am–5pm. Metro: Rosslyn.

If you've ever imagined being Dan Rather or Barbara Walters on television, you *can* be at this three-story, state-of-the-art museum dedicated to journalism and journalists. Its interactive newsrooms let you be a momentary anchorperson, reporter, editor, interviewer, or sportscaster. The control room staff will even make tapes of your "on the air" performance as a news anchor or sportscaster—and sell them to you at the gift shop. You'll also learn how journalists facing deadlines decide what's news and what isn't, and how they get it to you.

Pick up a self-guided tour brochure at the reception desk and proceed upstairs to Level II, where a 13-minute high-definition video in the dome-topped main theater explains what's news. You can punch in your birth date on computer screens under the News Globe, which bears the names of 1,841 newspapers, and find out what was happening during the month you were born. Then head up to Level III and rent an audiocassette tape guide for a walk through the News History Gallery, explaining 500 years of journalism. That will put today's news in perspective as you see programs being produced in the broadcast studio and watch historic broadcasts and other programming on the 126-foot-long Video News Wall. Back down on Level II, you can go on camera yourself in the interactive newsrooms, and you can meet journalists and famous newsmakers during special programs in the broadcast studio (call ahead for a schedule).

Outside, Freedom Park has a memorial to all journalists who have died in the line of duty, plus a piece of the Berlin Wall, the door from Martin Luther King, Jr.'s, jail cell in Birmingham, Alabama, and other mementos of famous news stories.

Allow at least 90 minutes to tour the building, longer if you attend one of the special programs. There's pay parking in the garage next to the Newseum.

Note: The Newseum was looking for larger quarters at presstime, so call to make sure it's still here.

The Pentagon. I-395 at Boundary Channel Dr. ☎ **703/695-1776.** Free admission. Open for time-assigned tours only, Mon–Fri 8:45am–3pm. Closed federal holidays. Metro: Blue or Yellow line to Pentagon.

After you've seen the other major attractions in this area, you can tour the immense five-sided headquarters of the American military establishment. Built during the early years of World War II, it houses approximately 24,000 employees—as well as a Metro subway station, an Amtrak ticket office, a post office, a beauty salon, a dry cleaner, banks, clothing boutiques, a jeweler, a florist, and more.

The only way to see the Pentagon is on a 1½-hour tour. The most interesting part is a brief introductory film about how the Pentagon was built. After that, you'll essentially spend more than an hour walking certain corridors whose walls are lined with military art. That's it: There's not much else to see in this security-clad building.

Reservations are taken only for groups of nine people or more; otherwise, tickets for each day's tours are given away on a first come, first served basis at the tour window in the Concourse area near the Metro station. The window opens at 8:45am, and the day's tickets usually are gone by 9:30am during the busy summer season from June to Labor Day, by 1pm in spring and fall. Once you have a ticket, you can go do something else and return at your appointed tour time (consider taking the Metro to the nearby Arlington National Cemetery or perhaps the Pentagon City shopping complex across I-395). You must bring a photo ID (a driver's license or passport) to be admitted, and you'll have to go through a metal detector and have your bags searched before the tour.

Note: No Pentagon dining facilities or rest rooms are open to the public, and despite signs to the contrary, there is no parking reserved for casual visitors. Your best bet is to take the subway here. You can park for free at the Arlington Visitor Center (see "Essentials," above), but you'll need to get a permit at the center, which opens at 9am.

Factoid

The world's largest office building, the Pentagon contains more than 6.5 million square feet of space, almost 18 miles of corridors, and enough phone cable to gird the globe three times.

From there, it's a 2-block walk to the Pentagon City Metro station. The first 2 hours of parking are free at Pentagon Centre, across I-395 (see "Shopping," below).

A SCENIC DRIVE ALONG THE POTOMAC RIVER

Skirting the south bank of the Potomac River for 30 miles (48km) between Mount Vernon in the south to the Capital Beltway (I-495) in the northwest, the **George Washington Memorial Parkway** is one of Virginia's most scenic drives. It's also a major commuter route, which means lots of congestion during weekday morning and evening rush hours. Other times, you can drive the entire route in about 45 minutes without stopping. The parkway runs through Old Town Alexandria via King Street (see section 2, below); otherwise, it's a four-lane road with neither traffic signals nor stop signs. Also, with the exception of the Lyndon Baines Johnson Memorial Grove, you cannot make a left turn; accordingly, it's best driven from south to north so you can pull off at designated areas (perhaps for a picnic) beside or overlooking the river.

Thrill-seekers congregate at **Gravelly Point,** just north of Ronald Reagan Washington National Airport, where jet planes roar overhead just a few feet off the ground. You'll get a view of the Washington, D.C., monuments across the river from the **Lyndon Baines Johnson Memorial Grove,** just north of the Pentagon, where 500 white pines and inscriptions carved into Texas granite commemorate the 36th president. Another good spot is on a hill north of Key Bridge at **Potomac Overlook Regional Park,** where you'll have a great view down over the capital city.

As noted in "Outdoor Activities," below, you can also run, hike, or bike along part of the parkway. One of the most pleasant places for a short stroll is on **Theodore Roosevelt Island,** an 88-acre wooded preserve and bird sanctuary connected to the parkway by a footbridge just south of Rosslyn. There's a statue of the Rough Rider in the middle of the island.

For more information, contact Headquarters, George Washington Memorial Parkway, c/o Turkey Run Park, McLean, VA 22101 (☎ **703/289-2500;** fax 703/ 289-2598; www.nps.gov/gwmp).

OUTDOOR ACTIVITIES

Two first-rate hiking, biking, and running trails begin in Arlington. A 17-mile paved trail starts at Memorial Bridge and borders the **George Washington Memorial Parkway** 17 miles south to Mount Vernon, passing through Old Town Alexandria on the way (see "A Scenic Drive Along the Potomac River," above). If you didn't bring your bike, you can rent one in Old Town from **Big Wheel Bikes,** 2 Prince St., at The Strand (☎ **703/739-2300**), which charges $5 an hour or $25 for all day. Open Monday to Friday 11am to 7pm, Saturday 10am to 6pm, Sunday 11am to 5pm.

Beginning in the Shirlington area, on I-395, the **Washington & Old Dominion (W&OD) Trail** follows Four Mile Run Drive and Glencarlyn Park northwest to an old railroad bed, which then proceeds 45 miles through Leesburg to Purcellville in the Hunt Country (see section 4, below). There are access points with parking at Walter Reed Drive and at Columbia Pike.

You'll have to drive about 15 miles (24km) northwest of Arlington to **Great Falls Park,** on Old Dominion Drive in Great Falls, Virginia (☎ **703/285-2966**), but you'll be rewarded with easy hiking trails along the rim of the dramatic Mather Gorge, cut by the Potomac River as it roars its way through the foothills before emerging as the broad tidal river separating Arlington from D.C. Some trails are open to mountain bikes, the cliffs are one of northern Virginia's best rock-climbing venues, and kayakers love these rushing waters (bring your own bike, ropes, or kayak). The park is open daily except Christmas from 8am to dusk. Admission is $4 per car, $2 for pedestrians and cyclists, good for 3 days. To reach the park, go west on I-66, north on I-495, west on Georgetown Pike (Va. 193), and north on Old Dominion Drive (Va. 738).

SHOPPING

Arlington's prime shopping area sits almost directly over the Pentagon Center Metro station between I-395 and U.S. 1. Anchored by Macy's and Nordstrom, the plush four-level **Fashion Centre at Pentagon City,** at South Hayes Street and Army Navy Drive (☎ **703/415-2400**), has more than 150 shops, including branches of Ann Taylor, Crate & Barrel, Banana Republic, Brentano's, the Disney Store, Record World, Crabtree & Evelyn, Godiva Chocolates, Hoffritz, Laura Ashley, Victoria's Secret, Lane Bryant, the Limited, the Body Shop, and the Gap. It's built around a soaring atrium that covers a food court and entry to a six-screen movie theater, and it adjoins the Ritz-Carlton Pentagon City (see "Where to Stay," below). Pay parking is available in a six-level garage, but you can park free for 2 hours on weekdays and all day weekends across South Hayes Street at **Pentagon Centre** (☎ **703/415-7612**), which houses Borders Books & Records, a Best Buy discount electronics and appliance store, a Marshall's discount clothing store, Linens 'N' Things, a huge Costco Wholesale, a Starbuck's coffee shop, and branches of California Pizza Kitchen, Chevy's Mexican Restaurant, and Sgt. Pepper's Market chain restaurants. Both complexes are open Monday to Saturday from 10am to 9:30pm and Sunday from 11am to 6pm (Costco's hours vary).

The county's other mall, the much smaller **Ballston Common,** Wilson Boulevard at North Glebe Road (☎ **703/243-8088**), is anchored by JCPenney and Hecht's. There's a food court, several restaurants, a six-screen cinema, and a multilevel pay parking garage. Mall shops are open Monday to Saturday from 10am to 9:30pm, Sunday from noon to 5pm.

✪ **Potomac Mills,** about 20 miles south of Arlington in Dale City, Virginia (☎ **800/VA-MILLS** or 703/643-1770), is not only one of the nation's largest outlet malls, but also one of Virginia's most visited tourist attractions. This huge complex of 250 factory and discount shops includes the Swedish retailer Ikea and a large branch of Waccamaw Pottery. Virtually every factory outlet store is represented here, as well as clearance outlets for the likes of Nordstrom, JCPenney, Saks Fifth Avenue, and Levi's. The mall is open Monday to Saturday from 10am to 9:30pm, Sunday from 11am to 6pm. It's 30 minutes south of Arlington at Exit 143 off I-95. A shuttle bus runs between the mall and the Rosslyn and Pentagon City Metro stations in Arlington, Wednesday to Sunday. Round-trip fare is $12. Call ☎ **703/551-1050** for schedule and reservations.

WHERE TO STAY

The larger hotels here are geared to weekday business travelers and conventions. Except during the height of the spring season and on the Marine Corps Marathon weekend in mid- to late October, rooms are easy to come by on weekends. If you'll be here on a Friday or Saturday night, be sure to ask about special weekend packages.

The Arlington Visitors Center's **reservations service** will help you find a place to stay (☎ **888/743-8292;** www.stayarlington.com).

CRYSTAL CITY & PENTAGON CITY

Less than 2 miles from Ronald Reagan National Airport, the Crystal City and Pentagon City neighborhoods have the vast majority of Arlington's 9,000-plus hotel rooms. These are the "airport" hotels for Washington, D.C., so they all offer free airport and Metro station transfers.

Among the mass of high-rises on the airport side of the Jefferson Davis Highway (U.S. 1) stand **Courtyard by Marriott Crystal City,** 2899 Jefferson Davis Hwy. (☎ **800/847-4775** or 703/549-0320), which actually lacks a courtyard but does offer a clublike elegance at a reasonable price; **Crystal City Marriott,** 1999 Jefferson Davis Hwy. (☎ **800/228-9290** or 703/413-5500), with 308 rooms; **Embassy Suites Crystal City,** 1300 Jefferson Davis Hwy. (☎ **800/EMBASSY** or 703/979-9799), where you'll get a virtual home away from home; **Holiday Inn Crowne Plaza National Airport,** 1489 Jefferson Davis Hwy. (☎ **800/HOLIDAY** or 703/ 416-1600), a recently upgraded property right over the Crystal City Metro stop; and **Hyatt Regency Crystal City,** 2799 Jefferson Davis Hwy. (☎ **800/233-1234** or 703/ 418-1289), with 685 units. Note that the Crystal City Metro station is on this side of the highway at South 15th Street, so the lower-numbered street addresses are closer to the subway.

Actually facing South Eads Street on the Pentagon City side of the highway are the **Days Inn Crystal City,** 2000 Jefferson Davis Hwy. (☎ **800/DAYS-INN** or 703/ 920-8600), and **Sheraton Crystal City,** 1800 Jefferson Davis Hwy. (☎ **800/ 862-7666** or 703/486-1111), with 200 rooms. So are the Americana Hotel and Crystal Gateway Marriott, both listed below.

Near to Pentagon City are **Doubletree Hotel National Airport,** 300 Army Navy Dr. (☎ **800/222-TREE** or 703/416-4126), with more than 600 rooms and suites in twin towers; and **Residence Inn by Marriott,** 550 Army Navy Dr. (☎ **800/ 331-3131** or 703/413-6630), whose units all have kitchens. Many rooms at both these hotels have great views out over Washington, D.C.; be sure to ask for one.

✪ **Americana Hotel.** 1400 Jefferson Davis Hwy. (U.S. 1), Arlington, VA 22202. ☎ **800/548-6261** or 703/979-3772. Fax 703/979-0547. 102 units. A/C TV TEL. $65–$80 double. AE, DC, DISC, MC, V. Free parking. Entry on S. Eads St. north of S. 15th St. Metro: Crystal City or Pentagon City.

A terrific value, this modest hotel is a holdover from the days when Crystal City had only roadside motels instead of the high-rises that now make a canyon of Jefferson Davis Highway. It also enjoys a very convenient location, just a block and 2 blocks, respectively, from the Crystal City and Pentagon City Metro subway stations, with their numerous restaurants and shops. Although it has been around since 1963, you'll find the Americana to be clean and extraordinarily well maintained, and its rooms equipped with all standard hotel features. Although it looks like a motel from the out-side, interior corridors make the four-story building seem more like a hotel. The friendly and helpful staff set out complimentary coffee, orange juice, and pastries in the lobby each morning. This is a very popular hotel in April and in summer, so reserve as far in advance as possible during those times. During the off-season, the Arlington Visitor Center (see "Essentials," above) may have coupons worth $20 off your first night's lodging here.

Crystal Gateway Marriott. 1700 Jefferson Davis Hwy. (U.S. 1), Arlington, VA 22202. ☎ **703/920-3230.** Fax 703/979-6332. 700 units. A/C TV TEL. $209–$249 double. Children under 18 stay free in parents' room. Weekend and other packages available. AE, DC, DISC, MC, V. Parking $10 per night. Entry is on S. Eads St. at S. 18th St. Metro: Crystal City.

Just 5 minutes from National Airport, this first-rate Marriott is connected by a short passageway under U.S. 1 to the Crystal City Metro stop and a subterranean mall with some 200 shops, restaurants, and facilities such as a bank and hair salon. A six-story atrium skylight lobby is adorned with Asian art objects. Almost up to Ritz-Carlton quality (see below), rooms here have elegant dark wood furniture. The 15th and 16th floors are the concierge level, where a private lounge (closed some weekends) serves a complimentary breakfast and evening cocktails with hors d'oeuvres. A concierge is on duty, and additional in-room amenities include nightly turndown, bathroom scales, electric shoe polishers, and magazines.

Dining/Diversions: The plushest of the hotel's three restaurants serves Northern Italian cuisine under the stars (through the skylight, that is). The lobby restaurant, with cushioned wicker furnishings amid lush greenery overlooking the pool, serves American fare. Pub fare is featured at lunch and dinner in a sports bar equipped with billiard tables and numerous TVs.

Amenities: Concierge, limited room service, laundry, free newspaper delivery, nightly turndown on request, complimentary airport shuttle. Indoor/outdoor pool, health spa, Jacuzzi, saunas, business center, lobby gift shop plus underground concourse shops.

✪ **Ritz-Carlton Pentagon City.** 1250 S. Hayes St. (at S. 12th St.), Arlington, VA 22202. ☎ **800/241-3333** or 703/415-5000. Fax 703/415-5061. 366 units. A/C TV TEL. $249–$279 double; $299–$500 suite. Weekend and other packages available. AE, DC, DISC, MC, V. Valet parking $22 per night. Metro: Pentagon City.

Across from the Pentagon, the Ritz-Carlton is located in the upscale Fashion Centre retail-office complex. It's hard to believe that this traditional-looking hostelry—decorated with massive polished china cabinets, graceful wing chairs, plush sofas, Oriental rugs, crystal sconces, and a $2.5-million collection of 18th- and 19th-century paintings and antiques—was built in 1990. The impeccable service also hearkens back to another era. Rooms are spacious and airy, with beautiful mahogany pieces (some have four-poster beds) and every amenity imaginable: TVs concealed in armoires, plush terry bathrobes, and marble bathrooms complete with phone.

Guests on Club floors have a private lounge where complimentary breakfast, light lunch, afternoon tea, and hors d'oeuvres and cocktails are served. Club guests also have a private concierge staff.

Dining/Diversions: The hotel's highly acclaimed Sunday brunch is served in the Grill, which feels like an English club with its green-marble mantel, equestrian-theme oil paintings and bronzes, and shaded table lamps and wall sconces. A popular luncheon buffet and afternoon tea are served daily in the Lobby Lounge.

Amenities: Multilingual concierge staff, 24-hour room service, nightly turndown, baby-sitting, complimentary shoeshine, and airport shuttle. Indoor pool, fitness and exercise center, Jacuzzi, steam room, sauna, business center, gift shop.

ROSSLYN

Right across Key Bridge from Georgetown in D.C., Rosslyn has several chain hotels in addition to the properties mentioned below. About half the 584 rooms at the **Marriott Key Bridge,** 1401 Lee Hwy. (☎ **800/331-3131** or 703/524-6400), overlook the river and Washington, as do its rooftop restaurant and lounge. Also here are the **Best Western Key Bridge,** 1850 N. Fort Myer Dr. (☎ **800/528-1234** or 703/ 522-0400), and the **Hyatt Arlington,** 1325 Wilson Blvd. (☎ **800/233-1234** or 703/ 525-1234). Both are high-rise properties that cater primarily to groups and business travelers.

Holiday Inn Rosslyn Westpark. 1900 N. Fort Myer Dr. (at I-66), Arlington, VA 22209. ☎ **800/368-3408** or 703/807-2000. Fax 703/522-8864. 276 units. A/C TV TEL. $117–$140 double; $150 suite. Free parking. AE, DC, DISC, MC, V. Free parking. Metro: Rosslyn.

Here's a property that offers good value and great convenience. This Holiday Inn is just a block from the Rosslyn Metro station and a 10-minute walk across the Key Bridge to Georgetown restaurants and nightlife. Many rooms in the 17-story property have balconies overlooking the Potomac and/or the Washington Monument. Local calls are free. The hotel's glass-enclosed rooftop restaurant features American fare, including moderately priced all-you-can-eat buffet lunches. Additional facilities include a coffee shop, swimming pool with sundeck, whirlpool, sauna, exercise room, coin-operated laundry, and gift shop. Room service is available during restaurant hours.

Motel 50 Rosslyn. 1601 Arlington Blvd. (U.S. 50), Arlington, VA 22209. ☎ **800/504-4888** or 703/524-3400. Fax 703/524-0220. 38 units. A/C TV TEL. $65 double. Rates include continental breakfast. AE, MC, V. Free parking. Metro: Rosslyn.

Owned and operated by the same family as the Americana Hotel (see above), the plain and simple Motel 50 is right on U.S. 50, so you're going to hear traffic from most of the rooms. Otherwise, it's a clean, well-run, and friendly property. An extensive continental breakfast is served in the lobby each morning, and free transport is provided to and from National Airport on request. Restaurants are nearby.

Quality Inn Iwo Jima. 1501 Arlington Blvd. (U.S. 50), Arlington, VA 22209. ☎ **800/ 228-5151** or 703/524-5000. Fax 703/522-5484. 141 units. A/C TV TEL. $79–$110 double. Children under 18 stay free. Weekend packages available. AE, DC, DISC, MC, V. Free parking. Metro: Rosslyn.

With a brick and white stucco facade, this pleasant Quality Inn also is situated on U.S. 50, although it's set back a bit, which makes a big difference in terms of traffic noise. Facilities include an indoor/outdoor swimming pool, a coin-operated laundry, and a small fitness room. A moderately priced restaurant decorated with World War II memorabilia serves American and Italian fare. *USA Today* is available free in the lobby, and room service is offered during restaurant hours. The Metro is about 3 blocks from the hotel.

BALLSTON

The 209-room **Arlington Hilton and Towers,** 950 N. Stafford St., at Fairfax Drive (☎ **800/HILTONS** or 703/528-6000), occupies the first three floors of a high-rise condo building right over the Ballston Metro station. Elevated walkways lead from the hotel to the Ballston Commons shopping mall.

Comfort Inn Ballston. 1211 N. Glebe Rd. (at Washington Blvd.), Arlington, VA 22201. ☎ **800/221-2222** or 703/247-3399. Fax 703/524-8739. E-mail: comfortinnballston@erols. com. 126 units. A/C TV TEL. $89–$149 double. Weekend and other packages available. AE, DC, DISC, MC, V. Free parking. From I-66, take Glebe Rd. exit and turn left. Metro: Ballston.

Housed in a three-story red-brick building, this Comfort Inn offers a convenient location off I-66, just 10 minutes from National Airport and a 5-block walk to the Metro and Ballston Common Mall. Rooms are exceptionally bright and spacious, with dark polished-wood furnishings and all the standard motel amenities. There's a gift shop in the lobby and an adjoining Italian restaurant, which provides limited room service.

Holiday Inn Arlington at Ballston. 4610 N. Fairfax Dr. (at N. Wakefield St.), Arlington, VA 22203. ☎ **800/HOLIDAY** or 703/243-9800. Fax 703/527-2677. E-mail: holidaybal@aol. com. 221 units. A/C TV TEL. $170 double. AE, DC, DISC, MC, V. Free parking. From I-66 eastbound, take Exit 71 to hotel on right. From I-66 westbound, take Exit 71; turn left on Glebe Rd., right on Fairfax Dr. to hotel on left. Metro: Ballston.

Although it lacks charm, this nine-story, utilitarian hotel is just 2 blocks from the Ballston Metro station and the many restaurants and shops surrounding it (the hotel provides a free shuttle to the station). Entered from interior corridors, the long rooms come equipped with two double beds or one king-size bed, plus either a sofa or a table and chairs. A restaurant at the lobby level serves three meals daily and provides room service during restaurant hours, while the lounge features a cozy, U-shaped bar.

Facilities include an outdoor pool (open Memorial Day to Labor Day), gift shop, and coin-operated laundry. Guests get discount membership at a nearby fitness center.

WHERE TO DINE
CRYSTAL CITY

In Crystal City, a row of one-story storefronts in the 500 block of South 23rd Street, between Jefferson Davis Highway (U.S. 1) and South Fern Street, houses a broad selection of inexpensive-to-moderate restaurants, most with sidewalk seating in fine weather. Overall, the selection isn't as diverse here—nor the quality quite as good—as at Clarendon (see below). The restaurants post their menus out front, and you can judge by the number of patrons who's serving the best food.

At the inexpensive end of the scale, **Akbar** (☎ 703/979-0777) offers home-style lamb kebabs, chicken curries, and other northern Indian fare. The pleasant **Bonsai Grill Sushi Bar** (☎ 703/553-7723) has both raw and cooked Japanese items in a setting graced with natural wood. **Saigon Crystal** (☎ 703/920-3822) adds a creative spin to Vietnamese fare and has Arlington's largest selection of dinner-size *pho* (noodle soup). **The Taco House** (☎ 703/979-7033) obviously offers Mexican cuisine.

A bit more expensive, the popular **Cafe Italia** (☎ 703/521-2565) is notable for its traditional pastas and other dishes from the old country, and **Stars and Stripes** (☎ 703/979-1USA) provides a tasty, eclectic collection of American fare.

You can get inexpensive burgers and other chow while watching the action or shooting pool at two sports bars, **Crystal City Sports Pub** (☎ 703/521-8215) and **The Fox Hole** (☎ 703/685-0555).

In Pentagon City, try the food court on the ground level of the **Fashion Centre at Pentagon City**, at South Hayes Street and Army Navy Drive (☎ 703/415-2400). Across South Hayes Street are the **California Pizza Kitchen** (☎ 703/412-4900), **Chevy's Fresh Mex Restaurant** (☎ 703/413-8700), and the cafeteria-style **Sgt. Pepper's Market Fresh Dining** (☎ 703/418-2203), which features all-you-can eat salads, soups, pizzas, pasta, and desserts for about $7 at lunch, $9 at dinner.

Ristorante Portofino. 526 S. 23rd St. (at S. Eads St.). ☎ **703/979-8200.** Reservations recommended. Main courses $15–$20. AE, DC, MC, V. Mon–Fri 11am–2pm; daily 5–10pm. Metro: Crystal City. ITALIAN.

A pretty downstairs garden room is just one of the dining spaces in this bustling Italian restaurant, a family-owned institution since 1970. The entrance is off the parking lot (a rarity in this neighborhood) at the rear of the converted three-story residence, and you'll know when you hear the taped arias of Enrico Caruso and Luciano Pavarotti that you're in for one of the best Italian meals hereabouts. Dinner begins with some tasty specialties, including fried calamari, ricotta-filled baked eggplant with creamy tomato sauce, and prosciutto with fresh mozzarella. Any of the pastas on the menu can be ordered as a half portion for an appetizer—linguine with green pesto sauce, fettucine Alfredo, and spaghetti carbonara are a few of the possibilities. Entrees include veal in all expected guises (parmigiana, piccata, marsala), plus a good variety of chicken and fish dishes. The house special dessert is a wonderful rum cake with whipped cream.

Top Thai. 523 S. 23rd St. (between S. Eads and S. Fern sts.). ☎ **703/521-1305.** Reservations accepted. Main courses $8–$10. DC, DISC, MC, V. Mon–Sat 11am–11pm, Sun 5–10pm. THAI.

My body was screaming at me to eat my vegetables when I came into this narrow storefront restaurant one evening. I chose widely, for not only does Top Thai offer six specifically vegetarian dishes, but you can substitute tofu for pork, chicken, beef, and seafood and still experience the exotic, almost flowery flavors of the red or green curries here. I opted for a mound of mixed vegetables in a mildly spicy sauce tamed by sweet coconut milk. Look in the front of the menu for house specials. For dessert, the sweet sticky rice with fresh mango, or just a plain slice of papaya, will soothe your palate.

ROSSLYN

✪ **Red Hot & Blue.** 1600 Wilson Blvd. (at N. Pierce St.). ☎ **703/276-7427.** Reservations not accepted. Sandwiches $5–$6; main courses $7–$17.50. AE, MC, V. Sun–Thurs 11am–10pm; Fri–Sat 11am–midnight. Metro: Rosslyn. AMERICAN.

Join the line of hungry diners waiting for tables at this casual, fun-filled, high-energy restaurant, the area's most popular barbecue joint. Some of the crowd gravitates to the bar for frosted steins of beer under the jolly eye of a blue-neon pig strumming a red guitar. The late Republican National Committee chairman Lee Atwater, along with a group of Tennessee politicians and a TV reporter, opened the restaurant and named it for a Memphis radio show (the surviving owners now have several other outlets). The decor here is a jumpy black, white, and red, and seating is in banquettes and at small tables jammed rather close together. But the food is just fine—ribs wet (with sauce) or dry (secret spices), barbecued beef brisket, smoked chicken and ham, fried catfish, and homemade trimmings like beans, coleslaw, potato salad, and fries. For dessert, try the Southern-style banana pudding or an Oreo cookie sundae. Naturally, the background music of choice here is the blues, and occasionally nationally known blues artists perform here.

Red Hot & Blue has a **carryout branch** at 3014 Wilson Blvd. in Clarendon (see below). The menu and prices are the same at both locations.

Tom Sarris' Orleans House. 1213 Wilson Blvd. (at N. Lynn St.). ☎ **703/524-2929.** Reservations not accepted. Main courses $10–$17. AE, DC, DISC, MC, V. Mon–Thurs 11am–10pm; Fri 11am–11pm; Sat 4–11pm; Sun 4–10pm. Metro: Rosslyn. PRIME RIB/STEAKS.

Within sight of the Newseum, this white pseudo-antebellum building, trimmed in wrought iron, is the home of this area's best beef bargain. The interior resembles a New Orleans garden, with iron chairs and railings, leaded-glass fixtures, and ceiling fans. The menu offers tender, well-seasoned steaks, baked chicken, and seafood, but locals and visitors alike flock here for the prime rib, especially the regular cut: It's ample for most appetites and costs $10.95—not inexpensive but a great value nonetheless. Heartier appetites can opt for the larger Louis XIV cut or the mammoth portion. With it, you get an oven-roasted potato and offerings from an exceptional salad bar that's decorated like a riverboat. Wine and other drinks are available. The restaurant is on the tour bus circuit, but it's large enough to accommodate most groups and still have room for independent travelers.

CLARENDON

Centered on North Highland Street and Wilson, Clarendon, and Washington boulevards, Clarendon is one of the prime places to dine in the Washington area, so diverse and so good are its multitude of inexpensive ethnic restaurants. You'll emerge from the Clarendon Metro station in the median strip dividing Wilson and Clarendon boulevards; the restaurants are on either side of the station, or within a 2-block walk.

There are so many Vietnamese restaurants here that locals have dubbed the area "Little Saigon." If the wait at Queen Bee (see listing below) is too long, you can get almost-as-good Vietnamese cuisine at several other restaurants, including **Cafe Dalat,** 3143 Wilson Blvd. (☎ **703/276-0935**), and **Cafe Saigon,** 1135 N. Highland St.

(☎ 703/243-6522); and also at **Nam Viet,** 1121 N. Highland St. (☎ 703/522-7110), and **Little Viet Garden,** 3012 Wilson Blvd. (☎ 703/522-9686), both of which have converted parts of parking lots to outdoor dining.

I've listed some of the better values below, but don't let my choices keep you from exploring **Atami,** 3155 Wilson Blvd. (☎ 703/522-4787), which sets an appropriately Japanese scene for fine sushi; the **Madhu Ban,** 3217 N. Washington Blvd. (☎ 703/528-7184), whose crispy, crepe-like masala dosas are the pick of its strictly vegetarian south Indian fare; **A Taste of Casablanca,** 3211 Washington Blvd. (☎ 703/527-7468), which will take you to Morocco; and **La Cantinita's Havana Cafe,** 3100 Clarendon Blvd. (☎ 703/524-3611), which will transport you to Miami's South Beach and its Cuban cuisine.

For some ethnic cuisine hailing from closer to home, a carryout branch (with seating but no table service) of **Red Hot & Blue** (see above) serves its Memphis-style barbecue at 3014 Wilson Blvd. (☎ 703/243-1510). You can get hearty breakfasts and many old American favorites at the **Silver Diner,** 3200 Wilson Blvd., at Washington Boulevard (☎ 703/812-8600).

The two most popular neighborhood pubs are **Witlow's on Wilson,** 2854 Wilson Blvd., at North Fillmore Street (☎ 703/276-9693), and the more yuppiefied **Clarendon Grill,** 1101 N. Highland St., between Clarendon Boulevard and North 11th Street (☎ 703/524-7455). Both are on the local music scene (see "Arlington After Dark," below).

When you're finished dining, stop by for a gourmet coffee or ice cream cone at the **Lazy Sundae,** 2925 Wilson Blvd., between Filmore and Garfield streets (☎ 703/525-4960).

Note: Parking can be difficult in Clarendon, but Cafe New Delhi, Cafe Dalat, Cafe Saigon, Clarendon Grill, Hard Times Cafe, Queen Bee, and Witlow's on Wilson have **free validated parking** after 6pm weeknights and all day weekends in the lot on North Highland Street in the block north of Wilson Boulevard. I usually find a metered street space (free after 6pm weekdays and all day Saturday and Sunday) beside the Silver Diner on North Irving Street, south of the intersection of Wilson, Clarendon, and Washington boulevards.

Aegean Taverna. 2950 Clarendon Blvd. (at N. Garfield St.). ☎ 703/841-9494). Reservations recommended. Main courses $8.50–$17. AE, MC. V. Mon–Thurs 11am–2:30pm and 5–10pm; Fri 11am–2:30pm and 5–11pm; Sat 5–11pm; Sun 11am–3pm and 5–9:30pm. GREEK.

During fine weather you can choose a patio table shaded by a real grape vine at this taverna. Inside will remind you of Greece, too, with stucco walls adorned with paintings and serving plates from the old country. The authentic fare includes gyro sandwiches (served as a platter with french fries), moussaka, pastitsio, dolmades (stuffed grape leaves), and braised lamb shank in a tomato sauce. You can try a little of everything on the Aegean special platter. Vegetarians can opt for the spinach pie, a Grecian-style eggplant dish, or a medley of sautéed vegetables served over pasta. Musicians play Greek tunes back by the big fireplace on Friday and Saturday evenings.

Cafe New Delhi. 1041 N. Highland St., at N. 11th St. ☎ 703/528-2511. Reservations accepted. Main courses $7–$14. AE, DC, MC, V. Daily 11:30am–2:30pm and 5–10pm. INDIAN.

"In India," goes the motto for this fine restaurant, "curry doesn't mean the yellow stuff that comes in a can." Indeed, here a variety of well-seasoned curries come in various colors, just like they do at better restaurants in India and Pakistan. My favorite is the chicken marsala, infused with smoky flavor from the tandoori oven and topped with a mild creamy tomato curry sauce. Also from the oven come excellent lamb, fish, and chicken (avoid the shrimp, which can come out of the clay oven a bit too dry). Old standby curries such as rogan josh are available, too, and there are several vegetarian selections. Look up at the unusual ceiling: It's painted like the sky, complete with white clouds and a pink and orange sunset just beginning at the front of the building.

✪ **Faccia Luna.** 2909 Wilson Blvd. (between Filmore and Garfield sts.). Reservations not accepted. Sandwiches $6; pizza $6.50–$19; main courses $10.50–$14. AE, MC, V. Sun–Thurs 11am–11pm, Fri–Sat 11am–midnight. ITALIAN.

This inviting trattoria is Clarendon's neighborhood favorite, so be prepared to grab a stool at the bar and wait for a table, especially on Friday and Saturday evenings. Wonderful aromas wafting from the open kitchen at the rear will surely whet your appetite as you're shown to your table out on the sidewalk or to your booth inside (charmingly set off by brick dividers and warmly lit by overhead spots). The pizzas are terrific, but you won't find spaghetti and meatballs offered here. Instead, imagine the creative likes of egg fettucine pesto (tossed with fresh basil, pine nuts, Parmesan cheese, olive oil, and garlic). And don't overlook the nightly special appetizers like bruschetta with smoked salmon, or main courses such as shrimp and penne pasta tossed in sauce of white wine, olive oil, and Romano cheese.

Hard Times Cafe. 3028 Wilson Blvd. (at N. Highland St.). ☎ **703/528-2233.** Reservations not accepted. Sandwiches and burgers $4–$6.50; main courses $5–$6.50. AE, MC, V. Mon–Thurs 11:30am–10pm; Fri–Sat 11:30am–11pm; Sun noon–10pm. Metro: Clarendon. CHILI.

A casual, laid-back hangout, the Hard Times Cafe is the kind of chili parlor you'd find in Texas. The bar is always crowded with young professionals, the jukebox plays country music, and the "bowls of red" are first-rate. The Lone Star State decor features Texas flags, plus a longhorn steer hide and historic photos of the Old West on the walls. Seating is in roomy oak booths as well as at tables. The restaurant cooks up three styles of chili: Texas (ground chuck simmered with secret spices and *no* tomatoes), Cincinnati (with hot and sweet spices, including cinnamon), and spicy vegetarian with peanuts. You can request your chili with beans or spaghetti. Homemade cornbread is included in the price; cheese and onions cost slightly more. Sandwiches (including burgers and hot dogs—covered with chili, of course), salads, and sides of onion rings and steak fries round out the offerings. Pecan pie is the logical dessert.

Mexicali Blues. 2933 Wilson Blvd. (at N. Garfield St.). ☎ **703/812-9352.** Reservations not accepted. Main courses $6.50–$11. MC, V. Mon–Thurs 11am–11pm, Fri–Sat 11am–midnight, Sun 4–10pm. SALVADORAN/MEXICAN.

Of many Central American restaurants in Arlington (reflecting the county's substantial population of immigrants from that region), this popular, lively storefront accented by gaudy lime green chairs is the most interesting. If you've never tried Salvadoran fare (it's not the same as Mexican), start with a *pupusa* (a soft tortilla stuffed with pork, cheese, or both) or a slightly sweet *tamal de elote* (yellow cornbread steamed in a husk and served with sour cream). For a main course, try *carne asada* (marinated steak strips sautéed with peppers and onions). Or you can opt for a combo platter of Salvadoran items and Mexican fare such as tacos, enchiladas, burritos, and flautas. Kids can dine here for $3.50. If you have to wait for a table, slake your thirst at the bar with a cold pilsner beer from El Salvador.

✪ **Queen Bee.** 3181 Wilson Blvd. (near Washington Blvd.). ☎ **703/527-3444.** Reservations not accepted. Main courses $7–$9. AE, DC, MC, V. Daily 11am–10pm. Metro: Clarendon. VIETNAMESE.

Clarendon's oldest and still best Vietnamese restaurant sits directly across Wilson Boulevard from the Clarendon Metro station. Mirrors lining one of the walls add an illusion of depth to the narrow room (forget having an intimate conversation here; the tables are elbow-distance apart). At lunch or dinner, start with the Queen Bee platter, a sampler of appetizers including a spring roll, shrimp tempura, charcoal-grilled pork, and house salad. Among the entrees, specials include steamed rice-flour meat rolls and shrimp cakes. Chicken is prepared in several delicious ways—curried, in ginger sauce, or with lemongrass. Roast duck and quail are also stellar entrees. Vegetarians can choose from a melange of vegetables sautéed in oyster sauce or fresh tofu sautéed with tomato and scallions. You may see me here on a cold winter day enjoying a meal-size bowl of Vietnamese-style *pho* (noodle soup), a house specialty.

BALLSTON

Several chain restaurants and an inexpensive food court grace **Ballston Common,** on Wilson Boulevard at North Glebe Road (☎ **703/243-8088**), the neighborhood's shopping mall.

Food Factory. 4221 N. Fairfax Dr. (entry at rear, off N. Stuart St.). ☎ **703/527-2279.** Reservations not accepted. Main courses $4–$7. MC, V. Mon–Fri 11am–10pm; Sat–Sun noon–10pm. Metro: Ballston. SOUTH ASIAN.

Plain and simple, with cafe chairs set at family-style tables, the Food Factory is famous hereabouts for its fine kebabs cooked in a tandoori oven. You can opt for Afghani-style sticks of beef, chicken, lamb, or spicy *chapli* (ground beef), or pick one of the Northern Indian–style samosas or meat and vegetable curries displayed at a cafeteria table. There's a free parking lot at the entry on North Stuart Street.

✪ **Rio Grande Cafe.** 4301 N. Fairfax Dr. (at N. Taylor St.). ☎ **703/528-3131.** Reservations not accepted. Main courses $8–$17.50. AE, DC, DISC, MC, V. Mon–Thurs 11am–10:30pm; Fri–Sat 11:30am–11:30pm; Sun 11:30am–10:30pm. Metro: Ballston. TEX-MEX.

Part of an excellent small chain (George Bush was a regular at the Bethesda, Maryland, branch when he lived in the White House), this casual, north-of-the-border roadhouse consistently serves some of the best Tex-Mex fare in northern Virginia. The dining room sets an appropriate scene with crumbling adobe walls bearing old advertising signs and photos from southwest Texas—although in warm weather you might want to wait for an umbrella table out on the sidewalk. You can start with old standbys such as nachos, quesadillas, or *ceviche* (South American–style marinated raw fish), then go on to tacos, enchiladas, burritos, or fajitas. Or you can choose from chicken, frog's legs, or quail grilled over mesquite, or perhaps a nightly special, such as rainbow trout sautéed with cilantro, white wine, and lemon butter.

ARLINGTON AFTER DARK

The best source of up-to-the-minute nighttime entertainment information is the daily "Style" and the Friday "Weekend" sections of the *Washington Post,* available at newsstands all over northern Virginia.

THE PERFORMING ARTS   All of northern Virginia is very much in the orbit of the John F. Kennedy Center for the Performing Arts, the National Theater, and other such first-rate venues across the Potomac in Washington, D.C. See *Frommer's Washington, D.C.* or *Frommer's Washington, D.C. from $70 a Day* for details.

On this side of the Potomac, ✪ **Wolf Trap Farm Park,** 1624 Trap Rd., Vienna, VA (☎ **703/255-1868;** www.wolf-trap.org or www.nps.gov/wotr), is the nation's only national park dedicated to the performing arts, with a star-studded summer season.

Performances are held in the open-air, 3,900-seat Filene Center II, but up to 3,000 patrons choose to picnic and watch the show from under the stars out on the sloping lawn (the sound system is great, but bring binoculars, and arrive early for a prime spot). A smaller venue, the **Barns of Wolf Trap,** offers performances indoors during the spring and fall. Tickets range from $12 to $26 on the lawn and up to $40 or more inside, depending on who's playing. The lawn opens 90 minutes before the performance. Take I-66 west and follow the signs for I-495 north to the Dulles Toll Road (Va. 267); stay on local exits (you'll see a sign) until you come to Wolf Trap. Toll is 50¢. Metro: West Falls Church, then take the Wolf Trap Express Shuttle ($3.50), which runs every 20 minutes beginning 2 hours before showtime at the Filene Center (not at the Barns).

THE BAR & MUSIC SCENE   Lively pubs along Wilson Boulevard have made Arlington a center of music for the entire national capital area. "Arlington's Wilson Boulevard used to be way out there, but now it's definitely in," the *Washington Post* said in describing this hip scene. Indeed, a number of noteworthy bands have formed here, including the nationally known alternative group Fugazi; the county even has its own record label, Dischord.

You can hear the music every weekend night along Wilson Boulevard between Rosslyn and Clarendon. Working west, alternative and pop prevail at the sprawling **Bardo Rodeo,** in a former automobile dealership at 2100 Wilson Blvd., near the Courthouse Metro station (☎ **703/527-9399**). In Clarendon, the pierced set takes in alternative and indie rockers at **Galaxie Hut,** a tiny hole-in-the-wall at 2711 Wilson Blvd. (☎ **703/525-9399**). **IOTA,** a block west at 2832 Wilson Blvd. (☎ **703/ 522-8340**), showcases roots rock, a blend of country, folk, and rock. Across the street, **Witlow's on Wilson,** 2854 Wilson Blvd., at North Filmore Street (☎ **703/ 276-9693**), specializes in frat rock and blues. More upscale is **Clarendon Grill,** a block south of the boulevard at 1101 N. Highland St. (☎ **703/524-7455**), which offers a mix of music. Depending on which bands are playing, these pubs draw twenty- and early-thirty-something professionals or the young pierced set.

2 Alexandria

5 miles S of Washington, D.C.; 95 miles N of Richmond

Founded by a group of Scottish tobacco merchants, the seaport town of Alexandria came into being on a sunny day in July 1749, when a 60-acre tract of land was auctioned off in half-acre lots. As you stroll the brick sidewalks and cobblestone streets of highly gentrified **Old Town,** the city's official historic district, you'll see more than 2,000 buildings dating from the 18th and 19th centuries. You can visit Gadsby's Tavern, where two centuries ago the men who created this nation discussed politics, freedom, and revolution over tankards of ale. You can stand in the doorway of the tavern where Washington reviewed his troops for the last time, walk past Lee's boyhood home, and sit in the pews of Christ Church, where both men worshiped.

Today Old Town Alexandria rivals Washington's Georgetown in its abundance of quaint shops, boutiques, art galleries, restaurants, and tourists (not to mention hordes of late-teens just hanging out on Friday and Saturday nights). But in this history-conscious "mother lode of Americana," the past is being ever-increasingly restored in an ongoing archaeological and historical research program. Indeed, if they weren't instantly shocked back to death by the cars jockeying for prized parking spaces, George Washington and Robert E. Lee would still recognize their old hometown.

ESSENTIALS
VISITOR INFORMATION

The Alexandria Convention & Visitors Association's **Ramsay House Visitor Center,** 221 King St., at Fairfax Street facing Market Square (☎ **703/838-4200;** 703/ 838-5005 for 24-hour Alexandria events recording; fax 703/838-4683; www. funside.com), is open daily from 9am to 5pm (closed New Year's Day, Thanksgiving, and Christmas). Here you can pick up maps and brochures, find out about special events taking place during your visit, and get information about accommodations, restaurants, sights, shopping, and whatever else. If you come by car, get a free **1-day parking permit** here for gratis parking at any 2-hour meter for up to 24 hours (the permits don't apply to 2-hour zones without meters).

Be sure to pick up a free copy of *Old Town Crier* (☎ **703/836-9132;** www. oldtowncrier.com), a monthly magazine packed with information and news about special events, dining, shopping, and entertainment.

GETTING THERE

BY PLANE   Ronald Reagan Washington National Airport (☎ **703/685-8000**) is just 2 miles north of Alexandria via the George Washington Memorial Parkway. See "Getting There & Getting Around" in chapter 2 and in the Arlington section, above, for more information. Washington's Metrorail (see below) provides easy transport to Alexandria via its Blue and Yellow lines (see below). SuperShuttle (☎ **800/ BLUE-VAN**) operates frequent van service daily from 6am to 10pm. Fares to Old Town start at $8.

**BY CAR   Going south from Washington, cross the 14th Street Bridge (I-395) and go south on the scenic George Washington Memorial Parkway, which becomes Washington Street, Alexandria's main north-south thoroughfare. A left turn on King Street will take you into the heart of Old Town. I-95 crosses the Potomac River at Alexandria; take Exit 1 (U.S. 1) and go north into Old Town.

On-street **parking** is severely limited here, but you can get a 1-day pass from the Alexandria Convention & Visitors Association (see "Visitor Information," above). There's a public garage under Market Square, virtually opposite the visitor center on Fairfax Street north of King Street.

BY TRAIN   The Amtrak passenger **rail station (☎ **703/836-4339**) is at 110 Callahan Dr., near King Street.

**BY WASHINGTON METRORAIL   From Arlington or Washington, take the Blue or Yellow lines to the King Street station (it's across the tracks from Amtrak's Alexandria station). From the Metro station, board DASH buses numbered AT-2 or AT-5 (85¢) down King Street to the corner of Fairfax Street and the door of the visitor center (see "Getting Around," below). It's a short ride from the station; in fact, you can walk it in about 15 minutes, but better to save your soles for sightseeing.

CITY LAYOUT

Old Town Alexandria is laid out in a simple grid system. Going west from the Potomac River, Union to Lee Street is the 100 block, Lee to Fairfax the 200 block, and so on. Numbers on the cross streets (more or less going north and south) are divided north and south by King Street. King to Cameron is the 100 block north, Cameron to Queen the 200 block north, and so on. King to Prince is the 100 block south, and so on.

As a glance at the walking-tour map later in this chapter will indicate, Old Town is contained within several blocks. Park your car for the day, don comfortable shoes, and start walking—it's the easiest way.

The Boyhood Home of Robert E. Lee

In 1812, American Revolution cavalry hero Gen. Henry "Light-Horse Harry" Lee moved his wife, Ann Hill Carter, and their family from Stratford Hall Plantation on the Northern Neck (see section 3 in chapter 5) to a Federal-style mansion at 607 Oronoco St. in Alexandria. One of the Lee's children was the then 5-year-old Robert E. Lee, future commander of the Confederate Army of Northern Virginia.

George Washington was an occasional guest of earlier occupants, Col. and Mrs. William Fitzhugh. In 1804, the Fitzhughs' daughter, Mary Lee, married Martha Washington's grandson, George Washington Parke Custis, in the drawing room. The Custises' daughter later married Robert E. Lee. In later years, the drawing room became known as the "Lafayette Room" to commemorate a visit by General Lafayette, a comrade-in-arms of Light-Horse Harry during the American Revolution, to Ann Hill Carter Lee in October 1824.

Built in 1785, the house was operated for many years as a museum known as "The Boyhood Home of Robert E. Lee."

GETTING AROUND

Old Town is compact, so you can easily see its historic sights on foot. From a visitor's standpoint, Alexandria's bus system, known as **DASH,** is primarily useful for getting from the King Street Metro station to the major sights. DASH provides service from 5am to 11pm daily except New Year's Day, Thanksgiving, and Christmas. Buses numbered AT-2 and AT-5 run between the King Street Metro station and the Ramsay House visitor center. Base fare is 85¢, with exact fare or tokens required. The visitor center gives away route maps (and sells DASH tokens), or call ☎ **703/370-3274** from 7:30am to 5pm Monday to Friday for schedule information.

All the major **car-rental firms** are based at Ronald Reagan Washington National Airport. For a taxi, call **Alexandria Yellow Cab Company** (☎ **703/549-2500**) or **Alexandria White Top Cab Company** (☎ **703/683-4004**).

EXPLORING OLD TOWN

Whenever you come, you're sure to run into some activity or other—a jazz festival, a tea garden or tavern gambol, a quilt exhibit, a wine tasting, or an organ recital. It's all part of Alexandria's *cead mile failte* (100,000 welcomes) to visitors.

Note: Many Alexandria attractions are closed on Mondays. The Potomac plantations (described later in this chapter) are 9 to 15 miles south of Alexandria and are most logically visited on day trips from here.

THE TOP ATTRACTIONS

The Ramsay House visitor center (see "Visitor Information," above) sells a money-saving **block ticket** for discounted admission to Gadsby's Tavern, the Carlyle House, and the Apothecary Shop (see below). The ticket, which can also be purchased at any of the three buildings, costs $9 for adults, $5 for students 11 to 17, free for children under 11.

Carlyle House. 121 N. Fairfax St. (near Cameron St.). ☎ **703/549-2997.** www. carlylehouse.org. Admission $4 adults, $2 children 11–17, free for children under 11. Tues–Sat 10am–4:30pm; Sun noon–4:30pm. Mandatory 40-minute tours depart on the hour and half hour.

Not only is Carlyle House regarded as one of Virginia's most architecturally impressive 18th-century homes, but it also figured prominently in American history. Patterned after Scottish-English manor houses, it was completed in 1753 by Scottish merchant John Carlyle for his bride, Sara Fairfax of Belvoir, who hailed from one of Virginia's most prominent families. Then a waterfront property with its own wharf (landfills have left the house 2 blocks inland), it became a social and political center visited by many great men of the time, George Washington among them. But its most important moment in history occurred in April 1755, when Maj. Gen. Edward Braddock, commander-in-chief of His Majesty's forces in North America, met here with five colonial governors and asked them to tax colonists to finance a campaign against the French and Indians. Colonial legislatures refused to comply, one of the first instances of serious friction between America and Britain. Nevertheless, Braddock made Carlyle House his headquarters during the campaign.

The house is furnished with period pieces, and the original large parlor and adjacent study have survived intact. An upstairs room houses an exhibit called "A Workman's View," which explains 18th-century construction methods with hand-hewn beams and hand-wrought nails.

There's seldom a wait for a tour, but if there is, you can kill the time by exploring the gardens or browsing the gift shop, which purveys jewelry, books, colonial toys, and other items. Call ahead for a schedule of special events and lectures.

✪ **Christ Church.** 118 N. Washington St. (at Cameron St.). ☎ **703/549-1450.** Free admission (contributions accepted). Mon–Sat 9am–4pm; Sun 2–4:30pm. Closed federal holidays.

This sturdy red-brick Georgian-style church, in continuous use since 1773, would be an important national landmark even if its two most distinguished congregants had not been Washington and Lee. There have, of course, been many changes since Washington's day. The bell tower, church bell, galleries, and organ were added by the early 1800s; the "wineglass" pulpit during an 1891 restoration. But much of what was changed later has since been unchanged. The pristine white interior with wood moldings and gold trim is colonially correct, though modern heating has obviated the need for charcoal braziers and hot bricks. For the most part, the original structure remains, including the hand-blown glass in the windows. The town has grown up around the building that was first called the "Church in the Woods" because of its rural setting.

Christ Church has had its share of historic moments. Washington and other early members fomented revolution in the churchyard, and Robert E. Lee met here with Richmond representatives, who offered him command of Virginia's army at the beginning of the Civil War. You can sit in either the Lee family pew or the pew where George and Martha sat with her two Custis grandchildren. In 1991, the **Old Parish Hall** was completely restored to its original appearance; it now houses a gift shop and an exhibit on the history of the church. Do walk in the weathered graveyard, Alexandria's first and only burial ground until 1805. The remains of 34 Confederate soldiers are also interred here.

Gadsby's Tavern Museum. 134 N. Royal St. ☎ **703/838-4242.** www.ci.alexandria.va. us/oha/gadsby. Admission $4 adults, $2 children 11–17, free for children under 11. Apr–Sept, Tues–Sat 10am–5pm, Sun 1–4:15pm; Oct–Mar, Tues–Sat 11am–3:15pm, Sun 1–3:15pm. Mandatory 30-minute tours begin 15 minutes before and after the hour.

Alexandria was at the crossroads of colonial America, and the center of life in Alexandria was Gadsby's Tavern. Consisting of two buildings—a tavern dating to about 1770 and the City Tavern and Hotel (ca. 1792)—it's named today for a memorable owner, Englishman John Gadsby, whose establishment was a "gentleman's tavern" renowned for elegance and comfort. The rooms have been restored to their

Factoid

The only brothers to sign the Declaration of Independence were Virginians Richard Henry "Light-Horse Harry" Lee and Francis Lightfoot Lee.

18th-century appearance. The second-floor ballroom with its musicians' gallery was the scene of Alexandria's most lavish parties, and since 1797 George Washington's birthday ball and banquet have been an annual tradition here.

A special tour called Gadsby's Time Travels is offered periodically. To cap off your colonial experience, you can dine at Gadsby's Tavern, which is still operating (see "Where to Dine," below).

Lee-Fendall House. 614 Oronoco St. (at Washington St.). ☎ **703/548-1789.** Admission $4 adults, $2 children 11–17, free for children under 11. Tues–Sat 10am–3:45pm; Sun 1–3:45pm. Closed mid-Dec to Jan. Mandatory 30-minute tours depart on the hour and half hour.

Light-Horse Harry Lee never actually lived in this handsome Greek Revival–style house, although he was a frequent visitor, as was his good friend George Washington. Light-Horse Harry sold the original lot to Philip Richard Fendall (himself a Lee on his mother's side), who built the house in 1785. It was home to 37 Lees of Virginia from then until 1903. John L. Lewis, the American labor leader, was its last private owner; his estate sold it to the Virginia Trust for Historic Preservation, which opened it as a museum in 1974. Today it's a treasure of Lee family furniture, heirlooms, and documents. Of special interest, especially to children, is the Lee collection of 18th-century and 19th-century dolls (making this Alexandria's only permanent doll museum).

You shouldn't have to wait long for a 30-minute guided tour, which will interpret the home as it was between 1850 and 1870 and offer much insight into Victorian family life. You'll also see the colonial garden with its magnolia and chestnut trees, roses, and boxwood-lined paths.

Stabler-Leadbeater Apothecary Museum. 105–107 S. Fairfax St. (between King and Prince sts.). ☎ **703/836-3713.** Admission $2.50 adults, $2 students 11–17, free for children under 11. Mon–Sat 10am–4pm; Sun 1–5pm. Closed New Year's Day, Thanksgiving, and Christmas. Guided tours Sun 1–5pm.

Beginning in 1792, this landmark drugstore was run for 5 generations by the same family. Its early patrons included George Washington and Robert E. Lee, who purchased the paint for Arlington House here. Gothic Revival decorative elements and Victorian-style doors were added in the 1860s. When it went out of business in 1933, it was the second-oldest pharmacy in continuous operation in America.

Today the apothecary shelves are lined with about 900 of the original hand-blown gold-leaf–labeled bottles (the most valuable collection of antique medicinal bottles in the United States), old scales stamped with the royal crown, patent medicines, and equipment for bloodletting. Among the shop's documentary records is an 1802 epistle from Mount Vernon: "Mrs. Washington desires Mr. Stabler to send by the bearer a quart bottle of his best Castor Oil and the bill for it."

Docent tours are offered Sundays from 1 to 5pm; other times, a 10-minute recording guides you around the displays.

MORE ATTRACTIONS

The Athenaeum. 201 Prince St. (at Lee St.). ☎ **703/548-0035.** Free admission (donations appreciated). Wed–Fri 11am–3pm; Sun 1–4pm. Call for Sat hours. Gallery shows Apr–Nov.

A handsome Greek Revival building with a classic portico and unfluted Doric columns, the Athenaeum is home to the Northern Virginia Fine Arts Association. Art exhibits here run the gamut from Matisse lithographs to shows of East Coast artists. The building, which dates from 1851, originally contained the Bank of the Old Dominion. The bank's operations were interrupted by the Civil War, when Yankee troops turned the building into a commissary.

Friendship Firehouse. 107 S. Alfred St. (near Alfred St.). ☎ **703/838-3891** or 703/838-4994. Free admission. Fri–Sat 10am–4pm; Sun 1–4pm.

Alexandria's first fire-fighting organization, the Friendship Fire Company, was established in 1774. As the city grew, the company attracted increasing recognition, not only for its fire-fighting efforts but also for its ceremonial and social presence at parades and other public occasions. As fate would have it, Friendship's building at 107 S. Alfred St. was destroyed by fire in 1855. Today's museum is in the brick building soon erected on the same spot in the fashionable Italianate style. A strong local tradition centers on George Washington's involvement with the firehouse as a founding member, active firefighter, and purchaser of its first fire engine, although extensive research does not bear out these stories. This interesting museum not only exhibits fire-fighting paraphernalia dating back to the 18th century, but also documents the Friendship Company's efforts to claim Washington as one of their own. There are no tours of the small building, so just walk in.

The Lyceum. 201 S. Washington St. ☎ **703/838-4994.** www.ci.alexandria.va.us/oha/lyceum. Free admission. Mon–Sat 10am–5pm; Sun 1–5pm.

Another distinguished Greek Revival building, the Lyceum is a museum focusing on Alexandria's history from colonial times through the 20th century. It features changing exhibits and an ongoing series of lectures, concerts, and educational programs. An adjoining nonprofit shop carries 18th-century reproductions and crafts.

Even without its manifold offerings, however, the brick-and-stucco Lyceum itself merits a visit. Built in 1839, it was designed in the Doric temple style (with imposing white columns) to serve as a lecture, meeting, and concert hall. The first floor originally contained the Alexandria Library and natural-science and historical exhibits. It was an important center of Alexandria's cultural life until the Civil War, when Union forces took it over for use as a hospital.

Old Presbyterian Meeting House. 321 S. Fairfax St. (at Duke St.). ☎ **703/549-6670.** Free admission. Mon–Fri 9am–4:30pm; services Sun at 8:30 and 11am.

Presbyterian congregations have worshiped in Virginia since Jamestown days, when the Rev. Alexander Whittaker converted Pocahontas. This brick church was established by Scottish pioneers in 1774. Though it wasn't George Washington's church, the Old Meeting House bell tolled continuously for 4 days after his death in December 1799, and memorial services were preached from the pulpit here by Presbyterian, Episcopal, and Methodist ministers.

Many famous Alexandrians are buried in the church graveyard—John and Sara Carlyle, Dr. James Craik (the surgeon who treated Washington, dressed Lafayette's wounds at Brandywine, and ministered to the dying Braddock at Monongahela), and William Hunter, Jr., founder of the St. Andrew's Society of Scottish descendants (bagpipers pay homage to him the first Saturday of each December). It's also the site of the Tomb of an Unknown Revolutionary Soldier. The original parsonage, or *manse,* is still intact. There's no guided tour, but there are recorded narratives in the church and graveyard.

OTHER ATTRACTIONS

Alexandria Black History Resource Center. 638 N. Alfred St. ☎ **703/838-4356.** Free admission. www.ci.alexandria.va.us/oha/bhrc. Tues–Sat 10am–4pm.

Located in a 1940s building that originally housed the black community's first public library, the Black History Resource Center exhibits historical objects, photographs, documents, and memorabilia relating to African Americans in Alexandria from the 18th century on. In addition to the permanent collection, the museum presents rotating exhibits.

Fort Ward Museum and Historic Site. 4301 W. Braddock Rd. ☎ **703/838-4848.** Free admission. Fort, daily 9am–sunset; museum, Tues–Sat 9am–5pm, Sun noon–5pm. From Old Town, follow King St. west; go right on Kenwood St., then left on W. Braddock Rd. Continue for ¾ mile to the entrance on the right.

If you're a Civil War buff, you will enjoy taking a short drive from Old Town to this 45-acre museum, park, and actual Union fort that President Lincoln ordered erected as part of a system called the "Defenses of Washington." About 90% of the earthwork walls are preserved, and the Northwest Bastion has been restored, with six mounted guns (there were originally 36) facing south waiting for the Confederates who never came. You can explore the fort as well as replicas of the Ceremonial Entrance Gate and an officer's hut. A museum on the premises houses Civil War memorabilia. Tours of the fort are given by guides in Union soldier costumes on selected Sundays.

   Picnic areas with barbecue grills are located in the park surrounding the fort, and evening concerts are presented from June to mid-September in the outdoor amphitheater.

George Washington Masonic National Memorial. 101 Callahan Dr. (at King St.). ☎ **703/683-2007.** www.gwmemorial.org. Free admission. Daily 9am–5pm. Guided tours available about every 45 minutes between 9:30am and 4pm. Metro: King St.

Visible for miles around, this imposing neoclassical shrine is modeled on the design of the lighthouse at Alexandria, Egypt, and dedicated to the most illustrious member and first Worshipful Master of Alexandria Lodge No. 22. It sits atop Shooter's Hill, overlooking the city and river. Emphasizing the panoramic view is an overlook with a wide-angle photograph pinpointing Civil War battle sites in Alexandria, taken by Matthew Brady during the Civil War. President Coolidge and former president Taft spoke at the cornerstone-laying in 1923. The pink-granite memorial was dedicated in 1932, with President Hoover assisting in the rites.

   You'll enter the ornate Memorial Hall, dominated by a colossal 17-foot-high bronze of Washington sculpted by Bryant Baker. On either side are 46-foot-long murals by Allyn Cox: One depicts Washington laying the Capitol cornerstone, and the other shows him and his officers in Christ Church, Philadelphia. A stained-glass window in the hall honors 16 patriots associated with Washington. A fourth-floor museum displays many valuable items, including the Washington family Bible, the bedchamber clock stopped by Washington's physician at 10:20pm (the time of his death), and a key to the Paris Bastille presented to the lodge by the Marquis de Lafayette. On the ninth floor, an observatory parapet offers a 360-degree view that takes in the Potomac, Mount Vernon, the Capitol, and the Maryland shore.

GUIDED TOURS

Though it's easy to see Alexandria on your own (see "Walking Tour: Old Town Alexandria," below), you may find your experience enhanced by the 1¼-hour **narrated walking tours** which begin at the Ramsay House Visitor Center (see "Visitor Information," above). The tours usually depart at noon Monday to Saturday, 2pm on Sunday, but call to make sure of the times. The tours cost $8 per person.

   You'll spend $4 to take a "Footsteps of George Washington" walking tour conducted by **Doorways to Old Virginia** (☎ **703/548-0100**), whose guides wear colonial costumes. The tours depart the Stabler-Leadbeater Apothecary Museum,

105 S. Fairfax St., Saturday at 11am, Sunday at 2pm, from March to November. Kids 11 and under are free. This company's interesting (but less-than-creepy) "Ghost and Graveyard" tours leave from the Ramsay House Visitor Center at 7:30 and 9pm Friday and Saturday. They cost $5 for adults, $3 for kids 7 to 17.

Alexandria Tours (☎ **703/329-1122**) has 1-hour walking tours at 2pm Friday, Saturday, and Sunday from March to November. They depart from the fountain in Market Square on King Street and cost $5 per person, free for kids 6 and under. Buy your tickets from the guide. Reservations are required for this company's "Ghosts, Legends & Folklore" walks, which depart nightly from the fountain and also cost $5 per person.

Walking Tour
Old Town Alexandria

Start: Ramsay House visitor center, King Street and Fairfax Street.
Finish: Torpedo Factory, Waterfront at Cameron Street.
Time: Allow approximately 2½ hours, not including museum and shopping stops.
Best Times: Anytime except Mondays (see below).
Worst Times: Monday, when many historic sites are closed.

You'll get a glimpse into the 18th century as you stroll Alexandria's brick-paved sidewalks, lined with colonial residences, historic houses and churches, museums, shops, and restaurants. This walk ends at the waterfront, no longer a center of commercial shipping but now home to a vibrant arts center along the Potomac riverfront park.

Begin your walk at the:

1. **Ramsay House visitor center,** 221 King St., at Fairfax Street, in the heart of the Historic District. It's a historic structure itself, with a Dutch barn roof and an English garden. This is a fine place to have your questions answered and to get your bearings before heading north on Fairfax Street to:

2. **Carlyle House,** an elegant 1753 manor house set off from the street by a low wall. Continue north on Fairfax to the corner. Turn left on Cameron, past the back of the old city hall, to the red-brick buildings across Royal Street, known as:

3. **Gadsby's Tavern Museum.** The original 18th-century tavern complex now houses a museum of 18th-century antiques, while the hotel portion is an Early American–style restaurant.

☕ **TAKE A BREAK**   If you're ready for lunch, the 18th-century atmosphere at Gadsby's Tavern is the perfect place for a sandwich or salad (see "Where to Dine," below).

From Gadsby's, continue west on Cameron Street and turn right on St. Asaph Street. At Queen Street, you can see:

4. **No. 523,** the smallest house in Alexandria. Continuing north on St. Asaph, you'll come to:

5. **Princess Street,** whose cobble paving stones are original (you'll see why heavy traffic is banned here). One block farther north on St. Asaph, turn left at Oronoco Street. The house on your right at number 607 was:

6. **The Boyhood Home of Robert E. Lee,** where he lived before he went to West Point in 1825. Across Oronoco Street, at the corner of Washington, is the:

Walking Tour—Old Town Alexandria

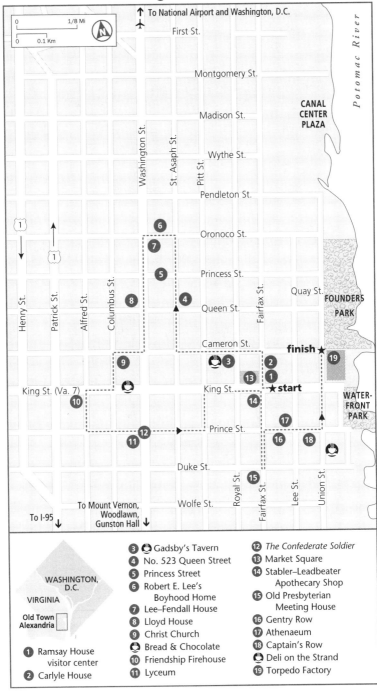

0   1/8 Mi

0   0.1 Km

To National Airport and Washington, D.C.

First St.

Montgomery St.

Madison St.

Washington St.

St. Asaph St.

Pitt St.

Wythe St.

Pendleton St.

6

7

Oronoco St.

5

Princess St.

Columbus St.

8

4

Queen St.

Fairfax St.

Quay St.

Henry St.

Patrick St.

Alfred St.

Cameron St.

finish ★

FOUNDERS
PARK

CANAL
CENTER
PLAZA

Potomac River

9

3

2

13

1

King St. (Va. 7)

10

King St.

★ **start**

14

WATER-
FRONT
PARK

19

12

11

Prince St.

17

16

18

Duke St.

15

Royal St.

Fairfax St.

Lee St.

Union St.

To Mount Vernon,
Woodlawn,
Gunston Hall

To I-95

Wolfe St.

WASHINGTON,
D.C.

VIRGINIA

Old Town
Alexandria

1 Ramsay House
   visitor center
2 Carlyle House

3 🍽 Gadsby's Tavern
4 No. 523 Queen Street
5 Princess Street
6 Robert E. Lee's
   Boyhood Home
7 Lee–Fendall House
8 Lloyd House
9 Christ Church
🍽 Bread & Chocolate
10 Friendship Firehouse
11 Lyceum

12 *The Confederate Soldier*
13 Market Square
14 Stabler–Leadbeater
   Apothecary Shop
15 Old Presbyterian
   Meeting House
16 Gentry Row
17 Athenaeum
18 Captain's Row
🍽 Deli on the Strand
19 Torpedo Factory

79

7. **Lee-Fendall House,** a gracious white clapboard residence that was home to several generations of Lees. Enter through the pretty colonial garden. Head south (left) on Washington, a busy commercial thoroughfare, to Queen Street and cross over to:

8. **Lloyd House,** a beautiful late-Georgian residence (1797) that is now part of the Alexandria Library and houses a fascinating collection of old documents, books, and records on the city and state. From here, proceed south on Washington Street to the quiet graveyard entrance behind:

9. **Christ Church,** where the Washingtons and Lees worshipped. Leave by the front entrance, on Columbus Street, and turn left to King Street.

☕ **TAKE A BREAK**   A cappuccino-and-pastry break at **Bread & Chocolate,** 611 King St. (see "Where to Dine," below), is guaranteed to revive flagging spirits. Sandwiches and salads are also available at this casual spot.

From King Street, turn left on Alfred Street, to the small but historic:

10. **Friendship Firehouse,** which has an extensive collection of antique fire-fighting equipment. Turn left at the corner of Prince Street and proceed to Washington. At the corner is the Greek Revival:

11. **Lyceum,** built in 1839 as the city's first cultural center. Today it's a city historical museum. The museum shop has a lovely selection of crafts, silver, and other gift items. At the intersection of Washington and Prince stands:

12. **The Confederate Soldier,** a sadly dejected bronze figure modeled after a figure in the painting *Appomattox* by John A. Elder. From here, continue walking east on Prince to Pitt Street, then turn left to King. Turn right and you'll see the fountain in the large open area called:

13. **Market Square,** along King Street from Royal to Fairfax in front of the modern but Williamsburg-style Town Hall. This open space has been used as a town market and meeting ground since 1749. Today the market is held once a week, on Saturday mornings. From here, turn right on Fairfax to the quaint:

14. **Stabler-Leadbeater Apothecary Shop,** housing a remarkable collection of early medical ware and hand-blown glass containers. Proceed south on Fairfax to Duke Street, to the:

15. **Old Presbyterian Meeting House,** the 18th-century church where George Washington's funeral sermons were preached in 1799. The graveyard has a marker commemorating the Unknown Soldier of the Revolutionary War. Retrace your steps back to Prince Street and turn right. Between Fairfax Street and Lee Street you'll see:

16. **Gentry Row,** named for the local leaders who made their homes in these three-story town houses in the 18th and 19th centuries. At the corner of Prince and Lee is the:

17. **Athenaeum,** a handsome Greek Revival structure that now houses contemporary art shows. Cross Lee Street to:

18. **Captain's Row,** a pretty cobblestone section of Prince Street. You're now in sight of the Potomac riverfront and may want to stroll down to the little waterfront park at the foot of Prince Street for a panoramic view of the river.

☕ **TAKE A BREAK**   The **Deli on the Strand,** on Union Street between Prince and Duke (see "Where to Dine," below), has delicious salads and sandwiches you can eat at picnic tables on their porch or carry out to the park.

Continue north on Union Street, where you can begin your shopping expedition at:

19. The Torpedo Factory, an arts-and-crafts center with studios and galleries open to the public.

POTOMAC RIVER CRUISES

An easy way to get to Mount Vernon is on a full-day cruise operated by **Potomac Riverboat Company** (☎ 703/548-9000), whose vessels dock at the city pier behind the Torpedo Factory Art Center, 105 N. Union St. See section 3, below, for details about the Mount Vernon cruise.

After you've seen Old Town's attractions on foot, you can cruise aboard the company's *Admiral Tilp,* which sails from Old Town up the Potomac to Washington, D.C., affording passengers super views of the capital and its monuments. Tour guides provide an entertaining commentary on both cities' history, legends, and sights. There are snack stands, or you can bring your own lunch. The *Admiral Tilp* makes several of the 1½-hour sightseeing cruises daily from June through September, weekends during May and October. The schedules change from year to year and season to season, so check at the wharfside booth or call for information and reservations. Prices range from $8 to $24 for adults, $7 to $22 for seniors, and $4 to $12 for children 2 to 12.

You can dine on the river aboard the ***Dandy*** or ***Nina's Dandy,*** restaurant cruise ships berthed at the foot of Prince Street (☎ 703/683-6090). They can carry 200 and 250 passengers, respectively, so you'll have lots of company. The ships make 2½-hour luncheon and 3-hour dinner cruises. Reservations are imperative, since you'll choose your entree when you call. Lunches have three courses; dinner is a multi-course affair. Lunch cruises range from $28 to $32 per person, and dinner trips from $52 to $63 per person, depending on the day of the week. Prices include the meal but not bar drinks, coffee, or gratuities. Music and a small dance floor round out the dinner cruise. They also offer midnight cruises.

OUTDOOR ACTIVITIES

The 17-mile biking, jogging, and hiking trail along the **George Washington Memorial Parkway** passes through Old Town Alexandria on the way to Mount Vernon (see "A Scenic Drive Along the Potomac River" and "Outdoor Activities" in the Arlington section, above). **Big Wheel Bikes,** 2 Prince St., at The Strand (☎ 703/739-2300), rents a wide range of bikes at $5 an hour or $25 for all day. Open Monday to Friday 11am to 7pm, Saturday 10am to 6pm, Sunday 11am to 5pm.

You can learn to paddle, explore local waters, or go on guided trips farther afield with **Atlantic Kayak,** 1201 N. Royal St. (☎ 703/838-9072; www.atlantickayak. com). Call or check their Web site for classes, demonstrations, day trips, and guided excursions along the Potomac River and as far away as the Eastern Shore.

SHOPPING

Old Town has hundreds of charming boutiques, antiques stores, art galleries, and gift shops selling everything from souvenir T-shirts to 18th-century reproductions. Plan to spend a fair amount of time browsing between visits to historic sites. A guide to the city's 50-plus antiques/collectibles stores is available at the visitor center. Here are some suggestions to get you started.

THE TORPEDO FACTORY ART CENTER   Built by the U.S. Navy in 1918 and operated as a torpedo shell-case factory until the early 1950s, then used as storage for dinosaur bones and various artifacts of the Smithsonian Institution, **The Torpedo**

Factory, 105 N. Union St., between King and Cameron streets on the Potomac River (☎ 703/838-4565; www.torpedofactory.org), now houses more than 150 artists and craftspeople, who create and sell their own works on the premises. You can see potters, painters, printmakers, photographers, sculptors, and jewelers among others at work in this block-long, three-story building. The shops and galleries are open daily 10am to 5pm. Closed New Year's Day, Easter, July 4, Thanksgiving, and Christmas.

KING STREET   Take your time as you stroll along King Street between the river and Washington Street. Beginning with the art galleries and studios in the Torpedo Factory at the water's edge (see "More Attractions," above), this main drag has many fascinating shops interspersed among its restaurants and offices.

One highlight here is the ✪ **Winterthur Museum Store,** 207 King St., between Lee and Fairfax streets (☎ 703/684-6092), an off-site venture of the renowned museum of decorative arts on the magnificent country estate of horticulturist Henry Francis du Pont, in Delaware's Brandywine Valley. It's a delightful browse, including the back garden, which features all sorts of garden plants and ornaments. You'll come across fine reproductions from the Winterthur collections, including lamps, prints, ceramics, brassware, jewelry, garden furniture, and statuary. Open Monday to Saturday 10am to 5pm, Sunday 11am to 5pm. At the corner of King and Lee streets, **The Pineapple's Collection** (☎ 703/836-3639) has two floors of gorgeous things for the home, including exquisite door handles and knobs, handmade antique quilts, period reproduction furnishings, candlesticks, hurricane lamps, picnic baskets, and the like. Open Monday to Saturday 10am to 9pm, Sunday noon to 5pm.

UNION STREET NEAR THE RIVER   Near the river on South Union Street between Duke and Prince streets, you'll come to the **Christmas Attic** (☎ 703/548-2829), where it's always the holiday season, complete with toy train sets choo-chooing along a track overhead and 20 or more decorated trees. Christmas decorations, gifts, toys, and ornaments are sold year-round, with festive items for other holidays available in their appropriate months. The **Carriage House,** 215 S. Union St., houses two interesting shops: **Rocky Road to Kansas** (☎ 703/683-0116) has on display more than 200 vintage and 20th-century patchwork quilts, antiques, gift items, and collectibles; and **Old Town Coffee, Tea & Spice** (☎ 703/683-0856) carries about 50 kinds of coffee and 175 varieties of tea, plus gourmet imports like German cornichons, Dundee preserves from Scotland, and imported cheeses and pâtés. Accessories such as teapots and cosies and coffeepots are sold here, too.

Around the corner on Prince Street, between South Union and Strand streets, you'll find **Olde Towne Gemstones** (☎ 703/836-1377), where rock and fossil enthusiasts Pat, Mike, and Marvin Young actually make jewelry from petrified dinosaur bones that come from their collection of fossils, some up to 500 million years old. There's also a wide-ranging collection of minerals, gemstones, petrified wood, and objets d'art. Banded-agate clocks are a popular item.

ANTIQUING NORTH OF KING STREET   There's an abundance of antiques and collectibles shopping in Old Town, although antiques tend to be so pricey here that many locals do their hunting in Fredericksburg (see chapter 5). The best place to look here is north of King Street on North Lee Street, between Cameron and Queen streets. The building known as **Old Town Market and Antique Mall,** 210 N. Lee St., houses **Teacher's Pet/Trojan Antiques** (☎ 703/549-9766), two adjoining shops offering a highly browsable mix of collectible dolls and stuffed animals, hand-painted birdhouses, antique and reproduction furnishings, antique silver, old books and postcards, and much more. While you're here, peek into two other antiques/collectibles shops: **Time Juggler** (☎ 703/836-3594) and **Old Town Antiques** (☎ 703/519-0009).

Also in this block, **Crilley Warehouse Mall,** 218 N. Lee St. (☎ 703/548-3330), is a mini-mall housing several shops on two levels in a turn-of-the-century bakery. **Hunt's III** (☎ 703/548-1111) is filled with antiques and collectibles—furniture, Herend hand-painted porcelain china and figurines, silver, jewelry boxes, crystal, and more. Also noteworthy is **Monday's Child** (☎ 703/548-3505), featuring lovely imported and domestic clothing for children.

Now walk west on Cameron to the corner of North Royal Street, where **La Cuisine** (☎ 703/836-4435) offers a seemingly endless supply of copperware, cookbooks, terrines, cooking implements, and hard-to-find ingredients, and **Gossypia** (☎ 703/836-6969) carries Mexican and Latin American fold art—masks, textiles, Nativity scenes, and jewelry. Some clothing is sold here as well.

WHERE TO STAY

The properties listed below are located in the historic district. In addition, the **Holiday Inn Hotel & Suites,** 625 1st St. (☎ 800/HOLIDAY or 703/548-6300), is on the north end of Old Town, next to the Best Western Old Colony (see below). The nearby **Executive Club Suites,** 610 Bashford Lane (☎ 800/535-CLUB or 703/739-2582), is a converted apartment building, so all units have kitchens. Another good bet if you want a kitchen is **Embassy Suites,** 1900 Diagonal Rd. (☎ 800/EMBASSY or 703/684-5900), across the street from the King Street Metro station on the western edge of Old Town. The high-rise **Radisson Hotel Old Town Alexandria,** 901 N. Fairfax St., at Montgomery Street (☎ 800/333-3333 or 703/683-6000), stands near the river, giving some of its 258 rooms water views.

The Alexandria Hotel Association provides a free **reservation service** (☎ 800/296-1000 or 703/836-6653) to help you find a room at these and other properties, including several chain motels near I-95 and I-395.

Best Western Old Colony. 615 1st St. (at Washington St.), Alexandria, VA 22314. ☎ 800/528-1234 or 703/739-2222. Fax 703/549-2568. 151 units. A/C TV TEL. $95 double. Rates include continental breakfast. AE, DC, DISC, MC, V. Free parking.

Encompassing some 7 acres on the northern edge of Old Town, a 15-minute walk from the prime attractions, this Best Western is the best value here. It's a rambling two-story red-brick motel built in 1958 but greatly improved over the years. Although the grounds are predominantly parking lots, the covered walkways, English ivy, and large shade trees break up the blacktop and lend a colonial ambience. The rooms are spacious, although the baths are dated and small. Limited facilities include an outdoor pool.

✪ **Holiday Inn Select Old Town.** 480 King St. (between Pitt and Royal sts.), Alexandria, VA 22314. ☎ 800/368-5047 or 703/549-6080. Fax 703/684-6508. www.oldtownhis.com. E-mail: oldtownhis@erols.com. 227 units. A/C TV TEL. $159–$179 double. Weekend and other packages available. AE, DC, DISC, MC, V. Parking $7 per night.

Right in the heart of Old Town (just a block from the visitor center), this six-story red-brick building is one of the finest of all Holiday Inns; in fact, it even feels more like an inn than a hotel. Entered via a quiet brick courtyard and Williamsburg-look lobby, the hotel occupies an entire block. Complimentary morning coffee and Danish and afternoon English tea are served in the lamp-lit lobby. Dark antique-look furniture lends colonial ambience to the guest rooms. Rooms with king-size beds have small seating areas with couches and coffee tables.

Dining/Diversions: The 101 Royal Restaurant features seafood and steaks, although you'll find better fare at the plethora of nearby restaurants. Annabelle's, an intimate lounge off the courtyard, is open for afternoon and evening drinks and light snacks.

Amenities: Concierge, room service (from 6:30am to midnight), same-day laundry, nightly turndown, complimentary baby-sitting and airport and Metro shuttles. Heated indoor pool, exercise room, sauna, beauty salon, gift shop.

✪ **Morrison House.** 116 S. Alfred St. (between King and Prince sts.), Alexandria, VA 22314. ☎ **800/367-0800** or 703/838-8000. Fax 703/684-6283. www.morrison-house.com. E-mail: mhresv@morrisonhouse.com. 45 units. A/C TV TEL. $150–$240 double; $295 suite. AE, DC, MC, V. Parking $10 per night.

Designed after the grand manor houses of the Federal period, Morrison House, in the heart of Old Town, is enchanting from the moment you ascend the curving staircase to its white-columned portico, where a butler greets you at the door of the marble foyer. The residential-style lobby divides into a series of beautifully appointed, cozy rooms: a mahogany-paneled library, a formal parlor, and two intimate restaurants. Afternoon tea is served daily from the sideboard in the library. Guest rooms are charmingly furnished with fine Federal-period reproductions, including mahogany four-poster beds, brass chandeliers, and decorative fireplaces. In-room amenities include two phones, TV and VCR, fresh flowers, and imported terry-cloth robes. The plush Italian marble baths are equipped with hair dryers.

Dining/Diversions: The Dining Room, with antique prints on the walls and fresh bouquets at every table, serves all three meals. The Elysium, with the look of an English club, is the inn's showpiece, offering fine Mediterranean-influenced cuisine. Serving both restaurants, the Grill bar offers more than 20 different wines and champagnes by the glass. Locals and guests alike gather to hear a resident pianist perform on the baby grand in the lounge on Thursday, Friday, and Saturday.

Amenities: Superb service begins with indoor valet parking and continues with the doorman, 24-hour butler and room service, concierge, free newspaper delivery, nightly turndown, and complimentary shoeshine. Privileges at nearby health club.

Sheraton Suites Alexandria. 801 N. St. Asaph St. (between Madison and Montgomery sts.), Alexandria, VA 22314. ☎ **800/325-3535** or 703/836-4700. Fax 703/548-4514. 247 suites. A/C TV TEL. $210 double. Weekend and holiday packages available. AE, DC, DISC, MC, V. Parking $8 per night.

A 10-minute walk north of the historic attractions, this very hospitable all-suite hotel provides a luxurious residential atmosphere. Each spacious suite has a full living room with a wet bar and fridge, an extra phone on the desk (equipped with call-waiting), a comfortable convertible sofa, big TVs in both rooms, and irons and ironing boards. Those on the corporate club level also have fax-copy-printer machines and two-line portable phones. Bedrooms are set off from the living rooms by curtained French doors, and most have king-size beds. Other in-room amenities include coffeemakers and hair dryers.

Dining: The Fin and Hoof Bar & Grill offers steaks and seafood specialties. Breakfast is served buffet-style in the lobby.

Amenities: Concierge, room service (from 6:30am to 11pm), same-day laundry/valet, complimentary newspaper, free shuttle to airport, Metro, historic district. Indoor pool, health club, Jacuzzi, gift shop.

BED & BREAKFASTS

More than 30 private Old Town homes, 90% of them historic properties dating from 1790 to 1895, offer B&B accommodations under the aegis of Evelyn Boxley, a former Old Town resident who now operates **Princely Bed & Breakfast Ltd.** from Roanoke (☎ **800/470-5588;** fax 540/343-6250; e-mail: princelybb@aol.com). The best time to call for reservations is Monday through Friday between 10am and 6pm. Rooms are nicely furnished, most with antiques and fireplaces, and all have private bathrooms.

Old Town Alexandria Accommodations & Dining

ACCOMMODATIONS
Best Western Old Colony 1
Holiday Inn Old Town 10
Morrison House 5
Sheraton Suites Alexandria 2

DINING
Bilbo Baggins 11
Bread & Chocolate 7
Chart House 13
Deli on the Strand 17

East Wind 3
Fish Market 16
Gadsby's Tavern 9
King St. Blues 8
La Bergerie 12
Landini Brothers 15
Le Refuge 6
South Austin Grill 4
Two–Nineteen 14

They cost $89 to $250 per night, including continental breakfast. There's a $20 surcharge on those rates if you stay only 1 night (a 2-night minimum applies in peak seasons). The most expensive are non-hosted houses; that is, you get the whole place to yourself.

Another booking agent is **Alexandria & Arlington Bed & Breakfast Network,** P.O. Box 25319, Arlington, VA 22202 (☎ **888/549-3415** or 703/549-3415; e-mail: aabbn@erols.com), which represents properties throughout the Washington, D.C., metropolitan area. Rates start at $60 a night.

WHERE TO DINE

One of the Washington area's most popular dining destinations, Old Town has more restaurants than it does historic attractions. You'll find cuisines from around the world offered in every price range along the full length of King Street and on Union Street south of King Street. Just stroll along. They all post their menus out front, and you'll know by the number of customers which restaurants get nods from the town's affluent citizenry. A few of the best are listed below.

EXPENSIVE

Chart House. 1 Cameron St. (on the Potomac River). ☎ **703/684-5080.** Reservations advised. Main courses $18–$29; Sun brunch $13–$22. AE, DC, DISC, MC, V. Mon–Sat 5–11pm; Sun 11am–2:30pm and 5–10pm. AMERICAN.

One of the few Washington-area restaurants actually on the Potomac River, this member of the national Chart House chain gives diners a view of the river, with alfresco patio dining in good weather. Under a soaring cathedral ceiling, the interior is decidedly tropical, featuring rattan furniture, potted palms, and a copper-covered salad bar. The ample, straightforward American fare includes seafood and thick, tender steaks and prime rib, supplemented by daily specials. All entrees come with freshly baked breads and unlimited trips to the salad bar, which usually features caviar. For dessert, try the house specialty of mud pie—Kona coffee ice cream in an Oreo cookie crust, topped with fudge, whipped cream, and diced almonds.

Gadsby's Tavern. 138 N. Royal St. (at Cameron St.). ☎ **703/548-1288.** Reservations advised. Main courses $17–$21. AE, DC, DISC, MC, V. Mon–Sat 11:30am–3pm and 5:30–10pm; Sun 11am–3pm and 5:30–10pm. AMERICAN.

Behind the portals where Washington reviewed his troops for the last time, period furnishings, wood-plank floors, fireplace, gaslight-style lamps, and costumed wait staff re-create an appropriate atmosphere for authentic if not outstanding colonial chow (view a meal here as an extension of your history tour, not a fine-dining experience). You'll dine off the same kind of pewter and china our ancestors used, and Sally Lunn bread is baked daily. Lunch might consist of an appetizer of shrimp and clams in puff pastry, chicken roasted on an open fire and served with fried potatoes, and a dessert of buttermilk pie. Dinner entrees usually include roast turkey, crab cakes, stuffed flounder, and colonial game pie. In winter, warm yourself with drinks like hot buttered rum and Martha's Remedy—coffee, cocoa, and brandy. Entertainers perform 18th-century style during dinner and at Sunday brunch. The courtyard serves as an outdoor dining area during fine weather (you can smoke out there but not inside the tavern).

La Bergerie. 218 N. Lee St. (in Crilley Shops, between Cameron and Queen sts.). ☎ **703/683-1007.** Reservations required. Main courses $17–$26. AE, DC, DISC, MC, V. Mon–Thurs 11:30am–2:30pm and 6–10pm, Fri–Sat 11:30am–2:30pm and 6–11pm. TRADITIONAL FRENCH/BASQUE.

Alexandria's most formal restaurant features traditional French and Basque specialties in a fittingly provincial setting, with crystal chandeliers, oil paintings of the Pyrenees countryside on exposed-brick walls, and big booths private enough for proposing marriage. White-linened tables, each adorned with a pink rose in a silver vase, add an elegant note. A large floral arrangement graces an antique dresser up front, and there are many hanging and potted plants. Owner-chefs Bernard and Jean Campagne's fare—including the likes of magret of duck, filet mignon in a port wine sauce, roast rack of lamb au jus, and luscious Basque-style chicken—lives up to the high standard set by their decorator. Exquisite desserts include a delicious fresh plum tart with homemade plum ice.

✪ **Landini Brothers.** 115 King St. (between Lee and Union sts.). ☎ **703/836-8404.** Reservations recommended. Main courses $15–$24. AE, DC, DISC, MC, V. Mon–Sat 11:30am–11pm; Sun 4–10pm. NORTHERN ITALIAN.

Old Town's finest Italian fare—or the classic, delicate cuisine of Tuscany, to be more precise—is featured at this rustic, almost grotto-like restaurant with stone walls, a flagstone floor, and rough-hewn beams overhead. It's especially charming at night by candlelight. There's additional seating in a lovely upstairs dining room. Everything is homemade—the pasta, the desserts, and the crusty Italian bread. Things might get underway with prosciutto and melon or Top Neck clams on the half shell, followed by prime aged beef tenderloin medallions sautéed with garlic, mushrooms, and rosemary in a Barolo wine sauce. Dessert choices include tiramisu and custard-filled fruit tarts.

Two-Nineteen. 219 King St. (between Fairfax and Lee sts.). ☎ **703/549-1141.** Reservations suggested, especially for dinner in the formal dining rooms. Main courses $15–$24. AE, DC, DISC, MC, V. Mon–Thurs 11am–10:30pm; Fri–Sat 11am–11pm; Sun 10am–4pm (brunch) and 5–10:30pm. AMERICAN/CREOLE.

Two-Nineteen comprises three formal Victorian-style dining rooms, a covered sidewalk patio, and the Bayou Room, a Rathskeller-like basement. Inside the main dining rooms, crystal chandeliers, rose-velvet upholstery, and a floral-patterned carpet re-create Victorian New Orleans for Creole cuisine, which is featured here along with less exciting Chesapeake Bay–style seafood. Begin with crabmeat royale (with artichoke bottoms and hollandaise sauce) or a version of creamy she-crab soup, which actually is spicier than the otherwise authentic gumbo. Seafood entrees include blackened gulf fish with blue crab claws, *poisson en papillote* (fish baked in parchment paper), and seafood-stuffed rainbow trout.

The covered patio, reminiscent of a New Orleans courtyard, is a delightful alternative in warm weather. In the Bayou Room, you'll find many of the same items featured upstairs, plus sandwiches and salads. The setting is highly atmospheric, with stone and brick walls, oak beams, a bar of leaded glass and oak, and a ceiling plastered with a collection of business cards from all over the country. You'll hear live jazz in the Basin Street Lounge Tuesday through Saturday evenings (you'll pay a cover charge on weekends).

MODERATE

✪ **Bilbo Baggins.** 208 Queen St. (between Fairfax and Lee sts.). ☎ **703/683-0300.** Reservations suggested, especially for dinner on weekends. Main courses $12–$16. AE, DC, DISC, MC, V. Mon–Sat 11:30am–2:30pm and 5:30–10:30pm; Sun 11am–2:30pm and 5:30–9:30pm. Closed Christmas Day. INTERNATIONAL.

Named for a character in Tolkien's *The Hobbit,* this charming two-story restaurant offers fresh homemade fare. The downstairs area has rustic wide-plank floors, wood-paneled walls, oak tables, and a brick oven centerpiece. Upstairs is another dining room with stained-glass windows and seating on old church pews. It adjoins a skylit wine bar with windows overlooking Queen Street treetops. Candlelit at night, it becomes an even cozier setting. Ranging the globe, the eclectic menu changes daily to reflect seasonal specialties, but lunch entrees usually include quiche Lorraine, gnocchi pesto, and spinach/bacon/mushroom salad. At dinner, you'll enjoy entrees such as salmon topped with crabmeat and red and black caviar, and lamb chops brushed with Dijon mustard and sautéed in bread crumbs. An extensive wine list is available (more than 30 boutique wines are offered by the glass and another 150 by the bottle). Homemade desserts like steamed dark-chocolate bread pudding topped with sliced bananas provide a delightful finish.

East Wind. 809 King St. (between Columbus and Alfred sts.). ☎ **703/836-1515.** Reservations suggested. Main courses $10–$15. AE, DC, DISC, MC, V. Mon–Fri 11:30am–2:30pm and 5:30–10:30pm; Sat 5:30–10:30pm; Sun 5:30–9:30pm. VIETNAMESE.

The decor of this Vietnamese restaurant is very appealing: Sienna stucco and knotty-pine-paneled walls are adorned with works by talented Vietnamese artist Minh Nguyen. There are planters of greenery, *faux* palm trees, and a lovely floral arrangement on each table. An East Wind meal might begin with an appetizer of delicate *cha gio* (Vietnamese egg rolls). *Bo dun*—beef tenderloin strips marinated in wine, honey, and spices, then rolled in fresh onions and broiled on bamboo skewers— is the most popular dish here. You'll have fun wrapping broiled minced pork skewers and the accompanying lettuce, sliced carrot, rice noodles, and parsley in thin rice paper and dipping the fajitas-style result in a peanut sauce laced with red chilies. Also excellent, the curried chicken is made sweet by coconut milk and comes with a refreshing lemongrass and cilantro sauce on the side. Vegetarians will find many selections here.

Fish Market. 105 King St. (at Union St.). ☎ **703/836-5676.** Reservations not accepted. Salads and sandwiches $4–$9.50; main courses $11.50–$16.50. AE, DC, MC, V. Sun–Thurs 11:15am–1am; Fri–Sat 11:15am–2am (kitchen closes at midnight). SEAFOOD.

Although the popular Fish Market has grown to include the building next door, its original corner location is a warehouse that's over 200 years old. Heavy beams, terracotta tile floors, exposed-brick and stucco walls adorned with nautical antiques, copper pots suspended over a fireplace, copper-topped bars, and saloon doors all lend a fittingly old-timey ambience. The newer Sunquest Room is bright, with light streaming in through floor-to-ceiling windows; its white walls are graced with musical instruments. If you're lucky in fine weather, you might get a table for two on a narrow balcony above King Street. Although not exceptional, the fare is quite passable (and reasonably priced) Chesapeake-style (broiled, fried, or grilled) fresh fish, shrimp, oysters, and crab. The rich seafood stew is a wonderful warmer-upper on a cold day. On weekends, there's live entertainment in the upstairs Main Dining Room and the Sunquest Room.

✪ **Le Refuge.** 127 N. Washington St. (at Cameron St.). ☎ **703/548-4661.** Reservations recommended, especially at dinner. Main courses $15–$25; special 3-course dinner $17. AE, DC, MC, V. Mon–Sat 11:30am–2:30pm and 5:30–10pm (early-bird dinner, Mon all evening, Tues–Thurs 5:30–7pm and 9–10pm). FRENCH.

A wicker model of the Eiffel Tower sits in the bowfronted window of Jean-François Chaufour's charming little restaurant. Reflecting the cooking style, the intimate setting is typically French country—stucco walls adorned with wine labels and provincial ceramics, bentwood chairs, black-leather banquettes, and tables covered with beige-and-brown napery. The special three-course dinner is a great buy: It includes soup or salad; fresh catch of the day, leg of lamb, or calf's liver; and crème brûlée or peach Melba for dessert. There's a lunch version for about $11. Regular house specialties include bouillabaisse, classic rack of lamb, rainbow trout amandine, and chicken Dijonnaise, and nightly specials feature produce fresh from the market.

INEXPENSIVE

It's a bit of a hoof from the Old Town historic attractions, but there's a **Hard Times Cafe** chili parlor at 1404 King St., near West Street (☎ **703/683-5340**). It has the same menu, hours, and low prices as the Arlington branch (see "Where to Dine" under "Arlington," above).

Stalls sell inexpensive chow in the **Food Pavilion** behind the Torpedo Factory, at King and Cameron streets. Best of the lot is **Radio Free Italy** (☎ **703/683-0361**), with a downstairs carryout counter and a fancier dining area on the mezzanine offering views of the boat-filled marina (in fact, this is a poor man's version of the very expensive Chart House, which blocks part of the view). Oak-fired pizzas feature California-style toppings, such as grilled chicken, goat cheese, spinach, and marinara sauce. Prices range from $7 to $13. Open daily from 11am to 9:30pm.

Bread & Chocolate. 611 King St. (between Washington and St. Asaph sts.). ☎ **703/548-0992.** Breakfast $2.50–$6; sandwiches and salads $2–$6; main courses $5.50–$7. AE, DC, DISC, MC, V. Mon–Sat 7am–7pm; Sun 8am–6pm. CONTINENTAL/BAKERY.

This cheerful European-style place has a counter up front displaying an array of fresh-baked breads, croissants, napoleons, chocolate truffle cakes, Grand Marnier cakes, Bavarian fruit tarts, and other goodies. The interior features a changing art show on white walls lit by gallery lights. At breakfast, you can get a cafe mocha and an almond croissant or opt for an omelet served with potatoes and a slice of melon. The rest of the day, entrees like a salad of peppered smoked salmon and citrus vinaigrette dressing, Hungarian goulash, or vegetarian strudel will keep you walking.

✪ **King Street Blues.** 112 N. St. Asaph St. (between King and Cameron sts.). ☎ **703/836-8800.** Reservations not accepted. Salads and sandwiches $6–$9; main courses $7.50–$13; blue plate specials $6. AE, DC, DISC, MC, V. Mon–Thurs 11:30am–10:30pm, Fri–Sat 11:30am–11:30pm, Sun 10:30am–10pm; blue plate specials Mon–Thurs; bar stays open later. AMERICAN/SOUTHERN.

This re-creation of a Virginia roadhouse is one of Alexandria's most charming restaurants–and one of its best values, too. It's easy to find, for it occupies all three floors of a small brick building with windows painted on its exterior brick wall, and has a blue entrance canopy adorned with a pig trumpeting the words "Good Food." Blue neon outlines the real window panes. Brian McCall, a local artist whose studio (called "The Barking Dog") is in the Torpedo Factory, has covered almost every inch of the interior walls with papier-mâché figures and murals. His colorful work is reminiscent of Red Grooms's constructions, created with a sly tongue-in-cheek good humor. A young crowd usually packs the place for the house beef stew (with a memorable accompaniment of garlic mashed potatoes), barbecued pork and chicken in a sweet yet spicy sauce, Southern-fried catfish filet, baked meat loaf, and house-smoked baby-back ribs. For something unusual, order the "American nachos"—they come with cheese, scallions, and either chicken or pork barbecue over potato chips instead of tortilla chips. The blue-plate special is an excellent money-saver.

South Austin Grill. 801 King St. (at Columbus St.). ☎ **703/684-8969.** Reservations not accepted. Main courses $8–$15 (most $8–$10). AE, DC, MC, V. Mon 11:30am–10pm; Tues–Thurs 11:30am–11pm; Fri 11:30am–midnight; Sat 11am–midnight; Sun 11am–11pm. TEX-MEX.

The big bar on the ground floor of this popular Texas roadhouse–style restaurant is likely to be crowded with thirty-something professionals sipping cold Pacifico beers from Mexico and Old Town's best frozen margaritas—made with lime, strawberry, or a mix thereof. Dining patrons sit at leatherette booths along the wall opposite the bar or at tables in two non-smoking dining rooms upstairs, where the best tables overlook King Street. The Tex-Mex fare comes in ample portions and is a good value, with steak tacos and chargrilled shrimp fajitas leading the list. You can also choose burritos and enchiladas. Be prepared for a long wait on Friday and Saturday nights, when the place is packed.

PICNIC FARE

Buy the fixings for a picnic at the **Deli on the Strand** (☎ 703/548-7222), a pleasant establishment on Union Street between Prince and Duke streets, a block south of King Street, and right on the George Washington Memorial Parkway bike path. They bake bread on the premises, so the aroma is divine, and you can get reasonably priced cold-cut sandwiches as well as croissants, muffins, and, on weekends, bagels. Also available are luscious homemade salads, cheeses, beer, and wine. There are a few picnic tables outside. Hours are daily from 8am to 6pm, until 7pm in summer.

ALEXANDRIA AFTER DARK

Like Arlington, Alexandria falls under the aegis of Washington, D.C., when it comes to the performing arts (see "Arlington After Dark" in the Arlington section, above). The monthly giveaway magazine *Old Town Crier* is one of the best sources of news about the local bar and music scene; pick up a copy at the Ramsay House Visitor Center and in hotel lobbies.

King Street restaurants are the center of Alexandria's ongoing club and bar scene. Especially noteworthy (and noticeable as you cruise the street) are the **Alamo,** 100 King St. (☎ 703/0555), which has live bands on weekend nights; **Two-Nineteen,** 219 King St. (☎ 703/549-1141), which features live jazz Tuesday to Saturday nights in the Basin Street Lounge; the **Fish Market,** 105 King St. (☎ 703/836-5676), with either a pianist or a guitarist from Thursday to Saturday nights; and both **Murphy's,** 713 King St. (☎ 703/548-1717), and **Ireland's Own,** 132 N. Royal St. but fronting King Street (☎ 703/549-4535), which have live Irish and Welsh bands on weekends.

An older crowd likes to sing along on Thursday, Friday, and Saturday evenings with the resident pianist in the lounge of the **Morrison House,** 116 S. Alfred St. (☎ 703/838-8000), between King and Prince streets (see "Where to Stay," above). You could hear wanna-be professional singers belt out some fine jazz and maybe even an aria or two.

The ✪ **Birchmere,** 3901 Mount Vernon Ave., south of Glebe Road (☎ 703/549-5919), is the Washington area's prime showcase for nationally known bluegrass, country, and folk stars. Call for the schedule and reservations, which are absolutely necessary when a top performer is on stage.

3 Mount Vernon & the Potomac Plantations

Mount Vernon: 9 miles S of Old Town Alexandria

With spacious lawns spread like carpets among the sprawling suburbs south of Alexandria, the Potomac River plantations at Mount Vernon, Woodlawn, and Gunston Hall beckon anyone with the slightest interest in early American thought, politics, sociology, art, architecture, fashion, and the decorative arts. One of Virginia's top tourist attractions, the Mount Vernon home of George and Martha Washington draws some 1.25 million visitors a year. The first president gave Woodlawn, on a hilltop 3½ miles

Mount Vernon & the Potomac Plantations

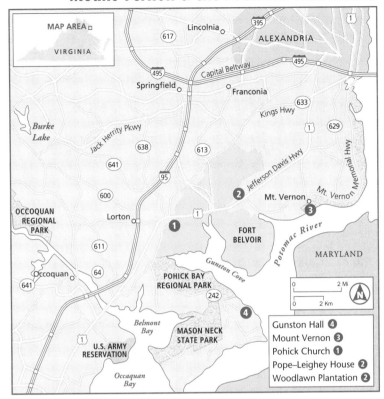

Legend:
Gunston Hall ④
Mount Vernon ③
Pohick Church ①
Pope–Leighey House ②
Woodlawn Plantation ②

down the road, as a 2,000-acre gift to his and Martha's adopted daughter, who was actually Martha's granddaughter via her first marriage. And at the less imposing but equally fascinating Gunston Hall lived their creative neighbor, George Mason, a revolutionary liberal whose words inspired Thomas Jefferson when he sat down in 1776 to pen the Declaration of Independence.

The plantations are best seen as a day excursion from Washington, D.C., or Old Town Alexandria. Start early and give yourself a morning to explore Mount Vernon, the most extensive and interesting of the plantations and the only one actually overlooking the Potomac River. Have lunch at Mount Vernon and then tour the other plantations. If you have time for just one more, make it Gunston Hall, where you will learn of Mason's valuable but less well-known contributions to the American Revolution and the principles for which it was fought.

GETTING THERE

You will need a car to get to Woodlawn, Gunston Hall, and the other attractions south of Mount Vernon, but you can get to the first president's home by public transportation.

BY CAR   It's a pleasant and picturesque drive to Mount Vernon, 9 miles south of Alexandria via the George Washington Parkway. After passing Mount Vernon, the same highway connects to U.S. 1 and the nearby attractions.

BY SUBWAY, BUS & TAXI   You can get to Mount Vernon via Washington's Metrorail and connecting bus. Take Metro's Yellow line subway (☎ **202/637-7000**) to

Huntington Station south of Alexandria. Exit to Huntington Avenue and catch the **Fairfax Connector** bus 101 (☎ 703/339-7200). The bus ride from Huntington to Mount Vernon takes about 20 minutes and costs 50¢ each way. Call for the bus schedules (they don't run on holidays). See "Getting There" in the Arlington section, above, for more information about Metrorail. You can also take a **White Top Cab** (☎ 703/644-4500) from the station; fares are about $11 each way.

BY TOUR BUS   From Arlington National Cemetery or from the Washington Monument and Lincoln Memorial in Washington, D.C., you can take the **Tourmobile** (☎ 202/554-5100) to Mount Vernon from April to October daily at 10am and noon. The fare is $20 for adults, $10 for children 3 to 11, free for children under 3, which includes admission to Mount Vernon. The trip takes about 4 hours; reservations are required in person at least 30 minutes before departure. Call for off-season departure times.

Grey Line tour buses depart from the Lyceum, 201 S. Washington St. in Old Town Alexandria, at 9am daily except New Year's Day, Thanksgiving, and Christmas, with return at 12:15pm. The fare is $18 for adults, $9 for children, including admission. Call Mount Vernon (☎ 703/289-1995) for reservations, which are required.

All About Town (☎ 202/393-3696) has 4-hour tours of Old Town Alexandria and Mount Vernon, departing year-round at 1:15pm on Monday, Wednesday, Friday, and Sunday. Call in advance for pickup at your hotel. Fares are $26 for adults, $13 for kids, including admission.

BY BOAT   From April to October, the **Potomac Riverboat Company,** at Union and Cameron streets behind the Torpedo Factory Art Center in Old Town Alexandria (☎ 703/548-9000), offers cruises down the river to Mount Vernon and back. They depart Tuesday to Sunday at 11:30am and 2pm from Memorial Day to Labor Day, on weekends during May, September, and October. Fares are $24 for adults, $22 for seniors, and $12 for children, including admission to Mount Vernon.

THE TOP ATTRACTIONS

Gunston Hall. 10709 Gunston Rd. (Va. 242). ☎ **703/550-9220.** www.gunstonhall.org. Admission $5 adults, $4 seniors, $1.50 students through 12th grade, free for children under 6. Daily 9:30am–5pm (30-minute tours on the hour and half hour 9:30am–4:30pm). Closed New Year's Day, Thanksgiving, and Christmas. From Woodlawn, drive 5.5 miles south on U.S. 1, turn left on Gunston Rd. (Va. 242), then drive 3.7 miles to plantation entry on left.

Some 550 acres remain of the original 5,000 acres belonging to George Mason (1725–92), a statesman and political thinker who, while shunning public office, played an important behind-the-scenes role in founding our nation. Mason drafted the Virginia Declaration of Rights, model for the Bill of Rights. Thomas Jefferson based the famous sentence of the Declaration of Independence on Mason's statement that "all men are by nature equally free and independent and have certain inherent rights . . . namely, the enjoyment of life and liberty, with the means of acquiring and possessing property, and pursuing and obtaining happiness and safety." A staunch believer in human rights, Mason refused to sign the Constitution (which he helped write) because it didn't abolish slavery or, initially, contain a Bill of Rights.

At the reception center, an 11-minute film introduces visitors to Mason and his estate. You must then take a 30-minute tour in order to enter the mansion. Allow 45 minutes for the total house tour, 1½ hours to see the house and gardens. En route to the house, you'll pass a small museum of Mason family memorabilia.

A fine example of colonial American architecture, the brick house is unusual hereabouts because it's only 1½ stories tall (the peaked roof has gables to let light into the upstairs rooms). Gunston knew what type of house he wanted but couldn't build it, so he asked his brother, who was studying law in England at the time, to find him an architect who would come to America as an indentured servant. The brother found William Buckland, an English craftsman in his early 20s, who worked on the house from 1755 to 1759. Buckland's great achievement was the Palladian Room, whose intricately carved woodwork was inspired by the 16th-century Italian architect Andrea Palladio. Another room features a chinoiserie interior, the latest London rage in the mid–18th century. In Mason's library and study is the writing table on which he penned the Virginia Declaration of Rights.

Containing only plants found in colonial days, the formal gardens focus on the 12-foot-high English boxwood allée planted by Mason (that's right: the shrubs are more than 250 years old!). Also on the premises is the family graveyard where George and Ann Mason are buried. If you have an extra hour for the round-trip stroll, you can take a nature trail down the Potomac past Mason's Deer Park and woodland area (you cannot see the river from the mansion).

Gunston Hall borders Pohick Bay Regional Park (see "Outdoor Activities," below).

✪ **Mount Vernon.** End of George Washington Memorial Pkwy., 9 miles south of Old Town Alexandria and I-95. ☎ **703/780-2000.** www.mountvernon.org. Admission $9 adults, $8.50 seniors, $4.50 children 6–11. Taped tour recording rentals $2. Mar–Aug daily 8am–5pm; Sept–Oct daily 9am–4pm; Nov–Feb daily 9am–4pm.

In 1784, George Washington wrote the Marquis de Lafayette, "I am become a private citizen on the banks of the Potomac, and under the shadow of my own Vine and my own Fig-tree, free from the bustle of a camp and the busy scenes of public life . . . I am not only retired from all public employments, but I am retiring within myself; and shall be able to view the solitary walk, and tread the paths of private life with heartfelt satisfaction."

Washington's announcement of retirement to his beloved ancestral plantation home was premature. In 1787, he once again heeded the call to duty, presiding over the Constitutional Convention in Philadelphia. In 1789, he became the first president of the United States and managed to visit Mount Vernon only once or twice a year during his 8-year term. It wasn't until 1797, 2 years before his death, that Washington was finally able to devote himself fully to the "tranquil enjoyments" of Mount Vernon.

The home and final resting place of George and Martha Washington has been one of America's most-visited shrines since 1858, when a group of women banded together to raise money to rescue the sadly deteriorated mansion. The organization they formed, the Mount Vernon Ladies Association of the Union, purchased the estate from Washington's great-grandnephew, John Augustine Washington, Jr., and continues to own and maintain the mansion and its beautifully kept grounds. For more than 100 years, there's been an ongoing effort to locate and return the estate's scattered contents and memorabilia, thus enhancing its authentic appearance (ca. 1799). About 30% of the contents actually belonged to the Washingtons.

With its tall white columns, the house is an outstanding example of Georgian architecture. Constructed of beveled pine painted to look like stone, it sits at the top of a lawn that slopes down to the river's edge.

Factoid

Virginia is known as the "Mother of Presidents" because eight U.S. presidents were born here: George Washington, Thomas Jefferson, James Madison, James Monroe, both William Henry and Benjamin Harrison, John Tyler, and Woodrow Wilson.

There's no formal tour of Mount Vernon, but attendants stationed throughout the house and grounds offer commentary explaining 18th-century plantation life.

The best time to visit is fall and winter, when the crowds are sparser. If you come in spring or summer, get here by 8am to beat the mobs. Buy your ticket, rent a helpful 40-minute taped audio tour, get a detailed map of the property, and head straight for the mansion, the most popular part of the complex. (The ticket office also sells the 132-page, full-color *Mount Vernon Handbook,* which is helpful and inexpensive, and makes a good souvenir.)

You'll enter the house by way of the "large dining room," which contains many of the original chairs, Hepplewhite mahogany sideboards, and paintings. Step outside on the long front porch and enjoy the view that prompted Washington to declare, "No estate in United America is more pleasantly situated than this."

A key to the Paris Bastille, which Lafayette presented to Washington in 1790 via messenger Thomas Paine, hangs in the central hall, the social center of the house in Washington's day. The "little parlor" contains the English harpsichord of Martha Washington's granddaughter, Nelly Custis. Martha's china tea service is laid out on the table in the "west parlor." In the "small dining room," the sweetmeat course set up on the original mahogany dining table is based on a description of an actual Mount Vernon dinner in 1799. The "downstairs bedroom" was used to accommodate the many overnight guests Washington mentions in his diary. Washington's study contains its original globe, desk, and dressing table.

Upstairs are five bedchambers, including the "Lafayette Room," named for its most distinguished occupant, and George and Martha's bedroom, in which Washington died.

After leaving the house, tour the outbuildings, including the kitchen, the smokehouse, the overseer's and slave quarters, and the Washingtons' graves. A museum on the property has many interesting exhibits and memorabilia, and a 4-acre exhibition area focuses on Washington's accomplishments off the battlefield and outside the government.

Allow at least 2 hours to tour the entire house and grounds.

If you have an extra 45 minutes to spare, the air-conditioned cruise boat *Potomac Spirit* makes **sightseeing trips on the river** from the plantation's wharf (the mansion is lovely when seen from out on the river, but you get almost as good a view from the water's edge). The cruises depart at 11:15am Tuesday to Sunday from Memorial Day to the first weekend in October, on weekends during the off-season. Available at the main gate or at the wharf, tickets cost $5 for adults, $4 for seniors, $3 for children.

There's an ongoing schedule of special activities at Mount Vernon, especially in summer. They run the gamut from special garden and history tours to colonial crafts demonstrations and treasure hunts for children. Call to find out what's going on during your visit. On Washington's Birthday (the federal holiday, not the actual date), admission is free and a wreath-laying ceremony is held at his tomb. Needless to say, the place is mobbed with visitors that day.

WHERE TO DINE AT MOUNT VERNON

The quaintly charming **Mount Vernon Inn** (☎ **703/780-0011**), to the right of the gift shop at the plantation's entrance, serves some of the same colonial-style fare George and Martha provided their multitudinous guests. It's not exceptional at lunch (the colonial turkey pie can be on a par with Stouffer's frozen version), but the atmosphere is great—period furnishings, working fireplaces, a wait staff in 18th-century costumes. And it's a fine place to cool off and relax after your morning's tour. At lunch, sandwiches and salads cost $5.25 to $7, while main courses go for $6 to $7.50. Dinner main courses cost $12 to $24, but there's a fixed-price meal for $14, including soup or salad, entree, homemade breads, and dessert. There's a full bar, and premium Virginia wines are offered by the glass. Lunch is first come, first served, but reservations are highly recommended at dinner (if for no other reason than to find out if the inn is closed for a wedding reception or other event). American Express, Discover, MasterCard, and Visa are accepted. Open Monday to Saturday 11am to 3:30pm and 5 to 9pm, Sunday 11am to 4pm.

For faster and less expensive fare, **A Quick Bite to Eat** snack bar at the entrance serves salads, sandwiches, burgers, and other light fare daily from 9am to 5:30pm in spring and summer, 9am to 4pm off-season. Prices range from $2 to $6. There are picnic tables outside. If you pack your own picnic, consider driving a mile north on the George Washington Memorial Parkway to **Riverside Park,** where picnic tables overlook the Potomac.

Pohick Church. 9301 Richmond Hwy. (U.S. 1, at Telegraph Rd.). ☎ **703/339-6572.** Free admission. Daily 9am–4pm; services Sun 8, 9:15, and 11:15am. From Woodlawn, drive 5.5 miles south on U.S. 1.

The seat of Mount Vernon Parish, Pohick Church was built between 1769 and 1774 from plans drawn up by George Washington. The interior was designed by his fellow vestryman, George Mason, owner of Gunston Hall (see above), with the pulpit to one side and box pews like those prevalent in England at the time. During the Civil War, Union troops stabled their horses in the church and stripped the interior. The east wall was used for target practice. Today the church is restored to its original appearance and still houses an active Episcopal congregation.

Woodlawn Plantation and Pope-Leighey House. 9000 Richmond Hwy. (U.S. 1, at Mount Vernon Memorial Pkwy. [Va. 235]). ☎ **703/780-4000.** Admission to each house $6 adults, $5 students and seniors, free for children under 5. Combination tickets $10 adults, $8 seniors and students, free for children under 5. Admission may be higher during special events. Daily 10am–4pm. Tours on the hour and half hour. Closed Jan–Feb, Thanksgiving, and Christmas. From Mount Vernon, drive 3 miles west on Mount Vernon Memorial Pkwy. (Va. 235) to U.S. 1. Entry is straight ahead.

On a hill overlooking the Potomac River valley, Woodlawn originally was a 2,000-acre section of Mount Vernon (some 130 acres remain). George Washington gave it as a wedding gift to his adopted daughter (and Martha's actual granddaughter), the beautiful Eleanor "Nelly" Parke Custis, and her husband, his nephew, Maj. Lawrence Lewis, when they married in 1799. Three years later, they moved into the Georgian-style brick mansion designed by William Thornton, first architect of the U.S. Capitol, and furnished it primarily with pieces from Mount Vernon (everything you see today dates to before 1840, with about 30% from the Lewises' time).

Under the auspices of the National Trust for Historic Preservation, the restored Woodlawn mansion and its elegant formal gardens reflect many periods of history. Post-Lewis occupants included antislavery Quaker and Baptist settlers from the North (1846–89); New York City playwright Paul Kester (1901–05); Elizabeth Sharpe of Pennsylvania (1905–25), who commissioned noted architect Waddy Wood to restore the house to a semblance of its original appearance; and finally Sen. Oscar Underwood of Alabama and his wife, Bertha, who retired here in 1924. The Underwood family occupied the house through 1948, retaining Waddy Wood to continue its restoration. With nature trails designed by the National Audubon Society, the grounds include the largest East Coast collection of 19th-century species of roses.

On the other side of the parking lot, you leap architecturally ahead 150 years to Frank Lloyd Wright's modernistic **Pope-Leighey House,** designed in 1940 for the

Loren Pope family of Falls Church. Built of cypress, brick, and glass, the flat-roof, Usonian house was created as a prototype of well-designed space for middle-income people. "The house of moderate cost," said Wright in 1938 (the house and lot cost $7,000 back then), "is not only America's major architectural problem but the problem most difficult for her major architects." In 1946, the house was purchased by the Robert A. Leigheys—hence the double name. After living in the house for 17 years, the Leigheys donated to the National Trust both the house and the money to dismantle and move it here.

You must take a 30-minute guided tour to go inside either house. Kill the wait in the excellent gift shop.

The paintings come off the walls here during March, when Woodlawn hosts one of the largest annual **needlework exhibits** in the United States. There are no house tours during that month.

4 The Hunt Country

Leesburg: 35 miles NW of Washington, D.C.; 115 miles NW of Richmond.
Middleburg: 45 miles W of Washington, D.C.; 95 miles NW of Richmond.

The colonial tradition of fox hunting continues today in Virginia's Hunt Country, the rolling hills of Loudon and Fauquier counties between the Washington, D.C., metropolitan area and the Blue Ridge Mountains. Despite rapid suburban development west of Washington Dulles International Airport (Loudon is the third fastest growing county in the United States), the Hunt Country west of Leesburg is studded with expansive horse farms bordered by stone fences, plantations with elegant manses, picturesque villages, historic country inns, and fine restaurants. You can see the rich and famous strolling the streets or having a bite of lunch in picturesque Leesburg and Middleburg, for some of the world's wealthiest people keep their thoroughbreds here.

This area also attracts Civil War buffs, for the North and the South fought two important battles here at Manassas, including the war's first great contest. Nearby in Harpers Ferry, John Brown's 1859 raid helped bring on that bloody conflagration. And along what is now U.S. 50 rode Col. John Singleton Mosby, the famous Confederate raider.

ESSENTIALS
VISITOR INFORMATION
Contact the **Loudon Tourism Council,** 108-D South St. SE, Leesburg, VA 22075 (☎ 800/752-6118 or 703/771-2170; www.visitloudon.com), whose **Leesburg Visitor Center** is on Loudon Street in Market Station, a renovated complex of shops and restaurants. The center is open daily from 9am to 5pm, to 6pm from Memorial Day to Labor Day. Be sure to pick up a copy of the walking tour guide to Waterford Village (see below). You can buy self-guided tour books for Leesburg ($2 a copy) and the county's Civil War sights ($3.50) at the **Loudon Museum** (see "Exploring Leesburg," below).

Middleburg has an information center in the Pink Box, 12 Madison St., Middleburg, VA 22117 (☎ 540/687-8888). It's open Monday to Friday from 11am to 3pm, Saturday and Sunday from 11am to 4pm. (Note the public pavilion next door: It's dedicated to the late Jacqueline Kennedy Onassis in honor of the contributions she made to the town while residing here.)

For Manassas, contact the **Prince William County/Manassas Conference & Visitor Bureau,** 14420 Bristow Rd., Manassas, VA 20112 (☎ 800/432-1792 or 703/792-4254; www.visitpwc.com).

The Hunt Country

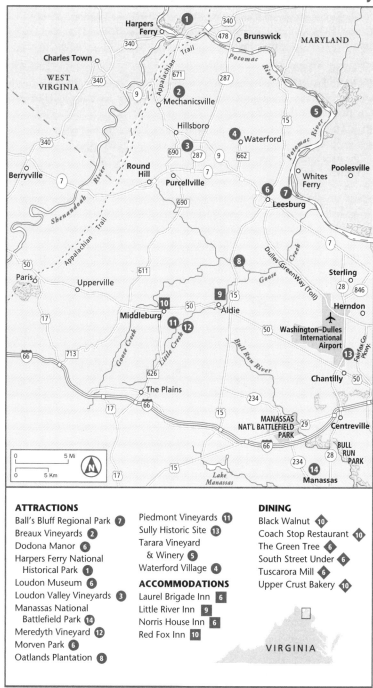

ATTRACTIONS
Ball's Bluff Regional Park **7**
Breaux Vineyards **2**
Dodona Manor **6**
Harpers Ferry National
   Historical Park **1**
Loudon Museum **6**
Loudon Valley Vineyards **3**
Manassas National
   Battlefield Park **14**
Meredyth Vineyard **12**
Morven Park **6**
Oatlands Plantation **8**

Piedmont Vineyards **11**
Sully Historic Site **13**
Tarara Vineyard
   & Winery **5**
Waterford Village **4**

ACCOMMODATIONS
Laurel Brigade Inn **6**
Little River Inn **9**
Norris House Inn **6**
Red Fox Inn **10**

DINING
Black Walnut **10**
Coach Stop Restaurant **10**
The Green Tree **6**
South Street Under **6**
Tuscarora Mill **6**
Upper Crust Bakery **10**

VIRGINIA

For Fauquier County, contact or visit the **Warrenton–Faquier County Visitor Center,** 183A Keith St., Warrenton, VA 20186 (☎ **800/820-1021** or 540/347-4414; fax 540/347-7510; e-mail: visctr@crosslink.net). It's open daily 9am to 5pm.

GETTING THERE

BY PLANE   Washington Dulles Airport is on the eastern edge of the Hunt Country, 14 miles east of Leesburg and 21 miles east of Middleburg. See "Getting There & Getting Around" in chapter 2 for details.

BY CAR   You'll need to travel the beautiful back roads to see the key sights, so a vehicle is the best way to explore the Hunt Country. Washington Dulles airport has all the major rental firms.

There are two routes from the Capital Beltway (I-495) to **Leesburg.** The free but slow way is Va. 7 to Leesburg. The fast way is via the Dulles Toll Road (Va. 267) between I-495 and Washington Dulles Airport; it feeds into the Dulles Greenway, a privately financed toll expressway connecting Dulles to Leesburg. The total toll from the I-495 to Leesburg is $1.75. Once in downtown Leesburg, you can leave your vehicle in the **municipal parking garage** on Loudon Street between King and Wirt streets (first 2 hours are free, then 50¢ an hour up to $4 maximum per day).

To get to **Middleburg** from Arlington or I-495, follow I-66 west to Va. 28 north to U.S. 50 west into town. U.S. 15 south from Leesburg intersects with U.S. 50 westbound 10 miles east of Middleburg.

LEESBURG

The largest town in the Hunt Country, Leesburg is a good base for exploring the region. It has considerable charm, with architecture ranging from pre-Revolutionary to late 19th century. The center of Leesburg and its historic district is at the intersection of Market Street (Va. 7 Business) and King Street (U.S. 15 Business). Everything you will want to see is within 2 blocks of this key crossroads, including one of the largest collections of antiques dealers in Virginia.

EXPLORING LEESBURG

At the Market Street–King Street intersection stands the brick **Loudon County Court House,** built in 1894 and a mix of Roman Revival and classical elements.

You can buy **block tickets** to several regional attractions, including the Loudon Museum, Dodona Manor, and Oatlands Plantation in the Hunt Country plus Belle Grove Plantation near Middletown and Glen Burnie in Winchester over in the Shenandoah Valley (see chapter 7). They cost $30 and are available at the Leesburg Visitor Center (see "Visitor Information," above) and the Loudon Museum.

Ball's Bluff Regional Park. Ball's Bluff Rd. (northeast Leesburg off U.S. 15 Bypass). ☎ **703/799-9372.** Admission is free. Daily from dawn to dusk.

The Grey Ghost

The Hunt Country was the stomping grounds of the famous Confederate raider Col. John Singleton Mosby, whose hit-and-run exploits earned him the nickname "The Grey Ghost." Today U.S. 50 is officially the John S. Mosby Highway, and local residents have dubbed it the John Singleton Mosby Heritage Area. You can get a driving tour brochure explaining historic sights along the highway from local tourist info offices (see "Visitor Information," above) or directly from the **Mosby Heritage Area,** P.O. Box 1178, Middleburg, VA 22117 (☎ **540/687-6681**).

On the northeastern outskirts of town, this regional park is best known for a little circle of stone markers in **Ball's Bluff National Cemetery,** the nation's second-smallest national cemetery. It holds the remains of soldiers felled during the Battle of Ball's Bluff, fought here in October 1861. Many more Union troops were shot dead trying to retreat across the Potomac River; their corpses floated down to Washington, bringing the grim realities of the war to the nation's capital. Call about ranger-led guided tours of the battlefield.

Dodona Manor, Home of George C. Marshall. 212 E. Market St., near east end of Loudon St. ☎ **703/777-1880.** www.georgecmarshall.org. Admission $5 adults, $2 seniors and students 7–17. Mon–Sat 10am–4pm. Mandatory 30-minute house tours on demand. Free parking on Edwards Ferry Rd.

Gen. George C. Marshall and his wife Katherine bought Dodona Manor, an early–18th century manse, in 1941, when he planned to retire from the U.S. Army. Those plans were interrupted by World War II, when Marshall was army chief of staff overseeing the victorious war effort. Later he served as secretary of state (during which he won the Nobel Peace Prize for the postwar Marshall Plan), president of the American Red Cross, and secretary of defense. The house was in Marshall's family until 1990, when a local group bought it and began restoring its 1940s and '50s appearance. The visitor center next door shows an 18-minute video about Marshall's career. This also is the home of the George C. Marshall International Center, a non-profit educational organization dedicated to world peace. If you're going to Lexington (see chapter 7), plan to spend more time at that town's George C. Marshall Museum than here.

Loudon Museum. 16 W. Loudon St., at Wirt St. ☎ **703/777-7427.** www.loudonmuseum. org. Admission $1 adults, 50¢ children 5–18. Mon–Sat 10am–5pm, Sun 1–5pm.

This small but interesting museum houses memorabilia about the county from American Indian days to the present. It also distributes free visitor information and sells helpful walking and driving tour booklets.

Morven Park. 17263 Southern Planter Lane, off Old Waterford Rd. ☎ **703/777-2414.** www.morvenpark.com. Admission to mansion, grounds, and carriage collection $6 adults, $5 seniors, $3 children 6–13; mansion and ground only, $5 adults, $4 seniors, $2 kids 6–13; carriage collection only, $2 adults, $1 seniors and children 6–13. Apr–Oct, Tues–Fri 10am–5pm, Sat 10am–4:30pm, Sun 1–4pm. Call for special events and Dec hours. Mandatory 45-minute house tours on the hour and half hour. Take Va. 7 Business west 1 mile from the center of town; turn right onto Morven Park Rd., left onto Old Waterford Rd. to park on right.

On the northwest edge of town, this 1,200-acre estate and its Greek Revival mansion are don't-misses for fox hunting fans. The manse, whose original part was built in the early 18th century as a simple farmhouse, is home to the **Museum of Hounds and Hunting,** while the carriage house protects the impressive **Winmill Carriage Collection.** It's all surrounded by rolling pastureland (there are picnic tables under shade trees at the parking lot, so bring the fixings). It's an 10-minute uphill walk through formal boxwood gardens from the parking lot to the mansion. Add another 45 minutes for the house tour and 15 minutes to see the carriages.

NEARBY ATTRACTIONS

✪ **Harpers Ferry National Historical Park.** Harpers Ferry, WV. ☎ **304/535-6298.** www.nps.gov/hafe. Admission $5 per car; $3 per pedestrian, bicyclist, bus passenger, and people ages 17–61. Daily 8am–5pm. Closed Christmas. From Leesburg, it's about 20 miles to Harpers Ferry. Take Va. 7 west and turn right at Va. 9 north, right at C.R. 671 north, left on U.S. 340 west; follow signs to Harpers Ferry and visitor center.

Thomas Jefferson wrote of Harpers Ferry in 1783, "The view is worth a voyage across the Atlantic." The National Historical Park that now preserves much of that breath-taking view where the Potomac and Shenandoah rivers converge and cut a gorge through the Blue Ridge Mountains is worth a visit from anyone interested in discovering a wealth of American history—and not just John Brown's famous raid against slavery in 1859, for Harpers Ferry also saw the arrival of the first successful American railroad, the largest surrender of Union troops during the Civil War, and the education of former slaves in one of the earliest integrated schools in the United States.

Nevertheless, Harpers Ferry is best remembered for John Brown's raid, which presaged the Civil War. After his friend, abolitionist editor Elijah Lovejoy, was murdered by a mob in 1837, Brown dedicated his life to the destruction of slavery. When the Supreme Court decreed in its infamous Dred Scott decision that Congress could not deprive slave owners of their human property, Brown led a raid into Missouri and freed 11 slaves. Seeking weapons, he captured the federal arsenal at Harpers Ferry on October 16, 1859. The next day, 90 U.S. Marines under the command of Col. Robert E. Lee surrounded the arsenal, and Col. J. E. B. Stuart twice delivered surrender demands to Brown. When he refused, a party of 12 Marines smashed the door and captured Brown and the surviving raiders. Brown was tried for treason and hanged in nearby Charles Town on December 2. Although both sides considered him certainly a zealot and possibly mad, his raid helped stir the anti-slavery passions that led to the Civil War.

Start at the **visitor center,** which is on U.S. 340 about a mile from the historic area. There are no guided tours of the town, so be sure to pick up a copy of the National Park Service brochure, which has an excellent map. Free shuttle buses run from the parking lot to the historic area, where the **John Brown Museum** vividly recounts the story with photographs, documents, and a slide show. Many original stone buildings are open, including a restored dry-goods store, a blacksmith shop, and the arsenal where Brown took refuge. A number of shops along Washington Street, the main drag, sell antiques, souvenirs, and Civil War memorabilia.

In addition, the area is a terrific place for **hiking** (pick up a trail map at the visitor center). Easy to follow, the most popular path crosses the old railroad bridge over the Potomac River and scales the mountain to the top of a cliff, where you'll look down over the village wedged between the two rivers. This view so loved by Jefferson is worth the strenuous 30-minute climb to the top (bring your camera and a roll of fresh film).

While here, enjoy a plain but hearty country-style buffet lunch or dinner at the **Hilltop House Hotel,** on Ridge Street (☎ 800/338-8319 or 304/535-2132). Overlooking the Potomac, this historic, creaky-floor hostelry dates from 1888 and has hosted Mark Twain, Alexander Graham Bell, Pearl S. Buck, Woodrow Wilson, and other luminaries. You can stay at the hotel (rooms are old-fashioned but have private bathrooms) or in the modern digs at the **Comfort Inn,** on U.S. 340 (☎ 800/228-5250 or 304/535-6391).

For more information, check out the Web site or write to the Superintendent, Harpers Ferry National Historical Park, P.O. Box 65, Harpers Ferry, WV 25425.

Oatlands Plantation. 20850 Oatlands Plantation Lane (on U.S. 15, 6 miles south of Leesburg). ☎ **703/777-3174.** Admission $8 adults, $7 seniors and students, $1 children 5–11, free for children under 5. Apr–Dec, Mon–Sat 10am to 4:30pm; Sun 1–4:30pm. Mandatory 40-minute house tours depart on the hour and half hour.

This 1803 Greek Revival mansion with a Corinthian portico and beautiful gardens is worth touring for its treasure trove of Federal period antiques. It hosts numerous events, such as the Hunt Country Antiques Show in January, annual sheepdog trials in May, a Celtic festival in June, and a Civil War weekend in August. In late December the mansion is all decked out in Victorian-era Christmas decorations, and tours are given by candlelight. You must take a tour to see the house, but you can wander the gardens on your own.

Sully Historic Site. 3601 Sully Rd. (Va. 28), Chantilly. ☎ **703/437-1794.** Admission to house $4 adults, $3 students, $2 seniors and children 5–15; grounds free. Mar–Dec, Wed–Mon 11am–4pm; Jan–Feb, Sat–Sun 11am–3pm. Grounds open until sunset. Mandatory 45-minute house tours depart on the hour. Closed New Year's Day, Thanksgiving, and Christmas. Sully is on Va. 28, ¾ mile north of U.S. 50, 9 miles south of Va. 7 in Leesburg.

Sully Plantation, a 2½-story farmhouse, was built in 1794 by Richard Bland Lee (northern Virginia's first congressman and brother of "Light-Horse Harry" Lee) for his wife, Elizabeth Collins Lee. The original plantation had more than 3,000 acres. Washington Dulles International Airport now occupies most of the land, leaving a small plot for the main house, dairy, smokehouse, kitchen building, and slave quarters. Now owned and operated by the Fairfax County Parks Authority, the house is furnished with antiques of the Federal period and looks much as it would have during the 1795–1842 era. Mahogany furniture, Wilton carpets, and imported silver approximate the style in which the Lees lived. You must take a tour of the house, but you can wander around the grounds and look into the outbuilding windows on your own. Living-history programs further re-create the era. Call for a schedule of special events, which include an antique car show in June and a quilt show in September.

✪ WATERFORD VILLAGE

Reached by a marvelous scenic drive, the enchanting hamlet of Waterford, with numerous 18th- and 19th-century buildings, is a National Historic Landmark. Surrounded by a rolling landscape of 1,420 acres, it offers vistas of farmland and pasture that unfold behind barns and churches. You'll feel as though you've entered an English country scene painted by Constable. A Quaker from Pennsylvania, Amos Janney, built a mill here in the 1740s. Other Quakers followed, and by 1840, most of the buildings now on Main Street and Second Street were in place. In 1870, the railroad bypassed Waterford, and because the pace of change slowed, much of the town was preserved. Affluent professionals who work in Washington, D.C., and the bustling northern Virginia suburbs now own many of the homes. In other words, it's a real town, not a theme park like Williamsburg, so don't traipse through their front yards.

Usually counted in the few hundreds, the population swells to the many thousands on the first weekend in October, when local residents stage the annual **Waterford Arts and Crafts Fair,** one of the best in the region.

Be sure to get a walking tour guide booklet from the **Waterford Foundation, Inc.,** P.O. Box 142, Waterford, VA 20197 (☎ **540/882-3018;** fax 540/882-3921). The foundation's office is in the Corner Store at Main and Second streets and is open Monday to Friday 9am to 5pm. The booklets also are available at the Leesburg Visitor Center and the Loudon Museum (see "Visitor Information," above).

Waterford is about 6 miles northwest of Leesburg. Don't take Old Waterford Road, which isn't paved. Instead, follow Va. 7 west, turn right onto Va. 9 for about a mile, then make a right on Clark's Gap Road (C.R. 662) into Waterford.

ON THE WINE TRAIL

You'll pass several small "farm" vineyards while driving around Loudon County. The most interesting is **Tarara Vineyard & Winery,** 13648 Tarara Lane (☎ **703/771-7100;** www.tarara.com), overlooking the Potomac River, where wines are aged in a 6,000-square-foot cave. Tours and tastings are daily 11am to 5pm (Saturday and Sunday only in January and February). From Leesburg drive north on U.S. 15 to Lucketts, then east on C.R. 662. On your way to Harpers Ferry, you'll pass the picturesque **Loudon Valley Vineyards,** on Va. 9 (☎ **540/882-3375**), which has tours Friday to Sunday from 11am to 5pm April to December, Saturday and Sunday only in winter, and **Breaux Vineyards,** north of Hillsboro on C.R. 671 (☎ **540/ 668-6299**), whose vintages you can taste Thursday to Monday from 11am to 6pm (to 5pm November to April). Try Breaux's viognier, one of Virginia's up-and-coming wines.

If you taste too many glasses of its vino, you can crash at Tarara Vineyard & Winery's bed-and-breakfast accommodations.

OUTDOOR ACTIVITIES

The Hunt Country's picturesque back roads and its portion of the 45-mile Washington & Old Dominion Railroad (W&OD) Trail bring bicyclists from all over the mid-Atlantic states. The W&OD follows an old railroad bed through the heart of the area, crossing South King Street in downtown Leesburg. You can rent wheels from **Bicycle Outfitters,** 19 Catoctin Circle NE, in the Leesburg Plaza Shopping Center (☎ **703/777-2148**).

Although there are many horse farms throughout these hills, surprisingly few of them rent mounts. One that does is **Greenway Stables,** P.O. Box 211, Leesburg, VA 22075 (☎ **703/327-6117**), which offers unguided trail rides over its property on Racefield Road, off U.S. 50 between I-66 and C.R. 629. Reservations are required; let them know your level of experience and whether you prefer English or Western.

SHOPPING

Leesburg's numerous **antiques shops** are within a block of the Market Street–King Street intersection and are easy to find. The visitor center (see "Visitor Information," above) has lists of the shops, both in town and throughout the Hunt Country.

Two miles east of downtown near the intersection of the U.S. 15 Bypass and Va. 7, the **Leesburg Corner Premium Outlets,** 241 Fort Evans Rd. (☎ **703/737-3071**), has more than 50 manufacturers' stores and a food court. Many well-known brands are present, including Banana Republic, Brooks Brothers, Burberry, DKNY, Bass, The Gap, Jockey, Jones New York, Liz Claiborne, London Fog, Nike, Saks Fifth Avenue, Polo Ralph Lauren, Reebok, Tommy Hilfiger, OshKosh B'Gosh, Rockport, L'eggs/Hanes/Bali/Playtex, Mikasa, Oneida, Pfaltzgraff, and WestPoint Stevens.

WHERE TO STAY

A mansion built atop a knoll in 1773 is the centerpiece of the **Holiday Inn at Historic Carradoc Hall,** on Va. 7 about 2 miles east of downtown (☎ **800/HOLIDAY** or 703/771-9200). The four suites on the mansion's second floor have a country inn–like ambience. The other 122 rooms are in standard motel buildings. Also on Va. 7 but only a half mile east of downtown are the **Best Western Leesburg-Dulles** (☎ **800/528-1234** or 703/777-9400) and the **Leesburg Days Inn** (☎ **800/ DAYS-INN** or 703/777-6622).

In addition to the inns mentioned below, Loudon has a dozen **bed-and-breakfasts** scattered around the county, including Tarara Vineyard & Winery (see "On the Wine Trail," above). Most belong to the Loudon County Bed & Breakfast Guild (no address or phone; www.vabb.com), which publishes a listing available from the Leesburg Visitor Center (see "Visitor Information," above).

Laurel Brigade Inn. 20 W. Market St., Leesburg, VA 22075. ☎ **703/777-1010.** 8 units. A/C. $60–$100 double. AE, DISC, MC, V.

The history of this two-story Federal-period inn goes back to 1766, when town records show that a tavern operator named John Miller became the owner of an "ordinary" (the colonial equivalent of a British pub) on this lot. In 1817, it was purchased by Eleanor and Henry Peers and became the Peers Hotel. The hotel's kitchen was so highly regarded that it was chosen to prepare the food for the collation on the courthouse green when Lafayette visited Leesburg in 1825. In 1949, the building became Laurel Brigade Inn, named for the Civil War brigade led by local Col. Elijah V. White. Today the inn does much of its business as a venue for weddings, receptions, and other special events in its dining room and lovely rear garden. Dated by today's standards, the guest rooms are furnished with wing chairs, chenille spreads, and hooked rugs. Some have fireplaces, and those facing the back overlook the garden. Air-conditioning is provided by window units, some of which can be noisy, so check yours out before checking in.

The **Laurel Brigade Restaurant** is open for lunch and dinner Tuesday to Sunday. Three-course meals feature entrees like crab imperial, baked scallops, and strip steak.

Norris House Inn. 108 Loudon St. SW, Leesburg, VA 20175. ☎ **800/644-1806** or 703/777-1806. Fax 703/771-8051. www.norrishouse.com. E-mail: inn@norrishouse.com. 6 units (none with private bathroom). $95–$150 double. Rates include breakfast. AE, DC, DISC, MC, V.

A charming 2½-story red-brick 1806 home, Norris House was renovated in the Eastlake style in the Victorian era. Its facade is bedecked with green shutters and a white-columned entrance porch, the whole capped by three pedimented dormer windows. The common rooms include a parlor and library, the former with an oak fireplace. Hosts Don and Pam McMurray serve full breakfasts in the formal dining room; they might feature fresh fruit or juice, quiche, home-baked muffins, and coffee or tea. Guest-room furnishings are a charming mix of antiques. All rooms share three bathrooms and have fireplaces, stenciled fireplace surrounds, four-poster beds (some with lace canopies), rockers, and framed botanical prints on the walls. You can have afternoon tea in the **Stone House Tea Room,** which the McMurrays operate next door.

WHERE TO DINE

The Green Tree. 15 S. King St. (between Market and Loudon sts.), Leesburg. ☎ **703/777-7246.** Reservations recommended, especially for dinner on weekends. Lunch $7–$12; main courses $15–$25. AE, DC, DISC, MC, V. Summer daily 11:30am–10pm. Off-season Mon–Thurs 11:30am–9:30pm; Fri–Sat 11:30am–10pm; Sun 11:30am–10pm. COLONIAL AMERICAN.

Not only is the decor colonial at this downtown restaurant; most of the dishes are made from faithfully reproduced 18th-century recipes gathered from the Library of Congress and the National Archives. Recipes for green-herb soup, Sally Lunn bread, roast prime rib with Yorkshire pudding, and rum-and-black-walnut pie are among the stellar results of this research. Both dining rooms have wide-plank floors, harvest dining tables, ladderback chairs, brass chandeliers, working fireplaces, and walls hung with hunting prints; servers are in period dress. A full dinner might start with cabbage pie or a sampling platter of smoked-sausage pie, seafood, mushroom canapés, pâté with rusks (a crusty colonial bread), and English beer cheese. Among the entrees are rabbit fricassee, crab, roast chicken, and broiled brook trout. Like Gadsby's Tavern in Alexandria (see "Where to Dine," section 2, above), The Green Tree is better viewed as an experience and not a place for fine dining, and it draws a considerable number of tourists, especially on weekends.

South Street Under. 203 Harrison St. (in Market Station, between Loudon and Harrison sts.), Leesburg. ☎ **703/771-9610.** Reservations not accepted. Most items $2–$6. AE, MC, V. Daily 7am–6pm. DELI/BAKERY.

Operated by the Tuscarora Mill (see below), this bright bakery and deli is housed in a renovated turn-of-the-century mill, one of the six historic buildings that make up the Market Station shopping and dining complex (the Leesburg Visitor Center is across the courtyard). It's the best place in town for a breakfast of gourmet coffee and hot-out-of-the oven pastries, or a lunch of curried chicken salad (among many selections in the chiller case) or a made-to-order sandwich on freshly baked bread. Order at the counter, and in good weather, grab a table out in the sunny courtyard.

✪ **Tuscarora Mill.** 203 Harrison St. (in Market Station, between Loudon and Harrison sts.), Leesburg. ☎ **703/771-9300.** Reservations recommended, especially at dinner. Main courses $12–$25. AE, DISC, MC, V. Daily 11:30am–2:30pm and 5:30–9:30pm; cafe serves light fare until 11pm Sun–Thurs, until midnight Fri–Sat. AMERICAN.

Leesburg's best restaurant has a casual ambience—a combination of light jazz music, flourishing plants suspended from wood-beamed high ceilings, skylights, fresh bouquets, and black wrought-iron street lamps. Red-metal exterior siding, grain bins, old belts and pulleys, and a grain scale evoke the mill's past. Delicious luncheon fare includes sandwiches, omelets, and hot entrees like sautéed shrimp over angel-hair pasta. At dinner, standouts include Santa Fe–style chicken or seared yellowfin tuna with a sauce of roasted shallots and Madeira wine. For dessert, warm strawberry napoleon with zabaglione is a seasonal favorite; chocoholics may opt for the double-chocolate torte with raspberry sauce.

MIDDLEBURG

One of Virginia's most beautiful small towns, Middleburg likes to call itself the unofficial capital of the Hunt Country. Indeed, jodhpurs and riding boots are *de rigueur* in this town that is home to those interested in horses, horse breeding, steeplechase racing, and fox hunting. Look carefully, because the person walking next to you could be very, very famous.

Middleburg is included on the National Register of Historic Villages, and it's about the same size today as when it was settled in 1731. You can't get lost here, in fact, for the entire town occupies just 6 blocks along Washington Street (U.S. 50).

Park anywhere on Washington Street and buy a copy of a walking tour brochure for $1 from the **Pink Box Visitor Information Center,** on Madison Street a block north of Washington Street (see "Visitor Information," above). Then stroll along Middleburg's brick sidewalks, poke your head into upscale shops with names like the Finicky Filly that sell "home embellishments," have lunch at one of several fine restaurants, or stop for a cone at Scruffy's Ice Cream Parlor. Note the small Gothic Revival **Emmanuel Episcopal Church** (1842) at Liberty Street; it was the first example of mid–19th-century architecture in the village.

NEARBY ATTRACTIONS

✪ **Manassas National Battlefield Park.** 6511 Sudley Rd. (Va. 234), Manassas. ☎ **703/361-1339.** www.nps.gov/mana. Admission (good for 3 days) $2 adults, free for children under 17. National Park Service passes accepted. Battlefield, daily dawn to dusk. Visitor center daily 8:30am–5pm. From Middleburg (about 11 miles), take U.S. 50 east, turn right onto U.S. 15 south, turn left at Va. 234, and continue southeast to Manassas. From I-66, take Exit 47B and go ½ mile north on Va. 234.

The first massive clash of the Civil War took place here on July 21, 1861. A well-equipped but poorly trained Union army of 35,000 under Gen. Irvin McDowell had marched from Washington, where cheering crowds expected them to return victorious within several days. Most of the men were 90-day volunteers who had little knowledge

---

Factoid ———————————————————————————————————————

Stonewall Jackson acquired his nickname in the first Battle of Manassas when Confederate General Bernard Bee, marveling at his persistence in standing his ground, exclaimed, "There stands Jackson, like a stone wall!"

---

of what war would mean. Their goal was Richmond, but to meet the oncoming army, Gen. P. G. T. Beauregard deployed his Confederate troops along a stream known as Bull Run to the north of the important railroad junction of Manassas. The 10 hours of heavy fighting on the first day stunned soldiers on both sides as well as onlookers who had ridden out from Washington to watch the fray. A surprise Confederate victory shattered any hopes that the war would end quickly. Historians later conjectured that had the Confederates not been too disorganized to follow the fleeing Union troops, an even more decisive victory perhaps could have ended the war, with the South victorious.

Union and Confederate armies met here again on August 28–30, 1862. The Second Battle of Manassas secured Gen. Robert E. Lee's place in history as his 55,000 men soundly defeated the Union army under Gen. John Pope.

Start your tour at the visitor center, where a museum, a 13-minute slide show, and a 5-minute video and battle map program tell the story. These rolling hills are excellent for hiking, and there are a number of self-guided walking tours that highlight Henry Hill, Stone Bridge, and the other critical areas of the two battles. Allow about 2 hours to take in the visitor center and the First Battle walking tour (it's about 1 mile long). The tour of the entire First Battle area is 6½ miles long. A 12-mile driving tour that covers Second Manassas (which raged over a much larger area) will take about 1½ hours if you get out of your car to examine the sites.

For more information, contact Manassas National Battlefield Park, 12521 Lee Hwy., Manassas, VA 20109-2005 (☎ **703/754-1861**).

ON THE WINE TRAIL

The more interesting of the local wineries is **Piedmont Vineyards,** on Halfway Road (C.R. 626) about 3 miles south of town (☎ **540/687-5528**), a former dairy farm whose barn now houses a tasting room and gift shop. Tours are given daily from 10am to 4pm. Just 5 minutes south of Middleburg on Logan's Mill Road (C.R. 628), **Meredyth Vineyard** (☎ **540/687-6277**) enjoys a beautiful setting in the Bull Run Mountains. Tours are given daily from 11am to 4pm. The 58-acre farm winery also has a picnic area and gift shop. Both wineries are closed New Year's Day, Thanksgiving, and Christmas.

WHERE TO STAY

Red Fox Inn. 2 E. Washington St. (P.O. Box 385), Middleburg, VA 20118. ☎ **800/ 223-1728** or 540/687-6301. Fax 540/687-6053. 24 units. A/C TV TEL. $140–$250 single or double. Rates include continental breakfast. AE, DC, DISC, MC, V.

The historic Red Fox Inn in the center of Middleburg maintains the romantic charm of early Virginia in its original 1728 stone structure. Later additions include the Stray Fox Inn building, so called because a misfired cannonball struck its foundation in the Civil War, and the McConnell House Inn building. The Red Fox has three rooms and three suites, all with wide-plank floors and 18th-century furnishings; several have working fireplaces. Rooms in the Stray Fox and McConnell also preserve a traditional character with hand-stenciled floors and walls, canopy beds, hooked rugs, and original fireplace mantels. Continental breakfast is served in the rooms, and extra amenities include terry-cloth bathrobes, bedside sweets, fresh flowers, and a morning newspaper.

The dark, cozy **Red Fox Inn Restaurant** occupies the first floor of the inn. It features a Hunt Country ambience—low beamed ceilings, pewter dishes, and equestrian prints lining the walls. The seasonal menu runs the gamut from pastas (such as angelhair with smoked salmon, smoked scallops, green onion, dill, and shiitake mushrooms) to dinner entrees like chicken breast stuffed with Boursin cheese. Across the back street, you'll find **Mosby's Tavern,** an English-style drinking establishment with a mixed menu for lunch and dinner, which you can enjoy at one of the wooden booths or, in good weather, on the small outdoor patio.

A Nearby Bed-and-Breakfast

✪ **Little River Inn.** 39307 John Mosby Hwy. (U.S. 50; P.O. Box 116), Aldie, VA 22001. ☎ **703/327-6742.** www.aldie.com. 5 units (2 with private bathroom), 3 cottages (with bathroom). A/C TV. $80–$210 double. Rates include full breakfast. AE, MC, V. Aldie is 5 miles east of Middleburg on U.S. 50.

The peaceful setting of this bed-and-breakfast is so appealing, it's almost worth coming to Aldie just to stay here. Farm animals, a small garden, and a patio are behind the main building, an early-19th-century farmhouse. The living room has polished wide-plank floors; in front of the fireplace are two antique wing chairs and a sofa, all upholstered in colonial-print fabrics. Fresh flowers, a basket of magazines, and a few decorative pieces of china add warmth to the setting. Accommodations range from one room to a cottage of your own. The main house has five bedrooms, all charmingly furnished with antique pieces and pretty quilts; one has a working fireplace. Three small houses are also on the property—both the log cabin and the Patent House, a small late-1700s domicile, have working fireplaces. Hill House (ca. 1870) sits on 2 acres of landscaped gardens and can be rented in its entirety, or its two bedrooms may be rented separately. Hosts Tucker and Mary Ann Withers serve full breakfasts including home-baked goodies like poppy-seed muffins and giant popovers filled with cooked apples, raisins, and cinnamon sauce.

If you're in Aldie on a Sunday afternoon between April and October, you can take a guided tour of **Aldie Mill** (☎ **703/327-6118**), the only grist mill in Virginia powered by twin waterwheels.

WHERE TO DINE

You may want to buy the fixings for a gourmet picnic before you set out on a day's excursion in Hunt Country. Try **Black Walnut,** 20 E. Washington St. (☎ **540/687-6833**), or the **Upper Crust Bakery,** 2 N. Pendleton St. (☎ **540/687-5666**).

Coach Stop Restaurant. 9 E. Washington St., Middleburg. ☎ **540/687-5515.** Reservations not necessary. Breakfast $3–$7; sandwiches and salads $4.50–$10; main courses $12.50–$18. AE, DC, DISC, MC, V. Mon–Sat 7am–9pm; Sun 8am–9pm. AMERICAN.

Locals flock to this country-style restaurant for good old-fashioned American fare—everything from a delicious breakfast of Virginia country ham and eggs or creamed chipped beef on buttermilk biscuits to a dinner of honey-dipped fried chicken. Seating is at the counter or at tables and booths set with hunting-themed place mats. Ceiling fans keep the breezes moving as you tuck into a hearty meal. You can order sandwiches served with french fries or pasta salad at lunch or dinner. Dinner entrees—comfort foods like pork chops or roast turkey with stuffing and gravy—are served with two vegetables.

Fredericksburg & the Northern Neck

Like Alexandria, Richmond, Williamsburg, and other early Virginia towns, Fredericksburg is steeped in American history. It came into being in 1728 as a 500-acre frontier settlement on the banks of the Rappahannock River, and its heritage spans colonial, Revolutionary, and Civil War events. George Washington, James Monroe, Thomas Jefferson, and George Mason are among the great names who walked Fredericksburg's cobblestone streets.

For Civil War buffs, Fredericksburg is almost a holy shrine. Heroes such as Lee and Stonewall Jackson fought a major battle in town and three others nearby at Chancellorsville, the Wilderness, and Spotsylvania Court House. Jackson was shot mistakenly by his own men at Chancellorsville; his amputated arm is buried at Ellwood Plantation, where the Battle of the Wilderness would be fought a year later. Each year hundreds of thousands of visitors come to the battlefields, now part of a national military park.

Both George Washington and Robert E. Lee were born east of Fredericksburg on the bucolic Northern Neck, a peninsula set apart by the broad Potomac on one side and the winding Rappahannock River on the other. At the end of the peninsula sits the Tides Inn, one of Virginia's finest resorts, and the tiny fishing village of Reedville, built in the Victorian era and still making its living from the Chesapeake Bay. Large and small creeks crisscross the neck, and bald eagles, blue heron, flocks of waterfowl, and an occasional wild turkey inhabit the unspoiled marshland.

1 Fredericksburg

50 miles S of Washington, D.C.; 45 miles S of Alexandria; 50 miles N of Richmond

Though George Washington always called Alexandria his hometown, he spent his formative years in the Fredericksburg area at Ferry Farm (where he supposedly never told a lie about chopping down the cherry tree). His mother later lived in a house he purchased for her on Charles Street, and she is buried on the former Kenmore estate, home of his sister, Betty Washington Lewis.

The town was a hotbed of revolutionary zeal in the 1770s. Troops drilled on the courthouse green on Princess Anne Street, and it was in Fredericksburg that Thomas Jefferson, George Mason, and other founding fathers met in 1777 to draft what later became the Virginia

Statute of Religious Freedoms, the basis for the First Amendment guaranteeing separation of church and state. James Monroe began his law career in Fredericksburg in 1786.

During the Civil War, Fredericksburg's strategic location—equidistant from two rival capitals, Richmond and Washington—turned the town into a fierce battlefield, scene of one of the war's bloodiest conflicts. Clara Barton and Walt Whitman nursed wounded Federal soldiers in Chatham mansion, just across the river. Cannonballs embedded in the walls of some prominent buildings, as well as the graves of 17,000 Civil War soldiers in the town's cemeteries, are grim reminders of that tragic era.

A 40-block area of the town is now a National Register Historic District, and most visitors come here today either to see the buildings in which Washington, Jefferson, Lee, Mason, Monroe, and their families lived and worked, or to explore the Civil War battlefields. Among the buildings are the Hugh Mercer Apothecary Shop and The Rising Sun Tavern, two of the more entertaining historic sites in Virginia.

ESSENTIALS
VISITOR INFORMATION
The **Fredericksburg Visitor Center,** at 706 Caroline St. (at Charlotte St.), Fredericksburg, VA 22401 (☎ **800/678-4748** or 540/373-1776; fax 540/372-587; www.fredericksburgva.com), offers free maps, menus of many restaurants, and a walking tour brochure following the 1862 Battle of Fredericksburg. It also sells a block ticket to the major sites (see "Exploring Fredericksburg," below). The center is open Memorial Day to Labor Day, daily from 9am to 7pm; the rest of the year, 9am to 5pm. Closed New Year's Day, Thanksgiving, and Christmas.

GETTING THERE
BY CAR   Fredericksburg is about an hour's drive via I-95 from Richmond or Arlington, a little less from Alexandria. From I-95, take Exit 130A and follow Va. 3 east. Bear left on William Street (Va. 3 Business), which takes you to the heart of town.

BY PLANE   The nearest airports are Ronald Reagan Washington National and Washington Dulles International (see "Getting There" in the Arlington section of chapter 4) and Richmond International (see "Orientation & Getting Around" in chapter 9).

BY TRAIN   Fredericksburg's **Amtrak** station (☎ **800/872-7245;** www.amtrak.com) is at Lafayette Boulevard and Princess Anne Street, 3 blocks south of the visitor center. Several Amtrak trains arrive daily from Washington, D.C., and New York City to the north, Richmond and Newport News to the south. **Virginia Railway Express** (☎ **800/743-3843** or 703/497-7777) operates a commuter rail link between Fredericksburg and Union Station in Washington, D.C., with stops at Arlington (Crystal City), Alexandria, Lorton, Woodbridge, Quantico, and Stafford.

EXPLORING FREDERICKSBURG
Make your first stop in town the **Fredericksburg Visitor Center** (see "Essentials," above), which is housed in a historic 1824 house on Caroline Street at Charlotte Street. Here you can see a 12-minute slide presentation on Fredericksburg's colonial history and get a pass for free parking anywhere in the city (including lots beside the center and across the street).

Except Belmont and Chatham, which are across the river, the historic sights are within walking distance of the visitor center.

Old Town Fredericksburg

Pitt Street

Hawke Street

Fauquier Street

Lewis Street

Amelia Street

William Street

George Street

Hanover Street

Charlotte Street

Washington Avenue

Prince Edward Street

Charles Street

Princess Anne Street

Caroline Street

Sophia Street

Fredericksburg•
VIRGINIA

Approximate Scale
0   0.1 Mi
0   0.1 Km

ATTRACTIONS
The Courthouse **17**
Fredericksburg Area
  Museum and
  Cultural Center **14**
Hugh Mercer
  Apothecary Shop **13**
Hugh Mercer Monument **3**
James Monroe Museum
  and Memorial Library **11**
Kenmore Plantation
  & Gardens **4**

Mary Washington House **8**
Masonic Lodge No. 4 **19**
Meditation Rock **1**
Presbyterian Church **16**
Rising Sun Tavern **6**
St. George's
  Episcopal Church **15**
Thomas Jefferson
  Religious Freedom
  Monument **2**
Visitor Center **21**

ACCOMMODATIONS
Fredericksburg
  Colonial Inn **5**
Kenmore Inn **9**
Richard Johnston Inn **20**

DINING
La Petite Auberge **12**
Le Lafayette **22**
Ristorante Renato **10**
Sammy T's **18**
The Smythe's Cottage
  and Tavern **7**

BLOCK TICKETS   The visitor center sells a **Hospitality Pass** ticket that includes admission to Belmont, Fredericksburg Area Museum and Cultural Center, Hugh Mercer Apothecary Shop, James Monroe Museum and Memorial Library, Kenmore, Mary Washington House, and The Rising Sun Tavern. It costs $19.75 for adults, $7 for students 6 to 18. If you're going to all seven, that's a savings of 30% over individual admissions. If you don't have time to see them all, the **Pick Four** ticket allows adults to choose any four of them for $13.75, students 6 to 18 for $5.50. Children under 6 are admitted free to all attractions. Tickets can also be purchased at any of these attractions.

Note: The seven block-ticket attractions listed below are closed New Year's Day, Thanksgiving, and December 24, 25, and 31.

TROLLEY TOURS   You can get an entertaining overview of the town with **Trolley Tours of Fredericksburg** (☎ 540/898-0737), which passes 35 historic sights. The 1¼-hour narrated tours leave the visitor center at 10am, noon, 1:30pm, and 3:30pm from June through September. During April, May, and October, they depart at 10:30am and 1:30pm. Fares are $10 for adults, $5 for children 6 to 12, and free for kids under 6. The visitor center sells tickets.

THE TOP ATTRACTIONS

✪ **Belmont.** Washington St. (Va. 1001), Falmouth. ☎ **540/654-1015.** Admission (without block ticket) $4 adults, $1 children 6–18, free for children under 6. Mar–Nov, Mon–Sat 10am–5pm, Sun 1–5pm; Dec–Feb, Mon–Sat 10am–4pm, Sun 1–4pm. Mandatory 45-minute house tours depart on the hour and half hour. From the visitor center, take U.S. 1 north across the Falmouth Bridge, turn left at the traffic light in Falmouth, and go ¼ mile up the hill; turn left on Washington St. (C.R. 1001) to Belmont.

Situated on 27 hillside acres overlooking the falls of the Rappahannock River, Belmont began as an 18th-century farmhouse (the central six rooms of the house date to the 1790s) and was enlarged to a 22-room estate by a later owner. The house is furnished with the art treasures, family heirlooms, and European antiques of famed American artist Gari Melchers, who lived here from 1916 until his death in 1932. His wife, Corinne, gave Belmont to the Commonwealth of Virginia in 1955. In addition to Melchers's own works, there are many wonderful paintings in the house—a watercolor sketch by Jan Brueghel, 19th-century paintings by Morisot, and works by Rodin. Tours begin in the Stroh Visitor Center (Melchers's former carriage house), where you can also view an orientation video. It'll take about 1 hour to see the video and tour the house. You can explore the gardens on your own. Call for a schedule of special exhibitions and lectures.

✪ **Hugh Mercer Apothecary Shop.** 1020 Caroline St. (at Amelia St.). ☎ **540/ 373-3362.** Admission (without block ticket) $4 adults, $1.50 children 6–18, free for children under 6. Mar–Nov, daily 9am–5pm; Dec–Feb, daily 10am–4pm. Mandatory 45-minute tours run continuously.

Dr. Hugh Mercer practiced medicine and operated this shop from 1761 to 1776. A much-admired patriot and scholar, he followed his close friend George Washington into the Revolution as a brigadier-general. His soldiering career was short-lived, for he met a violent death at the Battle of Princeton in 1776. The warrior tradition continued in his family, however—Gen. George S. Patton was his great-great-great-grandson. Today this is one of the most entertaining attractions in Virginia. Fascinating 45-minute **tours** are given by hostesses in colonial dress, who explain how the doctor treated patients in those days (see the "Little Shop of Horrors" box, below). The tours run more or less continuously, so you can join one when you get here and see what you missed on the next.

Little Shop of Horrors

You've only to visit Dr. Hugh Mercer's Apothecary Shop to realize the ghastliness of getting sick in the 18th century.

Patients didn't read magazines while waiting to see this doctor, for Mercer's waiting room doubled as his operating room. Since opium, the only known anesthesia, was too expensive and too difficult to obtain, those waiting for treatment were often put to work holding down the screaming wretch under the knife.

Even minor treatment seems ghoulish by today's standards, as displays in Mercer's shop attest. Leeches and other devices were used to bleed patients (George Washington may well have bled to death while undergoing treatment in his final days). A heated cup removed boils and carbuncles, a knife cut out cataracts, and an ominous-looking key extracted teeth (Dr. Mercer did it all).

You can also see Mercer's saw, used to amputate limbs. Such instruments gave rise to the early slang term for doctors: *sawbones.*

James Monroe Museum and Memorial Library. 908 Charles St. (between William and George sts.). ☎ 540/654-1043. Admission (without block ticket) $4 adults, $1 children 6–18, free for children under 6. Mar–Nov, daily 9am–5pm; Dec–Feb, daily 10am–4pm. Mandatory 30-minute tours given throughout the day.

James Monroe came to Fredericksburg in 1786 to practice law and went on to become a U.S. senator; minister to France, England, and Spain; governor of Virginia; secretary of state; secretary of war; and fifth president of the United States. His shingle hangs outside, while within, all the furnishings are originals from either the Monroes' White House years or their retirement home.

In a cozy office much like one Monroe might have used, you can peruse correspondence from Thomas Jefferson (a letter partially in code), James Madison, and Benjamin Franklin. Here, too, are the gun and canteen Monroe used in the American Revolution. Other than Washington, he was the only president to fight in the War of Independence and experience the grim winter at Valley Forge.

Also on display are two Rembrandt Peale portraits of Monroe, the outfits the Monroes wore at the court of Napoleon, silhouettes of the Monroes by Charles Willson Peale, his wife's teensy wedding slippers, his dueling pistols, and other memorabilia. The library of some 10,000 books is a reconstruction of Monroe's own personal collection. You must take one of the 30-minute guided tours, which have no fixed schedule but are given throughout the day as demand dictates.

✪ Kenmore Plantation & Gardens. 1201 Washington Ave. (between Lewis and Fauquier sts.). ☎ 540/373-3381. www.kenmore.org. Admission (without block ticket) $6 adults, $3 children 6–18, free for children under 6. Mar–Dec, Mon–Sat 10am–5pm; Sun noon–5pm; Jan–Feb, Mon–Fri by reservation only, Sat and Presidents' Day 10am–4pm, Sun noon–4pm. Mandatory 30-minute house tours depart on the hour and half hour.

This stately Georgian mansion was built in the 1770s for George Washington's only sister, Betty Washington, and her husband, Fielding Lewis, one of the wealthiest planters in Fredericksburg. According to legend, George involved himself considerably in the building, decoration, and furnishings of the estate. During the Revolution, Lewis financed a gun factory and built vessels for the Virginia navy. As a result of his large expenditures in the cause of patriotism, he had to sell Kenmore to liquidate his debts. He died soon after the victory at Yorktown.

Today the house is meticulously restored to its colonial appearance. The original exquisitely molded plaster ceilings and cornices are its most outstanding features. Most of the floors and all the woodwork and paneling are also original, and the authentic 18th-century English and American furnishings include several Lewis family pieces.

During the 30-minute tour of the house, you'll be fed spiced tea and ginger cookies in the kitchen, just as Betty Washington did for the Marquis de Lafayette when he visited during the revolution. Either before or after the tour, spend another 15 to 30 minutes on your own exploring the famous gardens (restored and maintained according to the original plans by the Garden Club of Virginia) and the excellent museum shop.

✪ **The Rising Sun Tavern.** 1306 Caroline St. (at Fauquier St.). ☎ **540/371-1494.** Admission (without the block ticket) $4 adults, $1.50 children 6–18, free for children under 6. Mar–Nov, daily 9am–5pm; Dec–Feb, daily 10am–4pm. Mandatory 30-minute tours run continuously.

The Rising Sun was originally a residence, built in 1760 by Charles Washington, George's youngest brother, but beginning in the early 1790s it served as a tavern for some 30 years. The building is preserved, not reconstructed, though the 17th- and 18th-century furnishings are not all originals. You'll be thoroughly entertained during the 30-minute tours led by a tavern wench—an indentured servant sentenced to 7 years for stealing a loaf of bread in England. The Rising Sun Tavern was a proper high-class tavern, she explains, not for riffraff. The gentlemen congregated over Madeira and cards in the Great Room or had a rollicking good time in the Taproom over multicourse meals and many tankards of ale (the tavernkeeper's son will serve you wassail—a delicious spiced drink—during the tour). Meanwhile, ladies were consigned to the Retiring Room, where they would spend the entire day gossiping, doing needlework, and reading the Bible (novels were verboten). You must take a tour, but as at Hugh Mercer Apothecary Shop, they run continuously so you can join the one in progress when you get here and see what you missed on the next.

MORE ATTRACTIONS

Chatham. 120 Chatham Lane. ☎ **540/371-0802.** www.nps.gov/frsp. Admission $3 per person, good for 7 days (includes Fredericksburg and Spotsylvania National Military Park). Daily 9am–5pm. Closed New Year's Day and Christmas. Take William St. (Va. 3) east across the river and follow the signs.

This pre-Revolutionary mansion built between 1768 and 1771 by wealthy planter William Fitzhugh has figured prominently in American history. Fitzhugh was a fourth-generation American who supported the Revolution both politically and financially. In the 18th century, Chatham was a center of Southern hospitality, often visited by George Washington. During the Civil War, the house, then belonging to J. Horace Lacy, served as headquarters for Federal commanders and as a Union field hospital. Lincoln visited the house twice, and volunteers Clara Barton, who later founded the American Red Cross, and poet Walt Whitman helped nurse the wounded here. Exhibits on the premises tell about the families who have owned Chatham and detail the role the estate played during the war. Plaques on the grounds identify battle landmarks. You can tour five rooms and the grounds on your own. The dining room and hallway have exhibits explaining Chatham's owners and its role in the Civil War. National Park Service employees are on hand to answer questions. A picnic area is on the premises. The mansion is headquarters of the Fredericksburg and Spotsylvania National Military Park, so your admission here will include the Civil War battlefields (see section 2, below).

The Courthouse. Princess Anne and George sts. ☎ **540/372-1066.** Free admission. Mon–Fri 9am–4pm.

If you're interested in architecture, be sure to see this Gothic Revival courthouse, built in 1853. Its architect, James Renwick, also designed St. Patrick's Cathedral in New York and the original Smithsonian "Castle" and Renwick Gallery in Washington, D.C. Exhibits in the lobby include copies of Mary Ball Washington's will and George Washington's address to the city council in 1784.

Fredericksburg Area Museum and Cultural Center. 907 Princess Anne St. (at William St.). ☎ **540/371-5668.** www.famcc.org. Admission (without block ticket) $4 adults, $1.50 children 6–18, free for children under 6. Mar–Nov, Mon–Sat 10am–5pm, Sun 1–5pm; Dec–Feb, Mon–Sat 10am–4pm, Sun 1–4pm.

This municipal museum and cultural center occupies the 1816 Town Hall located in Market Square. In existence since 1733, Market Square was the center of trade and commerce in Fredericksburg for over a century, while Town Hall served as the city's social and legal center. Lafayette was entertained at Town Hall in 1824 with lavish parties and balls, and the building continued to serve its original function until 1982.

The first level is a changing exhibit area for displays relating to regional and cultural history. The second floor houses permanent exhibits on Native American settlements and pre-English explorers (the earliest years); natural history; colonial settlement; the Revolution and Federal Fredericksburg, including architectural and decorative aspects of the period; the antebellum period (1825–61), focusing on the development of canals, early industry, railroads, and the cholera epidemic of 1833; the Civil War and its aftermath, graphically depicting the reality of the war as experienced by the local citizenry; Fredericksburg's evolution from town to city (1890–1920); and, finally, 20th-century Fredericksburg. Exhibits are enhanced by audiovisual presentations, crafts demonstrations, and symposiums. The hall's 19th-century Council Chamber on the third floor is also used for changing exhibits.

Mary Washington House. 1200 Charles St. (at Lewis St.). ☎ **540/373-1569.** Admission (without block ticket) $4 adults, $1.50 children 6–18, free for children under 6. Mar–Nov, daily 9am–5pm; Dec–Feb, daily 10am–4pm. Closed New Year's Eve, New Year's Day, Thanksgiving, and Dec 24–25. Mandatory 30-minute tours run continuously.

George Washington purchased this house for his mother, Mary Ball Washington, in 1772, and added a two-story extension. She was then 64 years old and had been living at nearby Ferry Farm since 1739. Lafayette visited during the Revolution to pay respects to the mother of the greatest living American, and Washington came in 1789 to receive her blessing before going to New York for his inauguration as president. He never saw her again, for she died later that year.

Masonic Lodge No. 4. 803 Princess Anne St. (at Hanover St.). ☎ **540/373-5885.** Admission $2 adults, $1 students, 50¢ children under 13. Mon–Sat 9am–4pm; Sun 1–4pm.

Not only is this the mother lodge of the father of our country, it's also one of the oldest Masonic lodges in America, established, it is believed, around 1735. Although the original building was down the street, Masons have been meeting at this address since 1812. On display are all kinds of Masonic paraphernalia and memorabilia, among them the Masonic punchbowl used to serve Lafayette, a Gilbert Stuart portrait of Washington in its original gilt Federalist frame, and the 1668 Bible on which Washington took his Masonic obligation (oath). **Tours** are given throughout the day.

Presbyterian Church. George and Princess Anne sts. ☎ **540/373-7057.** Free admission. Services Labor Day–June, Sun 8:30 and 11am; July–Aug, Sun 8:30 and 10am (go to church office at other times).

This Presbyterian church dates to the early 1800s, although the present Greek Revival building was completed in 1855—just in time to be shelled during the Civil War, and, like St. George's (see below), to serve as a hospital where Clara Barton nursed Union wounded. Cannonballs in the front left pillar and scars on the walls of the loft and belfry remain to this day. The present church bell replaced one that was given to the Confederacy to be melted down for making cannons.

St. George's Episcopal Church. Princess Anne St. (between George and William sts.). ☎ **540/373-4133.** Free admission. Mon–Sat 9am–5pm (unless a wedding is taking place Sat); Sun services Labor Day–May at 8 and 10:30am, June–Labor Day at 8 and 10am.

Martha Washington's father and John Paul Jones's brother are buried in the graveyard of this church, and members of the first parish congregation included Mary Washington and Revolutionary War generals Hugh Mercer and George Weedon. The original church on this site was built in 1732; the current Romanesque structure, in 1849. During the Battle of Fredericksburg, the church was hit at least 25 times, and in 1863 it was used by General Lee's troops for religious revival meetings. In 1864, when wounded Union soldiers filled every available building in town, it served as a hospital. Note the three signed Tiffany windows.

Washington Avenue

Washington Avenue, just above Kenmore, is the site of several notable monuments. A brochure detailing its historic buildings is available at the visitor center. Mary Washington is buried at **Meditation Rock,** a spot where she often came to pray and meditate; there's a monument there in her honor. Just across the way is the **Thomas Jefferson Religious Freedom Monument,** commemorating Jefferson's Fredericksburg meeting with George Mason, Edmond Pendleton, George Wythe, and Thomas Ludwell Lee in 1777 to draft the Virginia Statute of Religious Freedom. The **Hugh Mercer Monument,** off Fauquier Street, honors the doctor and Revolutionary War general.

SHOPPING

Fredericksburg is a treasure trove for antiques and collectibles shoppers, with more than 40 stores in the historic area. The selection is good here, and the prices are reasonable when compared to those in metropolitan areas such as Alexandria, Richmond, and Norfolk.

You'll pass most of the shops along Caroline Street, the city's main drag, north of the visitor center. Others are on Sophia and William streets. The visitor center has a brochure describing each store's specialty (see "Essentials," above).

WHERE TO STAY

Every major chain has motels just off I-95. The strip along Va. 3 at Exit 130 is Fredericksburg's major shopping area, with the Spotsylvania Mall, several strip centers, and an inexpensive Morrison's Cafeteria among a host of chain family restaurants. Here you'll find the **Best Western Fredericksburg** (☎ 800/528-1234 or 540/371-5050), the **Best Western Thunderbird** (☎ 800/528-1234 or 540/373-0000), the **Econo Lodge Central** (☎ 800/55-ECONO or 540/786-8374), a **Hampton Inn** (☎ 800/HAMPTON or 540/371-0330), a **Ramada Inn** (☎ 800/2RAMADA or 540/786-8361), the **Sheraton Fredericksburg Inn & Conference Center** (☎ 800/682-1049 or 540/786-8321), and a **Super 8** (☎ 800/800-8000 or 540/786-8881).

Another concentration of motels, restaurants, and shops is at Exit 126 (U.S. 1) south of town, where you'll find the Massaponax Factory Outlet Center (including Bass Shoes, Bugle Boy, Corning Revere, Dress Barn, and Oneida). Sitting among the factory shops, the **Comfort Inn Southpointe** (☎ 800/228-5151 or 540/898-5550) has an indoor pool. On U.S. 1 just north of I-95 are **Days Inn Fredericksburg South** (☎ 800/DAYS-INN or 540/373-5340), **Econo Lodge South** (☎ 800/55-ECONO or 540/898-5440), **Fairfield Inn by Marriott** (☎ 800/348-6000 or 540/891-9100), the independent and inexpensive **Heritage Inn** (☎ 800/787-7440 or 540/ 898-1000), and **Holiday Inn Fredericksburg South** (☎ 800/HOLIDAY or 540/ 898-1102).

The following inns are located in the historic area.

Fredericksburg Colonial Inn. 1707 Princess Anne St. (at Herndon St.), Fredericksburg, VA 22401. ☎ **540/371-5666.** Fax 540/371-5884. www.fci1.com. 40 units. A/C TV TEL. $59–$89 double. Rates include light continental breakfast. AE, MC, V. Free parking.

Victorian furnishings from the Civil War era make this attractive spot a natural hub for Civil War buffs, and people participating in local Civil War reenactments often drop by; don't be surprised to see musket-toting Blues and Grays in the lobby. In the Conference Room, you'll find a display of Civil War weaponry and Confederate dollars. The rooms are furnished with some reproductions but mostly with antiques (owner Alton Echols, Jr., is an avid collector), such as marble-top walnut dressers, rag rugs, canopied beds, Victorian sofas, and a bed that belonged to George Mason's son. The spacious lobby is furnished with comfortable wicker rocking chairs and a player piano. This is a non-smoking hotel.

✪ **Kenmore Inn.** 1200 Princess Anne St. (at Lewis St.), Fredericksburg, VA 22401. ☎ **540/371-7622.** Fax 540/371-5480. E-mail: keninn@fls.infi.net. 14 units. A/C TEL. $95–$125 double; $150 suite. Rates include continental breakfast. Packages available. AE, DC, MC, V. Street parking with free card from visitor center.

An elegant white pediment supported by fluted columns and a front porch with wicker chairs welcome you to this late 1700s mansion in Old Town on property originally owned by George Washington's brother-in-law, Fielding Lewis. Crystal chandeliers, Oriental rugs, polished Georgian side tables, and an enormous gold-framed mirror enhance the foyer. A sweeping staircase leads to the guest rooms—a handsome assortment of both cozy and spacious accommodations furnished with a mix of antiques, many in Regency style. Expect to find four-poster beds with pretty coverlets and lacy canopies, draperies framing louver-shuttered windows, antique chests, and walls hung with botanical prints and engravings. The house has eight working fireplaces, four in the bedrooms.

The inn serves lunch Tuesday through Saturday, dinner Monday through Saturday, and Sunday brunch. The Pub, a convivial spot, offers live music Friday and Saturday nights.

Richard Johnston Inn. 711 Caroline St. (between Hanover and Charlotte sts.), Fredericksburg, VA 22401. ☎ **540/899-7606.** E-mail: rjinn@aol.com. 8 units. A/C. $95–$145 double. Rates include continental breakfast. AE, MC, V. Free parking.

Two 18th-century brick row houses have been joined to form this elegantly restored inn directly across the street from the visitor center. The downstairs sitting rooms and dining room, where continental breakfast is served, are invitingly furnished. The Oriental rugs and mahogany furniture in the second-floor rooms in one house create a more formal atmosphere, while in the other house, braided rugs, rockers, oak dressers, and four-poster beds lend a country charm. Third-floor dormer rooms are cozy, with low ceilings. The inn's original summer kitchen exudes rural charm, with brick floors, two antique beds, and a private entrance off the courtyard. The spacious and comfortable suites each offer a private courtyard entrance as well as a separate living room with TV, wet bar, and refrigerator. The owners have dogs in the house, but your pets aren't allowed.

WHERE TO DINE

La Petite Auberge. 311 William St. (between Princess Anne and Charles sts.). ☎ **540/ 371-2727.** Reservations recommended, especially at dinner. Main courses $10–$26; early-bird dinner $14. AE, CB, DC, MC, V. Mon–Fri 11:30am–2:30pm and 5:30–10pm; Sat 5:30–10pm; early-bird dinner Mon–Thurs 5:30–7pm. FRENCH.

Christian Etienne Reanult's delightful La Petite Auberge was designed to look like a garden, an effect enhanced by white latticework and garden furnishings. Unpainted brick walls are hung with copper pots and cheerful oil paintings, and candlelit tables are adorned with fresh flowers. A cozy lounge adjoins. The menu changes daily. A recent visit included a salade Niçoise, soft-shell crabs amandine, poached salmon with hollandaise sauce, and sirloin steak with béarnaise sauce. The early-bird dinner here is an attractive offering—soup, salad, a choice of seven entrees from the regular dinner menu, and homemade ice cream.

✪ **Le Lafayette.** 623 Caroline St. (at Charlotte St.). ☎ **540/373-6895.** Reservations recommended. Main courses $9–$24; special prix-fixe dinner $14; Sun brunch $17.50. AE, DC, DISC, MC, V. Tues–Sat 11:30am–2:30pm and 6–9:30pm; Sun 11:30am–2:30pm and 4:30–9pm. FRENCH.

Owners Pierre and Edith Muyard have restored a Georgian-style private home, once called the Chimneys, to create Fredericksburg's best and most elegant restaurant, which they named for the famed French marquis. The interior retains much of its period character, with original wide-plank flooring, paneling, and dining-room fire-places. Tables are set with white cloths, gleaming china, and silver. During the day, sunlight pours in through the many-paned windows; at night, lamps on each table glow in crystal holders. Traditional French cuisine dominates the menu, but you'll also note many nouvelle innovations. Dinner might start with hearty onion soup gratinée. Specialties among the entrees are poached salmon filet with sea scallops in lobster bouillon; fresh trout sautéed with shrimp, tomatoes, and toasted almonds; and sautéed veal scallopine with morel and dry-sherry cream sauce. Duck à l'orange or catfish ther-midor are the main-course choices for a special three-course dinner served Tuesday to Friday evenings. An extensive wine list includes both French and domestic selections. The homemade desserts vary, but usually include a delectable chocolate mousse cake. Sunday brunch offers a bountiful buffet.

Ristorante Renato. 422 William St. (at Prince Edward St.). ☎ **540/317-8228.** Reserva-tions recommended, especially on weekends. Main courses $10–$22 (most under $16); lunch special $7; early-bird dinner $22 for 2 people. AE, MC, V. Mon–Fri 11:30am–2pm and 4:30–10pm; Sat–Sun 4:30–10pm; early-bird dinner Mon–Fri 4:30–7pm. ITALIAN.

This very good, reasonably priced Italian eatery offers homey decor—candlelit (at night) white-linened tables adorned with fresh flowers, ceramic candelabra chande-liers, oil paintings of Italy lining the walls, and a working fireplace. The booths in a small room to one side are especially cozy. In addition to its regular menu, Renato offers a complete luncheon featuring salad, home-baked bread, and a choice of such entrees as eggplant parmigiana, fettucine Alfredo, or steamed mussels in white sauce. A similar early-bird dinner adds dessert and a demicarafe of wine; a three-course meal with a bottle of wine is also available anytime Monday through Thursday evenings, at a cost of $50 for two persons.

Sammy T's. 801 Caroline St. (at Hanover St.). ☎ **540/371-2008.** Reservations not accepted. Sandwiches $4–$7; main courses $6.50–$9. DISC, MC, V. Sun–Thurs 11am–9pm; Fri–Sat 11am–10pm. AMERICAN/VEGETARIAN.

Located right in the middle of the historic business district, this popular, inexpensive pub offers a relaxed, tasteful setting and a creative health-food orientation. It has a rustic feel, with large overhead fans, a pressed-tin ceiling, roomy knotty-pine booths, a long oak bar, and painted wood walls adorned with framed art posters. Everything on the menu is made from scratch, with an emphasis on natural ingredients. The lunch and dinner menu offers many vegetarian items, such as a baked potato stuffed with mushrooms, tomatoes, walnuts, sunflower seeds, three cheeses, and sprouts, all topped with sour cream and served with soup. Other enticing entree possibilities are broiled salmon steak, vegetarian lasagna, and chicken Parmesan over fettucine.

The Smythe's Cottage and Tavern. 303 Fauquier St. (at Princess Anne St.). ☎ **540/ 373-1645.** Reservations suggested on weekends. Lunch $4–$7; main courses $11–$18. MC, V. Mon and Wed–Thurs 11am–9pm; Fri–Sat 11am–10pm; Sun noon–9pm. TRADITIONAL SOUTHERN.

At quaintly charming Smythe's Cottage, you can dine on the site of a blacksmith's stable once operated by George Washington's brother. The current building dates back to 1840. The original owner hailed from an old Virginia family, hence the photograph of General Grant upside down next to a photo of her great-great-grandfather, who was hanged by the Union army in the Civil War. The low-ceilinged interior is extremely cozy, decorated with colonial-style furnishings, old oil portraits, and family memorabilia. There's dining in a bright sunroom, and alfresco in a flower-bordered garden when the weather's clear and warm.

The menu offers reasonably good colonial-era Virginia fare like creamy peanut soup, delicious chicken or seafood potpie under a flaky crust, and quail with a bourbon sauce. The entrees are served with a basket of oven-fresh bread, soup or salad, and vegetable. The homemade desserts include hot cherry or apple turnovers. You can order vintages from Ingleside Plantation Winery on the Northern Neck (see section 3, below).

2 The Civil War Battlefields

Fredericksburg has never forgotten its Civil War victories and defeats in the battles of Fredericksburg, in town, and at Chancellorsville, The Wilderness, and Spotsylvania Court House, 12 to 15 miles west of the city. Today the sites are beautifully preserved in the National Park Service's **Fredericksburg and Spotsylvania National Military Park,** which also includes the Stonewall Jackson Shrine, where the great Confederate general died after being mistakenly shot by his own men.

SEEING THE BATTLEFIELDS

The starting point is in town at the **Fredericksburg Battlefield Visitor Center,** 1013 Lafayette Blvd. (U.S. 1 Business), at Sunken Road (☎ **540/373-6122**), where you can get detailed tour brochures and buy or rent the 3-hour-long auto-tour tapes ($2.85 per battlefield for cassette player and tape, $4.45 to buy each tape). I strongly recommend the tapes, since they definitely enhance the experience, and renting a player along with them will allow you to get out of your car and still hear the informative commentary. The center offers a 12-minute slide-show orientation and related exhibits. Be sure to pick up the park service's main brochure, which has a detailed map of the area, and specific pamphlets for each of the sites. If you want much more detailed information, a bookstore across the parking lot is packed with Civil War literature. The visitor center is open daily from 9am to 5pm, with extended hours in summer determined annually.

There's also a visitor information center at Chancellorsville (see below). The Wilderness and Spotsylvania Court House battlefields have shelters with exhibits explaining what happened.

Admission to the park is $3 per person, payable at the Fredericksburg and Chancellorsville battlefields or at Chatham plantation (see "Exploring Fredericksburg" in section 1, above). It's good for 7 days and includes Chatham. National Park Service passports are accepted.

Park rangers give **guided tours** of each battlefield on a seasonal basis. Call the visitor center to see if one is scheduled. You can also contact Greg Kurtz, a former park ranger who operates **Fredericksburg Area Battlefield Guides,** 718 Caroline St. (☎ 540/361-2090).

For advance **information,** contact the Superintendent, Fredericksburg and Spotsylvania National Military Park, 120 Chatham Lane, Fredericksburg, VA 22405 (☎ 540/371-0802; www.nps.gov/frsp).

ORGANIZING YOUR TIME   You'll need 2 days to take the full 75-mile-long audio-guided auto tours of the battlefields. Allow a minimum of 30 minutes at each of the two visitor centers and 3 hours for each of the four battlefield audio tours, plus driving times in between.

The battles happened over a 2½-year period from December 1862 to May 1864 and were part of three different Union attempts to advance from Washington, D.C., to Richmond (only the last one succeeded). Ideally, you should tour the battlefields in the order in which the conflicts occurred: Fredericksburg (December 11–12, 1862), Chancellorsville (April 27–May 6, 1863), The Wilderness (May 5–6, 1864), and Spotsylvania Court House (May 8–21, 1864). Spend the first day at Fredericksburg and Chancellorsville; the second, at The Wilderness and Spotsylvania Court House, where the battles happened within days of each other. The Stonewall Jackson Shrine at Guinea Station is 18 miles southeast of Spotsylvania Court House; go there last.

BATTLE OF FREDERICKSBURG

Lee used the Rappahannock River as a natural line of defense for much of the war, while the Union army's goal was to cross it and head for Richmond. The Battle of Fredericksburg took place from December 11 to 13, 1862, when the Union army under Gen. Ambrose E. Burnside crossed the river into Fredericksburg via pontoon bridges. Burnside made a major mistake when he sent the main body of his 100,000 men uphill against Lee's 75,000 troops, most of them dug in behind a stone wall along Sunken Road at the base of Marye's Heights. Firing from the hill, Lee's cannon mowed down the Yankees as they crossed the open space, turning the ground below into a bloody killing field. The stone wall—some parts original, some reconstructed—stands beside the visitor center at the base of Marye's Heights. Before setting out on the driving tour, examine the wall and follow the gently sloping pathway up the 40-foot-high heights for a fine view over the town. The stroll takes about 30 minutes.

BATTLE OF CHANCELLORSVILLE

President Lincoln fired Burnside after the Marye's Heights massacre. Under his replacement, Gen. Joseph Hooker, the Union forces crossed the river above Fredericksburg in late April 1863, and advanced to Chancellorsville, a crossroads 10 miles west of Fredericksburg on the Orange Turnpike (now Va. 3). When Lee rushed westward to meet him, Hooker dug in. In a surprise attack, Stonewall Jackson flanked Hooker's line on May 2 and won a spectacular victory. Unfortunately, Jackson was inadvertently shot by his own men that same night. Jackson was taken 5 miles west to Ellwood Plantation, where doctors amputated his arm and buried it in the family cemetery. They then moved him to Guinea Station, 27 miles away, where he could be evacuated by train. Pneumonia set in, however, and Jackson died there on May 10 (see

Civil War Battlefields & the Northern Neck

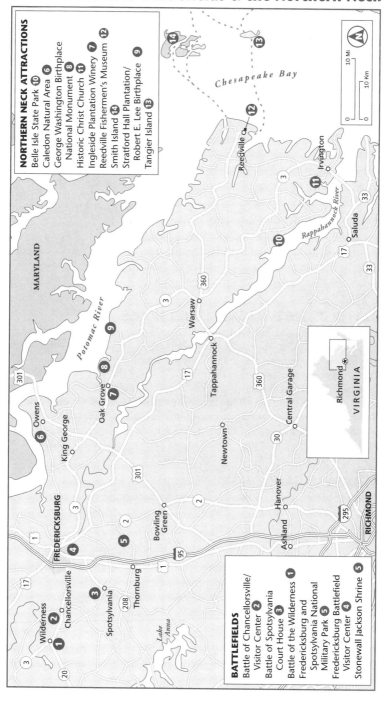

NORTHERN NECK ATTRACTIONS

Belle Isle State Park **10**
Caledon Natural Area **6**
George Washington Birthplace National Monument **8**
Historic Christ Church **11**
Ingleside Plantation Winery **7**
Reedville Fishermen's Museum **12**
Smith Island **14**
Stratford Hall Plantation/ Robert E. Lee Birthplace **13**
Tangier Island **13**

BATTLEFIELDS

Battle of Chancellorsville/ Visitor Center **2**
Battle of Spotsylvania Court House **3**
Battle of the Wilderness **1**
Fredericksburg and Spotsylvania National Military Park **5**
Fredericksburg Battlefield Visitor Center **4**
Stonewall Jackson Shrine **5**

MARYLAND

Potomac River

Rappahannock River

Chesapeake Bay

VIRGINIA

Richmond

RICHMOND

FREDERICKSBURG

Chancellorsville
Wilderness
Spotsylvania
Thornburg
Lake Anna
Bowling Green
Ashland
Hanover
Newtown
Central Garage
Tappahannock
Warsaw
Saluda
Irvington
Reedville
Oak Grove
King George
Owens

10 Mi
10 Km

"Stonewall Jackson Shrine," below). By then, Lee had driven the Union army back across the Rappahannock.

The **Chancellorsville Visitor Center** (☎ 540/786-2880) is 12 miles east of Fredericksburg on Va. 3. Stop there to see another 12-minute audiovisual orientation and related exhibits. Once again, an auto-tour tape is available. The center is open daily from 9am to 5pm, with extended hours in summer and autumn weekends.

BATTLE OF THE WILDERNESS

A year later, now under the direction of the aggressive Ulysses S. Grant, Union forces once again crossed the Rappahannock and advanced south to Wilderness Tavern, 5 miles west of Chancellorsville near what is now the junction of Va. 3 and Va. 20. Lee advanced to meet him, thus setting up the first battle between these two great generals. For 2 days (May 5 and 6, 1864), the armies fought in the tangled thickets of the Wilderness. The battle was a stalemate, but instead of retreating as his predecessors had, Grant backed off and went around Lee toward his ultimate target, Richmond, via the shortest road south (now Va. 208).

Ironically, the battle raged around Ellwood plantation, which had served as a Confederate hospital during the Battle of Chancellorsville the year before. You can see the grave of Stonewall Jackson's arm in the old family cemetery, which is open to the public Saturday and Sunday from 11am to 5pm between Memorial Day and Columbus Day.

BATTLE OF SPOTSYLVANIA COURT HOUSE

Lee quickly regrouped and tried to stop Grant 2 days later at Spotsylvania Court House, about 18 miles southeast of The Wilderness. Taking advantage of thick fog and wet Confederate gunpowder, Union troops breached the Southerners' line. When Lee's reinforcements arrived, the sides spent 20 hours in the war's most intense hand-to-hand combat at a site known as Bloody Angle. During the fighting, Lee built new fortifications to the rear, which he successfully defended. Instead of pushing the fight to the finish, however, Grant again backed off, flanked his entire army around Lee's, and resumed his unrelenting march toward Richmond. It was the end of major fighting in the Fredericksburg area, as the war moved progressively south to its ultimate conclusion 11 months later at Appomattox.

STONEWALL JACKSON SHRINE

Now part of the park, the **Stonewall Jackson Shrine** is in the plantation office where the general spent the last 6 days of his life. The wood-frame office was one of the outbuildings on Fairfield Plantation. Jackson's doctors chose it because it was quieter and more private than the manor house. They hoped that he would recover sufficiently to board a train at nearby Guinea Station for the ride to Richmond, but it was not to be. Jackson's body was taken to Lexington, where he was buried with full honors (see chapter 7).

The office is the only structure remaining at the plantation and appears as it did when Jackson died. About 45% of its contents are original.

The shrine is open 9am to 5pm, daily from Memorial Day to Labor Day, Friday to Tuesday in spring and fall, Saturday to Monday in winter. It's at the junction of C.R. 606 and C.R. 607, about 27 miles southeast of Chancellorsville, 18 miles southeast of Spotsylvania Court House. From I-95, take Exit 118 at Thornburg and follow the signs east on C.R. 606.

3 The Northern Neck

A peninsula between the Potomac and Rappahannock rivers, the Northern Neck stretches 90 miles (145km) east from Fredericksburg to the Chesapeake Bay. A popular weekend getaway and retirement retreat for residents of nearby metropolitan areas, this picturesque land of rolling hills serrated by quiet tidal creeks is the ancestral home of the Washingtons and the Lees, who created large plantations on the riverbanks. Its hills still are punctuated by agricultural and small fishing villages (they speak in terms of counties here, not towns).

From a visitor's standpoint, the Northern Neck has three areas of interest. Heading east from Fredericksburg on Va. 3, you first come to George Washington's Birthplace National Monument, where the first president was born in 1732 on Pope's Creek Plantation, and Stratford Hall, the magnificently restored Lee plantation. Nearby, the Ingleside Plantation Vineyards offer tours and tastings.

A left turn on Va. 202 will take you northeast to the end of the Northern Neck, at Smith Point on the Chesapeake. Here you can explore the quaint town of Reedville, founded as a menhaden fishing port in 1867 by Capt. Elijah Reed, a New England seafarer. Reedville soon became rich, and its captains and plant owners built magnificent Victorian-style homes (some are bed-and-breakfasts today). One plant still processes the small, toothless menhaden, a fish that's of little use for human consumption but extremely valuable as meal, oil, and protein supplements used in everything from Pepperidge Farm cookies to Rustoleum paint. You can learn all about the menhaden at the local fishing museum. From Reedville you can depart on cruises to remote Tangier and Smith islands out in the bay.

Va. 200 will take you south to the genteel riverfront hamlet of Irvington, home of the Tides Inn, one of Virginia's premier resorts, and Christ Church, perhaps the nation's best example of colonial church architecture.

You can easily see Washington's birthplace, Stratford Hall, and the Ingleside Plantation Winery as a day trip from Fredericksburg. Plan on 2 days if you go on to Reedville and Irvington, 3 days if you take an all-day cruise to Tangier or Smith islands.

ESSENTIALS

VISITOR INFORMATION   For advance information about the area, contact the **Northern Neck Tourism Council,** P.O. Box 1707, Warsaw, VA 22572 (☎ **800/ 393-6180;** www.northernneck.org; e-mail: nntc@northernneck.org). Ask for a copy of the council's annual visitor's guide. The walk-in **Virginia's Potomac Gateway Welcome Center** (☎ **540/633-3205**) is on U.S. 301 just south of the Potomac River bridge. It's open daily from 9am to 5pm. The **Westmoreland County Visitor's Center,** Courthouse Square (P.O. Box 996), Montross, VA 22520 (☎ **888/ 733-9282**), covers the area around George Washington's Birthplace and Stratford Hall plantation. It's open daily 9am to 5pm from April to October, daily 10am to 3pm during winter. The **Reedville Fishermen's Museum** (see "Exploring the Northern Neck," below) has information about Reedville and the Smith Point area. For the Irvington area, check with the **Lancaster County Chamber of Commerce & Visitor's Center,** P.O. Box 1868, Kilmarnock, VA 22482 (☎ **800/579-9102** or 804/ 435-6092), which is on Va. 3 in the Chesapeake Commons Shopping Center. Open Monday to Friday 8am to 5pm.

GETTING THERE   You'll need a **car** to get here. From Fredericksburg, go east on Va. 3, which traverses the length of the peninsula. From Fredericksburg, Washington's Birthplace is 40 miles; Irvington, 95 miles. You can make a scenic loop tour of the peninsula by taking Va. 3 past Montross, Va. 202 to Reedville, Va. 200 to Irvington, then Va. 3 back to Fredericksburg. You can get here from Richmond via U.S. 360, and from Williamsburg via U.S. 17 and Va. 3.

EXPLORING THE NORTHERN NECK

❂ **George Washington Birthplace National Monument.** 1732 Pope's Creek Rd. (Va. 204, off Va. 3). ☎ 804/224-1732. www.nps.org/gewa. Admission $2 adults, free for children under 17 (good for 7 days). National Park Service passports accepted. Daily 9am–5pm. Closed New Year's Day and Christmas.

Although it's a re-creation of Pope's Creek Plantation and not the real thing, this living-history display is like a tiny version of Williamsburg, with costumed guides showing you what 18th-century farm life was like. Washington's father, Augustine, established a tobacco plantation here in 1718. The first president was born on February 22, 1732, and lived here until the family moved to Mount Vernon when he was 3½. The manor house burned down on Christmas Day in 1779 and was never rebuilt. There are no historic records detailing what it looked like, but the outline of its foundation is marked on the lawn of Memorial House. Built in 1930–31 and furnished with antiques appropriate to the period, Memorial House is an accurate reproduction of a typical plantation home of that era. The kitchen, workshop, and other outbuildings also have been reconstructed.

You can see the site in 1½ to 2 hours. Start at the visitor center, where a 14-minute film explains plantation life, and a display case holds Washington family artifacts uncovered during archaeological digs here. A slightly uphill walk of some 300 yards along Pope's Creek leads to the actual birthplace (transportation is provided if you can't walk that distance). You'll first pass the outlines of the main house and then the kitchen building and Memorial House (a guide will take you through). Beyond are the spinning shed, workshop, vegetable gardens, hog pen, and paddocks holding cows, bullocks, horses, sheep, geese, and ducks. Guides demonstrate cooking, blacksmithing, spinning, and weaving from spring to fall. During winter, rangers conduct tours from the visitor center. The graves of 32 Washington family members, including George's father, are in a small burial ground on the property.

Admission is free on Presidents' Day in February (gingerbread and hot cider are served), and a multitude of activities take place on February 22, George's actual birthday.

❂ **Historic Christ Church.** C.R. 646, off Va. 200, 1 mile north of Irvington. ☎ 804/438-6855. Free admission (donations accepted). Church, daily 9am–5pm. Museum and guided tours, Apr–Nov, Mon–Fri 10am–4pm; Sat 1–4pm; Sun 2–5pm. Closed Christmas.

Elegant in its simplicity and virtually unchanged since it was completed in 1735, Christ Church was the gift of Robert "King" Carter, who offered to finance it if his parents' graves remained interred in the chancel. They are still here: John Carter, four of his five wives, and two infant children. Robert Carter's tomb is on the church grounds. Among the descendants of the Carters are eight governors of Virginia; two presidents of the United States (the two Harrisons); Gen. Robert E. Lee; and Edward D. White, a chief justice of the U.S. Supreme Court.

Listed on the National Register of Historic Places, the church is cruciform in shape, its brick facade laid in a pleasing Flemish bond pattern, with a three-color design that saves the expanse of brick from monotony. Inside, the three-decker pulpit is in excellent condition, and all 26 original pews remain. The building has no artificial heat or light and is now used for services only during the summer.

Volunteers are on hand in a small museum in the rectory next door to tell the church's story and show you through. Allow 30 minutes, or longer if you want to poke among the gravestones.

Ingleside Plantation Winery. 5872 Leedstown Rd., Oak Grove. ☎ **804/224-8687.** Free admission. Mon–Sat 10am–5pm; Sun noon–5pm. Closed major holidays. From Va. 3, turn right in Oak Grove on Leedstown Rd. (C.R. 638) and go about 2½ miles south.

This 2,500-acre plantation winery on the Rappahannock River side of the peninsula has winery tours, tastings, a gift shop selling wine-related items, and a small exhibit area displaying colonial wine bottles, Chesapeake waterfowl carvings, and Native American artifacts. If you're coming from Fredericksburg, you'll get here before Washington's birthplace and Stratford Hall, so go easy on tasting the Chardonnay and cabernet sauvignon.

Reedville Fishermen's Museum. 504 Main St., Reedville. ☎ **540/453-6529.** Admission $2 adults, free for children under 12. Jan by appointment; Feb closed; Mar–Apr, Sat–Sun 10:30am–4:30pm; May–Oct, daily 10:30am–4:30pm; Nov–Dec, Fri–Mon 10:30am–4:30pm. From Va. 3 east, take U.S. 360 east to Reedville.

On Cockrell's Creek, an inlet of Chesapeake Bay, the fishing village of Reedville provides a living image of the past with its Victorian mansions and seafaring atmosphere. The Fishermen's Museum consists of the 1875 William Walker House, the town's oldest building, which was restored to appear as it did in 1900. Almost as old, the Covington Building houses a permanent collection and special exhibits commemorating the watermen who participate in the town's leading industry, menhaden fishing, which dates to 1874, when Capt. Elijah Reed arrived here. There's a 5-minute video about the industry, and guides lead 10-minute tours of the Walker House.

✪ **Stratford Hall Plantation.** Va. 214, 2 miles north of Va. 3, Stratford. ☎ **804/ 493-8038.** www.stratfordhall.org. Admission $7 adults, $6 seniors, $3 children 6–18, free for children under 6. Daily 9am–4:30pm. Closed New Year's Day, Thanksgiving, and Christmas.

This is one of the great houses of the South, magnificently set on 1,600 acres above the Potomac, renowned not only for its distinctive architectural style but also for the illustrious family who lived here. Thomas Lee (1690–1750), a planter who later served as governor of the Virginia colony, built Stratford in the late 1730s. Five of his sons played major roles in the forming of the new nation, most notably Richard Henry Lee, who made the motion for independence in the Continental Congress in 1776. He and Francis Lightfoot Lee were the only brothers to sign the Declaration of Independence. Cousin Henry "Light-Horse Harry" Lee, a hero of the Revolution, was a friend of George Washington and father of Robert E. Lee, who was born here in 1807.

The H-shaped manor house, its four dependencies, coach house, and stables have been brilliantly restored.

One of the mansion's most striking features is its brick chimney groupings, which flank the roofline. The paneled Great Hall, one of the finest rooms to have survived from colonial times, runs the depth of the house and has an inverted tray ceiling. On the same floor are bedrooms and a nursery, where you can see Robert E. Lee's crib. The fireplace in the nursery is trimmed with sculpted angels' heads.

Start at the reception center, where a 13-minute video will set the stage. You can go inside the mansion and its dependencies only on 30-minute **tours** led by costumed guides, who will meet you at one of the outbuildings. The videos start on the hour and half hour. Allow 45 minutes to see the film and tour the house. You can easily spend another 2 hours strolling the gardens, meadows, and nature trails on this 1,600-acre estate, still operated as a working farm.

There aren't many places to dine hereabouts, so have lunch in the rustic, log cabin–style **Plantation Dining Room,** which has a screened-in terrace. It offers worthy Virginia-style cream of crab soup, crab cake and fried oyster sandwiches, salads topped with chicken or cured ham, ham biscuits, and meals of fried chicken, crab cakes, flounder, or ham. Sandwiches range from $5 to $8, meals cost $9 to $13, and children's portions are available. Chardonnay and cabernet sauvignon wines from Ingleside Plantation Winery are served by the glass or bottle. The dining room is open daily 11:30am to 8pm from April through October. Call ahead to see if it's open during winter.

BIKING, BIRDING, GOLFING, FISHING & KAYAKING

Country roads winding through gently rolling hills and crossing picturesque creeks make the Northern Neck a great place to ride your bicycle. One excellent route makes a loop from Reedville via U.S. 360 and county roads 652 and 644. On C.R. 644, you'll cross the Little Wicomico River via the free Sunnybank Ferry. Some bed-and-breakfasts and campgrounds provide bikes for the guests, but there are no places to rent them here, so bring your own.

The Northern Neck has more than 1,100 miles of shoreline and 6,500 acres of nature preserves, making it an important stop for birds migrating along the Atlantic Flyway. It also has a substantial population of bald eagles. One of the best places to view the migratory birds is at **Belle Isle State Park** (☎ 804/462-5030), off C.R. 354 on the Rappahannock River northwest of Irvington, which has guided canoe trips. To see the eagles, head to the **Caledon Natural Area,** on Va. 218 near King George (☎ 540/663-3861), which has observation tours along the Potomac River. The **Northern Neck Audubon Society,** P.O. Box 991, Kilmarnock, VA 22482 (no phone), organizes field trips.

Golfers come here to play the Golden Eagle course shared by the Tides Inn and the Tides Lodge (see "Where to Stay," below), one of Virginia's best. The Tides resorts have two other courses to keep you playing. Other less challenging—and less expensive—links are **Quinton Oaks Golf Course** near Callao (☎ 804/529-5367; www.quintonoaks.com); the 9-hole Windjammer course at **Windmill Point Resort** at White Stone near Irvington (☎ 804/435-1166); and another 9-holer at **Bushfield Golf Course** on Va. 202 at Mt. Holly (☎ 804/472-2602).

Reedville is the jumping-off point for fishing charters on the Chesapeake Bay, where you might hook a fighting bluefish or snag a succulent rockfish (sea bass). Call Capt. Jim Conner of the *Jennie C* (☎ 804/453-4021), Capt. Jim Hardy of *The Ranger II* (☎ 804/453-6635), or **Pittman's Charters** (☎ 804/453-3643).

The quiet backwaters are fine places to paddle a kayak while watching for the area's abundant birds and other wildlife. Near Reedville, John and Peggy Federhart of **RiverRats,** P.O. Box 247, Ophelia, VA 22530 (☎ 804/453-3064; fax 804/s453-3433; www.virginia.org/riverrats; e-mail: federar@crosslink.net), rent kayaks, teach courses, and organize tours on the Great Wicomico and Little Wicomico rivers.

You can learn to sail at **Chesapeake Bay Sailing School,** P.O. Box 779, Irvington, VA 22480 (☎ and fax **804/435-5019;** www.sailingschool.net), which is based at the Tides Inn. Two-day introductory classes for beginners cost $275 per person, while 4-day sessions for beginners or intermediate sailors go for $520 per person.

CRUISES TO TANGIER & SMITH ISLANDS

Out in the Chesapeake Bay lie quaint and still relatively remote ✪ **Tangier Island** and the nearby **Smith Island.** They were so remote until recent times, in fact, that inhabitants of both islands still speak in the Elizabethan brogue of their colonial ancestors. See "Onancock" under "Chincoteague & the Eastern Shore" in chapter 11 for more information about Tangier Island. Mostly in Maryland, Smith Island has three fishing villages, of which Ewell is the most often visited. Residents of both islands earn their livelihoods by crabbing, oystering, and raising soft-shell crabs in shallow pens. Smith Island has the distinction of being an entirely Methodist community.

 Tangier Island Cruises (☎ **800/598-2628** or 804/453-2628) leave from Buzzards Point Marina, off U.S. 360 east of Reedville. **Smith Island Cruises** (☎ **804/453-3430**) depart from Chesapeake Bay/Smith Island KOA Resort, on Campground Road near Smith Point, also off U.S. 360 east of Reedville. Both cruises depart at 10am daily from May to mid-October. Fares on both are about $20 for adults, $10 for children 4 to 13, free for kids 3 and under. The narrated voyages take 90 minutes each way, so they'll take a full day. Reservations are required.

WHERE TO STAY

This is a land of Victorian homes turned into bed-and-breakfasts, especially along Main Street in Reedville. In addition to those listed below, **The Morris House Bed and Breakfast Inn,** 826 Main St., Reedville, VA 22539 (☎ **804/453-7016;** www.eaglesnest.net/morrishouse; e-mail: morrish@crosslink.net), has two rooms (one with a fireplace), two suites with whirlpool baths, and one waterside cottage. Rates range from $70 to $170 for a double.

 Near the Tides Inn, **The Hope and Glory Inn,** 65 Tavern Rd., Irvington, VA 22480 (☎ **804/438-6053**), has seven rooms and four cottages. Double rates are $95 to $175.

 The only chain motel on the Northern Neck is the **Best Western Warsaw,** on U.S. 360 at Warsaw (☎ **800/528-1234** or 804/333-1700). Although centrally located, it's not particularly convenient to any of the major sights.

The Gables Bed & Breakfast Inn. 859 Main St., Reedville, VA 22539. ☎ **804/453-5209.** 2 units (neither with private bathroom). A/C. $75–$125 double. MC, V.

You won't have the modern amenities here, but architecturally this is the most fascinating of the area's B&Bs. Seafaring Capt. James Fisher used wood from his dismantled schooner to build the house about 1909. In fact, one of the masts extends from the center of a large room on the third floor up into the attic. Continuing the nautical theme, the eight gables (four are shaped like ship bells) extend from the center of the roof like the points on a compass, carvings on the stairs evoke sea waves, and the floors of the stairwell landings are laid to resemble the rising sun. Lots of Victorian period pieces adorn the two formal parlors and dining room downstairs as well as the two second-story bedrooms. Equipped with a double bed, the Rose Room at the rear of the house overlooks Cockrell's Creek. The Blue Room on the front lacks the view but is larger and has a double bed. Bring robes, since you'll have to walk across the hallway or upstairs to one of the bell-shaped gables to reach a bathroom. Only the bedrooms are air-conditioned, but a huge screened porch wraps three-quarters of the way around the house, and there are two sunrooms on the second floor for relaxing. Hosts Norman and Barbara Clark serve full breakfasts, including Barbara's noted apple fritters. The Clarks soon should have four more units available in the carriage house; they'll have their own bathrooms.

✪ **The Tides Inn.** 480 King Carter Dr. (P.O. Box 480), Irvington, VA 22480. ☎ **800/ 843-0480** or 804/438-5000. Fax 804/438-5552. www.the-tides.com. 110 units. A/C TV TEL. $135–$215 per person double. $22 per room daily service charge. Rates include breakfast and dinner. Golf packages available. Pets $10 per animal (in some rooms). AE, DC, DISC, MC, V. Closed early Jan to mid-Mar. Free parking. From Va. 3, take Va. 200 south 2 miles to Irvington, turn right at the sign to end of King Carter Dr.

One of Virginia's top resorts, the Tides Inn has maintained a tradition of gracious service since 1947 under the auspices of the Stephens family, which manages the inn together with the Tides Lodge (see below). A boat shuttles across Carter's Creek between the properties, and guests at one can use the facilities at the other. On the east side of the creek, the sprawling inn complex consists of several low-rise buildings encircling a nicely landscaped entrance. Guests can choose accommodations in the clapboard Main Building, where the dining room and gift shop are located, or in the cottagelike Windsor or Lancaster Houses, where the rooms are more spacious and feature dressing rooms, living areas, and, in some cases, balconies overlooking Carter's Creek. All rooms contain coffeemakers.

Dining/Diversions: Guests are assigned to a table in the lovely main dining room overlooking the creek (men must wear jackets at dinner). Food is also available at Cap'n B's, at the Golden Eagle golf course, and at Commodore's, an airy glass-enclosed room adjacent to the creekside pool that serves informal buffet luncheons. Menus feature seafood items like soft-shell crabs and fried-oyster sandwiches, along with prime rib and pork tenderloin. The very clubby Chesapeake Club lounge, next to the dining room, has exquisite wood paneling (including bottle lockers left from the days before Virginia allowed liquor-by-the-drink), panoramic views, music, and dancing Wednesday to Saturday evenings.

Amenities: Morning newspaper, nightly turndown, no surcharge for local or long-distance phone calls. Heated saltwater pool; complimentary nearby health club with aerobics classes, weights, sauna, and racquetball; unlimited tennis, sailing, paddle-boating, canoeing, bicycling, croquet; two 18-hole golf courses, one 9-hole par-three course plus driving range and putting green; game room with Ping-Pong, billiards, electronic games, and shuffleboard; gift and resort-wear shops; yacht cruises; sailing school.

The Tides Lodge Resort & Country Club. St. Andrews Dr. (P.O. Box 480), Irvington, VA 22480. ☎ **800/843-0480** or 804/438-5000. Fax 804/438-5552. www.the-tides.com. 60 units, 1 cottage. A/C TV TEL. $155–$175 double; $10 per room daily service charge in lieu of tipping. Golf and other packages available. AE, DC, DISC, MC, V. Closed Nov–Mar. Free parking. From Va. 3, take Va. 200 south 2 miles to Irvington, follow signs.

Taking a page from St. Andrews golf course in Scotland, a tartan motif prevails at this less-expensive sister of the Tides Inn (see above), in both the public areas and the comfortable, motel-style rooms, whose walls are adorned with hunting and fishing scenes. No jackets are required in the casual, seafood-oriented Binnacle Restaurant, which overlooks the creek. McD's Pub offers weekend entertainment. Guests here have their own Tartan Course, saltwater pool, games room, tennis courts, and exercise room, and they can take the water taxi across Carter's Creek to share the Tides Inn's dining room, Golden Eagle golf course, and other facilities.

WHERE TO DINE

Several marinas on Northern Neck creeks have low-key restaurants where you can have your fill of steamed crabs, spiced shrimp, and other fresh goodies from the Chesapeake Bay. The **Fairport Marina & Restaurant** (☎ **804/453-5002**) overlooks Cockrell's Creek near Reedville. It's open daily for lunch and dinner. Take U.S. 360

west and follow the signs at the turnoff to Tangier Island Cruises. **The Crab Shack,** 672 Painter Rd. (☎ **804/435-4500**), near Kilmarnock and Irvington, is open Thursday to Sunday for lunch and dinner. From Kilmarnock, take Va. 200 north, turn right on Bluff Point Road (C.R. 608) for 3 miles, then turn right on Oyster Shell Road.

If you're walking around Reedville, pop into **Peppermints,** 858 Main St. (☎ **804/453-6468**), in a little pink building near the marina, for ice cream sundaes and inexpensive homemade soups and sandwiches. It's open Monday to Saturday 11am to 7pm. You'll find the locals having their afternoon coffee break here.

The Crazy Crab. 902 Main St., Reedville (end of U.S. 360, at Reedville Marina). ☎ **804/453-6789.** Reservations not accepted. Main courses $8.50–$16. MC, V. Tues–Sun 11am–3pm and 5–9pm. SEAFOOD.

You can look out across the Reedville harbor to the menhaden processing plants from inside or outside this cafe-style restaurant. Best bets are the finely seasoned crab cakes made with premium back fin meat (I found not a shred of shell in mine—unusual at even expensive restaurants), which are available as sandwiches at lunch, main courses at dinner. Other temptations include soft-shell crabs, shrimp, and fried, broiled, or stuffed fresh flounder. Light eaters can turn to large salads, especially the shrimp or crabmeat versions.

Elijah's Restaurant. 729 Main St., Reedville. ☎ **804/453-3621.** Reservations recommended. Sandwiches $6–$10; main courses $10–$19. MC, V. Wed–Sat 5–9pm, Sun noon–8pm. REGIONAL/INTERNATIONAL.

Owned by a great-great-grandson of Capt. Elijah Reed, this attractive restaurant occupies an early-1900s waterfront building which housed a cannery and large general store. Lots of exposed beams and tongue-in-groove planking in several dining rooms evoke that era. Well-prepared seafood is offered traditionally, such as fried shrimp or oysters; more urbanely, such as scallops wrapped in bacon with a sherry sauce; blackened in the Cajun fashion; or with Italian touches, such as seafood in a marinara sauce over penne. Landlubbers can choose from chicken potpie, veal piccatta, and grilled steaks.

6

Charlottesville

With the serene Blue Ridge Mountains on the horizon to the west, the rolling hills of central Virginia reveal a scenic pastoral landscape. No wonder Peter Jefferson, coming here to survey the land, decided to settle and amassed hundreds of acres. His son Thomas Jefferson, America's third president, inherited not only his father's property but also an abiding attachment to the land where he, too, spent much of his life, and where his friends included James Madison and James Monroe, two other future presidents. His presence is very much felt today in what the locals call "Mr. Jefferson's Country." It was in Charlottesville that Thomas Jefferson built his famous mountaintop home, Monticello; selected the site for and helped plan James Monroe's Ash Lawn–Highland house near Monticello; designed his "academical village," the University of Virginia; and died at home. "All my wishes end where I hope my days will end," he wrote, "at Monticello."

Established in 1762 as the county seat for Albemarle, the town had its Court Square complete with courthouse, jail, whipping post, pillory, and stocks to keep fractious citizens in line. The courthouse doubled as marketplace in those early days and served as a church as well, with rotating services for different denominations (Jefferson called it the "Common Temple"). Elections were held in Court Square followed by raucous political celebrations. Needless to say, the taverns across the street were well patronized.

Along with James Madison, who lived at Montpelier 25 miles north of Charlottesville, Jefferson and Monroe were instrumental in developing the emerging nation. In addition to writing the Declaration of Independence, Jefferson advocated freedom of religion and public education. And although he never freed his own slaves (it's now established through DNA testing that he sired a son with Sally Hennings, his slave mistress), he believed that slavery should be abolished.

Charlottesville today is a growing cosmopolitan center, attracting an increasing number of rich and famous folks like author John Grisham. But its prime attractions are still Thomas Jefferson and his magnificent creations.

1 Orientation & Getting Around

VISITOR INFORMATION

For information, contact the **Monticello Visitor Center,** P.O. Box 178, Charlottesville, VA 22902 (☎ **804/977-1783;** fax 804/ 295-2176;

Charlottesville

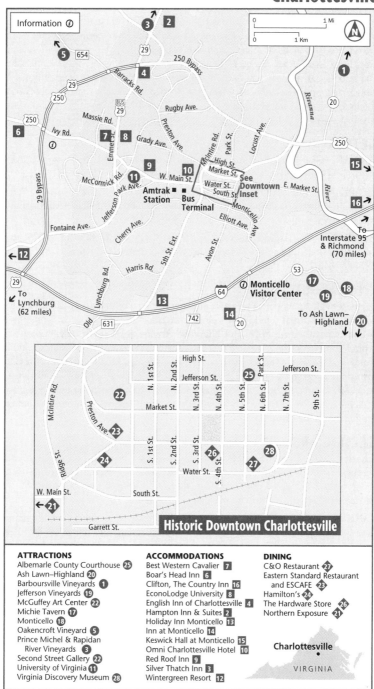

Information ⓘ

0 — 1 Mi
0 — 1 Km

N

2
3

1

5 654
4
29

250 Bypass
250
BUS 29
Barracks Rd.
250
Ivy Rd.
6
ⓘ
Massie Rd.
7 **8**
Grady Ave.
Rugby Ave.
Preston Ave.
Emmet St.
McCormick Rd.
Jefferson Park Ave.
McIntire Rd.
Park St.
Locust Ave.
High St.
Market St.
Water St.
South St.
9
10
11 W. Main St.
Amtrak Station
Bus Terminal
See Downtown Inset
Fontaine Ave.
Cherry Ave.
5th St. Ext.
Avon St.
Elliott Ave.
Monticello Ave.
E. Market St.
River
250
15
16
To Interstate 95 & Richmond (70 miles)
29 Bypass
12
29
To Lynchburg (62 miles)
Lynchburg Rd.
Harris Rd.
13
Old 631
742
14
20
64
53
ⓘ **Monticello Visitor Center**
17 **18**
19
To Ash Lawn–Highland
20
Rivanna
20
250

Historic Downtown Charlottesville

McIntire Rd.
Ridge St.
Preston Ave.
High St.
Jefferson St.
Market St.
N. 1st St.
N. 2nd St.
N. 3rd St.
N. 4th St.
N. 5th St.
N. 6th St.
N. 7th St.
9th St.
Jefferson St.
Park St.
25
22
23
24
S. 1st St.
S. 2nd St.
S. 3rd St.
S. 4th St.
Water St.
26
27
28
W. Main St.
South St.
21
Garrett St.

ATTRACTIONS
Albemarle County Courthouse **25**
Ash Lawn–Highland **20**
Barboursville Vineyards **1**
Jefferson Vineyards **19**
McGuffey Art Center **22**
Michie Tavern **17**
Monticello **18**
Oakencroft Vineyard **5**
Prince Michel & Rapidan
  River Vineyards **3**
Second Street Gallery **22**
University of Virginia **11**
Virginia Discovery Museum **28**

ACCOMMODATIONS
Best Western Cavalier **7**
Boar's Head Inn **6**
Clifton, The Country Inn **16**
EconoLodge University **8**
English Inn of Charlottesville **4**
Hampton Inn & Suites **2**
Holiday Inn Monticello **13**
Inn at Monticello **14**
Keswick Hall at Monticello **15**
Omni Charlottesville Hotel **10**
Red Roof Inn **9**
Silver Thatch Inn **3**
Wintergreen Resort **12**

DINING
C&O Restaurant **27**
Eastern Standard Restaurant
  and ESCAFE **23**
Hamilton's **24**
The Hardware Store **26**
Northern Exposure **21**

Charlottesville

VIRGINIA

www.charlottesvilletourism.org; e-mail: visitorcenter@charlottesvilletourism.org). The center is on Va. 20 at Exit 121 off I-64. It's open daily from 9am to 5:30pm, to 5pm from December to March. The center sells block tickets to Monticello and other key attractions (see "What to See & Do," below). It also provides maps and literature about local and state attractions, and can make same-day, walk-in hotel/motel reservations for you. The center is open March through October, daily from 9am to 5:30pm; the rest of the year, daily until 5pm. Closed New Year's Day, Thanksgiving, and Christmas.

GETTING THERE

BY CAR   Charlottesville is on I-64 from east or west and U.S. 29 from north or south. I-64 connects with I-81 at Staunton and with I-95 at Richmond.

BY PLANE   US Airways, Delta, and United fly commuter planes to **Charlottesville-Albemarle Airport,** 201 Bowen Loop (☎ **804/973-8341**), north of town off U.S. 29.

BY TRAIN   The **Amtrak** station is at 810 W. Main St. (☎ **800/872-7245;** www.amtrak.com), about halfway between the town's commercial district and the University of Virginia.

CITY LAYOUT

Charlottesville has not one but two commercial centers. Both are on Main Street (U.S. 250 Business), about a mile apart. On West Main Street, opposite the University of Virginia between 13th Street and Elliewood Avenue, the **Corner** neighborhood is a typical campus enclave, with student-dominated restaurants, bookstores, clothing stores, and a dearth of parking spaces. A mile to the east, **Historic Downtown Charlottesville** is centered on the Downtown Mall, an 8-block, pedestrian-only strip of Main Street between 2nd Street West and 8th Street East. The major suburban growth is along U.S. 29 north, which is lined with shopping centers, chain motels, and fast-food and family restaurants.

GETTING AROUND

Charlottesville Transit Service (☎ **804/296-RIDE**) provides bus service Monday through Saturday from 6:30am to 6:30pm throughout the city (but not to Monticello). Routes 2, 3, and 7 run along West Main Street between downtown and the university. Base fare is 75¢, with exact change required.

PARKING   On-street parking is extremely limited here. In the historic downtown area, you can park free for 2 hours with merchant validation in the garage on Market Street between 1st and 2nd streets, or in any of the lots and two garages along Water Street. The university's visitor parking garage is on the western side of the campus, on Emmet Street (U.S. 29 Business) a block south of University Avenue (which is the continuation of West Main Street). On the eastern side of campus, two public garages are located opposite the University Hospital on Lee Street, off Jefferson Park Avenue. The Corner has public parking on Elliewood Avenue, Wertland Street at 14th Street, and down the alleys behind the businesses fronting West Main Street. Most garages and lots cost $1 per hour.

2 Where to Stay

Wherever you choose to stay, make your reservations as far in advance as possible during University of Virginia events such as graduation, football games, and parents' weekends, when every property here will be full.

The commercial strip along U.S. 29 north of the U.S. 250 bypass has an abundance of chain motels, including a comfortable **Courtyard by Marriott** (☎ 800/321-2211 or 804/973-7100), which abuts the Fashion Square Mall. Others along U.S. 29 north include **Best Western Mount Vernon** (☎ 800/528-1234 or 804/296-5501), **Comfort Inn** (☎ 800/228-5150 or 804/293-6188), **Econo Lodge North** (☎ 800/55-ECONO or 804/295-3185), **Hampton Inn** (☎ 800/HAMPTON or 804/978-7888), **Holiday Inn North** (☎ 800/HOLIDAY or 804/293-9111), **Knights Inn** (☎ 800/843-5644 or 804/973-8133), **Sheraton Inn Charlottesville** (☎ 800/325-3535 or 804/973-2121), and **Super 8** (☎ 800/800-8000 or 804/973-0888).

EXPENSIVE

Boar's Head Inn at the University of Virginia. 200 Ednam Dr. (P.O. Box 5307), Charlottesville, VA 22905. ☎ **800/476-1988** or 804/296-2181. Fax 804/972-6019. www.boarsheadinn.com. 172 units. A/C TV TEL. $189–$219 double. Weekend and golf packages available. AE, DC, DISC, MC, V. Free parking. Resort is on U.S. 250 1 mile west of U.S. 29/250 bypass.

Named for the traditional symbol of hospitality in Shakespeare's England, this university-operated resort is a combination of rural charm and sophisticated facilities. The focal point is a reconstructed historic gristmill that was dismantled and brought here in the early 1960s. It houses the Tavern, the Garden Room, the Old Mill dining room, and some guest rooms. Adjoining low-rise wings are more modern, though furnishings throughout are colonial reproductions. Recently spiffed up during a $10 million renovation, rooms offer lake views, and some have working fireplaces. Each suite has a bedroom and a sitting room, with either a kitchenette or a wet bar.

The Boar's Head is one of the best places in the region to take off on a hot-air balloon ride.

Dining/Diversions: Open for all three meals, the Old Mill Room offers candlelit dining in a historic setting with beamed ceilings, multi-paned windows, and plank floors. Among its offerings are Virginia-accented dishes such as hunter's chili with beef and venison. The adjacent Terrace Lounge offers indoor and outdoor seating, an appetizer menu, and piano music from Wednesday to Saturday. Racquets Restaurant and Lounge offers healthy salads, sandwiches, and daily specials.

Amenities: Concierge, room service, complimentary morning newspaper, nightly turndown, free airport shuttle, in-room coffee/tea service. Concierge section has bathrobe, hair dryer, and computer hookup. Four pools (including an Olympic-size model), health club, indoor and outdoor tennis, squash, platform tennis, fishing, jogging trail, bicycle rental, adjacent 18-hole golf course, massages, facials, gift shop.

MODERATE

✪ **Hampton Inn & Suites.** 900 W. Main St. (P.O. Box 0) at 10th St., Charlottesville, VA 22903. ☎ **800/HAMPTON** or 804/923-8600. Fax 804/923-8601. 100 units. A/C TV TEL. $85–$108 double. Rates include continental breakfast. AE, DC, DISC, MC, V.

This five-story brick structure stands just east of the campus near the university's medical center. Murals of Monticello, the Rotunda, and other local scenes overlook a gas fireplace that stands in the center of an elegant, two-story lobby. Eight of the suites here also contain gas fireplaces, and all of them have separate bedrooms, VCRs, and kitchens complete with microwave ovens and dishwashers. The medium-size rooms also come well-equipped. Guests are treated to an extensive continental breakfast in a room off the lobby. Other facilities include an exercise room and free guest laundry.

The Omni Charlottesville Hotel. 235 W. Main St. (at McIntire St.), Charlottesville, VA 22901. ☎ **800/THE-OMNI** or 804/971-5500. Fax 804/979-4456. 204 units. A/C TV TEL. $124–$154 double. AE, DC, DISC, MC, V. Free parking. From I-64, take Exit 120 and follow Fifth Ridge St. (C.R. 631) north to McIntire St. and hotel on the right.

You can't miss this seven-story, brick-and-glass structure with a soaring atrium lobby, since its triangular shape towers above the western end of the Downtown Mall. Rooms are medium-size; those on the upper floors have views over the city. At the street level, a fountain bubbles amid a tropical forest in the atrium lobby. With a garden-like setting and a view of the mall, a Virginia wine country theme restaurant specializes in regional cuisine and local wines. You can get your exercise in the health club, which has both indoor and outdoor pools. The Omni has extensive meeting space and draws more conventions and groups than most hotels here.

INEXPENSIVE

Best Western Cavalier. 105 Emmet St. (P.O. Box 5647) at W. Main St., Charlottesville, VA 22905. ☎ **888/882-2129** or 804/296-8111. Fax 804/296-3523. 118 units. A/C TV TEL. $69–$99 double. Rates include continental breakfast. AE, DC, DISC, MC, V. Free parking. From U.S. 29 bypass, go east on Ivy Rd. (U.S. 250 Business) 1 mile to hotel on the left.

Exactly half a mile west of the Rotunda, this five-story glass-and-steel motel is popular with visiting athletic teams, since it's also close to Scott Stadium and University Hall, the two major sports venues here. Enter the spacious rooms through external walkways bordered by wrought-iron railings. Guests are served a basic continental breakfast in the small lobby with colonial decor, and there's an independently operated restaurant on the premises. During summer you can cool off in a small outdoor pool. The hotel provides complimentary shuttle service to and from the airport and the Amtrak and bus stations.

Econo Lodge University. 400 Emmet St. (U.S. 29 Business), Charlottesville, VA 22903. ☎ **800/55-ECONO** or 804/296-2104. Fax 804/977-5591. 60 units. A/C TV TEL. $45–$60 double. Small pets accepted ($5 fee). AE, DC, DISC, MC, V.

This Econo Lodge sits 2 blocks north of West Main Street and across Emmet Street from University Hall, the indoor sports arena. Recently renovated, the rooms are small but comfortable, and 15 of them are especially equipped for seniors (with special phones with oversized buttons, grab-bars in the bathtubs, and so forth). The best rooms, in the rear of the L-shaped building, face a hillside and get less street noise than those in the front. There's a small outdoor swimming pool here, and a reasonably good Italian restaurant is next door.

English Inn of Charlottesville. 2000 Morton Dr., Charlottesville, VA 22903. ☎ **800/ 786-5400** or 804/971-9900. Fax 804/977-8008. 88 units. E-mail: englishinn@ wytestone.com. A/C TV TEL. $65–$85 double. Rates include full breakfast. AE, DC, MC, V. Free parking. Follow U.S. 29 north to just south of the U.S. 250 bypass.

A traditional English Tudor–style building houses this hospitable inn. You'll feel as though you're in an English club when you enter the comfortable wood-paneled lobby, its floors strewn with Oriental rugs. Step down into the Conservatory, where cozy seating areas and an oversize fireplace make a perfect setting for the continental breakfast served daily. Rooms are variously decorated, many with Queen Anne–style reproduction pieces; others have a more contemporary look. The hotel offers no food service other than breakfast, but it does provide free airport transfers. Facilities include a pool, exercise room, and sauna.

Holiday Inn Monticello. 1200 5th St., Charlottesville, VA 22902. ☎ **800/HOLIDAY** or 804/977-5100. Fax 804/293-5228. 130 units. A/C TV TEL. $75–$90 double. AE, DC, DISC,

MC, V. Free parking. Take Exit 120 from I-64 and drive north on 5th St. over the highway; the hotel is on the right.

The most convenient hotel to Monticello, Ash Lawn–Highland, and Michie Tavern, this pleasant high-rise offers an easygoing atmosphere, a hospitable staff, and spacious accommodations. The more expensive executive-level rooms have access to a business center and lounge serving complimentary continental breakfast and evening hors d'oeuvres. A large outdoor pool is open seasonally. The on-premises restaurant has full-service dining nightly.

Red Roof Inn. 1309 W. Main St. (at 13th St.), Charlottesville, VA 22903. ☎ **800/THE-ROOF** or 804/295-4333. Fax 804/295-2021. 135 units. A/C TV TEL. $52–$100 double. AE, DC, DISC, MC, V. Free parking. From U.S. 29 bypass, go east on Ivy Rd. (U.S. 250 Business) 1½ miles to hotel on the left.

The clean and comfortable seven-story hotel is on the eastern edge of the Corner and right across West Main Street from the university. Interior hallways lead to medium-size guest rooms, which contain cherry-wood furniture. Despite being a bit small, the bathrooms have surprisingly ample vanity space. There are two restaurants in the building, and the Corner's multitude of food outlets are mere steps away.

BED & BREAKFAST ACCOMMODATIONS

Bed-and-breakfast accommodations in elegant homes and private estate cottages are handled by **Guesthouses Reservation Service, Inc.,** P.O. Box 5737, Charlottesville, VA 22905 (☎ **804/979-7264;** fax 804/293-7791; www.va-guesthouses.com). You can write, fax, or check out the Web site for information describing the properties, but reservations must be made by phone. Credit cards can be used for deposits. The office is open Monday through Friday from noon to 5pm.

The Inn at Monticello. 1188 Scottsville Rd. (Va. 20), Charlottesville, VA 22902. ☎ **804/ 979-3593.** Fax 804/296-1344. www.innatmonticello.com. E-mail: innatmonticello@ mindspring.com. 5 units. A/C. $110–$140 double. Rates include full breakfast. MC, V. Free parking. From I-64, take Va. 20 south and continue past the visitor center for about a third of a mile. The inn is on your right.

The most convenient accommodation to Monticello, Ash Lawn–Highland, and Michie Tavern, this beautiful two-story white-clapboard country house sits on 5 acres well back from Va. 20. The manicured lawn is ornamented in spring with blooming dogwood trees and azaleas. Boxwoods, tall shade and evergreen trees, shrubs, and a babbling brook provide an exceptionally lovely setting. Guests enter via the front porch into a double sitting room, dramatically furnished with crimson walls, two fireplaces, and a handsome collection of antiques. Guest rooms are individually decorated and have such special features as a working fireplace, private porch, or four-poster canopy bed. Guests can relax outdoors on the hammock or on the front verandah lined with wicker rockers. There's a croquet course on the sweeping lawn.

NEARBY COUNTRY INNS

✪ **Clifton, The Country Inn.** 1296 Clifton Inn Dr., Charlottesville, VA 22911. ☎ **888/971-1800** or 804/971-1800. Fax 804/971-7098. 14 units. A/C TEL. $150–$375 double; $225–$450 suite. Rates include full breakfast and afternoon tea. AE, MC, V. Minimum 2-night stay weekends. Packages available. From Charlottesville take U.S. 250 east 5 miles; turn right on N. Milton Rd. (C.R. 729) and go ¼ mile to Clifton Inn Dr. on left.

You'll think you've arrived at Tara in *Gone With the Wind* when you first see this stately, 1790-vintage manse, a combination of Federal and Colonial Revival styles. You can relax in the main house's formal parlor, browse through hundreds of titles shelved in its cozy library, or partake of homemade cookies and pastries in its tea room. Although Clifton is not as grand physically as Keswick Hall at Monticello (see below), you'll be attended by a young staff whose energy and informality make this inn much more casual than Keswick. And the food here is consistently among Virginia's finest.

Guest rooms and suites upstairs in the main house all have working fireplaces, and most have claw-foot tubs with separate showers. The estate's whitewashed stables now house three other units, and the old carriage house and another outbuilding have been converted into romantic outposts. The split-level carriage house sports a grand piano, while the even more remote honeymoon cottage has a glass-walled bathroom. Feather pillows, down comforters, plush robes, and other such amenities are *de rigueur* throughout.

Dining/Diversions: Not only is staying here a delight, chef Craig Hartman's award-winning gourmet cuisine makes this one of Virginia's finest places to dine. Craig and his assistants explain the preparation before presenting five courses Sunday through Thursday ($60 per person), six courses on Friday and Saturday ($70 per person). Reservations are required. Wine comes from one of the state's finest collections, kept in a 5,000-bottle cellar beneath the house.

Amenities: Nightly turndown with Perrier and roses; early morning coffee and tea delivered to rooms daily, plus newspapers on weekends; complimentary cookies and soft drinks available at all hours. Swimming pool (romantically lit at night); tennis and croquet; 20-acre lake stocked for fishing; hiking trails.

Keswick Hall at Monticello. 701 Country Club Dr., Keswick, VA 22947. ☎ **800/ 274-5391** or 804/979-3440. Fax 804/977-4171. www.keswick.com. 48 units. $375–$575 double. Rates include afternoon tea. AE, DC, MC, V. From Charlottesville take U.S. 250 or I-64 east to Shadwell (Exit 124), then take Va. 22 east and follow signs to Keswick.

This super-luxury estate was the creation of Sir Bernard Ashley, widower of famed designer Laura Ashley, but Orient Express Hotels bought it in 1999, added "at Monticello" to the name (it's not "at" Monticello but some 5 miles away), and promised to improve the bar and restaurant facilities and add 50 more guest quarters in a separate building. Many of the 1912 vintage Italianate Crawford villa's rooms and suites have fireplaces, claw-foot tubs, and views over a golf course redesigned by Arnold Palmer, but don't expect to find these in the 14 least expensive "house rooms." All guests can roam around the vast public rooms on the main level, including a main lounge with fireplace and terrace with golf course view. Compared to Clifton, The Country Inn (see above), the atmosphere here is formal to the point of being stuffy.

Dining: Although not at Clifton's high level, dining here usually is quite good, and a new main-floor dining room should eventually provide golf-course views. Dinners are fixed price at $58. English afternoon tea is free to guests, who can have lunch or dinner at the adjoining Keswick Club's bistro.

Amenities: Concierge, masseur, twice-daily maid service, social director, babysitting. Guests have complimentary use of the private Keswick Club's indoor/outdoor heated pool, Olympic-size outdoor pool, and fitness center, and they can pay to play on its tennis courts and golf course.

Silver Thatch Inn. 3001 Hollymead Dr., Charlottesville, VA 22911. ☎ **804/978-4686.** Fax 804/973-6156. www.silverthatch.com. 7 units. A/C. $125–$165 double. Rates include full breakfast. AE, DC, MC, V. Take U.S. 29 about 8 miles north of town; turn right at traffic signal onto Hollymead Dr. to inn on the right.

Occupying a rambling white-clapboard house, a section of which dates back to Revolutionary days, this charming hostelry is located on a quiet road and set on nicely landscaped grounds. Attractively decorated with authentic 18th-century pieces, the original part of the building now serves as a cozy common room, where guests are invited for afternoon refreshments. The 1812 center part of the house is now one of the dining rooms. Guest rooms are lovely, with down comforters on four-poster canopied beds, antique pine dressers, carved walnut-and-mahogany armoires, and exquisite quilts. Several rooms have working fireplaces. Telephones and TVs are available in the common areas.

Gourmet dinners are served in candlelit rooms open to the public (inn guests should reserve a table in advance, since this is one of the area's most popular dining venues). The list of Virginia and California wines is excellent.

A MOUNTAIN GETAWAY

Wintergreen Resort. P.O. Box 706, Wintergreen, VA 22958. ☎ **800/325-2200** or 804/325-2200. Fax 804/325-8004. www.wintergreenresort.com. 300 units. A/C TV TEL. $167–$182 double; $197–$739 condos and homes. Weekly rates and packages available. AE, MC, V. Take I-64 west to Exit 107 and follow U.S. 250 west; turn left onto C.R. 151 south, then right on C.R. 644 for 4½ miles to resort. It's about 43 miles from Charlottesville.

With 6,700 of its 11,000 acres dedicated to the remaining undisturbed forest land, this recreational real estate development offers year-round vacation activities in a magnificent Blue Ridge Mountain setting. While the big draws here include skiing, golf, horseback riding, mountain biking, swimming in the lake, and canoeing, Wintergreen also has a Nature Foundation that offers guided hikes, seminars, and camps for children.

The resort's focal point is the tastefully lodge-like Inn, which has a huge gristmill wheel occupying the two-story registration area. Most accommodations are in small enclaves scattered throughout the property, but there are also two- to seven-bedroom homes, one- to four-bedroom condos, and studios and lodge rooms. Since the homes and condos are privately owned, furnishings are highly individual, ranging from country quaint to sleek and sophisticated. Each condo is appointed with a modern kitchen, living area, bathroom for each bedroom, and balcony or patio (the mountain views are superb); most have working fireplaces.

Wintergreen has several full-service restaurants, so you won't go hungry. Recreational facilities include 17 ski slopes and trails, indoor and outdoor pools, health club, spa, massage, tennis courts, mountain bike rentals, 36 holes of golf, horseback riding, lake swimming and canoeing, fishing, children's center, hair salon, shops, and a grocery store.

3 Where to Dine

This area's most exceptional dining is at its country inns, especially Clifton, The Country Inn, and the Silver Thatch Inn (see "Nearby Country Inns," above).

Charlottesville has more than 200 restaurants—an enormous number for such a small city. For a complete rundown, pick up a copy of *Bites,* a free restaurant guide available at the Monticello Visitors Center (see "Visitor Information," above). There's also a list in *Cville Weekly* (www.cville.com), a free alternative newspaper available in boxes all over town.

In addition to some of those listed below, the Downtown Mall has several restaurants serving a variety of cuisines. In warm weather, some offer outdoor seating under the Mall's shade trees. Likewise, the Corner opposite the university has several restaurants catering to the college crowd (the best are on Elliewood Avenue, a block-long, alley-like street off University Avenue). Just stroll these neighborhoods and pick your place. You can tell by the crowds which are "in" and which aren't.

✪ **C&O Restaurant.** 515 E. Water St. (at 5th St. E.). ☎ **804/971-7044.** Reservations recommended (not accepted for smoking tables). Main courses $13–$20. MC, V. Mon–Thurs 11:30am–3pm and 5:30–10pm; Fri 11:30am–3pm and 5:30–11pm; Sat 5:30–11pm; Sun 5:30–10pm. INTERNATIONAL.

A block south of the Downtown Mall's east end, this unprepossessing brick front, complete with a faded Pepsi sign, might make you think twice, but don't be deterred, for the C&O provides the town's most unusual setting for highly acclaimed fare. Raved a *Food & Wine* reviewer: "I can assure you that not since Jefferson was serving imported vegetables and the first ice cream at Monticello has there been more innovative cooking in these parts." And from all appearances, the creaky floors in this charming old building were around in Jefferson's day. Changing monthly, the menu is basically country French but ranges across the globe—from Thailand to New Mexico and Louisiana—for additional inspiration. Many patrons stop downstairs, a rustic setting of exposed brick and rough-hewn barnwood, while others proceed upstairs to a more formal venue. Both dining areas have candlelight, white-clothed tables adorned with attractive flower arrangements, the same excellent menu choices, and premium wines by the glass.

Eastern Standard Restaurant and ESCAFE. 102 Old Preston Ave. (west end of the Downtown Mall). ☎ **804/295-8668.** Reservations accepted in restaurant. Main courses $16–$23 in restaurant, $7–$15 in cafe. AE, DC, DISC, MC, V. Restaurant, Thurs–Sat 5:30–10pm; cafe, Sun, Tues, Wed 5:30–10pm, Thurs–Sat 5pm–2am. AMERICAN/MEDITERRANEAN/ASIAN.

Sharing a kitchen, these sister restaurants offer a fusion of cuisines, all excellently prepared. Downstairs, the bistro-style ESCAFE is one of the town's most popular spots for an inexpensive yet fine meal (warm-weather seating is available on the Mall or out back). It features salads, sandwiches, and blue-plate specials like roasted eggplant rollatini and spicy Thai seafood. More expensive and more romantic, the upstairs Eastern Standard sports oak floors with antique carpets, potted birds of paradise, gold walls, and big arched windows overlooking the Mall. The upstairs fine-dining menu changes seasonally, but appetizers might include smoked trout with a beet salad, or perhaps warm California sushi rolls. There are usually 10 or so entree choices, such as lamb shank with orange, cinnamon, cumin, and ginger—an exciting combination of flavors. Desserts, made on the premises, include such delectables as Belgian chocolate truffles.

The Hardware Store. 316 E. Main St. (Downtown Mall). ☎ **804/977-1518.** Sandwiches and salads $4–$9; main courses $9–$13. AE, DC, MC, V. Mon 11am–5pm (to 9pm June–Oct); Tues–Thurs 11am–9pm; Fri–Sat 11am–10pm. AMERICAN.

Old rolling ladders; stacks of oak drawers that once held screws, nuts, and bolts; and vintage advertising signs—all display the old-time origins of this fun, high-energy spot popular with town and gown alike. A long, narrow space with an upstairs gallery, it provides comfortable seating in spacious leather-upholstered booths. Specialties include quiches and crepes, crab cakes, salads, an enormous variety of hamburgers, sandwiches, baked potatoes with great toppings, platters of fried fish, and barbecued ribs. There are soda-fountain treats, and pastries and cakes run the gamut from dense double-chocolate truffle cake to Southern pecan pie. There's a fully stocked bar.

✪ **Hamilton's.** 101 W. Main St. (at 1st St., midway along the Downtown Mall). ☎ **804/295-6649.** Reservations recommended. Lunch $7–$9; main courses $15–$24. AE, DC, MC, V. Mon–Sat 11:30am–3pm and 5:30–10pm. NEW AMERICAN/ASIAN.

Marble-top tables, crisp linen napkins, and fresh flowers let you know you're in for some high style at the urbane bistro in the heart of the Downtown Mall. It's the kind of place you'd take a special date, but not necessarily propose marriage. Like the C&O does with country French (see above), here American fare is enhanced with flavors from the Orient. The sesame-crusted crab cakes with pickled ginger vinaigrette will amply demonstrate what I mean. There also are some strictly Asian dishes, such as *nasi goreng*, the flavorful noodle dish from Indonesia. The daily vegetarian blue plate special actually is very tasty, too. In fine weather you can dine at wrought-iron umbrella tables out on the mall.

✪ **Northern Exposure.** 1202 W. Main St. (at 12th St.). ☎ **804/977-6002.** Reservations accepted only for groups. Lunch $5–$10; main courses $9–$18. AE, DC, DISC, MC, V. Sun 10am–10pm; Mon–Thurs 11am–10pm; Fri–Sat 11am–11pm. ITALIAN/ NEW AMERICAN.

You may have to wait for a table at this sophisticated bistro a block east of the Corner district, as it's Charlottesville's most popular dining spot. Patrons sit in one of four areas: a dining room decorated with old photos of New York City and a huge map of Gotham's subway system (guess where the owners are from); an enclosed patio; an open-air but heated patio; and a rooftop deck. Both lunch and dinner feature individual-size pizzas, either "red" with tomato sauce or "white" with olive oil, garlic, and cheese, with a choice of toppings both traditional and inventive. Likewise, you can order pasta with standard sauces like Alfredo or marinara, but the emphasis here is on creative concoctions like ginger sesame shrimp over linguine or Maine lobster ravioli with a cream sauce. The dinner menu offers main courses such as Cajun-style marinated steak with a pepper and Cognac cream sauce, Greek-style chicken, or a house special filet of salmon with sea salt, lemon juice, soy, and Dijon mustard. Big salads and burgers are available at all hours.

4 What to See & Do

Make your first stop the **Monticello Visitor Center** (see "Visitor Information," above). In addition to welcoming visitors and dispensing information, the center houses a marvelous permanent exhibit called "Thomas Jefferson at Monticello" and shows a free 30-minute video about Jefferson's life at 11am and 2pm daily.

THE TOP ATTRACTIONS

You'll need at least half a day to see **Monticello, Ash Lawn–Highland,** and **Michie Tavern,** all within 2 miles of each other on the southeastern outskirts of town, near the Monticello Visitor Center. You'll need a full day on spring and summer weekends and every day during the October "leaf season," when you can expect long lines waiting to go through Jefferson's Monticello home (plan to get there when it opens in the morning). Timed passes are given out when the wait exceeds 30 to 40 minutes; you can spend the time exploring Monticello's gardens and outbuildings on your own. Next head to nearby Michie Tavern, where you can spend 30 minutes touring the tavern and the Virginia Wine Museum, and then have a colonial-style lunch in the dining room (again, expect a wait on weekends and in October). In the afternoon head for Monroe's Ash Lawn–Highland, 2½ miles away, which will take about an hour to see.

If you have time left over, head for the University of Virginia. Otherwise, plan to tour the campus and see the town's other sights the next day.

The Monticello Visitor Center (see "Visitor Information," above) sells a **Presidents' Pass,** a discount block ticket combining admission to Monticello, Michie Tavern, and Ash Lawn–Highland. It costs $19 for adults but is not available for children.

✪ **Ash Lawn–Highland.** C.R. 795. ☎ **804/293-9539.** www.avenue.org/ashlawn. Admission $7 adults, $6.50 seniors, $4 children 6–11, free for children under 6. Mar–Oct, daily 9am–6pm; Nov–Feb, daily 10am–5pm. Mandatory 30-minute house tours depart every 10 to 15 minutes. From Va. 20, follow the directions to Monticello. Ash Lawn is 2½ miles past Monticello on James Monroe Pkwy. (C.R. 795).

Fifth president James Monroe fought in the Revolution, was wounded in Trenton, and went on to hold more public offices than any other president. Monroe's close friendship with Thomas Jefferson brought him to the Blue Ridge Mountains of Charlottesville, where Jefferson wished to create "a society to our taste." In 1793, Monroe purchased 1,000 acres adjacent to Monticello and built an estate he called "Highland" (the name *Ash Lawn* was added in 1838). Before he could settle in, however, Washington named him minister to France and sent him to Paris for 3 years. During his absence, Jefferson sent gardeners over to start orchards, and the Madisons made agricultural contributions as well. Nevertheless, by the time Monroe returned, he was suffering financial difficulties, and his "cabin castle" developed along more modest lines than originally intended. When he retired from office in 1825, his debts totaled $75,000, and he was forced to sell the beloved farm where he had hoped to spend his last days. A later owner, John Massey, built a two-story addition to the main house in 1884.

Today Monroe's 535-acre estate is owned and maintained as a working farm by his alma mater, the College of William and Mary. Livestock, vegetable and herb gardens, and colonial crafts demonstrations recall the elements of daily life on the Monroes' plantation. Horses, sheep, and cattle graze in the fields, while peacocks roam the boxwood gardens. Five of the original rooms remain, along with the basement kitchen, the overseer's cottage, restored slave quarters, and the old smokehouse. On a 30-minute house tour, you'll see some of the family's original furnishings and artifacts and learn a great deal about the fifth president. Allow another 30 minutes to explore the grounds and gift shop on your own.

Many special events take place at Ash Lawn–Highland: The outdoor **Summer Festival** features opera and contemporary music performances; a major colonial arts festival, **Plantation Days,** which takes place in July, showcases dozens of 18th-century crafts, historic reenactments, period music performances, and dressage.

✪ **Michie Tavern ca. 1784.** 683 Thomas Jefferson Pkwy. (Va. 683). ☎ **804/977-1234.** www.michietavern.com. Admission $6 adults, $5.50 seniors, $2 children 6–11, free for children under 6. Meals $11 adults, $5.50 children. Daily 9am–5pm (last tour 4:20pm). Restaurant daily 11:30am–3pm. Mandatory 30-minute tavern-museum tours depart as needed, Apr–Oct. Self-guided tours with recorded narratives, Nov–Mar. Closed New Year's Day and Christmas. From the visitor center, go south on Va. 20, turn left at Thomas Jefferson Pkwy. (Va. 683); Michie Tavern is about 1 mile on the right.

In 1746, Scotsman "Scotch John" Michie (pronounced "Mickey") purchased 1,152 acres of land from Patrick Henry's father, and in 1784, Michie's son, William, built this historic tavern on a well-traveled stagecoach route at Earlysville, 17 miles northwest of Charlottesville. A wealthy businesswoman, Josephine Henderson, saw its value as a historic structure and in 1927 had it moved to its present location and painstakingly reconstructed. Michie Tavern stands today as a tribute to early preservationists.

Included in the 30-minute tours are the **Virginia Wine Museum** and reproductions of the "dependencies"—log kitchen, dairy, smokehouse, ice house, root cellar, and "necessary" (note the not-so-soft corncobs). The general store has been re-created, along with an excellent crafts shop. Behind the store is a grist mill that has operated continuously since 1797.

Plan your visit to Michie Tavern to coincide with lunchtime, when an all-you-can-eat buffet of Southern fare is served to weary travelers for reasonable pence in the

Jefferson Survives

The phrase "Renaissance man" might have been coined to describe Thomas Jefferson. Perhaps our most important founding father, he was a lawyer, an architect, a scientist, a musician, a writer, an educator, and a horticulturist.

After writing the Declaration of Independence, Jefferson served as governor of Virginia, ambassador to France, secretary of state, and president for two terms, during which he nearly doubled the size of the United States by engineering the Louisiana Purchase from France. He also helped found of one of America's first political parties.

Yet despite all his national and international achievements, Jefferson ordered that his gravestone be inscribed: "Here Was Buried Thomas Jefferson/Author Of The Declaration Of American Independence/Of The Statute Of Virginia For Religious Freedom/And Father Of The University Of Virginia."

Jefferson was 83 when he died at Monticello on July 4, 1826, exactly 50 years to the day after his Declaration of Independence was signed at Philadelphia.

Ironically, as Jefferson died his fellow revolutionary—but later heated political enemy—John Adams lay on his own deathbed in Massachusetts. Unaware that Jefferson had expired a short time earlier, Adams's last words were: "Jefferson survives."

"Ordinary," a converted log cabin with original hand-hewn walls and beamed ceilings. Expect a short wait on summer weekends and during all of October.

✪ **Monticello.** Off Va. 53. ☎ **804/984-9822** for tickets, 804/984-9844 on weekends, or 804/984-9800 daily for recorded information. www.monticello.org. Admission $11 adults, $6 children 6–11, free for children under 6. Mar–Oct, daily 8am–5pm; Nov–Feb, daily 9am–4:30pm. Mandatory 25-minute house tours run continuously. From the visitor center go south on Va. 20, turn left on Va. 53, then proceed 2 miles to entrance.

Pronounced "Mon-ti-*chel*-lo," the home Thomas Jefferson built over 40 years from 1769 to 1809 is a highlight of any visit to Virginia. This architectural masterpiece was the first Virginia plantation manse to sit atop a mountain rather than beside a river. Because it was British, Jefferson rejected the Georgian architecture that characterized his time, opting instead for the 16th-century Italian style of Andrea Palladio. Later, during his 5-year term as minister to France, he was influenced by the homes of nobles at the court of Louis XVI, and after returning home in 1789, he enlarged Monticello, incorporating features of the Parisian buildings he so admired.

Today the house has been restored as closely as possible to its appearance during Jefferson's retirement years. Nearly all its furniture and other household objects were owned by Jefferson or his family. The garden has been extended to its original 1,000-foot length, and Mulberry Row—where slaves and free artisans lived and labored in light industrial shops such as a joinery, smokehouse-dairy, blacksmith shop–nailery, and carpenter's shop—has been excavated. Guided tours of the gardens and Mulberry Row are available from April through October.

Jefferson's grave is in the family burial ground, which is still in use. After visiting the graveyard, you can take a shuttle bus back to the visitor parking lot or walk through the woods via a delightful path. There is a lovely wooded picnic area with tables and grills on the premises, and, in summer, lunch fare can be purchased.

As noted above, traffic is heaviest here on spring and summer weekends and during all of October, when you can wait up to 3 hours to tour the house. Accordingly, get here as soon as possible after opening time in the morning, and immediately go get in line at the house. Attendants at the ticket office, about halfway up the mountain (vans shuttle from there to the mansion), will tell you how long the wait will be. Once it gets to 30 to 40 minutes, timed tickets are given to those already in line (they are not issued at the ticket office). You can kill the wait exploring the gardens and outbuildings.

✿ THE UNIVERSITY OF VIRGINIA

One of the world's most beautiful college campuses, Jefferson's **University Of Virginia** is graced with spacious lawns, serpentine-walled gardens, colonnaded pavilions, and a classical rotunda inspired by the Pantheon in Rome. Jefferson regarded its creation as one of his three greatest achievements—all the more remarkable since it was begun in his 73rd year. He was in every sense the university's father, since he conceived it, wrote its charter, raised money for its construction, drew the plans, selected the site, laid the cornerstone in 1817, supervised construction, served as the first rector, selected the faculty, and created the curriculum. His good friends Monroe and Madison sat with him on the first board, and Madison succeeded him as rector, serving for 8 years.

The focal point of the university is the **Rotunda** (on University Avenue at Rugby Road), today restored as Jefferson designed it. Some 600 feet of tree-dotted lawn extend from the south portico of the Rotunda to what is now Cabell Hall, designed at the turn of the 20th century by Stanford White. On either side of the lawn are pavilions still used for faculty housing, each of a different architectural style "to serve as specimens for the Architectural lecturer." Behind are large gardens (originally used by faculty members to grow vegetables and keep livestock) and the original student dormitories, used—and greatly coveted—by students today; though centrally heated, they still contain working fireplaces. The room Edgar Allan Poe occupied when he was a student here is furnished as it would have been in 1826 and is open to visitors.

Paralleling the lawn are more rows of student rooms called the Ranges. Equally spaced within each of the Ranges are "hotels," originally used to accommodate student dining. Each hotel represented a different country, and students dining in them would have to both eat the food and speak the language of that country. Although a wonderful idea on Jefferson's part, it lasted only a short while since everyone wanted to eat French but not German.

Students lead 45-minute **campus tours** daily at 10 and 11am and 2, 3, and 4pm, usually from the Rotunda. Self-guided walking tour brochures are available from the university's **Visitor Information Center** (☎ **804/924-7166**), which is located not on campus but in the University Police Headquarters, on Ivy Road (U.S. 250 Business) just east of the U.S. 29/U.S. 250 bypass. The visitor center is open 24 hours a day. See "Getting Around," above, for parking information.

Note: The university is closed 3 weeks around Christmas.

MORE ATTRACTIONS IN TOWN

The center of Charlottesville's historic district is the **Downtown Mall,** a pedestrian-only section of Main Street between 2nd and 6th streets (☎ **804/296-8548** for mall events). It's handy for visitors because it's lined by a host of restaurants and boutiques, and there's parking (see "Getting Around," above). It's all enhanced by fountains, park benches under shade trees, outdoor cafes, and buskers making music both day and night. On the west end, you'll find a six-screen movie theater, the Charlottesville Omni Hotel (see "Where to Stay," above), and the Charlottesville Ice Park, which offers an irregular schedule of ice-skating and pickup hockey games.

Albemarle County Court House. 501 E. Jefferson St. (at 5th St. E.). ☎ **804/296-5822.** Free admission. Mon–Fri 9am–5pm.

The center of village activity in colonial days, the Court House in the historic down-town area features a facade and portico dating from the Civil War. There's no tour offered, but you can take a glance at Jefferson's will in the County Office Building. It's easy to imagine Jefferson, Madison, and Monroe talking politics under the lawn's huge shade trees.

McGuffey Art Center. 201 2nd St. NW (at 2nd St. W.). ☎ **804/295-7973.** Free admission. Tues–Sat 10am–5pm; Sun 1–5pm.

At the center, in an early–20th century school building a block north of the Mall, local artists and craftspeople hold studio exhibits and sell their creations. The **Second Street Gallery,** showing contemporary art from all over the United States, is also located here.

Virginia Discovery Museum. 524 Main St. (at 6th St., east end of Downtown Mall). ☎ **804/977-1025.** www.vadm.org. Admission $4 adults, $3 seniors and children 1–13. Tues–Sat 10am–5pm; Sun 1–5pm.

The Virginia Discovery Museum is a place of enchantment, offering numerous hands-on exhibits and programs for young people. Here kids can dress up as firefighters, sol-diers, police, and other grownups. The Colonial Log House, an authentic structure that once stood on a site in New Bedford, Virginia, is outfitted with the simple fur-nishings appropriate to an early–19th century lifestyle. A series of fascinating exhibits appeals to the senses, and the Fun and Games exhibit offers a wonderful array of games, including bowling and giant checkers. An arts and crafts studio, an active bee-hive, and a changing series of traveling and made-on-site exhibits round out the fun.

MONTPELIER & OTHER NEARBY ATTRACTIONS

✪ **Montpelier.** 11407 Constitution Hwy. (Va. 20), Montpelier Station. ☎ **540/ 672-2728.** www.montpelier.org. Admission $7.50 adults, $6.50 seniors, $2.50 children 6–11, free for children under 6. Apr–Nov, daily 9:30am–5:30pm (last tour 4pm); Dec–Mar, daily 9:30am–4:30pm (last tour 3pm). Closed New Year's Day, first Sat in Nov (Race Day), Thanksgiving, Christmas Eve, Christmas, New Year's Eve. Montpelier is 25 miles northeast of Charlottesville. Take U.S. 29 north to U.S. 33 east at Ruckersville. At Barboursville, turn left onto Va. 20 north.

This 2,700-acre estate facing the Blue Ridge Mountains was home to President James Madison and his wife, Dolley. Madison was just 26 when he ensured that the 1776 Constitutional Convention in Williamsburg would include religious freedom in the Virginia Declaration of Rights, and his efforts at the federal Constitutional Conven-tion in 1787 earned him the title "Father of the Constitution." Madison became sec-retary of state under his good friend Thomas Jefferson in 1801, and succeeded Jefferson as president in 1809. He and Dolley fled the White House in the face of advancing British troops during the War of 1812. The sharp-tongued Dolley was famous in her own right, serving as White House hostess during bachelor Jefferson's two terms and First Lady during her husband's two.

Madison inherited Montpelier, which was then a modest two-story red-brick Geor-gian residence, from his father, who built it around 1760. With architectural advice from Jefferson, James Madison expanded its proportions. James and Dolley are buried here in the Madison family cemetery. Two structures remain from their time: the main house and the "Ice House Temple" (built over a well and used to store ice).

William du Pont, Sr., bought the estate in 1900. He enlarged the mansion and added barns, staff houses, a sawmill, a blacksmith shop, a train station, a dairy, and greenhouses, and his wife created a 2½-acre formal garden. Daughter Marion du Pont Scott later built a steeplechase course and initiated the **Montpelier Hunt Races,** which are still held here on the first Saturday in November. The National Trust for

Historic Preservation acquired the property following her death in 1984, and architectural historians have been carefully studying the house since then.

The house has changed significantly since the Madisons' time, and their personal possessions have been widely dispersed, so don't expect the usual historical mansion tour here. You'll start with a 14-minute video, which introduces James and Dolley Madison. A 45-minute audio cassette tape will then lead you through the "Discovering Madison" exhibit on the first floor of the mansion, and among key points on the grounds outside. Staffers are on hand in the house to answer questions.

Call ahead for a schedule of special events, such as the races in November, birthday celebrations for James (March 16) and Dolley (May 20), and the Montpelier Wine Festival in May.

Walton's Mountain Museum. Schuyler. ☎ **804/831-2000.** Admission $5 adults, $4 seniors, free for children under 12. Mar–Nov, daily 10am–4pm. Closed Easter, second Sat in Oct, and Thanksgiving. From I-64 take U.S. 29 south 18 miles. Turn left on Va. 6, go east 6 miles to C.R. 800, turn right on C.R. 800, and go south 2 miles to Schuyler and follow signs.

There is no real "Walton's Mountain," but Hollywood screenwriter Earl Hamner, Jr., based characters of the popular TV series *The Waltons* on real folks he knew growing up during the Depression in the picturesque hamlet of Schuyler (pronounced *Sky*-lar). Hamner worked closely with hometown residents to create this charming museum in the old elementary school across the street from his boyhood home. Photos of the real characters are displayed beside those of the actors who played them on television, and fans of the warmhearted series will get a kick out of seeing the set of John-Boy's bedroom. All profits are given back to the community, funding such things as a computer learning center in the old school.

While here, you can get a home-cooked meal or refreshment at **Schuyler Family Restaurant,** in what used to be a Victorian hotel next door to the museum (☎ **804/831-3333**).

ON THE WINE TRAIL

There have been vineyards in the Piedmont since the 18th century, and Jefferson hoped to someday produce quality wines in Virginia. His dream has come true, and today Charlottesville is in the middle of one of Virginia's prime winemaking regions. Many area wineries offer tours and tastings. **Jefferson Vineyards** (☎ **804/977-3042**) is on Va. 53 between Monticello and Ash Lawn–Highlands (consider stopping for a taste after your long day's sightseeing). **Oakencroft Vineyard** (☎ **804/296-4188;** www.oakencroft.com) is off Barracks Road, 3½ miles northwest of U.S. 29. If you're going to Montpelier, the award-winning **Barboursville Vineyards** (☎ **540/832-3824**) is on C.R. 177 near the intersection of Va. 20 and Va. 33. On U.S. 29 about 8 miles south of Culpepper, **Prince Michel & Rapidan River Vineyards** (☎ **800/869-8242** or 540/547-9720) is one of Virginia's largest; it has a wine museum, a fine-dining restaurant, and expensive bed-and-breakfast suites. Call the vineyards for business hours and admission prices, or check out the Virginia Wine Country Web site at www.vawine.com.

ATTRACTIONS IN THE LYNCHBURG AREA

When Jefferson wanted to get away from it all, he headed south to Poplar Forest, his beloved country retreat near the James River town of Lynchburg. Today Lynchburg is a base from which to explore not just Poplar Forest but Patrick Henry's plantation home and the tiny village of Appomattox Court House, where Robert E. Lee surrendered to Ulysses S. Grant.

✪ **Thomas Jefferson's Poplar Forest.** Va. 661, Forest. ☎ **804/525-1806.** www. poplarforest.org. Admission $7 adults, $6 seniors, $1 children 6–16, free for children under 6; grounds only, $3 per person. Apr–Nov, daily 10am–4pm (last tour begins at 4pm). Closed Thanksgiving and Dec–Mar. Mandatory 45-minute house tours depart on the hour and half hour. Entrance is about 6 miles southwest of Lynchburg. Take U.S. 221 south, go straight on Va. 811, turn left on Va. 661.

In 1806, while he was president, Thomas Jefferson himself assisted the masons in laying the foundation for this dwelling on what was then a 4,819-acre plantation and the source of much of his income. He designed the octagonal house to utilize light and air flow to the maximum in as economical a space as possible. It became his favorite place to escape from the parade of visitors at Monticello. Today his final architectural masterpiece is once again a work in progress, for it is being slowly and meticulously restored to the way it looked in the early 19th century. There is no furniture inside the house, only architectural historians going about their work. Outside, archaeologists dig about the grounds, trying to discover exactly how Jefferson landscaped the gardens. You can see relics from the buildings and grounds as they are brought to light and exhibited.

✪ **Appomattox Court House National Historical Park.** Va. 24, 2 miles north of Appomattox. ☎ **804/352-8987.** www.nps.gov/apco. Admission Memorial Day–Labor Day, $4 adults, free for children under 17 (maximum $10 per vehicle); rest of year, $2 adults, free for children under 17 (maximum $5 per vehicle). Memorial Day–Labor Day, daily 9am–5:30pm; rest of year, 8:30am–5pm. Take U.S. 460 east. The park is about 22 miles east of Lynchburg.

Here, in the parlor of Wilmer McLean's home, Robert E. Lee surrendered the Army of Northern Virginia to Ulysses S. Grant on April 9, 1865, thus ending the bitter Civil War. Today the 20 or so houses, stores, courthouse, and tavern that made up the little village called Appomattox Court House have been restored, and visitors can walk the country lanes in the rural stillness where these events took place.

At the visitor center, pick up a map of the park and a self-guided tour booklet. Upstairs, slide presentations and museum exhibits include fascinating excerpts from the diaries and letters of Civil War soldiers. Allow at least 2 hours to do that and visit McLean's house, Clover Hill Tavern, Meeks' Store, the Woodson Law Office, the courthouse (totally reconstructed), jail, and Kelly House. Surrender Triangle, where the Confederates laid down their arms and rolled up their battle flags, is outside Kelly House.

There's a full schedule of ranger programs during the summer months. For a schedule or more information, contact Superintendent, Appomattox Court House National Historical Park, P.O. Box 218, Appomattox, VA 24522 (☎ **804/352-8987;** www.nps.gov/apco).

Booker T. Washington National Monument. 12130 Booker T. Washington Hwy. (Va. 122), Hardy. ☎ **540/721-2094.** www.nps.gov/bowa. Free admission. Daily 9am–5pm. From Lynchburg, take U.S. 460 west to Va. 122 south.

At this memorial to one of America's great African-American leaders, visitors can conjure up the setting of Booker T. Washington's childhood in reconstructed farm buildings and demonstrations of farm life and slavery in Civil War–era Virginia. Although Washington called his boyhood home a plantation, the Burroughs farm was small, with just 207 acres and never more than 11 slaves. His mother was the cook, and the cabin where he was born was also the kitchen. His family left the farm in 1865, when he was 9. He determinedly sought an education and actually walked most of the 500 miles from his new home in West Virginia to Hampton Institute. He worked his way through school and achieved national prominence as an educator, founder of Tuskegee Institute in Alabama, author, and advisor to presidents. In 1956, a century after he was born, this national monument was established to honor his life and work.

Begin at the visitor center, which offers a slide show and a map with a self-guided plantation tour and nature walks that wind through the original Burroughs property.

For more information, write Booker T. Washington National Monument, 12130 Booker T. Washington Hwy., Hardy, VA 24101 (www.nps.gov/bowa).

Red Hill, Patrick Henry National Memorial. Brookneal. ☎ **804/376-2044.** www. redhill.org. Admission $3 adults, $2 seniors over 65, $1 students. Apr–Oct, daily 9am–5pm; Nov–Mar, daily 9am–4pm. Closed New Year's Day, Thanksgiving, and Christmas. Red Hill is 35 miles from Lynchburg. Take U.S. 501 south to Brookneal, then Va. 40 east and follow the brown signs.

Fiery orator Patrick Henry ("Give me liberty or give me death") retired to Red Hill plantation in 1794 after serving five terms as governor of Virginia. Failing health forced him to refuse numerous posts, including chief justice of the United States, secretary of state, and minister to Spain and France. He died at Red Hill on June 6, 1799, and is buried in the family graveyard.

Begin your tour at the visitor center, where you can see an enlightening 15-minute video about Henry's years here and visit the museum with the world's largest assemblage of Henry memorabilia. The centerpiece is Peter Rothermel's famous painting *Patrick Henry before the Virginia House of Burgesses,* depicting his "If this be treason, make the most of it" speech against the Stamp Act in 1765. The site contains his actual law office, an accurate reproduction of the main house, the carriage house, and other small buildings. You can't miss the most striking feature of the landscape: Standing 64 feet high and spanning 96 feet, the Osage Orange Tree is listed in the American Forestry Hall of Fame.

5 Golfing & Canoeing

If you can afford it, the best golfing here is at the Arnold Palmer–designed links at the private Keswick Club, which guests of Keswick Hall at Monticello can pay to play (see "Where to Stay," above). The University of Virginia's 18-hole **Birdwood Golf Course** (☎ **804/293-GOLF**), at the Boar's Head Inn (see "Where to Stay," above), is one of the top 10 collegiate courses in the country. You can play a round there for $42 on weekends, $32 weekdays. The 18-hole **Meadow Creek,** at Pen Park (☎ **804/ 977-0615**) costs a mere $23 on weekends, $12 weekdays. Call the courses to reserve tee times and get directions.

You can go canoeing on the James River at Scottsville, a quaint, 19th-century town 20 miles south of Charlottesville via Va. 20. The river can run swiftly here—class I or II if it has rained recently; tubing conditions if it hasn't. Contact **James River Runners** in Scottsville (☎ **804/286-2338;** www.jamesriver.com) for canoe and inner tube rentals.

For hiking and other outdoor activities, remember you're less than an hour's drive from Shenandoah National Park (see chapter 7).

6 Charlottesville After Dark

The University of Virginia has a constant and ever-changing parade of concerts, plays, lectures, exhibits, and other events. For a complete schedule, pick up copies of the slick monthly magazine *Charlottesville Arts & Entertainment* and the free newspaper *Cville Weekly* (www.cville.com) at the Monticello Visitors Center (see "Visitor Information," above).

Like most college towns, Charlottesville sees numerous bands performing at its student-oriented bars, especially on weekends. On the Downtown Mall, there's nighttime jazz or blues at **Miller's,** 109 W. Main St. (☎ **804/971-8511**).

The Shenandoah Valley 7

Extending north-south some 150 miles from Winchester to Natural Bridge, the famous Shenandoah Valley is one of the most beautiful areas of the eastern United States. The Blue Ridge Mountains flank it to the east; to the west rise the even taller Shenandoah and Allegheny ranges. Down on the rolling valley floor lay picturesque small towns steeped in American history dating to the early 1700s, when pioneers moved west from the Tidewater. Scottish-Irish and German emigrants later arrived from the north and built their farmhouses of stone, which makes the valley seem as much Pennsylvania as Virginia.

Most visitors come here to see the views from the Shenandoah National Park atop the Blue Ridge Mountains. The park offers spectacular landscapes and a plethora of hiking and riding trails, including a portion of the Maine-to-Georgia Appalachian Trail. The **Skyline Drive**—one of America's great scenic routes—runs the full length of the park and connects directly with the **Blue Ridge Parkway,** which continues south into North Carolina.

Down in the valley, outdoor enthusiasts can ride horses and go tubing, canoeing, or rafting.

In addition to its scenic grandeur and plethora of outdoor pursuits, history is a major reason to come here. Lord Fairfax sent George Washington west to survey the valley, and reminders of his visits are visible at Natural Bridge, where he carved his initials, and in Winchester, which has preserved the office he occupied during the French and Indian War.

During the Civil War, the Shenandoah's rich farmland served as the breadbasket for Robert E. Lee's Army of Northern Virginia, and Union armies staged several assaults to cut off Lee's supplies. Stonewall Jackson left Lexington's Virginia Military Institute to become one of the Confederacy's major generals. The entire VMI Corps of Cadets fought heroically in the legendary Battle of New Market. After the war, Lee settled in Lexington as president of what is now Washington and Lee University, and both he and Jackson are buried there.

Woodrow Wilson was born in Staunton in 1856, and a museum adjoining his restored birthplace pays tribute to this president's peace-loving ideals.

EXPLORING THE VALLEY

VISITOR INFORMATION   For information about attractions, accommodations, restaurants, and services in the entire region, contact the **Shenandoah Valley Travel Association (SVTA),** P.O. Box 1040, New Market, VA 22844 (☎ **877/847-4878** or 540/740-3132; fax 540/740-3100; www.shenandoah.org). The SVTA operates a visitor center in New Market, just off I-81 at U.S. 211 (Exit 264). The center, open daily from 9am to 5pm, has a free phone line for hotel reservations.

GETTING THERE & GETTING AROUND   The gorgeous scenery of the Shenandoah is best seen by **car,** since public transportation in the valley is almost nonexistent. At least part of your trip should include the spectacular Skyline Drive (see section 1, below). The fast way to and through the region is via I-81, which runs the entire length of the valley floor and has been designated one of America's 10 most scenic interstates. Running alongside I-81, the legendary Valley Pike (U.S. 11) is like a trip back in time at least 50 years, with its old-fashioned gas pumps, small motels, shops, and restaurants. Likewise, the old U.S. 340 follows the scenic western foothills of the Blue Ridge.

I-66 enters the valley from Washington, D.C., before ending at Strasburg. I-64 comes into the valley's southern end from both east and west, running contiguous with I-81 between Staunton and Lexington. Other major east-west highways crossing the valley are U.S. 50, 211, 33, 250, and 60.

Valley roads are open year-round, but snow and ice can close the Skyline Drive in midwinter.

The nearest major airport is Washington Dulles International, 50 miles east of Front Royal (see "Getting There & Getting Around" in chapter 2). **US Airways Express** (☎ **800/428-4322**) has commuter flights to and from **Shenandoah Valley Regional Airport** (☎ **540/234-8304**), off I-81 between Harrisonburg and Staunton. There also are airports in Charlottesville (see chapter 6) and Roanoke (see chapter 8).

Amtrak (☎ **800/872-7245;** www.amtrak) offers direct service to Staunton.

1 Shenandoah National Park & the Skyline Drive

Running for 105 miles down the spine of the Blue Ridge Mountains, Shenandoah National Park is a haven for plants and wildlife. Although long and skinny, the park encompasses some 300 square miles of mountains, forests, waterfalls, and rock formations. It has more than 60 mountain peaks higher than 2,000 feet, with Hawksbill and Stony Man exceeding 4,000 feet. Although high ozone levels frequently create obscuring smog during summer, on many spring and fall days you will have panoramic views from overlooks along the Skyline Drive over the Piedmont to the east and the Shenandoah Valley to the west. The drive gives you access to the park's visitor facilities and to more than 500 miles of glorious hiking and horse trails, including the Appalachian Trail.

Europeans began settling these slopes and hollows in the early 18th century. Plans for establishment of a national park got under way 200 years later, and it was President Franklin D. Roosevelt's Depression-era Civilian Conservation Corps that built the recreational facilities, guard walls, cabins, and many hiking trails. The corps completed the Skyline Drive in 1939, thus opening this marvelously beautiful area to casual visitors.

Today, over two-fifths of the park is considered wilderness. Animals like deer, bear, bobcat, and turkey have returned, and sightings of deer and smaller animals are frequent; the park also boasts more than 100 species of trees.

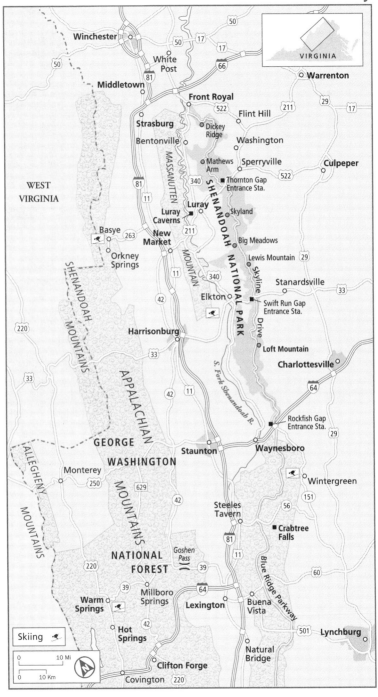

VIRGINIA

Winchester
White Post
Middletown
Warrenton
Strasburg
Front Royal
Flint Hill
Dickey Ridge
Bentonville
Washington
WEST VIRGINIA
Mathews Arm
Sperryville
Culpeper
Thornton Gap Entrance Sta.
MASSANUTTEN
Luray
Skyland
Basye
Luray Caverns
New Market
Orkney Springs
Big Meadows
Lewis Mountain
Stanardsville
SHENANDOAH MOUNTAINS
MOUNTAIN
Elkton
Skyline Drive
Swift Run Gap Entrance Sta.
Harrisonburg
SHENANDOAH NATIONAL PARK
Loft Mountain
Charlottesville
APPALACHIAN
S. Fork Shenandoah R.
Rockfish Gap Entrance Sta.
GEORGE
WASHINGTON
Staunton
Waynesboro
Monterey
ALLEGHENY MOUNTAINS
MOUNTAINS
Wintergreen
Steeles Tavern
NATIONAL
FOREST
Goshen Pass
Crabtree Falls
Blue Ridge Parkway
Warm Springs
Millboro Springs
Lexington
Buena Vista
Hot Springs
Natural Bridge
Lynchburg
Clifton Forge
Covington

Skiing

0   10 Mi
0   10 Km

ESSENTIALS

ACCESS POINTS & ORIENTATION   The park and its Skyline Drive have four entrances. Northernmost is at **Front Royal** on U.S. 340 near the junction of I-81 and I-66, about 1 mile south of Front Royal and 90 miles west of Washington, D.C. The two middle entrances are at **Thornton Gap,** 33 miles south of Front Royal on U.S. 211 between Sperryville and Luray, and at **Swift Run Gap,** 68 miles south of Front Royal on U.S. 33 between Standardsville and Elkton. The southern gate is at **Rockfish Gap,** 105 miles south of Front Royal at I-64 and U.S. 250, some 21 miles west of Charlottesville and 18 miles east of Staunton.

The Skyline Drive is marked with **Mile Posts,** starting at zero at the Front Royal entrance and increasing as you go south, with Rockfish Gap on the southern end at Mile 105.

DISTRICTS   The access roads divide the park into three areas: Northern District, between Front Royal and U.S. 211 at Thornton Gap (Mile 0 to Mile 31.5); Central District, between Thornton Gap and U.S. 33 at Swift Run Gap (Mile 31.5 to Mile 65.7); and Southern District, between Swift Run Gap and I-64 at Rockfish Gap (Mile 65.7 to Mile 105).

INFORMATION   For free information, call or write Superintendent, Shenandoah National Park, 3655 U.S. Hwy. 211 E., Luray, VA 22835 (☎ **540/999-3500;** www.nps.gov/shen). The headquarters is 4 miles west of Thornton Gap and 5 miles east of Luray on U.S. 211.

The best source from which to purchase information is the **Shenandoah Natural History Association,** at the park headquarters (☎ **540/999-3582**). The association has a bookstore at the park headquarters, where it sells maps, guidebooks, and other publications about the park's cultural and natural history (they are also available at the park's visitor centers, see below). The association regularly updates the enormously informative *Guide to Shenandoah National Park and Skyline Drive* by the late Henry Heatwole. The book is an indispensable aid for anyone who wants to thoroughly explore Shenandoah, as it gives a mile-by-mile description of the park, including most hiking trails.

For more books, contact the **National Park Bookstore,** 470 Maryland Dr., Suite 2, Ft. Washington, PA 19034-9684 (☎ **877/NAT-PARK;** fax 215/591-0303; www.nationalparkbooks.org).

For guide books and detailed topographic maps of the park's three districts, write or call the **Potomac Appalachian Trail Club (PATC),** 118 Park St., Vienna, VA 22180 (☎ **703/242-0315,** or 703/242-0965 for a recording of the club's activities; www.patc.net). The PATC helps build and maintain the park's portion of the Appalachian Trail, including trail cabins (see "Hiking & Other Sports," below). The PATC is part of the **Appalachian Trail Conference,** P.O. Box 807, Harpers Ferry, WV 25425-0807 (☎ **304/535-6331;** www.atconf.org), which covers the entire trail from Maine to Georgia.

EMERGENCIES   In case of emergencies, call the park headquarters (☎ **540/999-3500**).

FEES, REGULATIONS & BACKCOUNTRY PERMITS   Entrance permits good for 7 consecutive days are $10 per car, $5 for each pedestrian or bicyclist. A Shenandoah Passport ($20) is good for 1 year, as is the National Park Service's Golden Eagle Passport ($50). Park entrance is free to holders of Golden Access (for disabled U.S. citizens) and Golden Age (U.S. citizens 62 or older) passports. The former is free; the latter is available at the entrance gates for $10.

The **speed limit** on the Skyline Drive is 35 m.p.h., although given the number of camper vans and rubberneckers creeping along this two-lane road, you'll be lucky to go that fast.

Plants and animals are protected, so all hunting is prohibited. Pets must be kept on a leash at all times and are not allowed on some trails. Wood fires are permitted only in fireplaces in developed areas. The Skyline Drive is a great bike route, but neither bicycles nor motor vehicles of any sort are allowed on the trails.

Most of the park is open to backcountry camping. Permits, which are free, are required; get them at the entrance gates, at visitor centers, or by mail from park headquarters (see "Information," above). Campers are required to leave no trace of their presence. No permits are necessary for backcountry hiking, but the same "no-trace" rule applies.

VISITOR CENTERS   There are two park visitor centers. The **Dickey Ridge Visitor Center,** at Mile 4.6, is usually open daily from April through November and on an intermittent schedule in December. **Byrd Visitor Center,** at Mile 51 in Big Meadows, is open daily from early April through October and on an intermittent schedule through December. Both provide information, maps of nearby hiking trails, interpretive exhibits, films, slide shows, and nature walks. There is a small information center at **Loft Mountain** (Mile 79.5). In addition, the privately run **Rockfish Gap Information Center,** on U.S. 211 outside the park's southern gate, has information about the park and the surrounding area.

SEASONS   The park is most popular from mid- to late October, when the gorgeous fall foliage peaks and weekend traffic on the Skyline Drive becomes bumper-to-bumper. Days also tend to be clearer in fall than in summer, when lingering haze can obscure the views. In spring, the green of leafing trees moves up the ridge at the rate of about 100 feet a day. Wildflowers begin to bloom in April, and by late May the azaleas are brilliant and the dogwood is putting on a show. Nesting birds abound, and the normally modest waterfalls are at their highest during spring, when warm rains melt the highland snows. You'll find the clearest views across the distant mountains during winter, but many facilities are closed then, and snow and ice can shut down the Skyline Drive.

AVOIDING THE CROWDS   With its proximity to the sprawling Washington, D.C., metropolitan area, the park is at its busiest on summer and fall weekends and holidays. The fall foliage season in October is the busiest time, however, and reservations for October accommodations in or near the park should be made as much as a year in advance. The best time to visit, therefore, is during the spring and on weekdays from June through October. When the Central District around Big Meadows and Skyland is packed, there may be more space available in the Northern and Southern districts.

RANGER PROGRAMS   The park offers a wide variety of ranger-led activities—nature walks, interpretive programs, cultural and history lectures, campfire talks. Most are held at or near Dickey Ridge Visitor Center in the north; Byrd Visitor Center and the Big Meadows and Skyland lodges and campground in the center; and Loft Mountain campground in the south. Schedules are published seasonally in the Shenandoah Overlook, available at the entrance gates, at visitor centers, and from park headquarters.

SEEING THE HIGHLIGHTS
The most interesting and beautiful section of the park is its **Central District,** between Mile 31.5 and Mile 65.7 (that is, between U.S. 211 at Thornton Gap and U.S. 33 at

Swift Run Gap). It has the highest mountains, best views, nearly half of the park's 500 miles of hiking trails, and its only stables and overnight accommodations. You can see the views in a day, but plan to spend at least 2 nights here if you're doing extensive hiking, riding, or fishing. The lodges at Big Meadows or Skyland are the best bases of operations, but place your reservations as early as possible (see "Where to Stay," below). If you can't get a room at Big Meadows or Skyland, Luray is the nearest town with accommodations (see section 5, below).

Unless you're caught in heavy traffic on fall foliage weekends, you can drive the entire length of the **Skyline Drive** in about 3 hours without stopping. But why rush? Give yourself at least a day for this drive, so lovely are the views from its 75 designated scenic overlooks. Stop for lunch at a wayside snack bar, a lodge, or one of seven official picnic grounds (for that matter, any of the overlooks will do for an impromptu picnic). Better yet, get out of your car and take at least a short hike down one of the hollows to a waterfall.

SCENIC OVERLOOKS   Among the more interesting of the 75 designated overlooks along the drive are the **Shenandoah Valley Overlook** (Mile 2.8), with views west to the Signal Knob of Massanutten Mountain across the south fork of the river; **Range View Overlook** (Mile 17.1; elevation 2,800 feet), providing fine views of the central section of the park, looking south; **Stony Man Overlook** (Mile 38.6), offering panoramas of Stony Man Cliffs, the valley, and the Alleghenies; **Thoroughfare Mountain Overlook** (Mile 40.5; elevation 3,595 feet), one of the highest overlooks, with views from Hogback Mountain south to cone-shaped Robertson Mountain and the rocky face of Old Rag Mountain; **Old Rag View Overlook** (Mile 46.5), dominated by Old Rag, sitting all by itself in an eastern extremity of the park; **Franklin Cliffs Overlook** (Mile 49), offering a view of the cliffs and the Shenandoah Valley and Massanutten Mountain beyond; and **Big Run Overlook** (Mile 81.2), which looks down on rocky peaks and the largest watershed in the park.

WATERFALLS   Only one waterfall is visible from the Skyline Drive, at Mile 1.4, and it's dry part of the year. On the other hand, 15 other falls are accessible via hiking trails (see "Hiking," below).

HIKING & OTHER SPORTS

HIKING   The number one outdoor activity here is hiking. The park's 112 hiking trails total more than 500 miles, varying in length from short walks to a 101-mile segment of the Appalachian Trail running the entire length of the park. Access to the trails is marked along the Skyline Drive. There are parking lots at the major trailheads, but they fill quickly on weekends.

I strongly recommend that you get maps and trail descriptions before setting out—even before leaving home, if possible. Free maps of many trails are available at the visitor centers, which also sell the topographic maps, published by the Potomac Appalachian Trail Conference, as well as a one-sheet map of all the park's walks published by Trails Illustrated ($8). Also, the Shenandoah Natural History Association's *Guide to Shenandoah National Park and Skyline Drive* provides detailed descriptions of all the major hikes. (See "Information," above, for addresses and phone numbers.)

At the minimum, take one of the short hikes on nature trails at Dickey Ridge Visitor Center (Mile 4.6), Byrd Visitor Center/Big Meadows (Mile 51), and Loft Mountain (Mile 79.5). There's also an excellent 1.6-mile nature hike at Stony Man (Mile 41.7).

Here are a few of the best trails:

- **Limberlost Accessible Trail:** At Mile 43 south of Skyland, this 1.3-mile loop runs through an old-growth forest of ancient hemlocks. The trail has a 5-foot-wide, hard-packed surface; crosses a 65-foot bridge; and includes a 150-foot boardwalk. It's accessible to visitors in wheelchairs.
- ✪ **White Oak Canyon:** Beginning at Mile 42.6 just south of Skyland, this steep gorge is the park's scenic gem. The 7.3-mile trail goes through an area of wild beauty, passing no less than six waterfalls and cascades. The upper reaches to the first falls are relatively easy, but further down the track can be rough and rocky. Total climb is about 2,160 feet, so allow 6 hours.
- **Cedar Run Falls:** Several trails begin at Hawksbill Gap (Mile 45.6). A short but steep trail leads 1.7 miles round-trip to the summit of Hawksbill Mountain, the park's highest at 4,050 feet. Another is a moderately difficult 3½-mile round-trip hike down to Cedar Falls and back. You can also connect from Cedar Run to White Oak Canyon, a 7.3-mile loop that will take all day.
- **Dark Hollow Falls:** One of the park's most popular hikes is the 1.4-mile walk to Dark Hollow Falls, the closest cascade to the Skyline Drive. The trail begins at Mile 50.7 near the Byrd Visitor Center. Allow 1¼ hours for the round-trip.
- ✪ **Camp Hoover/Mill Prong:** Starting at the Milam Gap parking area (Mile 52.8), this 4-mile round-trip hike drops down the Mill Prong to the Rapidan River, where President Herbert Hoover, an avid fisherman, had a camp during his administration (sort of the Camp David of his day). The total climb is 850 feet; allow 4 hours.
- **South River Falls:** Third-highest in the park, South River Falls drops a total of 83 feet in two stages. From the parking lot at South River Overlook (Mile 62.7), the trail is a moderately easy 2.6 miles round-trip, with a total climb of about 850 feet. Allow 2½ hours.
- **Doyles River Falls:** Starting at a large parking lot at Mile 81.1, a trail drops to a small waterfall in a natural amphitheater surrounded by large trees. Continue another quarter of a mile to see an even taller falls (63 feet). This hike is 2.7 miles round-trip, with a few steep sections in its 850-foot climb; allow 3 hours.
- **Appalachian Trail:** Access points to the Appalachian Trail are well marked at overlooks along the Skyline Drive. Along the trail, five backcountry shelters for day use each offer only a table, fireplace, pit toilet, and water. The **Potomac Appalachian Trail Club,** 118 Park St. SE, Vienna, VA 22180 (☎ **703/242-0693;** www.patc.net), maintains huts and fully enclosed cabins that can accommodate up to 12 people. Use of the huts is free, but they are intended for long-distance hikers only. Cabins cost $10 to $20 on weekdays, $15 to $40 on weekends. You can reserve cabins in advance by contacting PATC Monday to Wednesday between 7 and 9pm, Thursday and Friday from noon to 2pm Eastern time (and *only* during these hours). You'll have to submit a signed form (available on PATC's Web site), so start the process as early as possible.

FISHING   The park's streams are short, with limited fishing, so it's hardly worth the time and effort. Only native brook trout may be taken, and some streams are "catch-and-release," meaning you must release your catch back into the water. Only artificial lures are allowed, and you must get a Virginia fishing license (5-day licenses are available at the entry gates, visitor centers, wayside facilities, and camp stores inside the park, or at sporting-goods stores outside). The park publishes a free recreational fishing brochure and an annual list of streams open for fishing; both are available at the Big Meadows and Loft Mountain waysides or at sporting-goods stores outside the park.

HORSEBACK RIDING   Horses are allowed only on trails marked with yellow, and even then only via guided expeditions with **Skyland Stables** (☎ **540/999-2210**), on the Skyland Lodge grounds (Mile 41.8). Rides cost $20 per hour during the week, $22 per hour on weekends. Pony rides for children are $3 for 15 minutes, $6 for 30 minutes. Children must be 4 feet, 10 inches tall to ride the horses (otherwise they can take a pony ride), and those under 12 must be accompanied by an adult. The stables operate from April to November. Call for reservations 1 day in advance.

CAMPING

The park has four campgrounds with tent and trailer sites (but no hookups anywhere): Mathews Arm (Mile 22.2), Big Meadows (Mile 51.2), Lewis Mountain (Mile 57.5), and Loft Mountain (Mile 79.5).

In the middle of the park's Central District, **Big Meadows** has the best location, and it has sites equipped for disabled campers. You can reserve Big Meadows sites in advance by calling ☎ **800/365-2267** daily between 10am and 10pm Eastern time, or by using the park service's reservation Web site at http://reservations.nps.gov (*note:* don't type "www" in this web address). They cost $17 per night. Big Meadows is open from early April to the end of October.

Sites at **Mathews Arm, Lewis Mountain,** and **Loft Mountain** campgrounds are on a first-come, first-served basis at $14 per site per night. They are open from mid-May to late October. Lewis Mountain has only 31 sites and is often full during summer and early fall. Mathews Arm and Loft Mountain have 100 and 200 sites, respectively, and usually only fill on summer and fall weekends.

The **Shenandoah Valley Travel Association,** P.O. Box 1040, New Market, VA 22844 (☎ **540/740-3132;** www.shenandoah.org), publishes a list of private campgrounds outside the park.

WHERE TO STAY

Big Meadows Lodge and Skyland Lodge (see below) are the only hotels in the park. They are managed by park concessionaire **Aramark Virginia Sky-Line Co.,** P.O. Box 727, Luray, VA 22835 (☎ **800/999-4714** or 540/743-5108; www.visitshenanoah. com), which also operates food and other services for park visitors. Lodge reservations should be made well in advance—up to a year ahead for the peak fall season. In addition, cottages are available at Lewis Mountain. Contact Aramark Virginia Sky-Line Co. for information.

Luray is the nearest town to the park's Central District (see section 5, below). The other sections that follow describe accommodations in other Shenandoah Valley towns.

Big Meadows Lodge. P.O. Box 727, Luray, VA 22835 (on Skyline Dr. at Mile 51.2). ☎ **800/999-4714** or 540/999-2221. Fax 540/999-2231. www.visitshenandoah.com. 92 units. $65–$115 double main lodge; $79–$100 double motel; $99–$137 double suite; $72–$84 double cabin rm. Highest rates charged in Oct. Weekday packages available. MC, V. Closed Nov to early May.

Accommodations at Big Meadows consist of rooms in the main lodge and in rustic cabins, and multi-unit lodges with modern suites. Many of them have great views, and some (though not most) have TVs, fireplaces, refrigerators, and balconies or terraces—discuss what's available when you call the reservations clerk. Right in the heart of the park's Central District, Big Meadows is a major recreational center, so it's a bit more convenient than Skyland Lodge (see below). Many hiking trails start here, and it's also the site of the Byrd Visitor Center. The resort is built near a large grassy meadow where families of deer often come to graze at dawn and dusk. A grocery store is nearby.

The dining room features traditional regional dishes like fried chicken, mountain trout, and country ham. Blackberry–ice cream pie with blackberry syrup is a dessert specialty. Wine, beer, and cocktails are available. During the season, live entertainment keeps the Taproom busy.

Skyland Lodge. P.O. Box 727, Luray, VA 22835 (on Skyline Dr. at Mile 41.8). ☎ **800/ 999-4714** or 540/999-2211. Fax 540/999-2231. www.visitshenandoah.com. 177 units. $79–$110 double in lodge; $50–$98 double cabin room; $111–$165 suite. Highest rates charged in Oct. Weekday packages available. AE, DC, DISC, MC, V. Free parking.

Skyland was built by naturalist George Freeman Pollock in 1894 as a summer retreat atop the highest point on the Skyline Drive. Encompassing 52 acres, the resort offers rustic wood-paneled cabins as well as modern motel-type accommodations with wonderful views (tell the reservations clerk if you want a view). Some of the buildings are dark-brown clapboard, others fieldstone, and all nestle among the trees. The central building has a lobby with a huge stone fireplace, comfortable seating areas, and a TV (TVs are also in some, but not all, rooms).

Complete breakfast, lunch, and dinner menus are offered at reasonable prices. Dinner entrees include vegetarian lasagna, steak, roast turkey, and pan-fried rainbow trout. There's a fully stocked taproom.

WHERE TO DINE

In addition to Big Meadows and Skyland lodges, there are daytime restaurants and snack bars at Elkwallow Wayside (Mile 24.1), Panorama–Thornton Gap (Mile 31.5), and Loft Mountain (Mile 79.5).

Picnic areas with tables, fireplaces, water fountains, and rest rooms are at Dickey Ridge (Mile 4.6), Elkwallow (Mile 24.1), Pinnacles (Mile 36.7), Big Meadows (Mile 51), Lewis Mountain (Mile 57.5), South River (Mile 62.8), and Loft Mountain (Mile 79.5).

2 Winchester: Apple Capital

76 miles W of Washington, D.C.; 189 miles NW of Richmond

Winchester is Virginia's present-day "Apple Capital," so-called because of the large number of apple orchards here in the northern end of the Shenandoah Valley. It was the site of a Shawnee Indian campground before it was settled by Pennsylvania Quakers in 1732. Later George Washington set up shop here during the French and Indian War. Thanks to its strategic location, Winchester changed hands no fewer than 72 times during the Civil War. Both Confederate Gen. Stonewall Jackson and Union Gen. Philip Sheridan made their headquarters here at one time or another.

In more recent years, Winchester was the birthplace of novelist Willa Cather and the hometown of country music great Patsy Cline. It's also famous for the Shenandoah Apple Blossom Festival in May, one of the region's most popular events.

You can spend a morning or afternoon here and see Washington's office and Stonewall Jackson's headquarters, Winchester's major attractions. And country music fans can visit Patsy Cline's grave site on the edge of town.

ESSENTIALS

VISITOR INFORMATION   The **Winchester/Frederick County Visitors Center,** 1360 S. Pleasant Valley Rd., Winchester, VA 22601 (☎ **800/662-1360** or 540/ 662-4135; fax 540/722-6365; www.winchesterva.org), is open daily from 9am to 5pm; closed major holidays. Take Exit 313 off I-81, go west on U.S. 50, and follow the signs. Another source of information is the **Old Town Welcome Center,** in the

I Fall to Pieces

Early life wasn't easy for a Winchester native named Virginia Hensley. Her family was poor, and she had to quit high school and take a job in a drugstore to make ends meet. But she had a great voice—a voice that would someday propel her into the Country Music Hall of Fame.

Only die-hard country music fans know her by her real name, of course, for at age 21 she married a man named Gerald Cline. It was under the name Patsy Cline that Virginia Hensley sang "Walkin' After Midnight" on the nationally televised "Arthur Godfrey's Talent Scouts." The record of that song sold a million copies.

Difficult times set in again, however, and Patsy Cline disappeared from the charts. Her marriage to Gerald Cline failed, she remarried, and she took two years off to have a baby. But then, in 1960, she won a spot on the Grand Ole Opry and recorded one of country music's all-time hits, "I Fall to Pieces." Her career took off, and she recorded definitive versions of such songs as "Crazy," "Leavin' on Your Mind," and "Imagine That."

It all came to an abrupt end in March 1963, when she, Hawkshaw Hawkins, and the Cowboy Copas were killed in a plane crash on their way back to Nashville. Winchester's own Patsy Cline was brought home and buried in Shenandoah Memorial Park, 3 miles south of town on U.S. 522.

The Winchester/Frederick County Visitors Center (see "Essentials," above) has a Patsy Cline Corner that includes her very own jukebox. Pick up a brochure that points the way to important sites in her life, including her home, Gaunt's Drug Store (where she worked), the high school she attended, GNM Music (where she cut her first record), the house where she married second husband Charlie Dick, and her grave.

Kurtz Cultural Center, Cameron and Boscawen streets (☎ **540/722-6367**), in the heart of Winchester's historic district. It's open Monday through Saturday from 10am to 5pm, Sunday from noon to 5pm. Both centers distribute free maps and walking-tour brochures of the Old Town historic district. The Kurtz Cultural Center also has small museum sections devoted to the valley's role in the Civil War and to Patsy Cline, Winchester's contribution to country music (see "I Fall to Pieces," above). Both centers sell books about the Civil War.

GETTING THERE   Winchester is on I-81, U.S. 11, U.S. 522, U.S. 50, and Va. 7.

EXPLORING THE TOWN

Begin your tour at the Winchester/Frederick County Visitors Center (see "Essentials," above), where you can pick up a detailed map and see an 18-minute film about Winchester and Frederick County.

After you've been through Abram's Delight next to the visitor center (see below), drive into Winchester's historic district. Start your tour at the visitor information desk in the **Kurtz Cultural Center,** at the corner of Cameron and Boscawen streets (see "Essentials," above).

The heart of the historic area is the **Old Town Mall,** a 4-block-long pedestrian mall along Loudon Street between Piccadilly and Cork streets. Here you can explore a number of boutiques and enjoy refreshment at a bookstore-cum-coffeehouse, a pastry shop, or several restaurants, some of which offer outdoor seating under the mall's shade trees in warm weather (see "Where to Dine," below).

Facing the mall, the imposing **Frederick County Court House** was built in 1840. By the time you arrive, it should be home to a Civil War museum whose main exhibit will be a fabulous collection of weapons and ammunition (the collection was on display in the Kurtz Cultural Center during my recent visit but was expected to move to the court house).

While walking between the George Washington and Stonewall Jackson museums (see below), you can't miss the elaborate, Beaux Arts–style **Handley Library,** at the corner of Braddock and Piccadilly streets (☎ **540/662-9041**). Built between 1907 and 1912, it's adorned with a full panoply of Classic Revival statues. A copper-covered dome covers the rotunda, which symbolizes the spine of a book, with the two flanking wings representing its open pages.

Across the street from the library is the white-columned **Elks Building,** headquarters of Union Gen. Philip Sheridan from 1864 to 1865.

If you don't believe this northern end of the valley was fought over during the Civil War, visit **Mt. Hebron Cemetery,** on Woodstock Lane east of downtown. Some 8,000 men killed in the battles are buried here—the Rebels in Stonewall Confederate Cemetery on the south side of the street, the Yankees in the National Cemetery on the north side.

Both visitor centers sell **block tickets** to Abram's Delight, Washington's Office Museum, and Stonewall Jackson's Headquarters for $20 for a family, $7.50 adults, $6.50 seniors, and $4 children 6 to 12 (free for children under 6). See "Essentials," above.

Abram's Delight. 1340 S. Pleasant Valley Rd. ☎ **540/662-6519.** www.visitthevalley.org. Admission (without the block ticket) $3.50 adults, $3 seniors, $1.75 children, $8.75 family. Apr–Oct, Mon–Sat 10am–4pm; Sun noon–4pm. Mandatory 30-minute house tours depart on the hour and half hour. Closed Nov–Mar.

Adjoining the visitor center is this native-limestone residence built in 1754 by Quaker Isaac Hollingsworth on a pretty site beside a lake. The house is fully restored and furnished with simple 18th- and 19th-century pieces.

Stonewall Jackson's Headquarters. 415 N. Braddock St. (between Peyton St. and North Ave.). ☎ **540/667-3242.** Admission (without block ticket) $3.50 adults, $3 seniors, $1.75 children, $8.75 family. Apr–Oct, Mon–Sat 10am–4pm, Sun noon–4pm. Nov–Mar, Fri–Sat 10am–4pm, Sun noon–4pm. Mandatory 30-minute house tours depart as needed.

Stonewall Jackson used this Victorian home as his headquarters in the winter of 1861–62. It's filled with maps, photos, and memorabilia, making it a must for Civil War buffs. Plan on taking a guided tour, as you aren't allowed to just walk through. Two guides are usually on hand, so there's seldom a wait.

Glen Burnie. 801 Amherst St. (U.S. 50 West). ☎ **540/662-1473.** Admission to house and gardens, $8 adults, $6 seniors and students, free for children 6 and under; gardens only, $5 per person. Apr–Oct, Tues–Sat 10am–4pm, Sun noon–4pm. Mandatory 30-minute house tours depart on the hour and half hour.

On the western side of town, Glen Burnie is a lovingly restored, red-brick Georgian plantation home with sections dating to 1755. It's appointed with a remarkable collection of 18th-century furniture and art—including paintings by Rembrandt Peale and Gilbert Stuart—amassed by the late Julian Wood Glass, Jr., whose family owns Glen Burnie. A 14-minute film will set the stage for your tour of the house. Afterwards you can easily spend another hour strolling though the magnificent formal gardens.

Washington's Office Museum. 32 W. Cork St. (at Braddock St.). ☎ **540/662-4412.** Admission (without block ticket) $3.50 adults, $3 seniors, $1.70 children. Apr–Oct, Mon–Sat 10am–4pm, Sun noon–4pm. Closed Nov–Mar.

George Washington used this small log cabin (since covered with clapboard) as his office in 1755 and 1756 when he was a colonel in the Virginia militia, charged with building Fort Loudon to protect the colony's frontier from the French and the Indians. The building itself is the highlight of this charming little museum, whose exhibits explain Washington's career from 1748 to 1758. You can see it all in 30 minutes. Informative staff members are on hand to answer questions, but there are no guided tours.

WHERE TO STAY

If you decide to stay over, the area along Millwood Avenue (U.S. 50) at I-81 (Exit 313), on the southeast side of town, has Winchester's major shopping mall and several national restaurants and chain motels. About half the rooms at the **Holiday Inn** (☎ **800/HOLIDAY** or 540/667-3300) face a pleasant courtyard with outdoor pool; the hotel is also home to Jimmy's Restaurant, one of the town's most popular lunch spots. Another winner here is the inexpensive **Baymont Inn & Suites** (☎ **800/ 482-3438** or 540/678-0800), a member of the fine little chain that provides extra-long beds and phone cords, free local calls, a desk, a coffeemaker, and juice and a Danish hung on your doorknob before dawn.

Also nearby are the **Best Western Lee-Jackson Motor Inn** (☎ 800/528-1234 or 540/662-4154); **Comfort Inn** (☎ 800/228-5150 or 540/667-5000); **Hampton Inn** (☎ 800/HAMPTON or 540/667-8011); **Quality Inn East** (☎ 800/221-2222 or 540/667-2250); **Shoney's Inn** (☎ 800/222-2222 or 540/665-1700), which has an indoor pool; the inexpensive **Super 8** (☎ 800/800-8000 or 540/665-4450); and **Travelodge of Winchester** (☎ 800/255-3050 or 540/665-0685).

A Nearby Country Inn with a French Flavor

✪ **L'Auberge Provençale.** U.S. 340 (P.O. Box 190), White Post, VA 22663. ☎ **800/ 638-1702** or 540/837-1375. Fax 703/837-2004. www.laubergeprovencal.com. E-mail: cborel@shentel.net. 11 units. A/C. $150–$275 double. Rates include full breakfast. AE, DC, MC, V. From I-81, take U.S. 50 east 7 miles, turn right on U.S. 340. The inn is 1 mile on the right.

Master chef Alain Borel and his vivacious wife, Celeste, have managed to re-create the look, feel, and cuisine of Provence in a 1750s fieldstone farmhouse romantically set on a hilltop with a view of the Blue Ridge. In the original main house are three intimate dining rooms and a comfortable parlor to which guests are invited for pre-dinner drinks in front of the fireplace. Three of the 10 guest rooms are in this building; antiques and beautiful fabrics complement the colonial farmhouse's fine features. The remaining cozy accommodations, in an adjoining gray-clapboard addition, are individually decorated with Victorian and European pieces and lovely French provincial print fabrics. Exceptional works of fine art—including prints by renowned artists and a unique selection of carved wooden animals and small handcrafted bird sculptures—adorn the guest rooms.

Dining: Chef Borel uses the finest-quality ingredients, many from his own garden or local farmers, to create his superb five-course prix-fixe dinners ($65 per person; reservations required). Even breakfast is a splendid repast at L'Auberge Provençale, and Alain will provide a gourmet picnic lunch on request.

WHERE TO DINE

Winchester's finest cuisine is at L'Auberge Provençale (see above).

The Old Town Mall along Loudon Street in the heart of downtown has a number of coffeehouses, bakeries, and restaurants. Best of the lot are **Violino Ristorante Italiano** (☎ **540/667-8006**) and the pub-like **Brewbalcor's** (☎ **540/535-0111**), both on the north end of the mall at Piccadilly Street. They offer outdoor seating in good weather. For inexpensive down-home fare, check out **Vivian's Country Cooking,** on the mall at 103 N. Loudon St. (☎ **540/667-7612**).

Cork Street Tavern. 8 W. Cork St. (at S. Loudon St.). ☎ **540/667-3777.** Reservations not accepted. Main courses $9–$14.50. AE, DC, DISC, MC, V. Mon–Sat 11am–midnight; Sun noon–11pm. AMERICAN.

Just around the corner from South Loudon Street—the pedestrian mall at the heart of Winchester—this pub with small, dark rooms, fireplace, trophies, and photos of modern movie stars makes a fine place for lunch or a snack while touring the downtown sites. The house specialty is barbecued ribs, but the menu offers a wide range of other main courses, sandwiches, burgers, and salads. A newer wing offers outdoor patio seating in warm weather.

3 Middletown & Strasburg: Antiques Galore

Middletown: 13 miles S of Winchester; 174 miles NW of Richmond; 76 miles W of Washington, D.C. Strasburg: 6 miles S of Middletown

Middletown's historic sites will interest both history and architecture buffs, while its Wayside Theatre will entertain anyone who loves live theater. An extraordinary collection of shops makes Strasburg a prime destination for antiquers and collectibles shoppers. Both hamlets have exceptional country inns offering antiques-filled accommodations and fine dining.

It was to Strasburg that Gen. Stonewall Jackson brought the railroad locomotives he stole from the Union during his daring Great Train Raid on Martinsburg, West Virginia. He rolled the iron beasts down the Valley Pike to the existing station at Strasburg, which is now a local museum.

ESSENTIALS

VISITOR INFORMATION   The **Winchester/Frederick County Visitors Center** (see "Essentials" under "Winchester: Apple Capital," above) has in-depth information about Middletown. For Strasburg, contact the **Chamber of Commerce,** P.O. Box 42, Strasburg, VA 22657 (☎ **540/465-9197**).

GETTING THERE   From I-81, take Exit 302 west to U.S. 11 into Middletown. Take Exits 298 or 300 into Strasburg.

A PLANTATION MANSE & MUSEUM OF PRESIDENTS

✪ **Belle Grove Plantation.** U.S. 11 South, Middletown. ☎ **540/869-2028.** Admission $7 adults, $6 seniors, $3 students 13–17, free for children under 13. Mon–Sat 10:15am–3:15pm; Sun 1:15–4:15pm. Closed mid-Nov to mid-Mar except candlelight tours at Christmas. From Winchester, take U.S. 11 south, or I-81 south to Exit 302 at Middletown, then U.S. 11 south 1 mile. Mandatory 45-minute house tours depart 15 minutes past the hour.

One of the finest homes in the Shenandoah Valley, this beautiful stone mansion was built in 1794 by Maj. Isaac Hite, whose grandfather, Joist Hite, first settled here in

1732. Thomas Jefferson was actively involved in Belle Grove's design, having been brought in at the request of James Madison, Hite's brother-in-law. The columns and Palladian-style front windows are just two examples of Jefferson's influence.

Now owned by the National Trust, Belle Grove is at once a working farm, a restored 18th-century plantation house, and a center for the study and sale of traditional rural crafts. The interior is furnished with period antiques. Below the front portico is the entrance to the crafts center and gift shop, featuring an outstanding selection of locally made quilts, pillows, small rugs, and other handworked items.

Belle Grove suffered considerable damage in 1864 during the Battle of Cedar Creek, which was fought on 4,000 acres surrounding the manor house. Across U.S. 11, the **Cedar Creek Battlefield Visitors Center** (☎ **540/869-2064**) honors the fight with Civil War weapons, a diorama depicting the Napoleonic tactics used, and changing exhibits such as reproductions of the works of James Taylor, an artist who followed the Union troops. The battle is reenacted each year on the weekend closest to October 19.

The Museum of American Presidents. 130 N. Massanutten St. (U.S. 11), Strasburg. ☎ **540/465-5999.** www.waysideofva.com. Admission $3 adults, $2 children 6–16, free for children under 6. Mon–Sat 10am–5pm; Sun noon–5pm.

Leo M. Bernstein, a former Washington, D.C., lawyer and banker who restored the Wayside Inn (see "Where to Stay & Dine," below), displays his monumental collection of presidential memorabilia at this well-designed small museum in the heart of Strasburg. Among the highlights are a lock of George Washington's hair, James Madison's writing desk from his bedroom at Montpelier, and doors removed from the White House when it was restored during the Truman administration. Kids can don costumes and play educational games in a room set up like a colonial-era schoolhouse, complete with a potbelly stove.

ANTIQUING

Antiques lovers will want to hunt in nearby Strasburg, which has a bevy of fine outlets at the intersection of U.S. 11 and Va. 55. The ✪ **Great Strasburg Antiques Emporium,** 110 N. Massanutten St. (☎ **540/465-3711**), is one of the state's largest shops, an enormous warehouse with vendors selling both antiques and a plethora of collectibles. It's open daily from 10am to 5pm, to 7pm Friday and Saturday from May to October; closed New Year's Day, Easter, Thanksgiving, and Christmas.

You can't buy them, but there are plenty of antiques to inspect at the **Strasburg Museum,** 440 E. King St. (Va. 55) (☎ **540/465-3175**), 2 blocks east of the emporium. It occupies the old train station where Stonewall Jackson brought his stolen locomotives. Admission is $2 for adults, $1 for teenagers, 50¢ for children under 12. The museum is open May through October, daily from 10am to 4pm.

WHERE TO STAY & DINE

Hotel Strasburg. 213 Holliday St., Strasburg, VA 22657. ☎ **800/348-8327** or 540/465-9191. Fax 540/465-4788. www.svta.org/thehotel. 28 units. A/C TV TEL. $74 double; $84–$165 suite. Weekend and other packages available. AE, DC, MC, V. From I-81, take Exit 298 and go south on U.S. 11 1½ miles to the first traffic light; turn right 1 block, left at the light onto Holliday St.

Strasburg likes to call itself the Antiques Capital of Virginia, and this restored Victorian hotel, built as a hospital in 1895, is furnished with an impressive collection of period pieces. Most are supplied by the Strasburg Emporium (see "Antiquing," above), and are for sale. Hence, the decor changes constantly. Some rooms have Jacuzzis.

Known for its Russian sauerkraut soup, the dining room is open for all three meals. Dinner entrees might include shrimp-and-scallop cassoulet, chicken breast with walnuts and bacon in cream sauce, or Bavarian pork chops with onions, apples, and sauerkraut. A first-floor pub offers friendly conversation and libation.

✪ **Wayside Inn.** 7783 Main St., Middletown, VA 22645. ☎ **877/869-1797** or 540/869-1797. Fax 540/869-6038. www.waysidein.com. 24 units. A/C TV TEL. $95–$145 double. Weekend and theater packages available. AE, DC, MC, V. From I-81, take Exit 302 to U.S. 11 (Main St.).

This rambling roadside inn first offered bed and board to Shenandoah Valley travelers in 1797. It became a stagecoach stop some 20 years later when the Valley Pike was hacked out of the wilderness, and has continued to function as an inn ever since. In the 1960s, a Washington financier and antiques collector restored it, and today rooms are beautifully decorated with an assortment of 18th- and 19th-century pieces. Each room's decor reflects a period style, from colonial to elaborate Victorian Renaissance Revival. Expect to find canopied beds, armoires, highboys, writing desks, antique clocks, and stenciled or papered walls adorned with fine prints and oil paintings.

Regional American cuisine is served in seven antiques-filled dining rooms. Dinner entrees include whole stuffed valley trout and smothered chicken in white wine. Breakfast and lunch are also available. Cocktails and light fare are served in the Coach-yard Lounge.

MIDDLETOWN AFTER DARK

Since 1961, the **Wayside Theatre,** on U.S. 11 in Middletown (☎ **540/869-1776;** www.waysidetheatre.org), has staged fine productions by contemporary dramatists, including Peter Shaffer, Neil Simon, Wendy Wasserstein, Garson Kanin, and Alan Ayckbourn. Peter Boyle, Susan Sarandon, Jill Eikenberry, and Donna McKechnie began their careers here. The Curtain Call Cafe offers light post-theater fare and a chance for audience members to mingle with the performers. Admission is $17 to the Wednesday and Saturday matinees; $19 to Wednesday, Thursday, and Sunday evening performances; and $23 on Friday and Saturday nights. Senior and student discounts are available. The box office is open Monday and Tuesday from noon to 4pm, Wednesday through Saturday from 11am to 9pm, and Sunday from 3 to 8pm.

4 Front Royal: A Spy's Home

20 miles SE of Strasburg; 174 miles NW of Richmond; 70 miles W of Washington, D.C.

At the northern end of the Skyline Drive, Front Royal offers easy access to Shenandoah National Park's Northern District and is a good place to stay either before or after touring the park. It lacks the charm of Staunton, Lexington, and other valley towns, but during the summer months this area is a hotbed for canoeing, rafting, kayaking, and inner-tubing on the sometimes lazy, sometimes rapid South Fork of the Shenandoah River (see "River Rafting & Canoeing," below). And if you didn't disappear into the caverns down in Luray, you can go underground here.

Front Royal was named for a royal oak that stood in the town square during the Revolutionary War. In those days, it was a wild and woolly frontier waystation at the junction of the two trails that later became U.S. 340 and Va. 55. During the Civil War, it was home to the infamous Confederate spy Belle Boyd, whose close (*very* close) contact with Union officers led to a surprise Southern victory at the Battle of Front Royal in 1862.

Across the mountains to the east are two fine inns and dining choices, including a nationally famous, five-star inn and restaurant in "Little" Washington.

ESSENTIALS

VISITOR INFORMATION   Contact the **Front Royal/Warren County Chamber of Commerce Visitors Center,** 414 E. Main St., Front Royal, VA 22630 (☎ **800/ 338-2576** or 540/635-3185; fax 540/635-9758; www.frontroyalchamber.com; e-mail: visitfr@shentel.net). The chamber's visitor center is located in the old yellow train station and is open daily from 9am to 5pm. From I-66, follow U.S. 340 into town and turn left on Main Street at the Warren County Courthouse. The center sells discounted tickets to Skyline Caverns (see "Exploring the Town & the Caverns," below).

GETTING THERE   From I-66, take Exit 6, U.S. 340/U.S. 522 south; it's 5 minutes to town. Front Royal is also easily reached from I-81 by taking I-66 east to Exit 6.

EXPLORING THE TOWN & THE CAVERNS

If you're interested in the Civil War, you'll find two mildly fascinating minor attractions on Chester Street, 1 block north of the visitor center (see "Essentials," above). The **Warren Rifles Confederate Museum** (☎ **540/636-6982**) has a collection of Civil War firearms, battle flags, uniforms, letters, diaries, and other personal effects; it's open mid-April through October, Monday to Saturday from 9am to 4pm, Sunday from 12:30 to 4pm, by appointment the rest of the year. Next door is the restored **Belle Boyd Cottage** (☎ **540/636-1446**), where the infamous Confederate spy pillow-talked with her unsuspecting Union lovers. It's open April through October, Monday, Tuesday, Thursday, and Friday from 12:30 to 3pm, weekends by appointment. Admission to either the museum or the cottage is $2 per person, free for children under 12 accompanied by an adult.

Skyline Caverns. 13440 Stonewall Jackson Hwy. (U.S. 340). ☎ **800/296-4545** or 540/ 635-4545. Admission $10 adults, $9 seniors, $5 children 7–13, free for children under 13. June 15–Labor Day, daily 9am–6:30pm; Mar 15–June 14 and Labor Day–Nov 14, Mon–Fri 9am–5pm, Sat–Sun 9am–6pm; Nov 15–Mar 14, daily 9am–4pm. Mandatory 1-hour tours run continuously. Entry is 2 miles south of downtown Front Royal, 1 mile south of the Shenandoah National Park's northern entrance.

Although neither as varied nor as interesting as Luray Caverns (see section 5, below), the highlights here are unique rock formations called anthodites—delicate white spikes that spread in all directions from their positions on the cave ceiling. Their growth rate is only about 1 inch every 7,000 years. A sophisticated lighting system dramatically enhances formations like the Capitol Dome, Rainbow Trail, and Painted Desert. A miniature train covering about half a mile is a popular attraction for kids. The temperature in the caverns is a cool 54°F (12°C) year-round, and the tours take an hour, so bring a sweater even in summer.

Note: Discounted tickets are available at the Front Royal visitor center (see "Essentials," above).

SPORTS & OUTDOOR ACTIVITIES

GOLF   Duffers are welcome at the 27-hole **Shenandoah Valley Golf Club** (☎ 540/635-3588), the 36-hole **Bowling Green Country Club** (☎ 540/635-2095), the 18-hole **Jackson's Chase** (☎ 540/635-7814), and the 9-hole **Front Royal Country Club** (☎ 540/636-9062). Call for directions, starting times, and greens fees.

HORSEBACK RIDING   The 4,500-acre **Marriott Ranch,** 5305 Marriott Lane, Hume, VA 22639 (☎ **540/364-2627**), offers 1½-hour guided trail rides, buggy rides, summer sunset rides, and full-moon rides. Serious equestrians can stay over in the ranch's bed-and-breakfast inn (☎ **540/364-3221**), which has 10 rooms (seven with private bathroom). Hume is on the eastern side of the Blue Ridge, about 15 minutes from Front Royal via U.S. 522, C.R. 635, and C.R. 726.

RIVER RAFTING & CANOEING   The streams flowing west down from Shenandoah National Park end up in the South Fork of the Shenandoah River, which winds its way through a narrow valley between the Blue Ridge and Massanutten mountains.

The switchbacks of the South Fork are the region's main center for river rafting, canoeing, and kayaking from mid-March to mid-November. The amount of recent rain will determine whether you go white-water rafting, canoeing, kayaking, or just lazily floating downstream in an inner tube.

Several outfitters are based along U.S. 340, which parallels the river between Front Royal and Luray. All require advance reservations, and all are closed from November through April.

Front Royal Canoe Company (☎ **800/270-8808** or 540/635-5440; www.frontroyalcanoe.com) provides equipment and guides from its location south of Front Royal. In Bentonville, a small village about 8 miles south of Front Royal, you'll find **Downriver Canoe Company** (☎ **800/338-1963** or 540/635-5526; www.downriver.com) and **Shenandoah River Trips** (☎ **800/RAPIDS-1** or 540/635-5050; www.shenandoah.com). The latter operates at the Raymond R. "Andy" Guest Jr./Shenandoah River Park, a state facility on the river bank north of Bentonville. Near Luray, you can go with **Shenandoah River Outfitters** (☎ **800/6CANOE2** or 540/743-4159; www.shenandoah-river.com).

WHERE TO STAY

On U.S. 522 east of U.S. 340, the **Quality Inn Skyline Drive** (☎ **800/228-5151** or 540/635-3161) is the largest and best-equipped motel here. The inexpensive **Scottish Inn** (☎ **800/251-1962** or 540/636-6168) and **Super 8** (☎ **800/800-8000** or 540/636-4888) are both at the junction of U.S. 340 and Va. 55. In addition, the modest **Twin Rivers Motel,** on U.S. 340 south of I-66 (☎ **540/635-4101**), is well-maintained and mindful of families.

Chester House Inn. 43 Chester St., Front Royal, VA 22630. ☎ **800/621-0441** or 540/635-3937. Fax 540/636-8695. www.chesterhouse.com. E-mail: chesthse@rma.edu. 6 units (5 with private bathroom), 1 carriage house. A/C. $65–$125 double room or suite; $190 carriage house. Rates include continental breakfast. AE, MC, V. Free parking in on-site lot.

Bill and Ann Wilson's stately 1905 Georgian Revival mansion B&B is a friendly place set on two pretty acres of gardens and attractively furnished with a mix of antiques and reproductions. The premier accommodation is the Royal Oak Suite, a spacious high-ceilinged unit with a fireplace, separate sitting room, and private bath; it overlooks formal boxwood gardens. Another charmer is the Blue Ridge Room, which has a wrought-iron king bed and an old coal stove. Or you can opt for the restored Carriage House, which has a whirlpool tub and its own kitchen. The inn has a dining room, game room, and TV parlor, as well as terraced gardens adorned with a fountain, statuary, and brick walls.

Two Fine Nearby Country Inns

The two establishments below are located in the eastern foothills of the Blue Ridge Mountains, but within an easy (and very picturesque) drive from Front Royal via U.S. 522.

Caledonia Farm–1812. 47 Dearing Rd., Flint Hill, VA 22627. ☎ **800/262**-**1812** or 540/
675-3693. Manual-start fax on both numbers. www.bnb-n-va.com/cale1812.htm. 4 units.
A/C. $80 single or double with shared bathroom; $140 suite. Rates include full breakfast.
DISC, MC, V. From Front Royal, take U.S. 522 south 12 miles to Flint Hill and turn right onto
C.R. 641, to C.R. 606 to C.R. 628; look for a sign indicating a right turn to the farm about
1 mile past the last intersection.

This 1812 Federal-style stone farmhouse is a delightful B&B set on a 52-acre working
cattle farm. A scenic old barn, livestock, and open pastureland make for a bucolic setting. The common rooms are furnished with country charm. In the spacious Captain
John's Room, a double bed is beautifully made up with floral sheets and a quilt, while
blue-velvet wing chairs and Oriental rugs add to the cozy decor. A breezeway connects
the main house with the romantic and private 2½-room guest house. All accommodations offer working fireplaces and lovely views of the Blue Ridge. TVs and VCRs are
available on request. There are bikes and a hot tub for guests' use, and host Phil Irwin
will arrange hayrides.

✪ **Inn at Little Washington.** Middle and Main sts. (P.O. Box 300), Washington, VA
22747. ☎ **540/675-3800.** Fax 540/675-3100. 14 units. A/C TEL. $340–$495 double;
$550–$640 suite. Add $100–$225 for all Sat, major holidays, Oct. Rates include continental breakfast and afternoon tea. MC, V. From Front Royal, take U.S. 522 south 16
miles, then head west on U.S. 211 to Washington.

The Inn at Little Washington is simply one of America's finest country inns. Located
in the sleepy village of Washington (pop. about 160), it was opened as a restaurant in
1978 by owners Patrick O'Connell, the chef, and Reinhardt Lynch, who serves as
maître d'hôtel. It's best known as an outstanding restaurant with rooms (as opposed
to an inn with a restaurant). Nevertheless, the rooms are magnificently furnished
according to the design of an English decorator, whose original sketches are framed
and hanging in the inn's upstairs hallways. The two bi-level suites have loft bedrooms,
balconies overlooking the courtyard garden, and bathrooms with Jacuzzi tubs. Sumptuous amenities include terry-cloth robes, thick towels, hair dryers, and elegant toiletries. Antiques and Oriental rugs add warmth to the rooms, distinguished by
extravagantly canopied beds and hand-painted ceiling borders.

Dining: The 65-seat restaurant pays homage to French cuisine but relies on
regional products for culinary inspiration—trout, Chesapeake Bay seafood, wild
ducks, cheese from nearby dairies. Patrick O'Connell constantly changes the menu for
his fabulous fixed-price dinners ($98 per person Sunday through Thursday, $108
Friday, $128 Saturday). An autumn evening might begin with a seared duck foie gras
on polenta with Virginia country ham and blackberries, followed by a main course of
local rabbit braised in apple cider with wild mushrooms and garlic mashed potatoes,
or sautéed venison medallions on tart greens with black currant sauce.

Dinner reservations are absolutely essential. They begin taking them exactly 30 days
in advance, and Saturdays are often fully booked 2 days later.

WHERE TO DINE

In addition to the **Inn at Little Washington** (see above) and the Main Street Mill
Restaurant and Pub (see below), there's the **14th Street Bistro,** 101 W. 14th St. (U.S.
340) north of the historic district (☎ **888/636-8414** or 540/636-8400; www.
14thstreetbistro.com), which opened right after I last visited Front Royal but which
has received excellent reviews. It's open Monday to Thursday 10:30am to 11pm,
Friday and Saturday 10:30am to midnight, and Sunday 10am to 10pm (Sunday
brunch from 10am to 2:30pm).

Main Street Mill Restaurant and Pub. 500 E. Main St. (next to visitor center). ☎ **540/ 636-3123.** Reservations not necessary. Sandwiches (lunch only) $4–$7; main courses $8–$18. AE, MC, V. Mon–Thurs 10:30am–9pm; Fri–Sat 10:30am–10pm; Sun 10:30am–9pm. AMERICAN.

Occupying a picturesque 1922 mill building, this establishment has massive supporting columns and ceiling beams of chestnut. The distinctive trompe l'oeil murals representing Front Royal's pioneer and 19th-century eras were executed by local artist Patricia Windrow. Lunch fare includes soups, spicy chili, salads, and overstuffed deli sandwiches. Main courses range from pastas to bacon-wrapped filet mignon to a Virginia ham dinner. Hearty breakfasts are served on weekend mornings.

5 Luray: An Underground Organ

6 miles W of Shenandoah National Park; 91 miles SW of Washington, D.C.; 135 miles NW of Richmond

Established in 1812 and named for Luray Caverns, the most visited caves in the eastern United States, this small town is surrounded by the lush, rolling farmlands of a picturesque valley between the Blue Ridge and Massanutten mountains. It's the closest town with accommodation to the Shenandoah National Park's popular Central District, which makes it the most convenient base in the valley if you can't get a room at one of the park's inns. The park headquarters and the Thornton Gap entry are up U.S. 211 just a few miles east of town.

ESSENTIALS

VISITOR INFORMATION   The **Page County Chamber of Commerce,** 46 E. Main St., Luray, VA 22835 (☎ **888/743-3915** or 540/743-3915; fax 540/743-3944; www.luraypage.com; e-mail: pagecofc@shentel.net), will supply information in advance and make same-day hotel reservations at its visitor center, which is open daily 9am to 7pm from Memorial Day through October, daily 9am to 5pm the rest of the year.

GETTING THERE   From Shenandoah National Park, take U.S. 211 west. From I-81, follow U.S. 211 east (this scenic road goes up and over Massanutten Mountain). From Front Royal, take U.S. 340 south.

EXPLORING THE CAVERNS

✪ **Luray Caverns.** U.S. 211 West (2 miles west of downtown). ☎ **540/743-6551.** www.luraycaverns.com. Admission to caverns and car museum, $14 adults, $12 seniors, $6 children 7–13, free for children under 7; to Garden Maze, $4 adults, $3 children. June 15–Labor Day, daily 9am–7pm; Mar 15–June 14 and day after Labor Day–Nov 14, daily 9am–6pm; Nov 15–Mar 14, Mon–Fri 9am–4pm, Sat–Sun 9am–5pm. Mandatory 1-hour tours depart every 20 minutes. Tours of car museum are self-guided.

This U.S. Registered Natural Landmark is the most visited underground attraction in the eastern U.S., and with good reason, for these caverns are the Shenandoah Valley's most interesting and entertaining. In addition to monumental columns in rooms more than 140 feet high, they're noted for the beautiful cascades of natural colors found on the interior walls. They also combine the works of man and nature into an unusual organ with a sound system directly connected to stalactites. Music is produced when the stalactites are tapped by rubber-tipped plungers controlled by an organist or an automated system.

Guided tours follow a system of brick and concrete walkways and take about an hour. It's about 55°F (13°C) down here all the time, so bring a jacket or sweater.

Admission to the caverns includes the **Historic Car and Carriage Caravan,** a collection of antique carriages, coaches, and cars—including actor Rudolph Valentino's 1925 Rolls-Royce. The complex also contains a snack bar, gift shop, and fudge kitchen. Separate admission is charged to get thoroughly confused in the outdoor **Garden Maze.**

Across U.S. 211 stands the **Luray Singing Tower,** a stone carillon with 47 bells. It was given to the town of Luray in 1937 as a memorial to one of its residents. Free concerts are given at sunrise on Easter, at noon Labor Day, at 4pm the Sunday before Christmas, and on most summer evenings (pick up a schedule at the Luray visitor center or at the caverns).

WHERE TO STAY

Just as bed-and-breakfasts proliferated during the 1980s and early 1990s, **mountain cabins** are the latest trend around Luray. Most require at least a week's rental. The visitor center (see "Essentials," above) can provide information about the area's many rental cabins and B&Bs, and will assist in making reservations.

The **Days Inn,** on U.S. 211 northeast of town (☎ **800/325-2525** or 540/743-4521), is surrounded by acres of farmland, giving most rooms mountain views. The **Best Western,** on West Main Street/U.S. 211 Business (☎ **800/528-1234** or 540/743-6511), is an older motel in town. Both have outdoor swimming pools.

Several Victorian-era houses here have been converted into bed-and-breakfasts. Two of them (plus two mountain cabins) are operated by Lucas and Deborah Woodruff as **The Woodruff Collection,** 330 Mechanic St., Luray, VA 22835 (☎ **540/743-1494;** fax 540/743-1722; www.bbonline.com/va/woodruff).

The Cabins at Brookside. 2978 U.S. 211 East, Luray, VA 22835. ☎ **800/299-2655** or 540/743-5698. Fax 540/743-1326. 9 cabins. A/C. $75–$185 double. AE, DC, DISC, MC, V. From Luray, go east 4½ miles on U.S. 211. From Shenandoah National Park Headquarters, go west ½ mile on U.S. 211.

Owners Bob and Cece Castle remodeled this 1940s roadside service station/motel into a collection of log-look cabins with comfortable Williamsburg-style furnishings throughout. This is the closest accommodation to the Shenandoah National Park. Although located along busy U.S. 211, the rear of the cabins open to decks or sunrooms overlooking a bubbling brook, and road noise dies down after dark. Three "honeymoon" units have whirlpool tubs, four have gas fireplaces, and one has a kitchen (the others have refrigerators only). Morning coffee is delivered to the cabins. The rustic **Brookside Restaurant** on the premises serves inexpensive home cooking.

✪ **The Cardinal Inn.** 1005 E. Main St. (U.S. 211 Business), Luray, VA 22835. ☎ **888/648-4633** or 540/743-5011. Fax 540/743-3407. www.mountain-lodging.com. E-mail: cardinal@shentel.net. 27 units. A/C TV TEL. $59–$79 double. AE, DISC, MC, V.

Built in the 1950s and '60s, this comfortable roadside motel got a major overhaul from owners Barry and Nancy Presgraves after they bought it in 1998. The choice unit here has a separate bedroom, a kitchen, and a screened porch overlooking a picnic area with barbecue grills at the rear of the property. Opening to the parking lot out front, most other rooms are spacious, with a queen or two double beds, and have front and rear windows to let in the breeze. Some of these are a bit smaller, with room for a queen-size bed, but they also have two windows. Least attractive are lower level rooms on the rear of the building; these have only one window, but they open to the picnic area. All units have bright furniture, including writing desks. Bathrooms have shower stalls instead of tubs, but most have ample vanity space.

Luray Caverns Motel West. U.S. 211 Bypass West (P.O. Box 748), Luray, VA 22835. ☎ **540/743-4536.** Fax 540/743-6634. 19 units, including 1 apt. A/C TV TEL. $59–$76 double; $116 apt. AE, DISC, MC, V.

Sitting opposite Luray Caverns, which owns and spotlessly maintains it, this older one-story motel with a plantation facade is dated, but the spacious rooms all have pleasant views across pastureland to the Blue Ridge Mountains.

A sister establishment, the less appealing but equally clean **Luray Caverns Motel East** (☎ **540/743-4531**), is a short distance to the east on U.S. 211 Business.

The Mimslyn Inn. 401 W. Main St. (U.S. 211 Business), Luray, VA 22835. ☎ **800/296-5105** or 540/743-5105. Fax 540/743-2632. www.svta.org/mimslyn. E-mail: mimslyn@aol.com. 46 units. A/C TV TEL. $69–$139 double; $99–$169 suite. AE, DISC, MC, V.

This three-story, colonial-style country inn has been well maintained but not substantially changed since it was built in 1931 on 14 acres of lawns and trees west of the business district. The brick building is fronted by a portico and porch with tall white columns and high-back rockers. New dark-wood furniture and modern amenities such as TVs and phones have been added to the medium-size rooms, but they still have their original floor-to-ceiling windows and 1930s bathroom fixtures. Although wear shows here and there, the Mimslyn retains a kind of old-fashioned charm, and the rooms are clean and comfortable. A few suites have living rooms with two walls of paned windows, letting in lots of light. "Family units" have a single bath between two bedrooms. A stunning dining room with large fan-topped windows offers regional fare for breakfast, lunch, and dinner. On the third floor, you'll find a sunroom opening onto a rooftop deck. In the basement, the **Mimslyn Gallery** exhibits the works of noted artist P. Buckley Moss; it's open daily from 10am to 6pm.

A NEARBY EQUESTRIAN INN WITH FINE DINING

Jordan Hollow Farm Inn. 326 Hawksbill Park Rd., Stanley, VA 22851. ☎ **888/418-7000** or 540/778-2285. Fax 540/778-1759. www.jordanhollow.com. 15 units. A/C TV TEL. $133–$190 double. AE, DC, DISC, MC, V. Closed first 2 weeks in Jan. From Luray, take U.S. 340 south 6 miles, turn left on Hawksbill Park Dr. (C.R. 624), left on Marksville Rd. (C.R. 689), right on Hawksbill Park Rd. (C.R. 629).

Both equestrians and hikers will enjoy this working farm and inn, which has a stable of horses and ponies and 5 picturesque miles of trails in the foothills of the Blue Ridge. Two types of guest quarters are offered. Those in the vine-entangled Arbor View are suites with separate living rooms and spacious, romantic bedrooms with two-person whirlpool tub in one corner, a realistic-looking electric fireplace in another. The bedrooms open to a long porch with high-backed rockers for taking in the mountain view. The units in the log-sided, cabin-like Mare Meadow Lodge sport heavy pine furniture.

Trail rides on horseback cost $22.50 for guests and non-guests alike, while the kids can take 15-minute pony rides for $7. Even if you don't ride, you can visit the barns and pet the horses and ponies.

✪ **The Farmhouse Restaurant,** housed in the original clapboard homestead with wraparound porches upstairs and down, offers some of this area's finest cuisine, along with the best vintages from Virginia wineries. The menu changes seasonally and features local products as much as possible. In autumn, it might include chargrilled chicken breasts with a "wild olive" (actually wild mountain currant) sauce. Main courses range from $14 to $23. The restaurant serves breakfast to house guests and is open to the public daily from 6 to 9pm, with a Sunday champagne brunch from 10am to 2pm. Reservations are recommended on Friday and Saturday.

WHERE TO DINE

The best cuisine here is in The Farmhouse Restaurant, at Jordan Hollow Farm Inn (see "A Nearby Equestrian Inn with Fine Dining," above). For inexpensive country cooking, drive out to the Brookside Restaurant, at the Cabins at Brookside (see "Where to Stay," above).

Parkhurst Restaurant. U.S. 211, 2½ miles west of Luray Caverns. ☎ **540/743-6009.** Reservations recommended. Main courses $9–$21. AE, DISC, MC, V. Daily 11am–10pm. INTERNATIONAL.

An inn-like ambience pervades Chef George Weddleton's cozy establishment, built in 1938 as a country motel but operated as a restaurant since 1978. A small central dining room has knotty pine paneling, but the choice tables here are in an enclosed verandah with views across the parking lot to the mountains. Plants and quiet music create a romantic atmosphere in which to enjoy a mix of cuisine ranging from Southern fried chicken to veal Oscar (with king crab). Colonial steak is a house variation on prime rib: partially roasted, then finished on the grill with seasoned butter.

A TRIP UP MASSANUTTEN MOUNTAIN

Between Luray and New Market, U.S. 211 climbs over Massanutten Mountain, which splits this part of the Shenandoah Valley in two. Most of the mountain is preserved from development by the **George Washington National Forest,** which has hiking, mountain-biking, and horseback-riding trails, plus campgrounds. You can get information—and take a stroll along a half-mile-long wildflower trail—at the **Massanutten Visitors Center,** atop the mountain on U.S. 211 (☎ **540/740-8310**). It's open from April 15 to early November, daily from 8am to 4:30pm. For advance information, contact the forest's Lee Ranger District, 109 Molinue Rd., Edinburg, VA 22824 (☎ **540/984-4101;** www.fs.fed.us/gwjnf).

If you're heading north toward Front Royal and Winchester, pick up a map at the visitor center for a driving tour down long, narrow Fort Valley, which splits the northern half of Massanutten Mountain into a fork-like shape. The drive begins near the visitor center on C.R. 678, which runs down to Va. 55. The first 7 miles are over hardpacked gravel; the rest is paved.

A MOUNTAIN RESORT WITH GOLF & SKIING

Massanutten Resort. P.O. Box 1227, Harrisonburg, VA 22801. ☎ **800/207-MASS** or 540/289-9441 for information, 540/289-4914 for hotel reservations, 540/289-4952 for condo rentals, 540/289-6762 for house rentals. www.massresort.com. E-mail: skimass@shentel.net. 140 rooms, 800 condos. A/C TV TEL. $75 double, $90–$200 for condo. AE, DC, DISC, MC, V. From I-81, take Exit 247A, follow U.S. 33 east 10 miles to resort entrance on left.

Primarily a time-share operation, this mountain resort offers year-round outdoor activities, with 27 holes of golf, tennis courts, indoor and outdoor swimming pools, a half-dozen downhill ski slopes, and areas for snowboarding and snow tubing (riding inner tubes down a gentle slope). The hotel rooms have a queen or two double beds, sitting areas, and balconies. Most of the 800-plus time-share units are equipped with kitchens, fireplaces, and decks, and many have whirlpool tubs. There's a full-service restaurant, a pizzeria, a bar, and a grocery store on site.

6 New Market: A Civil War Battlefield & the Endless Caverns

16 miles W of Luray; 110 miles SW of Washington, D.C.

The little village of New Market holds a hallowed place in the hearts of all Civil War buffs, for it was here in 1864 that the cadets of Virginia Military Institute distinguished themselves in battle against a much larger and more experienced Union force. New Market has been a way station on the Valley Pike (U.S. 11) since frontier times, and many buildings from that era still stand along Congress Street, the main drag. Congress Street is also a good place to browse for antiques.

ESSENTIALS

VISITOR INFORMATION   The **Shenandoah Valley Travel Association,** P.O. Box 1040, New Market, VA 22844 (☎ **877/847-4878** or 540/740-3132; fax 540/ 740-3100; www.shenandoah.org), operates a visitor center across I-81 from New Market (Exit 264). The center has a free phone line for hotel reservations, and is open daily from 9am to 5pm.

GETTING THERE   New Market is on U.S. 11 at the junction of U.S. 211 and I-81 (Exit 264).

EXPLORING THE BATTLEFIELD

Even if your knowledge of the Civil War doesn't extend much beyond distinguishing the troops in gray from the troops in blue, you'll be fascinated by what happened here in May 1864. In a desperate move to halt Union troops advancing up the valley, Confederate Gen. John Breckenridge ordered 257 Virginia Military Institute cadets to New Market. The teenagers marched in the rain for 4 days to reach the front line. They charged the enemy on May 15, won the day, and returned home victorious, with only 10 cadets killed and 47 wounded. Hearing of the battle, Grant exclaimed, "The South is robbing the cradle and the grave."

The battle took place over a 6-mile-long stretch of ground now bisected by I-81. Only a small portion has been preserved, and it's on the western side of I-81 (the village of New Market is on the eastern side). From the village, go under I-81 (Exit 264) and turn immediately right on Collins Drive (C.R. 305), which will take you to the three museums listed below.

Note: New Market Battlefield State Historical Park and its Hall of Valor Museum are operated by the Virginia Military Institute Museum in Lexington (see section 9, below). It's at the end of Collins Drive. You'll first pass the other museums, which sit on part of the battlefield but are privately owned and operated. You'll need at least 3 hours to examine all three museums.

Calvary Museum. 298 W. Old Cross Rd. (at Collins Dr.). ☎ **540/740-3959.** Admission $5 adults, $2.50 children 6–12, free for children under 6. Apr–Nov, daily 9am–5pm. Closed Dec–Mar.

This small museum occupies the basement of a brick home built in 1870 by a Confederate cavalry veteran. Exhibits tell the story of U.S. cavalry soldiers from colonial days, when they rode horses and shot muskets, to Operation Desert Storm, when they flew helicopters and fired rockets. The artifacts were collected by Peter Comtois, former curator of New York State's historic site system, who lives upstairs with his wife, Jane. They will sell you actual "minnie balls" uncovered on the battlefield.

Gentlemen . . . I trust you will do your duty.
—Gen. John Breckenridge, Battle of New Market (May 15, 1864)

I look back upon that orchard as the most awful spot on the battlefield.
—Cadet John C. Howard, Battle of New Market (May 15, 1864)

New Market Battlefield Military Museum. 9500 Collins Dr. ☎ **540/740-8065.** Admission $7 adults, $4 children 6–14, free for children under 6. Mid-Mar to Nov, daily 9am–5pm. Closed Dec to mid-Mar.

In a structure built to resemble Robert E. Lee's Arlington House at Arlington National Cemetery (see chapter 4), this privately owned museum arranges its exhibits of photos, small arms, uniforms, personal gear, and other artifacts to follow the buildup to the Civil War and the battle. Among the more interesting items: Stonewall Jackson's family Bible, a pair of spurs left behind when Gen. George Armstrong Custer was almost overrun by Confederate troops, and a bullet-pierced belt buckle worn by a Union soldier when he was killed at Gettysburg. Outside, monuments note troop placements on a small part of the battlefield.

✪ **New Market Battlefield State Historical Park/Hall of Valor Museum.** 8805 Collins Dr. ☎ **540/740-3101.** www.vmi.edu/museum/nm. Admission $5 adults, $2 children 6–15, free for children under 6. Daily 9am–5pm. Closed New Year's Day, Thanksgiving, and Christmas.

This lovely state park contains the largest preserved part of the battlefield. Begin at the Hall of Valor Museum, dedicated to the VMI cadets who fought here. You can see two films—one about the battle, the other about Stonewall Jackson's Shenandoah campaign—then walk through the museum, which further explains the battle with uniforms, small arms (Gen. Breckenridge's sword is among the exhibits), and paintings. Outside on the rolling, grassy fields, a self-guided 1-mile walking tour will take you along the final Confederate assault on the Union line. In the center of the battle line was the Bushong farmhouse, which served as a hospital. The farm today is a museum of 19th-century valley life.

EXPLORING THE TOWN & THE CAVERNS

Begin your visit at the Shenandoah Valley Travel Association's visitor center (see "Essentials," above), where you can pick up a walking-tour brochure. Most of the historic buildings, some of them dating to before 1800, are situated along Congress Street (U.S. 11), so you can walk down one side of the street and return on the other.

Be sure to poke your head into the many relic-filled shops you'll pass, including the multi-dealer **Nickelodeon Antique Mall,** in the old firehouse (☎ **540/740-3424**).

Endless Caverns. Endless Caverns Rd. (3 miles south of town off U.S. 11). ☎ **540/740-3993.** www.endlesscaverns.com. Admission $12 adults, $6 children 3–12, free for children under 3. Mar 15–June 14, daily 9am–5pm; June 15–Labor Day, daily 9am–7pm; day after Labor Day–Nov 14, daily 9am–5pm; Nov 15–Mar 14, daily 9am–4pm. Mandatory 1¼-hour tours depart every 30 to 40 minutes. From New Market, go 2 miles south on U.S. 11, turn left on Endless Caverns Rd.

Extending into the western flank of the Blue Ridge, these caverns use dramatic lighting to display spectacular rooms, each boasting a variety of stalactites, stalagmites, giant columns, and limestone pendants orchestrated into brilliant displays of nature's work. Endless Caverns maintains a year-round temperature of 55°F (12°C), so bring a sweater or jacket. Camping is available here.

A ROUND OF GOLF

On the south end of town, off Fairway Drive, **The Shenvalee Golf Resort** was originally part of a plantation whose name is a contraction of Shenandoah, Virginia, and Lee. During World War II, the U.S. State Department used the manor house to keep Italian detainees who had diplomatic rank. The 18-hole golf course, built in 1926, is now open to the public (☎ **540/740-8931**).

WHERE TO STAY

Near Exit 264 off I-81, the **Days Inn New Market** (☎ **800/325-2525** or 540/740-4100) is on Collins Drive next to the New Market Battlefield Military Museum and near the state park. On the town side of I-81 is the **Quality Inn Shenandoah Valley** (☎ **800/228-5151** or 540/740-3141).

The **Shenvalee Golf Resort,** P.O. Box 930, New Market, VA 22844 (☎ **540/740-3181;** fax 540/740-8931; www.shnvalee.com), has 42 standard-issue motel rooms. They cost $65 double, and golf packages are available. See "A Round of Golf," above.

Bed-and-breakfasts here include **Cross Roads Inn,** 9222 John Sevier Rd. (☎ **540/740-4157;** fax 540/740-4255; www.crossroadsinnva.com); **The Jacob Swartz House,** 574 Jiggady Rd. (☎ **540/740-9208;** www.shenwebworks.com/jshouse); and the **Red Shutter Farmhouse** (☎ **800/738-8BNB** or 540/740-4281), which is off Endless Caverns Road near the caves.

WHERE TO DINE

In addition to the Southern Kitchen, below, you'll find the usual national fast-food restaurants at the I-81 interchange.

Southern Kitchen. 9576 Congress St. (U.S. 11, ½ mile south of I-81 interchange). ☎ **540/740-3514.** Reservations not accepted. Main courses $6–$11.50. DISC, MC, V. Sun–Thurs 7am–9pm, Fri–Sat 7am–10pm. SOUTHERN.

You can get your arteries hardened in a hurry at this down-home restaurant sporting the same green leatherette booths and jukeboxes installed when it was built in the 1950s. Except for salads, there isn't a single nonfattening item on the menu, but the peanut soup, pan-fried chicken, barbecue pork, steaks, and cream pies warrant a caloric splurge.

7 Staunton: A Presidential Birthplace

42 miles S of New Market; 142 miles SW of Washington, D.C.; 92 miles NW of Richmond

Settled well before the Revolution, Staunton (pronounced "Stan-ton") was a major stop for pioneers on the way west. It was Virginia's capital for 17 days during June 1781, when then-Governor Thomas Jefferson fled Richmond in the face of advancing British troops. When the Central Virginia Railroad arrived in 1854, Staunton became a booming regional center.

Today the town is noted as the birthplace of Woodrow Wilson, our 28th president. Along with Wilson's first home, many of Staunton's 19th-century downtown buildings have been restored and refurbished, including the train station and its adjacent Wharf District (now a shopping and dining complex). The town is also home to a fascinating museum that explains the origins of the unique Shenandoah Valley farming culture. Country music lovers will find another shrine here in the hometown of the Statler Brothers, and Shakespeare aficionados can see the Bard's plays performed in striking new replicas of his English theaters.

ESSENTIALS

VISITOR INFORMATION   Contact the **Staunton/Augusta County Travel Information Center,** P.O. Box 810, Staunton, VA 24404 (☎ **800/332-5219** or 540/332-3972; www.staunton.va.us). There are two walk-in visitor centers here. One is at the **Frontier Culture Museum,** on U.S. 250 west of Exit 222 of I-81. It's open daily from 9am to 5pm. Downtown, the **Staunton Welcome Center** is on the grounds of the Woodrow Wilson Birthplace, 24 N. Coalter St. (☎ **540/332-3971**). The centers provide free walking-tour maps to Staunton's historic downtown. You can also tune your radio to AM 1620 for information.

GETTING THERE   Staunton is at the junctions of I-64 and I-81, and U.S. 11 and U.S. 250. Amtrak trains serve Staunton's station at 1 Middlebrook Ave. (☎ **800/872-7245;** www.amtrak.com).

EXPLORING THE TOWN

Downtown Staunton is a treasure trove of Victorian architecture, from stately residences to the commercial buildings downtown and in the adjacent Wharf District (actually along the railroad, not a river). Pick up a walking-tour brochure from one of the visitor centers (see "Essentials," above), and set out on your own. The brochure describes five tours, but be sure to take the "Beverly" and "Wharf" tours, which cover all of historic downtown.

Free guided tours of downtown depart from in front of the Woodrow Wilson Birthplace at 10am on Saturday from June to October.

Whether you do it yourself or take the guided tour, be prepared to work up a sweat: Staunton is built on the side of a steep hill, à la San Francisco.

Art lovers, too, will enjoy downtown, which has several galleries and working studios. Be sure to go upstairs at **The Frame Gallery,** 21 N. Market St. (☎ **540/885-2697**), which has works by many Virginia artisans. You can see painters, potters, porcelain artists, and glassblowers working at **Avery Studio Gallery,** 115 E. Beverly St. (☎ **540/885-3415**); **Naked Creek Pottery Gallery,** 112 S. New St. (no phone); **Heyward Cutting Jr. Porcelain,** 172-A Greenville Ave. (☎ **540/885-4500**); and **Trout Studios Glass,** 162 Greenville Ave. (☎ **540/885-3208**).

Frontier Culture Museum. Richmond Rd. (U.S. 250), half a mile west of I-81. ☎ **540/332-7850.** www.frontiermuseum.org. Admission $8 adults, $7.50 seniors, $4 children 6–12, free for children under 6. Mid-Mar to Nov, daily 9am–5pm; Dec to mid-Mar, daily 10am–4pm.

In light of its history as a major stopping point for pioneers, Staunton is a logical location for this museum, which consists of 17th-, 18th-, and 19th-century working farmsteads representing the origins of the Shenandoah's early settlers—Northern Irish, English, and German—and explaining how aspects of each were blended into a fourth farm, the typical colonial American homestead. Staff members in period costumes plant fields, tend livestock, and do domestic chores. A 15-minute film will set the stage for your self-guided exploration of the farms, which will take about 2 hours to thoroughly cover.

Statler Brothers Complex. 501 Thornrose Ave. (near Norfolk Ave.). ☎ **540/885-7927.** Free admission. Tours Mon–Fri 2pm. Souvenir shop Mon–Fri 10:30am–3:30pm.

The singing Statler Brothers grew up in Staunton, and after they made it big in Nashville, they bought the old neighborhood elementary school and turned it into their office complex. One tour a day takes visitors through the building and lets them see the brothers' awards and a mass of memorabilia sent to them by adoring fans.

✪ **Woodrow Wilson Birthplace.** 24 N. Coalter St. ☎ **888/496-6376** or 540/ 885-0897. www.woodrowwilson.org. Admission $6.50 adults, $6 seniors, $4 students, $2 children 6–12, free for children under 6. Mar–Oct, daily 9am–5pm; Nov–Feb, Mon– Sat 10am–4pm, Sun noon–4pm. Mandatory 30-minute house tours depart continuously.

This handsome Greek Revival building, built in 1846 by a Presbyterian congregation as a manse for their ministers, stands beside an excellent museum detailing Wilson's life. As a minister, Wilson's father had to move often, and so the family left Staunton when the future president was only 2. The house is furnished with many family items, including the crib Wilson slept in and the chair in which his mother rocked him. The galleries of the museum next door trace Wilson's Scottish-Irish roots, his academic career as a professor and president at Princeton University, and, of course, his 8 presidential years (1913–21). America's entry into World War I and Wilson's unsuccessful efforts to convince the U.S. Senate to participate in the League of Nations are also explored. Don't overlook the beautiful Victorian garden or Wilson's presidential limousine, a shiny Pierce-Arrow, in the museum. You must take the 30-minute tour of the house, but you can wander through the museum and gardens on your own. No more than 2 hours will be required to see it all.

WHERE TO STAY

On U.S. 250 at Exit 222 off I-81, you'll find the **Best Western Staunton Inn** (☎ 800/528-1234 or 540/885-1112), **Comfort Inn** (☎ 800/228-5150 or 540/ 886-5000), **Econo Lodge** (☎ 800/446-6900 or 540/885-5158), **Hampton Inn** (☎ 800/HAMPTON or 540/886-7000), **Shoney's Inn of Historic Staunton** (☎ 800/222-2222 or 540/885-9193), and **Super 8** (☎ 800/800-8000 or 540/ 886-2888). Near Exit 225 (Woodrow Wilson Parkway), the **Holiday Inn Golf & Conference Center** (☎ 800/HOLIDAY or 540/248-6020) is adjacent to the Country Club of Staunton, where guests can play. There also are several bed-and-breakfasts in the area; ask the visitor center for a list.

Bed-and-breakfasts in Staunton include **Ashton Country House,** 1205 Middlebrook Ave. (☎ 800/296-7819 or 540/885-7819; www.bbhost.com/ahstonbnb); **Montclair,** 320 N. New St. (☎ 877/885-8823 or 540/885-8832; www. bbonline.com/va/montclair); **The Sampson Eagon Inn,** 238 E. Beverley St. (☎ 800/ 597-9722 or 540/886-8200; www.eagoninn.com); and **Thornrose House at Gypsy Hill,** 531 Thornrose Ave. (☎ 800/861-4338 or 540/885-7026; www. bbhsv.org).

✪ **Belle Grae Inn.** 515 W. Frederick St. (Va. 254), Staunton, VA 24401. ☎ **888/ 541-5151** or 540/886-5151. Fax 540/886-6641. www.bellegrae.com. E-mail: bellegrae@sprynet.com. 18 units, including suites and small cottage. A/C. $109–$209 double; $159–$249 suite. Packages available. Rates include full breakfast. AE, MC, V. From I-81, take Exit 222 west and follow signs to Wilson Birthplace; once there, turn left on Frederick St. (Va. 254) to inn on right.

This beautifully restored 1873 Victorian house, with white gingerbread trim and an Italianate wraparound front porch, sits well back from the street atop a sloping lawn. The property now occupies an entire city block, and most accommodations are in the adjoining 19th-century houses, all of them beautifully restored. Rooms throughout are furnished with period antiques and reproductions, Oriental rugs, wicker pieces, and canopied four-poster, sleigh, and brass beds. All but two rooms have fireplaces, and most have phones and TVs. There are also TVs in the Garden Room and the main-house sitting room.

Staunton's finest (yet casual) dining is in the living and dining rooms of the main house. "You can eat fried chicken at home," says proprietor Michael Organ. "Here you can have quail." Indeed, the kitchen puts out fine continental cuisine with regional influences and ingredients. Dinner is served Tuesday to Sunday from 6 to 9pm. Main courses range from $14 to $22, very reasonable for this quality. The Garden Room next door offers a light-fare menu.

✪ **Frederick House.** 28 N. New St. (at Frederick St.), Staunton, VA 24401. ☎ **800/ 334-5575** or 540/885-4220. Fax 540/885-5180. www.frederickhouse.com. E-mail: ejharmon@frederickhouse.com. 23 units. A/C TV TEL. $85–$125 double; $110–$200 suite. Rates include full breakfast. AE, DC, DISC, MC, V. From I-81, take Exit 222 west and follow the signs to Wilson Birthplace; once there, turn left on Frederick St., left on Augusta St., and left into municipal parking lot to hotel entrance.

Back in 1984, innkeepers Joe and Evy Harmon began converting these seven historic town houses—dating from between 1810 and 1910—into a low-key, European-style hotel. The rooms and suites are individually decorated with authentic antiques and reproductions from the Victorian era. Most have hardwood floors covered by Oriental rugs, and seven units have fireplaces. All suites have separate living rooms, and three of them have two bedrooms. If you don't mind bright light early in the morning, the choice unit here is suite 35, whose bedroom once was a sun porch extending across the rear of one of the houses. Guests are treated to a full breakfast, which includes Evy's apple-raisin quiche, ham and cheese pie, or layers of sausages, cheese, and eggs (you'll find the menu printed on your coffee cup). Frederick House is across the street from Mary Baldwin College and just 2 blocks from the Wilson Birthplace.

WHERE TO DINE

Staunton's finest dining is at the Belle Grae Inn (see "Where to Stay," above). At the other extreme, **Wright's Dairy Rite,** 346 Greenville Ave. (U.S. 11), a block south of Richmond Road (☎ 540/886-0435), is a classic drive-in that has had car-hop service since it opened in 1952. Even if you dine inside this brick building, you must lift a phone to place your order with the kitchen and wait for it to be delivered to your red leatherette booth. Nothing here costs more than $6, and no credit cards are accepted. It's open Sunday through Thursday from 7am to 10pm, Friday and Saturday from 7am to 11pm.

Staunton Station, the town's old railway depot on Middlebrook Avenue between Augusta and Lewis streets in the Wharf District, has been restored and converted into a dining/entertainment complex. Here you'll find **The Depot Grille** (☎ 540/ 885-7332) and **The Pullman Restaurant** (☎ 540/885-6612), both moderately priced, pub-like establishments offering American fare. Nearby in the Wharf District, **Byers Street Bistro** (☎ 540/887-8100) is a lively restaurant-bar fronting a municipal parking lot on Byers Street at Central Avenue. Locals describe a visit to these three institutions as pub crawling.

The Beverly Restaurant. 12 E. Beverly St. (between Augusta and New sts.). ☎ **540/ 886-4317.** Reservations accepted. Sandwiches $4–$4.50; main courses $3.50–$6.50. MC, V. Mon–Fri 6:30am–7pm; Sat 6:30am–4pm. AMERICAN.

Family-owned and -operated since 1961, this storefront eatery in the heart of the business district hearkens back to that nearly bygone era when even hash-house cooks made everything from scratch. You won't find prepackaged mashed potatoes among the home cooking here. Says co-owner Paul Thomas, "We've got a potato peeler back there that came over on the *Mayflower*." The fresh fare is typically small-town Southern: rib-eye steaks, fried shrimp or fish, veal cutlets, and roast beef. The Beverly is famous hereabouts for English high tea at 3pm Wednesday and Friday.

L'Italia Restaurant. 23 E. Beverly St. (between Augusta and New sts.). ☎ **540/885-0102.** Reservations recommended. Lunch $5.50–$9; main courses $8.50–$15. AE, DISC, MC, V. Tues–Thurs 11am–10pm; Fri–Sat 11am–11pm; Sun noon–9pm. ITALIAN.

This pleasant establishment is run by accomplished cooks who moved here from Italy. You'll enter through a nondescript foyer in front of a small bar, but French doors lead to a sophisticated storefront dining room with modern art hung in lighted alcoves. Ceiling spots highlight the black tables and chairs set far apart for privacy. The well-prepared offerings range from Sicilian-style veal parmigiana to northern Italian veal piccata in a sauce of white wine, lemon, and capers.

✪ **Mill Street Grill.** 1 Mill St. (south of Johnson St./U.S. 250). ☎ **540/886-0656.** Reservations not accepted. Sandwiches and salads $5–$7; main courses $9–$17. AE, DC, DISC, MC, V. Mon–Sat 4–10pm, Sun 11:30am–10pm. AMERICAN.

In the basement of the old White Star mill, which produced Melrose flour from 1890 to 1963, this lively pub serves the region's best barbecued beef and pork ribs. Steaks and prime rib also are featured, with or without sauces, and the seafood—especially the shrimp steamed with spicy Old Bay seasoning—is worthy of a coastal town. You can also opt for dinner-size salads, a variety of sandwiches, a few chicken and pasta dishes, and vegetarian platters such as spicy Cajun-style vegetables over pasta. Nightly specials could include a tasty but not too spicy étoufée loaded with shrimp. Most main courses come with a fresh garden salad with homemade dressing and tricolor bread freshly baked in a muffin-style crock and accompanied by sweet fruit butter. Heavy support beams, cozy tables and booths, and back-lit stained glass windows portraying chefs at work all contribute to a warm and friendly atmosphere.

✪ **Mrs. Rowe's Family Restaurant and Bakery.** Richmond Rd. (U.S. 250), just east of I-81. ☎ **540/886-1833.** Reservations not accepted. Sandwiches $5–$7; main courses $5.50–$14. DISC, MC, V. May–Oct, Mon–Thurs 7am–8pm; Fri–Sat 7am–9pm; Sun 7am–7pm. Nov–Apr, Mon–Sat 7am–8pm; Sun 7am–7pm. Breakfast daily 7–11am year-round. AMERICAN.

Opened in 1947 by Mildred Rowe and still run by her family today, this is one of the better home-style restaurants in Virginia. Made from recipes from Mrs. Rowe's own cookbook, dishes here are very much in the Southern tradition, but tend to be lighter than the usual fare cooked elsewhere with ample portions of lard. Grilled steaks, country ham, pork chops, and fried chicken lead the regular items, but you can also choose from daily specials such as meat loaf and gravy or fried flounder filet, served with two veggies (corn pudding, spoon bread, baked tomatoes, and cucumber-and-onion salads are notable here). The freshly baked pies are so good that locals order slices along with their main courses, just to make sure they get their favorite flavors.

A PICNIC STOP

A good place to stop for a picnic lunch midway between Staunton and Lexington is the picturesque **Cyrus McCormick Farm** (☎ **540/377-2255**). In a lovely rural setting, it contains a small blacksmith shop, a gristmill, and other log cabins, where exhibits include a model of McCormick's 1831 invention, the first reaper. Open daily from 8am to 5pm; admission is free. From I-81, Exit 205 is well marked to the village of Steele's Tavern and the McCormick Birthplace, but the scenic way to get there from Staunton is via U.S. 11 South.

STAUNTON AFTER DARK

On the drawing board but about to break ground as we went to press, the 300-seat **Shenandoah Shakespeare Playhouse,** at 10 S. Market St., will be a re-creation of an early-17th-century London theater much like those in which the Bard staged his plays in Elizabethan times. Also coming will be the 1,500-seat, open-air **Shenandoah Shakespeare Globe,** an exact duplicate of the famous original. In other words, Staunton is Virginia's Shakespeare capital, and you can see his plays year-round here. For schedules, ticket prices, and other information, contact the **Shenandoah Shakespeare Express,** 11 E. Beverly St. (☎ 540/885-5588; www.ishakespeare.com), which until now has been strictly a touring company but will be based in the new theaters.

The pubs in and around **Staunton Station,** the old railway depot on Millwood Avenue, have live bands playing on weekend nights, and the city has a summertime program of outdoor concerts in Gypsy Hill Park and elsewhere (check with the visitor centers for a schedule).

OVER THE MOUNTAINS TO MONTEREY

You can scoot along I-81 from Staunton to Lexington, but a scenic detour will take you west across the mountains into Highland County, whose rugged beauty has given it the nickname "Virginia's Switzerland." In fact, the 50-mile drive on U.S. 250 from Staunton to the little town of **Monterey** is one of the state's most scenic excursions. The road first climbs over Shenandoah Mountain (elevation 3,760 feet), at the top of which you'll find a scenic hiking trail in the Confederate breast works park. The winding, two-lane highway then scales Bull Pasture Mountain (elevation 3,240 feet) before descending into Monterey, whose white clapboard churches and Victorian homes conjure up images of New England hamlets. Sitting at more than 2,500 feet elevation, Monterey enjoys a comfortable, spring-like climate during summer.

Start your visit here at the **Highland County Chamber of Commerce,** P.O. Box 223, Monterey, VA 24465 (☎ 540/468-2550; www.cfw.com/~highcc/; e-mail: highcc@cfw.com), whose office is on Main Street next to the Highland Inn. It's open Monday through Friday from 10am to 5pm. There's also an information board in front of the Highland County Court House on Main Street.

Pick up a walking-tour brochure, and then stroll along picturesque Main Street (U.S. 250) past the likes of **H&H Cash Store,** a holdover from the days when general stores sold a little bit of everything, and **Landmark House,** built of logs around 1790. You can also poke your head into several good arts and crafts stores.

The best (and most crowded) time to be here is on the second and third full weekends in March, when Monterey hosts the **Highland Maple Festival,** one of Virginia's top annual events. A smaller version, the Hands and Harvest Festival, is held on Columbus Day weekend in October.

Outdoor enthusiasts can contact **Highland Adventures,** P.O. Box 151, Monterey, VA 24465 (☎ 540/468-2722), a company specializing in caving, rock climbing, mountain biking, and other outdoor adventures in the Allegheny Highlands of Virginia and West Virginia (reservations are essential).

Accommodations are available at the charming **Highland Inn,** on Main Street (P.O. Box 40; ☎ 888/466-4682 or 540/468-2143; fax 540/468-3143; www.highland-inn.com; e-mail: highinn@cfw.com), a 17-unit, verandah-fronted resort hotel built in 1904 but significantly renovated and improved in the 1980s. Rooms and suites range from $55 to $85. Dinner is served in the dining room. The Black Sheep Tavern offers light fare Wednesday through Saturday from 6 to 8pm, and brunch is served on Sunday from 11:30am to 2pm. Even less expensive is the **Montvalle Motel,** also on Main Street (☎ 540/468-2500), a plain but comfortable 1950s facility. There are several B&Bs here (the chamber has a list).

From Monterey, another marvelously scenic drive on U.S. 220 takes you 30 miles south along the Jackson River to Warm Springs (see below). From there you can drive back across the mountains to Lexington via Va. 39 and the dramatic Goshen Pass.

8 Warm Springs & Hot Springs: Taking the Waters

Hot Springs: 220 miles SW of Washington, D.C.; 160 miles W of Richmond.
Warm Springs: 5 miles N of Hot Springs.

With temperatures ranging from 94 to 104°F (34.5 to 40°C), thermal springs rise throughout the mountains and valleys of Bath County, a fact that's made this highlands region a retreat since the 18th century, when Thomas Jefferson and other notables would stop at Warm Springs to "take the waters." The Homestead was founded in Hot Springs in 1766 and is still one of the nation's premier spas and golf resorts (the nation's oldest tee is here). After you've taken the waters, played the links, and had your pedicure, you can hear classical music at the Garth Newell Music Center.

Warm Springs today is a charming little hamlet which serves as the Bath County seat. The even smaller village of Hot Springs, 5 miles up this narrow valley, is virtually a company town: It lives to serve The Homestead. Hot Springs' Main Street begins where U.S. 220 circles around the resort and runs for 2 blocks south; here you'll find a country grocery store, several upscale art and clothing dealers (some in the old train depot), an interesting crafts outlet called the Bacova Guild Showroom (☎ **540/ 839-2105**), and a funky and very fine little restaurant that, surprisingly, is not part of The Homestead.

ESSENTIALS

VISITOR INFORMATION   The **Bath County Chamber of Commerce,** P.O. Box 718, Hot Springs, VA 24445 (☎ **800/628-8092** or 540/839-5409; e-mail: bathco@ va.tds.net), operates a visitor center 2 miles south of Hot Springs on U.S. 220 (it shares space with the U.S. Forestry Service's information center). The visitor center is open Monday through Friday 10am to 4pm. There's an unstaffed visitor center kiosk on U.S. 220 just south of the Va. 39 junction in Warm Springs. It usually has copies of a walking-tour brochure to the little village.

GETTING THERE   U.S. 220 runs north and south through Hot Springs and Warm Springs, with access to I-64 at Covington, 20 miles south of Hot Springs. The scenic route is via Va. 39 from Lexington, a 42-mile drive that follows the Maury River through Goshen Pass. You can also take the scenic loop through "Virginia's Switzerland," described at the end of the Staunton section, above.

The nearest regular air service is at Roanoke Regional Airport. Clifton Forge has an Amtrak station (☎ **800/872-7245;** www.amtrak.com).

TAKING THE WATERS & ENJOYING SUMMER MUSIC

The most famous of the thermal springs are the **Jefferson Pools** (☎ **540/839-5346**), which sit in a grove of trees in Warm Springs, at the intersection of U.S. 220 and Va. 39. The crystal-clear waters of these natural rock pools circulate gently and offer a wonderfully relaxing experience. Opened in 1761, they're still covered by the octagonal white clapboard bathhouses built in the 19th century, so the only luxuries you'll get are a clean towel and a rudimentary changing room. One pool is for men, one for women (I don't know about you gals, but us guys skinny-dip in ours). The Homestead manages them, but anyone can enjoy the pools for $12 an hour. Reservations aren't taken; just walk in. Hours are mid-April to November, daily from 10am to 6pm. Closed December to mid-April.

There's music in the mountain air at the **Garth Newel Music Center,** P.O. Box 240, Warm Springs, VA 24484 (☎ **540/839-5018;** fax 540/839-3154), on U.S. 220 between Warm Springs and Hot Springs. The center's summerlong chamber music festival has been drawing critical acclaim since the early 1970s, and concerts now go into the autumn months. Tickets cost about $20. Garth Newell also sponsors a series of unique Music Holiday Weekend Retreats in spring, fall, and winter, including Christmas and New Year's. Accommodations and dining at the on-site Manor House are part of the package. Call or write for details.

WHERE TO STAY

Other bed-and-breakfasts in Warm Springs include **Three Hills Inn & Cottages** (☎ 888/23-HILLS or 540/839-5381; fax 540/839-5199; www.3hills.com), and **Warm Springs Inn** (☎ 540/839-5351). In Hot Springs are **Kings Victorian Inn** (☎ 540/839-3134; fax 540/839-3134; www.inngetaways.com/va/kingvic.html), and **Vine Cottage Inn** (☎ 800/410-9755 or 540/839-2422; e-mail: charlton@ vatds.net). The latter is a block from The Homestead.

Anderson Cottage Bed & Breakfast. Old Germantown Rd. (P.O. Box 176), Warm Springs, VA 24484. ☎ **540/839-2975.** www.bbonline.com/va/anderson. 5 units (1 with shared bathroom), including 1 guest cottage. $60–$125 per night double. Rates include full breakfast. No credit cards. From Va. 39, turn left onto Old Germantown Rd. (C.R. 692), to fourth house on the left.

One of Bath County's oldest buildings, this log-and-white-clapboard cottage has been in owner Jean Randolph Bruns's family since the 1870s. She has welcomed guests into her home since 1983, and still operates it as "private home B&B" (in contrast to the more commercial operations which have sprung up all over Virginia more recently). The setting is an expansive lawn with a warm stream flowing through the property in the heart of the picturesque village. The house has appealing country charm, with many family heirloom pieces and photos, wide-board floors, Oriental rugs, working fireplaces, and lots of loaded bookcases. Accommodations are individually decorated and exceptionally spacious. Originally an 1820s brick kitchen, the Guest Cottage is ideal for families, with two bedrooms, two baths, a full kitchen/dining/sitting room with fireplace, and a living room.

✪ **The Homestead.** Hot Springs, VA 24445. ☎ **800/838-1766** or 540/839-1776. Fax 540/839-7670. www.thehomestead.com. 521 units. A/C MINIBAR TV TEL. $115–$248 double per person. Children under 5 stay free in parents' room, children 5–12 pay $46 per day extra, children 13–18 pay $65 extra. Higher rates charged during holidays. Rates include breakfast, dinner, and afternoon tea. Weekend, golf, and other packages available. AE, DC, DISC, MC, V. Main entrance is off U.S. 220 south of Main St.

With a prodigious reputation dating back to 1766, this famous spa and golf resort has been host to Presidents Jefferson, Wilson, Hoover, F.D.R., Truman, Eisenhower, Carter, and Reagan, plus social elites like the Henry Fords, John D. Rockefeller, the Vanderbilts, and Lord and Lady Astor.

Two mountains flank the hotel's main building of red Kentucky brick with white-limestone trim. Guests enter via the magnificent Great Hall, lined with 16 Corinthian columns and a 211-foot floral carpet. Two fireplaces, wing chairs, Chippendale-reproduction tables with reading lamps, and deep sofas create a warm atmosphere. Afternoon tea is served here daily, with classical piano playing in the background.

Guests have a variety of accommodations in rooms and suites with a Virginia country-manor ambience and custom-designed mahogany furniture. Most units offer spectacular mountain views, and the 81 suites in the South Wing have working fireplaces, private bars, sun porches, two TVs, and two phones.

This large property hosts conventions and other group meetings, so you'll have lots of company here.

Dining/Diversions: The Homestead's historic Dining Room is a lush palm court, in which an orchestra performs every evening during six-course dinners. The adjoining Commonwealth Room is adorned with murals of Virginia landmarks, such as Mount Vernon and Monticello. Tables throughout are elegantly appointed. Under the supervision of European-trained chefs, the cuisine features regional favorites like fresh rainbow trout, grilled lamb chops, and roast beef with Armagnac sauce. Cocktails, hors d'oeuvres, and after-dinner espresso are served in the View Lounge. Other dining options include The Homestead's signature restaurant, The Grille, and casual dining in the Casino and in Cafe Albert (named for the head chef, Albert Schnarwyler, who's been here since 1962). Across Main Street from the hotel, Sam Snead's Tavern is a lively pub serving traditional American fare (open Wednesday through Monday from 5 to 10pm). Evening entertainment includes live music, dancing, and free movies.

Guests may don casual resort wear during the day (including shorts of respectable length), but men must wear jackets and long pants after dark, with both jackets and ties required in the Dining Room.

Amenities: Concierge, room service, travel agency, children's programs. Three outstanding golf courses (Lanny Wadkins is the resident PGA pro), indoor and outdoor pools, spa with full health club facilities, 12 tennis courts, bowling, fishing, hiking trails, horseback and carriage rides, ice-skating on an Olympic-size rink, lawn bowling and croquet, billiards, sporting clays and skeet trap, downhill and cross-country skiing mid-December to March, horseshoes, volleyball, video-game room, board games, beauty salon, and 21 boutique and specialty shops.

Inn at Gristmill Square. C.R. 645 (Box 359), Warm Springs, VA 24484. ☎ **540/839-2231.** Fax 540/839-5770. www.vainns.com/grist.htm. E-mail: grist@va.tds.net. 17 units. A/C TV TEL. $80–$100 double. Rates include continental breakfast. Modified American Plan (also including 5-course dinner and gratuities) $155–$165 double. DISC, MC, V. From U.S. 220N, turn left onto C.R. 619 and right onto C.R. 645.

Five restored 19th-century buildings, including an old mill, make up this unique hostelry. It includes the Blacksmith Shop, which houses a country store; the Hardware Store, with seven guest units; the Steel House, with four units; and the Miller's House, with four rooms. Furnishings are charming period pieces, with comfortable upholstered chairs, brass chandeliers, quilts on four-poster beds, marble-top side tables, and working fireplaces. Breakfast is served in your room in a picnic basket. Other facilities include an outdoor pool, three tennis courts, and sauna.

The rustic Waterwheel Restaurant and Simon Kenton Pub are cozy spots in the old mill building. The restaurant features notably good American cuisine, with entrees like grilled trout, pork Calvados, and filet of salmon with béarnaise sauce. Wines are displayed among the gears of the waterwheel. The restaurant also serves Sunday brunch.

Roseloe Motel. U.S. 220 North (Rte. 2, Box 590), Hot Springs, VA 24445. ☎ **540/839-5373.** 14 units. A/C TV TEL. $48–$55 double. AE, DC, DISC, MC, V. From Hot Springs, go north 3 miles on U.S. 220.

At the opposite extreme from The Homestead, this brick-fronted, family-owned motel offers inexpensive, well-maintained, and clean rooms near the Garth Newel Music Center, between Warm Springs and Hot Springs. Four units have full kitchens, while two have kitchenettes. The others have refrigerators. It's very popular with leaf-watchers and deer hunters during fall, so book early.

AN UNUSUAL COUNTRY INN

✪ **Fort Lewis Lodge.** HCR 3, Box 21A, Millboro, VA 24460. ☎ **540/925-2314.** Fax 540/925-2352. www.fortlewislodge.com. E-mail: ftlewis@va.tds.net. 15 units, including 2 cabins. $150–$210 double. Rates include breakfast and dinner. MC, V. From Warm Springs, go 13 miles east on Va. 39, turn left on Indian Draft Rd. (C.R. 678) and drive north 10.8 miles, then turn left on River Rd. (C.R. 625) to entrance.

You'll discover one of Virginia's most unusual country inns at John and Caryl Cowden's farm beside the Cowpasture River, which cuts a north-south valley over the mountain from Warm Springs. Most guest quarters here are in a reconstructed barn, but an outside spiral staircase leads to three rooms inside the attached silo. One end of the rough-look barn is now a comfortable lounge with stone fireplace and large windows looking out to a Jacuzzi-equipped deck to the farmland and mountains beyond. Other guests stay in hand-hewn log cabins, each with a fireplace.

The Cowdens' summertime garden supplies flowers and vegetables for excellent meals served in the old Lewis Mill, whose upstairs has been turned into a game room. A screened porch to one side shelters Buck's Bar, which serves beer and wine. Activities include biking, hiking, swimming, and fishing for trout in the Cowpasture River. Fort Lewis Lodge is very popular with families getting away from Washington, D.C., and other nearby cities, so book early.

WHERE TO DINE

In addition to Chef Ed's (below), don't overlook the rustic **Waterwheel Restaurant** at the Inn at Gristmill Square in Warm Springs (see "Where to Stay," above).

✪ **Chef Ed's Community Market.** 3 Main St., Hot Springs. ☎ **540/839-3664.** Reservations required at dinner. Lunch $3–$8; main courses $15–$18. MC, V. Mon–Sat 10:30am–3:30pm, Thurs–Mon 6:30–8:30pm (2 seatings only). ECLECTIC.

This Main Street storefront half a block south of The Homestead doubles as a gourmet grocery and the domain of chef Ed McCardle, who busily whips up fine, eclectic cuisine in a kitchen behind the meat chiller at the rear. For lunch he offers salads, sandwiches, and tasty wraps made with red or green tortillas (go for his marvelous curry chicken salad made with apples and raisins), and three entrees. At night, Ed covers the folding tables at the rear with linen and offers an eclectic menu drawing from a number of cuisines. Grilled salmon with soba noodles, ginger-flavored bok choy, and a white-butter lime cilantro sauce is but one example of what he might offer at his two nightly seatings. To top things off, try his banana cream pie with roasted peanut crust.

9 Lexington: A College Town with a Slice of American History

36 miles S of Staunton; 180 miles SW of Washington, D.C.; 138 miles W of Richmond

A lively college atmosphere prevails in Lexington, which consistently ranks as one of America's best small towns. Fine old homes line tree-shaded streets, among them the house where Stonewall Jackson lived when he taught at Virginia Military Institute. A beautifully restored downtown looks so much like it did in the 1800s that scenes for the movie *Sommersby* were filmed on Main Street (Richard Gere was "hanged" behind the Jackson House while Jodie Foster looked on). After the Civil War, Robert E. Lee came to Lexington to serve as president of what was then Washington College; he and his horse Traveller are buried here. And Gen. George C. Marshall, winner of the Nobel Peace Prize for his post–World War II plan to rebuild Europe, graduated from VMI, which has a fine museum in his memory.

Washington and Lee University has one of the oldest and most beautiful campuses in the country. Built in 1824, Washington Hall is topped by a replica of a masterpiece of American folk art, an 1840 carved-wood statue of George Washington. Some of the massive trees dotting the campus are believed to have been planted by Lee.

Lexington

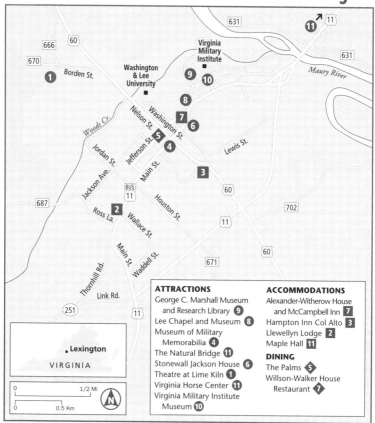

ATTRACTIONS

George C. Marshall Museum
and Research Library 9
Lee Chapel and Museum 8
Museum of Military
Memorabilia 4
The Natural Bridge 11
Stonewall Jackson House 6
Theatre at Lime Kiln 1
Virginia Horse Center 11
Virginia Military Institute
Museum 10

ACCOMMODATIONS

Alexander-Witherow House
and McCampbell Inn 7
Hampton Inn Col Alto 3
Llewellyn Lodge 2
Maple Hall 11

DINING

The Palms 5
Willson-Walker House
Restaurant 7

Sometimes called the West Point of the South, VMI opened in 1839 on the site of a state arsenal, abutting the Washington and Lee campus (W&L's buildings are like brick Southern manses; VMI's look like stone fortresses). The most dramatic episode in VMI's history took place during the Civil War at the Battle of New Market on May 15, 1864, when the corps of cadets helped turn back a larger Union army (see section 6, above). A month later, Union Gen. David Hunter got even, bombarding Lexington and burning down VMI.

If you have time to stop in only one Shenandoah Valley town, make it lovely Lexington.

ESSENTIALS

VISITOR INFORMATION   The **Visitor Center,** 106 E. Washington St., Lexington, VA 24450 (☎ **540/463-3777;** fax 540/463-1105; www.lexingtonvirginia. com; e-mail: lexington@rockbridge.net), is a block east of Main Street. Begin your tour of Lexington at this excellent source of information, for it offers museum-like displays about the town's history, makes same-day hotel reservations, and distributes free walking-tour brochures (you can park in the center's lot while touring the town). Be sure to see the engrossing slide show on Lexington's history. The center is open daily from 8:30am to 6pm June through August, from 9am to 5pm the rest of the year.

GETTING THERE   Lexington is on both I-81 and I-64, and U.S. 60 and U.S. 11 go directly into town.

EXPLORING THE TOWN

Be sure to pick up a free **walking-tour** brochure at the visitor center. It explains Lexington's many historic buildings and contains one of the best maps of downtown.

Seeing the sights is easy and enjoyable via **Lexington Carriage Company** (☎ 540/463-5647), whose horse-drawn carriages depart from the visitor center for 45-minute narrated tours daily from 9am to 5pm during the summer, from 10am to 4:30pm during April, May, September, and October. Fares are $12 for ages 14 to 64, $11 for seniors, $7 for ages 7 to 13, $4 for ages 4 to 6, and $1 for kids under 4.

Ghost Tour of Lexington (☎ 540/348-1080) conducts 1¼-hour nighttime walks through the streets, back alleys, and Stonewall Jackson Cemetery from late May to October. Cost is $8 for adults, $6 for children 4 to 10, and free for children under 4. Reservations are strongly recommended.

✪ **George C. Marshall Museum and Research Library.** VMI Parade. ☎ 540/463-7103. Admission $3 adults, $2 seniors, free for students and children. Museum, daily 9am–5pm; research library, Mon–Fri 8:30am–4:30pm.

Although it sits in the middle of a Civil War shrine, facing the VMI parade ground, this impressive stone structure is a terrific World War II museum, housing the personal archives of General of the Army George C. Marshall, a 1901 graduate of VMI. Marshall had an illustrious career, including service in France in 1917, when he was aide-de-camp to General Pershing. As army chief of staff in World War II, he virtually directed that conflict (it was Marshall who chose Gen. Dwight D. Eisenhower to command all Allied forces in Europe). After the war he served as secretary of state and secretary of defense under President Truman. He is best remembered for the Marshall Plan, which fostered the economic recovery of Europe after the war. For his role in promoting post-war peace, he became the first career soldier to be awarded the Nobel Peace Prize, in 1956.

The Nobel medal is on display in the museum, as is the script and best picture Academy Award won by the movie *Patton,* whose producers were advised by the museum and research library staff. A big electronic map charts the war and Marshall's decisions, and films explain his life. Allow at least an hour to explore the museum on your own.

By the way, the Marshall library and museum served as the prototype for modern presidential libraries, starting with President Truman's in Independence, Missouri.

✪ **Lee Chapel and Museum.** Washington and Lee University. ☎ 540/463-8768. Free admission. Mon–Sat 9am–5pm, Sun 2–5pm. Limited free parking on Jefferson St. opposite western end of Henry St. Follow signs from parking lot.

This magnificent Victorian-Gothic chapel of brick and native limestone, today used for concerts and other events, was built in 1867 at the request of General Lee. Start in the chapel upstairs. Walk up to the stage and Edward Valentine's striking white-marble sculpture, "Lee in Repose." A docent will explain the intricacies of the statue, which Valentine carved between 1871 and 1875, shortly after Lee's death. Charles Willson Peale's portrait of George Washington wearing the uniform of a colonel in the British Army and Theodore Pine's painting of Lee in Confederate uniform flank the statue. Then climb down the narrow rear steps to the basement, where the remains of the general and many other members of the Lee clan (including Light Horse Harry Lee of Revolutionary War fame) are entombed in a wall. Lee's beloved horse, Traveller, is buried in a plot outside the museum. Across the vestibule, Lee's office remains just as he left it when he died on September 28, 1870. The museum itself is devoted to the history of the Lee family. Allow 30 minutes to see the statue, the crypt, and Lee's office; another 30 for the museum.

Museum of Military Memorabilia. 122½ S. Main St. (in the driveway beside the Presbyterian Church). ☎ **540/464-3041.** Admission $3 per person. Apr–Oct, Wed–Fri noon–5pm, Sun 9am–5pm. Rest of year by appointment. Mandatory 45-minute tours run continuously.

This small but fascinating museum displays a collection of military uniforms and various bits of soldiers' gear, with the oldest dating from 1740 Prussia and the newest from the 1991 Persian Gulf War. The uniforms come from several different countries and represent a number of conflicts. You'll also see insignia, flags, a few weapons, trench art from World War I, and a piece of the Berlin Wall. If you miss the beginning, you can join the 45-minute guided tours in progress.

✪ **Stonewall Jackson House.** 8 E. Washington St. (between Main and Randolph sts.). ☎ **540/463-2552.** www.stonewalljackson.org. Admission $5 adults, $2.50 children 6–18, free for children under 6. Mon–Sat 9am–4:30pm, Sun 1–4:30pm; open until 5:30pm in summer. Mandatory 30-minute tours depart on the hour and half hour. Closed New Year's Day, Easter, Thanksgiving, and Christmas.

Maj. Thomas Jonathan Jackson came to Lexington in 1851 to take a post as teacher of natural philosophy (physics) and artillery tactics at VMI. Jackson lived here with his wife, Mary Anna Morrison, from early 1859 until he answered General Lee's summons to Richmond in 1861; it was the only house he ever owned. Photographs, text, and a slide show tell the story of the Jacksons' stay here. Appropriate period furnishings duplicate the items on the inventory of Jackson's estate made shortly after he died near Chancellorsville in 1863. His body was returned to Lexington and buried in Stonewall Jackson Memorial Cemetery on South Main Street.

Virginia Horse Center. Va. 39, west of U.S. 11 and north of I-64. ☎ **540/463-7060.** www.horsecenter.org. Admission varies by event; most are free. Open year-round. From downtown, take U.S. 11 north, turn left on Va. 39 a tenth of a mile north of I-64. The center is 1 mile on the left.

Sprawling across nearly 400 acres, the Virginia Horse Center offers horse shows, educational seminars, and sales of fine horses. Annual events include draft pulls, rodeos, various competitions, and competitive breed shows. In April, the center holds a Horse Festival showcasing the entire Virginia industry. For a full program of events, check the Web site or contact the center at P.O. Box 1051, Lexington, VA 24450.

✪ **Virginia Military Institute Museum.** Letcher Ave., VMI Parade (in Jackson Memorial Hall). ☎ **540/464-7232.** www.vmi.edu/museum. Free admission. Daily 9am–5pm. Closed New Year's Day, Thanksgiving, Christmas week.

This museum tracing VMI's history is in the basement of Jackson Memorial Hall, the school's auditorium. The structure was built in 1915 with federal funds paid in partial compensation for the Union army's burning the school after its cadets helped defeat federal troops at the Battle of New Market in May 1864 (see section 6, above).

Impressions ————————————————————————————

Let us cross the river and rest under the shade of the trees.
—Stonewall Jackson's last words (May 10, 1863)

Over the stage hangs B. West Clinedinst's oversized oil painting of the cadets' heroic Civil War charge. Downstairs, the museum displays uniforms, weapons, and memorabilia from cadets who attended the college and fought in numerous wars. You'll especially want to see the oil-slick raincoat Stonewall Jackson was wearing when his own men accidentally shot him at Chancellorsville (the bullet hole is in the upper left shoulder), and Jackson's unflappable war horse, Little Sorrel, who—thanks to taxidermy—stands nearby. Little Sorrel survived the war and died in 1886 at age 32. Also here are one of Gen. George S. Patton's pearl-handled pistols and his shiny helmet liner. Patton graduated from VMI in 1907.

THE NATURAL BRIDGE

Thomas Jefferson called this hugely impressive limestone formation "the most sublime of nature's works . . . so beautiful an arch, so elevated, so light and springing, as it were, up to heaven." The bridge was part of a 157-acre estate Jefferson acquired in 1774 from King George III. It was included in the survey of western Virginia carried out by George Washington, who carved his initials into the face of the stone. This geological oddity rises 215 feet above Cedar Creek; its span is 90 feet long and spreads at its widest to 150 feet. The Monocan Indian tribes worshipped it as "the bridge of God." Today it is also the bridge of man, as U.S. 11 passes over it.

I don't want to describe it as tacky, since the bridge itself is worth seeing, but Natural Bridge is now a small tourist-industry enclave, with a cavern (45-minute tours depart every 30 minutes), department-store-size souvenir shop, restaurant, hotel, campground, and wax museum. Nearby is a small, independently operated zoo.

There are no guided tours, but the bridge itself is an easy quarter-mile walk from the visitor center. From there, the 1-mile-long Cedar Creek Trail descends past a cave, a waterfall, and a 1,500-year-old arbor vitae tree. The bridge is open daily from 8am to dusk. During summer, a 45-minute sound-and-light show called "The Drama of Creation" begins at dusk beneath the bridge.

Admission to the bridge and show is $8 for adults, $4 for children 6 to 15. Combination tickets to the museum or caverns cost $7 adults, $3.50 children 6 to 15; to any 2 attractions, $12 adults, $5.50 children 6 to 15; to the bridge, wax museum, and caverns, $15 for adults, $7.50 for children 6 to 15. The bridge is located 12 miles south of Lexington on U.S. 11 (take Exit 175 off I-81). For more information, or to book a hotel room or campsite here, contact Natural Bridge, P.O. Box 57, Natural Bridge, VA 24578 (☎ **800/533-1410** or 540/291-2121; fax 540/291-1896; www.naturalbridgeva.com).

OUTDOOR PURSUITS

An avid outdoorsman, cohost John Roberts at **Llewellyn Lodge** organizes fly-fishing trips and hiking expeditions into the nearby hills and mountains (see "Where to Stay," below).

CANOEING, KAYAKING & RAFTING   The Maury River, which runs through Lexington, provides some of Virginia's best white-water rafting and kayaking, especially through the Goshen Pass, on Va. 39 northwest of town. The visitor center has information about several put-in spots, or you can rent equipment or go on expeditions on the Maury and James rivers with **James River Basin Canoe Livery,** U.S. 60 East (Route 4, Box 125), Lexington, VA 24450 (☎ **540/261-7334;** www.virtualcities.com/ons/va/r/varb501.htm; e-mail: canoeva@rockbridge.net). Call, write, or e-mail for schedules and reservations.

HIKING   Two linear parks connect to offer hikers and joggers nearly 10 miles of gorgeous trail between Lexington and Buena Vista, a railroad town 7 miles to the southeast. The major link is the **Chessie Nature Trail,** which follows an old railroad bed along the Maury River between Lexington and Buena Vista. No vehicles (including bicycles) are allowed, but you can cross-country ski the trail during winter. The Chessie trail connects with a walking path in **Woods Creek Park,** which starts at the Waddell School on Jordan Street and runs down to the banks of the Maury. Both trails are open from dawn to dusk. The visitor center has maps and brochures.

There are excellent hiking, mountain-biking, horseback-riding, and all-terrain-vehicle trails in the **George Washington National Forest,** which encompasses much of the Blue Ridge Mountains east of Lexington. Small children might not be able to make it, but the rest of the family will enjoy the 3-mile trail up to **Crabtree Falls,** a series of cascades tumbling 1,200 feet down the mountain (it's the highest waterfall in Virginia). Heartier hikers can scale on up to the Appalachian Trail at the top of the mountain. Crabtree Falls is on Va. 56 east of the Blue Ridge Parkway; from Lexington, go north on I-81 to Steeles Tavern (Exit 205), then east on Va. 56.

The National Forest Service has an **information office** at Natural Bridge (☎ **540/ 291-1806**), which offers free maps of trails and campgrounds. It's open daily from 9:30am to 5:30pm, April to mid-November. Or you can contact the Glenwood Ranger District, George Washington and Jefferson national forests, P.O. Box 10, Natural Bridge Station, VA 24579 (☎ **540/291-2188;** www.fs.fed.us/gwjnf).

SHOPPING

Lexington's charming 19th-century downtown offers about a dozen interesting shops and art galleries, most of them on Main and Washington streets. **Artists in Cahoots,** in the Alexander-Witherow House, at the corner of Main and Washington (☎ **540/ 464-1147**), is a cooperative venture run by local artists and craftspeople, featuring an outstanding selection of paintings, sculptures, wood and metal crafts, hand-painted silk scarves, handblown glass, Shaker-style furniture, photographs, prints, decoys, stained glass, and jewelry. **Virginia Born & Bred,** 16 W. Washington St. (☎ **540/ 463-1832**), has made-in-Virginia gifts.

Antiques hunters will find fascinating browsing at the **Lexington Antique & Craft Mall** (☎ **540/463-9511**), in which 250 dealers occupy 40,000 square feet of space. They offer country and formal furniture, glassware, books, quilts, folk art, and much more. The mall is located in the Kroger Shopping Center on U.S. 11, about half a mile north of downtown. It's open Monday through Thursday from 10am to 6pm, Friday and Saturday from 10am to 8pm, Sunday from 12:30 to 5pm; winter hours vary.

WHERE TO STAY

Lexington has several chain motels, especially at the intersection of U.S. 11 and I-64 (Exit 55), 1½ miles north of downtown. They include the **Best Western Inn at Hunt Ridge** (☎ 800/464-1501 or 540/464-1500), **Comfort Inn** (☎ 800/628-1956 or 540/463-7311), **Econo Lodge** (☎ 800/446-6900 or 540/463-7371), **Holiday Inn Express** (☎ 800/HOLIDAY or 540/463-7351), and **Super 8** (☎ 800/800-8000 or 540/463-7858).

✪ **Hampton Inn Col Alto.** 401 E. Nelson St., Lexington, VA 24450. ☎ **800/ HAMPTON** or 540/463-2223. Fax 540/463-9707. 86 units. A/C TV TEL. $78–$122 double motel room; $150–$225 in manor house. Rates include continental breakfast. AE, DC, DISC, MC, V.

This is certainly no ordinary Hampton Inn—Col Alto is an 1827 manor house built on a plantation that was then on the outskirts of town. The mansion now houses 10 bedrooms comparable to those found in deluxe country inns or B&Bs. An interior designer individually decorated these luxurious quarters with made-in-Virginia linens, reproduction antiques, and bright, vivid paints, wallpapers, and fabrics. Accommodations range in size from huge, light-filled rooms in the front of the house to smaller but more private ones in the rear. One unit even has a semi-round "fan" window of the style much favored by Thomas Jefferson. Two formal parlors on the first floor are available for mansion guests only, who can also choose to have breakfast and the morning newspaper delivered to their rooms. Rooms in the new, L-shaped motel wing next door are somewhat larger than average and have microwave ovens, coffeemakers, robes, and irons and ironing boards; some have balconies overlooking a courtyard with outdoor swimming pool and adjoining whirlpool. There's a small exercise room here, too. Guests in both wings get complimentary continental breakfasts in the original dining room, but it's standard Hampton Inn fare and doesn't live up to the gourmet breakfasts served at most bed-and-breakfasts. The hotel provides horse-drawn carriage rides to downtown from April through October ($3 per person round-trip).

HISTORIC COUNTRY INNS

Make reservations for Alexander-Witherow House, McCampbell Inn, and Maple Hall through **Historic Country Inns,** 11 N. Main St., Lexington, VA 24450 (☎ **877/ 463-2044** or 540/463-2044; fax 540/463-2044; www.innbook.com).

Alexander-Witherow House and McCampbell Inn. 11 N. Main St. ☎ **877/463-2044** or 540/463-2044. Fax 540/463-2044. www.innbook.com. 23 units. A/C TV TEL. $60–$125 double; $145 suite. Rates include extensive continental breakfast. DISC, MC, V. Free parking behind the McCampbell Inn.

The Alexander-Witherow House is a lovely late Georgian town house built in 1789 as a family residence over a store. The ground floor is occupied by Artists in Cahoots (see "Shopping," above). Accommodations are all homey suites with separate living rooms and small kitchens. Comfortable furnishings include wing chairs, four-poster beds, and hooked rugs on wide-board floors. The McCampbell Inn, across Main Street, houses the main office for Historic Country Inns; guests at both hostelries eat breakfast here. Begun in 1809, with later additions in 1816 and 1857, it occupies a rambling building, with rooms facing both Main Street and the quieter back courtyard. Furnishings are a pleasant mix of antiques and reproductions; all units have wet bars and refrigerators.

✪ **Maple Hall.** 3111 N. Lee Hwy. (U.S. 11), Lexington, VA 24450. ☎ **877/463-2044** or 540/463-6693. Fax 540/463-2044. www.innbook.com. 21 units. A/C TV TEL. $100–$165 double. Rates include breakfast. DISC, MC, V. Take U.S. 11, 7 miles north of town; house is near Exit 195 of I-81.

Set on 56 rolling acres, this handsome red-brick, white-columned 1850 plantation house offers a restful country retreat. Old boxwoods surround the inn, which consists of a main house, a restored Guest House, and a Pond House. Rooms are individually furnished, many with antiques, Oriental rugs, and massive Victorian pieces; 10 units have gas fireplaces. The Guest House has a living room, kitchen, and three bedrooms with baths. The Pond House, added in 1990, contains four suites and two mini-suites. Guests relax on the shaded patio, on porches with rocking chairs, and on back verandahs overlooking the fishing pond and nearby hills. A pool, tennis court, and 3-mile hiking trail are on-site.

Elegant dining in pretty garden-like surroundings attracts a good following to the Maple Hall restaurant, open daily for dinner. Specialties might include grilled quail, chicken breast sauté Provençale, and filet mignon wrapped in bacon and served with béarnaise sauce.

BED & BREAKFASTS

In addition to those mentioned below, Lexington has several other bed-and-breakfasts; the visitor center offers a complete list.

Llewellyn Lodge. 603 S. Main St., Lexington, VA 24450. ☎ **800/882-1145** or 540/463-3235. Fax 540/464-3122. www.llodge.com. E-mail: LLL@rockbridge.net. 6 units. A/C TV. $65–$98 double. Rates include full breakfast. AE, DC, DISC, MC, V. Free on-site parking.

A 55-year-old brick colonial-style house, the Llewellyn Lodge is within easy walking distance of all of Lexington's historic sites. On the first floor are a cozy sitting room with working fireplace and a TV room. Guest rooms are decorated in exceptionally pretty color schemes. All rooms have ceiling fans, and three have TVs. Cohost John Roberts has hiked just about every trail and fished every stream in the Blue Ridge Mountains, and organizes fly-fishing and hiking expeditions (see "Outdoor Pursuits," above).

WHERE TO DINE

While you're walking around town, stop in at Lexington's famous **Sweet Things,** 106 W. Washington St., between Jefferson Street and Lee Avenue (☎ **540/463-6055**), for a cone or cup of "designer" ice cream or frozen yogurt. It's open Monday to Saturday noon to 10:30pm, Sunday 2 to 9:30pm. Television weatherman Willard Scott raves about the fresh pastries at **Country Kitchen Bakery,** 8 N. Main St., between Washington and Henry streets (☎ **540/463-5691**). It's open Tuesday through Friday from 7am to 5pm, Saturday from 7am to 2pm, and is a great place for a sugar high.

The Palms. 101 W. Nelson St. (at Jefferson St.). ☎ **540/463-7911.** Sandwiches, burgers, and salads $4–$7; main courses $7–$15. AE, DC, DISC, MC, V. Mon–Tues 10am–1am; Wed–Sat 10am–2am; Sun 10am–11pm. AMERICAN.

With neon palms in its storefront window, this lively, popular pub draws town and gown alike with its substantial (if uninspired) fare, sports TVs, and friendly bar. At lunch or dinner, the hearty burgers will not disappoint. Deli sandwiches run the gamut from roast beef to smoked turkey. Mexican specialties like tacos and burritos spice up the menu. Dinner entrees, served with soup or salad, vegetable, and bread, include choices like baby-back ribs, grilled mahimahi, and fettucine Alfredo either plain or with shrimp, chicken, ham, or vegetables.

✪ **Willson-Walker House Restaurant.** 30 N. Main St. (between Washington and Henry sts.). ☎ **540/463-3020.** Reservations requested. Lunch $5–$9; main courses $10–$20. AE, MC, V. Tues–Sat 11:30am–2:30pm and 5:30–9pm. Closed for Sat lunch Jan–Mar. AMERICAN.

Occupying the first floor of an 1820 Greek Revival town house and furnished with period antiques, this distinctive restaurant offers some of the valley's finest cuisine. In good weather, the most popular tables are on first- and second-floor verandahs behind massive two-story white columns. At lunch, the $5 chef's special includes choice of soup or salad, entree, homemade muffins and rolls, and beverage. Changing weekly, the menu offers such tempting starters as crêpes filled with Scottish smoked salmon, dill cream cheese, capers, and red onions. Main courses might include potato crusted

North Carolina rainbow trout or Chesapeake Bay rockfish (sea bass) with tomato and chive sauce. The best of Virginia wines are available by the bottle.

LEXINGTON AFTER DARK

The ruins of an old limestone kiln provide the backdrop for the open-air **Theater at Lime Kiln,** Borden Road off U.S. 60W, which presents musicals, plays, and concerts from Memorial Day to Labor Day. Productions have ranged from a Civil War epic called *Stonewall Country,* based on Jackson's life, to Shakespeare, Appalachian folk-tales, and even water puppeteers from Vietnam. Tickets to plays and musicals cost $11 to $16; to concerts, $16 to $22. The in-town box office is at 14 S. Randolph St., between Nelson and Washington streets (☎ **540/463-3074;** www.cfw.com/limekiln). To reach the theater from downtown Lexington, take U.S. 11 south and turn right onto U.S. 60W.

Roanoke & the Southwest Highlands

8

You soon notice after leaving the vibrant, railroad-oriented city of Roanoke that I-81 begins to climb as it heads into Virginia's Southwest Highlands, the state's increasingly narrow "tail" hemmed in by West Virginia, Kentucky, Tennessee, and North Carolina. Down the center of the Highlands runs the rolling Great Valley of Virginia, whose floor averages 2,000 feet in altitude. Just as they delineate the Shenandoah Valley, the Blue Ridge Mountains form the eastern boundary of the Southwest Highlands, but here are dwarfed by the ridges to the west. While peaks above 4,000 feet are rare up in the Shenandoah, here they regularly exceed that altitude, with Mount Rogers reaching 5,729 feet, the highest point in Virginia.

Thousands of acres of this beautiful country are preserved in the Jefferson National Forest and in Mount Rogers National Recreation Area, which rivals the Shenandoah National Park with 300 miles of hiking and riding trails, including its own stretch of the Appalachian Trail. Two other major routes, the Virginia Creeper and New River Trails, lure both hikers and bikers to follow old railroad beds along river banks.

Like all Virginians, the Highlanders are justly proud of their history, which includes Daniel Boone's blazing the Wilderness Road through these mountains, plateaus, and hollows to Cumberland Gap and on into Kentucky. Gorgeous Abingdon and other small towns still have log cabins from those frontier days.

The Highlanders have also preserved their ancient arts, crafts, and renowned mountain music. Abingdon hosts both Virginia's official state theater and its Highlands Festival, one of America's top annual arts and crafts shows. The coal-mining town of Big Stone Gap has its own drama about mountain life. The famous Carter family makes mountain music at tiny Maces Spring, and fiddlers from around the world gather every August for their old-time convention at Galax.

Whether you love history, drama, music, arts, crafts, the great outdoors, or all of the above, you will be enchanted with Virginia's beautiful Southwest Highlands.

EXPLORING THE SOUTHWEST HIGHLANDS

VISITOR INFORMATION   A one-stop source for regional information is the **Highlands Gateway Visitor Center,** Drawer B-12, Max Meadows, VA 24360 (☎ **800/446-9670** or 540/637-6766; www.virginiablueridge.org; e-mail: vsbrh2@naxs.com). Funded by the state and the National Forest Service, this state-of-the-art center is located in the Factory Merchants Outlet Mall, 10 miles northeast of Wytheville at Exit 80 off the joint I-81/I-77. It offers brochures from all towns in the region, a touch-screen computer, and a small theater showing a video about the Highlands. It sells National Forest topographic maps, Appalachian Trail maps and guidebooks—even mountain music tapes and Smokey the Bear dolls. The center is open Monday through Saturday from 9am to 5pm (10am to 5pm in January and February), Sunday from noon to 5pm.

GETTING THERE & GETTING AROUND   Given the distances, the lack of public transportation, and the need to be able to explore the area's spectacular scenery at leisure, traveling by car is the only way to go. I-81 runs the entire length of the highlands and is its major thoroughfare. U.S. 11 follows I-81, and the Blue Ridge Parkway parallels it to the east. I-77 cuts north-south through the center of the region (the section from Wytheville north to Bluefield, West Virginia, is one of America's most dramatically scenic interstates). Otherwise, byways in the region are mountain roads—narrow, winding, and sometimes steep—so give yourself ample time to reach your destination.

The area's only air gateway is **Roanoke Regional Airport** (see "Getting There" under "Roanoke: City Below a Star," below). The nearest **Amtrak** (☎ **800/ 872-7245;** www.amtrak.com) station is in Clifton Forge, 45 miles northwest of Roanoke on I-64. Amtrak has a Thruway bus connection from Clifton Forge to Roanoke.

1 The Blue Ridge Parkway

Maintained by the National Park Service, the 469-mile Blue Ridge Parkway links the Shenandoah National Park in Virginia to the Great Smoky Mountains National Park in North Carolina. It begins at the southern terminus of the Skyline Drive and winds southwest through the Blue Ridge Mountains. Magnificent vistas and the natural beauty of the forests, wildlife, and wildflowers combine with pioneer history to make this a fascinating route.

Consider driving between Lexington and Roanoke via the northern section. Beyond Roanoke, the parkway runs through lower country, with more meadows and less mountain scenery. On the other hand, the 62-mile stretch between Otter Creek south to Roanoke Mountain crosses the James River Gorge; climbs Apple Orchard Mountain, the highest parkway point in Virginia (elevation 3,950 feet); and has the most spectacular overlooks and the best selection of visitor activities. At times, the road here follows the ridgeline, rendering spectacular views down both sides of the mountains at once. It also leads to the Peaks of Otter Lodge, the only place actually on the parkway where you can spend the night (see "Where to Stay," below).

There are about 100 **hiking trails** along the route, including the Appalachian Trail, which follows the parkway from Mile 0 to about Mile 103. Most trails are at or near the visitor centers (see below), which distribute free trail maps.

ESSENTIALS

ACCESS POINTS & ORIENTATION   The northern parkway entrance is near Waynesboro at the southern end of the Skyline Drive, on U.S. 250 at Exit 99 off I-64. The major access points in Virginia are U.S. 60 east of Buena Vista; U.S. 501 between Buena Vista and Lynchburg (Otter Creek and the James River Gorge); U.S. 460, Va. 24, and U.S. 220 near Roanoke; U.S. 58 at Meadows of Dan; and I-77 at Fancy Gap.

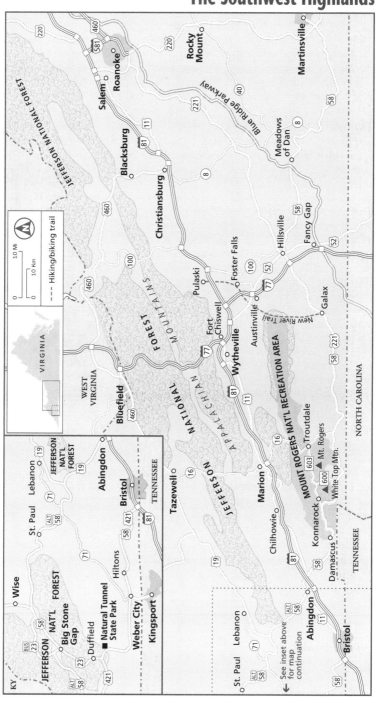

Unlike the Skyline Drive, which is surrounded by a national park, the parkway for most of its route runs through mountain meadows, private farmland, and forests (some but not all of them national forests). Nature hikes, camping, and other visitor activities are largely confined to the visitor centers and to more than 200 overlooks.

Mile Posts on the west side of the parkway begin with zero at the northern Rockfish Gap entry and increase as you head south. The North Carolina border is at Mile 218.

INFORMATION   For general information, contact the **National Park Service (NPS),** 400 BB&T Building, Asheville, NC 28801 (☎ **828/298-0398** for recorded information, or 828/271-4779; www.nps.gov/blri). The NPS sends out a brochure with an excellent map of the parkway, and can provide specific information about hiking trails, campgrounds, and bicycling as well. You can also get an information packet, including a copy of *The Blue Ridge Parkway Directory,* from the **Blue Ridge Parkway Association,** P.O. Box 2136, Asheville, NC 28802 (☎ **828/298-0398**). Also available at the parkway's visitor centers, the association's directory offers a wealth of information, including maps and descriptions of nearby attractions, shops, lodging, and restaurants, and a calendar showing when the wildflowers bloom. The visitor centers also sell books about the parkway (check out the park service's reading list at www.nps.gov/blri/bblgrphy.htm). Among the best are the detailed *Blue Ridge Parkway: Rockfish Gap to Grandfather Mountain* by William G. Lord (Menasha Ridge Press, Birmingham, AL, $6.95), and an excellent book for hikers, *Walking the Blue Ridge: A Guide to the Trails of the Blue Ridge Parkway,* by Leonard M. Adkins (University of North Carolina Press, Chapel Hill, $12.95).

For more books, contact the **National Park Bookstore,** 470 Maryland Dr., Suite 2, Ft. Washington, PA 19034-9684 (☎ **877/NAT-PARK;** fax 215/591-0303; www.nationalparkbooks.org).

EMERGENCIES   Call ☎ **1-800/PARK-WATCH** in case of emergencies anywhere along the parkway.

FEES, REGULATIONS & BACKCOUNTRY PERMITS   There is no fee for using the parkway. Maximum speed limit is 45 m.p.h. in rural areas, 35 m.p.h. in built-up zones. Bicycles are allowed only on paved roads and parking areas, not on any trails. Camping is permitted only in designated areas (see "Camping," below). Fires are permitted in campgrounds and picnic areas only. Hunting is prohibited. Pets must be kept on a leash. No swimming is allowed in parkway ponds and lakes.

VISITOR CENTERS   Several visitor centers are located along the parkway, including one at **Rockfish Gap** (Mile 0), which is open year-round. Others are closed from November to March. Since the centers are the focal points of most visitor activities, here's a rundown:

- **Humpback Rocks Visitor Center** (Mile 5.8) has picnic tables, rest rooms, and a self-guiding trail to a reconstructed mountain homestead.
- **James River Visitor Center** (Mile 63.6), near U.S. 501 northwest of Lynchburg, has a footbridge that crosses the river to the restored canal locks, exhibits, and a nature trail. Otter Creek wayside has a daytime restaurant and campground just up the road.
- **Peaks of Otter** (Mile 85.9), at Va. 43 northwest of Bedford, has a 2-mile hike to the site of a historic farm, wildlife and Native American exhibits, rest rooms, and the Peaks of Otter Lodge (see "Where to Stay," below), which looks across a picturesque little lake to the appropriately named Sharp Top Mountain. A trail leads to the top of this 3,875-foot peak, or you can take the campstore's **shuttle bus** (☎ **540/586-1614**) to within 1,500 feet of the peak (allow 1½ hours to

hike to the peak and back, and wear comfortable shoes). The bus runs May 1 through October, daily from 10am to 5pm, every hour on the hour. Round-trip fares are $3.75 for adults, $2.25 for children under 12.

- **Rocky Knob** (Mile 167.1), southeast of Va. 8, has some 15 miles of hiking trails (including the Rock Castle Gorge National Recreational Trail), a comfort station, and a picnic area.
- **Mabry Mill** (Mile 176), between Va. 8 and U.S. 58, has a picturesque gristmill with a giant wheel spanning a little stream. Displays of pioneer life, including crafts demonstrations, are featured, and the restored mill still grinds flour. A restaurant, open May through October, adjoins it.

SEASONS   The parkway is at its best during spring, when the wildflowers bloom and young leaves are multi-hued green, and during mid-October, when changing leaves are at their blazing best (and traffic is at its heaviest).

ON THE WINE TRAIL   At Mile 171.5, between Va. 8 and U.S. 58 north of Mabry Mill, you can turn off on C.R. 726 and follow the signs to **Chateau Morrisette** (☎ **540/593-2865;** www.chateaumorririsette.com), a vineyard which produces Black Dog and Our Dog Blue, two of Virginia's most popular red wines. It's open for tastings and sales Monday to Saturday 10am to 5pm, Sunday 11am to 5pm. There's a restaurant on the premises.

CAMPING

Campgrounds are at **Otter Creek,** Mile 60.8; **Peaks of Otter,** Mile 86; **Roanoke Mountain,** Mile 120.4; and **Rocky Knob,** Mile 174.1. The Roanoke Mountain campground is actually on Mill Mountain, about 1 mile west of the parkway above the city of Roanoke (see "Roanoke: City Below a Star," below).

Campgrounds are open from about May 1 to early November, depending on weather conditions. Drinking water and rest rooms are available, but shower and laundry facilities are not. There are tent and trailer sites, but none have utility connections. The charge per night for each site is $12 for two adults, $2 extra for each additional adult, and free for children under 18. Golden Age and Golden Access Passport holders are entitled to a 50% discount. Daily permits are valid only at the campground where purchased.

Cabins are available at **Rocky Knob Cabins,** Meadows of Dan, VA 24120 (☎ **540/593-3503**).

WHERE TO STAY

Peaks of Otter Lodge (see below) is the only concessionaire-operated accommodation right on the parkway. Hotels and motels are available a short distance away in Roanoke (see "Where to Stay" in section 2, below).

At Mile 189, near I-77 and the North Carolina border, **Doe Run Lodge,** P.O. Box 280, Fancy Gap, VA 24328 (☎ **800/325-6189** or 540/398-2212; fax 540/398-2833; www.dorerunlodge.com; e-mail: doerun@tcia.net), has hotel rooms, romantic suites with whirlpool tubs, a fine-dining restaurant, a swimming pool, tennis courts, and hiking trails.

Peaks of Otter Lodge. Milepost 86 (P.O. Box 489), Bedford, VA 24523. ☎ **800/542-5927** in Virginia and North Carolina, or 540/586-1081. www.peaksofotter.com. 63 units. A/C. $76 double; $98–$108 suite. MC, V.

At Peaks of Otter, everything is in harmony with nature, from the lakeside mountain setting to the rustic room decor of natural rough-grained wood with slate-top furnishings. Split-rail fences and small footbridges add to the picturesque beauty of this serene valley. The main lodge building has a restaurant, a crafts and gift shop, and a game and TV room with a view of the lake. Accommodations are in motel-like attached units on a grassy slope overlooking the lake. All rooms have private balconies or terraces to maximize the splendid view, but only suites have TVs and phones. Reservations are accepted beginning October 1 for the *following* year's fall foliage season. Winter and early spring are not overly crowded, but reservations should be made 4 to 6 weeks ahead for all good-weather months.

The lodge's dining room is low-key and pleasant, with a cathedral ceiling, hanging plants, and windows overlooking the lake. Reasonably priced American fare is served at all three meals; there is also a full bar. The parkway's Peaks of Otter visitor center is located here (see "Essentials," above).

2 Roanoke: City Below a Star

54 miles SW of Lexington; 74 miles NE of Wytheville; 193 miles SW of Richmond; 251 miles SW of Washington, D.C.

Sprawling across the floor of the Roanoke Valley, Virginia's largest metropolitan area west of Richmond likes to call itself the "Capital of the Blue Ridge." Roanoke is also known as "Star City," for the huge lighted star overlooking the city from Mill Mountain, which stands between it and the Blue Ridge Parkway.

There was no star on the mountain when colonial explorers followed the Roanoke River gorge through the Blue Ridge Mountains in the 17th century. They established several small settlements in the Roanoke Valley, including one named Big Lick. When the Norfolk and Western Railroad arrived in the 1880s and laid out a town for future development, it decided that *Roanoke*—a Native American word for "shell money"— was a much more prosperous-sounding name for its new city than Big Lick. Although Roanoke is still a major railroad junction (as the many tracks running through downtown will attest), its economy suffered when the interstate highway system shifted most freight from boxcars to trucks in the mid–20th century. Milestones in its recovery have been the construction of the Civic Center and a convention and cultural complex, and the restoration of the now trendy Market Square area around the Historic City Market.

With its zoo and its hands-on educational museums, Roanoke has special appeal for children. Families can easily spend a full day and more exploring its sights.

ESSENTIALS
VISITOR INFORMATION
Contact the **Roanoke Convention and Visitors Bureau,** 114 Market St., Roanoke, VA 24011 (☎ **800/635-5535** or 540/342-6025; fax 540/342-7119; www. visitroanokeva.com; e-mail: rvcvb@rbnet.com). Just a few doors north of Market Square, the bureau's visitor center is the best place to pick up maps and brochures for walking and biking tours before starting your exploration of Roanoke. It's open daily from 9am to 5pm.

If you're arriving via the Blue Ridge Parkway, there's a welcome center at **Virginia's Explore Park,** at Mile 115 (☎ **800/842-9163** or 540/427-3054). See "Attractions on or Near Mill Mountain," below. It's open during park hours from April through December.

GETTING THERE
BY PLANE   Roanoke Regional Airport (☎ **540/362-1999**), 5½ miles northwest of downtown off Hershberger Road (Exit 3E off I-581), is served by Delta Connection, Northwest Airlink, United Express, and US Airways. The major car-rental firms

Roanoke

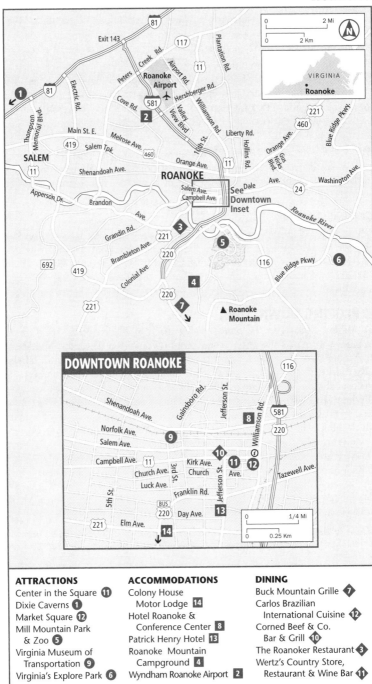

DOWNTOWN ROANOKE

ATTRACTIONS
Center in the Square ⓫
Dixie Caverns ❶
Market Square ⓬
Mill Mountain Park & Zoo ❺
Virginia Museum of Transportation ❾
Virginia's Explore Park ❻

ACCOMMODATIONS
Colony House Motor Lodge ⓮
Hotel Roanoke & Conference Center ❽
Patrick Henry Hotel ⓭
Roanoke Mountain Campground ❹
Wyndham Roanoke Airport ❷

DINING
Buck Mountain Grille ❼
Carlos Brazilian International Cuisine ⓬
Corned Beef & Co. Bar & Grill ❿
The Roanoker Restaurant ❸
Wertz's Country Store, Restaurant & Wine Bar ⓫

have booths on-site. **Roanoke Airport Limousine Service** (☎ 800/228-1958 or 540/345-7710) runs vans to downtown and to points as far away as Abingdon (see section 5, below) and throughout the Shenandoah Valley (see chapter 7). The fare to downtown is $12 for the first passenger, $2 for each additional person.

BY CAR   From I-81, take I-581 (Exit 143) south into the heart of Roanoke. I-581 becomes U.S. 220; together, they form an expressway which passes all the way through town. The Blue Ridge Parkway runs along the top of the mountains east of the city; the major Roanoke exits are at U.S. 460, Va. 24, the Mill Mountain Spur Road (at Mile 120), and U.S. 220.

BY TRAIN   Amtrak (☎ 800/872-7245; www.amtrak.com) provides Thruway bus connections daily between Roanoke and its stations in Lynchburg to the east and to the west at Clifton Forge, on I-64 west of Lexington. Either is about an hour's bus ride away.

GETTING AROUND

Yellow Cab (☎ 540/345-7711) is the largest taxi company here. **Valley Metro** provides public bus service Monday through Saturday from 5:45am to 8:45pm. The downtown transfer point is Campbell Court, 17 W. Campbell Ave. Call ☎ 540/982-2222 for schedules and fares. The visitor center distributes free Ride Guide route maps.

EXPLORING DOWNTOWN

✪ **Market Square,** in the center of downtown at Market Street and Campbell Avenue, is Roanoke's answer to Georgetown in Washington, D.C., and Shockoe Slip in Richmond. As they have for more than a century, stands and shops at the **Historic City Market** display plants, flowers, fresh fruits and vegetables, dairy and eggs, and farm-cured meats. Nearby, restored Victorian-era storefronts house trendy restaurants, gift shops, art galleries, clothiers, a book-and-music emporium, and an Orvis outdoor-wear outlet. Of special note are two spiffed-up relics from the past: **Agnew Seed Store,** which still uses its old-fashioned oak drawers, and **Wertz's Country Store,** carrying a gourmet selection of local produce which is converted into meals (see "Where to Dine," below).

Built of red brick in 1922, the **Market Building** now houses a food court offering the downtown lunch crowd an inexpensive international menu, from Chinese egg rolls to North Carolina–style barbecue. The market and food court are open Monday through Saturday.

Center in the Square. 1 Market Square SE (at Campbell Ave.). ☎ 540/342-5700. www.centerinthesquare.org. Free admission (see museums below). Museums, Tues–Sat 10am–5pm, Sun 1–5pm.

This five-story converted warehouse is home to the Mill Mountain Theatre (see "Roanoke After Dark," below) and three good local museums:

- **Art Museum of Western Virginia** (☎ 540/342-5760; www.artmuseumroanoke.org) focuses on 19th- and 20th-century American art from the region, including the decorative arts. There's an interactive art center and a museum store. Call or check the Web site for special exhibits. Admission is free (suggested donation $4 adults, $2 children under 18).
- **History Museum of Western Virginia** (☎ 540/342-5770; www.historymuseum.org) houses documents, tools, costumes, and weapons that tell the story of Roanoke from American Indian days 10,000 years ago through pioneer days 2 centuries ago to the present. The museum shop carries historic items, wooden

and tin toys, and locally made quilts. Admission is $2 for adults, $1 for seniors and children 6 to 12, free for children under 6.

- **Science Museum of Western Virginia** (☎ **540/342-5710;** www.smwv.org) will intrigue children with its high-tech interactive exhibits. A weather gallery features a tornado simulator and a Weather Channel–like studio; the Hopkins Planetarium offers programs related to the stars, planets, and galaxies; the MegaDome Theatre shows large format 70mm films; and you can surf the Internet in the SuperNet Gallery 350 times faster than normal. The museum store on the ground level offers a fascinating collection of educational toys. Admission to the exhibits is $6 for adults, $5 for seniors, $4 for children 3 to 12, and free for children under 3. Planetarium and MegaDome shows cost $5 adults, $4 children 3 to 12.

Virginia Museum of Transportation. 303 Norfolk Ave. (at 3rd St.). ☎ **540/342-5670.** www.vmt.org. Admission $5 adults, $4 seniors, $3 students 13–18, free for children under 13. Mon–Sat 10am–5pm, Sun noon–5pm.

In a restored freight depot 5 blocks west of Market Square, this museum is a work in progress, with aviation, space, and canal exhibits being added to an already fine collection of railroad rolling stock being restored on the tracks out back. You can climb aboard the steam and diesel locomotives, cabooses, and other cars. Inside, the automotive section has buggies, an 1895 horse-drawn hearse, and several automobiles, including a 1950 "bullet nose" Studebaker. The aviation section is due to be greatly expanded. In the meantime, there's a small but interesting "Eagles of the Valley" exhibit chronicling the history of local flyers, one of whom was Chauncey Spencer, son of Harlem Renaissance poet Anne Spencer of Lynchburg. He organized the first African-American air show in 1938 and was partially responsible for President Roosevelt's executive order banning racial discrimination in the military. There are no guided tours. You'll need at least an hour here, about 2½ to thoroughly digest all the exhibits.

ATTRACTIONS ON OR NEAR MILL MOUNTAIN

Situated between the city and the Blue Ridge Parkway, Mill Mountain offers panoramic views over Roanoke Valley. The two main attractions are in **Mill Mountain Park,** on the Mill Mountain Parkway Spur, a winding road that leaves the Blue Ridge Parkway at Mile 120. From the city, take Walnut Avenue, which becomes the J. P. Fishburn Parkway and intersects the Mill Mountain Parkway Spur at the entry to Mill Mountain Park.

Local citizens know they're home when they can see the white neon **Roanoke Star on the Mountain.** Erected in 1949 as a civic pride project, it stands 88½ feet tall, uses 2,000 feet of neon tubing, and is visible from most parts of the city. Stop at the base for a magnificent view over the city and valley.

Mill Mountain Zoo. Mill Mountain Pkwy. Spur (in Mill Mountain Park). ☎ **540/ 343-3241.** www.mmzoo.org. Admission $5 adults, $4.50 seniors, $3 children 3–11, free for children under 3. Train rides $1.50. Daily 10am–5pm.

This small zoo plans to expand from 3 acres to 11 acres and enlarge its enclosures by 2001—a much needed improvement, since most animals have lived in cages and small outdoor areas since the zoo was founded in the 1940s. Only the solitary Siberian tiger has had room to roam. More than 50 other animal species live here, including snow leopards, monkeys, prairie dogs, hawks, red pandas, and Japanese macaques (a bald eagle should be in residence by 2001). An open-air, narrow gauge train runs around the periphery, giving access to red wolves and deer, which you can't see from the walking paths.

✪ **Virginia's Explore Park.** Roanoke River Pkwy. ☎ **540/427-1800.** www. explorepark.com. Admission $8 adults, $7 seniors, $4.50 students 6–18, free for children under 6. Apr, Sat 10am–5pm, Sun noon–5pm; May–Oct, Wed–Sat 10am–5pm, Sun noon–5pm. Brugh Tavern, Apr, Sat 11:30am–2pm and 5–10pm, Sun 11:30am–2pm and 5–9pm; May–Oct, Sun–Thurs 11:30am–2pm and 5–9pm, Fri–Sat 11:30am–2pm and 5–10pm. From Mill Mountain, take Mill Mountain Pkwy. Spur to Blue Ridge Pkwy., turn left, go to Mile Post 115, turn right on Roanoke River Pkwy. to park.

It's a scenic 7-mile drive from Mill Mountain to this 1,300-acre reserve on the south side of the gorge cut by the Roanoke River on its way through the Blue Ridge. Like the Frontier Culture Museum in Staunton (see section 7 in chapter 7), the park sports reconstructed settlements which show what life was like in these parts circa 1671, 1740, and 1850. Down at the riverside are a bateau (a flat-bottomed boat like those used for river transport before railroads) and a cabin like those in which the bateaumen lived. Begin at the welcome center, where a 13-minute video will set the scene. Then allow about 2 hours for a self-guided tour of the historic areas. You can take a break at the moderately priced Brugh Tavern (appropriately pronounced "Brew"), which serves lunch and dinner.

More than 1,000 acres of the park's hills and wetlands have been set aside as a natural area. You can hike or mountain-bike on 8 miles of trails, and go canoeing on the river. On-site bike and canoe rentals are provided by **Appalachian Adventures** (☎ **540/342-2858;** www.zip2.com/roanoke/adventure; e-mail: tanmorgan@aol.com).

DIXIE CAVERNS

If you didn't go underground in the Shenandoah Valley, you can do so at **Dixie Caverns,** on U.S. 11/460 near Exit 132 off I-81 about 5 miles southwest of Salem (☎ **540/380-2085**). These caves are best known for a huge dome-like structure called the Wedding Bell (yes, a few couples actually get married here each year) and an underground lake called the Magic Mirror. Mandatory 45-minute guided tours depart every 20 minutes. Admission is $6.50 for adults, $3.50 for children 5 to 12. The caverns are open daily from 9:30am to 6pm in summer, daily from 9:30am to 5pm the rest of the year; closed Christmas Day.

Vendors sell antiques, collectibles, rocks, and minerals in the main building. You can also **camp** here, with wooded hookup sites going for $18 for two persons, tent spaces for $6 per person.

WHERE TO STAY

Downtown Roanoke has two older chain motels catering to groups attending functions at the adjacent Civic Center: the **Quality Inn Civic Center** (☎ 800/228-5151 or 540/342-8961) and **Days Inn** (☎ 800/325-2525 or 540/342-4551), both on Orange Avenue east of Exit 4 off I-581.

If you're coming off the Blue Ridge Parkway, convenient choices include the **Holiday Inn Tanglewood** (☎ 800/HOLIDAY or 540/774-4400) and **Hampton Inn Tanglewood** (☎ 800/HAMPTON or 540/989-4000), both on Franklin Road near U.S. 220 southeast of downtown.

Near the airport, Herschberger Road (Exit 3 off I-581) has the **Best Western at Valley View** (☎ 800/362-2410 or 540/362-2400), **Clarion Hotel** (☎ 800/ CLARION or 540/362-4500), and **Howard Johnson Express** (☎ 800/654-2000 or 540/563-0229). Farther out, Peters Creek Road (Exit 2 off I-581) has a **Hampton Inn** (☎ 800/HAMPTON or 540/265-2600), the **Holiday Inn Airport** (☎ 800/ HOLIDAY or 540/366-8861), and an inexpensive **Super 8 Roanoke** (☎ 800/ 800-8000 or 540/563-8888).

B&B accommodation is available in town at **Maridor Bed & Breakfast,** 1857 Grandin Rd. (☎ **540/982-1940**), and at **Walnuthill Bed & Breakfast,** 436 Walnut Ave. SE (☎ **540/427-3312;** fax 540/427-0273); and in Salem at **The Inn at Burwell Place,** 601 W. Main St. (☎ **800/891-0250** or 540/387-0250; fax 540/387-3279).

Colony House Motor Lodge. 3560 Franklin Rd. (U.S. 220 Business), Roanoke, VA 24014. ☎ **540/345-0411.** Fax 540/345-0411, ext. 459. 72 units. A/C TV TEL. $59 double. Rates include continental breakfast. AE, DC, DISC, MC, V. From I-581/U.S. 220, exit at Franklin Rd. (U.S. 220 Business), turn left at traffic signal to motel on right. From Blue Ridge Pkwy., take U.S. 220 Business west, exit on Franklin Rd. north to motel on right.

This clean, well-maintained motel enjoys a convenient suburban location in the Tanglewood shopping area, 2 miles south of downtown and 2 miles north of the Blue Ridge Parkway. A series of peaked roofs creates cathedral ceilings in some of the spacious rooms, all of which have unusual louvered screen doors that let in fresh air without sacrificing privacy. About half the rooms are at the rear of the property; they face a steep hillside and get less natural light but also less traffic noise. A small roadside outdoor swimming pool has a view of the Kmart across Franklin Road. Continental breakfast is served in the lobby, and there's a 24-hour Waffle House next door and other chain restaurants nearby.

✪ **Hotel Roanoke & Conference Center.** 110 Shenandoah Ave., Roanoke, VA 24016. ☎ **800/222-TREE** or 540/985-5900. Fax 540/853-8264. www.hotelroanoke.com. 332 units. A/C TV TEL. $99–$145 double; $159–$259 suite. Packages available. AE, DC, DISC, MC, V. Self-parking $5; valet parking $7. From I-581 south, take Exit 5, cross Wells Ave. into parking lot.

The Norfolk and Western Railroad built this grand Tudor-style hotel in a wheat field in 1882, even before it changed the name of Big Lick to Roanoke. Heated by steam from the railroad's maintenance shops and cooled by America's first hotel air-conditioning system (circulating ice water), it became a resort as well as a stopover. Some 26 passenger trains a day rolled into the station at the foot of the hill, and virtually every celebrity passing though Roanoke stayed here, among them William Jennings Bryan, Amelia Earhart, Joe DiMaggio, Jack Dempsey, Elvis Presley, and Presidents Eisenhower, Nixon, Ford, Reagan, and Bush. For the locals, it was *the* place for wedding receptions, reunions, beauty pageants, and other special events.

The hotel was closed from 1989 to 1995, when it reopened after a magnificent, $42 million restoration. Even if you don't stay here, it's worth a walk uphill just to see the rich, black walnut–paneled lobby with its Oriental rugs and leather lounge furniture; the oval-shaped Palm Court lounge with its pineapple central fountain and four lovingly restored murals of colonial and Victorian Virginians dancing the reel, waltz, minuet, and quadrille; and the elegant Regency Room, where waiters in starched tunics deliver the hotel's signature peanut soup.

The building was gutted and rebuilt above the public areas, so all the rooms and suites are completely modern. Given the odd shape of the building, there are now 92 room configurations, many with sloping ceilings and gable windows.

Dining/Diversions: In addition to peanut soup, the Regency Room serves venison, quail, pink speckled trout, sweet-potato chips, and other historic dishes, all at moderate prices. Pub fare is available in the knotty Pine Room, which has a large bar, sports TV, and billiards table.

Amenities: Concierge, room service, laundry, free newspaper, nightly turndown. Outdoor pool, fitness center.

The Patrick Henry Hotel. 617 S. Jefferson St. (at Bullit Ave.), Roanoke, VA 24011. ☎ **800/303-0988** or 540/345-8811. Fax 540/342-9908. www.patrickhenryroanoke.com. 117 units.

$109 double; $125–$185 suite. Packages available. Rates include continental breakfast. Parking $3.25 per day. AE, DC, DISC, MC, V. From I-585, take Elm St. (Exit 6) west, turn right on S. Jefferson St. to the hotel on the left.

A downtown Roanoke landmark since 1925, this mid-rise brick building is the kind of hotel where politicians once cut deals in smoke-filled rooms. The rooms and suites here are some of the largest you'll find anywhere at these prices. All rooms—not only the suites—boast kitchens and modern bathrooms. A marble staircase leads into the two-story lobby, which has massive windows, polished marble floors, Oriental rugs, period furnishings, and a brilliant bas-relief frieze embellishing its ceiling.

Dining: Hunter's Grille specializes in hand-cut steaks and provides room service during lunch and dinner hours.

Amenities: Free airport transportation, newspapers on weekdays, game room, coin-operated laundry. Guests can use the health-club facilities at the local YMCA.

Wyndham Roanoke Airport. 2801 Hershberger Rd. NW, Roanoke, VA 24017. ☎ **800/ WYNDHAM** or 540/563-9300. Fax 540/366-5846. 320 units. A/C TV TEL. $110–$159 double. Weekend rates available. AE, DC, DISC, MC, V. Free parking. From I-581 south, take Exit 3, Hershberger Rd. west; make a right U-turn at the first light; the hotel is on the service road.

With its hacienda-style public areas, the ambience at this eight-story hotel (the former Roanoke Airport Marriott) is much more like Santa Fe or Big Sur than Virginia. Its brick-accented lobby is adorned with decorative objects from Italy, France, and Spain, and Oriental rugs and a huge fireplace create a warm atmosphere. In two mid-rise buildings, the spacious guest rooms are conventionally decorated with inlaid traditional furnishings of dark wood. A concierge level offers upgraded amenities and a private lounge.

Dining/Diversions: Lily's, an inviting room with skylights and high ceilings, is open for all meals. There's also a lobby bar and entertainment lounge.

Amenities: Limited room service, free newspaper, courtesy airport shuttle, indoor and outdoor pools, fitness center, sauna, whirlpool, two lighted tennis courts, gift shop.

Note: Unlike most other properties, this and all other Wyndham hotels charge 95¢ for each outside call to a toll-free number, such as to your long-distance carrier or Internet provider.

A NEARBY MOUNTAIN RESORT

Mountain Lake. Mountain Lake, VA 24136. ☎ **800/346-3334** or 540/626-7121. Fax 540/ 626-7172. www.mountainlakehotel.com. E-mail: mtnlake@swva.net. 92 units, including 16 cottages. TEL. Main hotel $180 double; Chestnut Lodge $220 double. Children 13 and older in parents' unit are charged $35 per day; ages 4–12, $20; ages 3 and under free. Rates include breakfast and dinner. AE, DC, DISC, MC, V. Closed Nov–Apr. From I-81, take Exit 118, U.S. 460 west; turn right onto C.R. 700 and go 7 miles to Mountain Lake.

If you saw the movie *Dirty Dancing*, you're already familiar with this rustic mountaintop resort. Surrounded by a 2,600-acre wildlife conservancy, it consists of a main building (a stately lodge made from rough-cut stone) with clusters of small white-clapboard summer cottages nearby. The lobby has thick rugs over a terra-cotta tile floor and comfortable seating in front of a massive fireplace. Complimentary tea and coffee are kept hot on the sideboard. A stone archway separates the lobby from the adjoining bar and lounge.

The popular parlor suites have Jacuzzis and fireplaces, and some rooms offer full lake views. Dark-wood Chippendale-reproduction furnishings give the decor a warm, traditional look. Cottages are more simply furnished, although guests here enjoy porches with rockers. Chestnut Lodge, a recent addition, is a three-story gray-clapboard building set on the side of a hill. Rooms here are decorated in country style, with fireplaces and private balconies.

Dining: The spacious, stone-walled dining room has large windows offering panoramic lake views—a romantic evening setting. A recent dinner here began with an appetizer of sautéed mushrooms in burgundy sauce, followed by swordfish in sour cream–dill sauce, and chocolate mousse for dessert. There's also a snack bar in the Recreation Barn.

Amenities: Health club with sauna and weight room; tennis; hiking trails; boathouse with canoes and rowboats; fishing; Recreation Barn for Ping-Pong, billiards, and evening entertainment; summer program for children; clothing, souvenir, and sporting-goods shops.

WHERE TO DINE

Roanoke's finest dining is in the Regency Room at the Hotel Roanoke & Conference Center (see "Where to Stay," above).

Market Square (see "Exploring Downtown," above) is one of Virginia's most diverse dining scenes. The block of Campbell Avenue just east of Market Street offers beverages and pastries at **Mill Mountain Coffee & Tea** (☎ 540/342-9404), kebabs and curries at **Nawab Indian Cuisine** (☎ 540/345-5150), and fish and shrimp at **Awful Arthur's Seafood Company** (☎ 540/344-2997). Opposite the stalls on Market Street, **Ernie's Bar & Grill** (☎ 540/982-1131) is a popular spot for breakfast. All are closed on Sunday evening.

✪ **Buck Mountain Grille.** 5002 Franklin Rd. (U.S. 220) (at Blue Ridge Pkwy.). ☎ **540/776-1830.** Reservations recommended Fri and Sat evenings. Main courses $10–$19. AE, DC, DISC, MC, V. Tues–Thurs 11am–3pm and 5–9pm; Fri 11am–3pm and 5–10pm; Sat 5–10pm; Sun 11am–3pm and 5–9pm. From downtown, take Franklin Rd. (U.S. 220) south 7 miles to restaurant on left. From Blue Ridge Pkwy., exit U.S. 220 east, make a U-turn to restaurant on left. INTERNATIONAL.

This roadside, peaked-roof establishment is a fine place for lunch while driving the Blue Ridge Parkway or for dinner while overnighting in Roanoke. Some guests are seated at the counter or in booths, but most dine at glass-over-linen tables in a pleasant dining room. The menu offers a mix of cuisine, with innovative new American and Mediterranean dishes predominating. Nightly specials feature Roanoke's freshest seafood, including crab cakes made with all back fin meat. Vegetarians can choose from several offerings, and a children's menu is available.

✪ **Carlos Brazilian International Cuisine.** 312 Market St. (in Market Sq. south of Campbell St.). ☎ **540/345-7661.** Reservations recommended. Lunch $6–$8; main courses $8–$18. AE, MC, V. Mon–Thurs 11am–2pm and 5–9pm; Fri–Sat 11am–2pm and 5–10pm. BRAZILIAN/INTERNATIONAL.

Brazilian-born chef Carlos Amaral brings exceptional cuisine to downtown Roanoke's Market Square. You'll find both his bright storefront dining room and the darker spaces in the rear packed with patrons at both lunch and dinner. Small table lanterns and flower arrangements create an elegant ambience. The highlights are obviously Brazilian, and include *moquca mineira,* a blend of shrimp, clams, and fish in a slightly spicy tomato sauce and served over rice and thinly sliced onions and green peppers. Chicken sautéed with pineapple, grapes, and fried bananas is another winner. Vegetarians can pick from pastas, Brazilian black beans served with collard greens, or a meatless version of paella Valenciana (there's regular paella, too). Don't be in a hurry: Carlos prepares everything to order.

Corned Beef & Co. Bar and Grill. 107 Jefferson St. (between Campbell and Salem aves.). ☎ **540/342-3354.** Reservations accepted. Salads, sandwiches, burgers $6–$7.50; pizzas $8–$10; main courses $8–$15.50. AE, DC, DISC, MC, V. Mon 11:30am–10pm, Tues–Wed 11:30am–11pm, Fri–Sat 11:30am–2am. AMERICAN.

A block west of Market Square, this lively sports bar emporium—the largest of its kind I've ever seen—occupies almost an entire downtown city block. One room is a sophisticated billiards parlor; another room upstairs has a wall of monstrous TV screens for watching every game being televised at the moment. You can even watch from a rooftop patio during warm weather. There are other sports TVs throughout the building, but the mezzanine above the main entrance is the choice for dining, with less crowd noise. Although having a good time is the main reason to come here, the chow is better than average pub fare. Lunch sees more than 30 choices of deli sandwiches (including the namesake corned), a selection of salads, wood-fired pizzas, and smaller portions of main courses from the dinner menu, such as chicken "diablo" (a breast topped with chopped tomatoes, mushrooms, and cheddar, then piqued with Texas Pete hot sauce).

✪ **The Roanoker Restaurant.** 2522 Colonial Ave. (south of Wonju St.). ☎ **540/344-7746.** Reservations not accepted. Main courses $7–$9. MC, V. Mon–Thurs 7am–9pm; Fri–Sat 7am–10pm; Sun and holidays 8am–9pm. From downtown, go south on Franklin Rd., turn right on Brandon Ave., left on Colonial Ave. From I-581, go south to Colonial Ave. exit, turn left at traffic light on Colonial Ave. to restaurant on left. SOUTHERN.

A very popular local restaurant since 1941, the Roanoker occupies a colonial-style building surrounded by much-needed parking lots. Several dining rooms offer booth seating arranged to provide privacy. Antique signs from Roanoke businesses adorn the walls. Every Roanoker with a car seems to have breakfast here, so fluffy are the biscuits served with spicy sausage gravy. The lunch and dinner menus change daily, depending on available produce. Fresh vegetables may include skillet-fried yellow squash, a mouthwatering Southern favorite.

Wertz's Country Store, Restaurant & Wine Bar. 215 W. Market St. (between Campbell and Kirk aves.). ☎ **540/342-5133.** Reservations not accepted. Meals $7–$19. AE, DISC, MC, V. Mon 11am–3pm, Tues–Sat 11am–3pm and 6–9pm. REGIONAL.

Market Square's famous country store turns its gourmet products into fine salads, sandwiches, and soups at lunchtime (don't miss the rich gumbo if it's offered). In fact, all of the beef, top sirloin, turkey, lamb, and other sandwich meats are cooked on the premises. Dinner sees the addition of main courses such as portobello mushrooms stuffed with crab and shrimp in a puff pastry with a garlic cream sauce. Everything is tasty and fresh at this casual restaurant, a favorite lunch spot for downtown office workers. You can sample wines from Virginia and elsewhere at the downstairs wine bar.

ROANOKE AFTER DARK

Mill Mountain Theatre, in the Center in the Square building on Campbell Avenue (☎ **800/317-6455** or 540/342-5740; www.millmountain.org), offers children's productions, free lunchtime readings (October through May), and year-round matinee and evening performances on two stages. Productions range from Shakespeare to minstrels. Recent performances have included *The Sound of Music, West Side Story, Godspell, A Man For All Seasons,* and *The Tempest.* Tickets prices range from $5 to $25, depending on performance and venue.

Many of the restaurants and pubs at Market Square (see "Exploring Downtown," above) offer live music on weekends, some during the week. Available at the visitor center (see "Essentials," above), the free *City Magazine* has a rundown of who's playing where.

3 Wytheville: Crossroads of the Highlands

74 miles SW of Roanoke; 49 miles NE of Abingdon; 306 miles SW of Washington, D.C.; 247 miles SW of Richmond

Situated on a relatively flat plateau, Wytheville's strategic position in the center of the Highlands has made it a major crossroads since trappers and hunters came into the region in the early 1700s. After a treaty with hostile Native Americans opened Kentucky for settlement in 1775, Daniel Boone built the Wilderness Road through the Highlands to Cumberland Gap. Monroe Street in downtown Wytheville was part of that route, and a few log cabins left over from those days still stand on Main Street.

The Wilderness Road is long gone, but I-81 and I-77 meet here today, giving Wytheville a motel room for every family in town, plus a host of places to dine. Since accommodations are relatively scarce elsewhere in this sparsely populated region, these facilities make Wytheville a well-equipped base from which to explore the New River Trail State Park, Mount Rogers National Recreation Area, and other sights in the central portion of the Highlands.

ESSENTIALS

VISITOR INFORMATION   For advance information, contact the **Wytheville Convention and Visitors Bureau,** 150 E. Monroe St. (P.O. Drawer 533), Wytheville, VA 24382 (☎ **540/223-3355;** fax 540/223-3315; http://visit.wytheville.com; e-mail: info@wytheville.com), which supplies information about the town, including a walking-tour brochure to the historic district. It has a visitor information office in the Municipal Building, at Monroe and 1st streets. Roadside tourist information kiosks are also located at all interstate exits leading into town.

GETTING THERE   I-81 and I-77 meet on the outskirts of Wytheville. To get into town, take Exits 67, 70, or 73 off I-81. U.S. 11 (Main Street) and U.S. 21 meet in downtown.

EXPLORING THE TOWN

Stop at the convention and visitors bureau office in the Municipal Building for a walking-tour brochure explaining the town's historic buildings (see "Essentials," above). An 1830s mayor decided Wytheville needed wide streets to keep fires from spreading, so even though the town dates back to 1757, the broad avenues deprive it of some of the quaintness and charm of other old towns like Lexington and Abingdon.

Wytheville's proximity to the South's only salt mine and an important lead mine led Union troops to attack the crossroads village during the Civil War and burn many historic homes and businesses. One area remained untouched, however, and you will want to examine these **Old Log Houses,** on Main Street (U.S. 11) between 5th and 7th streets. Some of them now house shops and a restaurant, The Log House 1776 Restaurant (see "Where to Dine," below).

Another house that escaped Civil War destruction—but not bullet holes—was the **Rock House Museum,** at Monroe and Tazewell streets (☎ **540/223-3330**). A National and State Historic Landmark, this Pennsylvania-style stone structure was built in 1820. The museum has a collection of historic artifacts from the region. Admission is $2 for adults, $1 for children 6 to 12, and free for children under 6. It's open Tuesday through Friday from 10am to 4pm. Just behind the house on Tazewell Street, the **Thomas J. Boyd Museum** has exhibits on Wytheville's history, including an 1850s fire truck, Civil War relics, and farm equipment. (Same phone, hours, and admission as the Rock House Museum.)

Although it's not open to the public, upstairs in the building at 145 E. Main St., in the business district, was the **Birthplace of Edith Bolling Wilson,** second wife of Staunton-born President Woodrow Wilson.

NEW RIVER TRAIL STATE PARK

With its plethora of accommodations, Wytheville is an excellent base from which to hike, bike, or ride horses on the exceptional ✪ **New River Trail State Park,** which runs 57 miles between Galax and Pulaski. The trail follows an old railroad bed beside the picturesque New River, which despite its name is in geologic terms one of the oldest rivers in the United States (it predates the Appalachian Mountains). The river flows toward the Mississippi River, on its way carving the New River Gorge in southeastern West Virginia, the best white-water rafting spot in the eastern U.S.

The park's headquarters are at **Foster Falls,** an old mining hamlet on Foster Falls Road (C.R. 608), about 20 miles northeast of Wytheville, or 2 miles north of U.S. 52 (take Exit 24 off I-77 and follow the signs). You can enter the trail here daily from 8am to 10pm. Parking costs $2 per vehicle.

Other entries to the trail are at Shot Tower Historical State Park (see below); Draper, near Exit 92 off I-81; Allisonia and Hiwassee, both on C.R. 693; Barren Springs, on Va. 100; Austinville, on Va. 69; Ivanhoe, on Va. 94; Byllesby Dam, on C.R. 602; and Galax, on U.S. 58. There's also a branch trail to Fries, on Va. 94.

Foster Falls Livery (☎ **540/699-1034**) rents bicycles, canoes, inner tubes, and horses. Bikes cost $5 per hour or $18 per day. Canoes start at $7 an hour or $30 per day, plus $10 for a shuttle ride. Tubes go for $10 per day. Call for horse rental information. Overnight canoe and fishing trips are available, too. The livery is open from Memorial Day to Labor Day, Sunday to Thursday 8am to 5pm, Friday and Saturday 8am to 8pm; from April to Memorial Day and from Labor Day through October, Saturday and Sunday from 8am to 3pm. Foster Falls Livery is operated by the park's concessionaire, **New River Adventures, Inc.,** 1007 N. 4th St., Wytheville, VA 24382 (☎ **540/228-8311;** www.newriveradventires.com; e-mail: shackler@naxs.com).

Also check with **New River Bicycles** (☎ **540/980-1741**), **Allisonia Trading Post** (☎ **540/980-2051**), and **Cliffview Trading Post** (☎ **540/238-1530**). The latter is at the Cliffview Ranger Station near Galax and also rents horses. Horse-trailer parking is permitted only at Foster Falls, the Cliffview Ranger Station, and Draper.

For more information, write or call New River Trail State Park, 176 Orphanage Rd., Foster Falls, VA 24360 (☎ **540/699-6778**). The office is open Monday to Friday 8am to 4:30pm.

While in this area, you can also stop at **Shot Tower Historical State Park,** on U.S. 52 near Exit 5 off I-77, which features a stone shot tower built about 1807. Molten lead poured from the top of the tower fell 150 feet into a kettle, thus cooling and turning into round shot. The lead was mined at nearby Austinville, birthplace of Stephen Austin, the "Father of Texas." (There's a monument to Austin at the New River Trail State Park in Austinville.) Admission to the park is free, but there's a $2 per vehicle parking fee. The park is open April to November from 8am to dusk. Rangers conduct tours of the tower from Memorial Day to Labor Day on weekends and holidays from 10am to 6pm.

SHOPPING

Three log cabins in Old Town Square, Main Street at 7th Street, now house the **Wilderness Road Trading Post** (☎ **540/223-1198**), purveyor of Appalachian crafts, pottery, toys, and a wide range of gifts.

Near Fort Chiswell, about 10 miles northeast of Wytheville on the service road between Exits 77 and 80 off I-81, you'll find **Snooper's Antique & Craft Mall** (☎ **540/637-6441**) and **Old Fort Emporium Antique Mall** (☎ **540/228-GIFT**). Both are cooperatives, with vendors selling a wide range of antiques, collectibles, and gifts. Both are open from Memorial Day to Labor Day, daily from 10am to 8pm, to 7pm in spring and fall, to 6pm in winter.

Across I-81 at Exit 80, **Factory Merchants of Fort Chiswell** (☎ **540/637-6214**) has 35 outlet stores, including Polo Ralph Lauren, Bugle Boy, London Fog, Samsonite, Arrow, L'Eggs/Hanes/Bali, Reebok, Bass, Corning/Revere, Casual Corner, Dress Barn, and Hush Puppies. The Highlands Gateway Visitor Center is also located here (see "Exploring the Southwest Highlands" at the beginning of this chapter).

WHERE TO STAY

The Wytheville area has more than 1,200 motel rooms—one for every family in town, the locals joke. Most are in national chain establishments along I-81 and I-77.

The largest concentration is at Exit 73 off I-81 (U.S. 11), where the **Holiday Inn Wytheville** (☎ **800/HOLIDAY** or 540/228-5483) is the only motel in town with its own in-house restaurant. Also at Exit 73 is a **Days Inn** (☎ **800/325-2525** or 540/228-5500), **Motel 6** (☎ **800/446-8356** or 540/228-7988), and **Red Carpet Inn** (☎ **800/251-1962** or 540/228-5525). Note that some rooms in the Days Inn, Motel 6, and Red Carpet Inn are virtually beside I-81 and are subject to traffic noise. You can also take Exit 73 to reach a parking-lot-surrounded **Econo Lodge** (☎ **800/ 424-4777** or 540/228-5517), about 1 mile to the south on U.S. 11.

For less congested locations, consider Exit 70 off I-81 (North 4th Street), which has the modern **Comfort Inn Wytheville** (☎ **800/228-5150** or 540/228-4488), and Exit 41 off I-77 (Peppers Ferry Road), where the **Best Western Wytheville Inn** (☎ **800/528-1234** or 540/228-7300), **Hampton Inn** (☎ **800/HAMPTON** or 540/ 228-6990), and **Ramada Inn** (☎ **800/2-RAMADA** or 540/228-6000) are far enough away from the interstate to escape the road noise.

Boxwood Inn Bed & Breakfast. 460 E. Main St. (U.S. 11), Wytheville, VA 24382. ☎ **540/ 228-8911.** Fax 540/288-4274. www.newriveradventures.com/boxwood. E-mail: shackler@ naxs.com. 8 units. A/C. $69–$89 double. Rates include full breakfast. MC, V. Take Exit 73 off I-81, go 1½ miles south on U.S. 11 to inn on the right.

This renovated Georgian colonial home is just a few doors down from the historic log cabins on East Main Street. The rooms sport Victorian antiques and reproductions, such as solid oak sleigh beds. The units in the front of the house are enormous. A full breakfast is served family-style in the sunny country kitchen. The B&B shares owners with New River Adventures, the sports concessionaire at New River Trail State Park (see above), which boards its overnight trippers here.

WHERE TO DINE

✪ The Log House 1776 Restaurant. 520 E. Main St. (U.S. 11) (at 7th St.). ☎ **540/ 228-4139.** Reservations recommended. Lunch $3–$5; main courses $9–$17. AE, DISC, MC, V. Mon–Sat 11am–3pm and 4–10pm (to 9:30pm Jan–Apr). From I-81, take Exit 67 or 73 and follow U.S. 11 to the restaurant. AMERICAN.

Although clapboard additions to this historic building were made in 1804 and 1898, the main dining room is in a log house built in 1776. Modern gas logs now burn in the fireplaces, but antiques augment the colonial charm of the dining room. Offerings include Virginia fare such as peanut soup, Smithfield ham, Confederate beef stew (a very sweet concoction of beef, vegetables, and apples that General Lee fed his troops), and Thomas Jefferson's favorite, chicken Marengo, which he brought home from his stint as ambassador to France.

Scrooge's Restaurant. At Comfort Inn, Holston Rd. at E. 4th St. ☎ **540/228-6622.** Reservations not accepted. Main courses $10–$25. AE, DC, MC, V. Sun–Thurs 5–10pm; Fri–Sat 5–11pm. From downtown, take 4th Ave. north across I-81, turn right on Holston Rd. From I-81, take Exit 70, follow signs to Comfort Inn. INTERNATIONAL.

Cartoons of Dickens's Ebenezer Scrooge, especially those on the sports-bar walls showing him scowling his way through such modern activities as tennis and golf, make this English-style establishment a fun place. Recommended is the "pig and pepper soup," a spicy mixture of smoked sausage, potatoes, and peppercorns that will warm the innards after a cold day on the New River Trail. Otherwise, the menu takes a stab at fine dining with the likes of charbroiled steaks, chicken, and seafood dishes like flounder Florentine and shrimp Provençale. There's a "Tiny Tim" menu for kids.

Skeeter's E.N. Umberger Store. 165 E. Main St. (between 1st and Tazewell sts.). ☎ **540/228-2611.** Reservations not accepted. Breakfast $1–$2.50; sandwiches and hot dogs $1.10–$2.20. No credit cards. Mon–Fri 7am–5:50pm; Sat 7am–4:50pm. AMERICAN.

Established in 1920 and housed in an ancient storefront, this simple diner is the home of "Skeeter's World Famous Hotdogs," which are grilled on rollers and served on steamed buns, Southern-style. Other offerings include breakfast items and simple sandwiches. The diner hasn't changed since the 1940s, as the old advertisements and well-worn counter seats will attest.

4 Mount Rogers National Recreation Area

Noted for its 300 miles of hiking, mountain-biking, cross-country skiing, and horse trails, Mount Rogers National Recreation Area includes 117,000 forested acres running some 60 miles from the New River southwest to the Tennessee line. Included is its namesake, Virginia's highest peak at 5,729 feet. Nearby White Top is the state's second-highest point at 5,520 feet. Most of the land, however, flanks Iron Mountain, a long ridge running the area's length. Ranging the extensive upland meadows are wild ponies, introduced to keep the grasses mowed.

Not all of this remote expanse is pristine, for as part of the Jefferson National Forest it's subject to multiple uses such as hunting and logging. Nevertheless, you'll find three preserved wilderness areas and plenty of other backcountry to explore, with mountain scenery that's among the best in Virginia. The many trails include the Virginia Creeper Trail, the Virginia Highlands Horse Trail, and a stretch of the Appalachian Trail. A spur off the Appalachian Trail leads to the summit of Mount Rogers.

ESSENTIALS

ACCESS POINTS & ORIENTATION Access roads from I-81 are U.S. 21 from Wytheville; Va. 16 from Marion; C.R. 600 from Chilhowie; Va. 91 from Glades Spring; and U.S. 58 from Damascus and Abingdon. C.R. 603 runs 13 miles lengthwise through beautiful highland meadows from Troutdale (on Va. 16) to Konnarock (on U.S. 58).

INFORMATION Since the area is so vast and most facilities widespread, it's a good idea to get as much information in advance as possible. Contact the **Mount Rogers National Recreation Area,** 3714 Hwy. 16, Marion, VA 24354 (☎ **540/783-5196;** www.fs.fed.us/gwjnf). If you're driving from the north on I-81, stop at the **Highlands Gateway Visitor Center** in the Factory Merchants Outlet Mall at Exit 80 near Fort Chiswell (see "Exploring the Southwest Highlands" at the beginning of this chapter). Like the recreation area itself, both visitor centers are operated by the George Washington and Jefferson national forests. They offer free brochures describing the trails, campgrounds, and wilderness areas, and they sell a one-sheet topographic map of the area. The topographic map does not show the trails, however, so if writing or calling for information, specifically request brochures on trails, campgrounds, horseback riding, and recreation areas.

FEES, REGULATIONS & BACKCOUNTRY PERMITS   There is no charge to drive through the area, but day-use fees from $1 to $3 per vehicle apply to specific recreational areas, payable on the honor system. Except for the Appalachian Trail and some others reserved for hikers, mountain bikes are permitted but must give way to horses. Bikers and horseback riders must walk across all bridges and trestles. Hikers must not spook the horses. Fishing requires a Virginia license. The "No-Trace Ethic" applies: Leave nothing behind, and take away only photographs and memories.

VISITOR CENTER   The visitor center is at 3714 Va. 16, about 6 miles south of Marion (take Exit 45 off I-81 and go south on Va. 16). Exhibits and a 10-minute video describe the area. The center is open Memorial Day to October, Monday through Thursday from 8am to 5:30pm, weekends from 9am to 5pm. Off-season, it's open Monday through Friday from 8am to 4:30pm. Closed federal holidays.

SEASONS   The area gets the most visitors on summer and fall weekends and holidays. Spring is punctuated by wildflowers in bloom (the calendars published by the Blue Ridge Parkway are generally applicable here), while fall foliage is at its brilliant best in mid-October. Cross-country skiers use the trails during winter. Summer thunderstorms, winter blizzards, and fog any time of the year can pose threats in the high country, so caution is advised.

SEEING THE HIGHLIGHTS

If you don't have time to camp and hike, you can still enjoy the lovely scenery from your car. From Marion on I-81, take Va. 16 south 16 miles to the country store at Troutdale. Turn right on C.R. 603 and drive 13 miles southwest to U.S. 58. Turn right there and drive 20 miles down Straight Branch—a misnomer if ever there was one—through Damascus to I-81 at Abingdon.

An alternative route is to continue on Va. 16 south past Troutdale and turn west on U.S. 58. This will take you past Grayson Highlands State Park (see below). After you pass the park, turn right on C.R. 600 north. This road climbs almost to the summit of White Top Mountain. Up there, a dirt track known as Spur 89 branches off for 2 miles to the actual summit; it's the highest point in Virginia to which you can drive a vehicle, and has great views. C.R. 600 then descends to a dead-end at C.R. 603; turn right there and drive down to U.S. 58, then west to Damascus and Abingdon, as described above.

OUTDOOR PURSUITS

HIGH-COUNTRY HIKING   Almost two-thirds of the area's 300 miles of trails are on these routes: the local stretch of the **Appalachian Trail** (64 miles), the **Virginia Highlands Horse Trail** (66 miles), and the **Iron Mountain Trail** (51 miles). Many of the other 67 trails connect to these main routes, and many can be linked into circuit hikes.

You can walk for days on the white-blaze Appalachian Trail without crossing a paved road, especially on the central stretch up and down the flanks of Mount Rogers between C.R. 603 and C.R. 600. A spur goes to the top of the mountain. The blue-blaze **Mount Rogers Trail,** a very popular alternate route, leaves C.R. 603 near Grindstone Campground; a spur from that track heads down into the pristine Lewis Fork Wilderness before rejoining the Appalachian Trail.

Running across the southern end of the area, the **Virginia Creeper Trail** offers a much easier but no less beautiful hike (and bike ride). This 34-mile route follows an old railroad bed from Abingdon to White Top Mountain (see "Outdoors: The Virginia Creeper Trail" under " Abingdon: A Town with Beauty & Charm," below).

HORSEBACK RIDING   Riders can use 150 miles of the area's trails, including Iron Mountain, New River, and the Virginia Highlands Horse Trail, which connects Elk Garden to Va. 94. Horse camps are at Fox Creek, on Va. 603; Hussy Mountain, near Speedwell; and Raven Cliff, about 4 miles east of Cripple Creek. They have toilets and drinking water for horses (but no water for humans).

Mount Rogers High Country Outdoor Center, on C.R. 603 near Troutdale (☎ 540/677-3900), offers day rides and overnight pack trips by horse, pack mule, or covered wagon. Reservations are required, so phone for information and current prices.

✪ **GRAYSON HIGHLANDS STATE PARK**   On the southern edge of the national recreation area, 8 miles west of Va. 16 on U.S. 58, the lovely Grayson Highlands State Park sits almost at the summit of Haw Orchard Mountain (the visitor center is at 4,958 feet altitude). Here you'll find nine short hiking trails to panoramic vistas, waterfalls, and a 200-year-old cabin; bridle paths; a picnic area near a rebuilt frontier homestead; 73 campsites; horse stables; hunting; and fishing. Admission is $1 weekdays, $2 on weekends. Call ☎ 800/933-PARK to reserve a campsite, which costs $18 a night with electricity, $14 without.

Other activities include park ranger Buddy Emerson's guided fly-fishing trips ($50 half day, $75 full day). Contact Buddy at the park (see above). During summer, **Hopes and Dreams Unlimited** (☎ 800/899-6554) has covered wagon rides in the park and parts of Mount Rogers National Recreation Area; reservations are essential.

For more information, contact the park at 829 Grayson Highland Lane, Mouth of Wilson, VA 24363 (☎ 540/579-7092; www.state.va.us/~dcr/).

CAMPING

In addition to the horse camps mentioned above, the recreation area has several other campgrounds, all open from mid-March through December. A limited number of sites can be reserved in advance by calling ☎ 877/444-6777 or through the National Forest Service Web site (**www.fs.fed.us**).

On C.R. 603 between Troutdale and Konnaraock, **Grindstone** serves as a base camp for hikers heading up Mount Rogers. It has 100 sites with campfires, drinking water, a half-mile nature trail, and weekend ranger programs during summer. **Beartree Recreation Area,** a popular site 7 miles east of Damascus on U.S. 58, features a sand beach on a 12-acre lake stocked with trout for fishing. Both Grindstone and Beartree have flush toilets and warm showers but no trailer hookups. Fees are $10 per site from May through September; $4 during the months of March, April, October, and November.

WHERE TO STAY

There are no hotels, motels, or inns within Mount Rogers National Recreation Area. The nearest motels are in Wytheville on the north end (see above); Abingdon on the south (see below); and Marion in the center, where the **Best Western Marion** (☎ 800/528-1234 or 540/783-3193) and the **Econo Lodge Marion** (☎ 800/55-ECONO or 540/783-6031) stand side by side on U.S. 11 north of downtown. Both were recently renovated. Opposite them on U.S. 11 is the **Virginia House Inn** (☎ 800/505-5151 or 540/783-5112; fax 540/783-1007), a one-story motel built in 1952 but still in fine shape. It has an outdoor pool for cooling off after all that hiking in the mountains. The rooms, at $49 for a double, are small but clean and comfortable.

Fox Hill Inn. 8568 Troutdale Hwy. (Va. 16), Troutdale, VA 24378. ☎ **800/874-3313** or 540/677-3313. www.bbonlne.com/va/foxhill. 7 units. $75–$85 double; $130 suite. Rates include full breakfast. DISC, MC, V. From I-81, take Exit 45 at Marion, then Va. 16 south 20 miles. Inn is on the left, 2 miles south of C.R. 603 at Troutdale.

Situated on a secluded, 3,200-foot-high hilltop and surrounded on three sides by gorgeous mountain views, this comfortable country home offers spacious guest rooms and suites furnished in simple country style. The big living room has a fireplace, and guests can use the roomy country kitchen (the nearest restaurant is 20 miles away in Marion, so bring groceries). A basement game room has Ping-Pong. This is also a working farm, where sheep graze the meadows in the summer months. The hosts will arrange canoe trips on the New River, horseback riding, and mountain-biking, and they will pick you up if you're hiking the nearby Appalachian Trail (that's how they originally got here).

5 Abingdon: A Town with Beauty & Charm

49 miles SW of Wytheville; 133 miles SW of Roanoke; 437 miles SW of Washington, D.C.; 315 miles SW of Richmond

While on his first expedition to Kentucky in 1760, Daniel Boone tramped across the 2,000-foot-high Holston Valley and camped at the base of a hill near a small settlement known as Black's Fort. When wolves emerged from a cave and attacked his dogs, Boone named the place Wolf Hill. Boone and other pioneers opened the area for settlement, and by 1778, a thriving community named Abingdon had grown up around Black's Fort and Wolf Hill. The fort has been replaced by the Washington County Court House, but Boone's cave is still behind one of the historic homes on tree-shaded Main Street. Indeed, Abingdon today looks much as it did in those early years, making it one of Virginia's best small towns to visit.

Abingdon's beauty and historic charm have attracted more than its share of actors, artists, craftspeople, and even a few writers. Visitors drive hundreds of miles to attend shows at the Barter, Virginia's official state theater, and the town is crowded the first 2 weeks of August for the popular **Virginia Highlands Festival,** a display of the region's best arts and crafts.

Abingdon is also a convenient base for a scenic driving tour westward to Big Stone Gap in the Appalachian coal fields (where you'll find yet another fine theater), and for an evening's drive to the little community of Maces Spring, where the famous Carter family makes mountain music every Saturday night.

ESSENTIALS

VISITOR INFORMATION   Contact the **Abingdon Convention & Visitors Bureau,** 335 Cummings St., Abingdon, VA 24210 (☎ **800/435-3440** or 540/676-2282; fax 540/676-3076; www.abingdon.com/tourism; e-mail: acvb@abingdon.com). Located in a restored Victorian house, the **Abingdon Visitors Center** is on the left as you drive into town on U.S. 58; it's open daily from 9am to 5pm.

GETTING THERE & GETTING AROUND   Delta, United, and US Airways have commuter service to **Tri Cities Regional Airport** (☎ **423/325-6000**), about 30 miles southwest of Abingdon between Bristol and Kingsport, Tennessee. By road, Abingdon is at the junction of I-81 and U.S. 11, U.S. 19, and U.S. 58. From I-81, take Exit 17 and follow U.S. 58 west directly into town. U.S. 11 runs east-west along

Main Street (which has a phenomenal amount of traffic for such a small town). Both the **Greyhound/Trailways** bus station (☎ 800/231-2222; www.greyhound.com) and the local **taxi depot** (☎ 540/628-4409) are at 495 W. Main St..

WHAT TO SEE & DO

Stop at the visitor center (see "Essentials," above) and pick up a walking-tour brochure and map. With advance notice, the center can also arrange for guided tours. Horse-drawn carriage rides depart from Camberly's Martha Washington Inn (see "Where to Stay," below) on weekends during the summer, or call ☎ 540/669-6522 at other times.

Begin your sightseeing tour at the **Fields-Penn 1860 House Museum,** at the corner of Main and Cummings streets (☎ 540/676-0216), which depicts how Abingdon's elite lived in the mid–19th century. The museum is open Wednesday through Saturday from 1 to 4pm. Admission is free.

From there, stroll east along lovely Main Street, where Camberly's Martha Washington Inn, the Barter Theatre, and 30 other buildings and homes—with birth dates ranging from 1779 to 1925—wait to be observed. Lined with brick sidewalks, the historic part of Main Street runs for about three-quarters of a mile. It goes up and down two hills, so wear comfortable walking shoes.

After the second hill—where the 1869 Washington County Court House stands—you'll come to the **Cave House,** now home to a fine crafts shop (see "Shopping," below). Behind the house is the cave from whence emerged the wolves who attacked Daniel Boone's dogs. To reach it, take the alley to the left of the house to a stop sign, and turn right. You can peer through a lattice fence into the mouth of the cave, which is below a rickety old barn.

Across Main Street is **The Tavern,** considered the oldest building in Abingdon. Built around 1779 and used as a stagecoach inn and tavern, it's now home to one of the town's better restaurants (see "Where to Dine," below). You can still see the mail slot in the town's original post office, in an addition on the east side of the building.

Art lovers can head to the west side of town and the **William King Regional Arts Center,** 415 Academy Dr. (☎ 540/628-5005; www.wkrac.org), where three galleries host rotating exhibits, most with a cultural heritage theme and an emphasis on visual arts produced in Southwest Virginia. There's also a very good museum shop. The center is open Tuesday 10am to 9pm; Wednesday, Thursday, and Friday 10am to 5pm; Saturday 10am to 3pm; and Sunday 1 to 5pm. It's closed Labor Day weekend. Admission is $3. The center is housed in an old school building in an office complex (turn uphill off Main Street on Academy Street at the Chevron station and follow the signs for arts center parking).

NEARBY ATTRACTIONS

Check with the visitor center to find out if locals have raised enough funds to reopen **White's Mill** (☎ 540/676-0285), a grist-grinding facility built in 1790 and last "restored" in 1866. On the National Register of Historic Places, it's in a picturesque valley 3½ miles north of town via White's Mill Road. It's all downhill to the mill, but you'll have an arduous ride coming back.

Stock car racing fans will enjoy a stop at the **Morgan-McClure Motorsports Museum and Souvenir Gift Shop,** 26460 Newbanks Rd., at Exit 22 (Va. 75) off I-85 (☎ 888/494-0404; www.morgan-mcclure.com), about 5 miles north of town. The museum, which resembles an auto parts store, is home to the Kodak No. 4 NASCAR Winston Cup team. Highlights are a car that won two Daytona 500 races but "expired" during a third try when its engine quit, and another in which driver

Bobby Hamilton escaped injury during a serious crash in Japan (it gives new meaning to the term "rear-ender").

OUTDOORS: THE VIRGINIA CREEPER TRAIL

Take Pecan Street south off Main Street to the western head of the ✪ **Virginia Creeper Trail** (www.fs.fed.us/gwjnf or www.ehc.edu.vacreeper). This 34-mile hiking, biking, and horseback-riding route follows an old railroad bed between Abingdon and White Top Station, at the North Carolina line on the southern flank of White Top Mountain, just inside Mount Rogers National Recreation Area. Now on display at the Abingdon trailhead is the old steam engine, which had such a tough time with this grade that it became facetiously known as the "Virginia Creeper."

The trail starts at an elevation of 2,065 feet in Abingdon, drops to 2,000 feet at the town of Damascus (11 miles east on U.S. 58), then climbs to 3,675 feet. But most people approach it from top to bottom, since it's a fabulous downhill bike ride. You can get to the top via shuttle vans operated by **Highlands Ski & Outdoor Center** (☎ 800/735-4174 or 540/628-1329), on East Main Street near I-81 in Abingdon, or with **Blue Blaze Bike & Shuttle Service** (☎ 800/475-5905 or 540/475-5095), **Adventure Damascus** (☎ 888/595-2453; www.adventuredamascus.com), or **Mt. Rogers Outfitters** (☎ 877/475-5414 or 540/475-5416) in Damascus. The shuttles operate daily during the summer months, on Saturday and Sunday during spring and fall (reservations are essential). Fares are $12 from Abingdon to the top, $9 from Damascus. These firms also rent bikes, which start at $15 for a full day. They compete vigorously, so call them all to see who has the best shuttle and rental rates.

Highlands Bike Rentals (☎ 540/628-9672), a branch of Highlands Ski & Outdoor Center, rents bikes at the Abingdon trailhead on weekends between April and October.

Beginning 2 miles east of Damascus, the stretch between Green Cove Station and Iron Bridge crosses High Trestle (about 100 feet high) and has swimming holes in the adjacent stream. Green Cove is a seasonal forest service information post with portable toilets.

If you don't want to hike or bike up to the heights, you can get a bird's-eye view of the highlands from the basket of a hot-air balloon. **Sky High Balloon Promotions** (☎ 540/623-2306; e-mail: blunerbill@naxs.com) and **Balloon Virginia** (☎ 540/628-6353) fly just-after-sunrise and just-before-dusk rides. Call for prices and reservations, which are essential.

SHOPPING

Mountain arts and crafts are for sale in the **Cave House Crafts Shop,** 279 E. Main St. (☎ 540/628-7721), a 150-member cooperative housed in the 1858 Victorian home built in front of the famous wolf cave.

Original artworks are on display and for sale in the **Arts Depot,** located in the old freight station on Depot Square (☎ 540/628-9091); visitors are welcome to watch artists at work in their studios Thursday, Friday, and Saturday from 11am to 3pm.

Main Street has no fewer than 10 **antiques shops,** which you will pass during your walking tour.

Dixie Pottery, 5 miles south of Abingdon on U.S. 11 (half a mile south of Exit 13 off I-81), is a huge warehouse-style store that sells decorative objects and housewares from around the world. You'll find both cheap and high-quality china, porcelain figurines, candles, dried and artificial flower arrangements, baskets, and lots of brass, copper, pewter, enamel, and cast-iron ware. Open Monday to Saturday 9:30am to 6pm, Sunday 1 to 6pm.

WHERE TO STAY

I-81 has four chain motels: **Comfort Inn** at Exit 14 (☎ **800/221-2222** or 540/676-2222); **Hampton Inn** (☎ **800/HAMPTON** or 540/619-4600) and **Super 8** (☎ **800/800-8000** or 540/676-3310) at Exit 17; and **Holiday Inn Express** (☎ **800/HOLIDAY** or 540/676-2929) at Exit 19. The Hampton Inn is the newest and best of them.

In addition to the Summerfield Inn listed below, B&B accommodations are available in town at **The Love House** (☎ **800/475-5494** or 540/623-1281; www.abingdon-virginia.com; e-mail: lovehouse@naxs.com), **Shepherd's Joy** (☎ **540/628-3273**), **Silversmith Inn** (☎ **800/533-0195** or 540/676-3924; e-mail: bbhost.com/silversmithinn), **Victoria and Albert Inn** (☎ **888/645-5636** or 540/676-2797; www.naxs.com/victoria&albertinn), and **White Birches Inn** (☎ **800/BIRCHES** or 540/676-2140; www.whitebirchesinn.com).

You can also stay in **Crooked Cabin,** 303 E. Main St., Abingdon, VA 24210 (☎ **540/628-9583;** www.crookedcabin.com), a log cabin built in 1790. It has three bedrooms, a living room, and kitchen. Rates are $225 a night.

Alpine Motel. 882 E. Main St. (P.O. Box 615), Abingdon, VA 24212. ☎ **540/628-3178.** Fax 540/628-4217. 19 units. A/C TV TEL. $54 double. AE, DISC, MC, V.

Located just off Exit 19 of I-81 near several restaurants, this older but extraordinarily well maintained 1960s-vintage motel has mountain views from 15 of its 19 rooms. Owners Jim and Gloria Stroup keep their very spacious units spotlessly clean. Their rates are somewhat higher during the Highlands Festival.

☼ **Camberly's Martha Washington Inn.** 150 W. Main St., Abingdon, VA 24210. ☎ **800/555-8000** or 540/628-3161. Fax 540/628-8885. www.camberlyhotels.com. 61 units. A/C TV TEL. $129–$169 double; $179–$309 suite. AE, DC, DISC, MC, V.

In the heart of the historic district, the stately Greek Revival portico of the Martha Washington Inn creates a formal facade for this 2½-story red-brick hotel; its center portion was built as a private residence in 1832. White-wicker rocking chairs give the front porch the look of an old-time resort. The lobby and adjoining parlor are elegantly decorated, with original marble fireplaces and crystal chandeliers. Choose from regular or deluxe rooms, the latter more lavishly appointed with rich fabrics and fine antiques. Suites have museum-quality furnishings. Two executive-level suites have two fireplaces, whirlpool tubs, and steam showers.

Dining/Diversions: The dining room serves traditional Southern fare at breakfast, lunch, and dinner. The President's Club serves cocktails nightly.

Amenities: Concierge, room service (from 7am to 10pm), weekend turndown, shoeshine, antiques and gift shops.

☼ **Summerfield Inn Bed & Breakfast.** 101 W. Valley St., Abingdon, VA 24210. ☎ **540/628-5905.** Fax 540/628-7515. www.summerfieldinn.com. E-mail: Stay@summerfieldinn.com. 7 units. A/C TV TEL. $95–$135 double. Rates include full breakfast. AE, MC, V. Closed Dec–Feb.

Just 1 block from Main Street and the Barter Theatre, this gracious 1920s Colonial Revival residence is set back from the quiet street on an expansive lawn. The inviting verandah, bright with flower boxes, is lined with wicker rockers. A spacious foyer leads to a cozy library where guests can relax and watch TV. The dining room features a magnificent long oval table and period chairs. Adjacent is a cheerful sunroom. The living room is furnished with a player piano, a Queen Anne–period wing chair, and plush Regency-style sofas flanking the fireplace. The guest rooms offer both the ambience of a private home and the luxurious comfort of a fine hotel; each is elegantly furnished with antique pieces and reproductions. Beside the main building, the "Carriage House" has three deluxe units equipped with TVs and whirlpool tubs. Hosts Janice and Jim Cowan serve full breakfasts in the dining room and adjacent sunroom.

WHERE TO DINE

The Abingdon General Store and Gallery. 301 E. Main St. (at Tanner St.). ☎ **540/ 628-8382.** Reservations not accepted. Lunches $6–$7. MC, V. Bakery and deli Mon–Sat 9:30am–5:30pm; dining room Mon–Sat 11am–3pm. DELI/SANDWICHES/SALADS.

The front part of this restored old general store houses a shop that carries gifts, crafts, and decorative pottery; for food, head to the gourmet deli and bakery at the rear. From May through October, you can eat your salad, soup, or deli sandwiches outside in the courtyard known as the Plum Alley Eatery. When the weather turns cold, sit upstairs in the Dumwaiter Restaurant, or pick up a box lunch to take with you while biking, hiking, or riding the Virginia Creeper Trail.

Biscuit Connection. 798 W. Main St. (U.S. 11). ☎ **540/676-2433.** Reservations not accepted. Breakfast, sandwiches, and burgers $1.50–$4. No credit cards. Mon–Fri 6am–2:30pm; Sat 6am–1:30pm. Closed New Year's Day, Thanksgiving, and Christmas. Go west on Main St., look for the sign just west of the railroad overpass. AMERICAN.

This tiny (just five tables), down-home hole-in-the-wall specializes in big, light biscuits right out of the oven. You can order them at the counter either plain or with gravy, country ham, chicken, sausage, pork tenderloin, or bacon, egg, and cheese. This is the town's best bet for a fresh, inexpensive breakfast. Burgers and homemade sandwiches are available at lunch.

Hardware Company Restaurant. 260 W. Main St. ☎ **540/628-1111.** Reservations not accepted. Sandwiches and burgers $5.50–$10; main courses $8–$18. MC, V. Sun–Mon 11am–10pm; Tues–Sat 11am–midnight. Closed Mon Oct–Mar. AMERICAN.

Abingdon's favorite watering hole bears an appropriate name, for this building housed a hardware store from 1885 until 1983. Many of the old features remain: pressed-tin ceiling, rolling ladder, brick walls, and the old oak counter, now a long and friendly bar. The walls are hung with old-fashioned hardware-store memorabilia. Patrons sit at wooden booths upholstered in black leather or at oak tables in Windsor chairs. A balcony overlooking the main dining area and bar provides extra space. Although not in the same league as other restaurants here, the predominantly pub-fare menu offers a variety of decent piled-high sandwiches and assorted burgers, plus a limited list of main courses: pastas, steaks, chicken, and a moderately spicy Cajun concoction of shrimp, chicken, and crawfish.

✪ **Peppermill.** 967 W. Main St. ☎ **540/623-0530.** Reservations recommended. Main courses $10–$22.50. AE, DISC, MC, V. Mon–Sat 11am–9pm, Sun 11am–8pm. Restaurant is 1½ miles west of historic district, half-mile west of railroad overpass. SEAFOOD/INTERNATIONAL.

Along with the Starving Artist Cafe (see below), this little restaurant is the favorite hangout of local foodies who appreciate exciting flavors. Chef Jack Barrow honed his skills in Charleston, South Carolina, and he brings a deft touch to Low Country specialties such as crab cakes served with tartar sauce laced with spicy jalapeños, his most popular dish. Lightly breaded oysters are another favorite. I opted for shrimp Margherita; although the shrimp were a tad overdone, the flavors of olive oil, fresh tomatoes, basil, cracked pepper, and white wine combined excellently over fettucine. Choice tables are out on a deck built over the parking lot, where reed walls and potted palms lend a tropical ambience, and heaters extend the alfresco season well into autumn.

✪ **Starving Artist Cafe.** 134 Wall St. (Depot Sq.). ☎ **540/628-8445.** Reservations not accepted. Main courses $12–$21. AE, MC, V. Mon 11am–2pm; Tues–Sat 11am–3pm and 5–9pm. AMERICAN.

Despite its unpretentious location at Depot Square, this charming cafe lacks nothing in the way of culinary sophistication. The food is both innovative and delicious and is prepared using only the freshest ingredients. The setting is low-key: Seating is at silver-painted ice-cream-parlor chairs and tables, and walls are adorned with a changing display of artists' work, all for sale. In summer, there's outdoor dining on the patio. At lunch, the menu bestows artists' names on a gallery of sandwiches: The Leonardo da Vinci, for example, features spicy Italian meatballs on a hoagie with fresh tomato-basil sauce and melted provolone. French onion soup and smoked salmon with Dijon-horseradish sauce and garlic bread usually are among the appetizer choices. The chef makes superb pan-blackened prime rib with Cajun spices (Friday and Saturday nights only), steaks, and seafood dishes such as Norwegian salmon Oscar. Freshly baked desserts are excellent. The cafe doesn't lack for customers, and the small dining room is usually full; arrive off-hours or prepare for a wait—it's worth it.

✪ **The Tavern.** 222 E. Main St. ☎ **540/628-1118.** Reservations advised for outdoor seating at dinner. Main courses $16–$25. AE, MC, V. Mon–Sat 11am–3pm and 5–10pm, Sun 4–9pm. Closed New Year's Day, Thanksgiving, Christmas. GERMAN/AMERICAN.

The oldest building in Abingdon, The Tavern was built in 1779 as an overnight inn for stagecoach travelers. Exposed brick and stone walls, log beams, and hand-forged locks and hinges make for an appropriately rustic setting. Downstairs, you'll find an antique bar and a cozy waiting lounge with fireplace; upstairs, three dining rooms and a porch overlook a brick terrace under huge shade trees. The menu reflects the present owners' German and American backgrounds. Lunch offers bratwurst with German potato salad, as well as Reubens and smoked-turkey club sandwiches. At dinner, you can choose from Wiener schnitzel, kassler ripchen (German smoked pork loin), crab cakes, rack of lamb, or chicken saltimbocca.

ABINGDON AFTER DARK

✪ **Barter Theatre.** 127 W. Main St. (at College St.). ☎ **540/628-3991.** www. bartertheatre.com. Tickets $16–$25, depending on show and time.

The official policy still permits barter for admission (with prior notice), but theatergoers now pay cash to attend the State Theater of Virginia, America's longest-running professional repertory theater. The building itself was built around 1832 as a Presbyterian church, and later served as a meeting hall for the Sons of Temperance. It functioned as the town hall and opera house when Robert Porterfield brought his unemployed actors here in 1933 (see box, below). Recent productions, now performed by an Actor's Equity company, have included *Camelot, Alice . . . through the Picture Tube, Travels With My Aunt, The Bear Facts,* and *Don't Dress for Dinner.* The theater's impressive alumni include Hume Cronyn, Patricia Neal, Fritz Weaver, Ernest Borgnine, Gregory Peck, and Ned Beatty. Across Main Street, the **Barter's First Light Theatre** specializes in the classics. The season for both stages runs from April through December.

✪ **Carter Family Fold Music Shows.** C.R. 614, Maces Spring. ☎ **540/386-9480.** Music show tickets $4 adults, $1 children 6–12, free for children under 6. From Abingdon, take I-81 south 17 miles to Bristol, U.S. 58 west 19 miles to Hiltons, C.R. 614 east 3 miles to auditorium.

Mountain-music fans consider the 78-mile round-trip from Abingdon to the Carter Family Music Center well worth it, for here they can see and hear the best regional

Hams for Hamlet

The career of an aspiring Virginia-born actor named Robert Porterfield came to a screeching halt during the Great Depression. Giving up on Broadway, he and 22 other unemployed actors came to Abingdon during the summer of 1933 and began putting on plays and shows.

Their first production was John Golden's *After Tomorrow,* for which they charged an admission of 40¢, or the equivalent in farm produce—thus did their little operation become known as the Barter Theatre.

Playwrights who contributed—among them Noël Coward, Thornton Wilder, Robert Sherwood, Maxwell Anderson, and George Bernard Shaw—were paid with a token Virginia ham. Shaw, a vegetarian, returned the smoked delicacy and requested spinach instead; Porterfield and his crew obliged.

The first season ended with a profit of $4.30, two barrels of jelly, and a collective weight gain of 300 pounds!

artists every Saturday night. This is as pure as it gets—the descendants of country music legends A. P. Carter, wife Sara, and sister-in-law Maybelle won't allow electronic equipment in their unpretentious auditorium, which occupies a huge shed. Local residents are adept at traditional styles like buck dancing and clogging on a small dance floor in front of the stage. An annual festival that takes place during the first weekend in August (the same time as the Virginia Highlands Festival in Abingdon) draws many well-known singers and music groups, clog-dance performers, and local artisans who sell crafts. A family museum in A. P. Carter's country store is open on Saturday from 6 to 7pm, before the show.

AN EASY EXCURSION TO BIG STONE GAP

The mountains get steeper and the valleys narrower as you head west from Abingdon into Virginia's share of the Appalachian coal fields. Following I-81 south, U.S. 58 west, U.S. 23 north, and Alternate U.S. 58 east, you can make a scenic loop through these hollows.

NATURAL TUNNEL STATE PARK   From Abingdon, take I-81 south 17 miles to Bristol, then follow the winding U.S. 58 west across the mountains 40 miles to **Natural Tunnel State Park,** where you can take a cable-car ride down a 400-foot-deep gorge to railroad tracks emerging from the mouth of an 850-foot-long tunnel cut by an underground river. The park has nature trails, interpretive programs, a campground, a swimming pool, and a small but very good museum explaining the tunnel's geological formation. Admission to the park is free; cable-car rides cost $2 round-trip. The park is open daily from 8am to dusk; the cable car operates daily from 10am to 5pm during summer, weekends only in spring and fall. For information, contact the park at Route 3, Box 250, Duffield, VA 24244 (☎ **540/940-2674** or 800/933-PARK for campsite reservations; www.state.va.us/~dcr/).

CUMBERLAND GAP   From Duffield, you can make a side trip west 55 miles in each direction on U.S. 58 to **Cumberland Gap National Historical Park,** at the confluence of Virginia, Kentucky, and Tennessee. During the 1780s, more than 300,000 settlers followed Daniel Boone to Kentucky through the gap, at that time the only way to get wagons through the otherwise unbroken Allegheny Front. It is still a major local thoroughfare, with a four-lane highway through the gap. For more information, contact the park superintendent at P.O. Box 1848, Middlesboro, KY 40965 (☎ **606/ 248-2817;** fax 606/248-7276; www.nps.gov/cuga).

BIG STONE GAP   After Duffield, U.S. 23 climbs north through Jefferson National Forest into the mining town of Big Stone Gap. When coal was discovered here in the 1870s, northern businessmen dreamed of turning Big Stone Gap into the "Pittsburgh of the South." It never happened, but the influx of northerners was the inspiration for *Trail of the Lonesome Pine,* hometown writer John Fox, Jr.'s sentimental tale of a local lass who falls for a Yankee mining engineer and becomes a worldly woman. The play is staged every summer at the ✪ **Trail of the Lonesome Pine State Outdoor Drama,** on Clinton Avenue near East 4th Street (☎ **540/523-1235**). Shows are at 8pm Thursday through Saturday from late June to the last weekend in August. Tickets are $10 for adults, $7 for seniors and children. The playhouse is adjacent to the **June Tolliver House & Craft Shop** (☎ **540/523-4707**), real-life home of the woman upon whom Fox based his heroine.

Take the first U.S. 23 Business exit and follow it to the **Regional Tourist and Information Center,** where you can get a walking-tour brochure. The center is housed in Interstate Railroad Private Car Number 101, built in 1870. Visitors are welcome to poke through its staterooms and dining room. The center and car are open from Memorial Day to Labor Day, Tuesday to Wednesday 10am to 5pm, Friday and Saturday 10am to 7pm, and Sunday 1 to 5pm; the rest of the year, Tuesday to Friday 10am to 5pm. For information in advance, contact the center at P.O. Box 236, Big Stone Gap, VA 24219 (☎ **540/523-2060;** www.coalfield.com/touristinfo).

The **John Fox, Jr., Museum** (☎ **540/523-2747** or 540/523-1235), in the author's charming 1888 house on Shawnee Avenue between East 2nd and East 3rd streets, is filled with family furnishings and mementos. Admission is $3 for adults, $2 for seniors, and $1 for students. Open from Memorial Day to Labor Day, Tuesday and Saturday 2 to 5pm, Sunday 2 to 6pm.

The **Southwest Virginia Museum,** 10 W. 1st St. N., at Wood Avenue (☎ **540/ 523-1322**), is housed in a renovated 1888 residence and displays artifacts of the history and culture of the area. Admission is $3 adults, $1.50 for children. Open Monday to Thursday and Saturday 10am to 5pm, Friday 9am to 5pm, Sunday 1 to 5pm (closed Monday from Labor Day to Memorial Day and all of January and February).

The **Harry W. Meador, Jr., Coal Museum,** Shawnee Avenue at East 3rd Street (☎ **540/523-9209**), explains the industry that has been the backbone of the local economy for more than a century. Admission is free. It's open Wednesday to Saturday 10am to 5pm, Sunday 1 to 5pm (closed holidays).

From Big Stone Gap, take U.S. 23 north, then Alternate U.S. 58 east back to Abingdon. The rest of the trip is easy, since both highways have four lanes.

AN EASY EXCURSION TO CRAB ORCHARD

About 1 hour north of Abingdon on U.S. 19/460 just west of Tazewell, the **Crab Orchard Museum and Pioneer Park of Southwestern Virginia,** Crab Orchard Road (☎ **540/988-6755;** www.netscope.net/~histcrab) is an exceptionally interesting museum with exhibits devoted to prehistoric times, Native Americans, the Revolutionary War, the Civil War, and the domestic life and home industries of the area. Outdoors are original farm dwellings, shops, and barns outfitted in typical pioneer fashion. Admission is $6 for adults, $5 for seniors, $3 for children 12 to 18, $2 children 6 to 11, and free for kids under 6. The museum is open Monday through Saturday from 9am to 5pm; in summer, it's also open Sunday from 1 to 5pm.

Richmond

9

Although it has been Virginia's capital since 1780, Richmond isn't the state's largest metropolis (both Fairfax County in northern Virginia and sprawling Hampton Roads have larger populations), but it has been the stage for much of the state's history. It was in Richmond's St. John's Church that Patrick Henry concluded his address to the second Virginia Convention with the stirring words "Give me liberty, or give me death!" The traitorous Benedict Arnold led British troops down what is now Main Street in 1781 and set fire to many buildings, including tobacco warehouses—in those days, the equivalent of banks. Cornwallis briefly occupied the town, and Lafayette came to the rescue.

But it was in the role as capital of the Confederate States of America that Richmond made its mark on American history. Here Jefferson Davis presided over the Confederate Congress, and Robert E. Lee accepted command of Virginia's armed forces. For 4 years the Union army tried to capture the city. Troops often battled on its outskirts, and its tobacco warehouses overflowed with prisoners of war, its hospitals with the wounded, and its cemeteries with the dead. The city has a host of monuments, battlefields, and museums that recall the war, and an easy excursion to the south leads to historic Petersburg, the vital rail junction whose loss in 1865 led to Lee's surrender a week later.

Richmond also has many modern attractions to keep visitors busy, including an excellent fine-arts museum, a hands-on science museum with state-of-the-art planetarium, and a lovely botanical garden. And a short drive north of the city will take you to that most modern of all attractions, Paramount's Kings Dominion theme park, where you can ride exciting roller-coasters, splash around in a water park, and "visit" with Paramount's many movie and cartoon characters.

1 Orientation & Getting Around

VISITOR INFORMATION

The **Richmond Convention and Visitors Bureau,** 550 E. Marshall St. (Box C-250), Richmond, VA 23219 (☎ **800/365-7272** or 804/782-2777; fax 804/780-2577; www.richmondva.org; e-mail: mrcvb@richmonva.org), provides information in advance and operates a hotel reservation service (☎ **888/RICHMOND**). The bureau is open Monday through Friday from 8:30am to 5pm. In addition to its offices on the second floor of Sixth Street Marketplace, on Marshall Street at 6th Street, it operates the **Richmond Visitors Center,** 1710 Robin Hood Rd. near Boulevard and Exit 78 off I-95/I-64 (☎ **804/358-5511**). Opposite the Diamond baseball park, the center occupies an old railroad station and has a huge steam locomotive, a red caboose, and several other cars on display in a small park with picnic area. It will make same-day hotel reservations for walk-in visitors. Open daily from 9am to 5pm, until 7pm from Memorial Day to Labor Day.

The bureau's **Richmond International Airport Visitors Center** (☎ **804/ 236-3260**) is open Monday to Friday 9:30am to 4:30pm. It also will make same-day hotel reservations.

The state operates a visitor information center in the **Bell Tower** (☎ **804/ 648-3146**), on the State Capitol grounds near 9th Street and Marshall Avenue. It's open Monday to Friday 9am to 5pm.

GETTING THERE

BY PLANE Richmond International Airport, Airport Drive off I-64, I-295, and Williamsburg Road (U.S. 60) (☎ **804/226-3052**), locally known as Byrd Field, is about 15 minutes east of downtown. It's served by American, Continental, Delta, TWA, United, and US Airways.

The major car-rental companies have desks at the airport. **Groome Transportation** (☎ **800/552-7911** in Virginia, or 804/222-7222) offers 24-hour van service to downtown; the cost is $14.25 for one person, $18.50 for two people, $22.75 for three people, and $7 each for four or more. Groome also runs vans to Williamsburg ($29 for one person, $19 per person for two or more going to the same place).

Public bus service is available between downtown and the airport only during weekday morning and evening rush hours.

BY CAR   Richmond is at the junction of **I-64,** traveling east-west, and **I-95,** traveling north-south. **I-295** bypasses the city on its east and north sides. **U.S. 60** (east-west) and **U.S. 1** and **U.S. 301** (north-south) are other major arteries.

BY TRAIN   For the time being, several daily **Amtrak** trains pull into the station at 7519 Staples Mill Rd., north of Exit 185 off I-64 (☎ **800/872-7245;** www.amtrak. com), but plans are in the works to renovate the old Shockoe Bottom station. Meantime, Amtrak shuttle buses connect the Marriott and Omni hotels downtown to arriving and departing trains. Public bus Route 27 also runs to downtown (see "Getting Around," below).

BY BUS   The **Greyhound/Trailways** bus terminal is at 2910 N. Boulevard (☎ **800/231-2222;** www.greyhound.com), near the Richmond Visitors Center (see below).

CITY LAYOUT

Richmond is located at the fall line of the James River. Although the city has spread southward, all the hotels, restaurants, and historic sites of interest to visitors are north of the river. A series of bridges crosses the river, and there's also access to two islands, Brown's Island and Belle Isle, from the **Richmond Riverfront Canal Walk,** a promenade extending along the downtown riverfront beside the **James River & Kanawha Canal** (see "Attractions," below).

Foushee Street divides street numbers east and west, while **Main Street** divides them north and south. **Broad Street** is the major east-west thoroughfare, and it's one of the few downtown streets with two-way traffic.

Metropolitan Richmond

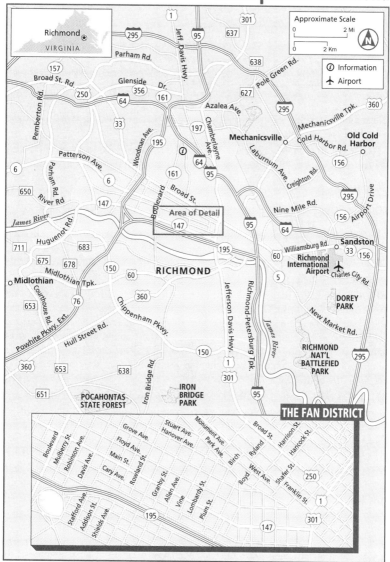

Neighborhoods in Brief

Metropolitan Richmond grew from east to west, along the banks of the James River. As you explore the neighborhoods described below (moving roughly from east to west), you'll get a good sense of Richmond's history.

CHURCH HILL   Named for St. John's Church, its outstanding landmark, this east Richmond neighborhood is largely residential, with an abundance of 19th-century Greek Revival residences. Bordering Church Hill is:

TOBACCO ROW   Paralleling the James River for about 15 city blocks between 20th and Pear streets, this is Richmond's latest urban redevelopment area. Handsome

Broad-streeted Richmond . . . The trees in the streets are old trees used to living with people. Family trees that remember your grandfather's name.
—Stephen Vincent Benet, *John Brown's Body*

old red-brick warehouses are being converted into apartment houses here, but the neighborhood has little of interest to visitors.

SHOCKOE BOTTOM   Shockoe Bottom is roughly bounded by Dock and Broad streets and 15th and 20th streets, with the heart at the 17th Street Farmer's Market between East Main and East Franklin streets. Richmond's first real business district, it once encompassed tobacco factories, produce markets (farmers still sell produce at stands on North 17th Street), slave auction houses, warehouses, and shops, and it retains much of its original character. Today, old-fashioned groceries with signs in their windows for fresh chitterlings stand alongside trendy shops and restaurants, making this Richmond's prime nightlife district. Shockoe Bottom is also home to the Edgar Allan Poe House. The area's old train station, whose spectacular clock tower is visible to motorists soaring above it on I-95, is slated to once again be the city's depot.

SHOCKOE SLIP   Bordering downtown roughly between 10th and 14th streets and Main and Canal streets, this warehouse and commercial area was reduced to rubble in 1865 and rebuilt as a manufacturing center after the war. Today it's a tourist mecca, with its quaint cobblestone streets, old-fashioned street lamps, and renovated warehouses and residences housing lively restaurants, art galleries, nightspots, fashionable shops, and two major hotels. The Richmond Riverfront Canal Walk promenade and its boat rides begin here.

DOWNTOWN   West and north of Shockoe Slip, downtown includes the old and new city halls, the state capitol, and other government buildings of Capitol Square; and the historic homes and museums of the Court End area, notably the Valentine Museum, Museum and White House of the Confederacy, and John Marshall House. The financial and business center of Richmond, downtown also encompasses the Coliseum, the Carpenter Center for the Performing Arts, and the Sixth Street Marketplace.

JACKSON WARD   Jackson Ward, north of Broad Street, is a downtown National Historic District and home to many famous African-Americans, including the first woman bank president in the United States, Maggie Walker, and legendary tap dancer Bill "Bojangles" Robinson, who donated a stoplight for the safety of children crossing the intersection of Leigh Street and Chamberlayne Avenue (where a monument to him stands today). Notable, too, is the fine ornamental ironwork gracing the facades of many Jackson Ward residences.

THE FAN   Just west of downtown, the Fan is named for the shape of the streets, which "fan" out from downtown. Bordered by West Broad and Boulevard and West Main and Belvidere, this gentrified area of turn-of-the-century town houses includes Virginia Commonwealth University and many restaurants and galleries. Monument Avenue's most scenic blocks, with the famous Civil War statues—and one of African-American tennis star Arthur Ashe—down its median strip, are in the Fan.

CARYTOWN   Just west of Boulevard, affluent Carytown has been called Richmond's answer to Georgetown. Cafes, restaurants, boutiques, antiques shops, and the restored Byrd Theater, an old movie palace, bring Saturday-afternoon crowds to stroll West Cary Street between Boulevard and Nasemond Street.

From Swords to Tennis Racquets

Since it fell to Grant's army in 1865, Richmond has changed in many ways—especially in its demographics. Many descendants of the defeated Confederate soldiers have fled to Richmond's sprawling suburbs, while descendants of the slaves those soldiers fought so hard to keep in bondage now make up a majority of the city's population—and of the city council.

The council set the city's old-line white residents off in 1995 by voting to place a statue of the late Arthur Ashe—the world's first African-American tennis star and Richmond's most famous modern son—among those of the Civil War heroes lining hallowed Monument Avenue. It was a hard-fought battle, but today at the corner of Monument Avenue and Roseneath Road stands Ashe's bronze likeness, holding not a sword, but a tennis racquet.

A similar controversy erupted in 1999, when an advisory committee of nine African-Americans, nine whites, and a Native American chief proposed placing an image of Confederate hero Robert E. Lee on the flood wall bordering the city's new Richmond Riverfront Canal Walk promenade along the river. Members of the city's African-American majority objected, but this time the city council voted to include Lee among 13 murals depicting 400 years of Richmond history.

GETTING AROUND

BY PUBLIC TRANSPORTATION   The Greater Richmond Transit Company (☎ 804/358-GRTC) operates the **public bus** system throughout the metropolitan area. Base bus fare is $1.25 (exact change only). Service on most bus routes begins at 5am and ends at midnight.

Of much more use to visitors are GRTC's motorized **Richmond Cultural Connection trolleys,** which run around downtown Monday to Saturday from June through November. The **Orange Line** operates every 45 minutes from Chimborazo Park, on East Broad Street at 33rd Street, across town to the Science Museum of Virginia, on West Broad Street at Robinson Street. It stops at all attractions in between. From the science museum, the **Blue Line** operates every 55 minutes along Boulevard to Maymount, passing Carytown on the way. Trolley fare is 25¢ per ride.

GRTC has an information booth in Sixth Street Marketplace, Marshall Street and 6th Street, where you can get trolley and bus maps (open Monday to Friday 9:30am to 5:30pm). The city's visitor centers also have trolley maps (see "Visitor Information," above).

BY CAR   Richmond is fairly easy to navigate by car, although all but a few streets are one-way. Left turns from a one-way street onto another one-way street may be made at red lights after a full stop.

BY TAXI   Call **Yellow Cab Service Inc.** (☎ **804/222-7300**) or **Veterans Cab Association** (☎ **804/329-1414**). Fares are approximately $1.50 per mile.

BY BICYCLE   Bikes can be rented at **Two Wheel Travel,** 2934 W. Cary St., at South Sheppard Street (☎ **804/359-2453**), in Carytown 2 blocks west of Boulevard. Bikes cost $20 for the first day, $10 per day thereafter. Open Monday to Friday 10am to 6pm, Saturday 9am to 4:30pm.

SAFETY

Richmond has a drug problem, so ask at the visitor centers or at your hotel desk if a neighborhood you intend to visit is safe. Avoid all deserted streets after dark. As in any city, it's wise to stay alert and be aware of your surroundings, whatever the time of day.

2 Where to Stay

The **Richmond Convention and Visitors Bureau** operates a free hotel reservation service (☎ **800/RICHMOND**). If you arrive without a reservation, the **Richmond Visitors Center,** 1710 Robin Hood Rd. near Boulevard and Exit 78 off I-95/I-64 (☎ **804/358-5511**), will make same-day reservations for walk-in visitors, often at a discount. See "Visitor Information," above.

The closest suburban chain motels to downtown—**Days Inn North** (☎ 800/DAYSINN or 804/353-1287) and **Holiday Inn Central** (☎ 800/HOLIDAY or 804/359-9441)—are near Robin Hood Road and I-95 (Exit 78), near the Richmond Visitors Center and the Diamond, home of baseball's Richmond Braves.

The Executive Center area, on West Broad Street (U.S. 33/250) at I-64 (Exit 183), about 5 miles west of downtown, has a wide selection of much newer properties. This pleasant, campus-like area also has many chain restaurants, including an inexpensive Morrison's Cafeteria. Best of the hotels is the redwood-and-brick **Hyatt Richmond at Brookfield** (☎ 800/233-1234 or 804/285-1234). Nearby are the colonial-look **Comfort Inn Executive Center** (☎ 800/228-5150 or 804/672-1108), a comfortable **Courtyard by Marriott** (☎ 800/321-2211 or 804/282-1881), a **Days Inn** (☎ 800/DAYS-INN or 804/282-3300), a **Fairfield Inn by Marriott** (☎ 800/228-2200 or 804/755-7155), the **Hampton Inn West** (☎ 800/HAMPTON or 804/747-7777), the **Holiday Inn West** (☎ 800/HOLIDAY or 804/285-9951), a **Shoney's Inn** (☎ 800/222-2222 or 804/672-7007), and a **Super 8** (☎ 800/800-8000 or 804/672-8128).

The Berkeley Hotel. 1200 E. Cary St. (at 12th St.), Richmond, VA 23219. ☎ **888/780/4422** or 804/780-1300. Fax 804/648-4728. www.berkeleyhotel.com. 55 units. A/C TV TEL. $140–$190 double. Weekend and other packages available. AE, DC, DISC, MC, V. Valet parking $10, no self-parking.

At this elegant little Shockoe Slip hostelry, a handsome red-brick facade opens into a seemingly old-world interior. Although established in 1988, the hotel creates the illusion that it was built hundreds of years ago. An innlike ambience and attentive personal service prevail here. Rooms are very residential in feel and luxuriously appointed with fine period-reproduction furnishings and walls hung with botanical prints; some have whirlpool tubs.

Dining/Diversions: Every chef in town says that the Berkeley has Richmond's finest dining. Virginia ingredients accent entrees such as venison with kale, stewed okra, and black-eyed peas, or breast of duck with creamy grits, wild mushrooms, and berries. Nightingale's Lounge adjoins.

Amenities: Valet parking, concierge, laundry, newspaper, turndown. Guest privileges at nearby health club.

Crowne Plaza Hotel. 555 E. Canal St. (at 6th St.), Richmond, VA 23219. ☎ **800/HOLIDAY** or 804/788-0900. Fax 804/788-7087. 299 units. A/C TV TEL. $129–$159 double. AE, DC, DISC, MC, V. Self-parking $5; valet parking $8.

You won't mistake this Crowne Plaza for any other building in town—it's a starkly modern, triangular 16-story high-rise with reflecting glass windows. Most rooms offer stunning river and city views. Guests on the executive level get their own concierge lounge and complimentary continental breakfast and evening hors d'oeuvres and cocktails.

Downtown Richmond Accommodations & Dining

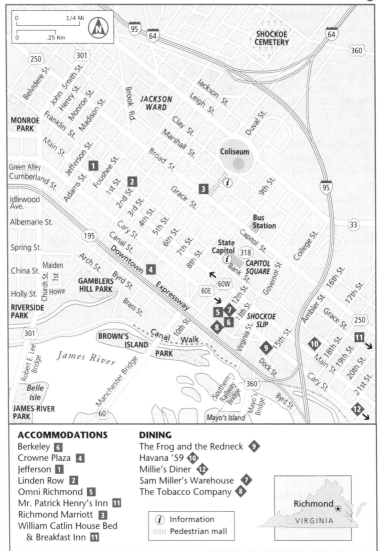

ACCOMMODATIONS
Berkeley **6**
Crowne Plaza **4**
Jefferson **1**
Linden Row **2**
Omni Richmond **5**
Mr. Patrick Henry's Inn **11**
Richmond Marriott **3**
William Catlin House Bed **11**
  & Breakfast Inn

DINING
The Frog and the Redneck **9**
Havana '59 **10**
Millie's Diner **12**
Sam Miller's Warehouse **7**
The Tobacco Company **8**

i Information
IIIII Pedestrian mall

Richmond
VIRGINIA

Dining & Diversions: The mezzanine-level Pavilion Cafe serves all three meals, while the 555 Club off the lobby offers drinks and light fare with a view of Canal Walk.

Amenities: Concierge, laundry, baby-sitting, indoor pool, health club.

✪ **Jefferson Hotel.** Franklin and Adams sts., Richmond, VA 23220. ☎ **800/484-8014** or 804/788-8000. Fax 804/225-0334. www.jefferson-hotel.com. 275 units. A/C MINIBAR TV TEL. $205–$275 double. Weekend and other packages available. Pets accepted ($25 fee). AE, DC, MC, V. Self-parking $9; valet parking $11.

A stunning Beaux Arts sightseeing attraction in its own right, the Jefferson was opened in 1895 by Maj. Lewis Ginter, who wanted his city to have one of the finest hotels in

America. He hired the architectural firm of Carrier & Hastings, which had designed the monumental New York Public Library. The magnificent limestone-and-brick facade here is adorned with Renaissance-style balconies, arched porticos, and an Italian clock tower. Two-story faux-marble columns, embellished with gold leaf, encircle the Rotunda, or lower lobby. Acres of Oriental area rugs define the central seating area, furnished with elegant tufted-leather sofas amid potted palms. The marble Grand Staircase, magnificently wide and red-carpeted, leads to the Palm Court upper lobby under a stained-glass domed skylight; 9 of its 12 panes are original Tiffany glass.

Furnished with custom-made 18th-century reproduction pieces, the rooms have hosted hundreds of notables, including Charles Lindbergh, Henry Ford, Charlie Chaplin, Elvis Presley, and Presidents Harrison, McKinley, Wilson, Coolidge, and both Roosevelts. F. Scott and Zelda Fitzgerald held glamorous parties here.

Dining: Sunday brunch in the Rotunda is a bountiful all-you-can-eat feast in opulent surroundings. T.J.'s (as in Thomas Jefferson) is a restaurant, bar, and oyster bar just off the Rotunda. Off the Palm Court, there's elegant dining at Lemaire (named for the real T.J.'s maître d'), a warren of seven handsome rooms, one with a library. Dinners here feature regional entrees such as roast pheasant stuffed with fresh oysters and Virginia ham in wine sauce.

Amenities: Concierge, 24-hour room service, same-day valet laundry, complimentary newspaper, nightly turndown, baby-sitting; shuttle to theaters and Shockoe Slip can be arranged. Access to nearby health club, indoor pool, business center, beauty salon, gift shop.

Linden Row Inn. 100 E. Franklin St. (at 1st St.), Richmond, VA 23219. ☎ **800/348-7424** or 804/783-7000. Fax 804/648-7504. www.lindenrowinn.com. E-mail: linden.inn@erols.com. 69 units. A/C TV TEL. $99–$149 double; $149–$189 suite. Rates include continental breakfast. AE, DC, MC, V. Valet parking $7.

This row of seven mid–19th century Greek Revival town houses and their garden dependencies (small, separate buildings) is within walking distance of Shockoe Slip, Capitol Square, and the financial center. Not only the facades have remained intact; original interior features such as fireplaces, marble mantels, and crystal chandeliers still grace the inn. In other words, the property has been renovated but not restored, so don't expect the quality—or services—you'll get at a place like the Jefferson Hotel.

Rooms in the main houses, all with windows nearly reaching the 12-foot ceilings, have a mix of late-Empire and early-Victorian pieces, with damask draperies, flower-patterned carpets, and marble-top dressers. Back rooms overlook a brick-walled garden and patio, and the garden dependencies of the original town houses have been restored and offer accommodations with private entrances, pine furniture, and handmade quilts.

Dining: The cozy dining room is not the inn's strong suit. Cheese, crackers, and drinks in the early evening and hot beverages after dinner are laid out buffet style in two parlors, handsomely furnished with leather couches and working fireplaces.

Amenities: Limo service and limited room service are available, and use of the YMCA Fitness Center is free to guests.

Omni Richmond Hotel. 100 S. 12th St. (at E. Cary St.), Richmond, VA 23219. ☎ **800/ THE-OMNI** or 804/344-7000. Fax 804/648-6704. 353 units. A/C MINIBAR TV TEL. $189 double; $239–$299 suite. Weekend and other packages available. AE, DC, DISC, MC, V. Valet parking $10.

The Omni is located in the James Center office towers, across the street from The Berkeley Hotel and Shockoe Slip's boutiques, restaurants, and clubs. It boasts a handsome pink-marble lobby, with green-velvet-upholstered chairs and sofas around a working fireplace. Rooms are decorated in soft pastels, and some have spectacular views of the nearby James River. Club-floor rooms offer access to a private lounge, where a complimentary continental breakfast and afternoon refreshments are served on weekdays.

Dining: Caffè Gallego is a casual restaurant that opens to the office tower's atrium, where The Market, a gourmet take-out deli, offers breakfast pastries and other bakery treats, sandwiches, and pizzas.

Amenities: Concierge, limited room service, laundry. Indoor/outdoor pool with sundeck, squash and racquetball courts, and Nautilus equipment, all on the premises, are available to Omni guests for $5 per day. James Center shops adjoin the hotel lobby.

Richmond Marriott. 500 E. Broad St. (at 5th St.), Richmond, VA 23219. ☎ **800/ 228-9290** or 804/643-3400. Fax 804/788-1230. 411 units. A/C TV TEL. $129 double; $200–$500 suite. Weekend and other packages available. AE, DC, DISC, MC, V. Self-parking $5; valet parking $7.

Ideally located for convention-goers at the Sixth Street Marketplace shops, the Marriott is connected via a skywalk to the Richmond Convention Center. Many of the exceptionally spacious and handsomely furnished accommodations offer panoramic city views.

Dining/Diversions: Allie's American Grille serves breakfast, lunch, and dinner in a cheerful atmosphere. Sporting events are aired on the big TV in Triplett's, the lobby lounge and cocktail bar.

Amenities: Concierge, limited room service, laundry, free newspaper. Indoor pool, health club, game room, gift shop.

BED & BREAKFASTS

Bensonhouse of Richmond, 2036 Monument Ave., Richmond, VA 23220 (☎ **804/ 353-6900;** fax 804/355-5050; www.bensonhouse.com; e-mail: be.our.guest@ bensonhouse.com), acts as agent for carefully chosen bed-and-breakfast accommodations. Administrator Lyn Benson offers listings within 5 to 15 minutes of major attractions, including her own lovingly restored **Emmanuel Hutzler House** (same address; ☎ 804/355-4885), an Italian Renaissance–style inn, built in the early 1900s with beautiful mahogany paneling, leaded-glass windows, and a coffered-beam ceiling. Her spacious guest rooms boast handsome antique furnishings, TVs, telephones, and private bathrooms, some with whirlpool tubs. Rates range from $95 to $155 for a double.

Mr. Patrick Henry's Inn. 2300–02 E. Broad St. (at 23rd St.), Richmond, VA 23223. ☎ **800/ 932-2654** or 804/644-1322. 4 suites. A/C TV TEL. $95–$125 double. Rates include continental breakfast for 2. AE, DC, DISC, MC, V.

One block west of historic St. John's Church, these two Greek Revival town houses are in Richmond's oldest neighborhood. The lower two floors are a tavern and colonial-style restaurant. The tavern on the basement level has low-beamed ceilings and whitewashed-brick walls; it serves up light fare. The outdoor garden patio offers alfresco dining in good weather. All accommodations have working fireplaces and kitchenettes, and one has a private balcony overlooking the garden. Furnishings are a mix of antiques and reproductions, featuring four-poster beds, wing chairs, and pretty ruffled curtains. St. John's landmark church is just a block away.

William Catlin House Bed & Breakfast Inn. 2304 E. Broad St. (between 23rd and 24th sts.), Richmond, VA 23223. ☎ **804/780-3746.** 5 units (3 with private bathroom). A/C. $95 double. Rates include full breakfast. DISC, MC, V. Free off-street parking.

Occupying an 1845 Greek Revival residence, this inn offers a comfortable home away from home. Sliding doors separate a plush first-floor parlor from the dining room, where breakfast is served. Guest accommodations are in the basement and on the second and third floors. They're tastefully furnished with period pieces, lace curtains, working fireplaces, and charming decorative objects like spinning wheels and dried-flower arrangements. Hosts Robert and Josephine Martin provide evening sherry.

3 Where to Dine

I've arranged the following restaurants by neighborhood, running from east to west across the city in the same order they're described under "Neighborhoods in Brief," above.

CHURCH HILL

✪ **Millie's Diner.** 2603 E. Main St. (at 26th St.). ☎ **804/643-5512.** Reservations not accepted. Main courses $14.50–$22. AE, DC, DISC, MC, V. Tues–Fri 11am–2pm and 5:30–10:30pm; Sat 10am–3pm and 5:30–10:30pm; Sun 9am–3pm (brunch) and 5:30–9:30pm. ECLECTIC.

Once Millie's really was a diner, and although it's been renovated, the counter, booths, and open kitchen from those days are still here. It's not a diner anymore, however, for now a talented young chef works the gas stove, turning out a variety of tasty dishes. His spicy Thai shrimp with asparagus, red cabbage, shiitake mushrooms, cilantro, lime, peanuts, and hot chilis over fettucine is always on the blackboard menu, which otherwise changes every 2 weeks. Sometimes he features Southern-influenced cooking, sometimes dishes from the Pacific Rim or the Caribbean. Regardless, he prepares everything from scratch—as you watch, if you grab a counter seat. Excellent fare, an entertaining wait staff, and hearty portions make this noisy eatery highly popular among Richmond's young professionals.

SHOCKOE BOTTOM

Havana '59. 16 N. 17th St. (between Main and Franklin sts.). ☎ **804/649-2822.** Reservations recommended on weekends. Main courses $15–$20. AE, DC, DISC, MC, V. Sun–Thurs 5:30–11pm; Fri–Sat 5:30–11:30pm; Sun brunch Mar–Oct, 10am–3pm. CUBAN.

This lively theme restaurant presents a strange sight across the street from the covered stalls of Richmond's ancient Farmer's Market, especially during warm weather when its big, garage-style storefront windows roll up to let fresh air in (and cigar smoke out). Then you might swear you're down in Havana in 1959 when Fidel Castro marched into town. Fake palms, ceiling fans, string lights, Cuban music, and adobe walls with gaping holes (where plaster ought to be) set a festive scene. The Cuban-accented cuisine, to which the chef gives eclectic twists, lives up to the ambience. I began with pork morsels with an exciting cilantro dipping sauce and went on to very tasty shrimp and chorizo sausage tossed with a mango cream sauce and served over pasta.

SHOCKOE SLIP

The strip of East Cary Street between 12th and 15th streets has a bevy of good-to-excellent restaurants. In addition to those listed below, you can get excellent Vietnamese cuisine at **Cafe Indochine,** 1209 E. Cary St. (☎ 804/225-1331); sushi, sashimi, and tempura at **Hana Zushi Japanese,** 1309 E. Cary St. (☎ 804/225-8801); Italian at **La Grotta Restaurant,** 1218 E. Cary St. (☎ 804/644-2466); excellent Chinese at **The Peking Pavilion,** 1302 E. Cary St. (☎ 804/649-8888);

crab, shrimp, and fish at **The Hard Shell,** 1411 E. Cary St. (☎ **804/643-2333**); and tapas and other Mediterranean fare at **Europa,** 1409 E. Cary St. (☎ **804/643-0911**).

Enormously popular with young professionals as a watering hole, **Siné Irish Pub & Restaurant,** 1327 E. Cary St. (☎ **804/649-7767**), is anything but a typical Irish pub, offering a wide selection of seafood, steaks, and chicken in addition to the usual corned beef and cabbage. In warm weather you can dine and drink on the deck out back.

✪ **The Frog and the Redneck.** 1423 E. Cary St. (between 14th and 15th sts.). ☎ **804/648-3764.** Reservations recommended. Main courses $14–$20; sampler meal $45. AE, DC, DISC, MC, V. Mon–Thurs 5:30–10pm, Fri–Sat 5–10pm. FRENCH/ AMERICAN.

This facetious name derives from co-owner and chef Jimmy Sneed, who grew up in the South and then worked as an under-chef at Jean-Louis Paladin's renowned French restaurant in Washington, D.C. Jimmy excellently blends the "Frog" style of cooking he learned there with local "Redneck" ingredients. For example, instead of Bayonne ham and melon, Jimmy offers Virginia ham and local cantaloupe as an appetizer. Some of the largest lumps of backfin Chesapeake crabmeat I've ever seen floated in his deliciously sweet red pepper soup. As his signature dish, Jimmy packs those giant lumps into the best sautéed crab cakes I've ever tasted. The menu changes daily to incorporate the freshest local produce. A suggestion: Try his five-course sampler menu, a deal at $45 per person. Meanwhile, co-owner Adam Steely presides over a spacious bistro-style dining room with mirrors on the posts supporting the upper floors of a converted warehouse. As would be expected, the wine list carries a good selection of both French and Virginian vintages.

Sam Miller's Warehouse. 1210 E. Cary St. (between 12th and 13 sts.). ☎ **804/ 643-1301.** Reservations suggested, especially for dinner on weekends. Sandwiches and burgers $5.50–$8; main courses $14–$25.50. AE, DC, MC, V. Daily 11:30am–4:30pm and 5–11pm; Sun brunch 10am–4pm; Fri–Sat entertainment until 2am. AMERICAN.

Although it has been eclipsed in popularity by Siné Irish Pub & Restaurant (see above), this pub has been in business since the Slip's revival in 1975 and still draws a faithful following. At lunch, terrific sandwiches include beef barbecue with coleslaw, crab cakes, and a juicy 5-ounce hamburger. Chesapeake Bay seafood and prime rib are dinner-menu highlights. The seafood entrees, all served with vegetable du jour and wild rice or baked potato, include broiled or blackened fresh fish du jour; shrimp stuffed with crab imperial; and an enormous seafood platter piled high with scallops, oysters, clams, shrimp, fresh fish, and crab cakes.

The Tobacco Company. 1201 E. Cary St. (at 12th St.). ☎ **804/782-9431.** Reservations accepted. Main courses $16–$22. AE, MC, V. Mon–Fri 11:30am–2:30pm and 5:30–10:30pm; Sat 11:30am–2:30pm and 5–11pm; Sun 11am–2:30pm and 5:30–10pm. AMERICAN.

Appropriately, this dining-entertainment complex is housed in a former tobacco ware-house that's been converted into a sunny, plant-filled three-story atrium. An exposed antique elevator carries guests from the first-floor cocktail lounge to the two dining floors above. Nostalgic touches abound—brass chandeliers, a cigar-store Indian, Tiffany-style lamps, white porch-style banisters, even an old ticket booth that now serves as the hostess desk. Exposed-brick walls are festooned with antiques collectors' items. Contemporary American cuisine is featured. Lunch specialties could be as light as a vegetarian stir-fry or as hearty as chicken chimichangas. Also available are omelets, salads, sandwiches, and burgers. At dinner, you might begin with shrimp and Virginia ham with papaya or an innovative pairing of mushrooms and escargots, then move on to the house special: slow-roasted prime rib with seconds on the house. There's live music in the Club downstairs Tuesday through Saturday nights, with dancing Thursday through Saturday.

THE FAN

✪ **Joe's Inn.** 205 N. Shields Ave. (between Grove and Hanover sts.). ☎ **804/355-2282.** Reservations not accepted. Breakfast $3–$5.50; sandwiches $2.50–$5.50; main courses $6.50–$11. AE, MC, V. Mon–Thurs 9am–midnight; Fri–Sat 8am–2am; Sun 8am–midnight. ITALIAN.

This very popular neighborhood hangout has been serving terrific Greek-accented Italian fare since 1952, including veal parmigiana, fish, pizzas, and pasta. The house specialty is gargantuan portions of spaghetti. Two can easily share an order of somewhat rubbery spaghetti à la Joe, which arrives steaming hot en casserole, bubbling with a layer of baked provolone between the pasta and heaps of rich meat sauce. Soups, salads, omelets, and sandwiches are also options. Stop by for a mouthwatering stack of hotcakes or French toast at breakfast. Joe's occupies two storefronts: a dining room side and a bar side with sleek mahogany booths and ornate brass-trimmed ceiling fans.

Strawberry Street Café. 421 N. Strawberry St. (between Park and Stuart aves.). ☎ **804/353-6860.** Reservations needed only for large groups. Sandwiches and burgers $4.50–$7; main courses $6–$13; weekend brunch buffet $8. AE, MC, V. Mon–Thurs 11:30am–3pm and 5–10:30pm; Fri 11:30am–3pm and 5pm–midnight; Sat 11am–midnight; Sun 10am–10:30pm. AMERICAN.

The chic but casual Strawberry Street Café is decorated in turn-of-the-century style, with a beautiful oak bar, *Casablanca*-inspired fan chandeliers, and a plant-filled cafe-curtained window. Flower-bedecked tables (candlelit at night) add a cheerful note. At lunch or dinner, you can help yourself to unlimited offerings from a bountiful salad bar displayed in a claw-foot bathtub. At lunch, you might get a broccoli quiche or a 6-ounce burger. At dinner, the menu offers several pastas plus London broil, steaks, chicken Oscar, and homemade chicken potpie with a flaky crust. There's luscious chocolate cake for dessert. The weekend unlimited brunch bar lets you create a memorable meal from an assortment of fresh fruits, yogurt, baked ham, pastries, hot entree, salads, homemade muffins, and beverage.

CARYTOWN

✪ **Acacia.** 3325 W. Cary St. (at Dooley Ave.). ☎ **804/354-6060.** Reservations required at dinner. Lunch $4–$8; main courses $16–$24. AE, DC, MC, V. Tues–Sat 11:30am–2:30pm and 5:30–9:30pm. REGIONAL.

You can't miss this fine restaurant as you stroll through Carytown, for it occupies the front portico and part of the late 19th-century First Baptist church, now converted into a small shopping complex. It's the domain of The Frog and The Redneck (see above) alums Dale Reitzer, his wife Aline, and partner Jim O'Toole. Using the skills he learned there under Jimmy Sneed, Dale presides over the kitchen and concocts a nightly dinner menu to reflect the produce they've been able to directly procure from the region's farmers and fishers that day. He often accompanies the fresh fish with a mouthwatering ragout of Maine lobster, country sausage, and potatoes. He always prepares one vegetarian and one chicken main course. In autumn, look for venison and buffalo. Lunch doesn't reflect the quality of the dinner fare, but you'll still enjoy the sandwiches, wraps, soups, and salads aimed at Carytown's office workers and shoppers.

Ristorante Amici. 3343 W. Cary St. (between Freeman Rd. and S. Dooley St.). ☎ **804/353-4700.** Reservations recommended. Main courses $13–23. AE, DC, DISC, MC, V. Mon–Thurs 11:30am–2:30pm and 5:30–10pm; Fri–Sat 11:30am–2:30pm and 5:30–11pm; Sun 5:30–10pm. NORTHERN ITALIAN.

This delightful establishment seats diners upstairs in a formal, coral-stucco room. On the street floor are a small bar and seating at several additional tables for dinner; during good weather, patrons vie for umbrella tables on a sidewalk patio. The owners of Amici (which means "friends" in Italian) hail from Cervinia, a small resort in the Italian Alps, where they perfected their craft—and perfection in the culinary arts is certainly what they have achieved here. The menu changes seasonally, but you might begin with grilled portobello mushroom caps with garlic, basil, and olive oil; and thin slices of veal loin with delicate tuna sauce. Among the entree highlights is a superb veal scaloppini with mushrooms and Barbera wine sauce. From the grill come fresh salmon, jumbo shrimp and scallops, chicken breast, lamb chops, steaks, and bison. Stunning desserts include a wicked tiramisu. The wine list, with many Italian vintages, is surprisingly affordable.

PICNIC FARE

In Carytown, **Coppola's Delicatessen,** 2900 W. Cary St., at South Colonial Avenue (☎ **804/359-NYNY**), evokes New York's Little Italy with an aromatic clutter of cheeses, sausages, olives, pickles, and things marinated. Behind-the-counter temptations include pasta salads, antipasti, cannoli, specialty sandwiches, and pasta dinners. Coppola's is so New York that it "imports" Thuman's low-fat, low-salt deli meats from New Jersey. Prices are low; this is a down-to-earth deli, not a pretentious gourmet emporium, though the fare is as good as any the latter might offer. There are some tables inside and a few out on the street. Hours are Monday through Wednesday from 10am to 8pm, Thursday through Saturday from 10am to 9pm.

4 What to See & Do

For a free overall view of the city, start at the observation deck of the **New City Hall,** 900 Broad St. at 9th Street, for a magnificent panorama of Richmond and the James River. You'll also get a fine bird's-eye view of the 1894 **Old City Hall,** diagonally across Broad Street between 9th and 10th streets, a dramatic Victorian Gothic with gray-stone walls 3 feet thick. Now a private office building, it has an interior court-yard that's a three-story marvel of painted cast iron. Visitors are welcome to enter the first floor during business hours. It's well worth the stop.

ORGANIZED TOURS

Richmond has too many attractions covering too many fields of interest—American Revolution, Civil War, literature, art, science, houses and gardens, even cemeteries—for me to tell you what you *must* see. I will advise you, however, that before striking out on your own, take a guided van tour offered by ✪ **Historic Richmond Foundation Tours,** 707-A E. Franklin St. (☎ **804/780-0107;** fax 804/788-4244; www. historicrichmond.com). Trained historians lead the foundation's tours, so you'll get a wealth of information. You'll also see where everything is, which will help you decide how to schedule your in-depth sightseeing.

Spend your first morning here on the foundation's 2½-hour **"Old Richmond Today" van tour,** which provides an excellent overview of the city. It goes through the historic neighborhoods and stops at the State Capitol. This tour is offered year-round, daily in the morning (pickup times vary by hotel). They cost $18 for adults, $10 for students 6 to 18, free for kids under 6.

The 1½-hour **"Richmond Highlights" tour** is somewhat less informative. It drives by Monument Avenue, St. John's Church, Capitol Square, and along the James River without stopping. It's offered Monday through Saturday afternoons from April to October and costs $15 for adults, $10 for students 6 to 18, free for kids under 6.

The 3½-hour **"Civil War Sampler"** goes past wartime prisons, hospitals, slave markets, cemeteries, the White House of the Confederacy, and east of the city for stops at Cold Harbor and Gaines' Mill battlefields. It runs on Friday to Sunday afternoons from April to October and costs $22 for adults, $10 for students 6 to 18, free for kids under 6.

The foundation also offers a program of Sunday afternoon **walking tours.** Call for a schedule and prices. Reservations are required for all foundation tours.

RICHMOND RIVERFRONT CANAL WALK

As envisioned by George Washington, a system of canals would link America's eastern seaboard with the Ohio and Mississippi rivers in the west. In Richmond, construction was begun in 1789 on the James River & Kanawha Canal, which was to run alongside the James River and connect it to the Kanawha River. It reached as far as Buchanan, Virginia, before the railroads made canal transportation obsolete in the early 19th century (its towpath was later sold to the Richmond and Allegheny Railroad, which laid tracks along it).

In 1999, more than 2 centuries later, the city opened its new ✪ **Richmond Riverfront Canal Walk,** a promenade running along the waterway and its locks for 1 mile between 14th Street in Shockoe Slip and Brown's Island and the Tredegar Iron Works at the foot of 5th Street downtown. Brochures with maps are available at the city's visitor centers (see "Visitor Information," above).

From a visitor's viewpoint, the ends of the walk are the most interesting parts to see. Near the eastern end, at the foot of Virginia Street in Shockoe Slip, you can take a 35-minute ride on the canal in a bateau boat. Operated by **Kanawha Cruises** (☎ **804/649-2800**), these motorized passenger boats operate daily from 9am to 10pm in summer, Wednesday to Sunday from 11am to 9pm in spring and fall. Rides cost $4 for adults, $3 seniors and children 5 to 12, free for kids under 5. Buy tickets at the booth beside the turning basin at the foot of Virginia Street.

You can cross the canal on the 14th Street Bridge, a block away, and see the **Floodwall Picture Gallery,** whose mural of Robert E. Lee stirred up much controversy (see "From Swords to Tennis Racquets" box, above). The wall was built after the James flooded during Hurricane Agnes in 1972, causing some $350 million in damages to Shockoe Slip (and its eventual revival as a dining-entertainment area).

At the western end of the walk, at the foot of 5th Street, the **Tredegar Iron Works** on Brown's Island was the South's largest industrial complex during the Civil War, producing about half of the Confederacy's armaments. The restored brick building now houses the Richmond National Battlefield Park's visitor center (see "Top Historical Attractions," below). There's a turning basin here, where you can rent boats to explore the canal on your own.

TOP HISTORICAL ATTRACTIONS

Several of Richmond's attractions are included in the **Historic Downtown Richmond Ticket,** which includes admission to any five of them for $15 per person, regardless of age. Buy the block tickets at any of the Richmond visitor centers (see "Visitor Information," above).

✪ **John Marshall House.** 818 E. Marshall St. (at 9th St.). ☎ **804/648-7998.** Admission $3, $2.50 seniors, $1.25 children 7–12, free for children under 7. Apr–Sept, Tues–Sat 10am–5pm; Oct–Dec, Tues–Sat 10am–4:30pm. Jan–Mar, by appointment only. Mandatory 45-minute tours run continuously.

This historic property is the restored home of John Marshall, a giant in American judicial history. As its chief justice from 1801 to 1835, Marshall essentially established the

Downtown Richmond Attractions

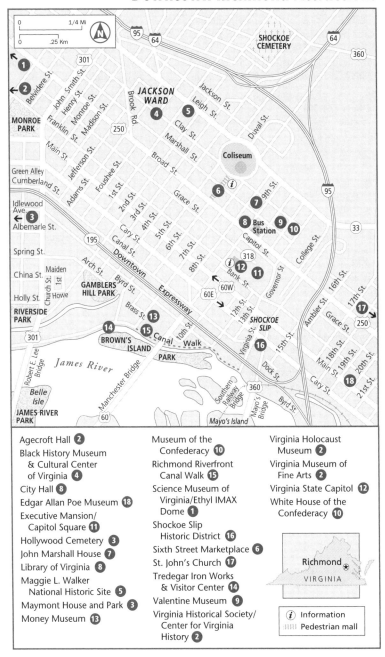

Attraction	#	Attraction	#	Attraction	#
Agecroft Hall	2	Museum of the Confederacy	10	Virginia Holocaust Museum	2
Black History Museum & Cultural Center of Virginia	4	Richmond Riverfront Canal Walk	15	Virginia Museum of Fine Arts	2
City Hall	8	Science Museum of Virginia/Ethyl IMAX Dome	1	Virginia State Capitol	12
Edgar Allan Poe Museum	18			White House of the Confederacy	10
Executive Mansion/Capitol Square	11	Shockoe Slip Historic District	16		
Hollywood Cemetery	3	Sixth Street Marketplace	6		
John Marshall House	7	St. John's Church	17		
Library of Virginia	8	Tredegar Iron Works & Visitor Center	14		
Maggie L. Walker National Historic Site	5	Valentine Museum	9		
Maymont House and Park	3	Virginia Historical Society/Center for Virginia History	2		
Money Museum	13				

(i) Information
▦ Pedestrian mall

power of the United States Supreme Court through his doctrine of judicial review, under which federal courts can overturn acts of Congress. Earlier, Marshall served in the Revolutionary Army, argued cases for George Washington (his close personal friend), served as ambassador to France under John Adams, and had a brief term as secretary of state. He was a political foe of his cousin, Thomas Jefferson.

Largely intact, the house Marshall built between 1788 and 1790 is remarkable for many original architectural features—exterior brick lintels, interior wide-plank pine floors, wainscoting, and paneling. Marshall's own furnishings and personal artifacts have been supplemented by period antiques and reproductions. A 9-minute video about Marshall's life precedes the 45-minute guided tours, so allow an hour here.

Maggie L. Walker National Historic Site. 110½ E. Leigh St. (between 1st and 2nd sts.). ☎ **804/771-2017.** www.nps.gov/malw. Free admission. Wed–Sun 9am–5pm. Closed New Year's Day, Thanksgiving, and Christmas. 30-minute tours depart as necessary.

The daughter of a former slave, Maggie L. Walker was an unusually gifted woman who achieved success in the world of finance and business and rose to become the first woman bank president in the country. Originally a teacher, Walker, after her marriage in 1886, became involved in the affairs of a black fraternal organization, the Independent Order of St. Luke, which grew under her guidance into an insurance company, and then into a full-fledged bank, the St. Luke Penny Savings Bank. The bank continues today as the Consolidated Bank and Trust, the oldest surviving African-American–operated bank in the United States. Walker also became editor of a newspaper and created and developed a department store. Her residence from 1904 until her death in 1934, this house remained in her family until 1979. It has been restored to its 1930 appearance by the National Park Service. Park rangers are on hand to lead 30-minute guided tours.

✪ **Museum of the Confederacy.** 1201 E. Clay St. ☎ **804/649-1861.** www.moc.org. Museum admission $5 adults, $4 seniors, $3 students, free for children under 7. Combination ticket (White House and museum) $8 adults, $7 seniors, $5 students. White House and museum, Mon–Sat 10am–5pm; Sun noon–5pm. Mandatory 40-minute White House tours depart continuously Mon, Wed, and Fri–Sat 10:30am–4:30pm; Tues and Thurs 11:30am–4:30pm; Sun 12:30–4:30pm. Free parking in MCVH patients parking deck next door.

This fine museum houses the largest Confederate collection in the country, much of it contributed by veterans and their descendants. All the war's major events and campaigns are documented, and exhibits include period clothing and uniforms, a replica of Lee's headquarters, the role of African Americans in the Civil War, Confederate memorabilia, weapons, and art.

Next door is the **White House of the Confederacy.** When the rebels moved their capital to Richmond, the city government leased this 1818 mansion as a temporary home for President Jefferson Davis. It was the center of wartime social and political activity in Richmond. In 1891, a group of civic-minded Richmond women acquired the property and began a long restoration. The entrance hall is notable for its bronzed classical Comedy and Tragedy figures holding exquisite gas lamps. Formal dinners, luncheons, and occasional cabinet meetings were held in the dining room, a Victorian chamber with ornate ceiling decoration; some of the furniture in this room is original to the Davis family. Guests were received in the center parlor, interesting now for its knickknacks produced by captured Confederate soldiers and for an 1863 portrait of Davis. Upstairs are the bedrooms and the office in which Davis conducted the business of war.

You can explore the museum on your own, but you must take a guided tour to see the house (tours depart from the museum lobby). You'll need about 2 hours to see both.

✪ **Richmond National Battlefield Park.** Visitor Center in Tredegar Iron Works, on Richmond Riverfront Canal Walk at Tredegar and 5th sts. Headquarters, 3215 E. Broad St. (at 33rd St.). ☎ **804/226-1981.** www.nps.gov/rich. Free admission. Audio tape tours $5.40. Visitor Center, daily 9am–5pm. Closed New Year's Day, Thanksgiving, and Christmas.

As the political, medical, and manufacturing center of the South and the primary supply depot for Lee's Army of Northern Virginia, Richmond was a prime military target throughout the Civil War. Seven major drives were launched against the city between 1861 and 1865. The bloody battlefields ring Richmond's eastern side, now mostly suburbs, for some 60 miles.

Before setting out on a driving tour, stop at the **Tredegar Visitor Center,** which was being established as we went to press from the old Chimborazo Visitor Center on East Broad Street (see below) to the restored Tredegar Iron Works building, on Richmond Riverfront Canal Walk at the foot of 5th Street. Here, a 12-minute movie about the Civil War is shown every 30 minutes throughout the day, as is *Richmond Remembers,* a 22-minute film documenting the socioeconomic impact of the Civil War on the Confederate capital. If you're planning to drive around the battlefields, be sure to buy a 3-hour auto-tape tour that covers the Seven Days Campaign of 1862. (In other words, this complete tour takes a minimum of 3 hours without stops, so give yourself half a day to do it in comfort.) Park rangers are on hand to answer all questions.

The former **Chimborazo Visitor Center,** on East Broad Street at 33rd Street, was the site of one of the Confederacy's largest hospitals (about 76,000 patients were treated here). Plans call for this building to become a medical museum (check the Tredegar Visitor Center for details). Park headquarters will continue to be located here.

There are smaller visitor centers at **Cold Harbor,** about 10 miles northeast, and at **Fort Harrison,** about 8 miles southeast. Cold Harbor was the scene of a particularly bloody 1864 encounter during which 7,000 of Grant's men were killed or injured in just 30 minutes. Programs with costumed Union and Confederate soldiers reenacting life in the Civil War era take place during the summer. The Cold Harbor visitor center is open year-round, daily 9am to 5pm, and rangers lead 45-minute walking tours of the battlefield during summer. The Fort Harrison visitor center is open daily 9am to 5pm in summer, on weekends during spring and fall.

It's convenient to combine a battlefield tour with visits to the James River plantations (see chapter 10), since Fort Harrison and some other sites are near Va. 5, the plantations route.

Valentine Museum. 1015 E. Clay St. ☎ **804/649-0711.** www.valentinemuseum.com. Admission $5 adults, $4 seniors, $3 children 7–12, free for children under 7. Mon–Sat 10am–5pm; Sun noon–5pm. Mandatory 30-minute tours depart on the hour 11am–4pm. Free parking on premises.

Named for Mann S. Valentine II, a 19th-century businessman and patron of the arts whose fortune was based on a patent medicine called Valentine's Meat Juice, this museum documents the history of Richmond from the 17th to the 20th centuries. It includes the elegant Federal-style Wickham House, built in 1812 by attorney John Wickham, Richmond's wealthiest citizen who had helped defend Aaron Burr in 1807. Wickham assembled the finest talents of his day to design and decorate his mansion and entertained Richmond's social elite here, along with such visiting notables as Daniel Webster, Zachary Taylor, John Calhoun, Henry Clay, and William Thackeray.

Impressions

As the sun rose on Richmond, such a spectacle was presented as can never be forgotten by those who witnessed it. . . . All of the horrors of the final conflagration, when the earth shall be wrapped in flames and melt with fervent heat, were, it seemed to us, prefigured in our capital.

—An observer (April 3, 1865)

Highlights include spectacular decorative wall paintings, perhaps the rarest and most complete set in the nation; the Oval Parlor, designated as "one of the hundred most beautiful rooms in America"; and the circular Palette Staircase. Slave and servant quarters have been restored to reveal the lives of the residents who supported the Wickhams' lavish lifestyle. Guided house **tours,** included in the price of admission to the museum, are given hourly.

Valentine purchased the house in 1882, converted it into a private museum, and left it to the public when he died. Exhibits cover social and urban history, decorative and fine arts, textiles, architecture, and more. An ongoing display, "Shared Spaces, Separate Lives," uses touch-screen audiovisual elements and surround-sound special effects to explore the history of Richmond's complex race relationships. Lunch in Wickham's Garden Café is offered weekdays.

✪ **Virginia State Capitol.** 9th and Grace sts. ☎ **804/698-1788.** Free admission. 30-minute tours depart continuously Apr–Nov, daily 9am–5pm; Dec–Mar, Mon–Sat 9am–5pm, Sun 1–5pm.

Thomas Jefferson was minister to France when he was commissioned to work on a capitol building for Virginia. He closely patterned the Classical Revival building on the Maison Carrée, a Roman temple built in Nîmes during the 1st century A.D., which he greatly admired. The colonnaded wings on either side were added between 1904 and 1906. Today the building is the second-oldest working capitol in the United States, in continuous use since 1788.

The central portion is the magnificent Rotunda, its domed skylight ceiling ornamented in Renaissance style. The room's dramatic focal point is Houdon's life-sized statue of George Washington, said to be a perfect likeness. "That is the man, himself," said Lafayette. "I can almost realize he is going to move." A Carrara-marble bust of Lafayette by Houdon also graces the Rotunda, as do busts of the seven other Virginia-born presidents.

Resembling an open courtyard, the old Hall of the House of Delegates, where the Virginia House of Delegates met from 1788 to 1906, is now a museum. Here, in 1807, Washington Irving took notes while John Marshall tried and acquitted Aaron Burr of treason. The room was also a meeting place of the Confederate Congress. In the former Senate chamber, now used for occasional committee meetings, Stonewall Jackson's body lay in state after his death in 1863.

You can wander around the hallways on your own, but you'll actually learn something on the 30-minute guided tours. After the tour, explore the **Capitol grounds.** To the east is the **Executive Mansion,** official residence of governors of Virginia since 1813. Another historic building is the old **Bell Tower,** built in 1824, often the scene of lunch-hour entertainment in summer. The Bell Tower houses a visitor center, where you can get information about Richmond and other Virginia destinations.

Edgar Allan Poe Museum. 1914–1916 E. Main St. ☎ **804/648-5523.** www. poemuseum.org. Admission $6 adults, $5 seniors and students, free for children under 6. Sun–Mon noon–5pm; Tues–Sat 10am–5pm. Mandatory 45-minute tours depart on the hour (last tour daily 4pm). Free parking on premises.

Enclosing an "Enchanted Garden," the Poe Museum consists of four buildings in which the poet's rather sad life and career are documented. The museum complex

---

A Lifelike Washington

The Houdon statue of George Washington in the Rotunda of the Virginia State Capitol is the only one ever made of the first president from life.

centers on the Old Stone House, the oldest building in Richmond, dating to about 1736. Poe didn't live in this house, but as a 15-year-old he was part of a junior honor guard that escorted Lafayette when the famous general was entertained here in 1824. Today the Old Stone House contains a shop and a video presentation that initiates guided tours of the museum. The other three buildings were added to house the growing collection of Poe artifacts and publications, now the largest in existence.

Poe was orphaned at age 2 and taken into the home of John and Frances Valentine Allan, thus his middle name. As a young man, Poe worked as an editor, a critic, and a writer for the *Southern Literary Messenger*. The desk and chair he used at the *Messenger* are among the artifacts, photos, portraits, documents, and other memorabilia on display. Most fascinating is the Raven Room displaying artist James Carling's evocative illustrations of "The Raven." You must take a guided tour of the museum, but you can examine the Enchanted Garden and see some of the memorabilia on your own.

✪ **St. John's Church.** 2401 E. Broad St. (at 24th St.). ☎ **804/648-5015.** Admission $3 adults, $2 seniors, $1 children 7–18, free for children under 7. Mandatory 25-minute tours given Mon–Sat 10am–3:30pm, Sun 1–3:30pm; services Sun at 8:30 and 11am.

Originally known simply as the "church on Richmond Hill," St. John's dates to 1741, but its congregation was established in 1611. Alexander Whitaker, the first rector, instructed Pocahontas in Christianity, baptized her, and married her to John Rolfe. The church building is best known as the 1775 meeting place of the second Virginia Convention. In attendance were Thomas Jefferson, George Wythe, George Mason, Benjamin Harrison, George Washington, Richard Henry Lee, and many other historic personages. In support of a bill to assemble and train a militia to oppose Great Britain, Patrick Henry stood up and delivered his incendiary speech: "Is life so dear, or peace so sweet, as to be purchased at the price of chains or slavery? Forbid it, Almighty God! I know not what course others may take; but as for me, give me liberty, or give me death!"

You'll see the original 1741 entrance and pulpit, the exquisite stained-glass windows, and the pew where Patrick Henry sat during the convention. From the last Sunday in May to the first Sunday in September, there's a living-history program at 2pm re-creating the second Virginia Convention (admission is free but donation plates are passed).

THE "BOULEVARD MUSEUMS"

The following museums are either on or near Boulevard, the major north-south avenue. The city's **Blue Line** trolley operates every 55 minutes along Boulevard between the science museum and Maymount (see "Getting Around," above).

Science Museum Of Virginia/Ethyl IMAX Dome. 2500 W. Broad St. (3 blocks east of Boulevard). ☎ **800/659-1727** or 804/367-6552. www.smv.mus.va.us. Admission $5 adults, $4.50 seniors, $4 children 4–12. Tickets to films, $4 per person, free for children under 5. Exhibits, summer, Mon–Thurs 9:30am–5pm, Fri–Sat 9:30am–7pm, Sun 11:30am–5pm; winter, Mon–Sat 9:30am–5pm, Sun 11:30am–5pm. Theater, Mon–Thurs 10:30am–5pm; Fri–Sat 10:30am–9pm; Sun noon–5pm. Free parking.

There are few DO NOT TOUCH signs in the galleries here, as hands-on exhibits are the norm in this science museum and state-of-the-art planetarium, making it ideal for youngsters. For example, in "Computer Works," visitors create programs, discuss their problems with a computer shrink, and play "assistant" for a computer magician. One wing features exhibits on aerospace technology, energy and electricity, chemistry, and physics. Elsewhere, you'll learn about optical illusions inside a giant kaleidoscope, try to get your bearings in a full-size distorted room, and crawl into a space capsule.

Not to be missed are the shows at the 275-seat Ethyl Universe Planetarium/Space Theater, which shows spectacular Omnimax films as well as the most sophisticated special-effects multimedia planetarium shows. The building itself merits attention, too: It's the Beaux Arts former Broad Street Station, designed in 1919 by John Russell Pope (architect of the Jefferson Memorial, the National Archives, and the National Gallery of Art in Washington). With a soaring rotunda, classical columns, vaults, and arches, Pope created it to evoke a sense of wonder—very fitting for a museum of science.

Virginia Historical Society/Center for Virginia History. 428 N. Boulevard (at Kensington Ave.). ☎ **804/358-4901.** www.vahistorical.org. Admission $4 adults, $3 seniors, $2 students and children. Mon–Sat 10am–5pm; Sun 1–5pm.

Housed in the neoclassical Battle Abbey, built in 1913 as a shrine to the state's Civil War dead, the South's oldest historical society (founded in 1831) has the world's largest collection of Virginia artifacts. Touring the major permanent exhibit, "The Story of Virginia, an American Experience," is like rummaging through the state's attic: You'll see gold buttons from Pocahontas's hat, Patrick Henry's eyeglasses, and much, much more. Changing exhibits cover a wide range of subjects, from Civil War armaments to a history of the Negro baseball leagues. Genealogists will find a treasure trove of family histories in the library of some 125,000 volumes and 7 million manuscripts.

✪ **Virginia Museum of Fine Arts.** Boulevard and Grove Ave. ☎ **804/367-0844.** www.vmfa.state.va.us. Admission by suggested donation $4. Tues–Sun 11am–5pm; Thurs 11am–8pm. Free parking.

Any city would be proud of this museum, noted for the largest public Fabergé collection outside Russia—more than 300 objets d'art created at the turn of the century for czars Alexander III and Nicholas II. The jewel-encrusted Imperial Easter eggs evoke what art historian Parker Lesley calls the "dazzling, idolatrous realm of the last czars."

Highlights include the Goya portrait *General Nicholas Guye,* a rare life-size marble statue of Roman emperor Caligula, Monet's *Iris by the Pond,* and six magnificent Gobelin *Don Quixote* tapestries. That's not to mention the works of de Kooning, Gauguin, van Gogh, Delacroix, Matisse, Degas, Picasso, Gainsborough, and others; antiquities from China, Japan, Egypt, Greece, Byzantium, Africa, and South America; art from India, Nepal, and Tibet; and an impressive collection of contemporary American art.

The museum also contains the 500-seat **TheatreVirginia** (see "Richmond After Dark," below) and a low-priced cafeteria overlooking a waterfall cascading into a pool with a Maillol sculpture.

HOUSES, GARDENS & CEMETERIES

Agecroft Hall. 4305 Sulgrave Rd. ☎ **804/353-4241.** www.agecrofthall.com. Admission $5 adults, $4.50 seniors, $3 students; half price for gardens only. Tues–Sat 10am–4pm; Sun 12:30–5pm. Mandatory 30-minute tours depart on the hour and half hour.

In an elegant neighborhood overlooking the James River, Agecroft Hall is an authentic late–15th century Tudor manor house built in Lancashire, England, and brought here in the 1920s. Today it serves as a museum portraying the social history and material culture of an English gentry family of the late Tudor and early Stuart eras. Typical of its period, the house has ornate plaster ceilings, massive fireplaces, rich oak paneling, leaded- and stained-glass windows, and a two-story great hall with a mullioned window 25 feet long. Furnishings authentically represent the period. Adjoining the mansion are a formal sunken garden, resembling one at the English royals' Hampton Court Palace, and a formal flower garden, an Elizabethan knot garden, and an herb garden. Visitors see a 12-minute slide show about the estate before taking the house tour. Plan time to explore the gardens as well.

Hollywood Cemetery. 412 S. Cherry (at Albemarle St.). ☎ **804/648-8501.** Free admission. Cemetery, daily 8am–5pm; office, Mon–Fri 8:30am–4:30pm.

Perched on the bluffs overlooking the James River not far from Maymont (see below), Hollywood Cemetery is the serenely beautiful resting place of 18,000 Confederate soldiers, two American presidents (Monroe and Tyler), six Virginia governors, Confederate president Jefferson Davis, and Confederate Gen. J.E.B. Stuart (one of 22 Confederate generals interred here). Designed in 1847, it was conceived as a place where nature would remain undisturbed. Its winding scenic roads, flowering trees, stone-bridged creeks, and ponds are largely intact today. The section in which the Confederates are buried is marked by a 90-foot granite pyramid, a monument constructed in 1869. A 20-minute film about the cemetery is shown in the office.

Lewis Ginter Botanical Garden. 1800 Lakeside Ave. ☎ **804/262-9887.** www.lewisginter.org. Admission $5 adults, $4 seniors, $3 children 2–12, free for children under 2. Daily 9am–5pm (to 8pm Sun–Mon in summer). Take I-95 North to Exit 80 (Brook Rd.) and turn left at Hilliard Rd. to Lakeside.

In the 1880s, self-made Richmond millionaire, philanthropist, and amateur horticulturist Lewis Ginter (a founder of the American Tobacco Company) built the Lakeside Wheel Club as a summer playground for the city's elite. The resort boasted a lake, a nine-hole golf course, cycling paths, and a zoo. At Ginter's death in 1897, part of his vast fortune went to his niece, Grace Arents, who converted the property to a hospice for sick children and named it Bloemendaal for Ginter's ancestral village in the Netherlands. An ardent horticulturist, she imported rare trees and shrubs and constructed greenhouses. A white gazebo and trellised seating areas were covered in rambling roses and clematis. Large beds on the front lawn were planted with shrubs and flowers. Grace died in 1926, leaving her estate to the city of Richmond to be maintained as a botanical garden and public park. An admissions brochure suggests routes through the gardens and highlights significant aspects of the collection. There's a delightful Tea House on the premises for lunch.

Maymont House and Park. Just north of the James River between Va. 161 and Meadow St. ☎ **804/358-7166** or 804/358-7167 for tram ride information. www.maymont.org. Free admission (donations suggested). Apr–Oct, daily 10am–7pm; Nov–Mar, daily 10am–5pm. Mandatory 25-minute house tours depart every hour and half hour Tues–Sun noon–4:30pm. Go south 2 miles to the end of Boulevard; follow signs to the parking area.

In 1886, Maj. James Henry Dooley, one of Richmond's self-made millionaires, purchased a 100-acre dairy farm and built this 33-room mansion surrounded by beautifully landscaped grounds. The house is in the Romanesque Revival style, with colonnaded sandstone facade, turrets, and towers. The architectural details of the formal rooms reflect various periods, most notably 18th-century French. The dining room has a stunning coffered oak ceiling; the library, a stenciled strapwork ceiling. A grand stairway leads to a landing from which two-story-high stained-glass windows rise. The house is elaborately furnished with pieces from many periods chosen by the Dooleys—Oriental carpets, an art nouveau swan-shaped bed, marble and bronze sculpture, porcelains, tapestries, and Tiffany vases.

The Dooleys lavished the same care on the grounds. They placed gazebos wherever the views were best, laid out Italian and Japanese gardens, and planted horticultural specimens and exotic trees culled from the world over. The **Nature and Visitor Center** has interactive exhibits interpreting the James River. There are outdoor animal habitats for birds, bison, beaver, deer, elk, and bear. At the **Children's Farm,** youngsters can feed chickens, piglets, goats, peacocks, cows, donkeys, and sheep. A collection of late 19th- and early 20th-century horse-drawn carriages—surreys, phaetons, hunting vehicles—is on display at the **Carriage House.** Carriage rides are a weekend afternoon option from April to October and at Christmas.

You can see everything else on your own, but you must take a guided tour in order to visit the house (enter the park via Hampton Street). There's a parking lot off Spottswood Road near the Children's Farm, and another at Hampton Street and Pennsylvania Avenue near the house and gardens.

Wilton House. S. Wilton Rd. ☎ **804/282-5936.** Admission $5 adults, $4 seniors and students, free for children under 6. Mar–Jan, Tues–Sat 10am–4:30pm, Sun 1:30–4:30pm; Feb, by appointment only. Closed national holidays. Mandatory 40-minute tours depart continuously. Take Va. 147 (Cary Street Rd.) west and turn south on Wilton Rd.

Originally built on the James River about 14 miles below Richmond, the stately 1753 Georgian mansion was painstakingly dismantled and reconstructed on this bluff overlooking the river in 1933. Most of the original brick, flooring, and paneling were saved. Wilton's design has been attributed to a leading Williamsburg architect, Richard Taliaferro. It was part of a 2,000-acre plantation where William Randolph III entertained many of the leading figures of the day, including George Washington, Thomas Jefferson, and Lafayette. The house has a fine collection of period furnishings throughout. All rooms feature handsome pine paneling, some with fluted pilasters and denticulated cornices.

SPECIAL INTEREST MUSEUMS

The **Black History Museum & Cultural Center of Virginia,** 00 Clay Street, at Foushee Street (☎ **804/780-9093**), houses documents, limited editions, prints, art, and photos emphasizing the history of the state's African-American community. It resides in a Federal/Greek Revival–style house built in 1832 and purchased a century later by the Council of Colored Women under the leadership of Maggie L. Walker. Admission is $4 for adults, $3 seniors, $2 for children under 12. Open Tuesday to Saturday 10am to 5pm, Sunday 1 to 5pm.

Two museums celebrate Richmond's Jewish heritage. The **Virginia Holocaust Museum,** 213 Roseneath Rd. (☎ **804/673-6341**), pays tribute to those who died in or lived through the Holocaust. Among the exhibits are a mock ghetto surrounded by barbed wire and a model of an underground hiding place. It's open by appointment only. Operated by the nation's sixth-oldest Jewish congregation, the **Congregation Beth Ahabah Museum & Archives Trust,** 1109 W. Franklin St. (☎ **804/353-2668**), houses an extensive collection of records, letters, documents, and photos relating to Jewish history. It's open Sunday through Wednesday from 10am to 3pm. Admission is free ($2 donation suggested).

Numismatists will enjoy the small but interesting **Money Museum,** in the Federal Reserve Bank lobby, 701 E. Byrd St., between 7th Street and the Manchester Bridge (☎ **804/679-8108**). Exhibits trace the history of money, from the bartering of corn to an uncut sheet of $100,000 gold certificates. Admission is free. Open Monday to Friday from 9:30am to 3:30pm.

The lobby of the **Library of Virginia,** 800 Broad St., between 8th and 9th streets (☎ **804/692-3919**), has changing exhibits of state documents and published works, some of them more than 400 years old. For example, one recent exhibit documents from the Jamestown period, including a copy of Capt. John Smith's history of the colony published in 1624. The library is open Monday through Saturday from 9am to 5pm; admission is free.

Anyone who loves old airplanes can see some beautifully restored craft at the small but impressive **Virginia Aviation Museum,** 5701 Huntsman Rd. (☎ **804/236-3622**), off Airport Drive on the grounds of Richmond International Airport. The planes all date from 1916 to 1946, often called the golden age of aviation. Included is a World War II Spad, one of the few still airworthy. Admission is $5 adults, $4 seniors, $3 for kids 4 to 12. Open daily 9:30am to 5pm except Thanksgiving and Christmas.

A RIVERBOAT CRUISE

Modern technology's answer to an 1850s riverboat, the paddle wheeler *Annabel Lee* (☎ **800/752-7093** or 804/664-5700) offers a variety of lunch, dinner, and sightseeing cruises down the James River, some as far as the famous plantations. She operates from April to mid-October. Call for all prices and departure times. Reservations are a must, especially on weekends.

NEARBY ATTRACTIONS

About 14 miles north of Richmond on I-95 is the small community of Ashland in Hanover County, which has deep historical roots. Patrick Henry once tended bar at Hanover Tavern, built in 1723, and argued cases in the Hanover County Courthouse, dating from 1735.

✪ **Scotchtown.** 16120 Chiswell Lane, Beaverdam. ☎ **804/227-3500.** Admission $6 adults, $5 seniors, $3 children 6–12, free for children under 6; grounds only, $3 per person. Apr–Oct, Tues–Sat 10am–4:30pm, Sun 1:30–4:30pm. Nov–Mar, open by appointment only. Closed Easter. Mandatory 1-hour house tours depart on demand. From Ashland, follow Va. 54 west, turn right on Scotchtown Rd. (C.R. 671) north, take right fork on C.R. 685.

One of Virginia's oldest plantation houses, Scotchtown is a charming one-story white-clapboard home, located in a park-like setting of small dependencies and gardens. The house was built by Charles Chiswell of Williamsburg, probably around 1719. Patrick Henry bought the house in 1770 and lived here from 1771 to 1778 with his wife, Sarah, and their six children. Henry served as governor of Virginia during those years, but sadly, Sarah was mentally ill during much of that time and was eventually confined to a room in the basement. Although Henry last lived at Red Hill near Lynchburg (see chapter 6), this is the only house he ever occupied that is still standing. It has been beautifully restored and furnished with 18th-century antiques, some associated with the Henry family. In the study, Henry's mahogany desk-table still bears his ink stains, and bookshelves still contain his law books. A walnut cradle used by several of his children now sits in the guest bedroom. Scotchtown also has associations with another historical figure, Dolley Madison. Her mother was a first cousin to Patrick Henry, and Dolley and her mother lived here while their family moved back to this area from North Carolina.

Unlike many historic houses open to the public, none of the rooms here are roped off, so you can go into all of them during the leisurely and informative guided tours, which emphasize 18th century plantation life in addition to the specific Henry story.

Paramount's Kings Dominion. Doswell. ☎ **804/876-5000.** www.pkd4fun.com. Admission changes from year to year, usually about $35 adults and children 7 and over; $30 seniors 55 and over; $25 children 3–6. Parking $6 per vehicle. Consecutive 2-day passes and season passes available. Hours may vary a bit from year to year, but generally park is open Memorial Day–Labor Day, daily 9:30am to 8 or 10pm; Apr–May and Labor Day to early Oct, Sat–Sun 9:30am to 8 or 10pm. Take Va. 30 (Exit 98) off I-95.

One of the most popular theme parks in the East, this fanciful 400-acre, family-oriented facility offers a variety of rides and entertainment, many with themes from Paramount movies and TV shows. A ride simulator combines moving seats, a giant-screen image, digital audio technology, and other special effects with actual film footage from the movie *Days of Thunder.* A totally enclosed, multiple-inversion launch roller coaster is named "Outer Limits: Flight of Fear," after the popular TV series *Outer Limits.* Another attraction, "Volcano, The Blast Coaster," uses electromagnetic energy to blast riders out of a volcano.

And that's just the beginning, as the park also has an ice-skating show featuring music from Paramount movies; a walk-of-fame salute to Paramount's movie history; several walk-around characters, including Klingons, Vulcans, and Romulans from *Star Trek;* and an outdoor laser-and-fireworks show portraying adventure scenes from Paramount movies and TV programs such as *Mission: Impossible, Top Gun,* and *Beverly Hills Cop.* There's an area called *Wayne's World,* featuring the aptly named "Hurler" roller-coaster, and a children's fantasy area called "Hanna-Barbera Land." Kids also can meet the Rugrats in "Nickelodeon Splat City," and everyone can be part of the action in *James Bond 007: A Licence to Kill.*

Almost like its own theme park, the splash-happy WaterWorks features Big Wave Bay, a 650,000-gallon wave pool. White Water Canyon is a wet-and-wild ride simulating white-water rafting. Hurricane Reef offers more watery fun, with 15 water slides, a refreshing raft ride, and Splash Island, designed for younger children with a wading pool and pint-sized slides.

5 Sports & Outdoor Activities

SPECTATOR SPORTS

AUTO RACING   See NASCAR racing at **Richmond International Raceway,** located at the Virginia State Fairgrounds, between Laburnum Avenue and the Henrico Turnpike/Meadowbridge Road (☎ **804/329-6796**). The Raceway is Virginia's largest sports facility, attracting crowds of 70,000 or more.

BASEBALL   The **Richmond Braves** (☎ **804/359-4444;** www.rbraves.com), the top minor-league club in the Atlanta Braves' organization, compete in the 10-team International League from April to mid-September. All home games are played at the Diamond, a 12,500-seat modern baseball stadium located at 3001 N. Boulevard (Exit 78 off I-95).

COLLEGE SPORTS   The **University of Richmond's** Spiders play football and basketball in the Colonial Athletic Association (☎ **804/289-8388**). **Virginia Commonwealth University** fields a basketball team, the Rams, that plays at the Coliseum (☎ **804/282-7267**).

HORSE RACING   Virginia's first pari-mutuel racetrack, **Colonial Downs,** opened in 1997 on Va. 155, between I-64 (Exit 205) and U.S. 60 in New Kent County, 25 miles east of Richmond (☎ **804/966-7223**). Call for schedule. Admission is $5.

ICE HOCKEY   Richmond's pro hockey team, the **Renegades,** belongs to the East Coast Hockey League and plays home games October through March at the Coliseum, 601 E. Leigh St., at 7th Street (☎ **804/643-7825**).

SOCCER   The **Richmond Kickers** play professional soccer games at the University of Richmond Soccer Complex (☎ **804/282-6776**).

OUTDOOR ACTIVITIES
GOLF   Golf courses abound in the Richmond area. Among them are the **Belmont Park Recreation Center,** 1800 Hilliard Rd. (☎ **804/266-4929**), and **Glenwood Golf Club,** Creighton Road (☎ **804/226-1793**).

WHITE-WATER RAFTING   You don't have to trek to the remote mountains to ride the rapids, since **Richmond Raft Company,** 4400 E. Main St., at Water Street (☎ **804/222-7238;** www.richmondraft.com), offers trips on the James through the heart of Richmond. Water levels aren't always predictable, but the James is usually high and fast enough from March to November, with spring best for fast water.

6 Shopping

Richmond's neighborhoods have a number of specialty shops, including those mentioned below. The visitor centers provide brochures that cover these and many other stores around the city and out in the suburbs.

For distinctive souvenirs, don't forget museum gift shops, especially those at the Science Museum, Art Museum, Museum and White House of the Confederacy, Valentine Museum, and Children's Museum.

✪ **CARYTOWN**   The best place in town for a shopping stroll, the 7 blocks of West Cary Street between Boulevard and Nasemond Street—known collectively as Carytown—are lined with a mix of small stores and interesting cafes. The old **First Baptist Church,** 3325 W. Cary St., has been transformed into an inviting retail complex, with the high-fashion Annette Dean's, Karina beauty salon, and fine Acacia restaurant (see "Where to Dine," above).

Antiques hunting is good here, especially at **The Antiques Gallery,** 3140 W. Cary St. (☎ **840/358-0500**); **Martha's Mixture Antiques,** 3445 W. Cary St. (☎ **804/358-5827**); **Thomas-Hines Antiques,** 3027 W. Cary St. (☎ **804/355-2782**); and **Mariah Robinson Antiques,** 3455 W. Cary St. (☎ **804/355-1996**). **Ten Thousand Villages,** 2820 W. Cary St. (☎ **804/358-5170**), carries handcrafts from around the world, with lots of baskets and primitive pottery. **In the Company of Cats,** 3421 W. Cary St. (☎ **804/359-6369**), offers unusual gifts and objets d'art for feline lovers. You'll also find gourmet food shops, ethnic restaurants, secondhand clothing stores, and the landmark **Byrd Theater,** which now shows second-run films at discount prices.

SHOCKOE SLIP   On East Cary Street, from 12th to 14th streets, the converted warehouse district has a profusion of trendy clothing stores, restaurants, art galleries, and entertainment venues along its cobblestone streets. Among the special shops here are Toymaker of Williamsburg and Beecroft & Bull, a fine men's clothier.

WEST END   The fashionable West End neighborhood features the **Shops at Libbie and Grove,** at the intersection of the 5700 block of Grove and the 400 block of Libbie, an enclave of distinctive women's fashions and specialty shops. It's especially worth browsing here for decorative items—anything from needlepoint pillows to an abstract wall hanging. Low-scale buildings and a relaxed atmosphere give this area its casual charm.

A short drive north, **West End Antiques Mall,** 6504 Horsepen Rd. (☎ **800/280-1916** or 804/285-1916), has more than 85 dealers offering a wide range of antiques and collectibles. From Libbie and Grove avenues, drive north on Libbie and turn left on Broad Street, then left on Horsepen Road. The mall is on the right.

7 Richmond After Dark

Richmond is no New York or London, so you won't be attending internationally recognized theaters and music halls here. Nevertheless, you might be able to catch visiting productions and artists at several large venues. The city also has its own ballet company and theater groups, and live music usually rocks Shockoe Bottom after dark.

Current entertainment schedules can be found in the Thursday "Weekend" section of the *Richmond Times-Dispatch,* the city's daily newspaper. The tabloid newspaper *Style Weekly* has details on theater, concerts, dance performances, and other happenings. It's free and widely available at the visitor centers and in hotel lobbies.

MAJOR CONCERT HALLS & ALL-PURPOSE AUDITORIUMS

Built in 1928 as a Loew's Theater, the **Carpenter Center for the Performing Arts,** 600 E. Grace St., at Sixth Street Marketplace (☎ 804/782-3900), was restored in 1983 to its Moorish splendor, complete with twinkling stars and clouds painted on the ceiling overhead. The center hosts national touring companies for dance, orchestra, and theater performances, including Broadway shows. The **Richmond Ballet** (see "The Performing Arts," below), the **Virginia Opera** (☎ 804/643-6004), and the **Richmond Symphony** (☎ 804/788-1212) perform here as well.

In the summer months, Richmond goes outdoors to **Dogwood Dell,** in Byrd Park, Boulevard and Idlewild Avenue (☎ 804/780-8683), for free Festival of Arts music and drama performances under the stars in this tiered grassy amphitheater. Bring the family, spread a blanket, and enjoy a picnic.

Adjacent to the bustling campus of Virginia Commonwealth University, **The Mosque,** Main and Laurel streets (☎ 804/780-4213), a 3,500-seat hall, is decorated with exotic mosaics and pointed-arch doorways. Offerings range from stage productions to nationally known musicians. The Mosque is also home to the **Richmond Forum** (☎ 804/330-3993), which presents stimulating discussions of current topics by figures such as Gen. Norman Schwarzkopf, H. Ross Perot, and talk-show host Larry King.

The **Richmond Coliseum,** 601 E. Leigh St. (☎ 804/780-4970), hosts everything from the Ringling Bros. and Barnum & Bailey circus to rock concerts. It's the largest indoor entertainment facility in Virginia and seats about 12,000. Major sporting events—wrestling, ice hockey, basketball—are also scheduled here.

THE PERFORMING ARTS

The state's leading professional theater is the 535-seat **TheatreVirginia,** in the Virginia Museum of Fine Arts, 2800 Grove Ave. (☎ 804/367-0831), which offers a variety of productions such as *Gypsy, Sylvia, Arcadia, Lost in Yonkers,* and *A Closer Walk with Patsy Cline.* The season runs from October to the end of April.

You can catch family plays and musicals at **Theatre IV,** 114 W. Broad St. (☎ 804/344-8040), which performs in the Empire Theater, at Broad and Jefferson streets.

The **Richmond Ballet** (☎ 804/359-0906), the official State Ballet of Virginia, performs from mid-October to May. Their productions run the gamut from classical to modern, from *The Nutcracker* to commissioned world premieres. Call for schedule, prices, and locations.

THE CLUB & MUSIC SCENE

Shockoe Bottom is the city's funky nightlife district. It occupies the square block beginning with the 17th Street Farmer's Market and going east along East Main and East Franklin streets to 18th Street. Its joints attract the "let's see your ID" crowd, and they go up and down in popularity, so those I visited recently may not be in vogue by the time you get here. If you can find a parking space, you can easily see for yourself what's going on by bar-hopping around Shockoe Bottom's busy block (but *do not* wander off onto deserted streets). Note that many Shockoe Bottom establishments are closed on Sunday and Monday.

Up Cary Street in the more affluent (and well-behaved) Shockoe Slip, **The Tobacco Company,** 1201 E. Cary St. (☎ **804/782-9555**), has acoustic jazz upstairs Tuesday through Saturday and dancing downstairs Wednesday through Saturday from 8pm to 1am.

8 An Easy Excursion to Petersburg

In the 1860s, Petersburg was a vital rail junction, which Grant recognized as the key to his quest to take Richmond. When every effort to capture the Confederate capital failed, Grant, in an inspired move, crossed the James River south of Richmond and advanced on Petersburg. Lee's forces weren't cooperative, however, and a tragic 10-month siege ensued. Finally, on April 2, Grant's all-out assault smashed through Lee's right flank, and that night Lee retreated west. A week later came the surrender at Appomattox Court House.

Today, Petersburg is a quiet southern town on the banks of the Appomattox River 23 miles south of Richmond on I-95. Its downtown has a few museums of the Civil War period, which you can see in a few hours. The more interesting sights are on the outskirts, where the battles took place.

VISITOR INFORMATION

When you arrive, take Washington Street (Exit 52) west and follow the Petersburg Tour signs to the **visitor center,** 425 Cockade Alley (P.O. Box 2107), Petersburg, VA 23804 (☎ **800/368-3595** or 804/733-2400; www.petersburg-va.org), where you can get a complimentary parking permit (valid for 1 day), maps, and literature. The center is open daily from 9am to 5pm.

EXPLORING DOWNTOWN

During the summer months, the visitor center, in the basement of the 1815 McIlwaine House, sells **block tickets** to several area museums. The best deal is the "Pass to the Past," which includes the Siege Museum, Centre Hill Mansion, Old Blandford Church, Petersburg National Battlefield Park, and Pamplin Park, all for $23 per person. Another version includes the Siege Museum, Trapezium House, Centre Hill Mansion, Farmers Bank, and Old Blandford Church for $11 for adults, $9 for seniors and children 7 to 12. Or, choose three attractions for $7 adults, $5 seniors and children. Otherwise, admission to each is $3 adults, $2 seniors and children. Active-duty military personnel pay the seniors/children rate.

The **Siege Museum,** 15 W. Bank St. (☎ **804/733-2400**), tells the story of everyday life in Petersburg up to and during the siege in displays and an exceptionally interesting 18-minute film narrated by actor Joseph Cotten, whose family lived in Petersburg during the Civil War. Give yourself another 30 minutes to see the museum, in the old Merchant Exchange, a magnificent Greek Revival temple-fronted building. It's open daily from 10am to 5pm.

The **Trapezium House,** at Market and High streets (☎ **804/733-2400**), is an amusing curiosity built without any right angles, supposedly because its owner was frightened by tales of ghosts who lurked in them. It's open March to October, daily from 10am to 5pm. You must take a 30-minute tour (they depart every hour on the half hour).

Centre Hill Mansion, 1 Centre Hill Circle (☎ **804/733-2400**), between Adams and Tabb streets, is a nicely restored 1823 mansion furnished with Victorian pieces. Hours are daily from 10am to 5pm. You'll have to take a 30-minute tour (departing every hour on the half hour).

ATTRACTIONS SOUTH OF DOWNTOWN

Old Blandford Church, about 2 miles south of downtown on Crater Road (U.S. 301) at Rochelle Lane (☎ **804/733-2400**), boasts one of the largest collections of Tiffany-glass windows in existence and is noted for the first observance of Memorial Day. The church was constructed in 1735 but abandoned in the early 1800s when a new Episcopalian church was built closer to the town center. During the Civil War, the building became a hospital for troops wounded on nearby battlefields, and many of them were later buried in the church graveyard. After the war, a group of Petersburg schoolgirls and their teacher came here to decorate the soldiers' graves. The ceremony inspired Mary Logan, wife of Union Gen. John A. Logan, who was head of the major organization of Union army veterans, to campaign for a national memorial day, which was first observed in 1868. The 13 Confederate states each sponsored one of the Tiffany windows as a memorial to its Confederate dead. The 14th was commissioned by the local Ladies Memorial Association. The artist himself, Louis Comfort Tiffany, gave the church the 15th window, a magnificent "Cross of Jewels" that is thrillingly illuminated at sunset. To get to the church, take Bank Street east and turn right on Crater Road (U.S. 301). It's open daily 9am to 5pm, with 30-minute tours departing on the hour and half-hour.

Not far from the church, the **Softball Hall of Fame Museum,** 3935 S. Crater Rd. (U.S. 301; ☎ **804/733-1005**), celebrates the stars and history of softball throughout America. Admission is $2 for adults, $1 for seniors and students. It's open Monday to Friday 9am to 4pm, Saturday 10am to 4pm, Sunday noon to 4pm. Closed all holidays.

THE CIVIL WAR BATTLEFIELDS

Together, the sites below will take about a day to tour. Start in the morning at the national battlefield's visitor center east of town, follow the battlefield tour to the Crater (you can also stop at Old Blandford Church and the National Softball Hall of Fame Museum, both near the Crater), have lunch at King's Barbeque No. 2 (see "Where to Dine," below), and spend the afternoon at Pamplin Historical Park.

✪ **Pamplin Historical Park & The National Museum of the Civil War Soldier.** 6125 Boydton Plank Rd. (U.S. 1). ☎ **877/PAMPLIN** or 804/861-2408. www. pamplinpark.org. Admission $10 adults, $9 seniors, $5 children 7–11, free for children under 7. Daily 9am–5pm (to 6pm Memorial Day to Labor Day). Park is 6 miles south of downtown, 1 mile south of I-85.

The battleground where Union troops actually broke through on April 2, 1865, to end the siege is in this fine, privately owned park, where more than a mile of interpretive trails lead through some of the best-preserved Confederate earthen-work fortifications. There's a re-created Military Encampment with costumed interpreters on hand, and a Battlefield Center with high-tech displays explaining the final conflict. Guides lead 45-minute guided walking tours of the battlefield twice a day; call for times. The park also includes Tudor Hall, a plantation home built in 1812, which you can see on your own or via a 40-minute guided tour. You start all this at The National Museum of the Civil War Soldier, which is dedicated to the common foot soldier (no famous generals need apply). The museum is best explored with an audiocassette, which will explain the exhibits and what a soldier's life was like between 1861 and 1865. Allow an hour in the museum, another 2 to see the battlefield and Tudor Hall.

✪ **Petersburg National Battlefield Park.** 1539 Hickory Hill Rd. (2½ miles east of downtown via E. Washington St./Va. 36). ☎ **804/732-3531.** www.nps.gov/pete. Admission June–Aug, $10 per vehicle; Sept–May, $5 per vehicle; $3 per pedestrian or bicyclist year-round. Daily 8am–5pm; battlefield, daily 8am–dusk.

Encompassing some 2,646 acres, this park preserves the key sites of the siege that lasted from mid-June 1864 to early April 1865. A multimedia presentation at the visitor center tells the story, and a 4-mile battlefield driving tour has wayside exhibits and audio stations; some stops have short walking trails. Most fascinating is the site of the Crater, literally a huge depression blown into the ground when a group of Pennsylvania volunteer infantry, including many miners, dug a passage beneath Confederate lines and exploded 4 tons of powder, creating the 170- by 60-foot crater. The carnage was sickening; thousands of men on both sides were killed or wounded during the ensuing battle. An extended 16-mile driving tour follows the entire siege line, from the visitor center to the Crater, on U.S. 301 south of Petersburg.

At Fort Lee, a mile east of the visitor center on Va. 36, the U.S. Army's **Quartermaster Museum** (☎ **804/734-4203**) has uniforms and equipment from all of America's wars, including a Jeep with a luxurious Mercedes car seat specially installed for Gen. George S. Patton during World War II. The Quartermaster Museum is open Tuesday through Friday from 10am to 5pm and Saturday, Sunday, and federal holidays from 11am to 5pm; admission is free. Take the first right into Fort Lee (no pass required), then the first left to the museum.

WHERE TO STAY

National chain motels near I-95 and Washington Street (Exit 52) include **Best Western** (☎ 800/528-1234 or 804/733-1776), **Howard Johnson** (☎ 800/654-2000 or 804/732-5950), **Knights Inn** (☎ 800/843-5644 or 804/732-1194), **Ramada Inn** (☎ 800/272-6232 or 804/733-0730), **Super 8** (☎ 800/800-8000 or 804/861-0793), and **Travelodge** (☎ 800/578-7878 or 804/733-0000).

Mayfield Inn. 3348 W. Washington St. (P.O. Box 2265), Petersburg, VA 23804. ☎ **800/538-2381** or 804/861-6775. Fax 804/863-1971. www.mayfieldinn.com. 4 units. A/C. $69–$95 double. Rates include full breakfast. AE, MC, V. From I-95 take Exit 52 and go west 3 miles on Washington St. (U.S. 1) to inn on the left.

You'll think you're in Williamsburg at this stately Georgian-style brick manse, built as a plantation home around 1750 by a member of the House of Burgesses and moved to this 4-acre plot of land in 1969. General Lee is thought to have spent the night here before going on to Appomattox. The present owners, Jamie and Dot Caudle, acquired it in 1979 and spent 5 years restoring it and furnishing it with antiques and period reproductions. Much of the interior is original, including seven working fireplaces. Rooms are spacious and luxurious; the largest has a four-poster canopied bed, dormer windows, a love seat, and a small table with a pewter tea service cozily set in front of the fireplace. Hearty country breakfasts are served downstairs in a formal dining room. Guests can stroll in a lovely colonial herb garden or lounge at the pool or in the gazebo.

WHERE TO DINE

✪ **King's Barbeque.** 3221 W. Washington St. (U.S. 1 South). ☎ **804/732-5861.** Main courses $5–$9.50. AE, MC, V. Tues–Sun 7am–9pm. Follow U.S. 1 south 3 miles from downtown. AMERICAN.

Open since 1946, this Petersburg institution supplies some of the best barbecue in the entire South. The setting is a pine-paneled room with colonial-style tables and Windsor chairs. Notice the shelves over the lunch counter and booths: They're lined with an extraordinary collection of pig dolls and figurines, including a Miss Piggy bank. Pork, beef, ribs, and chicken smoke constantly in an open pit right in the dining room. Unlike at most other barbecue emporia, the pork and beef are served just as they come from the pit. Aficionados can enjoy the smoked flavor *au naturel* or apply vinegary sauce from squeeze bottles. The menu also offers such Southern standbys as crispy fried chicken, ham steak, and seafood items like salmon cakes and fried oysters. Side orders include barbecued beans, yam puffs, and fried potato cakes. Fluffy home-made biscuits and hot apple pie are house specialties.

If you're going to the Crater, Old Blandford Church, and the Softball Hall of Fame Museum, **King's Barbeque No. 2,** 2910 S. Crater Rd. (☎ **804/732-0975**), has the same menu and is just as good.

Williamsburg, Jamestown & Yorktown

Stretching from Richmond to the shores of Hampton Roads and the Chesapeake Bay, the narrow peninsula between the James and York rivers saw the very beginnings of colonial America and the rebellion that eventually created the United States. Today you can get an extensive lesson in that early history at the beautifully restored 18th-century town of Colonial Williamsburg. You can see where the first permanent English settlers in North America landed at Jamestown in 1607 and visit re-creations of the ships they came on and the village they built. You can walk the actual ramparts where Washington decisively defeated Cornwallis, thus turning the colonists' dream of a new nation into a reality. Along the James River you can tour the tobacco plantations that created Virginia's first great wealth. And at the eastern end of the peninsula, you can visit Hampton, America's oldest continuously English-speaking town, which now has a modern air and space museum, and take in one of the country's best maritime museums in the shipbuilding city of Newport News.

More than history makes this one of America's family vacation meccas, for here the Busch Gardens Williamsburg theme park brims with entertainment and thrilling rides, and Water Country USA offers summertime fun with watery rides and attractions. There's also world-class shopping in the numerous factory outlet stores near Williamsburg, and golf to be played on some of Virginia's finest courses.

With so much to see and do—for all ages—you'll find this "Historic Triangle" a wonderful place to explore. You'll need at least 3 days to absorb it all: 2 in Colonial Williamsburg and another split between Jamestown and Yorktown. Make it a week if you add the theme parks, shopping, Hampton, Newport News, and a few rounds of golf on Virginia's best courses.

1 Williamsburg

150 miles S of Washington, D.C.; 50 miles E of Richmond

"I know of no way of judging the future," said Patrick Henry, "but by the past." That particular quotation couldn't be more apt as an introduction to Williamsburg. For one thing, Patrick Henry played a very important role here when, as a 29-year-old backcountry lawyer, he spoke out against the Stamp Act in the House of Burgesses in 1765. Many considered him an upstart and called the speech traitorous; others were inspired to revolution.

Another reason the quote is so apt: If you can judge the future by the past, you'll never have a better opportunity of doing so. Williamsburg is unique even in history-revering Virginia. It's gone beyond restoring and re-creating important colonial sites. Most of the year (except May 15 to July 4) a British flag flies over the Capitol. Here women wear long dresses and ruffled caps, men don powdered wigs, taverns serve colonial fare, blacksmiths and harnessmakers produce 18th-century wares, the local militia drills on Market Square, and clip-clopping horses draw carriages just as their ancestors did when George Washington rode these cobblestone streets. Though the Thomas Jefferson you meet may be a modern actor, your casual conversation with him about the rights of man will seem almost real.

ESSENTIALS
VISITOR INFORMATION

COLONIAL WILLIAMSBURG For information specific to the Historic Area, contact the **Colonial Williamsburg Foundation,** P.O. Box 1776, Williamsburg, VA 23187 (☎ 800/HISTORY or 757/220-7645; www.history.org).

Off U.S. 60 Bypass, just east of Va. 132, the foundation's **Colonial Williamsburg Visitor Center** is the beginning of every tour of this area (see "Exploring the Historic Area," below). The center is open 365 days a year, from 8:30am to 7pm in summer, to 5pm the rest of the year. It has two **reservations services** for Colonial Williamsburg Foundation operations: one for the foundation's **hotels** (☎ 800/HISTORY or 757/220-7645), the other for its four colonial **taverns** (☎ 800/TAVERNS or 757/229-2141). In summer it's essential to make these reservations well ahead of time.

WILLIAMSBURG AREA Contact the **Williamsburg Area Convention & Visitor Bureau,** 201 Penniman Rd., Williamsburg, VA 23187 (☎ 800/368-6511 or 757/253-0192; fax 757/229-2047; www.visitwilliamsburg.com), for general information about both the historic attractions and the many hotels, restaurants, and activities here. The bureau sells one of the best maps of the area. It shares offices with the Williamsburg Area Chamber of Commerce. Open Monday to Friday 8:30am to 5pm.

GETTING THERE

BY PLANE Newport News/Williamsburg Airport (☎ 757/877-0221), 14 miles east of Williamsburg, is served by AirTran, United Express, and US Airways Express. More flights (and certainly more jets) arrive at **Richmond International Airport** (see chapter 9), about 45 miles west of town via I-64. **Norfolk International Airport** (see chapter 11) is about the same distance to the east, but traffic on I-64 can cause delays in ground transport to Williamsburg during rush hours and especially on summer weekends when heavy beach traffic funnels through the Hampton Roads Bridge Tunnel.

BY CAR I-64 passes Williamsburg on its way between Richmond and Norfolk. For the historic area, take Exit 238 (Va. 143) off I-64 and follow the signs south to Va. 132 and Colonial Williamsburg. U.S. 60 is the old highway paralleling I-64; it's known as Richmond Road west of Williamsburg, and as York Street/Pocahontas Trail to the east. The scenic John Tyler Highway (Va. 5) runs between Richmond and Williamsburg, passing the James River plantations (see section 4, below). Va. 199, which forms a beltway around the southern side of the city, joins I-64 at Exit 242 east of town; this is the quickest way to get to Busch Gardens Williamsburg and Water Country USA. The Colonial Parkway, one of Virginia's most scenic routes, connects Williamsburg to Jamestown and Yorktown (it runs through a tunnel under the Historic Area).

Williamsburg Area

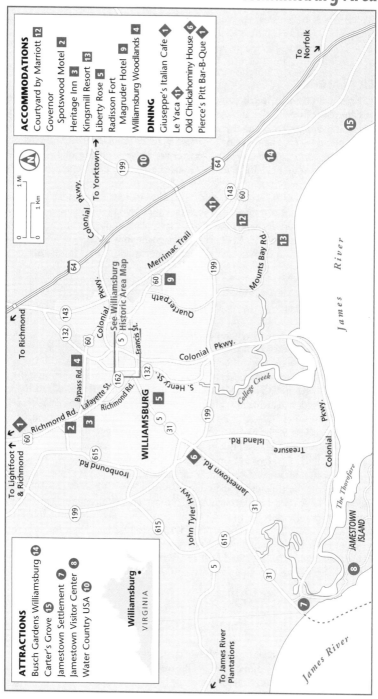

ACCOMMODATIONS
Courtyard by Marriott **12**
Governor
Spotswood Motel **2**
Heritage Inn **3**
Kingsmill Resort **13**
Liberty Rose **5**
Radisson Fort
Magruder Hotel **9**
Williamsburg Woodlands **4**

DINING
Giuseppe's Italian Cafe **1**
Le Yaca **11**
Old Chickahominy House **6**
Pierce's Pitt Bar-B-Que **1**

ATTRACTIONS
Busch Gardens Williamsburg **14**
Carter's Grove **15**
Jamestown Settlement **7**
Jamestown Visitor Center **8**
Water Country USA **10**

Williamsburg
VIRGINIA

BY TRAIN & BUS   Both **Amtrak** trains (☎ 800/872-7245; www.amtrak.com) and **Greyhound/Trailways** buses (☎ 800/231-2222; www.greyhound.com) arrive at the local Transportation Center, Boundary and Lafayette streets (☎ 757/229-8750), which is within walking distance of the historic area.

CITY LAYOUT

The restored **Historic Area** is at the center of Williamsburg. The 99-foot-wide **Duke of Gloucester Street** is this area's principal east-west artery, with the Capitol building sitting at the eastern end, and the Wren building of the College of William and Mary at the western end. The other two major streets are **Francis Street** and **Nicholson Street.** Merchants Square shops and services are between the Historic Area and the college, on the western end of Duke of Gloucester Street. The Visitor Center is north of the Historic Area.

   Richmond Road (U.S. 60 West) runs northwest from the Historic Area and is Williamsburg's main commercial strip, with a wide selection of motels, restaurants, and shopping centers, including the area's outlet malls. On the east side of town, **York Street/Pocahontas Trail** (U.S. 60 East) goes out to Busch Gardens Williamsburg. **By-Pass Road** joins these two highways on the north side of the Historic Area.

GETTING AROUND

Since few cars are allowed into the Historic Area between 8am and 10pm daily, you must park elsewhere. The Colonial Williamsburg Visitor Center (see "Exploring the Historic Area," below) has ample parking and operates a **shuttle bus** to and from the Historic Area. The service begins at 8:50am, with frequent departures until 10pm. It's free to holders of tickets to the Historic Area attractions.

   There's also a footpath from the visitor center to the Historic Area.

   Since traffic as well as the heat can be stifling here during the summer months, the easiest way to get around outside the Historic Area is by the air-conditioned **Relax & Ride Visitors Shuttle,** which runs from Memorial Day to Labor Day, daily from 9am to 9pm. These buses follow U.S. 60 from the Williamsburg Pottery Factory in the west to Busch Gardens Williamsburg in the east, with a detour to the hotels on By-Pass Road. They run through the Historic Area on Henry and Lafayette streets. Fare is $1 per ride. Call ☎ 757/259-4111 for more information.

   Bike rentals are available from Easter through October at the Williamsburg Woodlands hotel, at the Colonial Williamsburg Visitor Center (☎ 757/229-1000). The outdoor stand is open June through August from 9am to 9pm, from 9am to 5pm in spring and fall. Rates range from $7 an hour to $25 a day. **Tazewell Club Fitness Center,** at the Williamsburg Lodge (☎ 757/220-7690), rents bikes and strollers for $25 and $10.50 a day, respectively. It's open year-round, daily 9am to 5pm.

   Colonial Cab (☎ 757/220-1214) and **Williamsburg Taxi** (☎ 757/565-1240) are based at the Transportation Center (see "Getting There," above).

HISTORY & BACKGROUND

In 1699, after nearly a century of famine, fevers, and battles with neighboring American Indian tribes, the beleaguered Virginia Colony abandoned the mosquito-infested swamp at Jamestown for a planned colonial city 6 miles inland. They named it Williamsburg for the reigning British monarch, William of Orange.

   Royal Gov. Francis Nicholson laid out the new capital with public greens and a half-acre of land for every house on the main street. People used their lots to grow vegetables and raise livestock. Most houses were whitewashed wood frame (trees being more abundant than brick), and kitchens were in separate structures to keep the houses from burning down. A "palace" for the royal governor was completed in 1720.

The town prospered and soon became the major cultural and political center of Virginia. The government met here four times a year during "Publick Times," when rich planters and politicos (one and the same in most cases) converged on Williamsburg and the population, normally about 1,800, doubled. Shops displayed their finest imported wares, and there were balls, horse races, fairs, and auctions.

Until the government was moved to Richmond in 1780 to be safer from British attack, Williamsburg played a major role as a seat of royal government and later as a hotbed of revolution. Here occurred many of the seminal events leading up to the Declaration of Independence. Thomas Jefferson and James Monroe studied at the College of William and Mary. Jefferson was also the second state governor and last occupant of the Governor's Palace before the capital moved to Richmond (Patrick Henry was the first). During the Revolution, Williamsburg served as the wartime capital for 4 years and was variously the headquarters of Generals Washington (he planned the siege of Yorktown in George Wythe's house), Rochambeau, and Cornwallis.

A REVEREND, A ROCKEFELLER & A REBIRTH   Williamsburg ceased to be an important political center after 1780, but it remained a quaintly charming Virginia town for another 150 years or so, unique only in that it changed so little. As late as 1926, the colonial town plan was virtually intact, including numerous original 18th-century buildings. Then the Reverend W. A. R. Goodwin, rector of Bruton Parish Church, envisioned restoring the entire town to its colonial appearance as a tangible symbol of our early history. He inspired John D. Rockefeller, Jr., who during his lifetime contributed some $68 million to the project and set up an endowment to help provide for permanent restoration and educational programs. Gifts and bequests by thousands of Americans sustain the project Goodwin and Rockefeller began.

Today the Historic Area covers 173 acres of the original 220-acre town. A mile long, it encompasses 88 preserved and restored houses, shops, taverns, public buildings, and outbuildings that survived to the 20th century. More than 500 additional buildings and smaller structures have been rebuilt on their original sites after extensive archaeological, architectural, and historical research. Williamsburg set a very high standard for other Virginia restorations. Researchers investigated international archives, libraries, and museums and sought out old wills, diaries, court records, inventories, letters, and other documents. The architects carefully studied every aspect of 18th-century buildings, from paint chemistry to brickwork. And archaeologists recovered millions of artifacts while excavating 18th-century sites to reveal original foundations. The Historic Area also includes 90 acres of gardens and greens, and 3,000 surrounding acres serve as a "greenbelt" against commercial encroachment.

The Historic Area and its visitor center, hotels, and taverns are all operated by the Colonial Williamsburg Foundation, a nonprofit educational organization whose activities include ongoing restoration.

EXPLORING THE HISTORIC AREA

There is so much to see and do in the Historic Area that you should consider spending at least 2 days here—with evening retreats to Busch Gardens Williamsburg or Water Country USA to please the kids.

THE VISITOR CENTER   You and the other four million persons who come here every year will begin your visit at the **Colonial Williamsburg Visitor Center,** off U.S. 60 Bypass, just east of Va. 132 (☎ **800/HISTORY** or 757/220-7645). You can't miss it; bright-green signs point the way from all access roads to Williamsburg.

Here you can get maps, guidebooks, and information about lodgings, dining, and evening activities; book hotel rooms; make reservations for lunch and dinner at the

Learning Lord's Lines

You'll see a familiar face in *Williamsburg—the Story of a Patriot,* the 35-minute film shown continuously at the Colonial Williamsburg Visitor Center and on TVs in hotels operated by the Colonial Williamsburg Foundation. It's Jack Lord, who later became famous as the chief detective in the 1970s TV series *Hawaii Five-O.* Students at the College of William and Mary consider the 1950s film to be so campy that they learn every one of Lord's lines by heart.

town's historic taverns, for many tours and evening programs, and for the Orientation Walk (a good way to get an overview of the village); and buy tickets to the dozens of attractions that make up Colonial Williamsburg (see "Tickets," below).

It's imperative to pick up a copy of **Colonial Williamsburg Companion,** a weekly newspaper that gives the hours the attractions are open and the times and places of the week's special presentations, exhibits, and events, and has a detailed map of the Historic Area. It will be invaluable in helping you make the best use of your time.

The center continuously shows a free 8-minute video about Williamsburg, and once you've bought your ticket, you can watch the 35-minute orientation film, *Williamsburg—the Story of a Patriot,* which also runs continuously throughout the day.

The visitor center is open 365 days a year, from 8:30am to 7pm in summer, to 5pm the rest of the year. **Parking** costs $6 a day if you buy a pass, $12 a day if you don't. Once you have bought your pass, you can take a shuttle bus to the Historic Area (see "City Layout" and "Getting Around," above).

TICKETS   It costs nothing to stroll the streets of the Historic Area, and perhaps debate revolutionary politics with the actors playing Thomas Jefferson or Patrick Henry, but you will need a **ticket** to enter the key buildings and all the museums, see the 35-minute orientation film at the visitor center, use the Historic Area shuttle bus, and take a 30-minute Orientation Walk through the restored village (reservations required).

Adults pay $30 for the first day and $5 for each additional day up to 7 days. Youths ages 6 to 17 pay $18, which is good for 7 days. Children under 6 are admitted free when accompanied by a ticket-holding adult. An annual pass costs $65 for adults, $22.50 for youths 6 to 17. Guests at the Colonial Williamsburg Foundation's hotels pay $18 for tickets regardless of age.

Tickets are available at the Colonial Williamsburg Visitors Center and at a **ticket booth** at the Merchants Square shops, on Henry Street at Duke of Gloucester Street.

American Express, Diners Club, MasterCard, and Visa credit cards are accepted at all Colonial Williamsburg ticket outlets, attractions, hotels, and taverns.

HOURS   You can stroll the Historic Area streets anytime, but in general, its attractions are open from April to October daily from 9am to 5pm, to 6pm from Memorial Day to Labor Day. Some attractions are closed on specific days, and hours can vary, so check the *Colonial Williamsburg Companion* for current information.

THE COLONIAL BUILDINGS

Brush-Everard House

One of the oldest buildings in Williamsburg, the Brush-Everard House was occupied without interruption from 1717 (when Public Armorer and master gunsmith John Brush built it as a residence-cum-shop) through 1946. Charged not only with maintaining and repairing weaponry, Brush also had to take part in various ceremonies

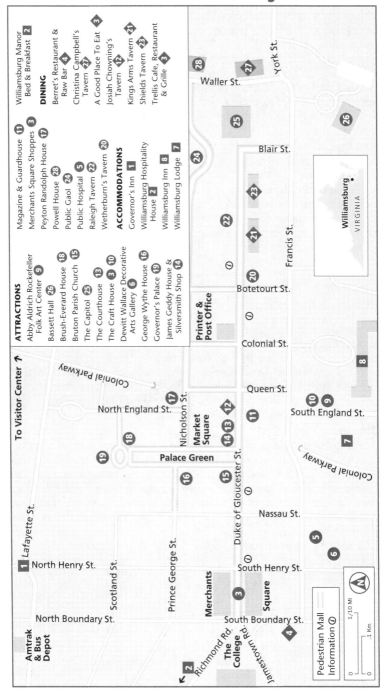

requiring gun salutes, such as royal birthdays. At one of these he wounded himself slightly and applied—without success—to the House of Burgesses for damages. Little else is known about him. He died in 1726. The most distinguished owner was Thomas Everard, clerk of York County from 1745 to 1771 and two-time mayor of Williamsburg. Though not as wealthy as Wythe and Randolph, he was in their elite circle. He enlarged the house, adding the two wings that give a U shape. Today the home is restored and furnished to its Everard-era appearance. The smokehouse and kitchen out back are original. Special programs here focus on African-American life in the 18th century.

✪ The Capitol

Virginia legislators met in the H-shaped Capitol at the eastern end of Duke of Gloucester Street from 1704 to 1780. America's first representative assembly, it has an upper house, His Majesty's Council of State, made up of 12 members appointed by the king for life. The lower body, the House of Burgesses, was elected by the free-holders of each county (there were 128 burgesses by 1776). They initiated legislation, then sent it to the Council for approval or rejection. The House of Burgesses became a training ground for patriots and future governors such as George Washington, Thomas Jefferson, Richard Henry Lee, and Patrick Henry. As 1776 approached, the Burgesses passed increasing petitions and resolutions against acts of Parliament, especially the Stamp Act and the levy on tea—in Henry's words, "taxation without representation," a phrase that became a motto of the Revolution.

All civil and criminal cases (the latter punishable by mutilation or death) were tried in the General Court. Since juries were sent to deliberate in a third-floor room without heat, light, or food, there were very few hung juries. Thirteen of Blackbeard's pirate crew were tried here and sentenced to hang.

The original Capitol burned down in 1747, was rebuilt in 1753, and succumbed to fire again in 1832. The reconstruction is of the 1704 building, complete with Queen Anne's coat-of-arms adorning the tower and the Great Union flag flying overhead. **Tours** (about 25 minutes) are given continuously.

The Courthouse

An intriguing window on colonial life, criminal justice division, is offered in the courthouse, which dominates Market Square. An original building, the courthouse was the scene of widely varying proceedings, ranging from dramatic criminal trials to the prosaic issuance of licenses. Wife beating, pig stealing, and debtor and creditor disputes were among the cases tried in this restored building. Visitors can participate in the administration of colonial justice at the courthouse by sitting on a jury or acting as a defendant. In colonial times convicted offenders were usually punished immediately after the verdict. Punishments included public flogging at the whipping post (conveniently located just outside the courthouse) or being locked in the stocks or pillory, where they were subjected to public ridicule. Jail sentences were very unusual—punishment was swift and drastic, and the offenders then returned to the community, often bearing lifelong evidence of their conviction.

George Wythe House

On the west side of the Palace Green is the elegant restored brick home of George Wythe (pronounced "With"), foremost classics scholar in 18th-century Virginia, noted lawyer and teacher (Thomas Jefferson, Henry Clay, and John Marshall were his students), and member of the House of Burgesses. A close friend of Royal Governors Fauquier and Botetourt, Wythe nevertheless was the first Virginia signer of the Declaration of Independence. On principle, Wythe did not sign the Constitution, however, because it did not contain the bill of rights or antislavery provisions. The house, in which he lived with his second wife, Elizabeth Taliaferro (pronounced "Tolliver"), was Washington's headquarters prior to the siege of Yorktown, and Rochambeau's after the surrender of Cornwallis. Open-hearth cooking is demonstrated in the outbuilding.

❂ Governor's Palace

This meticulous reconstruction is of the Georgian mansion that was the residence and official headquarters of royal governors from 1714 until Lord Dunmore fled before dawn in the face of armed resistance in 1775, thus ending British rule in Virginia. As at other Williamsburg sites, where authentic period pieces were not available, reproductions have been crafted to exacting standards by artisans thoroughly schooled in 18th-century methods. The final 5 years of British rule is the period portrayed. Though the sumptuous surroundings, nobly proportioned halls and rooms, 10 acres of formal gardens and greens, and vast wine cellars all evoke splendor, the king's representative was by that time little more than a functionary of great prestige but limited power. He was more apt to behave like a diplomat in a foreign land than an autocratic colonial ruler.

Tours, given continuously throughout the day, wind up in the gardens, where you can explore at your leisure the elaborate geometric parterres, topiary work, bowling green, pleached allées, and holly maze patterned after the one at Hampton Court. Plan at least 30 minutes to wander these stunning grounds and visit the kitchen and stable yards.

James Geddy House & Silversmith Shop

This two-story L-shaped 1762 home (with attached shops) is an original building. Here visitors can see how a comfortably situated middle-class family lived in the 18th century. Unlike the fancier abodes you'll visit, the Geddy House has no wallpaper or oil paintings; a mirror and spinet from England, however, indicate relative affluence.

The Geddy dynasty begins with James Sr., an accomplished gunsmith and brass founder who advertised in the *Virginia Gazette* of July 8, 1737, that he had "a great Choice of Guns and Fowling Pieces, of several Sorts and Sizes, true bored, which he will warrant to be good; and will sell them as cheap as they are usually sold in England." He died in 1744, leaving his widow with eight children. His enterprising oldest sons, David and William, took over, offering their services as "Gunsmiths, Cutlers, and Founders," and on the side they did a little blacksmithing and engraving and sold cures for "all Diseases incident to Horses." A younger son, James Jr., became the town's foremost silversmith; he imported and sold jewelry, and was a member of the city's Common Council involved in furthering the patriot cause. At a foundry on the premises, craftsmen cast silver, pewter, bronze, and brass items at a forge.

The Magazine & Guardhouse

The magazine is a sturdy octagonal brick building constructed in 1715 to house ammunition and arms for the defense of the British colony. It has survived intact to the present day. In colonial Williamsburg every able-bodied freeman belonged to the militia from the ages of 16 to 60, and did his part in protecting hearth and home from riots, slave uprisings, pirate raids, and attack by local tribes. The high wall and guardhouse were built during the French and Indian War to protect the magazine's 60,000 pounds of gunpowder. Today the building is stocked with 18th-century equipment—British-made flintlock muskets, cannons and cannonballs, barrels of powder, bayonets, and drums, the latter for communication purposes.

A 15-minute **horse-drawn carriage ride** around the Historic Area departs from a horse post in front of the magazine; cost is $7 per person.

Peyton Randolph House

The Randolphs were one of the most prominent—and wealthy—families in colonial Virginia. Sir John Randolph was a highly respected lawyer, Speaker of the House of Burgesses, and Virginia's representative to London, where he was the only colonial-born Virginian ever to be knighted. When he died he left his library to a 16-year-old Peyton, "hoping he will betake himself to the study of law." Peyton Randolph did follow in his father's footsteps, studying law in London after attending the College of William and Mary. He served in the House of Burgesses from 1744 to 1775, the last 9 years as Speaker of the House. Known as the great mediator, he was unanimously elected president of 1774's First Continental Congress in Philadelphia, and though he was a believer in nonviolence who hoped the colonies could amicably settle their differences with England, he was a firm patriot. When he died in 1775, his cousin, Thomas Jefferson, purchased his books at auction; they eventually became the nucleus of the Library of Congress.

The house (actually, two connected homes) dates to 1715. It is today restored to reflect the period around 1770. Robertson's Windmill, in back of the house, is a post mill of a type popular in the early 18th century. The house is open to the public for self-guided tours, with period-costumed interpreters in selected rooms.

The Public Gaol

They didn't coddle criminals in the 18th century, when punishments included not only public ridicule (stocks and pillories) but also whipping, branding, mutilation, and hanging, the latter invoked not only for murder and treason but for burglary, forgery, and horse stealing. Imprisonment was not the usual punishment for crime in colonial times, but persons awaiting trial (at the Capitol in Williamsburg) and runaway slaves sometimes spent months in the Public Gaol. In winter, the dreary cells were bitterly cold; in summer, they were stifling. Beds were rudimentary piles of straw; leg irons, shackles, and chains were used frequently; and the daily diet consisted of "salt beef damaged, and Indian meal." In its early days, the gaol doubled as a madhouse, and during the Revolution redcoats, spies, traitors, and deserters swelled its population.

The gaol opened in 1704. Debtors' cells were added in 1711 (though the imprisoning of debtors was virtually eliminated after a 1772 law made creditors responsible for their upkeep), and keeper's quarters were built in 1722. The thick-walled red-brick building served as the Williamsburg city jail through 1910. The building today is restored to its 1720s appearance.

The Public Hospital

Opened in 1773, the "Public Hospital for Persons of Insane and Disordered Minds" was America's first lunatic asylum. Before its advent, the mentally ill were often thrown in jail or confined to the poorhouse. From 1773 to about 1820, "treatment" involved solitary confinement and a grisly course of action designed to "encourage" patients to "choose" rational behavior (it was assumed that patients willfully and mistakenly chose a life of insanity). So-called therapeutic techniques included the use of powerful drugs, submersion in cold water for extended periods, bleeding, blistering salves, and an array of restraining devices. On a self-guided tour you'll see a 1773 cell, with a filthy straw-filled mattress on the floor, ragged blanket, and manacles.

During what is called the Moral Management Period (1820–65), patients were seen to have an emotional disorder and were treated with kindness. The high point of the Moral Management Period was the administration of John Minson Galt II, from mid-1841 to his death in 1862. Galt created a carpentry shop, a shoemaking shop, a games room, and sewing, spinning, and weaving rooms. He conducted reading and music

Strange Bedfellows

Williamsburg's taverns were crowded establishments during the busy Publick Times, when they offered accommodations, food, and libation to the wealthy planters and others who thronged the town.

Some things are almost like they were when Thomas Jefferson wrote after a night at the Raleigh Tavern: "Last night, as merry as agreeable company and dancing with Belinda in the Apollo the Raleigh's ballroom could make me, I never could have thought the succeeding Sun would have seen me so wretched."

On the other hand, the degree of comfort found at Williamsburg's hosteleries has changed immeasurably since then. In those days, the taverns' upstairs bedrooms offered nothing in the way of privacy. Often five or more grown men would share a bed, sleeping cross-ways in a half-sitting position. A smelly pig farmer might sleep next to a wealthy planter, thus giving rise to the expression, "Politics makes strange bedfellows."

---

classes and organized evening lectures, concerts, and social gatherings. For all his good intentions, however, Galt admitted that "practice invariably falls short of theory." His rate of cure was not notable.

After Galt's death, the hospital was administered by nine different superintendents. Confidence in reform and government intervention on behalf of the unfortunate diminished in this age of Social Darwinism, when the survival of the fittest was the new ethic. Though some of the improvements initiated during the Moral Management Period were extended, restraining devices once more came into vogue. This final period, when patients were essentially warehoused with little hope of cure, is known as the Custodial Care Period.

The self-guided tour sets one thinking about our often equally ineffective methods of treating the mentally ill today. The Public Hospital is open daily.

Raleigh Tavern

This most famous of Williamsburg taverns was named for Sir Walter Raleigh, who personally launched the "Lost Colony" which disappeared in North Carolina some 20 years before Jamestown was settled. After the Governor's Palace, it was the social and political hub of the town, especially during crowded Publick Times. Regular clients included George Washington and Thomas Jefferson, who met here in 1774 with Patrick Henry, Richard Henry Lee, and Francis Lightfoot Lee to discuss revolution. Patrick Henry's troops gave their commander a farewell dinner at the Raleigh in 1776.

The original tavern was destroyed by fire in 1859. The present building was reconstructed on the original site in 1932. Its facilities include two dining rooms; the famed Apollo ballroom, scene of elegant soirees; a club room that could be rented for private meetings; and a bar where ale and hot rum punch were the favored drinks. In the tavern bakery you can buy 18th-century confections like gingerbread and Shrewsbury cake as well as cider to wash them down.

Wetherburn's Tavern

Though less important than the Raleigh, Wetherburn's also played an important role in Colonial Williamsburg. George Washington occasionally favored the tavern with his patronage. And, like the Raleigh, it was mobbed during Publick Times and frequently served as a center of sedition and a rendezvous of Revolutionary patriots. The heart-of-yellow-pine floors are original, so you can actually walk in Washington's footsteps; windows, trim, and weatherboarding are a mixture of old and new; and the outbuildings, except for the dairy, are reconstructions. Twenty-five-minute **tours** are given throughout the day.

THE MUSEUMS

Abby Aldrich Rockefeller Folk Art Center

The works of folk art displayed at Bassett Hall (below) are just a small sampling of enthusiast Abby Aldrich Rockefeller's extensive collection. This delightful museum contains more than 2,600 folk-art paintings, sculptures, and art objects. Mrs. Rockefeller was a pioneer in this branch of collecting in the 1920s and 1930s. Folk art is of interest not only aesthetically but as visual history; since colonial times untutored artists have creatively recorded everyday life.

The Folk Art Center collection includes household ornaments and useful wares (hand-stenciled bed covers, butter molds, pottery, utensils, painted furniture, boxes), mourning pictures (embroideries honoring departed relatives and national heroes), family and individual portraits, shop signs, carvings, whittled toys, calligraphic drawings, weavings, quilts, and paintings of scenes from daily life.

Bassett Hall

Though colonial in origin (built between 1753 and 1766 by Col. Philip Johnson), Bassett Hall was the mid-1930s residence of Mr. and Mrs. John D. Rockefeller, Jr., and it is restored and furnished to reflect their era. The mansion's name, however, derives from the ownership of Burwell Bassett, a nephew of Martha Washington who lived here from 1800 to 1839. The Rockefellers purchased the 585-acre property in the late 1920s and moved into the restored two-story dwelling in 1936. In spite of changes they made, much of the interior is original, including woodwork, paneling, mantels, and yellow-pine flooring. Much of the furniture is 18th- and 19th-century American in the Chippendale, Federal, and Empire styles. There are beautifully executed needlework rugs made by Mrs. Rockefeller herself, and six early 19th-century prayer rugs adorn the morning room. Hundreds of examples of ceramics and china are on display, as are collections of 18th- and 19th-century American and English glass, Canton enamelware, and folk art.

Reservations are required; make them at the Special Programs desk at the visitor center.

DeWitt Wallace Decorative Arts Gallery

The Public Hospital serves as entrance to this 62,000-square-foot museum housing some 10,000 17th- to 19th-century English and American decorative art objects. In its galleries you'll see period furnishings, ceramics, textiles, paintings, prints, silver, pewter, clocks, scientific instruments, mechanical devices, and weapons.

In the upstairs Masterworks Gallery, you will see a coronation portrait of George III of England and a Charles Willson Peale study of George Washington. Surrounding the atrium are some 150 objects representing the highest achievement of American and English artisans from the 1640s to 1800. At the east end of the museum, a 6,000-square-foot area with four galleries around a skylit courtyard is used for changing exhibits. On the first level you'll see small exhibits of musical instruments, objects related to European conquest and expansion in the New World, and 18th-century dining items. A small cafe here offers light fare, beverages, and a limited luncheon menu.

The Lila Acheson Wallace Garden, on the upper level, centers on a pond with two fountains, a trellis-shaded seating area at one end, a 6-foot gilded bronze statue of *Diana* by Augustus Saint-Gaudens at the other. The garden is surrounded by a 19-foot-high, plum-colored brick wall embellished (in season) with flowering vines.

Apart from the support of the Rockefellers, the $14 million for this project, provided by *The Reader's Digest* owners DeWitt and Lila Acheson Wallace, represents the largest gift in the history of Colonial Williamsburg.

SHOPS, CRAFTS & TRADE EXHIBITS

Numerous 18th-century crafts demonstrations are on view throughout the Historic Area. Such goings-on were a facet of everyday life in this pre-industrial era. Several dozen crafts are practiced in cluttered shops by over 100 master craftspeople. They're an extremely skilled group, many having served up to 7-year apprenticeships both here and abroad. The program is part of Williamsburg's efforts to present an accurate picture of colonial society, portraying the average man and woman as well as more illustrious citizens. Crafts displays are open 5 to 7 days a week, with evening tours of candlelit shops available (visitors carry lanterns).

Here you can see at work a cabinetmaker, a wig maker, a silversmith, a printer and bookbinder, a maker of saddles and harnesses, a blacksmith, a shoemaker, a gunsmith, a milliner, a wheelwright, housewrights, and a candlemaker, all carrying on—and explaining—their trades in the 18th century fashion.

Interesting in a morbid way is the apothecary shop, where sore feet were treated with leeches between the toes, a headache with leeches across the forehead, and a sore throat with leeches on the neck.

CARTER'S GROVE & THE ROCKEFELLER ARCHEOLOGY MUSEUM

The magnificent plantation home at ✪ **Carter's Grove,** on U.S. 60 about 8 miles east of the Historic Area, has been continuously occupied since 1755 on a site that was settled over 3½ centuries ago. Searching for traces of lost plantation outbuildings on the banks of the James, archaeologists have discovered here the "lost" 17th-century village of Wolstenholme Towne, site of a 20,000-acre tract settled in 1619 by 220 colonists who called themselves the Society of Martin's Hundred. The great Native American uprising of March 22, 1622, destroyed most of the settlement and left only about 60 living inhabitants, who fled to Jamestown.

Over a century later, Robert "King" Carter (Virginia's wealthiest planter) purchased the property for his daughter, Elizabeth. Between 1751 and 1754, Elizabeth's son, Carter Burwell, built the beautiful two-story, 200-foot-long mansion that is considered "the final phase of the evolution of the Georgian mansion." The West Drawing Room with its exquisite 1750 fireplace mantel and carved frieze panel is often called the "Refusal Room"; legend has it that southern belle Mary Cary refused George Washington's proposal of marriage in this room and Rebecca Burwell said "no" to Thomas Jefferson. In 1781, British cavalryman Banastre Tarleton headquartered at Carter's Grove and is said to have ascended the magnificent carved walnut stairway on his warhorse while hacking at the balustrade with his saber.

Despite Tarleton's abuse, Carter's Grove remains one of the best-preserved old houses in America.

A fascinating Carter's Grove site is the reconstruction of the slave quarters. Though wattled circular enclosures to house chickens and a cabin's stick-and-mud chimney reflect African traditions, by the 1770s (the period here portrayed) most slaves were at least second-generation Virginians. Some 24 slaves would have lived in these few pine-log cabins, sleeping on straw pallets placed on dirt floors. There are few possessions or furnishings, except in the foreman's (or senior slave's) house, wherein an actual bed, a chair and table, a mirror, and a piece of Delft china indicate favored status.

At the reception/orientation center, housed in a cedar building, you can view a 14-minute slide presentation on Carter's Grove, and an exhibit area displays historic photographs and documents.

Designed by famed architect Kevin Roche, the **Winthrop Rockefeller Archeology Museum,** nestled into a hillside southeast of the mansion, identifies and interprets the Martin's Hundred clues and artifacts discovered on the site of the partially recon-structed Wolstenholme Towne. A permanent exhibit tells the story of the lost town's discovery through archaeological research. The first two intact 17th-century helmets found in North America are displayed outside the small theater where a film recounts the story of their recovery and preservation. The museum also displays excavation photographs, audiovisual exhibits interpreting the weapons collection, agricultural tools, ceramics, and domestic artifacts. Both the plantation and museum are open mid-March through the Christmas season, Tuesday to Sunday from 9am to 4pm. Allow at least 3 hours here.

Colonial Williamsburg ticket holders can get here via the **Carter's Grove bus,** which usually departs the visitor center at 12:50pm; it costs $10 round-trip. If you drive here, you can return to the Historic Area via a stunningly scenic one-way country road traversing streams, meadows, woodlands, and ravines. A re-creation of a colonial carriage pathway, the road is dotted with markers indicating old graveyards, Indian encampments, plantation sites, and other points of interest. The one-way country road is open Tuesday to Sunday from 9am to 5pm.

ESPECIALLY FOR KIDS

In addition to the excitement at Busch Gardens Williamsburg and Water Country USA (see below), families can enjoy many hands-on activities at the historic sites. At the **Powell House,** on Waller Street near Christiana Campbell's Tavern, families can participate in keeping a garden and managing a kitchen; here kids can dress up in 18th-century style. Another fun activity is at the **Governor's Palace,** where the dancing master gives lessons. During the summer kids can "enlist" in the militia and practice marching and drilling at the **Magazine and Guardhouse** (I still have a snapshot of me holding a flintlock when I was a boy). Inquire at the Visitor Center for special themed tours in areas of your children's specific interest.

✪ **Busch Gardens Williamsburg.** 1 Busch Gardens Blvd. (3 miles east of Williamsburg on U.S. 60). ☎ **757/253-3350.** www.buschgardens.com. Admission and hours vary from year to year so call ahead, check Web site, or get brochure at visitor centers. Admission at least $37 adults, $30 children 3–6, children under 3 free for unlimited rides, shows, and attractions. Annual passes available. Mid-Apr to June, daily 10am–6pm (to 8, 9, or 10pm weekends and holidays); July–Aug, Sun–Fri 10am–11pm; Sept–Oct, Fri 10am–6pm, Sat–Sun 10am–7pm. Closed Nov to late-Mar. Parking $6 cars, $4 motorcycles.

At some point you'll want to take a break from early American history, especially if you have kids in tow, and head over to Busch Gardens Williamsburg, a 360-acre family entertainment park. Here you can get a peek at European history, albeit fan-ciful, in authentically detailed 17th-century hamlets from England, Scotland, France, Germany, and Italy. But little mental effort is required to enjoy the villages, the rides, the shows, and the festivities here.

Each village has its own shops, crafts demonstrations, restaurants, rides, shows, and other entertainment. Your one-price admission entitles you not only to unlimited rides but to top-quality musicals, bird shows, ice-skating revues, and more. Get a show schedule when you come in and plan your day accordingly. Trains pulled by reproduc-tions of European steam locomotives connect the villages, so you can easily skip around.

The usual starting place is the Elizabethan English hamlet of Banbury Cross, where a replica of Shakespeare's Globe Theatre presents a 3-D film trip through ancient cas-tles. From there you proceed to Heatherdowns, Scotland, home of the famous

Anheuser-Busch Clydesdale horses and the serpentine Loch Ness Monster, a terrifying roller-coaster with two interlocking 360° loops and a 130-foot drop. Then it's back to England and Hastings, where kids can play 13th-century games and challenge King Arthur in a 3-D simulator, and the whole family can see "Rocking the Boat," a song and dance revue.

Next comes Aquitaine, France, where you and the kids can test your driving skills on the hairpin turns of Le Mans Raceway. The Royal Theatre here is the venue for the park's nighttime entertainment and special events. Now it's on to Rhinefeld, Germany, where Land of the Dragons lets the kids explore a three-story tree house and ride a flume and a dragon-themed Ferris wheel. Both you and kids can drop your hearts on Alpengeist, the world's tallest and fasted inverted roller coaster (195 feet tall, 67 m.p.h. fast). Dancers and an oompah band entertain in Das Festhaus, a 2,000-seat festival hall.

From Germany, a 300-foot bridge crosses the "Rhine River" to Fiesta Italia, a Renaissance-style Italian village where the water ride Escape from Pompeii will whisk you to the smoldering ruins of the ancient Italian city destroyed by a volcano, and Roman Rapids will speed you to a watery splash in front of the ruins. Here also is Apollo's Chariot, a "hypercoaster" with nine vertical drops of up to 210 feet. Tamer rides pay tribute to Leonardo da Vinci's inventions.

Water Country USA. Va. 199, north of Exit 242 off I-64. ☎ **757/229-9300.** www. 4adventure.com. Admission and hours vary from year to year so call ahead, check Web site, or get brochure at visitor centers. Admission at least $28 adults, $20.50 children 3–6, free for children 2 and under. Annual passes available. May, Sat–Sun 10am–5pm; June 1 to mid-June, daily 10am–5pm; mid-June to mid-Aug, daily 10am–8pm; mid-Aug to Labor Day, daily 10am–6pm, Labor Day to mid-Sept, Sat–Sun 10am–6pm. Parking $6. Take Va. 199 north of I-64 and follow the signs.

Virginia's largest water-oriented amusement park features exciting water slides, rides, and entertainment set to a 1950s and '60s surf theme. The largest ride—Big Daddy Falls—takes the entire family on a colossal river-rafting adventure. Or, they twist and turn on giant inner tubes through flumes, tunnels, and water "explosions," and down a waterfall to "splashdown." And there's much more, all of it wet and sometimes wild. It's a perfect place to chill out after a hot summer's day in the Historic District.

OUTDOOR PURSUITS

BICYCLING   Not only is a bike the easiest way to get around the Historic Area, the 23-mile-long **Colonial Parkway** between Jamestown and Yorktown is one of Virginia's most scenic bike routes. You'll pedal along the banks of the James and York rivers (where there are picnic areas) and through a tunnel under Colonial Williamsburg. The 7 miles between Williamsburg and Jamestown are relatively flat, but you'll have more automobile traffic to contend with here than on the more rolling 13-mile journey to Yorktown. Rentals are available at the Williamsburg Lodge and Williamsburg Woodlands (see "Getting Around" under "Essentials," above).

GOLF   The Williamsburg area is *the* place to play golf in Virginia—if you can afford it, since a round here can cost $90 and up during the prime summer months. It all started in 1947 with the noted Golden Horseshoe course at the **Williamsburg Inn** (☎ **757/229-1000**), which has two other 18-holers to play. On the James River, **Kingsmill Resort** (☎ **800/832-5665** or 757/253-3998) has three top-flight 18-hole courses of its own, including the world-famous River Course, home of the PGA Michelob Classic each October. See "Where to Stay," below, for more about the Williamsburg Inn and Kingsmill Resort.

Ford's Colony (☎ 757/258-4130) has two Dan Maples–designed courses, the challenging Blue-Gold (12 of 18 holes bordered by water) and the more forgiving White-Red. Another Maples-designed course is in the works. Golf carts here have satellite global positioning equipment, so you know exactly how long you have to hit your next shot. **Williamsburg National Golf Club** (☎ 800/826-5732 or 757/258-9642) has Virginia's only Jack Nicklaus–designed course, which *Golf Digest* magazine considers one of the state's top 10 links.

Royal New Kent Golf Club (☎ 888/253-4363 or 804/966-7023) has "a succession of you've-never-seen-this-before holes," according to *Golf Digest.* Its sister course at **Stonehouse Golf Club** (☎ 888/253-4363 or 757/566-1138) is more like a mountain course, with great vistas to please your eyes and deep bunkers to test your skills. Also pleasing to the eye, **Kiskiack Golf Club** (☎ 800/989-4728 or 757/566-2200) has two lakes nestled among its rolling hills.

Call the courses for current greens fees, directions, and tee times.

SHOPPING
IN THE HISTORIC AREA

Duke of Gloucester Street is the center for 18th-century wares created by craftspeople plying the trades of our forefathers. The goods offered include hand-wrought silver jewelry from the Sign of the Golden Ball, hats from the Mary Dickenson shop, pomanders to ward off the plague from McKenzie's Apothecary, hand-woven linens from Prentis Store, books bound in leather and hand-printed newspapers from the post office, gingerbread cakes from the Raleigh Tavern Bake Shop, and everything from foodstuffs to fishhooks from Greenhow and Tarpley's, a general store. In fine weather, check out the fair-like outdoor market next to the Magazine.

Not to be missed is **Craft House,** also run by the Colonial Williamsburg Foundation. There are two locations, one in Merchants Square, the other near the Abby Aldrich Rockefeller Folk Art Center. Featured at Craft House are exquisite works by master craftspeople and authentic reproductions of colonial furnishings. There are also reproduction wallpapers, china, toys, games, maps, books, prints, and souvenirs aplenty.

The modern, independently owned and operated **Merchants Square** "shoppes" at the west end of Duke of Gloucester Street offer a wide range of merchandise: antiques, antiquarian books and prints, 18th century–style floral arrangements, candy, toys, handcrafted pewter and silver items, needlework supplies, country quilts, and Oriental rugs. It's not all of the "ye olde" variety, however; you can also find a Baskin-Robbins ice-cream parlor, a drugstore that offers aspirin in lieu of leeches, a camera shop, and clothing stores. Merchants Square has free 2-hour parking for its customers.

ON RICHMOND ROAD

Shopping in the Historic Area is fun, but the biggest merchandising draws are along Richmond Road (U.S. 60) between Williamsburg and Lightfoot, an area 5 to 7 miles west of the Historic Area. If you like outlet shopping, Richmond Road is for you.

Driving west from town (or taking the Relax & Ride Visitors Shuttle during summer), you'll come first to **Patriot Plaza Premium Outlets,** between Ironbound and Airport roads (no phone), with Dansk, Fila, Leather Loft, Lenox fine china and crystal, Polo Ralph Lauren, Samsonite/American Tourister, Villeroy & Boch, Westpoint Pepperell, and the Prince Michel Wine Shop, where one of Virginia's premier vintners has a tasting room and bistro. Shops here are open Monday to Saturday 9am to 9pm, Sunday 9am to 6pm.

Next comes **Berkeley Commons Outlet Center,** Airport and Lightfoot roads (☎ **800/866-5900** or 757/565-0702), an outdoor mall with more than 80 shops including Anne Klein, Bass, Bose, Brooks Brothers, Capezio, Coach Leather, Crabtree & Evelyn, Eddie Bauer, Etienne Aigner, Harvé Bernard, J. Crew, Jones New York, Jos. A. Bank, Lladro, Maidenform, Mikasa, Naturalizer, Nike, Reebok/Rockport, Royal Doulton, Seiko, Van Heusen, and Waterford Wedgewood. Open March to December, Monday to Saturday 10am to 9pm; January and February, Monday to Thursday 10am to 6pm, Friday and Saturday 10am to 9pm, Sunday 11am to 6pm.

Many of these same outlets are among the 60 stores in the area's largest enclosed mall, **The Williamsburg Outlet Mall** (☎ **888/SHOP-333** or 757/565-3378), at the intersection of U.S. 60 Lightfoot Road (C.R. 646). Open March to December, Monday to Saturday 10am to 9pm, Sunday 10am to 6pm. Call for winter hours.

Just up the road is **Williamsburg Pottery Factory** (☎ **757/564-3326**), a 200-acre shopping complex with over 31 tin buildings selling merchandise from all over the world. It's all bought in large volume and sold at competitive prices. Shops on the premises sell Christmas decorations, garden furnishings, lamps, art prints, dried and silk flowers, luggage, linens, baskets, hardware, glassware, cookware, candles, wine, toys, crafts, clothing, food, jewelry, plants (there's a large greenhouse and nursery)— even pottery. There's plenty of quality and plenty of kitsch. It even has its own **Pottery Factory Outlets,** with discount offerings of 20 major manufacturers under one roof. They include Black & Decker, Van Heusen, Fieldcrest-Cannon, Izod, Oneida, and Pfaltzgraff. Open daily from 8am to 7pm in summer, daily from 9am to 5pm the rest of the year.

Continue west 1½ miles on U.S. 60 and you'll come to the **Williamsburg Doll Factory** (☎ **757/564-9703**), with limited-edition porcelain collector's dolls. You can observe the dollmaking process and even buy parts to make your own. Other items sold here are stuffed animals, dollhouses and miniatures, clowns, and books on dolls. Open daily from 9am to 5pm.

Lastly you'll come to the **Williamsburg Soap & Candle Company** (☎ **757/ 564-3354**). Here you can see a narrated video presentation on candlemaking while watching the process through viewing windows that look out on the factory. There are interesting shops adjoining, and a cozy country-style restaurant is on the premises. It's open daily from 9am to 5pm, with extended hours in summer and fall.

WHERE TO STAY
COLONIAL WILLIAMSBURG FOUNDATION HOTELS

The Colonial Williamsburg Foundation operates four hotels in all price categories: Williamsburg Inn (very expensive), Williamsburg Lodge (expensive), Williamsburg Woodlands (moderate), and the Governor's Inn (inexpensive), all in the Historic Area. For advance reservations at any of these, call the **Visitor Center reservations service** (☎ **800/HISTORY;** www.history.org). You also can make walk-in reservations at the Colonial Williamsburg Visitor Center.

Rooms in a modern building called **Providence Hall,** adjacent to the Williamsburg Inn and its golf courses, are furnished in a contemporary blend of 18th-century and Asian style, with balconies or patios overlooking tennis courts and a beautiful wooded area. Services are provided by the inn. Rates, from $110 to $225, offer exceptionally good value.

The foundation has some 84 rooms close by and within the Historic Area in its **Colonial Houses.** Tastefully furnished with 18th-century antiques and reproductions, they are variously equipped with canopied beds, kitchens, living rooms, fireplaces,

---

Reader's Comment

Colonial Houses and Taverns. *"We made reservations to stay in one of the restored houses in the colonial area. My husband had requested two beds and we had two beds all right, but they were in a tiny box of a room. Our private bathroom was across the hall, so we had to wear robes and keep our door locked at all times. Also our little house was on a street that allowed regular traffic, and since the restored houses have little if any insulation, we could hear cars and buses at all hours of the day and evening. If people want to stay in a restored house, specify what they expect in their accommodations. I never dreamed I'd need to say 'bathroom en suite.' We were very lucky that the Williamsburg Inn had an unexpected vacancy and were able to move to a wonderful, large, elegant room there."*

—Mrs. Tom Mason, Harlingen, Texas.

---

and/or sizable gardens. Some of the rooms are tiny, and not all have private bathrooms, so be sure to specify you want your bathroom to be "en suite," and tell the reservation clerk precisely what size room and what bed configuration you want (see "Reader's Comment"). Rates range from $100 to $400.

Rates at the foundation's accommodations can vary widely, depending on the time of year and how many guests may be booked on a given night. Try to reserve as far in advance as possible for the busy summer season. You might get a bargain during other times, especially if business is slow. And be sure to ask about the multitude of special package deals.

Governor's Inn. Henry St. (Va. 132), at Lafayette St. (P.O. Box 1776), Williamsburg, VA 23187. ☎ **800/HISTORY** or 757/229-1000. Fax 757/220-7480. www.history.org. 200 units. A/C TV TEL. $50–$99 double. AE, DC, DISC, MC, V.

Least charming and least expensive of the foundation's hotels, the Governor's Inn is a two- and three-story brick motel surrounded by parking lots. Natural wood furniture brightens the standard motel-style rooms, which were all spiffed up after the foundation recently bought the property. There's a small outdoor swimming pool for cooling off. It's near the visitor center on the northwest edge of the Historic Area. Some rooms are "pet friendly."

✪ **Williamsburg Inn.** 136 Francis St. (P.O. Box 1776), Williamsburg, VA 23187. ☎ **800/HISTORY** or 757/229-1000. Fax 757/220-7096. www.history.org. 102 units. A/C TV TEL. $250–$375 double. AE, DC, DISC, MC, V. Free parking.

One of the nation's most distinguished hotels, this rambling white-brick Regency-style inn has played host to hundreds of VIPs, including heads of state from 17 countries and U.S. presidents Truman, Eisenhower, Nixon, Ford, and Reagan. It is considered one of the country's finest golf resorts, with three top-flight courses to play, including the noted Golden Horseshoe (see "Outdoor Pursuits," above).

The lobby lounge is graced with Federal-style furnishings and two working fireplaces. Complimentary tea is served every afternoon in the East Lounge. Rooms are exquisitely furnished in Regency reproductions, and guests are pampered with French-milled soap, hair dryers, and terry-cloth robes in the bath, plus fresh flowers. A special reduced-price ticket to the Historic Area is sold at the concierge desk daily. All guests staying in official Colonial Williamsburg hotels are invited to a special 2-hour guided walking tour of the Historic Area.

Dining/Diversions: The inn's Regency Lounge offers cocktails, light suppers, and entertainment nightly and hosts Felicity's Tea for children each afternoon. The

Regency Dining Room features classic American cuisine at its finest. After 6pm, coats and ties are required in the Regency Dining Room, jackets in the Regency Lounge. Regency Sunday brunch is served from noon to 2pm.

Amenities: Concierge, room service, baby-sitting. Croquet, Tazewell Club Fitness Center in Williamsburg Lodge (see below) available for inn guests, two 18-hole and one 9-hole golf courses, lawn bowling, two outdoor pools, eight tennis courts, nature trail, croquet, family programs.

Williamsburg Lodge. S. England St. (P.O. Box 1776), Williamsburg, VA 23187. ☎ **800/ HISTORY** or 757/229-1000. Fax 757/220-7685. www.history.org. 315 units. A/C TV TEL. $140–$235 double. Extra person $12. Children under 18 stay free in parents' room. AE, DC, DISC, MC, V. Free parking.

The Williamsburg Lodge is located across the street from the Williamsburg Inn and offers all the sports facilities of the inn and a pleasantly rustic interior. The flagstone-floored lobby is indeed lodgelike, with cypress paneling and a large working fire-place. And there's a covered verandah with rocking chairs overlooking two pools and a golf course. Accommodations are contemporary but warm and homey, with pretty print bedspreads, polished wood floors, and hand-crafted furniture. American folk art—decoys, samplers, and such—highlights the decor. West Wing rooms have window walls overlooking duck ponds or a wooded landscape. They're furnished in oak, cane, and bamboo, and 12 have working fireplaces. Rooms in the Tazewell Wing have balconies facing landscaped courtyards. Guest rooms are attractively furnished with reproductions inspired by pieces in the Abby Aldrich Rockefeller Folk Art Center.

Dining/Diversions: The attractive Bay Room overlooks a garden and fountain. On Friday and Saturday nights it features a Chesapeake Bay Feast, and on Sunday an omelet brunch buffet is the draw. The Garden Lounge has drinks and musical enter-tainment from early afternoon.

Amenities: All inn facilities are available to lodge guests. The Tazewell Club Fitness Center has an indoor lap pool, Keiser exercise machines, and aerobic classes, and rents bicycles and strollers.

Williamsburg Woodlands. Va. 132, off U.S. 60 Bypass (P.O. Box 1776), Williamsburg, VA 23187. ☎ **800/HISTORY** or 757/229-1000. Fax 757/565-8728. www.history.org. 315 units. A/C TV TEL. $75–$125 double. Extra person $8. Children under 18 stay free in parents' room. AE, DC, DISC, MC, V. Free parking.

Set on 40 wooded acres with picnic tables under the pines, this sprawling, one-story motel offers a lot for your money. You're right behind the visitor center, so you hop the shuttle bus to the Historic Area. You can park right outside the rooms, which are cheerful and attractive, and have big window walls looking out to the woods. Facili-ties include a jogging path, golf putting green, miniature golf course, shuffleboard, playground, horseshoes, volleyball, badminton, seasonal bike rentals, and a large swimming pool complex with a toddlers' pool and a lifeguard during summer. The Cascades restaurant serves all meals, and there's a Burger King on the premises.

OTHER ACCOMMODATIONS

The **Williamsburg Hotel/Motel Association** (☎ **800/446-9244** or 757/220-3330) will make reservations for you in any price range. It's a free service, and their listings include most of the accommodations mentioned below.

Most national chains are represented here, including Best Western, Comfort Inn, Days Inn, Econo Lodge, Hampton Inn, Holiday Inn, Marriott, Motel 6, Quality Inn, Ramada Inn, and Travelodge.

Courtyard By Marriott. 470 McLaws Circle, Williamsburg, VA 23185. ☎ **800/321-2211** or 757/221-0700. Fax 757/221-0741. 151 units. A/C TV TEL. $99–$139 double; $119–$199 suite. Weekend rates available. AE, DC, DISC, MC, V. Free parking. From Williamsburg, follow U.S. 60 east about 2 miles to Busch Corporate Center, turn right at light and bear right on McLaws Circle.

This four-story member of the fine chain designed for business travelers (and very comfortable for the rest of us) enjoys an attractively landscaped setting of trees and shrubs. A plant-filled lobby looks out to the courtyard and its good-size pool. Furnished with substantial oak pieces, the guest quarters feature large desks, separate seating areas, and long phone cords. Suites have full sofa-bedded living rooms with extra phones and TVs, plus wet bars with small refrigerators. The lobby restaurant offers a breakfast buffet. There's an exercise room with Jacuzzi.

Governor Spotswood Motel. 1508 Richmond Rd. (just east of Ironwood Rd.), Williamsburg, VA 23185. ☎ **800/368-1244** or 757/229-6444. Fax 757/253-2410. E-mail: spottswood@widomaker.com. 86 units, including 8 cottages. A/C TV TEL. $32–$160 double. AE, DC, DISC, MC, V.

Opened and operated by the same family for two generations, this older but well-maintained motel offers rooms in one-story buildings facing a parking lot and cottages set back among magnolias, camellias, and towering pines on the property's 10 acres. The smallish but comfortable rooms have tub-shower combination baths; some sport brass or canopy beds, and 19 of them have kitchens. Capable of accommodating up to seven persons, each of the cottages has two bedrooms, a living room, a kitchen, and a bath. There's an outdoor pool and a playground area for kids here.

✪ **Heritage Inn.** 1324 Richmond Rd. (at Mt. Vernon Ave.), Williamsburg, VA 23185. ☎ **800/782-3800** or 757/229-6220. Fax 757/229-2774. www.heritageinnwmsb.com. 54 units. A/C TV TEL. $40–$86. Rates include continental breakfast. AE, DC, DISC, MC, V.

An impressive, colonial-style brick building houses the lobby and a beautiful, light-filled dining room at this family-owned motel, convenient to the Historic Area. Although the rooms are next door in a nondescript, two-story motel block, they are spacious and comfortable. Most have two double beds, desks, TVs hidden in armoires, and tiled shower-tub combination bathrooms with unusual knickknack shelves built in above the vanities. Three rooms also have sitting areas. There's an outdoor pool.

Radisson Fort Magruder Hotel. U.S. 60 East (P.O. Box KE), Williamsburg, VA 23187. ☎ **800/333-3333** or 757/220-2250. Fax 757/220-9059. 303 units. A/C TV TEL. $89–$169 double, $175–$300 suites. AE, DC, DISC, MC, V. From I-64, take Va. 199 west to U.S. 60 west.

Sitting between the Historic Area and Busch Gardens, this modern hotel draws lots of conventions and meetings but is also a good choice for families with children who want a location convenient to both attractions. Two-story glass walls create an atrium lobby, but lots of brick and antique-look furniture remind you that this is Williamsburg and not California. Guest rooms in the curving building are spacious, with wing chairs, writing desks, and balconies looking out on gardens that surround a swimming pool and lighted tennis courts (there's also a fitness center here). Looking out on the landscaped pool area, the Veranda Room serves breakfast, lunch, and dinner, while J.B.'s Lounge provides evening cocktails and music for dancing.

Williamsburg Hospitality House. 415 Richmond Rd., Williamsburg, VA 23185. ☎ **757/229-4020.** Fax 757/299-0731. www.williamsburghosphouse.com. 308 units. A/C TV TEL. $79–$169 double; $375 1-bedroom suite; $475 2-bedroom suite. AE, DC, DISC, MC, V.

Just 2 blocks from the Historic Area opposite William and Mary College, this four-story brick hotel is built around a central courtyard with flowering trees and plants and umbrella tables. Guest rooms and public areas are appointed with a gracious blend of 18th-century reproductions. The Colony dining room specializes in colonial fare. Christopher's Tavern serves lunch, dinner, and light fare. Facilities include an outdoor pool, health club, games room, and gift shop.

BED & BREAKFAST INNS

In addition to those mentioned below, Williamsburg has at least 16 more B&Bs. The Williamsburg Area Convention & Visitors Bureau has a list (see "Essentials," above).

✪ **Liberty Rose.** 1022 Jamestown Rd., Williamsburg, VA 23185. ☎ **800/545-1825** or 757/253-1260. www.libertyrose.com. 4 units. A/C TV TEL. $145–$205 double. Rates include full breakfast. AE, MC, V. On-site parking.

Williamsburg's most romantic B&B, Brad and Sara Hirz's home enjoys a premier location on a wooded hilltop just 1¼ miles from the Historic Area. Housed in a charming 1920s two-story white-clapboard residence with a dormered slate roof flanked by chimneys, Liberty Rose is furnished in delightful style; you'll find Victorian, French- and English-country, and 18th-century antiques and reproductions.

The elegant parlor, complete with grand piano that guests may play, has a working fireplace and comfortable chairs for relaxing. The accommodations are luxurious, each distinctively decorated. Although the smallest, the Savannah Lace guest room has peach-colored wallpaper, an antique carved-mahogany queen-size bed with a pink goosedown duvet, a TV, bathrobes, and a bowl of chocolates; the bathroom, tucked into the side dormer room, is papered with roses, and has a claw-foot tub (most rooms here have both a glass-enclosed shower and a claw-foot tub). A full breakfast is served on the morning porch or in the courtyard; a typical menu might include fresh orange juice, eggs with bacon, French toast, and coffee or tea. An overall feeling of graciousness makes the Liberty Rose a real delight, a tranquil refuge from the rigors of sightseeing.

Williamsburg Manor Bed & Breakfast. 600 Richmond Rd., Williamsburg, VA 23185. ☎ **800/422-8011** or 757/220-8011. Fax 757/220-0245. www.williamsburg-manor.com. 5 units. A/C TV. $95–$129 double. Rates include full breakfast. AE, MC, V. On-site parking.

Right in the heart of Williamsburg, 2 blocks from the Historic Area, this gracious 1928 Georgian Revival brick residence offers traditional comfort in nicely appointed rooms. Guests are invited to congregate in the living room, where there is a TV, magazines, and a great cookbook collection. In addition to the full breakfasts, host Laura Sisane offers, by prior reservation only, dinners for guests. Accommodations vary in size and furnishings, but you can expect to find four-poster beds, pretty wallpapers, white bedspreads, brass lamps, Oriental rugs, and wing chairs. The breakfast table, set with Villeroy & Boche china, might include fresh fruit, eggs in puff pastry with Surry bacon, homebaked breads or pastries, and coffee and tea.

A NEARBY RESORT WITH CHAMPIONSHIP GOLF

Kingsmill Resort. 1010 Kingsmill Rd., Williamsburg, VA 23185. ☎ **800/832-5665** or 757/253-1703. Fax 757/253-3993. www.kingsmill.com. 400 units. A/C TV TEL. $129–$259 double, $185–$864 suite. Packages available. AE, DC, DISC, MC, V. From I-64, take Exit 242 and follow Va. 199 west past U.S. 60 to sign for Kingsmill on the James.

Nestled in a peaceful setting on beautifully landscaped grounds on the James River, the gray-clapboard Kingsmill resort complex is very much like a country club, with 2,900 acres of resort facilities, including the world-famous River Course, home of the Michelob Classic; the Plantation Course designed by Arnold Palmer; and the Bray Links Par Three (complimentary to guests). Kingsmill accommodations—guest rooms and one-, two-, and three-bedroom units—are in tastefully furnished villas overlooking the James River (most expensive), golf-course fairways, or tennis courts. They're in individually owned and furnished condos, so decors vary from handsome colonial reproductions to sophisticated contemporary settings. Most suites have complete kitchens and living rooms with fireplaces. Daily housekeeping service, including fresh linens, is included.

Dining: All four dining rooms feature panoramic views of the James. In the Bray dining room, breakfast, lunch buffets, and à la carte evening meals are reasonably priced. More casual dining spots are Moody's Tavern, Peyton Grille, and Kingsmill Cafe in the golf clubhouse.

Amenities: Concierge, limited room service, laundry, newspaper delivery, babysitting, complimentary shuttle to Colonial Williamsburg and Busch Gardens Williamsburg, children's activity programs. Golf, 15 tennis courts (two lighted), indoor and outdoor pools, racquetball courts, children's program, full-service spa, Nautilus exercise room, saunas, Jacuzzi, billiards, marina, gift shop, pro shop, bike rentals.

WHERE TO DINE

Williamsburg abounds in restaurants catering to tourists. Most national-chain fast food and family restaurants have outlets on Richmond Road (U.S. 60) on the west side of town.

COLONIAL WILLIAMSBURG FOUNDATION TAVERNS

In addition to the restaurants in its accommodations (see "Where to Stay," above), the Colonial Williamsburg Foundation runs four popular reconstructed colonial taverns. If you're planning on dinner at any of them except Josiah Chowning's Tavern (which is first come, first served), make your reservations first thing in the morning—if not a day or two before—by going to or calling the **visitor center** (☎ **800/TAVERNS** or 757/229-2141). In the spring-to-fall season it's a good idea to reserve even prior to arrival (you can do so up to 60 days in advance). Their business hours can vary slightly from those given below, especially in January and February when they can be closed for annual upkeep.

All are reconstructed 18th-century "ordinaries" or taverns, and aim at authenticity in fare, ambience, and costuming of the staff. Their seasonal menus are posted out front and at the ticket booth on Henry Street at Duke of Gloucester Street, and are available at the visitor center, so you can see what's being served before making your reservations. All offer tasty, interesting colonial fare such as peanut soup, salad with chutney dressing, Brunswick stew, sautéed backfin crabmeat and ham topped with butter and laced with sherry, Sally Lunn bread, and deep-dish Shenandoah apple pie. They all have alfresco dining in good weather on brick patios under grape arbors. Low-priced children's menus are available.

Christina Campbell's Tavern. Waller St. ☎ **757/229-2141.** Reservations required at dinner. Main courses $19–$24. AE, DC, DISC, MC, V. Seatings Tues–Sat 5, 5:30, 7, 7:30, 9 and 9:15pm. COLONIAL.

Almost hidden behind the Capitol, Christina Campbell's Tavern is "where all the best people resorted" circa 1765. George Washington was a regular (in 1772, he recorded in his diary that he dined here 10 times over a 22-month period). After the capital moved to Richmond, business declined and operations eventually ceased. In its heyday, however, the tavern was famous for seafood, and today that is once again the specialty. Campbell's is an authentic reproduction with 18th-century furnishings, blazing fireplaces, and flutists and balladeers to entertain diners.

Josiah Chowning's Tavern. Duke of Gloucester St. ☎ **757/229-2141.** Reservations not accepted. Lunch $6–$8; main courses $14–$22. Gambols Pub, $3 cover charge. AE, DC, DISC, MC, V. Mon–Sat breakfast 8–10am, lunch 11am–5pm, dinner 5–9pm; Gambols Pub, daily 9pm–midnight. COLONIAL.

In 1766, Josiah Chowning announced the opening of a tavern "where all who please to favour me with their custom may depend upon the best of entertainment for themselves, servants, and horses, and good pasturage." It's very charming, with low beamed ceilings, raw pine floors, and sturdy country-made furnishings. There are two working fireplaces, and at night one dines by candlelight. One of the best things to do here after 9pm is to take in the 18th-century music, magic, and games, when the tavern becomes Gambols Pub. Note that this is the only tavern open for breakfast.

Kings Arms Tavern. Duke of Gloucester St. ☎ **757/229-2141.** Reservations required at dinner. Lunch $6–$12; main courses $18–$26. AE, DC, DISC, MC, V. Daily 11:30am–2:30pm; dinner, with 12 nightly seatings, 5:15–9:30pm. COLONIAL.

The Kings Arms Tavern, on the site of a 1772 establishment, is actually a re-creation of the tavern and an adjoining home. Outbuildings—including stables, a barbershop, laundry, smokehouse, and kitchen—have also been reconstructed. The original proprietress, Mrs. Jane Vobe, was famous for her fine cooking, and her establishment's proximity to the Capitol made it a natural meeting place during Publick Times. Today the 11 dining rooms (eight with fireplaces) are painted and furnished following authentic early Virginia precedent. The Queen Anne and Chippendale pieces are typical appointments of this class of tavern, and the prints, maps, engravings, aquatints, and mezzotints lining the walls are genuine examples of colonial interior decorations. Balladeers wander the rooms during dinner and entertain.

Shields Tavern. Duke of Gloucester St. ☎ **757/229-2141.** Reservations required at dinner. Lunch $6–$7; main courses $14.50–$22. AE, DC, DISC, MC, V. Daily 11:30am–3pm and 5–9:30pm. Garden, daily 11:30am–dusk. COLONIAL.

With 11 dining rooms and a garden under a trumpet-vine-covered arbor that seats 200, Shields is the largest of the Historic Area's tavern/restaurants. It's named for James Shields who, with his wife, Anne, and family, ran a much-frequented hostelry on this site in the mid-1700s. Using a room-by-room inventory of Shields's personal effects—and as a result of detailed archaeological investigation—the tavern has been furnished with items similar to those used in the mid-18th century, and many of the rooms have working fireplaces. A specially designed rotisserie unit in the kitchen allows chefs here to approximate 18th-century roasting techniques. Strolling balladeers entertain at night.

OTHER HISTORIC AREA RESTAURANTS

Berret's Restaurant & Raw Bar. 199 S. Boundary St. ☎ **757/253-1847.** Reservations recommended for dinner. Main courses $17.50–$25. AE, DISC, MC, V. Restaurant, Apr–Dec, daily 11:30am–3:30pm and 5–10pm. Jan–Mar, Tues–Sun 11:30am–5pm and 5:30–9pm. Outdoor raw bar, Apr–Oct, Mon–Fri 5–11pm, Sat–Sun noon–11pm. SEAFOOD.

A congenial, casual place, Berret's has a popular outdoor raw bar that seems to be busy all day long in warm weather, especially on weekends. The adjoining restaurant is bright and airy, with several dining rooms. Seating is at booths upholstered in a nautical-blue leather and at light-wood tables covered with matching blue cloth. Canvas sail-cloth shades, blue-trimmed china, and marine artifacts on the walls make an appropriate backdrop for the excellent seafood specialties. Oysters or clams raw or steamed on the half shell do nicely as starters. For a main course, the crab cakes here

are pan-fried and served with a sweet bell pepper sauce and an apple and pear salad—
a far cry from those dished up at fried seafood joints. The menu also features some
incredible desserts, among them chocolate-marble cheesecake with raspberry filling
and whipped cream. Berret's has an interesting selection of beers and specialty wines.

A Good Place To Eat. 410 Duke of Gloucester St., Merchants Sq. ☎ **757/229-4370.**
Breakfast $3–$4.50; lunch/dinner $2.60–$6.50. MC, V. Mid-Mar to Aug, daily 8am–10pm;
Sept–Oct, daily 8am–8pm; Nov–Dec, daily 8am–6:30pm; Jan to mid-Mar, daily 8am–5pm.
AMERICAN.

The Historic Area's only fast-food emporium is an especially good place for family
meals. The food is high quality—burger meat is prepared from the best cuts of chuck
and round, breads and cakes are fresh baked, and even the ice cream is homemade—
and the setting is rather attractive. There's a big indoor dining room with terra-cotta
tile floors, imitation-oak Formica tables, and many hanging plants. Better yet is the
outdoor seating at umbrella tables on a flower-bordered brick patio. Stop by for an
inexpensive breakfast of scrambled eggs and ham with homemade biscuits, or a sweet-
potato muffin and coffee. At lunch or dinner you can get a ham-and-Swiss sandwich
on French bread, a hamburger, or a chef's salad. Leave room for a sundae with homemade ice cream and fresh whipped cream.

✪ **Trellis Cafe, Restaurant & Grill.** Duke of Gloucester St., Merchants Sq. ☎ **757/
229-8610.** Reservations suggested at dinner. Sandwiches $7–$10; main courses
$13–$26; fixed-price dinners $20–$26. AE, MC, V. Mon–Sat 11:30am–9:30pm, Sun
11:30am–3pm and 5–9:30pm. AMERICAN.

Executive chef Marcel Desaulniers has brought national recognition to this fine restaurant, whose decor evokes delightful establishments in California's wine country. He
was the first chef from the South to be honored by the James Beard Foundation,
whose awards are considered the Oscars of the culinary industry, and was named to
Food and Wine magazine's honor roll of American chefs and to *Who's Who of Cooking
in America.* Marcel changes the menu every season to take advantage of local produce,
which he imaginatively combines with the best in foods from different regions of the
United States. If it's offered, try his exciting combination of grilled fish, thinly sliced
Virginia country ham, pine nuts, and Zinfandel-soaked raisins.

Near the front of the building, the casual Cafe has its own less expensive menu,
including sandwiches (not available in the restaurant). A highlight up here is a complete dinner for $20. During my visit, it consisted of a salad or a bowl of hearty, sage-
laced sausage and corn chowder; a mixed grill of duck's leg, chicken breast, and
country sausage with a side of perfectly steamed green beans and onions; and ice
cream or sorbet. I upgraded the dessert to Marcel's sinful Death by Chocolate, which
is the title of one of several cookbooks he has authored.

If the weather is fine, you might partake alfresco on the planter-bordered brick
terrace, but even indoors the ambience is extraordinarily informal and relaxed for
a restaurant offering such fine food.

NEARBY DINING

✪ **Giuseppe's Italian Cafe.** 5601 Richmond Rd. (U.S. 60), in Ewell Station Shopping
Center. ☎ **757/565-1977.** Reservations not accepted. Main courses $4.50–$17. AE,
DISC, MC, V. Mon–Thurs 11:30am–2pm and 5–9pm, Fri–Sat 11:30am–2pm and
5–9:30pm. From Historic District, go 4 miles west on U.S. 60 to shopping center on left.
ITALIAN.

This pleasant local favorite may be difficult to see from Richmond Highway (it's at the
end of a strip mall with a Food Lion supermarket at its center), but it's a great place

for a meal during or after a shopping expedition. The chef's lentil-and-andouille soup won justified raves from *Bon Appetit* magazine, and he's also adept at the likes of chicken Antonio in a subtly spicy pepper pesto sauce. Also on the menu: heaping plates of spaghetti, a page full of vegetarian pastas, and single-size pizzas with some unusual toppings such as smoked oysters. All entrees come with a salad or a bowl of the hearty soup. There are two dining rooms here plus heated sidewalk seating.

Le Yaca. U.S. 60E, in the Village Shops at Kingsmill. ☎ **757/220-3616.** Reservations recommended. Fixed-price dinners $21–$42. AE, DC, MC, V. Mon–Sat 6–9:30pm. From the Historic Area, go east on U.S. 60 to Va. 199; the shops are just east of the interchange. FRENCH.

Centered on a large open hearth, on which a leg of lamb is often roasting during cold weather, this quality French restaurant is charmingly provincial, with glossy oak floors, rough-hewn beams overhead, and romantic soft lighting from oil candles and shaded lamps. On the walls, prints of Paris scenes add an urban touch. A fixed-price dinner might begin with mountain-style onion soup, an entree of salmon in parchment, an array of fresh vegetables, salad, and then a marquise au chocolate—rich chocolate truffles afloat on crème anglaise.

✪ Old Chickahominy House. 1211 Jamestown Rd., at Va. 199. ☎ **757/229-4689.** Reservations not accepted. Breakfast $3–$8; lunch $2.50–$7.25. MC, V. Daily 8:30–10:15am and 11:45am–2:15pm. Closed Easter, July 4, Thanksgiving, Christmas. TRADITIONAL SOUTHERN.

The Old Chickahominy House is a reconstructed 18th-century house with mantels from old Gloucester homes and wainscoting from Carter's Grove. Floors are bare oak, and walls, painted in traditional colonial colors, are hung with gilt-framed 17th- and 18th-century oil paintings. Three adjoining rooms house an antiques/gift shop. The entire effect is extremely cozy and charming, from the rocking chairs on the front porch to the blazing fireplaces within. Authentic Southern fare is featured at breakfast and lunch. The house specialty in the morning is the plantation breakfast—real Virginia ham with two eggs, biscuits, cured country bacon and sausage, grits, and coffee. At lunch, Miss Melinda's special is a cup of Brunswick stew with Virginia ham on hot biscuits, fruit salad, homemade pie, and tea or coffee. After dining it's fun to roam through the warren of antiques-filled rooms. Also check out the Shirley Pewter Shop next door.

Pierce's Pitt Bar-B-Que. Rochambeau Dr., Lightfoot (beside I-64). ☎ **757/565-2955.** Reservations not accepted. Sandwiches $2.50–$3.50; main courses $6–$13. MC, V. Sun–Thurs 7am–9pm, Fri–Sat 7am–10pm. From Historic Area, go west on Richmond Rd. (U.S. 60), right on Airport Rd. (C.R. 645) 2 miles toward I-64; follow signs to restaurant on Rochambeau Dr., about 2 miles. BARBECUE.

Visible from I-64, this gaudy yellow-and-orange barbecue joint has been dishing up pulled pork, chicken, and smoked ribs for decades, as the walls hung with old photos of the owners and their family and staff will attest. The pulled pork here comes soaked in a smoky-flavored, tomato-based sauce. All platters are accompanied by creamy coleslaw, french fries, and hush puppies. Order at the counter and take your meal (served in plastic containers) to a table inside or outdoors under cover.

PICNIC FARE & WHERE TO EAT IT

There are benches throughout the restored area (lots of grass, too), and if you have a car you can drive to nearby scenic overlooks along Colonial Parkway (the parking areas along the James and York rivers are best, but they don't have picnic tables or other facilities).

The Cheese Shop, 424 Prince George St. in Merchants Square, between North Boundary and North Henry streets (☎ 757/220-0298), is a good place to purchase take-out sandwiches and other fixings. Open Monday to Saturday from 10am to 6pm, Sunday 11am to 4pm. Out on Richmond Road, a good choice is **Padow's Hams & Deli,** in the Williamsburg Shopping Center at Monticello Avenue (☎ 757/220-4267). It's open Monday to Friday 10am to 8pm, Saturday 10am to 5pm. Both delis have tables.

2 Jamestown: The First Colony

9 miles SW of Williamsburg

The story of Jamestown, the first permanent English settlement in the New World, is documented here in a national park on the Jamestown Island site where they landed. You'll learn the exploits of Capt. John Smith, the colony's leader who was rescued from execution by the American Indian princess Pocahontas; the arrival of the first African-American slaves; and how life was lived in 17th-century Virginia. Archaeologists have excavated more than 100 building frames, evidence of manufacturing ventures (pottery, winemaking, brickmaking, and glassblowing), early wells, and old roads, as well as scores of artifacts of everyday life—tools, utensils, ceramic dishes, armor, keys, and the like.

Next door at Jamestown Settlement, a state-run living-history museum complex, you can see re-creations of the three ships in which the settlers arrived in 1607, the colony they built, and a typical Native American village of the time.

Allow at least half a day for your visit and consider packing a lunch. Other than a cafe at Jamestown Settlement, there are no restaurants, so you may want to take advantage of the picnic areas at the National Park Service site.

The scenic way here from Williamsburg is via the picturesque Colonial Parkway, or you can take Jamestown Road (Va. 31).

✪ **Jamestown Island.** At the western terminus of the Colonial Pkwy., at Jamestown Rd. (Va. 31). ☎ **757/898-2410** or 757/229-1773. www.nps.gov/colo. Admission $5 per person over 16 years, free for children under 16. Combination ticket with Yorktown Battlefield $7 per person over 16, free for children under 16. Both admissions good for 7 days. National Park Service passports accepted. Audiotape tours $2. Main gate, daily 8:30am–4:30pm; park daily 8:30am–dusk; visitor center daily 9am–5pm. Closed Christmas.

Now part of the Colonial National Historical Park, this is the site of the actual colony, separated by an isthmus from the mainland. Begin at the visitor center, which contains an information desk, an exhibit area, and a theater in which a 15-minute orientation film tells the story of Jamestown from its earliest days to 1698, when the capital of Virginia moved to Williamsburg and Jamestown became a sleepy little village. Be sure to inquire at the reception desk about ranger-led walking tours, costumed interpretive programs, and other special programs offered that day.

Allow at least 2 hours for this special attraction. Rent a recorded tour at the visitor center and follow the footpaths to the actual site of **"James Cittie,"** where rubbly brick foundations of 17th-century homes, taverns, shops, and statehouses are enhanced by artists' renderings, text, and audio stations. Most complete are the remains of the tower of one of the first brick churches in Virginia (1639). Directly behind the tower is the Memorial Church, a 1907 re-creation built by the Colonial Dames of America on the site of the original structure, which, in 1619, housed the first legislative assembly in English-speaking North America. You can rent a tape recording at the visitor center to accompany your walk.

A fascinating **5-mile loop drive** begins at the Visitor Center parking lot and winds through 1,500 wilderness acres of woodland and marsh that have been allowed to return to their natural state in order to approximate the landscape as 17th-century settlers found it. Illustrative markers interpret aspects of the colonists' daily activities and industries—tobacco growing, lumbering, silk and wine production, potterymaking, farming, and so on.

For more information contact **Colonial National Historical Park,** P.O. Box 210, Yorktown, VA 23690 (☎ **757/898-2410;** www.nps.gov/colo).

✪ **Jamestown Settlement.** Jamestown Rd. (Va. 31), at James River. ☎ **888/593-4682** or 757/253-4838. www.historyisfun.org. Admission $10.25 adults, $5.75 children 6–12; free for children under 6. Combination ticket with Yorktown Victory Center $14 adults, $6.75 children 6–12. Daily 9am–5pm. Closed New Year's Day and Christmas.

At Jamestown Island (above) you'll see where the colonists actually landed and what little is left of their village. Here, at this living history museum operated by the Commonwealth of Virginia, you can see what their three ships, their colony, and a typical Powhatan Indian village looked like, and costumed interpreters will show you what colonial life was like in the early 1600s.

Before or after watching a 20-minute film about Jamestown, examine the permanent museum galleries featuring artifacts, documents, decorative objects, dioramas, and graphics relating to the Jamestown period. Leaving the museum complex, you'll come directly into the **Powhatan Indian Village,** representing the culture and technology of a highly organized chiefdom of 32 tribes that inhabited coastal Virginia in the early 17th century. There are several mat-covered lodges, or "longhouses," which are furnished as dwellings, as well as a garden and a ceremonial dance circle. Historical interpreters tend gardens, tan animal hides, and make bone and stone tools and pottery.

Triangular **James Fort** is a re-creation of the one constructed by the Jamestown colonists on their arrival in the spring of 1607. Inside the wooden stockade are primitive wattle-and-daub structures with thatched roofs representing Jamestown's earliest buildings. Interpreters are engaged in activities typical of early 17th-century life, such as agriculture, animal care, carpentry, blacksmithing, and meal preparation.

A short walk from James Fort are reproductions of the three **ships,** the *Susan Constant, Godspeed,* and *Discovery,* that transported 104 colonists to Virginia in 1607. Visitors can board and explore one or more of the ships.

A fast-food restaurant is on the premises.

For more information, contact **Jamestown Settlement,** P.O. Box 1607, Williamsburg, VA 23187 (☎ **888/593-4682** or 757/253-4838; www.historyisfun.org).

While here, you can take a 1½-hour narrated nature cruise on the *Jamestown Explorer,* a covered pontoon boat moored at the Jamestown Yacht Basin directly behind the settlement (☎ **757/259-0400**). It costs $12.50 for adults, $8 for children (kids under 4 free).

3 Yorktown: Revolutionary Victory

14 miles NE of Williamsburg

Yorktown was the setting for the last major battle of the American Revolution. Here, on October 19, 1781, George Washington wrote to the president of the Continental Congress, "I have the Honor to inform Congress, that a Reduction of the British Army under the Command of Lord Cornwallis, is most happily effected." Though sporadic fighting would continue for 2 years before a peace treaty was signed, the Revolution, for all intents and purposes, had been won.

Today the decisive battlefield is a national park, and the Commonwealth of Virginia has built the Yorktown Victory Center, an interpretive museum explaining the road to revolution, the war itself, and the building of a new nation afterward. Predating the revolution and overlooking the picturesque York River, the old town of Yorktown itself is worth a stroll.

To get here from Williamsburg, drive to the eastern end of the Colonial Parkway. From Norfolk, take I-64 west to U.S. 17 north and follow the signs to Yorktown.

You'll need at least half a day to digest all this history.

HISTORY

Though tourist attention focuses to a large degree on the town's role as the final Revolutionary battlefield, Yorktown is also of interest as one of America's earliest colonial towns.

BEFORE THE REVOLUTION   Though a number of settlers lived and farmed in the area by the 1630s, Yorktown's history really dates to 1691, when the General Assembly at Jamestown (then Virginia's capital) passed the Port Act creating a new town on the site. To encourage the development of the town, 50 acres were purchased from Benjamin Read for 10,000 pounds of "merchantable sweet-scented tobacco and cask," then broken into 85 half-acre lots and sold for 180 pounds of tobacco each. By the end of the century, Yorktown was on the way to becoming a principal mid-Atlantic port and a center of tobacco trade.

In the 18th century, Yorktown was a thriving metropolis with a population of several thousand planters, innkeepers, seamen, merchants, craftsmen, indentured servants, and slaves. After the waterfront officially became part of the town in 1738, Water Street, paralleling the river, was lined with shops, inns, and loading docks.

THE VICTORY AT YORKTOWN   The siege began on September 28, 1781, when Washington's American troops and their French allies occupied a line encircling the town within a mile of the British army led by Cornwallis. Washington's allied army of 17,000 men, spread out in camps extending 6 miles, dug siege lines and bombarded the redcoats with cannonfire. When a French fleet sailed up from the Caribbean and defeated the British navy off the Virginia Capes, thereby blocking any escape, Cornwallis's fate was sealed.

Cornwallis compounded his tactical errors by evacuating almost all his positions except for Redoubts (forts) 9 and 10 in order to concentrate his troops closer to town and better defend it. Washington was thus able to move his men to within 1,000 yards of British lines. By October 9, the allies were ready to respond to British artillery. But they didn't wait to respond. The French were the first to fire, and 2 hours later George Washington personally fired the first American round. By October 10, the British were nearly silenced. On October 11, the allies moved up about another 500 yards.

On October 14, the French stormed Redoubt 9 while the Americans made short work of Redoubt 10. Both columns began their assaults at 8pm. The Americans were through by 8:10pm; the French, whose target was stronger, by 8:30pm.

On October 16, following a last-ditch and fruitless attempt to launch an attack on the allies, a desperate Cornwallis tried to escape with his troops across the York River to Gloucester Point, but a violent storm scattered his boats. On October 17 at 10am, a British drummer appeared on the rampart. He beat out a signal indicating a desire to discuss terms with the enemy. A cease-fire was called, and a British officer was led to American lines where he requested an armistice. On October 18, commissioners met at the house of Augustine Moore (see "The Top Attractions," below) and worked out the terms of surrender.

At 2pm on October 19, 1781, the French and Continental armies lined Surrender Road, each stretching for over a mile on either side. The French were resplendent in immaculate white uniforms, their officers plumed and decorated; the Americans were in rags and tatters. The British army (about 5,000 British soldiers and seamen), clad in new uniforms, marched between them out of Yorktown to a band playing a tune called "The World Turned Upside Down." Gen. Charles O'Hara of the British Guards represented Cornwallis who, pleading illness, did not surrender in person.

The battle marked the end of British rule in America and made a permanent place for Yorktown in the annals of American history.

THE TOP ATTRACTIONS

✪ **Yorktown Battlefield.** End of Colonial Pkwy. ☎ **757/898-2410** or 757/898-3400. www.nps.gov/colo. Admission $4 per person over 16 years, free for children 16 and under. Combination ticket with Jamestown Island $7 per person over 16, free for children 16 and under. Both admissions good for 7 days. Audiotape tours $2. National Park Service passports accepted. Battlefield daily 8:30am–dusk. Visitor center Apr to mid-June and mid-Aug to Oct, daily 8:30am–5pm; mid-June to mid-Aug, daily 8:30am–5:30pm. Visitor center closed Christmas.

Today most of Yorktown and the surrounding battlefield areas are included in this 9,300-acre section of the Colonial National Historical Park. You can drive around the key battle sites, which have interpretive markers, but begin at the visitor center, where the 16-minute documentary film *Siege at Yorktown* is shown on the hour and half hour. Museum displays in the center include Washington's actual military headquarters tent; a replica (which you can board and explore) of the quarterdeck of H.M.S. *Charon;* additional objects recovered during excavations; exhibits about Cornwallis's surrender and the events leading up to it; and dioramas detailing the siege. Upstairs, an "on-the-scene" re-creation of the Battle of Yorktown offers taped narration by a 13-year-old soldier in the Revolutionary army, his narrative accompanied by a sound-and-light show.

National Park Service Rangers are on hand to answer questions. They give free **tours** of the British inner defense line on a seasonal basis (call the visitor center for times).

Most important, get a copy of the 60-minute audio driving tour tape, which will lead over the 7-mile Battlefield Route and the 10.2-mile Encampment Route. You'll be given a map indicating both routes and detailing major sites. The taped commentary, formulated as a narrative between British and American colonels whose polite hostilities to each other are most amusing, further elucidates the battlefield sites. You won't stay in your car the whole time; it's frequently necessary to park, get out, and walk to redoubts and earthworks. A lot of the drive is very scenic, winding through woods and fields abundant with bird life. The Encampment route is especially beautiful. If you rent the cassette, listen to the introduction in the parking lot; it will tell you when to depart.

On the Battlefield Route you'll see the **Grand French Battery,** where French soldiers manning cannons, mortars, and howitzers fired on British and German mercenary troops; the **Moore House,** where British and American representatives hammered out the surrender document on October 18, 1781; and **Surrender Field,** where the British laid down their arms and marched out of Yorktown.

The Encampment route will take you to the sites of Washington's and Rochambeau's headquarters, a French cemetery and Artillery Park, and allied encampment sites.

For more information, contact **Colonial National Historical Park,** P.O. Box 210, Yorktown, VA 23690 (☎ **757/898-2410;** www.nps.gov/colo).

✪ **Yorktown Victory Center.** Colonial Pkwy., ½ mile west of Yorktown. ☎ **888/ 593-4682** or 757/887-1776. www.historyisfun.org. Admission $7.25 adults, $3.50 children 6–12; free for children under 6. Combination ticket with Jamestown Settlement $14 adults, $6.75 children 6–12. Daily 9am–5pm. Closed New Year's Day and Christmas.

This state-operated multimedia museum offers an excellent orientation to Yorktown. After watching an 18-minute film, *A Time of Revolution,* you'll follow an open-air timeline walkway known as the "Road to Revolution," which illustrates the relationship between the colonies and Britain beginning in 1750. Aspects of the American Revolution are explored in its gallery exhibits. "Witnesses to Revolution" focuses on ordinary individuals who recorded their observances of the war and its impact on their lives. "Yorktown's Sunken Fleet" uses artifacts recovered from British ships sunk during the siege of Yorktown to describe shipboard life.

Outdoors, costumed interpreters in the Continental army encampment re-create the lives of men and women who took part in the American Revolution. There are presentations on weaponry, military drills and tactics, medicine, and cookery. Nearby, an 18th-century farmsite demonstrates how "middling" farmers—no wealthy plantation owners here—lived and worked.

For more information, contact **Yorktown Victory Center,** P.O. Box 1607, Williamsburg, VA 23187 (☎ **888/593-4682** or 757/253-4838; www.historyisfun.org).

TOURING THE TOWN

Though it is doubtful that Yorktown would have recovered from the destruction and waste that accompanied the Siege of 1781, it received the coup de grace in the Great Fire of 1814 and declined steadily over the years, becoming a quiet rural village. In fact, like Williamsburg, it changed so little that many of its picturesque old streets and buildings have survived intact to this day.

Self-guided or ranger-led walking tours of Old Yorktown—which include visits to some places of interest not related to the famed battle—are available at the Yorktown Battlefield visitor center (call for times; see listing above). Begin your ramble close to the visitor center at:

THE VICTORY MONUMENT News of the allied victory at Yorktown reached Philadelphia on October 24, 1781. On October 29, Congress resolved "that the United States . . . will cause to be erected at York, in Virginia, a marble column, adorned with emblems of the alliance between the United States and his Most Christian Majesty; and inscribed with a succinct narrative of the surrender of Earl Cornwallis to his excellency General Washington, Commander in Chief of the combined forces of America and France."

All very well in theory, but due to financial difficulties no action was taken for a century. Finally, on October 18, 1881, the cornerstone for the monument was laid by Masons as an appropriate opening to the Yorktown Centennial Celebration. The highly symbolic 98-foot marble shaft overlooking the York River was completed in 1884. The podium is adorned with 13 female figures hand in hand in a solemn dance to denote the unity of the 13 colonies; beneath their feet is the inscription "One Country, One Constitution, One Destiny," a moving post–Civil War sentiment. The column itself symbolizes the greatness and prosperity of the nation, and its stars represent the "constellation" of states in the Union in 1881. Atop the shaft is the figure of Liberty.

A footpath leads from the monument into town, where you can explore:

CORNWALLIS CAVE According to legend, Cornwallis lived here in two tiny "rooms" during the final days of the siege when he hoped to withdraw to the river and escape overland to New York. The two rooms were carved out by various occupants of the cave—which may at one time have included the pirate Blackbeard—and Confederate soldiers later enlarged the shelter and added a roof. A taped narrative at the entrance tells the story. The cave is at the foot of Great Valley, right on the river.

THE DUDLEY DIGGES HOUSE   You can view the restored 18th-century white weatherboard house on Main Street and Smith Street only from the outside, since it's a private residence and not open to the public. Its dormer windows set in the roofline, and surrounding outbuildings, are typical of Virginia architecture in the mid-1700s. Owner Dudley Digges was a Revolutionary patriot who served with Patrick Henry, Benjamin Harrison, and Thomas Jefferson on the Committee of Correspondence. After the war he was rector of the College of William and Mary.

THE NELSON HOUSE   Scottish merchant Thomas Nelson made three voyages between Great Britain and Virginia before deciding to settle in Yorktown in 1705. He proceeded to sire a dynasty, and by 1707 he had acquired two lots, along with a number of slaves, and built himself a house at Main and Nelson streets. Between 1711 and 1723, he obtained title to several other lots and became co-operator of a ferry, charter member of a trading company, builder of the Swan Tavern, trustee of York's port land, and a large-scale planter. By 1728, he had added 600 acres, a private warehouse and wharf, and a mill to his holdings. He died in 1745, leaving a vast estate, which his descendants—who included several prominent Revolutionary leaders, one of them a signer of the Declaration of Independence—further enlarged.

Though damaged (cannonballs remain embedded in the brickwork), the house survived the Battle of Yorktown (Cornwallis seized it for a command post during part of his occupation) and Nelson's descendants continued to occupy the house through 1907. The National Park Service acquired the house in 1968 and restored it to its original appearance.

It is open daily from 10am to 4:30pm in summer (check at the visitor center for off-season hours). Ranger-guided tours take 30 to 45 minutes.

THE SESSIONS HOUSE   Just across from the Nelson House, this is the oldest house in Yorktown, built in 1692 by Thomas Sessions. At least five U.S. presidents have visited the house, today a private residence off-limits to the public. You may, however, stare at it.

THE CUSTOMHOUSE   Dating to 1721, this sturdy brick building at the corner of Main and Read was originally the private storehouse of Richard Ambler, collector of ports. It became Gen. J. B. Magruder's headquarters during the Civil War. Today it is maintained as a museum by the Daughters of the American Revolution.

GRACE EPISCOPAL CHURCH   Located on Church Street near the river, Grace Church dates to 1697 and has been an active house of worship since then. Its first rector, the Rev. Anthony Panton, was dismissed for calling the secretary of the colony a jackanapes. Gunpowder and ammunition were stored here during the siege of Yorktown. And during the Civil War the church served as a hospital. It's open to visitors daily from 9am to 5pm. The original communion silver, made in England in 1649, is still in use. Thomas Nelson (II) is buried in the adjacent graveyard.

THE SWAN TAVERN   For over a century the Swan Tavern, at the corner of Main and Ballard streets (☎ **757/898-3033**), was Yorktown's leading hostelry. Originally owned by Thomas Nelson, it was in operation 20 years before Williamsburg's famous Raleigh Tavern. The Swan was demolished in 1863 by an ammunition explosion at the courthouse across the street, rebuilt, and destroyed again by fire in 1915. Today it is reconstructed as per historical research, and the premises house a fine 18th-century antiques shop. It's open Tuesday to Saturday 10am to 5pm, Sunday noon to 5pm.

WHERE TO DINE

Consider a **picnic** lunch in a large tree-shaded area at the Victory Center or at a riverside picnic area with tables and grills on Water Street at the foot of Comte de Grasse Street. There's another gorgeous area called **Ringfield,** 7 miles northeast of Williamsburg on the Colonial Parkway.

Nick's Seafood Pavilion. Water St. ☎ **757/887-5269.** Reservations not accepted. Main courses $8–$35. AE, DC, MC, V. Daily 11am–10pm. AMERICAN/GREEK.

Almost under the bridge over the York River, Nick's interior is an exuberant surprise. Several spacious dining rooms are bedecked with reproductions of classic stone statuary, mosaic tiles, plants, fountains, and oil paintings. If you can stand a heavy portion of butter, the best dish here is a lobster-and-rice combination known as *din bien.* Soft-shell crabs sautéed in butter, broiled tuna or mahimahi, and broiled lobster tail also are menu standbys, along with nonseafood entrees ranging from pork tenderloin Greek-style to prime beef shish kebabs. There's baked Alaska for dessert.

4 James River Plantations

While Williamsburg was the political capital of Virginia during the 18th century, its economic livelihood depended on the great tobacco plantations like Carter's Grove. Several more of the mansions built during that period of wealthy landowners still stand today along the banks of the James River between Williamsburg and Richmond, some occupied to this day by the same families that have produced generals, governors, and two presidents. They provide an authentic feel for 18th-century plantation life.

SEEING THE PLANTATIONS

The plantations are on John Tyler Highway (Va. 5) between Williamsburg and Richmond. From Williamsburg, take Jamestown Road and bear right on Va. 5. From Richmond, take Main Street east, which becomes Va. 5.

This so-called Plantation Route covers a distance of 55 miles between Williamsburg and Richmond and makes an excellent scenic driving tour between the two cities. Allow a full day to visit all the plantations and to take a break for lunch. I list them here east-to-west as you come to them from Williamsburg. If you're driving from Richmond, start at Shirley and work backwards.

The owners of Sherwood Forest, Evelynton, Berkeley, and Shirley offer a **block ticket** for admission to all of their homes. They cost $28 for adults. There's no children's ticket (it's less expensive to pay for them at each home). Block tickets can be purchased at any of the four plantations.

The plantations' **mailing address** is Charles City, VA 23030. They have a joint **Web site** at www.jamesriverplantations.org.

✪ **Sherwood Forest.** 14501 John Tyler Hwy. (Va. 5), 20 miles west of Williamsburg. ☎ **804/829-5377.** www.sherwoodforest.org. Admission $9 adults, $8 seniors, $6 students, $4.50 grounds only. Daily 9am–5pm. Closed Thanksgiving and Christmas. Mandatory 30-minute house tours depart on the hour and half hour.

Owned by President William Henry Harrison in the 1790s, this long, white clapboard house was the home of President John Tyler after he retired from the White House in 1845. It has been continuously occupied by Tyler family members ever since. Then in his sixties, Tyler brought with him a young second wife and commenced to start a new family. The son of that marriage was in his own seventies before be began a family, and his son—grandson of President Tyler—still lives upstairs. Built in 1730, the original house is now part of the Main Hall. Tyler extended the one-room-deep home to its present length of 301 feet, making it the longest wood-frame house in America. All furnishings are family heirlooms or similar period pieces. A walking tour of the grounds features numerous ancient trees and a number of original plantation outbuildings.

☕ **TAKE A BREAK** You can break your driving tour of the plantations at **Indian Fields Tavern,** 9220 John Tyler Hwy. (Va. 5), between Sherwood Forest and Evelynton (☎ **804/829-5004**). This fine restaurant in a restored Victorian farmhouse, with screened porches open during warm weather, offers salads of tarragon chicken or burgers, and entrees including quiche, crab cakes, and an unusual mixed grill of local sausages and marinated duck. The signature dish at dinner is crab cakes served over Virginia ham. Reservations are required at dinner. Open Monday to Saturday from 11am to 3:30pm, Sunday to Thursday 5 to 9pm, Friday and Saturday 5 to 9:30pm. American Express, Discover, MasterCard, and Visa are accepted.

Evelynton. 6701 John Tyler Hwy. (Va. 5), 25 miles west of Williamsburg. ☎ **800/473-5075** or 804/829-5075. www.evelyntonplantation.org. Admission $8.50 for adults, $7 seniors, $3.50 children 6 to 12, under 6 free. Daily 9am to 5pm. Closed Thanksgiving and Christmas. Mandatory 30-minute house tours on demand.

Adjacent to and part of the original 1619 Westover Plantation land grant (see "Berkeley," below), this tract was named for William Byrd's daughter Evelyn (pronounced "EVE-lyn"). She is said to have died of a broken heart because her father refused to let her marry her chosen suitor. According to legend, her ghost still roams both houses. Since 1847, Evelynton has been home to the Ruffin family, whose patriarch, noted agriculturist Edmund Ruffin, fired the first shot of the Civil War at Fort Sumter, S.C. The original house was destroyed in 1862, when Gen. George McClellan's Union troops skirmished with Confederates led by J. E. B. Stuart and John Pelham in the fierce but short-lived Battle of Evelynton Heights. The present structure, a magnificent example of Colonial Revival style, was designed by renowned Virginia architect Duncan Lee and built in 1935.

✪ **Berkeley.** 12602 Harrison Landing Rd. (off Va. 5), 30 miles west of Williamsburg. ☎ **800/921-6003** or 804/829-6018. www.berkeleyplantation.com. Admission $9 adults, $6.50 children 13–16, $4 children 6–12, children under 6 free. Daily 8am–5pm. Closed Christmas. Mandatory 30-minute house tours on demand.

On December 4, 1619, 38 English settlers sent by the Berkeley Company put ashore after a 3-month voyage. They fell on their knees in a prayer of thanksgiving. If you're here on the first Sunday of November, you can participate in the annual celebration commemorating that first official Thanksgiving in the New World.

The aristocratic Harrison family bought Berkeley in 1691. Benjamin Harrison III made it a prosperous operation, and in 1726 his son, Benjamin Harrison IV, built the three-story Georgian mansion. Benjamin Harrison V was a signer of the Declaration of Independence and thrice governor of Virginia. The next generation produced William Henry Harrison, the frontier fighter whose nickname "Old Tippecanoe" helped him get elected as our ninth president. His grandson, another Benjamin Harrison, took the presidential oath 47 years later. George Washington was a frequent guest, and every president through Buchanan enjoyed Berkeley's gracious hospitality.

Berkeley was twice occupied by invading troops. A British army under Benedict Arnold burned the family portraits, practiced target shooting on the cows, and went off with 40 slaves. General George McClellan's Union army trampled the gardens and chopped up the elegant furnishings for firewood. It was during the Yankee occupancy that Gen. Dan Butterfield composed "Taps." After the war, the Harrisons never returned to live at Berkeley.

John Jamieson, a Scottish-born New Yorker who had served as a drummer boy in McClellan's army, purchased the disfigured manor house and 1,400 acres in 1907. His son, Malcolm, has completely restored the house and grounds to their glorious appearances of the early days of the Harrisons' tenure. Following a 10-minute slide presentation, 30-minute guided **tours** of the house are given throughout the day by guides in colonial dress. Allow at least another half hour to explore the magnificent grounds and gardens on your own.

Sharing Berkeley's lane off Va. 5, **Westover** (☎ **804/829-2882**) is the beautiful 1730s Georgian manor house built by Richmond's founder, William Byrd II, directly on the banks of the James. The interior is open to the public only for 5 days during Garden Week (last week in April), although visitors are invited to walk around the grounds and gardens year-round, daily from 9am to 6pm. Admission is $2.

☕ **TAKE A BREAK**   Berkeley is a good place to stop for lunch, as moderately priced sandwiches, soups, and salads are served in the old carriage house, now appropriately named the **Coach House Tavern** (☎ **800/921-6003** or 804/ 829-6003). It's open for lunch Monday to Saturday 11am to 4pm during summer, to 3pm off-season, and for dinner Friday and Saturday 6 to 9pm. Reservations are required for dinner. American Express, Discover, MasterCard, and Visa are accepted. There also are picnic grounds on Berkeley's premises.

✪ **Shirley.** 502 Shirley Plantation Rd. (off Va. 5), Charles City, 35 miles west of Williamsburg. ☎ **800/232-1613** or 757/829-5121. www.shirleyplantation.com. Admission $9 adults, $8 seniors, $6 students 13–21, $5 children 6–12, children under 6 free. Mid-Feb to mid-Jan, daily 9am–4:15pm; mid-Jan to mid-Feb, Sat–Sun 9am–4:15pm. Closed Thanksgiving and Christmas. Mandatory 45-minute house tours depart continuously.

Another historic James River plantation, Shirley was founded in 1613 and has been in the same family since 1660. The present mansion, built by Edward Hill III or his son-in-law, John Carter (historians are not sure), dates to 1723. Since that time two very distinguished Virginia families—the Hills and the Carters—have occupied Shirley. Because of this continuous ownership, many original furnishings, portraits, and memorabilia remain, making this one of the most interesting plantations open to public view. The carved-walnut staircase, rising three stories with no visible means of support, is the only one of its kind in America. The house survived the Revolution, the Civil War, and Reconstruction, as did the dependencies—a group of superb brick outbuildings, including a large two-story kitchen, a laundry house, and two barns, that form a unique Queen Anne forecourt. Other original structures are the stable, smokehouse, and dovecote. After the tour, allow at least another 30 minutes to explore the grounds and dependencies.

5 An Easy Excursion to Hampton & Newport News

Jamestown was barely 2 years old when Capt. John Smith sent a contingent of men to build America's first fort on the Hampton River, strategically located on the western shore of Hampton Roads. There's been a town here since 1610, making Hampton the nation's oldest continuously English-speaking settlement. It was the colony's first seaport, and it was here in 1718 that British troops displayed the head of Edward Teach, better known as Blackbeard the Pirate, whom they killed during a furious battle on the North Carolina Outer Banks (his captured crew were tried and hanged in Williamsburg).

Unfortunately, there are few remaining structures from those early days other than Fort Monroe, for during the Civil War a Confederate general ordered the town burned to the ground rather than permit Union forces holding Fort Monroe to quarter troops and former slaves here. You can visit the dank Fort Monroe room where Confederate president Jefferson Davis was imprisoned after the war; the fine museum at Hampton University, founded in 1868 to educate the newly freed slaves (Booker T. Washington was an alumnus); and the very modern Virginia Air and Space Center, a smaller but excellent rendition of the Smithsonian Institution's National Air and Space Museum in Washington, D.C.

Named for Christopher Newport, skipper of the *Discovery*, which brought some of the Jamestown settlers to Virginia, Newport News dates back to the early 1600s and has a long maritime tradition. Many of America's most formidable warships have rolled down the ways of Newport News Shipbuilding & Dry Dock Company, the region's largest private employer. It's appropriate that the city is home to the Mariners' Museum, the largest maritime museum in the Western Hemisphere.

Hampton has enough interesting sights to take up most of a day trip from Williamsburg. The Mariners' Museum is on the way to Hampton, so you can spend part of the morning there on the way. You can also visit both cities on day excursions from Norfolk and Virginia Beach.

ESSENTIALS

VISITOR INFORMATION   Your visit to Hampton should start at the **Hampton Visitor Center,** 710 Settlers Landing Rd., Hampton, VA 23669 (☎ **800/800-2202** or 757/727-1102; fax 757/727-1310; www.hampton.va.us/tourism). The center is on the waterfront, a block from the Virginia Air and Space Center (see below). Open daily 9am to 5pm except New Year's Day, Thanksgiving, and Christmas.

For advance information about Newport News, contact the **Newport News Tourism Development Office,** 2400 Washington Ave., Newport News, VA 23607 (☎ **888/493-7386** or 757/926-3561; fax 757/926-6901; www.newport-news.org).

GETTING THERE   From Williamsburg, take I-64 east. To reach downtown Hampton, take Exit 267 and turn right on Settlers Landing Road and cross the Hampton River to the visitor center (a left turn at the exit will take you to Fort Monroe and the Casemate Museum via the village of Poquoson). To reach the Mariners' Museum, take Exit 258 and follow J. Clyde Morris Boulevard (U.S. 17) south; the museum is at the southern end of the boulevard. From Norfolk and Virginia Beach, take I-64 west through the Hampton Roads Bridge Tunnel to these exits.

You can also get to Hampton from downtown Norfolk (or vice versa) on the **Harbor Link** (☎ **757/722-9400**), a passenger ferry which shuttles between NAUTICUS (The National Maritime Center; see section 1 in chapter 11) and the Hampton Visitor Center. The ride takes 30 minutes each way and goes across Hampton Roads, where the famous ironclads *Monitor* and *Merrimac* fought to a stalemate during the Civil War. The ferry operates Monday to Friday 7:15am to 7:30pm, weekends and holidays 9:15am to 9:30pm, but call in advance to make sure of the schedule. One-way fare is $5 for adults, $4 for seniors and children under 12.

Amtrak (☎ **800/872-7245;** www.amtrak.com) has daily service to its station in Newport News.

ATTRACTIONS IN HAMPTON

Casemate Museum. Fort Monroe. ☎ **757/727-3391.** Free admission. Daily 10:30am–
4:30pm. Closed New Year's Day, Thanksgiving, and Christmas. From downtown Hampton
take Settlers Landing Road east across Hampton River bridge and under I-64 (Exit 267) into
Phoebus; take right fork onto County St. and turn right on Mallory St., left on Mellen St.,
straight to Fort Monroe and museum.

Fort Monroe's Casemate Museum is a must-see for Civil War buffs, as it's where Confederate President Jefferson Davis was imprisoned in 1865 after being captured in
Georgia (the accusation that he had participated in Lincoln's assassination was
disproved, and Davis was released in 1867). Located at the tip of a peninsula and
surrounded by a moat, the stone fort was built between 1819 and 1834. Robert E. Lee
served as second in command of the construction detachment in 1831 when he was a
young officer in the Army Corps of Engineers, and Edgar Allan Poe spent 16 months
here in 1828–29 as an enlisted man. The fort was so strong that it never fell to the
Confederates during the Civil War. The dungeon-like *casemates*, or rooms, were originally designed as storage for seacoast artillery. After 1861, they were modified to serve
as living quarters for the soldiers and their families stationed at the fort. You'll need
about 45 minutes in the dank rooms to view displays of military memorabilia and
Davis's sparsely furnished quarters (his intricately carved pipe—an egg-shaped bowl
clenched in an eagle's claw—is outside the door).

Tours can be arranged in advance by contacting the museum. The mailing address
is P.O. Box 341, Fort Monroe, VA 23651.

Hampton University Museum. Huntington Building, Hampton University campus.
☎ **757/727-5308.** www.hamptonu.edu. Free admission. Mon–Fri 8am–5pm; Sat–Sun
noon–4pm. From downtown Hampton, take Settlers Landing Road across the Hampton River
and follow signs to the university and museum.

Across the river from downtown, Hampton University was founded in 1868 to provide an education for newly freed African Americans. It boasts among its graduates
Booker T. Washington, who founded Tuskegee Institute in Alabama and whose birthplace is preserved near Lynchburg (see chapter 6). Four landmarks are nearby,
including the imposing Memorial Chapel (1886). The museum is noted for its African
collection, comprising more than 2,700 art objects and artifacts representing 887
ethnic groups and cultures. Rivaling the African collection in quality and importance,
the Native American collection includes works from 93 tribes; it was established in
1878, when the federal government began sending young Native Americans from
reservations in the West to be educated at Hampton. The museum also has notable
holdings in works by Harlem Renaissance artists, as well as an extensive number of
Oceanic and Asian objects.

✪ **Virginia Air and Space Center/Hampton Roads History Center.** 600 Settlers
Landing Rd. (at King St.). ☎ **757/727-0900.** www.vasc.org. Admission $6 adults, $5
seniors and military, $4 children 3–11, free for children under 3. Combination tickets
including the IMAX film $3 more. Memorial Day–Labor Day, Mon–Wed 10am–5pm,
Thurs–Sun 10am–7pm; off-season, daily 10am–5pm.

A stunning glass-fronted futuristic structure perched on the edge of Hampton's riverfront, this museum chronicles the history of aviation and space travel and also serves
as the official visitor center for NASA's Langley Research Center. The vast interior is
separated into bays that hold individual exhibits on rockets, satellites, and space exploration. In the main gallery, about 10 air vehicles are suspended from the 94-foot
vaulted ceiling, and below sits the *Apollo 12* command module, complete with reentry
burn marks. In the Space Gallery, you can don an astronaut's helmet and see yourself

on a TV monitor. An IMAX theater shows 45-minute films, usually about flying and space. Behind the air vehicles, you'll find a gallery devoted to Hampton Roads history, highlighted by a fascinating collection of Civil War photos. There are no guided tours; allow about 2 hours to explore it all on your own.

RIVER CRUISES

The most popular harbor cruises in Virginia are on the ***Miss Hampton II,*** a 65-foot passenger boat that sails from downtown across Hampton Roads to the huge U.S. Naval Base at Norfolk. You'll pass the landing site of the Jamestown settlers and Blackbeard's Point, where the pirate's head was displayed in 1718. Weather permitting, you'll go ashore for a 45-minute guided tour of pre–Civil War Fort Wool, on a 15-acre island out in the Chesapeake. The narrated 3-hour cruises depart from a dock next to the Hampton Visitor Center daily at 10am and 2pm from Memorial Day to Labor Day, at 10am only in April, May, September, and October. Fares are $14.50 for adults, $12.50 for seniors and military, $8 for children 6 to 12, free for kids under 6. The company also has sunset and daylong Intercoastal Waterway cruises.

ATTRACTIONS IN NEWPORT NEWS

✪ **Mariners' Museum.** 100 Museum Dr. ☎ **757/596-2222.** Admission $5 adults, $4 seniors, $3 students. Daily 10am–5pm. From I-64, take Exit 258A and follow J. Clyde Morris Blvd. (U.S. 17) south to its intersection with Warwick Blvd. (U.S. 60); go straight on Museum Dr.

Dedicated to preserving the culture of the sea and its tributaries, this is the largest maritime museum in the Western Hemisphere, situated in a pleasant 550-acre park setting with a lake, picnic areas, and walking trails. Inside, handcrafted ship models, scrimshaw, maritime paintings, decorative arts, working steam engines, and more are displayed in spacious galleries. Particularly interesting are exhibits highlighting the history and culture of the Chesapeake Bay and the Age of Exploration. Out back, the propeller from the Union ironclad U.S.S. *Monitor* is stored in a seawater tank; it was recovered from the Atlantic Ocean off Cape Hatteras in 1998. Shown on the hour and half hour, an 18-minute film narrated by actor James Earl Jones discusses maritime activity the world over. There usually are two guided tours a day Monday to Friday (call for schedule). Otherwise, allow about 2 hours here.

Virginia Living Museum. 524 J. Clyde Morris Blvd., Newport News. ☎ **757/595-1900.** Museum admission $6 adults, $4 children 3–12, free for children under 3. Planetarium admission $2.50 per person. Memorial Day to Labor Day, Sun–Wed and Fri 9am–6pm, Thurs 9am–9pm; rest of year, Mon–Wed and Fri–Sat 9am–5pm, Thurs 9am–5pm and 7–9pm, Sun noon–6pm. Nature trail closes daily at dusk. From I-64, take Exit 258A and follow J. Clyde Morris Blvd. (U.S. 17) south to its intersection with Warwick Blvd. (U.S. 60); go straight to museum on left.

If you're going to the Virginia Marine Science Museum in Virginia Beach (see chapter 11), you can skip this zoo-like nature preserve near the Mariners' Museum. If you're not, then here you can learn about the environment of the James River area. A touchtank lets youngsters handle turtles and other small river animals. Outdoors, a boardwalk nature trail winds along the banks of a picturesque lake. Enclosures contain local wildlife such as otters, beavers, turtles, and birds (including two bald eagles grounded by a gunshot wounds). A state-of-the-art planetarium presents shows explaining the southern skies.

11

Norfolk, Virginia Beach & the Eastern Shore

When they arrived in 1607, the Jamestown colonists first set foot in the New World on the sandy shores of Cape Charles. Although they didn't stay on the banks of Hampton Roads, one of the world's largest natural harbors, later generations did. Norfolk and Portsmouth became major seaports—they were fought over often during the Civil War, including the famous battle between the first ironclads, USS *Monitor* and CSS *Merrimac,* out on Hampton Roads. Today the cities of Norfolk, Virginia Beach, Portsmouth, and Chesapeake sprawl over the harbor's southern shores.

The area's population swells significantly during the summer months, when the sand and surf of Virginia Beach draw vacationers from around the globe. With a host of activities, a multitude of hotels, and close proximity to the other cities, "The Beach" makes a fine base of operations for a visit to this area.

The population here also goes up and down depending on deployments by the U.S. Navy, as this area has America's largest concentration of naval bases. The sailors once made Norfolk a bawdy seaport, but the city has rebuilt itself into a vibrant urban center of the New South. A ferry crosses the Elizabeth River to the neighboring city of Portsmouth, whose architecturally rich Olde Town may remind you of Charleston and Savannah.

From Virginia Beach, the 17-mile-long Chesapeake Bay Bridge-Tunnel whisks visitors north to a very different world: Virginia's rural Eastern Shore. There on the Delmarva Peninsula beckon ancient fishing villages like Chincoteague, a renowned wildlife refuge teeming with birdlife and wild horses, and the gorgeous Assateague Island National Seashore with 37 miles of pristine, totally undeveloped beach.

1 Norfolk

190 miles SE of Washington, D.C.; 93 miles E of Richmond; 17 miles W of Virginia Beach

Although it's still a major seaport and naval base, Norfolk has replaced its notorious waterfront sailor bars and burlesque houses with a vibrant, modern downtown of high-rise offices, condominiums, marinas, museums, shops, nightspots, and a 12,000-seat minor league baseball park. The biggest recent addition is the MacArthur Center, a huge shopping mall just a few blocks from the riverfront.

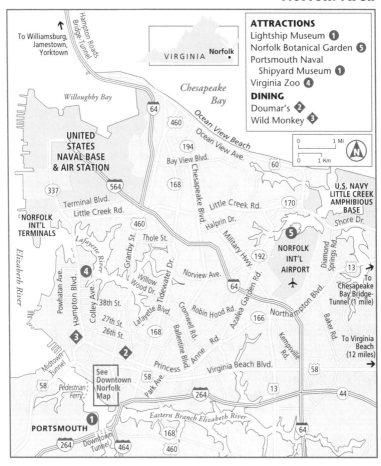

Interspersed in this revitalized downtown are reminders of Norfolk's past, such as historic houses and the old City Hall, now converted into a museum and memorial to World War II hero Gen. Douglas MacArthur. Here also is one of Virginia's finest art museums, the state's official zoo, and a beautiful botanical garden. And for foodies, hip new restaurants have brought great tastes to downtown and the gentrified old residential neighborhoods of Freemason and Ghent.

ESSENTIALS
VISITOR INFORMATION

For advance information, contact the **Norfolk Convention & Visitors Bureau,** 252 E. Main St., Norfolk, VA 23510 (☎ **800/368-3097** or 757/441-1852; fax 757/ 622-3663; www.norfolk.va.us). The bureau has a walk-in information desk at its offices, which are across Main Street from the Norfolk Marriott. It's open Monday to Friday 8:30am to 6pm. If you're arriving from the west via I-64, the **Norfolk Visitor Center** is on Fourth View Street at Exit 273 in the Ocean View section (☎ **757/441-1852**). It's open during the summer daily from 9am to 6pm, the rest of the year daily from 9am to 5pm. Another information booth is in NAUTICUS (see "The Top Attractions," below).

Information also is available at the **Freemason Street Reception Center,** 401 Freemason St. (☎ 757/441-1526), behind the MacArthur Center. It serves as host for tours of the Moses Myers and Willoughby-Baylor houses, which flank it (see "The Top Attractions," below).

GETTING THERE

BY PLANE   Norfolk International Airport, on Norview Avenue 1½ miles north of I-64 (☎ 757/857-3351), is served by American, Continental, Delta, Midway, Northwest, TWA, United, and US Airways. The major car-rental firms have desks here. **Groome Transportation** (☎ 800/552-7911 in Virginia, or 757/857-1231) runs vans to points between Williamsburg and Virginia Beach. One-way fares to downtown Norfolk are $13.50 for one passenger, $18.50 for two; to Virginia Beach or Hampton, $20 for one passenger, $26.75 for two; to Williamsburg, $29 for one passenger, $19 per passenger for two or more.

BY CAR   From the west, I-64 runs directly from Richmond to Norfolk, then swings around the eastern and southern suburbs, where it meets I-664 to form a beltway around the area. U.S. 460 also runs the length of Virginia to Norfolk, and U.S. 13 and 17 lead here from north or south. If you're coming from Virginia Beach, the Norfolk–Virginia Beach Expressway (Va. 44) becomes I-264, which goes through downtown and Portsmouth. Norfolk is linked to Portsmouth by ferry, bridge, and tunnel, and to Hampton and Newport News by the Hampton Roads Bridge-Tunnel (I-64).

BY TRAIN & BUS   Amtrak (☎ 800/872-7245; www.amtrak.com) has bus connections to and from its station in Newport News. **Greyhound** (☎ 800/231-2222; www.greyhound.com) has bus service to downtown Norfolk.

CITY LAYOUT

Norfolk occupies two peninsulas formed by the Chesapeake Bay and the Elizabeth and Lafayette rivers. **Downtown** is on the southern side of the city, on the northern bank of the Elizabeth River. Bordering downtown to the northwest, **Freemason** is Norfolk's oldest residential neighborhood, with most of its 18th- and 19th-century town houses now restored as private homes, businesses, and restaurants. You'll still find a few cobblestone streets here. Northwest of Freemason, across a semicircular inlet known as The Hague, **Ghent** was the city's first subdivision and is now its trendiest enclave. Most houses in "old" Ghent, near The Hague and the Chrysler Museum of Art (see "The Top Attractions," below), were built between 1892 and 1912. Today, the area is home to everyone from well-heeled professional types to writers, aspiring artists, and college students. The heart of Ghent's business district is on **Colley Avenue** between Baldwin Avenue and 21st Street, a strip of antiques shops and chic restaurants interspersed with an Irish tavern, a wine-and-cheese emporium, the artsy NORA Cinema, dry cleaners, shoe-repair shops, a 7 Eleven, and a public school.

GETTING AROUND

A **car** is the easiest way to get around this spread-out area, although traffic can back up in the bridge-tunnels under Hampton Roads, especially at weekday rush hours and summer weekends. To check traffic conditions, call ☎ 757/640-5555, ext. 7874. **Parking** is available downtown at the MacArthur Center and in four municipal garages (the most convenient is on Atlantic Avenue between Waterside Drive and Main Street).

The **Tidewater Regional Transit System (TRT)** (☎ 757/222-6100) operates public buses throughout Norfolk, Virginia Beach, Portsmouth, and Chesapeake. Bus fare is $1.50, with exact change required.

In addition to its buses and the Elizabeth River Ferry (see "A Ferry Ride to Olde Town Portsmouth," below), TRT operates **trolley tours** of downtown Norfolk, the Norfolk Naval Base, and Olde Town Portsmouth. You can get schedules and tickets at TRT's ticket kiosk on Waterside Drive in front of The Waterside (see "Seeing the Sights," below).

The **Norfolk Explorers Trolley Tour** provides a good overview of downtown, and it's a convenient way to get around. It starts at The Waterside and stops at attractions downtown and in the trendy Ghent neighborhood. You can get off at any stop and reboard a later trolley. It operates from Memorial Day to Labor Day, daily at 10:30am, noon, 1:30pm, and 3pm. Departures in September are at noon, 1:30pm, and 3pm. Fare is $3.50 for adults and $1.75 for seniors and children under 12, with free reboarding.

TRT's **Discover Tidewater Passport** permits 3 days of unlimited use of the trolley tours, the ferry, and the Virginia Beach trolleys; it costs $8.50 for adults and $4.75 for seniors, children under 12, and disabled passengers. Or you can buy an **Adventure Pass,** which allows 3 days of tours and transportation and includes admission to the Chrysler Museum of Art in Norfolk, the Children's Museum of Virginia in Portsmouth, and the Virginia Science Museum in Virginia Beach. It costs $26.50 for adults and $20 for seniors, children under 12, and disabled passengers.

For taxis, call **Yellow Cab** (☎ 757/622-3232).

SEEING THE SIGHTS

Downtown Norfolk is dominated by the **MacArthur Center** (☎ 757/627-6000), a $300-million shopping mall covering the 9 square blocks bordered by Monticello and City Hall avenues, Freemason Street, and St. Paul's Boulevard (the main entry is on Monticello Avenue at Market Street). Anchored by Nordstrom and Dillard's department stores, it has a host of the mall regulars, an 18-screen cinema, a food court, and full service restaurants (see "Where to Dine," below).

Before the mall opened in 1998, **The Waterside** (☎ 757/627-3300), a steel-and-glass pavilion built in 1983 between Waterside Drive and the Elizabeth River, was the centerpiece of Norfolk's revitalized downtown. Like Baltimore's Inner Harbor, Boston's Faneuil Hall, and New York's South Street Seaport, The Waterside houses shops, food outlets, and full-service restaurants, and the Elizabeth River Ferry and harbor cruises leave from the dock outside. With so much of its shopping business now going to the MacArthur Center, the city has announced plans to make The Waterside strictly a dining-and-entertainment complex.

Town Point Park's amphitheater, between The Waterside and NAUTICUS, features a full schedule of free special events throughout the year—concerts, children's theater, magic shows, puppetry, and more. East of The Waterside, **Harbor Park,** a 12,000-seat stadium, is home to the Norfolk Tides, the New York Mets AAA International League team (☎ 757/622-2222).

THE TOP ATTRACTIONS

✪ **The Chrysler Museum of Art.** 425 W. Olney Rd. (at Mowbray Arch). ☎ **757/644-6200.** www.chrysler.org. Admission $5 adults, $3 seniors and students 12–18, free for children under 12. Combination tickets with Moses Myers/Willoughby houses $8 adults, $5 seniors and students, free for children under 5. Tues–Sat 10am–5pm; Sun 1–5pm. Closed New Year's Day, Independence Day, Thanksgiving, and Christmas.

Originally built in 1932 as the Norfolk Museum of Art, this imposing Italian Renaissance building on The Hague inlet was renamed in 1971 when Walter P. Chrysler, Jr., gave a large portion of his collection to the city. It spans artistic periods from ancient

Recommending Ike

On display in Norfolk's Douglas MacArthur Memorial is a yellowing copy of an army "efficiency report" filled out by Gen. Douglas MacArthur in 1937. In it, he grades the performance of a member of his staff and recommends that in time of war, the subordinate should be immediately promoted to general. The staffer was Lt. Col. Dwight D. Eisenhower.

Egypt to the 1980s and includes one of the finest and most comprehensive glass collections in the world. Adjoining is an outstanding collection of art nouveau furniture. Other first-floor galleries exhibit ancient Indian, Islamic, Asian, African, and pre-Columbian art. Most second-floor galleries are devoted to painting and sculpture, particularly Italian baroque and French, including works by Picasso, Renoir, Matisse, Braque, Bernini, and Rouault. American art holdings include 18th- and 19th-century paintings by Charles Willson Peale, Benjamin West, John Singleton Copley, and Thomas Cole, and 20th-century works by Thomas Hart Benton, Calder, Kline, Warhol, Rauschenberg, and Rosenquist. A permanent gallery is devoted solely to photography, showcasing everyone from Walker Evans to Diane Arbus.

Pick up a free telephone-like audio tour at the front desk, which will explain some of the key items as you walk along. Allow at least 2 hours here, half a day to do it complete justice.

The museum administers the Moses Myers and Willoughby-Baylor houses (see below) and sells money-saving combination tickets covering admission here and there.

✪ **Douglas MacArthur Memorial.** MacArthur Sq. (between City Hall Ave. and Plume St., at Bank St.). ☎ **757/441-2965.** www.whro.org/c1/mac. Free admission (donations encouraged). Mon–Sat 10am–5pm; Sun 11am–5pm. Closed New Year's Day, Thanksgiving, and Christmas. Validated 3-hour parking at MacArthur Center or any City of Norfolk lot.

Along with excerpts from his other speeches, Gen. Douglas MacArthur's immortal words "I shall return" are engraved on a bronze plaque at his final resting place in Norfolk's old city hall, an imposing domed structure with a columned front portico. In a scene a bit reminiscent of the Taj Mahal in India, the dome towers over the side-by-side marble crypts of the general and his wife, Jean. Shown every half hour in a theater next door, a 22-minute film will give you a perspective on MacArthur's life and help you understand the exhibits. Filled with his personal memorabilia, the chronologically arranged galleries trace U.S. history during MacArthur's life and his role in specific events up to his ringing "Old Soldiers Never Die" speech to Congress after President Truman fired him during the Korean War. Of particular interest: MacArthur's famous corncob pipe, his omnipresent sunglasses, his field cap with its sides rolled down, and a replica of the plaque marking the spot on the USS *Missouri* where MacArthur presided over the surrender of Japan. A short film of the surrender ceremony includes his famous remark, "These proceedings are closed."

Moses Myers House and Willoughby-Baylor House. 331 Bank St. (at E. Freemason St.). ☎ **757/664-6283.** www.chrysler.org. Admission $4 adults, $2.50 seniors and seniors, free for children under 5. Combination tickets with The Chrysler Museum $8 adults, $5 seniors and students, free for children under 13. Tues–Sat 10am–5pm, Sun noon–5pm. Mandatory 1-hour tours of both houses depart on the hour. Closed New Year's Day, Independence Day, Thanksgiving, and Christmas.

It has the massive MacArthur Center as its backyard these days, but this handsome early-Federal brick town house was in Norfolk's oldest residential neighborhood when

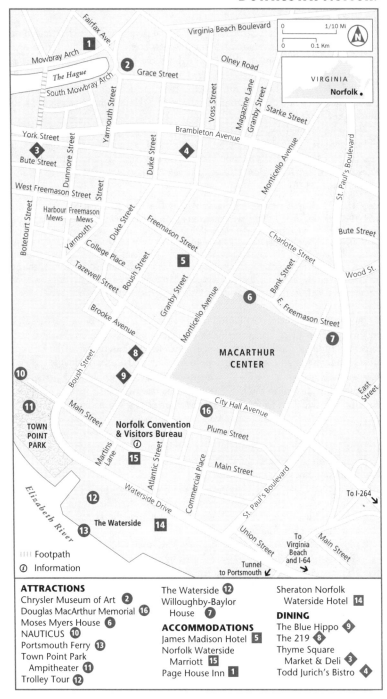

Downtown Norfolk

Virginia Beach Boulevard

Fairfax Ave.

1

Mowbray Arch

The Hague

South Mowbray Arch

2 Grace Street

Olney Road

Yarmouth Street

Voss Street

Magazine Lane

Granby Street

Starke Street

Brambleton Avenue

York Street

3

Bute Street

Dunmore Street

Duke Street

4

Monticello Avenue

St. Paul's Boulevard

West Freemason Street

Street

Botetourt Street

Harbour Mews

Freemason Mews

Duke Street

Freemason Street

Charlotte Street

Bute Street

Yarmouth

College Place

Tazewell Street

Boush Street

Granby Street

5

Monticello Avenue

Bank Street

Wood St.

Brooke Avenue

6

E. Freemason Street

7

Boush Street

8

9

MACARTHUR CENTER

East Street

10

11

TOWN POINT PARK

Main Street

City Hall Avenue

16

Norfolk Convention & Visitors Bureau
i

Plume Street

Martins Lane

15

Atlantic Street

Commercial Place

Main Street

St. Paul's Boulevard

To I-264

Elizabeth River

12

Waterside Drive

13 The Waterside **14**

Union Street

To Virginia Beach and I-64

Main Street

|||| Footpath

i Information

Tunnel to Portsmouth

1/10 Mi

0.1 Km

VIRGINIA

Norfolk •

ATTRACTIONS

Chrysler Museum of Art **2**

Douglas MacArthur Memorial **16**

Moses Myers House **6**

NAUTICUS **10**

Portsmouth Ferry **13**

Town Point Park Ampitheater **11**

Trolley Tour **12**

The Waterside **12**

Willoughby-Baylor House **7**

ACCOMMODATIONS

James Madison Hotel **5**

Norfolk Waterside Marriott **15**

Page House Inn **1**

Sheraton Norfolk Waterside Hotel **14**

DINING

The Blue Hippo **9**

The 219 **8**

Thyme Square Market & Deli **3**

Todd Jurich's Bistro **4**

it was built by Moses Myers and his wife, Eliza, who came to Norfolk in 1787. They were the first Jews to settle here, and special programs in observance of Jewish holidays are among the museum's annual events. Some 70% of the furniture and decorative arts collections displayed throughout the house are original to the first generation of the family, which lived here until 1930. Two Gilbert Stuart portraits of Mr. and Mrs. Myers hang in the drawing room, which contains some distinctive Empire pieces. The fireplace surround has unusual carvings depicting a sun god—with the features of George Washington.

Also administered by The Chrysler Museum, the **Willoughby-Baylor House,** a block away at 601 E. Freemason St., was built in 1794 and is furnished with Georgian and Federal pieces. One-hour tours covering both houses depart from the **Freemason Street Reception Center,** between the houses at 401 E. Freemason St. (☎ 757/441-1526).

NAUTICUS, The National Maritime Center. 1 Waterside Dr. (at Boush St.). ☎ **800/ 664-1080** or 757/664-1000. www.nauticus.org. Free admission to first deck and naval museum. Admission to upstairs exhibits and theaters $7.50 adults, $6.50 seniors, $5 children 4–17, free for children under 4. Naval Museum, free. Tugboat Museum, $2 adults, $1 children under 12. NAUTICUS, Memorial Day–Labor Day, daily 10am–5pm; rest of year, Tues–Sat 10am–5pm, Sun noon–5pm. Naval Museum, Mon 9am–4pm, Tues–Sun 10am–5pm (extended hours in summer). Tugboat Museum, Memorial Day–Labor Day, daily 7am–7pm; rest of year, Tues–Sun 10am–5pm (closed Jan–Mar). Entire complex closed Thanksgiving and Christmas.

By the time you get here, the 888-foot-long battleship USS *Wisconsin* will be berthed on the Elizabeth River (and presumably open for tours) alongside this large, battleship-gray building. Entered by its own gangplank, the building itself looks like an artist's rendering of a futuristic warship. Inside, kids and adults of all ages can entertain themselves with a plethora of hands-on interactive exhibits, theaters, and a museum, all dedicated to the U.S. Navy and the sea over which it sails. Visitors can stand on the actual bridge of the USS *Preble,* or pilot a submarine in search of the Loch Ness Monster in one of the world's first virtual-reality adventures. The Aegis Theater lets you participate in running a battle aboard a destroyer, while in another area you can learn navigation by piloting a ship into San Francisco Harbor. Meanwhile, the Living Sea theater shows films about sea life in the briny depths, simulating a swim among thousands of jellyfish.

On the second floor is the **Hampton Roads Naval Museum** (☎ 757/444-8921), in which the U.S. Navy tells the story of its presence here. It's worth walking in to see the exhibit describing the Civil War battle between the ironclads *Monitor* and *Merrimac* out on Hampton Roads.

Moored beside the building is the **Tugboat Museum** (☎ 757/627-4884), actually the *Huntington,* a tug built in 1933 and used by the navy to dock its ships for more than 50 years. Admission is $2 for adults, $1 for children under 12. It's open Memorial Day to Labor Day, daily from 7am to 7pm; the rest of the year, Tuesday through Sunday, from 10am to 5pm. Closed January to March.

✪ **Norfolk Botanical Garden.** 6700 Azalea Garden Rd. (off Norview Ave., near airport). ☎ **757/441-5385.** www.pilot.infi.net/~nbgs. Admission $4 adults, $3 seniors, $2 children 6–18, free for children under 6. Daily 8:30am–sunset. Garden Cafe, daily 10am–5pm. Take I-64 to Exit 279 (Norview/Airport), go east on Norview Ave., turn left on Azalea Garden Rd.

About 4 miles northeast of downtown, this quiet haven can be seen by trackless train, by canal boat, or on foot (more than 12 miles of floral pathways). From early April to mid-June, the grounds are brilliantly abloom with a massive display of azaleas. The

Statuary Vista is a beautiful setting for Moses Ezekiel's heroic-size statues (originally intended for the Corcoran Gallery in Washington) of great painters and sculptors—Rembrandt, Rubens, Dürer, and da Vinci, among others. Notable, too: the rose garden, with a terrace overlook; a classic Japanese hill-and-pond garden; a fragrance garden; and an Italian Renaissance garden with terraces, statuary, a fountain, and a reflecting pool. Behind the pool is the coronation court where April's Azalea Festival queen is crowned. Garden lovers can easily spend half a day here. You can have lunch or refreshment at the Garden House Cafe.

The Virginia Zoo. 3500 Granby St. (at 35th St.). ☎ **757/441-5227.** Admission $3.50 adults, $1 seniors, $1.75 children 2–11. Daily 10am–5pm. Closed New Year's Day, Thanksgiving, Christmas. From downtown, go north on Monticello Ave., which merges with Granby St., to the zoo on the right.

Virginia's official state zoo is noted for one of the finest tiger habitats in the country, part of an ambitious expansion plan that should make this one of the country's finest zoos (no more caged animals pacing back and forth). More than 350 other animals live here, including monkeys, baboons, elephants, rhinos, reptiles, and colorful birds.

A TROLLEY TOUR OF THE NAVAL BASE

The best way to see the U.S. Navy's giant facility is on the ✪ **Norfolk Naval Base Trolley Tour,** which includes admission to NAUTICUS (The National Maritime Center). Enhanced by informed commentary by naval personnel, the tour goes dockside for looks at aircraft carriers, destroyers, submarines, and other naval ships (there may be visits to selected ships on weekends from 1 to 4:30pm). It also passes Admiral's Row, a strip of Colonial Revival houses built at the turn of the century for the Jamestown Exposition and now inhabited by the Atlantic Fleet's top brass. You can board at NAUTICUS and at the base's visitor center, 9809 Hampton Blvd. (☎ **757/444-7955**), but you'll be assured of a seat if you board at the TRT kiosk in front of The Waterside. The tour costs $12 for adults, $9 for seniors and disabled riders, and $7.50 students 6 to 18, free for children under 6. For more information, check with **Tidewater Regional Transit** (☎ 757/222-6100) or its Waterside kiosk.

HARBOR CRUISES TO WHERE THE IRONCLADS FOUGHT

Three cruise boats docked at The Waterside offer cruises on the Elizabeth River, Hampton Roads, and the Chesapeake Bay. You will pass the naval base with nuclear subs and aircraft carriers and cross the site of the Civil War battle between the *Monitor* and the *Merrimac.*

The *Carrie B* (☎ 757/393-4735), a reproduction of a 19th-century Mississippi riverboat, offers daily cruises from April to October. A noon sailing takes 1½ hours and costs $9.95 for adults, $4.95 for children. A 2pm tour goes out for 2½ hours and costs $11.95 for adults, $5.95 for children. From June to Labor Day, there's also a 2½-hour sunset cruise leaving at 6pm. It costs $14 for adults, $7 for children.

Also departing from The Waterside, the enclosed, air-conditioned *Spirit of Norfolk* (☎ 757/627-7771) is like an oceangoing cruise ship, complete with dancing, good food, and entertainment. Offerings include lunch cruises ($24 to $27 per person), dinner cruises ($40 to $50), and moonlight party cruises with cocktails ($20) from midnight to 2am Friday and Saturday. Call for the schedule and to make reservations.

From April to October, there are 3-hour cruises on the *American Rover* (☎ 757/627-7245), a graceful schooner modeled after 19th-century Chesapeake Bay schooners. Prices for these sail-powered cruises along the Elizabeth River are $14 for adults, $7 for children.

Dismal Dirt & Nastiness

When the early English settlers fanned out from Jamestown, they found their way south blocked by a "vast body of dirt and nastiness." So wrote Col. William Byrd II, who in 1728 surveyed the Virginia–North Carolina border through this impenetrable region appropriately dubbed the **Great Dismal Swamp.**

George Washington came to the swamp in 1763 and organized a company to drain and log some 40,000 acres. A 5-mile ditch still bears his name, but Washington's investment went for naught. At the urging of then-governor Patrick Henry, slaves dug the 22-mile-long Dismal Swamp Canal from the Elizabeth River to North Carolina between 1793 and 1805. Still operating, it is America's oldest man-made waterway. A road constructed on the spoil is now U.S. 17 between Portsmouth and Elizabeth City, North Carolina.

Although much of the swamp was drained over the years, the **Great Dismal Swamp National Wildlife Refuge** still contains black bears, bobcats, white-tailed deer, otters, and a plethora of bird life. The last remnants of the swamp's great cypress forest stand along the haunting shores of Lake Drummond, center-piece of the refuge.

The refuge headquarters, off Va. 32 south of Suffolk, provides a boardwalk nature walk and hiking and biking trails to Lake Drummond. For information, contact the refuge at P.O. Box 349, Suffolk, VA 23434 (☎ 757/986-3705).

South of the North Carolina line on U.S. 17, the **Dismal Swamp Canal Welcome Center** (☎ 252/771-8333) is open from Memorial Day through October, daily from 9am to 5pm; the rest of the year, Tuesday through Saturday from 9am to 5pm. It has a car-top boat ramp where you can launch canoes and kayaks for trips to Lake Drummond via the Federal Feeder Ditch.

A FERRY RIDE TO OLDE TOWN PORTSMOUTH

When I first visited here in the early 1950s, ferries ran constantly across the Elizabeth River between Norfolk and Portsmouth. Today, the paddle-wheel **Elizabeth River Ferry** still makes that short but picturesque trip. Operated by Tidewater Regional Transit (☎ 757/226-6100), it departs the Waterside marina every 30 minutes Monday through Thursday from 7:15am to 9:45pm, Friday from 7am to 11:35pm, Saturday from 10am to 11:35pm, and Sunday from 10:15am to 9:45pm. Fare is 75¢ for adults, 50¢ for children, and 35¢ for seniors and disabled passengers.

Get off the ferry at the **Portside Visitor Center,** on Harbor Court (☎ 757/393-5111), and pick up a walking tour brochure and map. The center is open daily 9am to 5pm. Then stroll through Portsmouth's quaint **Olde Town** section, which traces its roots back to 1752. Like those in Charleston and Savannah, the homes and buildings here present a kaleidoscope of architectural styles: Colonial, Federal, Greek Revival, Georgian, and Victorian. Plaques mounted on imported English street lamps point out their architectural and historical significance.

If you're not up to walking or are short on time, you can take a **Portsmouth Discovery Trolley Tour,** which departs the visitor center daily at 10:45am, noon, 1:15pm, and 2:30pm from Memorial Day to Labor Day. Fare is $3.50 for adults, $1.75 for seniors and children under 12. Check at the visitor center, or call ☎ 757/226-6100 for more information.

At the **Lightship Museum,** in Riverfront Park at the foot of London Boulevard (☎ 757/393-8741), you can tour the *Portsmouth,* built in 1915 and anchored offshore until the 1980s to warn mariners of the dangerous shoals on the approach to Hampton Roads. Also in the park, the **Portsmouth Naval Shipyard Museum,** 2 High St. (☎ **757/393-8591**), houses many ship models and relics of Portsmouth's military past, including a cannon mount possibly from the Confederate ironclad *Merrimac,* which fought the Union's turret-topped *Monitor* on Hampton Roads during the Civil War. Admission to either is $1 per person. Both museums are open Tuesday to Saturday 10am to 5pm, Sunday 1 to 5pm.

You can keep the kids busy at a number of interactive educational exhibits in **Children's Museum of Virginia,** 221 High St. (☎ **757/393-8393**), but you must supervise them at all times. Admission is $5 per person. Open during summer from Monday to Saturday 10am to 5pm, Sunday 1 to 5pm. Closed Monday off-season.

Also here is the **Virginia Sports Hall of Fame,** 420 High St. (☎ **757/393-8031**), whose most famous inductees are golfers Sam Sneed and Lanny Wadkins, tennis pro Arthur Ashe, and basketball players Ralph Sampson and Nancy Lieberman Cline. Admission is free. Open Tuesday to Saturday 10am to 5pm, Sunday 1 to 5pm.

You can have lunch at the local branch of **The Jewish Mother,** 1 High St., at the river (☎ **757/398-3332**). See "Where to Dine" in section 2, below, for menu and prices.

For more information, contact the **Portsmouth Convention and Visitors Bureau,** 801 Crawford St., Portsmouth, VA 23704-3822 (☎ **800/PORTS-VA** or 757/393-8481; www.ci.portsmouth.va.us).

SHOPPING FOR ANTIQUES

Norfolk is one of the better places in Virginia to search for antiques, with at least 32 shops selling a wide range of furniture, decorative arts, glassware, jewelry, and many other items, from both home and overseas. The best place to look is in Ghent, where nine shops sit along the 4 blocks of West 21st Street between Granby Street and Colonial Avenue (four of them are at the corner of Llewellyn Avenue). Granby Street has another 13 shops of its own, including the **Ghent Market & Antique Center,** which occupies an entire city block between 14th and 15th streets and Monticello Avenue (☎ **757/625-2897**). The "market" part of this huge establishment is actually a farmer's market, where you can load up on farm-fresh produce.

The visitor centers have a complete list and description of the shops.

WHERE TO STAY

The hotels recommended below are within walking distance of the downtown attractions. A short drive east of downtown, the **Best Western Center Inn,** on Military Highway just north of I-264 (☎ **800/523-1234** or 757/461-6600), is a tasteful two-story light-gray-stucco complex set around a nicely landscaped courtyard and garden with park benches and old-fashioned street lamps. All rooms face the courtyard and Olympic-size pool.

DOWNTOWN

James Madison Hotel. 345 Granby St. (at W. Freemason St.), Norfolk, VA 23510. ☎ **888/408-6682** or 757/622-6682. Fax 757/623-5949. www.jamesmadisonhotel.com. 124 units. A/C TV TEL. $80–$110 double. Weekend and other packages available. AE, DC, DISC, MC, V. Free validated city garage parking.

Built in 1906 at the corner of Granby and Freemason streets as the Southland Hotel and later known as the Madison, this was the first hostelry in Norfolk to provide indoor plumbing for its guests. Although the Marriott and Sheraton have eclipsed it, the lobby reflects the hotel's status as Norfolk's grande dame landmark, with polished walnut columns, wing chairs, and a medallion-printed carpet. The rooms were recently renovated and decorated in colonial style with pale floral-print fabrics and mahogany furnishings. The least expensive rooms are small and cramped. Although long and narrow, the so-called king rooms are the largest here, with space for king-size beds, sofas, easy chair, coffee tables, desks, and wet bars. A few units have two double beds and two bathrooms. Most rooms have combination tub-shower bathrooms, but 30 have showers only.

Off the lobby, Basil's serves breakfast, lunch, and the city's best Italian-style seafood dinners daily. There is a nominal charge for use of a nearby health and racquetball club.

✪ **Norfolk Waterside Marriott.** 235 E. Main St. (between Atlantic St. and Martins Lane), Norfolk, VA 23510. ☎ **800/228-9290** or 757/627-4200. Fax 757/628-6452. 404 units. A/C TV TEL. $99–$179 double. Weekend packages available. AE, DC, DISC, MC, V. Self-parking $10; valet parking $12.

Norfolk's best hotel is an elegantly appointed 24-story high-rise conveniently connected to The Waterside via a covered skywalk. Its mahogany-paneled lobby is a masterpiece of 18th-century European style, with fine paintings, a crystal chandelier, potted palm trees, comfortable seating areas with gleaming lamps, and one-of-a-kind antiques. A magnificent staircase leads to the restaurants and lounges.

Rooms are sumptuously furnished with traditional dark-wood pieces. Be sure to ask for an upper floor room with a river view. Guests on the concierge levels enjoy a private lounge where complimentary continental breakfast and afternoon snacks are served.

Dining/Diversions: The second-level Dining Room is open for breakfast and dinner. Stormy's Sports Bar offers light fare and evening entertainment. The Piano Lounge adjoining the Dining Room has a cozy fireplace and serves cocktails from 4pm.

Amenities: Room service, same-day laundry/valet, baby-sitting, valet parking. Atrium-enclosed pool, health club with Universal equipment, saunas, whirlpools and sundeck overlooking waterfront, business services, gift shop.

Sheraton Norfolk Waterside Hotel. 777 Waterside Dr., Norfolk, VA 23510. ☎ **800/325-3535** or 757/622-6664. Fax 757/625-8271. 465 units. A/C TV TEL. $99–$185 double. Weekend and other packages available. AE, DC, DISC, MC, V. Self-parking $3 in adjacent Dominion Tower garage; valet parking $10.50.

Overlooking busy Norfolk Harbor, this former Omni hotel is next door to The Waterside. Its three-story atrium lobby is enhanced by stunning floral arrangements, and 30-foot windows overlook the river in the sunken Riverwalk restaurant and bar. The concierge level on the 10th floor offers such special amenities as complimentary continental breakfast, afternoon hors d'oeuvres, free daily newspaper, and nightly turndown with chocolates.

The Riverwalk offers American fare at all three meals, while the Lobby Bar has dancing on Friday and Saturday nights. Services include concierge, limited room service, and valet laundry. There's an outdoor pool, business center, gift and sundries shop, and nearby health club.

IN GHENT

✪ **Page House Inn.** 323 Fairfax Ave. (at Mowbray Arch), Norfolk, VA 23507. ☎ **757/625-5033.** Fax 757/623-9451. www.pagehouseinn.com. E-mail: innkeeper@ pagehouseinn.com. 7 units. A/C TEL. $120–$145 double; $150–$200 suite. Rates include full breakfast. MC, V.

Centrally located in the historic Ghent district and across the street from The Chrysler Museum, this splendid B&B was built in 1899 by Herman L. Page, a Welsh immigrant who made good in Norfolk. It's a grand three-story brick Colonial Revival mansion with a dormered roof and double columns punctuating the expansive verandah. New Yorkers Stephanie and Ezio DiBelardino masterfully restored its golden-oak paneling, sliding doors, and moldings on the first floor; the hand-carved fireplace in the living room; and the soaring staircase that ascends to the rooftop skylight. Guest quarters are beautifully furnished with four-poster beds and one-of-a-kind antiques. Five units have gas-log fireplaces. The most expensive also has a sunken whirlpool tub and a steam shower with his-and-her heads. Stephanie serves a gourmet European-style breakfast in the large dining room, set with Lenox china. Charlie, a friendly Boston terrier, keeps an eye on things, but don't bring your own pet.

Stephanie and Ezio also provide "boat-and-breakfast" aboard their 43-foot motor sailer *Bianca,* which can accommodate two couples who want to sail the Chesapeake. Rates are $200 for one couple, $275 for two, with a 2-night minimum stay required.

WHERE TO DINE
DOWNTOWN

In the MacArthur Center, on Monticello Avenue at Market Street, are branches of the elegant but informal **Kincaid's Fish, Chop & Steak House** (☎ 757/622-8000), offering exactly what its name says (downtown professionals turn the bar into a favorite Friday evening "meet" market); and the entertaining **Rainforest Cafe** (☎ 757/627-8440), always a hit with children with its fake birds, animals, rain, and fog. There's a Starbucks coffee outlet on the first level and a very good and inexpensive **food court** up on the third.

✪ **The Blue Hippo.** 147 Granby St. (between City Hall Ave. and Plume St.). ☎ **757/533-9664.** Reservations recommended. Main courses $16.50–$25. AE, MC, V. Mon–Thurs 11:30am–2:30pm and 5:30–10pm, Fri 11:30am–2:30pm and 5:30–11pm, Sat 5–9pm. ECLECTIC.

Owners Lee Bozeman and Scott Shearer named this urbane bistro, a block from both the MacArthur Center and The Waterside, after a 12th dynasty Egyptian sculpture, and adopted the motto "Life is too short to eat boring food." Indeed, executive chef Calvert Johnson's kitchen produces food that is anything but boring, creatively blending local produce with flavors from Thailand, Jamaica, and other spice-oriented locales. The menu changes frequently and always has a couple of surprises. For example, the crab cakes here are coated with a Parmesan cheese and black-bean crust, then served over a wild rice salad or sometimes with a caviar remoulade. You get the idea. The dining room is a bit cramped but it's nicely decorated with colorful works by local artists.

The 219. 219 Granby St. (at Brooke Ave.). ☎ **757/627-2896.** Reservations recommended. Pizzas $9–$10; main courses $11–$16. AE, DC, DISC, MC, V. Mon–Thurs 11:30am–3pm and 5–10pm, Fri 11:30am–3pm and 5–11pm, Sat 5–11pm, Sun 5–9pm. PIZZAS/ECLECTIC.

A block north of The Blue Hippo, this casual storefront cafe also offers an eclectic mix of cuisines but with more noise—and less expensive prices. A hit here is the pecan-crusted Chesapeake Bay rockfish (sea bass) sautéed in butter, finished with a tomato concassé, and accompanied by garlic mashed potatoes. Asian flavors crop up in fried catfish subjected to a sauce of soy, ginger, and chives. You can opt for one-person pizzas with unusual toppings like prosciutto ham, spinach, and portobello mushrooms.

IN FREEMASON

Thyme Square Market & Deli. 509 Botetourt St. (at York St. and Brambleton Ave.). ☎ **757/623-5082.** Reservations not accepted. Main courses $8–$17. DISC, MC, V. Mon–Fri 11:30am–3pm and 5–9pm. DELI/INTERNATIONAL.

Plants and wrought-iron patio chairs lend a garden ambience to this corner storefront, whose chiller cases offer a variety of gourmet deli items for stacked-high sandwiches. They go like hotcakes at lunch, but come evening, everyone's attention turns to chef Ethel Pangborn's cuisine, which ranges from her famous meat loaf to her impressive crab cakes—jumbo hunks of sweet backfin meat delicately seasoned with just a hint of traditional Old Bay spice. She serves them with real mashed potatoes and slices of huge, home-grown tomatoes topped with silver queen corn pared off the ear and sided by a roasted remoulade dressing.

✪ **Todd Jurich's Bistro.** 210 W. York St. (between Boush and Duke sts.). ☎ **757/ 622-3210.** Reservations recommended. Lunch $6–$9.50; main courses $15–$22. MC, V. Mon–Thurs 11:30am–2:30pm and 5:30–10pm; Fri 11:30am–2:30pm and 5:30–11pm; Sat 5:30–11pm. CREATIVE AMERICAN.

Actor Donald Sutherland dined regularly at this elegant, intimate bistro while filming a movie here, and you'll see why when you partake of chef Todd Jurich's creative twists on Southern traditions, such as his all-lump-meat crab cakes on brioche with lemon mayonnaise—a far cry, indeed, from the fried cakes dispensed at many Chesapeake Bay seafood shacks. Todd uses only fresh produce, drawn whenever possible from local farms that practice "ecologically sound agriculture." For example, the roasted chicken he serves on a seasonal risotto with crispy mustard greens was most likely allowed to range free rather than confined to a cage. For lunch, you can choose from sandwiches such as crab cakes or Todd's own version of Smithfield barbecue.

In Ghent

Doumar's. 19th to 20th sts. and Monticello Ave. ☎ **757/627-4163.** Sandwiches $1–$2.50. No credit cards. Mon–Thurs 8am–11pm; Fri–Sat 8am–12:30am. AMERICAN.

Doumar's is no modern re-creation of a 1950s drive-in with carhops, curb service, and a 1950s menu; in business since the 1930s, it's the real thing, which makes it a very hip historical attraction. The specialties here are sweet, waffle-like ice-cream cones, some of them from the original cone-making machine invented by Abe Doumar at the St. Louis Exposition in 1904. Abe's great-nephew, present owner Al Doumar, keeps his uncle's invention oiled and working. Barbecue sandwiches, burgers and hot dogs, sundaes, and milk shakes round out the menu.

✪ **Wild Monkey.** 1603 Colley Ave. (between Spotswood and Brandon aves.). ☎ **757/ 627-6462.** Reservations not accepted. Lunch $5–$7.50; main courses $8–$14. AE, MC, V. Mon–Fri 11:30am–2:30pm and 5:30–10pm; Sat 5:30–10pm, Sun 11am–3pm. AMERICAN/CAJUN.

I have a conflict of interest in recommending the Wild Monkey since my cousin Nancy Cobb owns a piece of the action (she's the short blonde cooking back in the open kitchen). Nevertheless, I really like this exciting, totally casual storefront restaurant in the heart of the Ghent business district. You likely will have to wait for a table, so popular is the Wild Monkey with Norfolk's young set. A huge blackboard on one side of the dining room advertises the offerings, while another on the opposite wall explains a limited but fine selection of California wines and displays the actual bottles. You can dine on old standbys such as "Ten Dollar" meat loaf or liver and onions, or treat your taste buds to the spicy likes of mahimahi with a mango relish or Cajun pasta with andouille sausage. If it's up on the board, you'll thoroughly enjoy a piping-hot bowl of spicy yet sweet crawfish étouffée over white and wild rice with corn-on-the-cob and slices of juicy fresh tomato on the side.

NORFOLK AFTER DARK

For a rundown on evening events, pick up a free copy of *Port Folio,* an entertainment weekly available at the visitor information offices, most hotel lobbies, and The Waterside. In addition to entertainment at hotel lounges and outdoors in Town Park on the Elizabeth River, you may be here during performances by several outstanding companies. The **Virginia Stage Company** puts on five productions annually, October through April, at the restored Wells Theatre, on Monticello Avenue opposite the MacArthur Center (☎ 757/627-1234). The Harrison Opera House, at Virginia Beach Boulevard and Llewellyn Avenue (☎ 757/627-9545), is home to the **Virginia Opera.**

SCOPE, Brambleton Avenue and St. Paul's Boulevard (☎ 757/441-2161), seats 12,000 for major events—including the circus, ice shows, and concerts. Part of the SCOPE complex, **Chrysler Hall,** Charlotte Street and St. Paul's Boulevard (☎ 757/441-2161), is home to the **Virginia Symphony** and the annual Pops series.

2 Virginia Beach

20 miles E of Norfolk; 110 miles E of Richmond; 207 miles S of Washington, D.C.

Given its more than 20 miles of unbroken sand and surf, it's not surprising that Virginia Beach comes alive during the summer months, when vacationers flock here. Although big hotels line the beachfront and block off ocean views from everywhere except their own rooms, the Boardwalk boasts immaculate landscaping, wood benches, small parks, a bike-skating path, public rest rooms, and attractive white colonial-style street lamps.

Adding to Virginia Beach's allure as a family vacation destination is the Virginia Marine Science Museum, the most popular museum in the state. History lovers will find several sites of interest, including the First Landing Cross at the spot where the Jamestown settlers first came ashore. Nature lovers can drive a few miles south to the Back Bay National Wildlife Refuge, which attracts migrating birds and protects several miles of beach and marshlands from encroaching development.

This is a major regional beach vacation destination from Memorial Day to Labor Day, and especially on holiday weekends, so expect lots of company.

ESSENTIALS

VISITOR INFORMATION

For information on planning your trip, or assistance while you're here, contact the **Visitor Information Center,** 2100 Parks Ave., Virginia Beach, VA 23451 (☎ 800/446-8038 for information or 800/VA-BEACH for hotel reservations; www.vbfun.com). A large board has phones connected to the reservations desks of major hotels and resorts. Particularly helpful is a free **map** showing public rest rooms and municipal parking lots in the resort area. The center's annual "Vacation Guide" is a no-nonsense listing of every hotel, restaurant, and activity here. The center is at the eastern end of the Va. 44 expressway. It's open daily from 9am to 5pm, to 8pm from mid-June to Labor Day.

A small satellite office is in First Landing State Park's **Chesapeake Bay Center,** 2500 Shore Dr. (U.S. 60) (☎ 757/412-2316). It's open April to November, daily 9am to 5pm. There are also **information kiosks** at the beach on Atlantic Avenue at 17th, 24th, and 30th streets from late spring through October. (*Note:* These are the only official visitor information booths at the beach; most others with "tourist information" signs are come-ons for time-share sales operations.) Racks at the visitor information center and elsewhere contain several slick give-away tourist publications that are packed with information and money-saving coupons.

GETTING THERE

BY CAR   Follow I-64 to Va. 44 east (the "44 Expressway" in local parlance), an Interstate-grade highway that runs straight to the heart of the oceanfront resort area. Also from the west, U.S. 60 becomes the scenic Shore Drive, which dead-ends at Atlantic Avenue on the northern end of the ocean beach; a right turn takes you along this main north-south drag through the resort area. From the north or south, U.S. 13 and 17 will take you to I-64.

BY PLANE   Virginia Beach is served by **Norfolk International Airport,** about 30 minutes (15 miles) west of the oceanfront resort area (see "Essentials" under "Norfolk," above).

CITY LAYOUT

At the southeastern corner of the state, Virginia Beach is bordered by the Chesapeake Bay and the Atlantic Ocean. They meet at Cape Henry, home to **Cape Henry Lighthouse, Fort Story,** and **First Landing State Park.** There's no real downtown in Virginia Beach; instead, most of the action is at the oceanfront **resort area,** where you'll find a solid line of big hotels, restaurants, beachwear and souvenir shops, video-game arcades, and the **Boardwalk** and its adjacent bike-skating path, which run along the beach. The resort area extends from 1st Street at Rudee Inlet north to 42nd Street (the boardwalk ends at 39th Street). Behind the beachfront hotels, **Atlantic Avenue** runs north-south between Rudee Inlet and Cape Henry. It's paralleled a block inland between Rudee Inlet and 43rd Street by the wider **Pacific Avenue,** a speedier way through the resort area. At Rudee Inlet, Pacific Avenue gives way to **General Booth Boulevard,** which runs southwest past the Virginia Marine Science Museum.

A less congested area with hotels and restaurants is at **Lynnhaven Inlet,** along Shore Drive (U.S. 60) on the Chesapeake Bay 6 miles west of the oceanfront.

Some 12 miles south of the resort area, **Sandbridge** is an oceanfront enclave of cottages and a relatively undeveloped public beach. From Sandbridge south to the North Carolina line, the **Back Bay National Wildlife Refuge** and **False Cape State Park** offer undisturbed beach and marshland for hikers, bikers, bird watchers, and sun worshippers.

GETTING AROUND

There are a few pay lots along Pacific Avenue (the visitor information center has free maps that show them), but **parking spaces** near the beach can be as scarce as hen's teeth between mid-June and Labor Day, especially on weekends. Your best bet then is to stay at the shore and get around on the **Beach Trolleys,** which run from May through September (no service off-season). The Atlantic Avenue Trolley runs daily, every 10 to 15 minutes from noon to midnight along the entire length of Atlantic Avenue.

The North Seashore Trolley runs Monday through Friday, every 30 minutes from 6:30am to 6:30pm along Pacific Avenue between 19th and 68th streets.

The Museum Express Trolley runs daily, every 15 to 30 minutes from 8am to 10pm, to midnight on weekends, between Atlantic Avenue at 40th Street and the Virginia Science Museum and Ocean Breeze Amusement Park on General Booth Boulevard.

Virginia Beach

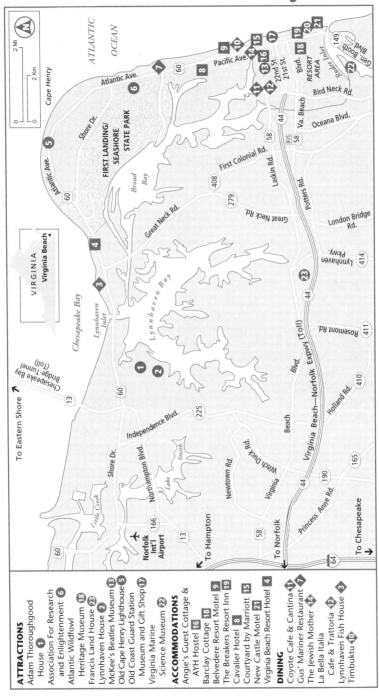

Fares on any of these trolleys are 50¢ per ride for adults and children, 25¢ for seniors and disabled persons. Or you can buy a Trolley Pass, which costs $3.50 for adults and children, $1.75 for seniors and disabled persons; it's good for 3 days of unlimited rides.

In addition, the Lynnhaven Mall Trolley also runs during summer, from Atlantic Avenue at 25th Street to Lynnhaven Mall, the city's main shopping center on Lynnhaven Parkway south of Va. 44. The fare is $1.50 per person.

The trolleys are operated by **Tidewater Regional Transit** (☎ 757/222-6100), which also provides public bus service in the region. TRT has a **ticket kiosk** on the oceanfront at Atlantic Avenue and 24th Street, where you can also buy its Discover Tidewater Passports and Adventure Passes (see "Getting Around" under "Norfolk," above).

OUTDOOR PURSUITS

Virginia Beach offers a wonderful variety of water sports, starting, of course, with its fine-sand beach. But note that between Memorial Day and Labor Day, no ball playing, fishing, and other sports are allowed on the beach between 2nd Street and 42nd Street from 10am to 5pm.

Boating and fishing are centered at marinas at Rudee Inlet, which empties into the ocean, and at Lynnhaven Inlet, where the Lynnhaven River meets the Chesapeake Bay.

BIKING, JOGGING & SKATING   You can walk, jog, or run on the Boardwalk, or bike and skate on its adjoining bike path. There are biking and hiking trails in **First Landing State Park** (which rents bikes) and in **Back Bay National Wildlife Refuge** (see "Parks & Wildlife Refuges," below). Bikes and in-line skates are available during summer from **Cherie's Bicycle Rentals** (☎ 757/437-8888), which has stands on the oceanfront at 8th, 22nd, 24th, and 37th streets. Cherie's also has clinics if you want to learn how to in-line skate.

FISHING   Deep-sea fishing aboard a party boat can be an exciting day's entertainment for novices and dedicated fishermen alike. Both party and private charter boats are based at the **Virginia Beach Fishing Center,** 200 Winston-Salem Ave. (☎ 757/422-5700), at the Rudee Inlet bridge. At Lynnhaven Inlet, party boats leave from the **D and M Marina,** 3311 Shore Dr. (☎ 757/481-7211).

You can also drop a line from several piers. The **Virginia Beach Fishing Pier,** between 14th and 15th streets, oceanfront (☎ 757/428-2333), open April through October, has bait for sale and rods for rent. On the Chesapeake Bay, **Lynnhaven Inlet Fishing Pier,** Starfish Road off Shore Drive (☎ 757/481-7071), open 24 hours a day in summer, rents rods and reels and sells crab cages.

GOLF   Next to Williamsburg, Virginia Beach offers more good golfing than any other Virginia destination. Sand, water, and wind make up for the area's flat terrain to provide plenty of challenges at the **Tournament Players Club (TPC) of Virginia Beach** (☎ 877/484-3872 or 757/563-9440), designed by Pete Dye and Curtis Strange for the Professional Golfer's Association (PGA), which owns and operates it. The course opened in 1999.

Elevated tees and strategically placed water and bunkers pose problems at **Heron Ridge Golf Club** (☎ 757/426-3800), another new course. Sharp fairway angles at the Rees Jones–designed **Hell's Point Golf Course** (☎ 757/721-3400) have been described as "devilish." Another Rees Jones project, **Honey Bee Golf Course** (☎ 757/471-2768) is shorter (par-70) but presents challenges for beginners and experts alike. You can also play the **Red Wing Lake Municipal Golf Course** (☎ 757/437-4845). Call the courses for greens fees, tee times, and directions.

KAYAKING   Tidewater Adventures (☎ **888/669-8368** or 757/480-1999; www.tidewateradventures.com) rents kayaks from May to September in front of the Cavalier Hotel, on the oceanfront at 42nd Street. Rentals range from $10 per hour to $80 for a full day. They also lead dolphin-watching trips and guided tours of Back Bay National Wildlife Refuge, into the Dismal Swamp (see the "Dismal Dirt & Nastiness" box, earlier in this chapter) and to other nearby locations. Tour prices range from $35 to $70. **Wild River Outfitters** (☎ **877/431-8566** or 757/431-8566; www.wildriveroutfitters.com) also has backcountry tours.

SCUBA DIVING   The Atlantic Ocean off Virginia Beach is colder and less clear than it is below Cape Hatteras, North Carolina, but that's not to say you can't dive here. For information about dive trips, contact **Atlantic Dive Charters Ltd.,** 1324 Teresa Dr., Chesapeake, VA 23322 (☎ **757/482-9777**); or **Lynnhaven Dive Center,** 1413 Great Neck Rd., Virginia Beach, VA 23454 (☎ **757/481-7949**).

SWIMMING   During the summer season, lifeguards are on duty along the resort strip from 2nd to 42nd streets; they also handle raft, umbrella, and beach-chair rentals.

You can get away from the summer crowds by driving 12 miles south of Rudee Inlet to **Little Island City Park,** in the residential beach area of Sandbridge. To really escape the crowds, take the tram from there to **False Cape State Park** (see "Parks & Wildlife Refuges," below).

TENNIS   The city has some 200 public tennis courts, most of which are lighted and free. If you call the city's **Parks Department** (☎ **757/437-4804**), they'll be happy to steer you to the nearest one. The major facility is **Owl Creek Municipal Center,** 928 South Birdneck Rd. (☎ **757/422-4716**), which has a pro shop, children's play area, and 12 hard-surface and two tournament courts.

WAVE RUNNING & PARASAILING   You can rent exciting wave runners from several operators along Winston-Salem Avenue, including **Rudee Inlet Jet Ski Rentals,** which has locations at the Virginia Beach Fishing Center (☎ **757/428-4614**), 31st Street at the oceanfront (☎ **757/491-1117**), and 1284 Laskin Rd. (☎ **757/428-6156**). At Lynnhaven Inlet, **Wave Runners Water Sports Center** (☎ **757/481-4747**) rents jet skis and jet boats and also offers parasailing over the Chesapeake.

PARKS & WILDLIFE REFUGES
You don't have to go far from the busy resort area to find open spaces ideal for hiking, biking, camping, and bird watching.

✪ **FIRST LANDING STATE PARK**   Most convenient to the resort area, these 2,270 preserved acres run between Back Bay and the Chesapeake Bay to within 2 blocks of the ocean. Rabbits, squirrels, and raccoon are among the many species inhabiting this urban park, which boasts 28 miles of hiking trails. The main entrance is on Shore Drive (U.S. 60), where the visitor center is open daily 9am to 6pm from April to Labor Day, daily 9am to 5pm in September, and daily 9am to 4pm the rest of the year. The ground and trails are open daily from 8am to sunset. The 64th Street entry, off Pacific Avenue, leads to a quiet-water beach on Broad Bay. Admission to the park is $2 per person on weekdays, $3 on weekends; it's free at all times for hikers and bikers. Bikes are prohibited except on the paved, 6-mile Cape Henry Trail, which runs between the 64th Street entrance and the visitor center.

Twenty two-bedroom cabins can be rented for $94 to $105 a day, $572 a week during summer, or $56 to $63 a night, $343 a week off-season, with a 2-night minimum stay required (Virginia residents get a discount). Across Shore Drive, a bayside campground has 200 sites for tents and RVs (no hookups) for $20 a night in summer, $14 off-season. For reservations call ☎ **800/933-PARK.** The campground is in a wooded area beside a fine bay beach, which is reserved for campers on summer weekends. The camp store (☎ **757/412-2302**) rents bicycles ($15 a day) and beach equipment and supplies.

On the north side of Shore Drive by the bay, the **Chesapeake Bay Center** (☎ **727/412-2316**) has a small exhibit about the Jamestown settlers' landing here in 1607. It also shows a short video and has a small exhibit about the local ecology, both put together by the Virginia Marine Science Museum, but skip it if you are going to the main museum (see "The Top Attractions," below). There's a visitor information desk here, and a beachside amphitheater hosts musical concerts during the summer (call for a schedule). The center is open daily 9am to 5pm from April through November.

For more information, contact the park at 2500 Shore Dr., Virginia Beach, VA 23451 (☎ **757/412-2320;** www.state.va.us/~dcr/).

BACK BAY & FALSE CAPE   Especially inviting for bird watchers is ✪ **Back Bay National Wildlife Refuge,** in the southeastern corner of Virginia near the North Carolina line. Its 7,732 acres of beaches, dunes, marshes, and backwaters are on the main Atlantic Flyway for migratory birds. No swimming or sunbathing is allowed on the pristine beach here, but you can collect shells, surf-cast for fish, and bird watch. There are also nature trails and a canoe launching spot with marked trails through the marshes. Daily admission is $4 per vehicle, $2 per pedestrian or biker. The visitor contact station (☎ **757/721-2412**) is open Monday through Friday from 8am to 4pm, weekends from 9am to 4pm. It offers nature programs by reservation only. From Rudee Inlet, go south on General Booth Boulevard and follow the signs 12 miles to Sandbridge and the refuge. For more information, contact the Refuge Manager, 4005 Sandpiper Rd., Virginia Beach, VA 23456 (☎ **757/721-2412**).

Swimming and sunbathing are permitted on the beach in ✪ **False Cape State Park,** 4 miles south of the Back Bay visitor contact station via hiking and biking trail. Here you'll find an interpretive trail as well as more than 3 miles of hiking trails. Primitive camping is by permit only, which you can get by calling ☎ **800/933-PARK.** There are no other visitor facilities here, however, so bring your own drinking water. The park is open daily from sunrise to sunset.

You can't park in the national wildlife refuge lot while visiting False Cape, so leave your vehicle at Little Island City Park in Sandbridge. From there, you can either hike or bike the 6 miles to False Cape, or take an **electric tram** that runs from April through October, departing daily at 9am and returning at 12:45pm (giving you 2 hours at False Cape). The tram is operated by volunteers, so call ☎ **757/498-2473** to make sure it's running. Fares are $6 for adults, $4 for seniors and children under 12, free for kids under 6 accompanied by adults.

Sandbridge Outfitters, on the beach road north of the wildlife refuge (☎ **757/721-6461**), offers rental equipment and nature tours of the area. You can rent bicycles and sea kayaks from **Ocean Rentals,** on Sandbridge Road 2 miles inland from the beach (☎ **757/721-6210**).

THE TOP ATTRACTIONS
Association for Research and Enlightenment (A.R.E.). 215 67th St. (at Atlantic Ave.). ☎ **757/428-3588.** Free admission. Mon–Sat 9am–8pm; Sun 11am–8pm. 1-hour guided tours depart at 2pm.

The international headquarters carrying on the work of the late psychic Edgar Cayce offers a host of free activities daily. Cayce's psychic talent first manifested itself when, as a young man, he found he could enter into an altered state of consciousness and answer questions on any topic. His answers, or "discourses" (now called "readings"), number some 14,305. Guided tours begin daily at 2pm and are followed at 3pm by a 30-minute movie about Cayce's life and a lecture on such topics as health, dreams, prophecies, meditation, and reincarnation. The A.R.E. Bookstore on the first floor has an excellent selection of books and videos about holistic health, parapsychology, life after death, dreams, and even cooking. The Meditation Room on the third floor offers a spectacular view of the ocean and is painted with special colors chosen because Cayce readings suggest they can help you attain higher consciousness. Outside the center is the Meditation Garden. Inside, the health services department offers steam baths, facials, and massages to the public.

Atlantic Wildfowl Heritage Museum. 1113 Atlantic Ave. (at 12th St.). ☎ **757/437-8432.** www.awhm.org. Free admission (donations encouraged). Mon–Sat 10am–5pm, Sun noon–5pm (closed Mon Nov–May).

This small but excellent museum displays a collection of intricately carved decoys—some of them a century old—and decorative wildlife, plus paintings of ducks, geese, and other wildfowl. It occupies the lovely white-brick-and-clapboard DeWitt beach cottage built in 1895 by Virginia Beach's first mayor. The cottage alone is worth a stop as you stroll the Boardwalk. It's operated by the Back Bay Wildfowl Guild, which applies the donations and profits from the gift shop (which carries excellent decoys) to its conservation efforts.

McKee's Beatles Museum. 205 25th St. (between Atlantic and Pacific aves.). ☎ **757/491-0491.** www.beatlemuseum.com. Admission $7, free for children under 12. Memorial Day–Labor Day, daily 11am–11pm. Off-season, daily 11am–7pm.

If you are a Beatles fan, you'll get a kick out of this little museum. You can have your picture taken with the star attractions: one of George's guitars, John's 1964 Volkswagen camper van (it sat in a field for 18 years and still looks like it), a set of Ringo's drumsticks, and a 1965 tour jacket. The gift shop sells Beatles tapes, CDs, photos, and other souvenirs.

Old Cape Henry Lighthouse. 583 Atlantic Ave. (in Fort Story). ☎ **757/422-9421.** Admission $2 adults, $1 seniors and students. Mid-Mar to Oct, daily 10am–5pm; Nov to mid-Mar, daily 10am–4pm. Closed Dec 5–Jan 4.

This picturesque brick structure was the first lighthouse authorized by the new U.S. Congress. It was built in 1791–92 and marked the southern entrance to Chesapeake Bay until 1881, when a new lighthouse nearby took over. If you're in shape, you can climb the 189 steps to the top for a spectacular view over Cape Henry, the bay, and the ocean.

Nearby, the Jamestown colonists' **First Landing Site** is marked by a cross and plaque where they "set up a Crosse at Chesapeake Bay and named that place Cape Henry" for Henry, Prince of Wales. Also here are a monumental relief map showing the French and British naval engagement off Cape Henry during the Revolutionary War and a statue of the French commander. Now known as the **Battle of the Capes,** this decisive battle effectively trapped Cornwallis at Yorktown and helped end British dominion in America.

This is all part of the U.S. Army's Fort Story, whose unguarded gates are open to the public.

Old Coast Guard Station Museum and Gift Shop. 24th St. and Atlantic Ave. ☎ **757/422-1587.** Admission $3 adults, $2.50 seniors, $1 children 6–18, free for children under 6.

In the heart of the oceanfront resort area, this small museum is housed in the white-clapboard building constructed in 1903 as a life-saving station. Its exhibits recall rescue missions and shipwrecks along the coast. An excellent gift shop carries clocks, drawings, books, and other things nautical.

✪ **Virginia Marine Science Museum.** 717 General Booth Blvd. (southwest of Rudee Inlet). ☎ **757/425-FISH.** Admission $8.95 adults, $7.95 seniors, $5.95 children 4–11, free for children under 4. IMAX tickets $6.95 adults, $5.95 children 4–11, free for children under 4. Combination museum-IMAX tickets $11.95 adults, $10.95 seniors, $9.95 children 4–11, free for children under 4. Daily 9am–5pm (with extended summer hours). Closed Thanksgiving and Christmas.

A wonderful place to take the kids, especially on a rainy beach day, this entertaining and educational facility focuses on Virginia's marine environment. It's fittingly located on 45 acres beside Owl Creek salt marsh, a wildlife habitat in its own right. You can easily spend half a day here, a full day to see—and learn—it all. Plan to spend at least half of your time in the main building, where touch tanks will fascinate both you and the kids (bet you don't know a horseshoe crab's mouth feels like a toothbrush). In one tank, rays willingly swim over to have their leathery hides petted. Kids also will love playing with the switches and dials in a dark room designed like a submarine, complete with sonar "pings." The sub looks out into one of several room-size aquariums holding a myriad of sea turtles, sharks, rays, and other species of sea life usually found in Virginia waters.

As you leave the main building, take a look at the salt marsh room, which will prepare you for a one-third-mile nature hike along the creek. There's an observation tower out here, from which you might see some of the wild animals living on an island across the creek. The boardwalk nature trail leads to the smaller Owl Creek Marsh Pavilion, were river otters play in an outdoor tank and more than 50 species of birds fly about an aviary (the really big, noisy birds passing overhead are fighters taking off and landing at nearby Oceana Naval Air Station). It also houses the fascinating "Macro Marsh" display in which everything is enlarged 10 times normal size to give you a crab's eye view of the world.

The Museum Trolley stops at both buildings, so you can get on at the pavilion; otherwise, you'll have to walk back to your car outside the main building.

The museum offers offshore **dolphin-watching cruises** (daily June to October), **whale-watching cruises** (Monday in January and February), and **sea life collecting trips** (Wednesday from June to August). They usually cost $12 for adults, $10 for children under 12. The cruises leave from Rudee Inlet, and reservations are required (☎ 757/437-**BOAT**).

HISTORIC HOMES

While the beachfront resort area is a modern development, settlers carved out inland homesteads and plantations starting in the 17th century. Dating to 1680 and 1725, respectively, the Adam Thoroughgood and Lynnhaven houses are interesting because they were both built in the fashion of medieval English farm cottages of Elizabethan times, 150 years before the Georgian architecture so prevalent elsewhere in colonial Virginia. Allow half a day to see them all, including driving times in between.

Adam Thoroughgood House. 1636 Parish Rd. (at Thoroughgood and Parrish drives). ☎ **757/460-0007.** $3.50 adults, $3 seniors, $2.50 children 13–18, $2 children 6–12, free for children under 6. Tues–Sat 10am–4:30pm, Sun 1–4:30pm. Mandatory 30-minute tours depart on the hour and half hour. From oceanfront, take Va. 44 west to Exit 3, go north on Independence Blvd. (Va. 225), turn right on Pleasure House Rd. and right on Thoroughgood Dr., follow the very small signs to house at Parish Rd.

One of the oldest homes in Virginia, this picturesque medieval English–style cottage sits on 4½ acres of lawn and garden overlooking the Lynnhaven River. It was constructed around 1680 by one of Adam Thoroughgood's grandsons (architectural historians believe its namesake never occupied the house). The interior has exposed wood beams and whitewashed walls, and although the furnishings did not belong to the Thoroughgoods, they are original to the period and reflect the family's English ancestry.

Francis Land House. 3131 Virginia Beach Blvd. (just west of Kings Grant Rd.). ☎ **757/ 431-4000.** Admission $3.50 adults, $3 seniors, $2 children 6–12, free for children under 6. Tues–Sat 9am–5pm, Sun noon–4:30pm. Mandatory 30-minute house tours depart on demand.

Built as a plantation manor in the mid–18th century (but now beside one of the region's busiest highways), this Georgian-style brick house is a restoration work in progress. Only the first floor rooms are open, and they are minimally furnished with a few period pieces. Meantime, the highlight here are 7 acres of herb, vegetable, and pleasure gardens and a one-eighth-mile wetlands nature trail.

Lynnhaven House. 4405 Wishart Rd. (off Independence Blvd.). ☎ **757/460-1688.** Admission $3.50 adults, $1.50 students 12–17, $1 children 5–11, free for children under 5. June–Sept, Tues–Sun noon–4pm; May–Oct, Sat–Sun noon–4pm. Mandatory 30-minute tours depart on demand. From the beach, take Va. 44 west to Exit 3, then head north on Independence Blvd. (Va. 225) and right on Wishart Rd.

Built in 1725 by a Huguenot family, this medieval cottage was occupied by tenant farmers for 271 years and still doesn't have running water or electricity. When the Association for the Preservation of Virginia Antiquities took the house over in 1971, it stripped away plaster and discovered the Champford ceiling beams to be in original condition (note the chalk marks carpenters made 1725). Tours led by costumed docents explain the house and interpret colonial lifestyles. Us moderns won't find Lynnhaven oysters as gigantic as the shells excavated from the trash pit and displayed in the kitchen.

WHERE TO STAY

The hotels and B&Bs listed below are just the tip of the iceberg in Virginia Beach, which has more than 11,000 hotel rooms. Even with that many places to stay, you should reserve as far in advance as possible for the busy summer season, from mid-June to Labor Day weekend. Room rates rise steeply then, so both summer and off-season rates are listed below.

The visitor information center maintains a **reservations service** (☎ **800/ VA-BEACH**) that will help you find accommodations in any price range. The center's annual "Vacation Guide" lists all the local hotels and their current rates. It also distributes an annual accommodations directory published by the **Virginia Beach Hotel/Motel Association,** 968 S. Oriole Dr., Virginia Beach, VA 23451.

All but a few of the major chains are represented here. For example, there are three high-rise Holiday Inns on the oceanfront, including the **Holiday Inn Sunspree Resort on the Ocean,** Atlantic Avenue at 39th Street (☎ **800/HOLIDAY** or 757/ 428-1711), which is away from the maddening crowds at the north end of the boardwalk. Nearby is the **Sheraton Oceanfront Hotel,** at 36th Street (☎ **800/325-3535** or 757/425-9000), which offers whirlpool tubs in some rooms. Even more removed from the busy resort scene is the **Ramada Plaza Resort,** sitting by itself beside the beach at Atlantic Avenue and 57th Street (☎ **800/365-3032** or 757/428-7025).

HOTELS

✪ **Belvedere Resort Motel.** Oceanfront at 36th St. (P.O. Box 451), Virginia Beach, VA 23458. ☎ **800/425-0612** or 757/425-0612. Fax 757/425-1397. 50 units. A/C TV TEL. Summer $86–$105 double; off-season $48–$95 double. AE, MC, V. Closed mid-Oct to Mar.

One of the least expensive and cleanest of the smaller, family-operated oceanfront hotels, this five-story building justifiably attracts lots of repeat guests, so book early. The motel-style rooms have screen doors that swing open to balconies facing the ocean. The combo tub-shower bathrooms are small, but compensate with separate sinks and vanities. A few rooms have king-size beds (most have two doubles). The 10 units at the ends of the building are somewhat larger and have cooking facilities. There's a small swimming pool, sundeck, and the Belvedere Coffee Shop (see "Where to Dine," below). Guests also get free use of bicycles.

✪ **The Breakers Resort Inn.** 1503 Atlantic Ave. (oceanfront at 16th St.), Virginia Beach, VA 23451. ☎ **800/237-7532** or 757/428-1821. Fax 757/422-9602. www.breakersresort.com. E-mail: breakersvb@aol.com. 57 units. A/C TV TEL. Summer $140–$180 double; winter $50–$110 double. Weekend and other packages available. AE, DC, DISC, MC, V. Free parking.

One of the more reasonably priced oceanfront hostelries, The Breakers is another small family-operated hotel. Located in a white, box-like, nine-story building, its rooms are comfortably furnished with contemporary pieces. All have oceanfront balconies and refrigerators; some rooms with king-size beds contain whirlpool tubs. Efficiency apartments have a bedroom with two double beds, a living room with a Murphy bed, and a sitting area. Kitchens are fully equipped. Additional amenities include an outdoor heated pool, coffee shop for poolside dining, and free bicycles.

Cavalier Hotel. Oceanfront at 42nd St., Virginia Beach, VA 23451. ☎ **800/446-8199** or 757/425-8555. Fax 757/428-7957. www.cavalierhotel.com. 425 units. A/C TV TEL. Summer $90–$185 double; winter $55–$95 double. Weekend and other packages available. AE, DC, DISC, MC, V. Parking $5.

This venerable resort consists of two hotels—the original Cavalier built in 1927 on the hill across Atlantic Avenue from the beach, and the Cavalier on the ocean, which opened in 1973. Open from Memorial Day to Labor Day, the original building's enclosed verandah with white-wicker furnishings, potted plants, and great ocean views evokes images of the days when F. Scott and Zelda Fitzgerald danced here and lunches were black-tie. Its guest rooms have Williamsburg-quality Chippendale reproductions, colonial-print fabrics, gilt-framed artwork, and museum-quality decorative objects. Some feature European-style baths with black and white tile, pedestal sinks, whirlpools, lighted makeup mirrors, and bidets. The heated indoor Olympic-size pool is magnificently tiled and illuminated by a grand skylight. Open all year, the newer beachside building has nicely decorated contemporary-style rooms, all with oceanfront balconies.

The dining room in the hotel on the hill is open seasonally. In the new building, the elegant Orion rooftop restaurant is open year-round for cocktails and dinner, and the dining room on the lobby floor serves all three meals. Services include a concierge, room service, baby-sitting, valet parking, and shuttle service between hotels. The resort boasts indoor, outdoor, and kiddie pools; a 20-station aerobic fitness course; a health club; four tennis courts; bike rentals; a putting green; croquet, volleyball, shuffleboard and basketball courts; two playgrounds and a summertime children's activities program; and a gift shop.

Courtyard by Marriott. 2501 Atlantic Ave. (oceanfront at 25th St.), Virginia Beach, VA 23451. ☎ **800/321-2211** or 757/491-6222. Fax 757/491-7774. www.courtyard.com. 141 units. A/C TV TEL. Summer $199–$259; off-season $79–$99.

This 11-story member of the chain designed for business travelers opened in 1999 near the Old Coast Guard Museum, McKee's Beatles Museum, and other attractions. The beach substitutes for an actual courtyard here, and big window walls look right out to the boardwalk, sand, and waves from the plush, fireplace-equipped lobby and the bright, casual dining room, which provides much better than average hotel fare for breakfast, lunch, and dinner (you can dine outside in fine weather). They're not at all resorty (Marriott's standard mahogany furniture prevails), but the spacious guest quarters all have balconies overlooking the ocean. Ten units have whirlpool tubs, and eight suites have French doors between their living rooms and bedrooms. A small indoor pool on the first floor and a fitness room on the second both look out to the beach. This hotel is ideal for business travelers and couples, but families who want myriad in-house beach activities should look elsewhere.

New Castle Motel. 1203 Atlantic Ave. (oceanfront at 12th St.), Virginia Beach, VA 23451. ☎ **800/346-3176** or 757/428-3981. Fax 757/491-4394. 83 units. A/C TV TEL. Summer $125–$275; off-season $50–$275. AE, DC, DISC, MC, V.

Situated beside the Atlantic Wildfowl Heritage Museum (see "The Top Attractions," above), the 10-story, family-operated New Castle offers the most unusual mix of rooms on the beach, ranging from standard motel units to romantic deluxe models with canopy beds, gas fireplaces, his-and-her shower heads, and wooden Venetian blinds to keep passersby from watching you frolic in big whirlpool tubs. All units have balconies, refrigerators, microwave ovens, and spa tubs. There's an indoor pool, fitness center, free bicycles for guests' use (in summer), and coin-operated laundry. The Cabana Cafe to one side offers reasonably priced meals under a big, beachside awning.

Virginia Beach Resort Hotel. 2800 Shore Dr. (U.S. 60), Virginia Beach, VA 23451. ☎ **800/468-2722**, 800/422-4747 in Virginia, or 757/481-9000. Fax 757/496-7429. www.virginiabeachresort.com. 295 units. A/C TV TEL. Summer $179–$365 double; winter $104–$285 double. Weekly and other packages available. AE, DC, MC, V. Free parking.

Situated beside the Chesapeake Bay 3 miles from the oceanfront resort area, this self-contained mid-rise resort is very popular with groups, but there's a host of activities to keep anyone busy without leaving the 4 acres surrounding the hotel. All units here are suites whose balconies have bay views. They're furnished with sophisticated, contemporary wood pieces in pleasing pastel hues. Kitchen areas are equipped with a refrigerator and microwave. Utensils are available for an extra charge, or you may bring your own.

Dining: The Tradewinds Restaurant beside the pool offers wonderful water views and good American fare; the Cafe by the Bay is for more casual dining.

Amenities: Limited room service, nightly turndown on request. Indoor and outdoor pools, 30 lighted tennis courts (six indoor), health club, sauna, water-sports equipment rental, volleyball, children's activities, business center, meeting facilities, coin-op laundry, beauty salon, gift shop.

BED & BREAKFASTS

Angie's Guest Cottage & AYH Hostel. 302 24th St. (between Atlantic and Pacific aves.), Virginia Beach, VA 23451. ☎ **757/428-4600**. www.bbinternet.com/angies. 6 units (1 with private bathroom), 36 dorm beds. A/C. $66–$94 double room; $10.50–$13 dorm bed. Rates for rooms include continental breakfast. No credit cards. Closed mid-Oct to mid-Mar.

You'll find a delightful mix of American and international young folks staying at innkeeper Barbara Yates's quaint white-clapboard cottage, built a block from the beach in 1918 as family housing for the nearby life-saving station, now the Old Coast Guard Station Museum and Gift Shop (see "The Top Attractions," above). An avid traveler during the winter months, when she closes the place up, Barbara keeps her small guest rooms spotlessly clean and freshly painted. Rooms are air-conditioned but lack other modern amenities (however, she does have a portable black-and-white TV for anyone suffering from tube withdrawal). At the rear of the cottage, one of Virginia's few official AYH hostels offers men's, women's, and co-ed dorm rooms. They aren't air-conditioned, but lots of fans kick up a breeze. Outside, there's a covered country kitchen for guests to use, plus a sundeck and table tennis under a sprawling shade tree. Barbara rents linens to her dorm guests. Non-AYH members can stay in the dorms if space is available.

Barclay Cottage. 400 16th St. (at Arctic Ave.), Virginia Beach, VA 23451. ☎ **757/ 422-1956.** www.barclaycottage.com. 5 units (3 with private bathroom). A/C. $78–$108 double. Rates include full breakfast. AE, MC, V. Closed Nov–Mar.

Innkeepers Peter and Claire Cantanese have turned this two-story, white-clapboard Victorian with wraparound verandahs into a comfortable and charming bed-and-breakfast. Peter and Claire may hail from New Jersey, but their house is *very* coastal Southern, with rocking chairs on the porches and green shutters trimming tall windows hung with lace curtains. The guest rooms are adorned with Victorian pieces, and you'll find pieces from Peter's antique trunk collection placed throughout the premises. Guests gather in the lounge promptly at 9am for a full breakfast served family style. Peter and Claire have a pet dog, but don't bring yours. The beach is a 2-block walk away.

WHERE TO DINE

Just as Virginia Beach has thousands of hotel rooms, so it also has hundreds of restaurants, especially establishments serving up bountiful harvests of seafood. We've picked a few of the best to get you started.

For breakfast by the sea, head for the **Belvedere Coffee Shop,** an old-fashioned diner at the Belvedere Motel, Oceanfront at 36th Street (☎ **757/425-1397**). It's small, noisy, and busy, with cooks scurrying around the stove behind the counter, but big windows look right out on the boardwalk, beach, and surf. You'll have local company for eggs, omelets, pancakes, made-to-order sandwiches, salads, and a few inexpensive hot meals such as crab cakes. Prices range from $3 to $8, but don't plan to pay by credit card. It's open daily in summer from 7am to 3pm; off-season, daily from 7:30am to 2:30pm.

If you have kids in tow, another good breakfast bet is **Pocahontas Pancake & Waffle Shop,** a block away at Atlantic Avenue at 35th Street (☎ 757/428-6352), which has plenty of reminders of the American Indian princess, including a teepee in one corner of the dining room. The menu offers a wide range of inexpensive pancakes and waffles. Hours are daily from 7am to 1pm.

✪ **Coyote Cafe & Cantina.** 972 Laskin Rd. (in Linkhorn Shops, 1 block east of Birdneck Rd.). ☎ **757/425-8705.** Reservations strongly advised at dinner. Lunch $6–$8; main courses $10–$16. AE, DC, DISC, MC, V. Mon–Sat 11:30am–2:30pm and 5–10:30pm, Sun 5–10:30pm. SOUTHWESTERN.

The best Southwestern-style food in Virginia makes this lively cantina the beach's most popular restaurant with local residents. The cuisine is influenced by Mexico, but here the beef and chicken in the fajitas are grilled over mesquite with tequila and Cajun spices, and the enchiladas are stuffed with chicken and smoked Gouda cheese. If you like duck, go for it roasted in olive oil and served with an apple and rosemary demi glace. The menu offers lots more to choose from, all of it served in gargantuan portions. Lunch sees salads, sandwiches, fajitas, and a few other main courses (the spicy chicken wrap served with cinnamon dusted sweet potato chips is a winner). The front dining room here is refined, with long benches down the walls, over-stuffed booths down the center, and eclectic works by local artists on the walls. The back room is more like a Texas roadhouse, with widely spaced wooden tables and chairs, a big bar on one side, and the open kitchen in the rear. The Coyote is in a little shopping center (look for Eckerd's Drugs) on the north side of Laskin Road about a mile from the oceanfront.

Gus' Mariner Restaurant. Atlantic Ave. at 57th St. (in Ramada Plaza Resort). ☎ **757/ 425-5699.** Reservations recommended. Main courses $12–$20, early-bird specials $10. AE, DC, DISC, MC, V. Sun–Thurs 7am–9pm, Fri–Sat 7am–10pm. Early-bird specials daily 3–6pm. SEAFOOD.

One of the few hotel restaurants popular with local residents, Gus's award-winning establishment sits right beside the beach, with gorgeous sea views from its windowed walls (there's no guarantee of a window table even with a reservation, but they're worth waiting for). The crisp table linen, padded chairs, and candlelight add a touch of elegance. Seafood reigns, with excellent renditions of old standbys like crab cakes and crab Norfolk augmented by seafood linguine and other pasta dishes. The daily catch is offered with a variety of sauces, from spicy Cajun to cucumber-dill. Early-bird specials include choices of seafood or meat entrees.

The Jewish Mother. 3108 Pacific Ave. (north of Laskin Rd.). ☎ **757/422-5430.** Reservations not accepted. Breakfast $3–$6; sandwiches $4–$6.50; other items $3–$9. AE, DISC, MC, V. Daily 8:30am–3am. DELI/AMERICAN.

The Jewish Mother has been fixture on the Virginia Beach dining and nightlife scene since 1975. The decor is charmingly dilapidated, like a down-at-the-heels bar, but it's well loved locally for its outstanding deli sandwiches, oversize egg and omelet platters, and fresh salads (either by itself or stuffed into a pita pocket, the chicken salad with apples, raisins, and walnuts is terrific). Bagels, blintzes, and potato latkes start at breakfast and run all day. The entrance looks more like a neighborhood grocery store, with take-out food items and a bakery case displaying an eclectic variety of desserts, ranging from Key lime pie to baklava to Black Forest cake. The food is top drawer, and after about 9:30pm there's solid entertainment. Live music performances run the gamut from rock and blues to country, bluegrass, and zydeco. Depending on the performers, there may be a cover, especially on weekends. A huge bar offers a wide selection of microbrews on tap, and arguably the largest array of bottled waters in town.

✪ **La Bella Italia Cafe & Trattoria.** 1065 Laskin Rd. (1 block east of Birdneck Rd.). ☎ **757/422-8536.** Reservations highly recommended for dinner. Sandwiches $5.50–$7.50; main courses $9–$17. AE, MC, V. Mon–Thurs 9am–10pm; Fri–Sat 9am–11pm. ITALIAN.

Virtually across Laskin Road from the Coyote Cafe & Cantina (see above), this deli here is an excellent place to pick up sandwiches or Italian breads, pastries, and cookies for a day at the beach. After dark, you had best reserve a table, for a roaring, mesquite-fired oven produces the area's best pizzas, calzones, and exquisite marinated shrimp, fish, and steaks. In addition, the open kitchen serves up steaming bowls of homemade pasta. For starters, order the caprese salad with homemade mozzarella and fresh tomatoes and basil.

✪ **Lynnhaven Fish House.** 2350 Starfish Rd. (on Lynnhaven Fishing Pier). ☎ **757/ 481-0003.** Reservations not accepted. Main courses $14–$22. AE, DC, DISC, MC, V. Daily 11:30am–10:30pm. Closed Thanksgiving and Christmas. From the resort area, take Shore Dr. (U.S. 60); turn right on Starfish Rd. to Lynnhaven Fishing Pier, east of Lynnhaven Inlet bridge. SEAFOOD.

There are many water-view restaurants offering traditional Chesapeake Bay seafood here, but this venerable institution is worth a 20-minute drive from the oceanfront. Perched over the beach on Lynnhaven Fishing Pier, it has fabulous bay views from its wraparound windows. At lunch, a good bet is half a dozen fresh-shucked clams on the half shell with cocktail sauce. Other choices include a crab-cake sandwich, shrimp salad on a croissant, seafood pasta salad, or seafood stir-fry. The dinner menu starts off with oysters Rockefeller and selections from the chowder pots. Fresh fish of the day (flounder, sea trout, salmon, red snapper, tuna, swordfish, or rainbow trout) is offered broiled, grilled, steamed, or poached, accompanied by one of nine sauces. All dinners come with a choice of baked potato, sweet potato, french fries, or black beans and rice; coleslaw, house salad, or Caesar salad; and corn muffins and hush puppies. For dessert, try the moist carrot cake, lavishly frosted, or a refreshing peach Melba. A cafe to the side has outdoor dining beside the fishing pier.

Timbuktu. Atlantic Ave. at 32nd St. (in Days Inn Oceanfront). ☎ **757/491-1800.** Reservations recommended. Main courses $14–$20. AE, DC, DISC, MC, V. Daily 7–10am and noon–3pm; Sun–Thurs 5–9pm; Fri–Sat 5–10pm. Closed Mon dinner off-season. Valet parking at dinner during summer and off-season weekends. NEW AMERICAN.

Although Timbuktu offers breakfast and lunch as part of the Days Inn Oceanfront's services to its guests, at night it turns into a venue for fine dining. As befits the name, palm-shaped ceiling fans and camel caravans engraved in glass table dividers set a North African scene behind big windows overlooking the ocean. There the similarity ends, for chef Dru Rennée offers inventive twists to old favorites, such as his crab cakes, which are filled not just with backfin crab meat but lobster and shrimp, and encrusted not with flour but with potato chips. Every offering is expertly seasoned and accompanied by fresh local vegetables.

VIRGINIA BEACH AFTER DARK

The prime performing-arts venue here is the 20,000-seat, open-air **GTE Virginia Beach Amphitheater,** inland at Princess Anne and Dam Neck roads (☎ 757/ 368-8888 for schedule, Ticketmaster at **757/671-8100** for tickets). Big-name stars appear here (Jimmy Buffett, James Taylor, Cyndi Lauper, Tina Turner, Hank Williams, Jr., and The Who helped inaugurate its first season in 1997), as well as more highbrow acts like the Virginia Symphony. About 7,500 seats are under cover, with some 12,500 spaces available out on the lawn. Big TV screens and a state-of-the-art sound system let everyone see and hear what's going on. The season runs from April through October.

During summer there are frequent outdoor concerts on stages at 7th, 17th, and 24th streets along the Boardwalk (the visitor information center can tell you when and where). The biggest of all is the annual **American Music Festival,** over Labor Day weekend on the beach at 5th Street. You might catch the Beach Boys or Randy Travis on one stage, the Average White Band or Wilson Pickett on another. Tickets are sold on a first-come, first-served basis, or as part of special hotel packages (☎ 800/ 446-8038).

Hotels and restaurants all along the beach have live music for nighttime dancing during the summer season. Just follow your ears along the Boardwalk. Of particular note are **The Jewish Mother** (see "Where to Dine," above); **Abbey Road Pub &**

Restaurant, 22nd Street between Atlantic and Pacific avenues (☎ **757/425-6330**), rated the best acoustic club here; and the **Duck-In & Gazebo,** on Shore Drive (U.S. 60) at Lynnhaven Inlet (☎ **757/481-0201**), a seafood restaurant with sunset beach parties every Wednesday and Friday during summer.

3 Chincoteague & the Eastern Shore

Chincoteague, 83 miles N of Virginia Beach and Norfolk; 185 miles SE of Washington, D.C.

Miles of uncrowded beaches, countless waterways, abundant wildlife, and down-home cooking and hospitality welcome visitors to Virginia's tranquil Eastern Shore. Whether you'd like to take a day cruise to a quaint island out in the Chesapeake Bay, bike along traffic-free back roads, go bird watching in a wildlife refuge, sun and swim on one of America's great undeveloped beaches, or browse little villages with Native American names like Chincoteague, Wachapreague, or Onancock, you'll enjoy the gentle pace of this serene area.

Virginia's 70-mile-long end of the Delmarva Peninsula is bordered on one side by the Atlantic Ocean, on the other by the Chesapeake Bay. The ocean side is shielded by a string of barrier islands, many of them now happily preserved in their natural state by the Nature Conservancy (thus making them impossible to visit without a boat). Fishing towns like Chincoteague and Wachapreague sit inside the barrier islands. On the bay side, creeks cut into the land, creating natural harbors for towns like Onancock, jumping-off point for cruises to the most quaint destination of all, Tangier Island.

SEEING THE EASTERN SHORE

VISITOR INFORMATION   For information about the area, contact **Virginia's Eastern Shore Tourism Commission,** P.O. Box 460, Melfa, VA 23410 (☎ **757/ 787-2460;** www.esva.net/~esvatourism). The commission shares office space with Virginia's Eastern Chamber of Commerce, on U.S. 13 about 4 miles south of Onancock. It's open Monday to Friday 8:30am to 5pm, and Saturday 9am to 4pm, from May through October.

There's a **Virginia Welcome Center** on U.S. 301 just south of the Maryland state line. It's open daily from 9am to 5pm.

GETTING THERE   There is neither airport nor public transportation on the Eastern Shore, so you'll need a car. From Norfolk and Virginia Beach take U.S. 13 north across the Chesapeake Bay Bridge-Tunnel, a beautiful 17.6-mile drive across and under the bay ($10 toll per car). U.S. 13 runs north-south down the center of the Eastern Shore. To reach Chincoteague, turn east on Va. 175, about 65 miles north of the bridge-tunnel and 5 miles south of the Maryland line.

CHINCOTEAGUE & ASSATEAGUE ISLANDS

With its many motels, inns, restaurants, and proximity to Assateague Island, **Chincoteague Island** is the most popular base for exploring the Eastern Shore. It sits just south of the Maryland line and is 7 miles long by 1½ miles wide. Settled by the English in the late 1600s, Chincoteague is famous for its surrounding bays full of flounder, oyster beds, and clam shoals. Marguerite Henry's children's book, *Misty of Chincoteague* (later made into a film), aroused wide interest in the annual pony penning and swim in late July, when pony-size wild horses are rounded up on Assateague Island, forced to swim across to Chincoteague, and sold to benefit the local fire department.

While the town of Chincoteague has its share of tourist facilities, it retains much of its old fishing-village charm. Rickety old piers still jut out into the water next to modern motels, and watermen in work boats still outnumber tourists on jet skis. Of the nationally recognized chain names, only McDonald's will be seen on this quaint island—and that occurred only after a long and sometimes bitter fight.

For us humans, wonderful **Assateague Island** is just a short bridge away from Chincoteague. This barrier island is the site of both the Chincoteague National Wildlife Refuge and Assateague Island National Seashore, which together protect the wild ponies' habitat and 37 miles of pristine beach. Assateague is on the main Atlantic Flyway, and its population of both migratory and resident birds is simply astounding.

ESSENTIALS

VISITOR INFORMATION   The **Chincoteague Chamber of Commerce,** P.O. Box 258, Chincoteague, VA 23336 (☎ **757/336-6161;** fax 757/336-1241; www. chincoteaguechamber.com; e-mail: pony@shore.intercom.net), operates a visitor center in the traffic circle on Maddox Boulevard, about a mile before the Assateague bridge. It's open from June to October, Monday through Saturday from 9am to 4:30pm, Sunday from noon to 4:30pm. Off-season, it's open Monday through Friday from 9am to 4:30pm.

AREA LAYOUT   Va. 175 crosses the Chincoteague Channel and dead-ends in the old village at Main Street, which runs north-south along the island's western shore. Turn right at the stoplight to reach the motels, marinas, and bait shops which line Main Street south of the bridge. Turn left at the light for Maddox Boulevard, which heads east from Main Street 9 blocks north of the bridge and goes to Assateague Island. Maddox Boulevard is Chincoteague's prime commercial strip, with a plethora of shops, restaurants, and motels. Church Street goes east 2 blocks north of the bridge and turns into East Side Drive, which runs along the island's eastern shore. Ridge Road and Chicken City Road together run north-south down the middle of the island. On Assateague, there's only one road other than a wildlife drive, and it goes directly to the beach.

GETTING AROUND   This flat land is great biking terrain, and you can rent bicycles at several shops on Maddox Boulevard. **The Bike Depot,** at the Refuge Motor Inn (☎ **757/336-5511**), and **Jus' Bikes,** at the traffic circle (☎ **757/336-6700**), are closest to Assateague Island. Both charge $3 a hour, $10 a day.

SPECIAL EVENTS   In the last 2 weeks of July, the **Chincoteague Fireman's Carnival,** a fun fest with rides, live entertainment, and food, climaxes with the famous **pony swim** across the Assateague Channel to Chincoteague Memorial Park. There is no charge for parking or watching the ponies swim. The ponies are herded to Memorial Park on East Side Drive, where the first colt to come ashore is given away, and many are then sold at auction. The swim takes place on the last Wednesday in July; the remaining ponies swim back to Assateague the following Friday. It's all for a good cause—proceeds go to the fire company's ambulance fund. Another top event is the **Chincoteague Oyster Festival,** when you can get your libido going by gorging on fresh oysters during the first week of October. This event is always sold out in advance, so call ☎ 757/336-6161 for ticket information.

ASSATEAGUE ISLAND

A barrier island protecting Chincoteague Island from the Atlantic Ocean, Assateague Island boasts over 37 miles of pristine **beaches** on its east coast, the northern 25 miles of which are in Maryland. The island is administered by two federal agencies, with the highest degree of protection afforded to wildlife on the Virginia side.

The Eastern Shore

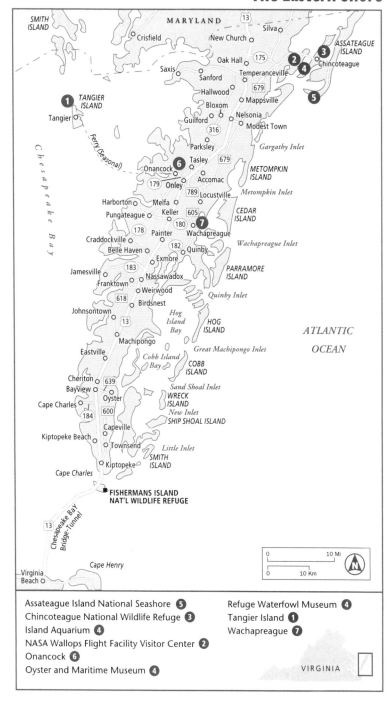

MARYLAND

SMITH ISLAND

Crisfield
New Church
Silva
ASSATEAGUE ISLAND
Oak Hall
175
Chincoteague
Saxis
Temperanceville
Sanford
Hallwood
679
Mappsville
Bloxom
Guilford
Nelsonia
Modest Town
316
Parksley
Gargathy Inlet
Tasley
679
METOMPKIN ISLAND
Onancock
Accomac
179
Onley
789
Locustville
Metompkin Inlet
Harborton
Melfa
Pungateague
Keller
605
CEDAR ISLAND
180
Painter
Wachapreague
178
Wachapreague Inlet
Craddockville
182
Quinby
Belle Haven
Exmore
Jamesville
183
Nassawadox
PARRAMORE ISLAND
Franktown
Weirwood
618
Birdsnest
Quinby Inlet
Johnsontown
13
Hog Island Bay
HOG ISLAND
Machipongo
Great Machipongo Inlet
ATLANTIC OCEAN
Eastville
Cobb Island Bay
COBB ISLAND
Cheriton
639
Sand Shoal Inlet
Bayview
WRECK ISLAND
Cape Charles
Oyster
New Inlet
184
600
SHIP SHOAL ISLAND
Capeville
Kiptopeke Beach
Townsend
Little Inlet
Kiptopeke
SMITH ISLAND
Cape Charles
FISHERMANS ISLAND NAT'L WILDLIFE REFUGE
Chesapeake Bay Bridge-Tunnel
13
Cape Henry
Virginia Beach

TANGIER ISLAND
Tangier
Ferry (Seasonal)
Chesapeake Bay

0   10 Mi
0   10 Km

Assateague Island National Seashore ⑤
Chincoteague National Wildlife Refuge ③
Island Aquarium ④
NASA Wallops Flight Facility Visitor Center ②
Onancock ⑥
Oyster and Maritime Museum ④

Refuge Waterfowl Museum ④
Tangier Island ①
Wachapreague ⑦

VIRGINIA

Bird watchers know Assateague Island as a prime Atlantic Flyway habitat where there have been sightings of peregrine falcons, snow geese, great blue heron, and snowy egrets. The annual Waterfowl Week, generally held around Thanksgiving, takes place when a large number of migratory birds use the refuge.

The famous **wild horses**—called "ponies"—have lived on Assateague since the 17th century. Local legend says their ancestors swam ashore from a shipwrecked Spanish galleon, but most likely English settlers put the first horses on Assateague, which formed a natural corral. Separated by a fence from their cousins in Maryland, the Virginia horses are now owned by the Chincoteague Volunteer Fire Department, which rounds them up and sells the foals at auction during the last week of July (see "Special Events," above).

THE WILDLIFE REFUGE   You first enter the **Chincoteague National Wildlife Refuge** (☎ 757/336-6122), which is open May 1 to September 30, daily from 5am to 10pm; April and October, daily from 6am to 8pm; November 1 to March 31, daily from 6am to 6pm. Owned and managed by the U.S. Fish and Wildlife Service, the refuge accepts the annual entrance passes issued at national parks; otherwise, admission is $5 per car for 1 week, free for pedestrians and bikers.

The refuge's visitor center, on the left quarter-mile east of the bridge, shows a video about the refuge on request and is the departure point for the paved **Wildlife Drive,** which runs through the marshes and is the best place to see the horses. This one-lane, one-way road is open to pedestrians and bicyclists all day, to motorized vehicles after 3pm.

Assateague Island Tours (☎ **757/336-6155** or 757/336-3700 for recorded information) conducts 1½-hour wildlife tours of the refuge, daily from Memorial Day to Labor Day at 10:30am and 5pm, at least once a day in April, May, and September. These tours cover 14½ miles and are usually the only way to visit most areas of the refuge other than on foot (the sole exception is the refuge's open house on Thanksgiving weekend, when 7 miles of service roads are open to vehicles). The tours cost $8 for adults, $4 for children. Book at the refuge visitor center.

Assateague Island Lighthouse, near the visitor center, is open to the public one weekend each month during the summer. Call the local U.S. Coast Guard station (☎ **757/336-2822**) for the schedule.

For **information** about the refuge and visitor-center seasons and programs, contact the Refuge Manager, Chincoteague National Wildlife Refuge, P.O. Box 62, Chincoteague, VA 23336 (☎ **757/336-6122**).

THE NATIONAL SEASHORE   The beach itself is in the **Assateague Island National Seashore,** operated by the National Park Service (☎ **757/336-6577**). You'll find a visitor center, bathhouses, and summertime lifeguards. In addition to swimming and sunning, activities at the beach include shell collecting (most productive at the tip of the Tom's Cove spit of land, on the island's southern tip) and hiking. Biking is allowed on the paved roads and along a bike path beside the road from Chincoteague to the refuge visitor center, then along Wildlife Drive to the Tom's Cove visitor center.

Note: Only a certain number of vehicles are allowed on the island at any given time. When that number is reached, park rangers stop traffic before the bridge to the island and allow one vehicle to cross only when another departs. Accordingly, it's best to arrive early in summer and on some fall weekends.

Several other **regulations** apply. Pets and alcoholic beverages are prohibited, even in your vehicle. In-line skating is not allowed, and off-road vehicles are permitted only at Tom's Cove. Surf fishing with a Virginia state license is allowed except on the lifeguard beach at Tom's Cove. Climbing and digging in the sand dunes is illegal. No overnight sleeping is allowed anywhere (backcountry camping is permitted on the Maryland end, a 12-mile hike from the Virginia-side visitor centers). And finally, thou shalt not feed the horses.

For information about the national seashore, contact the Superintendent, Assateague Island National Seashore, P.O. Box 38, Chincoteague, VA 23336 (☎ 757/ 336-6577; www.nps.gov/asis).

CRUISES & OUTDOOR PURSUITS

CRUISES   While most visitors head for the beach on Assateague, don't overlook the broad bays and creeks that surround Chincoteague. A good way to get out on them is with **Captain Barry's Back Bay Cruises** (☎ 757/336-6508), which depart Landmark Plaza on Main Street. Barry Frishman moved from upstate New York to Chincoteague and set about learning everything he could about the water and what's in it. Now he shares his knowledge by taking guests out on his pontoon boat for 1½-hour early-morning bird-watching expeditions ($15 per person); 4-hour morning or afternoon "Back Bay expeditions" in search of crabs, fish, shells, and clams ($30 per person); champagne sunset cruises ($20); moonlight excursions ($10); and just plain old "Fun Cruises" in spring and fall ($15).

Operated by Assateague Island Tours, which runs the wildlife tours in Chincoteague National Wildlife Refuge (see "Assateague Island," above), **Misty Boat Tours** (☎ 757/336-6155 or 757/336-3700 for recorded information) has 1½-hour nature cruises, departing from the Chincoteague Inn on South Main Street. Call for the seasonal schedule. Fares are $12.50 adults, $10 seniors, $8 kids 5 to 12.

FISHING   Before it became a tourist mecca, Chincoteague was a fishing village for centuries—and it still is. Both work and pleasure boats prowl the back bays and ocean for flounder, croaker, spot, kingfish, drum, striped bass, bluefish, and sharks, to name a few species. Among the pontoon party boats fishing the back bays are *Daisey's Dockside II,* at Daisey's Dockside Pier, South Main Street (☎ 757/336-3345), and the *Chincoteague View,* operating out of East Side Rentals & Marina on East Side Drive (☎ 757/336-3409). They charge $30 per person. More expensive are the charter boats that go oceanside, including the *Bucktail* (☎ 757/336-5188), the *Patty Wagon II* (☎ 757/336-1459), and the *Mar-shell* (☎ 757/336-1939). Reservations are essential, so call ahead.

Of course, you can do it yourself, either from a rented boat or by throwing your line from a dock. For equipment, supplies, free tide tables, and advice, check in at **Barnacle Bill's Bait & Tackle** (☎ 757/336-5188) or **Capt. Bob's** (☎ 757/ 336-6654), both on South Main Street. Marinas on East Side Drive that sell bait and rent boats and equipment include **East Side Rentals & Marina** (☎ 757/ 336-3409), **Snug Harbor Marina** (☎ 757/336-6176), and **Sea Tag Boat Rentals** (☎ 757/336-5555).

JET SKIING & PARASAILING   You can rent noisy but exciting jet skis at **Snug Harbor Marina** on East Side Drive (☎ 757/336-6176). For a bird's eye view of the islands, check with **Capt. Mike's Parasailing** (☎ 757/336-2760), at Capt. Fish's Steaming Wharf & Deck Bar on South Main Street.

KAYAKING   The waters around Chincoteague are ideal for sea kayaking, and **Tidewater Expeditions** has early morning and evening trips and an all-day sea clinic, all departing from its shop at 7729 East Side Dr. (☎ 757/336-6811 or 757/336-3159;

www.shol.com/seakayak). Costs for the excursions range from $37 for one-person kayaks to $42 for two-person kayaks. The clinic costs $65 per person. The company also rents kayaks for $10 an hour or $40 a day, and canoes for $12 an hour or $48 a day.

MUSEUMS

You'll pass a large airstrip as you drive to Chincoteague on Va. 175; this is NASA's Wallops Flight Facility, a research and testing center for rockets, balloons, and aircraft. The facility also tracks NASA's spacecraft and satellites, including the space shuttles. Across the highway is the **NASA Visitor Center** (☎ 757/824-1344), which explains the facility's history and role in the space program. Kids will get a kick out of seeing a practice space suit from the Apollo 9 moon mission. Admission is free. The visitor center is open from July 4 to Labor Day, daily from 10am to 4pm; March to June and September to November, Thursday through Monday from 10am to 4pm. The center is 5 miles west of Chincoteague.

On Maddox Boulevard, between the traffic circle and the bridge to Assateague, are two small marine-themed museums. The **Oyster and Maritime Museum** (☎ 757/336-6117) tells the area's history and the role played by the vital seafood industry from the 1600s to the present, with examples of marine life (some of them live). The fossil collection is worth a quick look here. Open Memorial Day to Labor Day, Monday to Saturday 10am to 5pm, Sunday noon to 4pm. Admission is $3 for adults, $1 for children 12 and under.

Virtually next door, the **Refuge Waterfowl Museum** (☎ 757/336-5800) has an interesting variety of antique decoys, boats, traps, art, and carvings by outstanding craftspeople. There's very good shopping here, although it's difficult to tell what's for sale and what's not. Open Memorial Day to Labor Day, Thursday through Monday from 10am to 5pm. Admission is $3 for adults, $1.50 for children under 12.

In the Landmark Plaza on North Main Street, the small **Island Aquarium** (☎ 757/336-6508) contains a marsh exhibit and touch tanks, where children can handle some of the marine life from local waters. It's a good place for kids on a rainy day, but you'll learn much, much more at the Virginia Marine Science Museum in Virginia Beach (see section 2, above). Admission is $3 for adults, $2 for children under 15. Open Memorial Day to Labor Day, Monday to Friday 10am to 9pm, Sunday 1 to 5pm. Call for off-season hours.

WHERE TO STAY

If you're looking for a longer-term rental on Chincoteague Island, contact **Vacation Cottages,** 6282 Maddox Blvd., Chincoteague, VA 23336 (☎ 800/457-6643 or 757/336-3720); **Island Property Rentals,** 7065 Main St., Chincoteague, VA 23336 (☎ 800/346-2559 or 757/336-3456); and **Bay Company, Inc.,** 6207 Maddox Blvd., Chincoteague, VA 23336 (☎ 800/221-5059 or 757/336-5490). They all have fully furnished cottages in various locations, including some on the waterfront.

Motels

The only chain motel here is the **Comfort Suites,** 4195 Main St. (☎ 800/228-5150 or 757/336-3700; fax 757/336-5452; www.chincoteaguechamber.com/comfortsuites), a three-story, V-shaped building beside Chincoteague Channel. Built and opened in 1999, it has 60 suites (all with balconies or patios facing the water) and an indoor pool. Rates range from $100 to $160 double in summer, $80 to $130 off-season.

Beach Road Motel. 6151 Maddox Blvd. (P.O. Box 557), Chincoteague, VA 23336. ☎ 800/699-6562 or 757/336-6562. Fax 757/336-1839. www.beachroad.com. 23 units. A/C TV TEL. Summer $63–$93 double; off-season $40–$63 double. AE, DC, DISC, MC, V. Turn left at the bridge on Main St., right on Maddox Blvd. to motel on left.

This owner-operated motel offers comfortable rooms in two one-story white-masonry buildings, one with a long front porch. The rooms are immaculate and contain all the basics, including refrigerators, microwave ovens, and beverage hot pots. Three efficiencies include a studio, a 1-bedroom cottage, and a 2-bedroom mobile home with full kitchen facilities. There's an outdoor pool on the property.

Driftwood Motor Lodge. 7105 Maddox Blvd. (P.O. Box 575), Chincoteague, VA 23336. ☎ **800/553-6117** or 757/336-6557. Fax 757/336-6558. E-mail: driftwood@shore. intercom.net. 53 units. A/C TV TEL. Summer $83–$96 double, $110 suite; off-season $55–$65 double, $75–$85 suite. AE, DC, DISC, MC, V. From the bridge, turn left on Main St., right on Maddox Blvd.

Along with the Refuge Motor Inn across the road (see below), this gray, three-story shiplap building is the closest accommodation to Assateague Island. Entered from the rear, the motel-style rooms all have balconies facing the road (those on the third floor overlook the marshes). Most contain two double beds, tables and chairs, and full tiled baths. The one suite has two bedrooms, one bath, and a microwave, refrigerator, and coffeemaker. There's an outdoor pool surrounded by shrubs and a picnic area with a barbecue grill.

✪ **Island Motor Inn.** 4391 N. Main St., Chincoteague, VA 23336. ☎ **757/336-3141.** Fax 757/336-1483. 60 units. A/C TV TEL. Summer $92–$150; off-season $68–$140. AE, DC, DISC, MC, V. From the bridge, turn left on Main St. to motel on left.

The top motel here, the Island Motor Inn sits right on Chincoteague Channel just north of the business district, giving its spacious rooms great views across the bay to the mainland. Reception is in a new, three-story building whose rooms are better appointed than the standard units in an older, two-story motel block adjoining. In fact, rooms at the ends of this new building have bay windows in their sides, giving them two-way views. All rooms have private balconies, desks, 27-inch TVs, and custom-made furniture. Some also have reclining sofas and baths with phones and pedestal sinks. On the water side of the property, you'll find a 600-foot boardwalk and boat dock, a covered barbecue area with hammock for lounging, an outdoor pool, and a glass-enclosed indoor pool and fitness center (with a trainer on duty during summer). On the road side, owners Reggie and Anna Stubbs have built a charming landscaped garden with lily ponds and benches for relaxing. There's also a guest laundry and a cafe that serves breakfast and lunch.

✪ **Refuge Motor Inn.** 7058 Maddox Blvd., Chincoteague, VA 23336. ☎ **888/ 868-6400** or 757/336-5511. Fax 757/336-6134. www.refugeinn.com. E-mail: refugeinn@ esva.net. 72 units. A/C TV TEL. Summer $85–$195 double; off-season $55–$110 double. AE, DC, DISC, MC, V. Free parking.

Between the traffic circle and the bridge to Assateague, this very attractive motel with weathered gray siding nestles on beautifully landscaped grounds shaded by tall pines. Like the Driftwood Motor Lodge across the street (see above), this is as close to Assateague Island as you can stay. You won't even have to go across the bridge to see the ponies, since several live in a small corral on the grounds here. The care and attention lavished on decor and facilities at this family-owned spot are evident everywhere. Furnishings are charming: Some rooms have colonial-style pieces, bleached-pine headboards, decoys, handmade wall hangings, and all the elements of country style. All rooms have refrigerators. First-floor rooms facing the back have sliding doors to private patios where guests can use outdoor grills. One of the two suites is a one-bedroom apartment with a fully equipped kitchen, a screened porch across the front, a spacious bathroom with whirlpool tub, and a spiral staircase leading to a loft with a double bed–size convertible futon (the apartment can sleep up to six persons). Other facilities here include an observation sundeck on the roof, an exercise room with sauna, a glass-enclosed pool and whirlpool, a children's playground, a coin-op laundry, and an excellent gift/crafts shop. The Bike Depot is here, so you can rent a cycle virtually at your front door.

Waterside Motor Inn. 3761 Main St. (P.O. Box 347), Chincoteague, VA 23336. ☎ **757/336-3434.** Fax 757/336-1878. www.intercom.net/local/chincoteague/hot/water.html. 45 units. A/C TV TEL. Summer $95–$150 double; off-season $68–$98 double. AE, DC, DISC, MC, V. Free on-site parking. At the bridge entering Chincoteague, turn right; the motel is on the right, about half a mile from the bridge.

All the accommodations at this three-story property feature private wooden balconies overlooking Chincoteague Channel, guaranteeing some breathtaking sunset views. Cream clapboard siding with slate-blue trim has a properly nautical look. Rooms are decorated in comfortable contemporary style. All have coffeemakers and refrigerators. The Waterside also offers a Jacuzzi, an exercise room, a tennis court, and a swimming pool, and it's located right on a fishing and crabbing pier.

Bed & Breakfasts

✪ **Cedar Gables Seaside Inn.** 6095 Hopkins Lane (P.O. Box 1006), Chincoteague, VA 23336. ☎ **888/491-2944** or 757/336-6860. Fax 757/336-1096. www.intercom.net/user/cdrgbl. E-mail: cdrgbl@shore.intercom.net. 4 units. A/C TV TEL. $130–$185 double. Rates include full breakfast. AE, DISC, MC, V. From the bridge, turn left on Main St., right on Maddox Blvd., left on Deep Hole Rd., right on Hopkins Lane.

Innkeepers Fred and Claudia Greenway offer Chincoteague's most luxurious accommodations at their modern house, which looks out to Assateague Island from beside a marsh-lined creek (this is the only B&B here that enjoys a waterfront location). The building doesn't actually have gables, although an irregularly shaped roof creates gable-like ceilings in the guest quarters. Each guest room has a gas fireplace, ceiling fan, TV with VCR, refrigerator, phone with data port, individual heating and air-conditioning controls, embroidered robes and Egyptian-cotton bed linens, and a bathroom with whirlpool tub and its own phone. Most intriguing (and expensive) is the Captain's Quarters, a spacious top-level room with its own deck and winding stairs leading up to a private tower with 360° views over the waterways and islands. Every unit has both inside and outside entrances, so you don't have to traipse through the house to get into and out of your room. Served on a screened porch in good weather, three-course breakfasts begin with fresh fruit and Claudia's homemade granola. Out on the lawn, a swimming pool is completely surrounded by screens to keep the mosquitoes away. The Greenways also rent canoes and kayaks to their guests. *Note:* Kids 14 and older can stay in the one downstairs room; otherwise, this is an all-adult establishment.

Inn at Poplar Corner. 4248 Main St. (at Poplar St.), Chincoteague, VA 23336. ☎ **800/336-6787** or 757/336-6115. Fax 757/336-5776. www.poplarcorner.com. 4 units. A/C. Summer $139–$149; off-season $109–$129. Rates include full breakfast and afternoon tea. MC, V. From the bridge, turn left on Main St. to inn on right.

This three-story house with wraparound verandah looks like it's been here since Victorian times, but it was actually built from scratch a few years ago by Tom and Jacque Derrickson, owners of the Watson House across the street (see below). Floral wallpaper, period antiques, and lace curtains add to the atmosphere. A central hallway is flanked by a formal parlor and a dining room, whose French doors open to the verandah, thus permitting guests of both B&Bs to enjoy full gourmet breakfasts outside during good weather. The two rooms on the front of the second story have bay windows, while the one to the rear has its own private balcony. But the star here is the third story, which has a unique lounge (you have to stoop under the roof to reach a small reading area) and a bedroom with three gables and French doors leading to a huge bathroom. All rooms have window air-conditioning units, ceiling fans, and whirlpool tubs, but none has a phone or TV.

Island Manor House. 4160 Main St., Chincoteague, VA 23336. ☎ **800/852-1505** or 757/336-5436. Fax 757/336-1333. www.chincoteague.com/b-b/imh.html. E-mail: imn@shore.intercom.net. 8 units (6 with private bathrooms). A/C. Summer $85–$130 double; off-season $80–$110 double. Rates include full breakfast and afternoon tea. MC, V. Free parking. From the bridge into Chincoteague, turn left onto Main St. and continue about 1½ blocks; the inn is on the right.

This older B&B consists of two white-clapboard houses joined by a one-story, light-filled garden room with a lovely brick patio and fountain outside (where guests enjoy breakfast in good weather). Originally, there was only one house, built before the Civil War by two young men. They eventually married sisters, who did not enjoy living under the same roof, so they split the structure and moved one half next door. Today, both houses have been handsomely restored and are furnished mainly in Federal style, along with 17th-, 18th-, and 19th-century pieces collected by hospitable owners Charles and Carol Kalmykow. In the two first-floor sitting rooms are fireplaces and telephones for guest use.

Miss Molly's Inn Bed & Breakfast. 4141 Main St., Chincoteague, VA 23336. ☎ **800/221-5620** or 757/336-6686. Fax 757/336-0600. www.missmollys-inn.com. 7 units (5 with private bathroom). A/C. Summer $89–$155 double; off-season $69–$125 double. Rates include full breakfast and afternoon tea. AE, DISC, MC, V. Closed early Jan to Feb. From the bridge into Chincoteague, turn left onto Main St. and continue about 1½ blocks to the inn, on the left.

This charming 1886 Victorian, with a wide wraparound porch, is named for the daughter of the builder J. T. Rowley, known as "the clam king of the world." Miss Molly, who lived in this house until the age of 84, was a resident when Marguerite Henry stayed here to write *Misty of Chincoteague*. Although this is the least upscale of the B&Bs in the area, innkeepers David and Barbara Wiedenheft have decorated all rooms with an agreeable mix of Victorian and earlier antiques, lace curtains, pretty coverlets, Tiffany-style lamps, and bibelots adorning mantels and dresser tops. The parlor and dining room have exceptionally fine Victorian pieces—marble-top tables, a curved sofa, original newel-post lamps, and Oriental carpets. There are five porches, including a screened one at the rear of the house.

If you want larger rooms, the Wiedenhefts also operate the **Channel Bass Inn,** around the corner at 6228 Church St. (☎ **800/249-0818** or 757/336-6148; fax 757/336-0600; www.channelbass-inn.com). They serve full breakfasts and English-style afternoon tea here.

The Watson House. 4240 Main St. (at Poplar St.), Chincoteague, VA 23336. ☎ **800/336-6787** or 757/336-1564. Fax 757/336-5776. www.watsonhouse.com. 6 units. A/C. Summer $89–$109; off-season $69–$99. Rates include full breakfast and afternoon tea. MC, V. From the bridge, turn left on Main St. to inn on right.

Unlike its sibling, the Inn at Poplar Corner (see above), the Watson House actually dates back to the Victorian era, having been built before 1874. You'll pay less on this side of Poplar Street, but you'll also get a much simpler room and a bath just large enough to accommodate a toilet and shower stall (pedestal sinks stand in the sleeping quarters). Nevertheless, Victorian oak furniture and lace curtains supply charm, and two of the rooms have small sitting areas. Guests breakfast at the Inn at Poplar Corner, but afternoon tea is served here, either in the formal dining room or on the wraparound verandah.

Campgrounds

Chincoteague has several family-oriented campgrounds. Most convenient to Assateague Island is the **Maddox Family Campground,** 6742 Maddox Blvd. (at the traffic circle; ☎ **757/336-3111;** fax 757/336-1980), which has 550 campsites, some with views of the Assateague Lighthouse. On the grounds are a pool, playground, pavilion, grocery store with RV supplies, rec hall, laundry room, bathhouses, dump station, and propane filling station. Shuffleboard, a duck pond, horseshoes, crabbing, and bird watching are on-site. Rates range from $20 for a tent site to $26 for full hookup. Discover, MasterCard, and Visa are accepted.

WHERE TO DINE

You won't find fine dining here, but you will be served seafood fresh from the boat. The famous Chincoteague oysters are harvested from September to March. The area is also known for flounder, caught year-round.

Winter is not a good time for dining here, since most restaurants close after Columbus Day weekend in October and reopen just before Easter weekend the next spring.

The best breakfast place in town is the **Island Cafe,** a cottage in front of the Island Motor Inn, 4391 Main St. (☎ **757/336-3141**). The French toast with honey and vanilla extract is outstanding. It's open Monday to Friday 6:30 to 11am, Saturday 6:30am to noon, Sunday 6:30am to 2pm.

AJ's by the Creek. 6585 Maddox Blvd. ☎ **757/336-5888.** Reservations not accepted. Lunch $3–$10; main courses $11–$25. AE, DC, DISC, MC, V. Mon–Sat 11:30am–10pm; Sun 4:30–10pm. ITALIAN/SEAFOOD.

A favorite with locals, AJ's offers dining either on a screened-in patio beside a narrow creek or inside, where candles and dried-flower arrangements adorn a mix of tables and booths (romantically inclined couples can wait for the one private table sitting alone in a corner). The menu offers a mix of Italian-style pastas (the house specialty) and traditional dishes such as fried or steamed shrimp and Chincoteague oysters, plus hand-cut aged steaks. A popular local hangout, the friendly and cozy bar to one side offers sports TVs and its own lunch and snack menu (including sandwiches, shrimp baskets, and small orders of pasta).

✪ **Capt. Fish's Steaming Wharf & Deck Bar.** 3855 Main St. ☎ **757/336-6986.** Reservations not accepted. Sandwiches $5–$7; main courses $10–$28. MC, V. Easter to mid-Oct, daily 11am–9pm (bar open later). Closed mid-Oct to Easter. SEAFOOD.

Like P.T. Pelican's Intercoastal Deck Bar at the Chincoteague Inn (see below), this casual, open-air bar beside Chincoteague Channel is a great place to unwind while watching spectacular sunsets over the marshes. The building was an old seafood packing plant until owners Mike and Linda McGee went on vacation to Aruba and decided they could make more money by converting it into a waterside bar like those in the Caribbean islands. Judging from the crowds packed around the *Osprey* (an old cruise-boat-turned-bar) during Pony Penning week and other special events, they're doing just fine. Watermen still dock their boats next door, and their flounder, shrimp, crabs, clams, oysters, and other morsels go straight into the McGee's steamer. You also can get them fried or grilled. You'll eat with plastic utensils off paper plates. Live bands play Thursday to Saturday nights during summer and during special events.

✪ **Chincoteague Inn/P.T. Pelican's Intercoastal Deck Bar.** Marlin St. (off Main St., south of the bridge). ☎ **757/336-6110.** Reservations not accepted. Sandwiches and salads $4–$9; main courses $10–$19. DISC, MC, V. Easter to mid-Oct, deck bar daily 11am–10pm, dining room daily 4–10pm. Closed mid-Oct to Easter. SEAFOOD.

Sitting beside the channel, the Chincoteague Inn has been a seafood mainstay here for generations, offering traditional preparations and fine water views from big window walls. The delicately seasoned crab cakes are first-rate, with large lumps of backfin meat. But the fun part of this establishment is outside at P.T. Pelican's rustic and funky deck bar right on the Intercoastal Waterway. Its well-weathered lean-to tin roof covers a spacious square bar and beat-up stools. Like Capt. Fish's Steaming Wharf & Deck Bar (see above), it's a most interesting place for a lazy waterside lunch—or for whiling away an afternoon chatting with the local watermen who take libation here after crabbing and oystering. You can sit by the water at green plastic tables and order either from the Inn's dinner menu or from the all-day bar menu, which features burgers, crab-cake sandwiches, sautéed soft-shell crabs, steamed or raw oysters and clams on the half shell, small pizzas, and tasty shrimp and crab salads.

✪ **Village Restaurant.** 7576 Maddox Blvd. ☎ **757/336-5120.** Reservations suggested on weekends. Main courses $10–$19.50. AE, DISC, MC, V. Daily 5–9pm. Closed 1 day a week off-season. SEAFOOD.

The garden-like Village Restaurant, with white trellises and floral wallpaper, is one of the fanciest restaurants here. It looks out to Assateague Island over a creek and a marsh. You'll enjoy some of the best traditionally prepared seafood in town here, whether you choose fried oysters, or flounder or shrimp stuffed with crab imperial. The house seafood platter is piled with fish filet, shrimp, scallops, oysters, clams, and lobster tail. Avoid the blackened fish, which is simply coated with Cajun spices. Non-seafood main dishes include veal or chicken Parmesan, fried chicken, and filet mignon. All entrees are served with home-baked bread, either potato or rice, and a choice of slaw, salad, or vegetable of the day.

ONANCOCK

In contrast to Chincoteague's somewhat scruffy fishing-town image, the picturesque town of Onancock, 1 mile west of U.S. 13 and Olney, has a more genteel charm dating back to 1690. Situated on Onancock Creek some 2½ miles from the Chesapeake Bay, it has always made its money from agriculture and trading as well as from the bay. The great ferries and ships that once plied between Norfolk and Baltimore put in here, helping to make Onancock a wealthy town. As a consequence, it has stately churches (many with fish-scale shingle exteriors) and fine historic homes built by wealthy traders and bankers.

Today Onancock is the most sophisticated town on Virginia's Eastern Shore. Many retirees and others have settled here, bringing with them good restaurants, boutiques and craft shops (search along Market Street), and, soon, a little theater. It's worth a short detour off U.S. 13 just to look around, and perhaps have a creekside lunch. And if you take a cruise from here to quaint Tangier Island, plan to do some sightseeing in town after the boat returns.

WHAT TO SEE & DO

If you like old houses, it's also worth a stop here to visit **Kerr Place,** a stately Federal mansion built in 1799 by Scottish merchant John Shepherd Kerr on Market Street (Va. 179). This two-story brick manor house, now headquarters for the Eastern Shore of Virginia Historical Society (☎ **757/787-8012**), is beautifully furnished with 18th- and 19th-century antiques. Admission is $4 for adults, free for children. Open March to December, Tuesday through Saturday from 9am to 4pm (closed holidays).

While here, linger for a bit at the **Town Dock,** at the foot of Market Street, and take a look at **Hopkins & Bro. General Store,** built in 1842. This clapboard building has been fixed up into a restaurant (see "Where to Dine," below) and a gift shop selling Virginia products.

A Cruise to Tangier Island
The wharf behind Hopkins & Bro. General Store is the departure point for cruises to tiny ✪ **Tangier Island** and its picturesque village of 750 souls out in the Chesapeake Bay. There are no cars on the narrow streets, which seems appropriate to this unspoiled island, discovered by Capt. John Smith in 1608. In fact, the local accent actually hearkens back to Elizabethan English. Out here, when someone says "Hoi toide onda soun soide tonoit," they mean there's high tide on the sound side tonight.

This is no glitzy resort: Entertainment consists of walking around the island, perhaps chatting with local watermen, and just enjoying the serenity and fresh sea air. In any case, you'll want to eat at **Hilda Crockett's Chesapeake House,** where down-home meals are served boardinghouse-style from mid-April to mid-October, 11:30am to 5pm daily, for $12.75 a head. You can also stay overnight at Mrs. Crockett's for a very reasonable $40 per person, including family-style dinner and full country breakfast the next morning. For details and reservations, the address is P.O. Box 194, Tangier Island, VA 23440 (☎ **757/891-2331**).

Weather permitting, the **Tangier Island Ferry** (☎ **757/891-2240**) operates May 15 to October 15, daily at 10am, returning at 3:30pm. Round-trip fare is $20 for adults, $10 for children 6 to 11, and free for children 5 and under. Reservations are not accepted.

WHERE TO STAY
The town of Olney, 1 mile east of Onancock on U.S. 13, has a modern **Comfort Inn** (☎ **800/228-5150** or 757/787-7787), one of only two chain motels between Charles City, Virginia, and Pocomoke City, Maryland.

Spinning Wheel Bed & Breakfast. 31 North St., Onancock, VA 23417. ☎ **757/787-7311.** Fax 757/787-8555. www.downtownonancock.com. E-mail: b&b@downtownonancock.com. 5 units. A/C. $75–$95. Rates include full breakfast. MC, V. Closed Nov–Mar. From Market St., turn north on North St.

Every room in this three-story wood-frame Victorian, built around 1890, has an antique spinning wheel, part of an extraordinary collection belonging to innkeeper Karen Tweedie. She and husband David have added other Eastern Shore antiques throughout, including iron and brass beds. Dormer windows contribute unique shapes to the top-level rooms. Free bikes are available for guests' use.

WHERE TO DINE
✪ **Armando's.** 10 North St., Onancock. ☎ **757/787-8044.** Reservations not accepted. Main courses $8–$16. AE, MC, V. Sun and Tues–Thurs 5–9pm; Fri–Sat 5–10pm. INTERNATIONAL.

Argentine-born Armando Suarez settled in Onancock in 1988 and opened a pizza and sandwich shop. So popular did it quickly become that he opened this fun storefront restaurant adorned with an eclectic mix of pottery, plants, and photos of jazz musicians. Armando's menu is equally eclectic, with some inventive twists such as crab crêpes, shrimp margarita (a slightly piquant tequila sauce), and lobster ravioli "drizzled" with sage, butter, and tomato cream sauce. Armando constantly spins jazz CDs and occasionally has live jazz on weekends.

Eastern Shore Steamboat Co. Restaurant. 2 Market St. (in Hopkins & Bro. General Store). ☎ **757/787-3100.** Reservations not accepted. Lunch $4.50–$11; main courses $10–$17. MC, V. Memorial Day–Labor Day, daily 11:30am–9pm; mid-Apr to May and Sept–Oct, Wed–Sun 11:30am–9pm. Closed Nov to mid-Apr. SEAFOOD.

You'll have a view of Onancock Creek either upstairs or on the downstairs deck of the historic Hopkins & Bro. General Store, where vessels of this restaurant's namesake docked during the 19th century. Naturally the fare is seafood, with mostly backfin meat crab cakes leading the list. You'll find more sophisticated restaurants on the Eastern Shore, but few with this much charm.

WACHAPREAGUE

Appearing much like Chincoteague must have looked before tourism arrived, the tiny village of Wachapreague, with 290 permanent residents, sits on the Atlantic coast mainland just 10 miles from Onancock. It overlooks the marshes and waterways that lie between town and an inlet between **Cedar Island** and **Parramore Island,** which protect the bays and marshes here as Assateague does for Chincoteague. At the turn of the 20th century, Wachapreague was a major resort for the likes of Walter Chrysler, actor Ronald Coleman, and former president Herbert Hoover. Excellent hunting and fishing drew them here, and they stayed at the grand Hotel Wachapreague, a four-story Victorian palace surrounded by verandahs and topped by gabled windows. Unfortunately, the hotel burned down in 1978, but the fishing and hunting here are as good as ever.

Seaside Boat Rentals at the Wachapreague Marina on the waterfront (☎ 757/787-4110) will rent boats for do-it-yourself trips for $60 a day, including fuel and a chart. The marina's bait shop or **Capt. Zed's Bait & Tackle** (☎ 757/787-8060) next door will advise on where the fish are biting. If you decide to go out on your own, do it at high tide, since many channels here are very shallow.

WHERE TO STAY

✪ **Hart's Harbor House and Burton House Bed & Breakfast.** 9 Brooklyn Ave., Wachapreague, VA 23480. ☎ 757/787-4848. E-mail: bnbbysea@shore.intercom.net. 10 units (4 with private bathroom, 6 with toilet and hand basin). A/C. $65–$95 double. Rates include full breakfast. MC, V. From Va. 180, turn left on Brooklyn Ave. 1 block before waterfront.

Born-and-bred Wachapreaguers Tom and Pat Hart have turned these two adjacent Victorian houses into a first-rate bed-and-breakfast operation with direct access to the waterfront. Tom salvaged some railing from the Hotel Wachapreague's verandahs and used them to build a charming, gazebo-like screened porch on the rear of Burton House (Hart's Harbor House also has a screened porch overlooking the water). Hart's Harbor House's rooms are larger than its neighbor's, but all have baths and attractive Eastern Shore antiques. Guests in the main houses are treated to Tom's country breakfast. The Harts provide free bikes for their guests' use and will arrange cruises, island trips, and hunting and fishing guides. They also have three cottages and a cabin for rent in their back lot, between the houses and the waterfront.

WHERE TO DINE

Island House Restaurant. 17 Atlantic Ave. (on the waterfront). ☎ 757/787-4242. Reservations accepted. Lunch $5–$8.50; main courses $10–$18. MC, V. Feb–Apr and Nov–Dec, Fri–Sun noon–9pm; May–Oct, daily noon–9pm. Closed 2 weeks in late Dec. SEAFOOD.

With a grand view of the marshes, channels, and barrier islands, this shingle-sided building gets its inspiration from the old Parramore Island Life Saving Station, which was built in the 1890s. Raw bar items include fresh Wachapreague oysters from September to March. The broiled or fried favorites such as soft-shell crabs, crab cakes, and fish are passable but don't live up to the view.

Appendix:
Virginia in Depth

The sections below take a look at modern Virginia and examine the state's illustrious past. The history of English-speaking America began here, the fires of independence were flamed here, the American Revolution was won here, and much of the Civil War was fought here. Indeed, Virginia's history will play a very important role in your visit, for many of the state's major attractions are houses, buildings, monuments, sites, and battlefields marking more than 3 centuries of America's past.

1 Virginia Today

The memory of the state's past still exerts its influence, as it surely must in towns where descendants of America's first patriots still live and where the homes, monuments, and battlefields that shaped the country's history comprise their daily landscape. So revered is history here that sometimes you would think George Washington still stands siege outside Yorktown, Thomas Jefferson still writes great political prose up at Monticello, and Robert E. Lee and Stonewall Jackson still ride at Fredericksburg and Chancellorsville.

Of all the memories, the Civil War lives strongest here, as witnessed by the recent civic battles in Richmond—whose population is now majority African-American—over whether to place a statue of black tennis star Arthur Ashe among those of Civil War generals along hallowed Monument Avenue, or to draw a mural of Robert E. Lee on the flood wall bordering the city's new Canal Walk park.

Prominent in Virginia Tidewater plantation society since the 1600s, the Byrd family dominated the state's politics from World War I until the 1980s. Under their conservative control, Virginia, the "Mother of Presidents," virtually withdrew from national leadership. The state government vigorously fought federally mandated public school integration in the 1950s, with one county actually closing its schoolhouse doors rather than admit African-Americans to previously all-white institutions. Although racial relations have improved greatly since then, the old animosities still raise their ugly heads from time to time.

Virginia's politics are about evenly split between Democrats and Republicans these days, although the Republicans have been slowly getting the upper hand (neither state party can be considered to be "liberal" by national standards). Democrat L. Douglas Wilder became the nation's first elected African-American governor in 1989, and in

1994 Democrat Charles Robb—son-in-law of President Lyndon B. Johnson—withstood a tough challenge for his U.S. Senate seat from Republican Oliver North, the controversial Iran-Contra figure. Republican George Allen—son of the famous professional football coach—took the governor's mansion back in 1997 (it's still in Republican hands), and the Republicans gained their first majority in the state legislature in 1999. At press time, no one would predict the result of a race between Republican Allen and Democrat Robb for the U.S. Senate in 2000.

Economically, most of the state is doing well. Although colonist John Rolfe is best remembered today for marrying Pocahontas, the tobacco industry he helped found is still important to Virginia's economy despite its recent legal setbacks. Farm income has been good from the apple orchards of the Shenandoah Valley; livestock, dairying, and poultry raising in the Piedmont; the state's famous Smithfield hams and peanuts from the Tidewater country; and seafood from the Chesapeake Bay. Industry continues to grow as well, notably in the manufacturing of clothes, chemicals, furniture, and transportation equipment. And northern Virginia's high-tech corridor has seen an outright boom.

2 A Look at the Past

Dateline

- **1607** First permanent English settlement in New World established at Jamestown.
- **1612** John Rolfe begins cultivation of tobacco for export.
- **1619** House of Burgesses—first representative legislative body in New World—meets in Jamestown. First Africans arrive at Jamestown as indentured servants.
- **1624** Virginia becomes a royal colony.
- **1652** Burgesses affirm that only they have right to elect officers of Virginia colony.
- **1682** Tobacco riots protest falling crop prices.
- **1699** Virginia's government moves to Williamsburg.
- **1754** French and Indian War begins as George Washington leads Virginia troops against French in Ohio Valley.
- **1755** Washington takes command of Virginia army on frontier.
- **1765** Patrick Henry protests Stamp Act, saying, "If this be treason, make the most of it."

continues

Virginia's history began on April 26, 1607, when 104 English men and boys arrived at Cape Henry on the Virginia coast aboard the *Susan Constant,* the *Godspeed,* and the *Discovery.* The expedition—an attempt to compete with profitable Spanish encroachments in the New World—was sponsored by the Virginia Company of London and supported by King James I.

A MODEST BEGINNING Although the colonists were heartened to find abundance of fish and game, if not streets paved with gold, their optimism was short-lived, for Native Americans attacked them on their very first day in the New World. Fleeing Cape Henry, they settled on Jamestown Island, which offered greater protection from the Spanish and the Indians. Unfortunately, most were gentlemen unaccustomed to work of any kind and with little inclination or aptitude for it. As one on-the-scene chronicler described it, "a world of miseries ensewed." An unfamiliar climate, contaminated water, famine, disease, and Indian attacks left only 50 alive by autumn.

When Capt. John Smith tried to barter for corn and grain, they took him prisoner and carried him to Chief Powhatan. According to legend, they would have killed him, but Powhatan's teenage daughter, the beautiful princess Pocahontas, interceded and saved his life. However, Smith was not much of a diplomat in dealing with natives; he helped sow seeds of dissension that would result in

- **1774** First Virginia Convention meets, sends delegates to Continental Congress.
- **1775** Patrick Henry incites rebellion with his "Liberty or Death" oration at Virginia Convention in Richmond. Washington chosen leader of army by Continental Congress.
- **1776** Patrick Henry elected first governor of self-declared free state of Virginia. Thomas Jefferson's wording for Declaration of Independence adopted by Congress.
- **1779** State capital moved to Richmond.
- **1781** Cornwallis surrenders at Yorktown.
- **1787** Washington elected president of Constitutional Convention.
- **1788** Virginia ratifies Constitution.
- **1789** Washington inaugurated as first president. Virginia cedes area to U.S. for seat of government.
- **1801** Thomas Jefferson inaugurated president.
- **1803** Jefferson sends James Monroe to France for purchase of Louisiana Territory.
- **1809** James Madison inaugurated president.
- **1814** President and Dolley Madison flee to Virginia as British enter Washington.
- **1831** Nat Turner's slave rebellion.
- **1832** House of Delegates bill to abolish slavery in Virginia loses by seven votes.
- **1859** John Brown hanged after failed raid on Harpers Ferry Arsenal.
- **1861** Richmond chosen Confederate capital. First battle of Manassas.
- **1862** First ironclad ships, *Monitor* and *Merrimac,* battle in Hampton Roads harbor. Confederate victories at Second Manassas, Fredericksburg.

continues

centuries of hostility between the tribes and the European settlers.

In 1613, John Rolfe (who later married Pocahontas) brought from the New World a new aromatic tobacco that proved popular in England. The settlers had discovered not the glittery gold they expected, but the "golden weed" that would be the foundation of Virginia's fortunes.

The year 1619 was marked by several important happenings: The Virginia Company sent a shipload of 90 women to suitors who had paid their transportation costs; 22 Burgesses were elected to set up the first legislative body in the New World; and 20 Africans arrived in a Dutch ship to work as indentured servants, a precursor of slavery.

In 1699, the capital of the colony was moved from Jamestown, which had suffered a disastrous fire, to the planned town of Williamsburg, and it was from Williamsburg that colonial patriots launched some of the first strong protests against Parliament.

COLONIAL LIFE   By the mid–18th century, the growth of vast tobacco plantations along Tidewater Virginia's rivers brought with it a concurrent increase in the importation of slaves from Africa as the base for the "plantation economy."

The French and Indian War in the 1750s proved to be a training ground for America's Revolutionary forces. When the French built outposts in territory claimed by Virginia, Governor Dinwoody sent George Washington to protect Virginia's claims. In the field Washington acquitted himself with honor, and after General Braddock's defeat, he was appointed commander-in-chief of Virginia's army on the frontier.

UNREST GROWS   Expenses from the war and economic hardships led the British to increase taxes in the colonies, and protests in Virginia and Massachusetts escalated. The 1765 Stamp Act met with general resistance. Patrick Henry inspired the Virginia General Assembly to pass the Virginia Resolves, setting forth colonial rights according to constitutional principles. The young orator exclaimed, "If this be treason, make the most of it." The Stamp Act was repealed in 1766, but the Revenue Acts of 1767, which included the hated tax on tea, exacerbated tensions.

Ties among the colonies were strengthened when Virginia's Burgesses, led by Richard Henry Lee, created a standing committee to communicate their problems in dealing with England to similar committees in the other colonies. When the Boston Post Bill closed that harbor in punishment for the Boston Tea Party, the Virginia Assembly moved swiftly. Although Governor Dunmore had dissolved the legislature, they met at Raleigh Tavern and recommended that a general congress be held annually. Virginia sent seven representatives to the First Continental Congress in 1774, among them Lee, Patrick Henry, and George Washington.

The following year, Patrick Henry made a fiery plea for arming Virginia's militia. He concluded his argument in these now-familiar words, "Is life so dear or peace so sweet as to be purchased at the price of chains and slavery? Forbid it, Almighty God! I know not what course others may take, but, as for me, give me liberty, or give me death!"

Later in 1775, upon hearing news of the battles of Lexington and Concord, the Second Continental Congress in Philadelphia voted to make the conflict near Boston a colony-wide confrontation and chose Washington as commander of the Continental Army. War had begun.

BIRTH OF THE NATION

On June 12, 1776, the Virginia Convention, meeting in Williamsburg, adopted George Mason's Bill of Rights and instructed Virginia's delegates to the Continental Congress to propose independence for the colonies. Mason's revolutionary document stated that "all power is vested in, and consequently derived from, the people," and that "all men are created free and independent, and have certain inherent rights. . . : among which are the enjoyment of life and liberty, with the means of acquiring and possessing property. . . ." He also firmly upheld the right of trial by jury, freedom of the press, and the right of all people to freedom of religion. When the Congress meeting in Philadelphia adopted Thomas Jefferson's Declaration of Independence (based on Mason's bill) on July 4, 1776, the United States of America was born.

The Revolution was a bloody 7-year conflict marked by many staggering defeats for the patriots. Historians believe it was only the superb leadership and pertinacity of Gen. George Washington that inspired the Continental Army (a ragtag group of farmers, laborers, backwoodsmen, and merchants) to continue so long in the face of overwhelming odds.

- **1863** Stonewall Jackson fatally wounded at Chancellorsville.
- **1864** Confederacy wins Battle of the Wilderness at Spotsylvania Court House near Fredericksburg. Grant's siege of Petersburg begins.
- **1865** Richmond evacuated. Lee surrenders at Appomattox.
- **1867** Virginia put under military rule of Reconstruction Act. Confederate President Jefferson Davis imprisoned for treason in Fort Monroe.
- **1870** Virginia readmitted to Union.
- **1900** Legislature passes "Jim Crow" segregation laws.
- **1902** Poll tax in new state constitution effectively keeps African-Americans from voting.
- **1913** Woodrow Wilson inaugurated president.
- **1917** Wilson leads America into war against Germany. Growth of Hampton Roads naval and military installations.
- **1954** Supreme Court school integration ruling leads to school closings to avoid compliance with law.
- **1989** L. Douglas Wilder, nation's first African-American governor, takes office in Richmond.
- **1994** Senator Charles Robb reelected, defeating controversial Republican Oliver North.
- **1999** Republicans gain historic majority in state legislature.

VICTORY AT YORKTOWN Although many Virginians were in Washington's army, it was not until the war's final years that the state became a major battleground. The turning point came in March 1781, when British general Lord Cornwallis established a base at the York River.

Two weeks after Cornwallis settled into Yorktown for the winter, General Washington received word from a French admiral, the Comte de Grasse, that he was taking his squadron to the Chesapeake and that his men and ships were at Washington's disposal through October 15. "I shall be obliged to you," wrote de Grasse, "if you will employ me promptly and effectually during that time." After conferring with the Comte de Rochambeau, commander of the French troops in America, Washington decided to march 450 miles to Virginia with the object of defeating Cornwallis.

Meanwhile, on September 5, 1781, a fleet of 19 British ships under Adm. Thomas Graves appeared at the entrance to Chesapeake Bay with the aim of reinforcing Cornwallis's Yorktown entrenchment. They were met by 24 French ships under de Grasse. Though the battle ended in a stalemate, Graves was forced to return to New York to repair his ships. The French remained to block further British reinforcements or the possibility of their escape by water, while the French and American armies under Washington neared Yorktown to block aid or escape by land.

The siege began on September 28 when 17,000 men under Washington occupied a line encircling the town. The allied army, spread out in camps extending 6 miles, dug siege lines and bombarded the redcoats with heavy cannon fire. British defeat was inevitable. On October 17, a cease fire was called and a British officer was led to American lines, where he requested an armistice. Although the war was not officially over until the Treaty of Paris was signed 2 years later, Cornwallis's defeat effectively marked the colonists' victory.

FRAMING THE CONSTITUTION The new nation's governmental powers were weak, resting on the inadequate provisions of the Articles of Confederation. To remedy the situation, a Constitutional Convention met in Philadelphia, and Washington was elected president of the Convention. He and fellow Virginian James Madison fought to have the new Constitution include a Bill of Rights and gradual abolition of the slave trade. Although both measures were defeated, the two Virginians voted to adopt the Constitution, feeling that its faults could be amended later.

In 1788, Virginia became the 10th state to ratify the Constitution, and by 1791 the first 10 amendments—the Bill of Rights—had been added. Madison was author of the first 9 amendments, Richard Henry Lee the 10th.

THE COUNTRY'S EARLY VIRGINIAN PRESIDENTS

Washington was elected president under the new Constitution and took office on April 30, 1789.

As third president of the United States, Thomas Jefferson nearly doubled the size of the country by purchasing the Louisiana Territory from Napoléon.

James Madison took office as president in 1809. Unable to maintain Jefferson's peacekeeping efforts in the face of continued provocations by England, Madison was swayed by the popular demand for armed response, and in 1812 Congress declared war. Although some coastal plantations were attacked by British warships, the only suffering Virginia witnessed was the burning of nearby Washington, D.C.

James Monroe followed as president, having already served Virginia and the nation in many capacities. During his two terms the nation pushed westward, and he faced the first struggle over the slavery question (which resulted in the Missouri Compromise), established the Monroe Doctrine, and settled the nation's boundary with Canada.

THE CIVIL WAR

It was not long before the United States became a nation divided. The issues were states' rights, slavery, and the conflicting goals of an industrial North and an agricultural South. In 1859, John Brown and his small band of followers raided the arsenal at Harpers Ferry (now West Virginia) to obtain arms for a slave revolt he hoped to instigate. Brown was captured and hanged. In the North, his execution rallied support for the abolitionist cause; in the South, people shuddered at the threat of a slave revolt.

The election of 1860 was crucial. The Republicans nominated Abraham Lincoln, whom the South vowed it would not accept; but the Democrats split and Lincoln was elected. Seven states seceded—Texas, Louisiana, South Carolina, Alabama, Georgia, Florida, and Mississippi. At his inauguration, Lincoln declared, "In your hands, my dissatisfied fellow countrymen, and not in mine, is the momentous issue of civil war. You can have no oath registered in heaven to destroy the government, while I have the solemn one to preserve, protect, and defend it."

On April 12, 1861, guns sounded at Fort Sumter in Charleston harbor. Secession had become war.

FIRST MANASSAS   In May 1861, the Confederate capital was transferred to Richmond, only 100 miles from Washington. Virginia was doomed to become the first major battleground of the Civil War. The first of six heavy offensives by the North against Richmond was decisively repulsed on July 21, 1861, at the battle of First Manassas (Bull Run). Union Gen. Irvin McDowell's 35,000 ill-trained federal volunteers marched southward to the cry "Onward to Richmond," and the following Union attacks were successful. Later, however, a stonewall-like stand by the Virginia Brigade of Gen. Thomas J. Jackson swept McDowell's forces back to Washington. In addition to the victory, the South had found a new hero—"Stonewall" Jackson. Casualties in this first major engagement of the war totaled 4,828 men. It was apparent that this would be a long and bitter conflict.

THE PENINSULA CAMPAIGN   The second major offensive against Richmond, the Peninsula Campaign, devised by Union Gen. George B. McClellan, was the setting for the most famous naval engagement in the western hemisphere. On March 9, 1862, two ironclad vessels, the USS *Monitor* and the CSS *Virginia* (formerly the *Merrimac*) pounded each other with cannon. Although the battle was a draw, the advent of ironclad warships heralded a new era in naval history.

Two months later Yorktown was reduced to rubble and the Union army advanced up the peninsula. The Confederates retreated until they were only 9 miles from Richmond. At that point they fought, and the Confederate leader, General Johnson, was badly wounded. Robert E. Lee, grandson of colonial patriot Richard Henry Lee, was appointed head of the army of Virginia. Personally opposed to secession, Lee had sadly resigned his commission in the U.S. Army when Virginia joined the Confederacy, saying, "My heart is broken, but I cannot raise my sword against Virginia." In a series of victories beginning on June 26, 1862, Lee finally defeated the Union armies. Richmond had again been saved.

SECOND MANASSAS, FREDERICKSBURG & CHANCELLORSVILLE

The third Union drive against Richmond was repulsed at Manassas, where Gen. Robert E. Lee secured his place in history by soundly defeating 70,000 Union troops under Gen. John Pope with a Confederate army of 55,000 men in three days. On December 13, 1862, Gen. Ambrose Burnside, newly chosen head of the Army of the Potomac, crossed the Rappahannock and struck Fredericksburg while Lee's army was scattered in northern Virginia. The federal advance was so slow that by the time the Union armies moved, Lee's forces were firmly entrenched in the hills south of the city. Burnside was unsuccessful, and the fourth Union drive against Richmond was turned back.

Gen. Joseph Hooker took command of the Union army early in 1863, and, once again, federal forces attempted to take Richmond. Fighting raged for 4 days. The Union army retreated, and the fifth drive on Richmond failed. But Lee's victory was costly. In addition to heavy casualties, the Confederacy lost Stonewall Jackson, who was wounded by his own troops and later died of complications resulting from the amputation of his arm. Without Jackson, Lee began his second invasion of the North, which would end in the small Pennsylvania town of Gettysburg.

A WAR OF ATTRITION In March 1864, Ulysses S. Grant was put in command of all federal armies. His plan for victory called for a war of attrition, total unrelenting warfare that would put constant pressure on all points of the Confederacy. The first great confrontation between Lee and Grant, the Battle of the Wilderness, resulted in a Confederate victory, but the South's casualties were high, 11,400. The Richmond campaign was the heaviest fighting of the Civil War. Three times Grant tried and failed to interpose his forces between Lee and Richmond. More than 80,000 men were killed and wounded.

LAYING SIEGE AT PETERSBURG Still determined, Grant secretly moved his army across the James River toward Petersburg, an important rail junction south of Richmond. Improvised Southern forces managed to hold the city until Lee arrived. Grant then resorted to ever-tightening siege operations. Blocked in his trenches, Lee could not leave Grant's front. To do so would be to abandon Petersburg and Richmond. Subjected to hunger and exposure, the Confederate will to resist began to wane and periodic skirmishes further weakened Confederate morale.

Lee, hoping to divert Grant's attention, dispatched a small army under Jubal Early to the Shenandoah Valley. Grant instructed Union Gen. Philip Sheridan: "The Shenandoah is to be so devastated that crows flying across it for the balance of the season will have to bring their own provender." The second valley campaign resulted in the destruction of Early's army and the Shenandoah Valley.

LEE'S RETREAT Back in Petersburg, Grant's attrition strategy was succeeding. For the army of Northern Virginia the 10-month siege of that city meant physical hardship, disease, filth, dwindling morale, and tedious waiting for the inevitable onslaught. It came on April 1, 1865, when federal forces smashed through weakened Confederate lines at Five Forks; Petersburg fell, and Richmond was occupied by federal forces. Lee's last hope was to rendezvous with Joe Johnson's army, which was retreating through North Carolina before Sherman's advance. However, on April 8 the vanguard of Grant's army succeeded in reaching Appomattox Court House ahead of Lee, thus blocking the Confederates' last escape route.

On April 9, 1865, the Civil War ended in Virginia at Appomattox in Wilbur McLean's farmhouse. Grant, so uncompromising in war, proved compassionate in peace. All Confederate soldiers were permitted to return home on parole, cavalrymen could keep their horses, and officers could retain their sidearms. Rations were provided at once for the destitute Southerners. Accepting these generous terms, Lee surrendered his 28,000 soldiers, the ragged remnants of the once-mighty Army of Northern Virginia. Lee's farewell was moving in its simplicity: "I earnestly pray that a merciful God will extend to you his blessing and protection. With an unceasing admiration of your constancy and devotion to your country, and a grateful remembrance of your kind and generous consideration for myself, I bid you all an affectionate farewell."

RECOVERY, RENEWAL & THE 20TH CENTURY

To a state devastated by a conflict that pitted brother against brother, recovery was slow. Besides the physical and psychological damages of the conflict, the Reconstruction era brought Virginia under federal military control until 1870.

However, by the turn of the century, Virginia's economic growth was characterized by new railroad lines connecting remote country areas in the west with urban centers. Factories were bringing more people to the cities, and the economy, once based entirely on agriculture, now had a growing industrial base. The great ports enjoyed growing importance as steamship traffic carried an increasing volume of commercial freight. During this period the great scholar, author, and educator Booker T. Washington, who had been born in slavery, studied at Virginia's Hampton Institute and achieved fame as an advisor to presidents.

Although he was serving as governor of New Jersey at the time, Virginia-born Woodrow Wilson was elected president in 1912. Although noted for his peace-loving ideals, Wilson saw the entry of the United States into World War I in 1917. War brought prosperity to Virginia with new factories and munitions plants and the expansion of military-training camps throughout the state.

World War II brought a population explosion, with men and women of the armed forces flocking to northern Virginia suburbs near Washington, D.C., and the port area of Hampton Roads. Many of these people stayed after the war, and by 1955 the majority of Virginians were urban dwelling. Today, the state's population is about 6^1/$_2$ million.

Index

Index

FROMMER'S® COMPLETE TRAVEL GUIDES

FROMMER'S® DOLLAR-A-DAY GUIDES

Australia from $50 a Day
California from $60 a Day
Caribbean from $70 a Day
England from $70 a Day
Europe from $60 a Day
Florida from $60 a Day

Hawaii from $70 a Day
Ireland from $50 a Day
Israel from $45 a Day
Italy from $70 a Day
London from $85 a Day
New York from $80 a Day

New Zealand from $50 a Day
Paris from $85 a Day
San Francisco from $60 a Day
Washington, D.C.,
   from $60 a Day

FROMMER'S® PORTABLE GUIDES

Acapulco, Ixtapa &
   Zihuatanejo
Alaska Cruises & Ports of Call
Bahamas
Baja & Los Cabos
Berlin
California Wine Country
Charleston & Savannah
Chicago

Dublin
Hawaii: The Big Island
Las Vegas
London
Maine Coast
Maui
New Orleans
New York City
Paris

Puerto Vallarta, Manzanillo
   & Guadalajara
San Diego
San Francisco
Sydney
Tampa & St. Petersburg
Venice
Washington, D.C.

FROMMER'S® NATIONAL PARK GUIDES

Family Vacations in the
   National Parks
Grand Canyon

National Parks of the
   American West
Rocky Mountain

Yellowstone & Grand Teton
Yosemite & Sequoia/
   Kings Canyon
Zion & Bryce Canyon

FROMMER'S® GREAT OUTDOOR GUIDES

New England
Northern California

Southern California & Baja
Washington & Oregon

FROMMER'S® MEMORABLE WALKS

Chicago
London

New York
Paris

San Francisco
Washington D.C.

FROMMER'S® IRREVERENT GUIDES

Amsterdam
Boston
Chicago
Las Vegas

London
Los Angeles
Manhattan

New Orleans
Paris
San Francisco

Seattle & Portland
Vancouver
Walt Disney World
Washington, D.C.

FROMMER'S® BEST-LOVED DRIVING TOURS

America
Britain
California

Florida
France
Germany

Ireland
Italy
New England

Scotland
Spain
Western Europe

THE UNOFFICIAL GUIDES®

Bed & Breakfast in
New England
Bed & Breakfast in
the Northwest
Beyond Disney
Branson, Missouri
California with Kids
Chicago

Cruises
Disneyland
Florida with Kids
The Great Smoky &
Blue Ridge
Mountains
Inside Disney
Las Vegas

London
Miami & the Keys
Mini Las Vegas
Mini-Mickey
New Orleans
New York City
Paris
San Francisco

Skiing in the West
Walt Disney World
Walt Disney World
for Grown-ups
Walt Disney World
for Kids
Washington, D.C.

SPECIAL-INTEREST TITLES

Born to Shop: France
Born to Shop: Hong Kong
Born to Shop: Italy
Born to Shop: New York
Born to Shop: Paris
Frommer's Britain's Best Bike Rides
The Civil War Trust's Official Guide
to the Civil War Discovery Trail
Frommer's Caribbean Hideaways
Frommer's Europe's Greatest Driving Tours
Frommer's Food Lover's Companion to France
Frommer's Food Lover's Companion to Italy
Frommer's Gay & Lesbian Europe
Israel Past & Present
Monks' Guide to California

Monks' Guide to New York City
The Moon
New York City with Kids
Unforgettable Weekends
Outside Magazine's Guide
to Family Vacations
Places Rated Almanac
Retirement Places Rated
Road Atlas Britain
Road Atlas Europe
Washington, D.C., with Kids
Wonderful Weekends from Boston
Wonderful Weekends from New York City
Wonderful Weekends from San Francisco
Wonderful Weekends from Los Angeles